THE ILLUSTRIOUS
HUGO GROTIUS
OF THE LAW OF
WARRE
AND
PEACE
WITH
ANNOTATIONS.
III. PARTS.
AND
Memorials of the Author's Life and Death.

See you not Learning in his Lookes?
See it more lively in his Bookes.

Tho. Cross Sculpsit

THE ILLUSTRIOUS
HUGO GROTIUS
OF THE LAW OF
WARRE
AND
PEACE
WITH
ANNOTATIONS.
III. PARTS.
AND
Memorials of the Author's Life and Death.

Tranſlated by *C. B.* Maſter of Arts.

Ὁ ἀδικῶν ἀσεβεῖ M. Antonin. Imp. l. 9.

With a new introduction by William E. Butler

John Edward Fowler Distinguished Professor of Law, Pennsylvania State University; Academician, National Academy of Sciences of Ukraine; National Academy of Legal Sciences of Ukraine; and Russian Academy of Natural Sciences

THE LAWBOOK EXCHANGE, LTD.
Clark, New Jersey

ISBN 978-1-61619-279-2

Lawbook Exchange edition 2013

The quality of this reprint is equivalent to the quality of the original work.

THE LAWBOOK EXCHANGE, LTD.
33 Terminal Avenue
Clark, New Jersey 07066-1321

Please see our website for a selection of our other publications and fine facsimile reprints of classic works of legal history:
www.lawbookexchange.com

Library of Congress Cataloging-in-Publication Data

Grotius, Hugo, 1583-1645.
[De jure belli ac pacis libri tres. English]
The illustrious Hugo Grotius of the law of warre and peace : with annotations, III. parts. and memorials of the author's life and death / translated by C.B., Master of Arts ; new introduction by William E. Butler, John Edward Fowler Distinguished Professor of Law, Pennsylvania State University Dickinson School of Law and Emeritus Professor of Comparative Law at University College London; Academician of the National Academy of Sciences of Ukraine. -- Lawbook exchange edition.
pages cm
Includes bibliographical references.
ISBN-13: 978-1-61619-279-2 (hardcover : alk. paper)
ISBN-10: 1-61619-279-8 (hardcover : alk. paper)
1. International law. 2. War (International law) 3. Natural law. 4. Grotius, Hugo, 1583-1645. De jure belli ac pacis libri tres. English. I. Barksdale, Clement, 1609-1687, translator. II. Butler, William Elliott, 1939- Barksdale translation of Hugo Grotius. III. Title. IV. Title: Of the law of warre and peace.
KZ2093.A3D313 2013
341--dc23 2013005158

Printed in the United States of America on acid-free paper

THE BARKSDALE TRANSLATION OF HUGO GROTIUS

W. E. Butler

Hugo Grotius was a formidably productive writer whose works ranged from the law of nations to Dutch law, poetry, history, theology, philosophy, literature, and other disciplines. Throughout the remainder of the seventeenth century following his death, a veritable "Grotiana factory" devoted to translations of his works into English and the other principal European vernacular languages operated throughout Europe. Latin editions continued to find an audience, however. One of those contributions is the present work, the first English translation of Hugo Grotius, *De jure belli ac pacis* (1625), completed ca. 1654 and published in London that year.

The Author

Hugo Grotius (1583–1645) remains after more than four and a quarter centuries from his birth perhaps the single most recognizable name in the history of international law. Sometimes (quite wrongly) labeled the "father of international law", his works on the subject – above all the present work – became classics in the field even during his lifetime.[1] In some works on the history of international law, "Grotius" is singled out as a period in its development.[2] A first edition of *De jure belli ac pacis* (1625) brings upwards of $120,000 and is included among the 500 most important books ever printed.

[1] See L. E. van Holk, "Hugo Grotius, 1583–1645: A Biographical Sketch", in L. E. van Holk and C. G. Roelofson (eds.), *Grotius Reader: A Reader for Students of International Law and Legal History* (1983), pp. 23–44; J. L. de Burigny, *The Life of the Truly Eminent and Learned Hugo Grotius* (London, 1754); E. Dumbauld, *The Life and Legal Writings of Hugo Grotius* (1969); W. S. M. Knight, *The Life and Works of Hugo Grotius* (1925).

[2] See W. E. Butler, "Periodization and International Law", in A. Orakhelashvili (ed.), *Research Handbook on the Theory and History of International Law* (2011), pp. 379–393.

Grotius was born at Delft into a Calvinist family. His intellectual abilities manifested themselves early on, composing Latin verses at the age of seven (said by Eyffinger[3] to be "… the only man in world history acclaimed a child prodigy by virtue of his juvenile poetry") and entering the University of Leiden at the age of eleven. He graduated at the age of fourteen, having satisfactorily performed in the fields of law, philosophy, and mathematics. By the age of fifteen he accompanied a Dutch Embassy to Henry IV of France. The King described him as the "miracle of Holland"; the University of Orléans conferred the degree of Doctor of Laws on him. Admitted to legal practice at the age of sixteen, he continued to excel in the humanities, publishing a dramatic tragedy in 1601. At twenty years of age he was appointed Historiographer of Holland.[4]

His first known work on the law of nations originated in a commission from the Dutch East India Company to prepare an opinion of the legality of the seizure of a Portugese ship, the carrack *Sta. Catarina*, by the Company flotilla during the war in February 1603 between the Netherlands and Spain. A substantial manuscript was produced, one chapter of which was published in 1609 as *Mare liberum*[5] (the full text was not discovered until 1864 and published in 1868).[6] Grotius rose rapidly in the Dutch firmament, being appointed to influential legal posts and continuing his sundry writings on history, theology, and Dutch law.

---

[3] A. Eyffinger, "In Quest of Synthesis: An Attempted Synopsis of Grotius's Works According to Their Genesis and Objective", *Grotiana*, IV (N.S., 1983), pp. 76–88.

[4] See A. Nussbaum, *A Concise History of the Law of Nations* (rev. ed., 1954; reprint ed. Gryphon, 2008).

[5] We are blessed with two recent published versions, one originally made by Richard Hakluyt but never fully published in its time. See Grotius, *The Free Sea*, transl. R. Hakluyt; ed. D. Armitage (2004); and Grotius, *Mare Liberum 1609–2009*, ed. R. Feenstra (2009), a sumptuous edition. Also see on this book W. E. Butler, "Grotius and the Law of the Sea", in H. Bull, B. Kingsbury, and A. Roberts (eds.), *Hugo Grotius and International Relations* (1990), pp. 209–220. On Hakluyt in this connection, see D. Pirillo, "Balance of Power and Freedom of the Sea: Richard Hakluyt and Alberico Gentili", in D. Carey and C. Jowitt (eds.), *Richard Hakluyt and Travel Writing in Early Modern Europe* (2012), pp. 177–186.

[6] The most recent edition, attended in several instances by new supporting materials, is H. Grotius, *Commentary on the Law of Prize and Booty*, ed. & intro. Martine Julia van Irtersum (2006).

His political career in Holland ended when he was sentenced to life imprisonment for his role in a dispute among Calvinists in 1619 that Prince Maurice equated to treason.[7] His tenure in prison and ultimate escape were known to every schoolboy throughout Europe.[8] During two years of confinement, he wrote two major works, one an introduction to Dutch jurisprudence and the other an exposition of the central doctrines of the Christian faith intended for seafarers. He was allowed to have books in quantity and the companionship of his wife. He trained himself to lie in a closed chest and was eventually removed clandestinely in that receptacle in March 1621 to the safety of friends, who assisted him in escaping to France in disguise. There he was received by the King of France, awarded an allowance, and, during 1622–1624, commenced and completed the Latin version of the monumental work here reproduced.[9] Dedicated to Louis XIII, the book, it was hoped, might contribute to a resolution of the Thirty Years War, then fully in progress.[10]

The work, well received at the time, disappointed in that its appearance did not enable him to return home or to secure a position consistent with his stature and ambition. Eventually, in 1634 he was appointed by the Court of Sweden to become the Swedish Ambassador to Paris. He held the post for a decade, but not without difficulties. In manner he was not diplomatic, and his continued preoccupations with matters of theology and literature

---

[7] On a later assessment of the trial based on access to sealed records of the proceedings, see G. G. Brandt, *Brandts Historie van de Rechtspleging gehouden in de Jaeren 1618 en 1619. Ontrent de dry gevangene Heeren Mr. Johan van Oldenbarnevelt Mr. Rombout Hoogerbeets Mr. Hugo de Groot* (Rotterdam, 1708). On Oldenbarnevelt's defense of his conduct, see Jan van Barnevelt, *Barnevelt's Apology of Holland's Mysterie, with Marginall Castigations* (1618). Also see John L. Motley, *The Life and Death of John of Barneveld, Advocate of Holland; with a View of the Primary Causes and Movements of the Thirty Years' War* (London, 1874). 2 vols.

[8] Recounted in Burigny, note 1 above and greatly embellished by "that literary larcenist", Charles Butler in what one reviewer called his "indifferent life" of Grotius. See C. Butler, *The Life of Hugo Grotius with Brief Minutes of the Civil, Ecclesiastical, and Literary History of the Netherlands* (London, 1826).

[9] Intellectually, Tuck suggests, *De Iure Belli ac Pacis* really grew out of Grotius's time in prison". See R. Tuck, "Introduction", in H. Grotius, *The Rights of War and Peace* (2005), p. xv.

[10] On that War and references to Grotius, see P. H. Wilson, *The Thirty Years War: Europe's Tragedy* (2009), pp. 134, 318, 389, 463, 553, and 675.

were seen by his Swedish patrons as detracting from the proper performance of his duties. In 1645 he perished in the aftermath of a shipwreck on the coasts of modern Germany.

There have been more than fifty editions of the original Latin text, including several during Grotius' lifetime with his emendations. There are translations into Chinese, Dutch, French, German, Japanese, Russian,[11] Spanish, Swedish, and Church Slavonic,[12] among others. Although well regarded in France and Spain, Grotius' fame was greatest in Protestant countries. The Vatican placed his book on the Index in 1626, where it remained until 1899.

There are several translations of Grotius's work in English. William Whewell referred to a "small and worthless abridgement" published in 1654 by C.B., whom he believed (correctly) to be Clement Barksdale.[13] Whewell is actually referring to a biography of Grotius cobbled together by Barksdale. Published in its own right in 1654, it was appended to the full translation of Grotius *De Jure Belli ac Pacis* published under the initials "C.B." in 1654 and 1655. Apparently Whewell was unaware of the full 1654 translation. A second version, in folio, appeared three decades later,

---

[11] The most comprehensive bibliography of foreign translations of Grotius is Jacob Ter Meulen and P. J. J. Diermanse, *Bibliographie des écrits imprimés de Hugo Grotiius* (The Hague, 1950). Published more than six decades ago, it requires some correction and augmentation. With respect to the Russian versions, for example, it is unaware of the 1902 St. Petersburg edition, which seems to be so far the first appearance of Grotius' treatise on the law of war and peace in printed form in Russia, although heavily censored. The later editions mentioned are not editions at all, but merely an enumeration of the table of contents from Grotius or extremely abbreviated extracts on certain topics (for example, ambassadorial immunity). The first full edition of Grotius in Russian appeared in 1956, after the Ter Meulen/Diermanse bibliography appeared. It is entirely possible that the reaction of the Russian Orthodox Church to Grotius was not dissimilar from that of the Vatican.

[12] See W. E. Butler, "Grotius' Influence in Russia", in Bull, et al., note 5 above, pp. 257–266.

[13] See Hugo Grotius, *De jure belli ac pacis libri tres. The Illustrious Hvgo Grotius Of the Law of Warre and Peace. With Annotations. III. Parts. And Memorials of the Author's Life and Death* (London, 1654). 39 p. A fuller edition appeared in 1654 and a second printing in 1655: [78], 660, [98] p. Harvard Law School has both printings which, but for the designation of dates, are much the same, together with the extremely short version.

translated by William Evats.[14] Another, also in folio, was published in 1738.[15] However, Whewell was unaware of the 1715 version, whose text differed to some extent from that of 1738, although both are now known to have been translated principally by John Morrice (1686–c. 1740).[16] There was also an 1814 London edition with notes by A. C. Campbell.[17] Given the wealth of translations of Grotius over the centuries, it remains to collate and compare them to determine how much our comprehension of Grotius may depend upon the particular merits of one or the other.

The Translator

The early English translations of the works of Grotius on the law of nations are not the product of legal scholars or legal scholarship. They are indebted primarily to theologians for their appearance, either because Grotius figured prominently in theological discourse at various periods after his death or because his legal writings were espoused by dons dedicated to the cause of peace who considered the Grotian contributions to the law of nations to be a constructive step in the direction of a more peaceful world community.

Clement Barksdale (1609–1687), born the same year that Grotius published his brief on the freedom of the seas, devoted a considerable portion of his translation activities to Grotius.[18] Born

---

[14] H. Grotius, *Three Books Treating of the Rights of War and Peace. In the First is handled, Whether Any War be Just. In the Second is shewed, The Causes of War, both Just and Unjust. In the Third is declared, What in War is Lawful; that is, Unpunishable. With the Annotations Digested into the Body of Every Chapter*, transl. William Evats (London, 1582). 572 p.

[15] H. Grotius, *The Rights of War and Peace, in Three Books: Wherein are Explained, the Law of Nature and Nations, and the Principal Points Relating to Government* (London, 1738).

[16] See R. Tuck, "A Note on the Text", in Grotius, note 9 above, p. xxxv.

[17] H. Grotius, *The Rights of War and Peace: Including the Law of Nature and of Nations*, transl. from the Original Latin of Grotius, with Notes and Illustrations from Political and Legal Writers by A. C. Campbell, A. M. (London, 1814). 3 vols. This version, with notes by Archibald Colin Campbell, was reprinted in 1901 with an introduction by David Jayne Hill and the 1901 version again in 1979.

[18] See J. A. Barksdale, *Barksdale Family History and Genealogy (with Collateral Lines)* (1940), p. 4. This volume is devoted to the American branch of the family. However, the Parish Registers examined in Winchcomb, Glos., show that on 22

at Winchcombe, Gloucestershire, on 23 or 26 November (the sources differ), Barksdale[19] attended grammar school in Abingdon and later studied at Merton and Worcester colleges, Oxford University, graduating BA in 1629 and MA in 1632. At a time unknown but prior to 1637, Barksdale was ordained and in 1637 acted as chaplain of Lincoln College, proceeding that same year to Hereford. In 1641 he became vicar choral and rector of St. Nicholas in Hereford. A stalwart royalist, Barksdale maintained his rectorship until the Cromwellian forces occupied Hereford in 1646. Support from the Chandos family, who had retained Barksdale as chaplain, enabled him to seek refuge in Sudeley Castle. After the Restoration, he established himself at Naunton, near Hawling, and Stow-on-the-Wold in Gloucestershire, where he remained for the rest of his life, becoming in 1660 Rector of Naunton and Stow on the Wold.

Contemporaries had little time for his work. Anthony Wood described Barksdale as "a good Disputant, a great admirer of Hugo Grotius, a frequent Preacher, but very conceited and vain, a great pretender to Poetry, and a Writer and Translator of several little Tracts, most of which are meer Scribbles".[20]

Alexander Balloch Grosart, echoing Wood, was equally dismissive of his contributions. "His only approach to poetic faculty is in his verse-translations of some of Crashaw's Latin epigrams. Otherwise he was a mere book-maker. As a biographer he is perfunctory and untrustworthy. His translations are usually paraphrastic and inelegant".[21]

In a far more sympathetic assessment of Barksdale, his biographer in the *Oxford Dictionary of National Biography* sees

---

May 1647 Clement Barksdale, "Minister of God", acted as a witness for the testament of William Barksdale.

[19] The surname "Barksdale" is believed to be a combination of the Scandinavian word "bark", meaning the rind of a tree, and "dale", meaning a vale, or a low place between the trees and perhaps originated from the barkers or tanners who lived in a valley were bark could be found for the tanning of hides.

[20] Anthony á Wood (1632–1695), *Athenae Oxenienses: An Exact History of All the Writers and Bishops Who Have Had Their Education in the Most Ancient and Famous University of Oxford* ... (2d ed.; 1721), II, pp. 811–814.

[21] A. B. Grosart, in *Dictionary of National Biography* (1885–1901), I, p. 1136. See also G. W. Williams, "Clement Barksdale's Translations of Richard Crashaw's Epigrams", in *John Donne Journal*, XXIV (2005), pp. 353–357.

Barksdale's "greatest significance" in "his work as a translator of Grotius". A "man with a clear sense of mission", Barksdale used Grotius primarily and some other writers secondarily to "foster the development of a moderate latitudinarian Anglicanism" and to introduce the English public to "less dogmatic figures within the Reformed tradition".[22] Mission notwithstanding, however, Barksdale envisaged a far broader readership for Grotius' work on the law of war and peace. In his appeal "To the Reader", he anticipated that the "Divine shall here behold the Evangelical Law …", the jurist "shall here read the most Common Law, that of Nature and Nations", the Civilian may find some "footsteps of the Goodly Body of his Law", the Statesman and the Soldier will see the value of the book in the Title, and the "Philosopher, the Poet, the Orator, and Historian" will meet with the choicest flowers gather "by a most skillful hand" (p. [vii]). The potential readership for the book, in other words, went far beyond those interested in the Grotian theology.

Clement Barksdale was related in some way to John Barksdale, a printer, bookseller, and book-binder based in London for some time and, evidently from 1678, in Cirencester, where he became the first bookseller.[23] John Barksdale published several of Clement Barksdale's translations from Grotius between 1675 and 1678.[24]

The Book

The Barksdale translation of Grotius exists in two printings that appeared a year apart, the first in 1654, the second in 1655. We have not compared the two, but we expect that they are identical

---

[22] John Coffey, "Barksdale, Clement (1609–1687), *Oxford Dictionary of National Biography* (available online). Barksdale's translations are evidence of "the renewal of interest in Grotius and his English disciples". H. Trevor-Roper, *Catholics, Anglicans and Puritans: Seventeenth-Century Essays* (1987), p. 223.

[23] H. R. Plomer, *A Dictionary of the Printers and Booksellers Who Were at Work in England, Scotland and Ireland from 1668 to 1725* (1922), pp. 20–21.

[24] Several were extracts from Grotius, *De veritate religionis christianae,* the outline of which was drafted while Grotius was imprisoned in Holland. The first edition appeared in 1627 in Latin. Sir Isaac Newton had a copy of the 1669 Amsterdam edition, recently rediscovered. See P. Rålamb, "An Unexpected Isaac Newton Provenance", in G. T. Tanselle (intro.), *Other People's Books: Association Copies and the Stories They Tell* (2011), pp. 45–49.

except for the possible adjustment of typographical infelicities. The 1655 version is reproduced here, together with the biographical sketch of Grotius.

Although international lawyers are well aware that Grotius wrote widely in theology, philosophy, history, and other components of the humanities, they are inclined to treat his works on the law of nations quite separately from his other writings.[25] Recent approaches to Grotian intellectual history suggest any such "compartmentalization" may be misleading and that the seventeen English translations of Grotius on the law of nations in aggregate were part of a dialogue quite different in nature and direction. Barksdale's version of Grotius is perceived to be part of a larger movement in England aimed partly at setting out an ideological alternative to reformation proposals under discussion and to clarifying the relations between civil and ecclesiastical authority in England.

The first English translation of *De veritate religionis Christianae* (1629) appeared in an English version by Franciscus a Sancta Clara (1598–1680)[26] under the title *True Religion Explained and Defended Against ye Archenemies Thereof in These Times* (London, 1632). Given Grotius' close association with the law of the sea, it is entirely appropriate, if not serendipitous, that *De Veritate* should have been intended for the ordinary seaman with time on his hands during lengthy voyages to fortify his Christian faith or, if opportunity presented itself, to convert pagans, Muslims, or Jews.[27]

Barksdale became a veritable "Grotian" factory, the full measure of which has never been appreciated. In his own collection of verses, *Nympha Libethris, or, The Cotswold Muse* (London, 1651), Barksdale praised Grotius. That same year Barksdale pursued the cause of disseminating Grotius' thinking with his translation of *De*

---

[25] A pioneering effort to synthesize the totality of Grotius is found in A. Eyffinger, note 3 above, pp. 76–88.

[26] Born Christopher Davenport, he entered the Franciscan order of friars in 1617 and eventually after periods of time in France and Spain, returned to England as a missionary, where he became chaplain to Queen Henrietta Maria (1609–1666), wife of King Charles I. Franciscus a Sancta Clara devoted himself to reconciling the Church of England with Rome. Author of more than ten major works on theology, his translation of Grotius is commonly ignored in many Grotian circles.

[27] Maria Rose Antognazza (intro.), to H. Grotius, *The Truth of the Christian Religion,* transl. J. Clarke with Notes by J. Le Clerc (2012), p. xiii.

Imperio Summarum Potestatum Circa Sacra (1647). Grotius had begun to compose the work as early as 1614, completing the first draft by 1617, but its appearance in print was posthumous, in 1647. John Selden was greatly impressed with the version, which he first read in manuscript ('that golden book' which he praised as 'than which there is nothing more learned').[28] Copies were circulating in manuscript as early as 1617 in England, and John Selden acquired at least two manuscript versions.[29] Although widely seen as a theological work and included in an early collection of Grotian theological writings,[30] *De Imperio* has been characterized as "a political response of the Dutch Arminian party led by Oldenbarnevelt, and to the independent and decentralized system of churches advocated by the 'Counter-Remonstrants'". In this perception, Grotius was said to have conceived his role and his work as a "manifesto of State-sponsored Erastian Arminianism,[31] whose main purpose was to affirm the supremacy of the State of Holland in the Dutch Government, and of the Arminian party in the Dutch church".[32] These are both facets of Grotius's works that would have appealed to the reconciliation inclinations of Barksdale within an English milieu.

Shortly after publication of his translation of *De Imperio*, Barksdale entered into a public disputation with Carnsew Helme (1622–1669), whose pamphlet account of the controversy portrayed

---

[28] Grotius shared a high opinion of Selden. Upon learning that Selden was walking about London and mistakenly believing him to have been released from prison. Grotius wrote in 1630 that Selden was "the best of men and a very brave citizen". G. J. Toomer, *John Selden: A Life in Scholarship* (2009), I, p.333.

[29] Toomer, ibid., II, p. 717.

[30] H. Grotius, *Opera omnia theologica* (London, 1679). 3 vols.

[31] "Erastian" refers to Thomas Erastus (1524–1583), a Swiss medical doctor and religious figure whose name is associated with a doctrine which he never supported, namely, that the State is superior to the Church in ecclesiastical matters. "Arminianism" has in view the teachings of Jacobus Arminius (1560–1609), who attempted to reform certain tenets of Calvinism. His followers became known as Remonstrants after issuing Five Theses disagreeing with central tenets of Calvinism. Arminian teachings continue to have vitality through their acceptance by mainstream Methodism.

[32] M. Barducci, "Clement Barksdale, Translator of Grotius: Erastianism and Episcopacy in the English Church, 1651–1658", *The Seventeenth Century*, XXV, no. 2 (2010), p. 270. On Erastian elements and influences in Grotian thought, see E. Nelson, *The Hebrew Republic: Jewish Sources and the Transformation of European Political Thought* (2010), pp. 97–107.

Barksdale as a defender of the Church of England with an Erastian vision of church-State relations expressly drawn from Grotius (Helme was ejected for non-conformity in 1662). Barksdale having quoted Grotius' *De Iure Belli ac Pacis* in the introduction to his 1651 translation, thought it was a logical step to undertake a full translation, which is the work presented here. Seen against this background, Barksdale assumes the mission of presenting the full spectrum of Grotian thought in accessible English-language versions; it was not his mission, or at least his principal mission, to further the development of international legal doctrine.[33]

It is instructive for international lawyers to consider the larger proposition that Barksdale's translations of Grotius, including the present work,

> publicized the idea expounded in it, and by placing it in a context other than the one in which it had been originally written, imparted a different meaning to it ... in doing so, the translator evaded authorial responsibility and the risk of being charged for positions put forward in the edited work ... By selecting from Grotius' output of over fifty works and translating his selection, Barksdale implicitly imparted his ideological interpretation of their meanings and purposes ... The study of translations and editions of texts should therefore be a feature of the philological approach to the history of ideas, pointing to the link between the author, the work, and its social and cultural circulation or reception ... .[34]

[33] Barksdale did not pursue Grotius' works on the origin of the American peoples, which although primarily theological and even polemical, would have implications for the status of American Indian tribes as subjects of the law of nations. See H. Grotius, *De origine Gentium Americanarum dissertatio* (1642). Manuscript versions were being circulated by late 1641 through Willem Grotius, the brother of Hugo Grotius and a jurist in The Hague. For an English translation, see H. Grotius, *On the Origin of the Native Races of America*, transl. Edmund Goldsmid (1884). More generally, see Joan-Pau Rubiés, "Hugo Grotius's Dissertation on the Origin of the American Peoples and the Use of Comparative Methods", *Journal of the History of Ideas*, LII, no. 2 (1991), pp. 221–244.

[34] Barducci, note 32 above, pp. 268–269.

THE ILLUSTRIOUS
HUGO GROTIUS
OF THE LAW OF
WARRE
AND
PEACE
WITH
ANNOTATIONS.
III. PARTS.
AND
Memorials of the Author's Life and Death.

Tranflated by *C. B.* Mafter of Arts.

Ὁ ἀδικῶν ἀσεβεῖ. M. Antonin. Imp. l. 9.

LONDON,
Printed by *T. Warren*, for *William Lee*, And are to be fold at his fhop, at the figne of the *Turks-head* in *Fleet-ftreet*, M. DC. LV.

TO THE

ENGLISH GENTRY,

WITH ALL

DUE HONOUR

TO THEIR

WISEDOM

AND

VALOUR,

THIS WORK IS

HUMBLY DEDICATED

BY THEIR SERVANT

THE TRANSLATOR.

TO THE READER.

THat This Book may obtein General Acceptance, I have somewhat to say to every sort of Readers. The Divine *shall here behold the* Evangelical Law *shining above all other in the perfect Glory of Charity and Meekness. The* Gentlemen *of our Noble Innes of Court shal here read the most* Common Law, *that of Nature and Nations. The* Civilian *may here observe some footsteps of the* Goodly Body *of his Law.* (*To the* Statesman *and the* Soldier *'twill be enough to see the Title*, *Of* War *and* Peace.) *The* Philosopher, *the* Poet, *the* Orator, *and* Historian, *shall here meet with the choicest Flowers gathered out of their spatious Gardens by a most skilful hand, the hand of Him that was excellent in all these kinds of good Learning, the Incomparable* HUGO GROTIUS. *This Great Name, as well as the* Usefulness *of the Argument*,

ment, we hope, will commend the Book to every Ingenuous Reader; to whose candid Cenſure *it is in all humility ſubmitted by*

C. B.

The

The Author's Dedication to the most Christian KING.

THis Book, Most Eminent of Kings, is bold to bear Your Royal Name in the Front, in Confidence, not of It self, not of the Author, but of the Argument. Because it is written for Justice. Which Vertue is so properly Yours, that, by your own Merits, and by the Suffrage of Mankind, You have thence received a Title most worthy of so Great a King: being known every where now, no less by the Name of JUST, than of LUDOVIC. The *Roman* Commanders esteemed the Titles very specious, which were deriv'd from *Crete*, *Numidia*, *Afric*, *Asia*, and

and other conquer'd Nations: How much more Illustrious is Yours, whereby you are declared both the Enemy every where, and all ways the Conquerour (of no people, of no man, but) of that which is Unjust? The *Egyptian* Kings thought it a great matter, if One were called the Lover of his Father, Another of his Mother, a Third of his Brother: How small parts are These of Your Name, which comprehendeth not only those things, but whatsoever can be imagined fair and honorable? You are Just, when, by Imitation of Him, you honour the Memory of your Father, a King Great, above all that can be said; Just, when you instruct your Brother every way, but no way more than by your

your example; Juſt, when you grace your Siſters with Higheſt Matches; Juſt, when you revive the Laws almoſt buried, and, as much as you can, oppoſe your ſelf againſt the declining Age: Juſt, but withal Clement, when you take away nothing from your ſubjects (whom Ignorance of your goodneſs had tranſported beyond the limits of their Duty) beſide the licence to offend; and offer no Violence to Souls of a different perſwaſion in matter of Religion: Juſt, and withall Merciful, when, by your Authority you relieve oppreſſed Nations, afflicted Princes, neither permit Fortune to be too inſolent. Which ſingular Beneficence of yours, and as neer like to God, as human Nature ſuffers, compells me, on my own behalf

behalf alſo, to make this pub-
lick thankfull Acknowledg-
ment. For, as the Heavenly Stars do not only communicate their Influence to the greater parts of the world, but vouchſafe it to every living Creature; So you, being the moſt beneficent Star on earth, not content to raiſe up Princes, to eaſe people, have been pleaſed to be a ſafeguard, and a Comfort, even to me, ill uſed in my own Country. Here is to be added, to fill up the Orb of Juſtice, after your publick Actions, the Innocency and Purity of Your private life, worthy to be admir'd, not by Men alone, but by the Angels too. For, how Few of the Inferiour ſort, yea of thoſe that have ſecluded themſelves from the Fellowſhip of the world, keep themſelves

themselves so untoucht by all faults, as You, being placed in such a Fortune, which is surrounded with innumerable allurements to sin? And how Admirable a Thing is This, among Business, in the Throng, in the Court, among so many Examples of Those that sin so many ways, to attain unto that, which solitude scarce, yea often not at all, affordeth others? This is indeed, to merit, even in this life, not only the name of JUST, but of **SAINT**, which was given by the consent of pious men, to *Charles the Great* & *Ludovic* your Ancestors, after their Death; that is, to be, not by a Gentilitious, but by your own proper right, *Most Christian*. Now, as every part of Justice is Yours, so is that which concerns

cerns the Matter of this Book, about the Counsells of War and Peace, yours peculiarly, as you are a King, and King of *France*: This your Kingdom is great, which ſtretcheth it ſelf to both Seas, through ſo many ſpaces of ſo happy Lands: but it is a greater Kingdom than This, that You do not covet other Kingdoms. This is worthy of Your Piety, worthy of that eminency, not to Invade the Right of any Other by your Arms, not to remove antient Bounds; but to do the Buſineſs of Peace in the time of War; neither to begin War, but with this Deſire, to bring it to a ſpeedy end. And, How Brave, How Glorious is This, How Joyful to Your conſcience, that, when God ſhal call you up to His Kingdom, which alone

alone is better than yours, you may confidently ſay, *This ſword have I receiv'd from Thee, for the ſafeguard of Juſtice; This I render to Thee pure and unſtained with the blood of any man, raſhly ſhed?* Thus it ſhall come to paſs, that the rules we now look for in books, hereafter may be taken from Your actions, as from a moſt perfect Exemplar. It is a very great matter, This; Yet doth the world of Chriſtians dare to exact ſomething more at Your Hands; Namely, that, the Flames of War being every where extinguiſhed, not only Empires, but Churches may ſee their Peace returning to them by Your procurement: and, that Our Age may learn to ſubmit to the Judgment of That Age, which All Chriſtians profeſs to have

been

been truly & sincerely Christian. The minds of Good men, weary of Discords, are raised to this Hope by the Friendship newly made 'twixt you & the *King of Great Britain* (a most wise Prince, & exceedingly studious of that Holy Peace) and confirmed by the most Auspicious Marriage of your Sister. Difficult is the Business, by reason of Partial Affections, inflamed and exasperated more and more: but Nothing is worthy of so excellent Kings, but That which is Difficult, but That which is Despaird of by all others, The God of Peace, the God of Justice, O Just & peaceable King, Crown your Majesty (neerest to His) as with all other happiness, so with this also, the procuring of a Just & Universal Peace. 1625.

THE PREFACE OF THE AUTHOR.

THE Civil Law, whether Roman, or that which is proper to any other Countrey, many Writers have attempted either to illustrate with Commentaries, or in a more compendious way to propose unto their Readers: But, that Law which is between many Nations, or their Rulers, whether proceeding from Nature it ſelf, or conſtituted by divine precepts, or introduced by cuſtoms and tacit agreement, Few have touched, None have hitherto

* handled

handled universally, and in a certain order: when yet the Doing hereof is of much Concernment to Mankind. For, *Cicero* truly call'd this an excellent Science, in Leagues, Covenants, and Agreements of several people, Kings and forein Nations, and in all Rights of War and Peace. *Euripides* also † prefers this science before the knowledge of divine and humane things. 1. This Work is the more necessary, because, both in our age there are, and in former times there have been some, who so contemned this part of Right and Law, as if it were onely an empty word, and had no real existence. That saying of *Euphemus* in *Thucydides*, is almost in all mens mouths, * *That nothing is unjust, which is profitable to a King or Common-wealth having power.* Whereto that is like, *In the highest Fortune that is more right, which is more prevalent.* And, *A Common-*

† Sic enim Theoclymenem compellari facit: *Nam turpe id esset, cum scias hominum ac Deûm Quod est eritque, justa te haud cognoscere.*

* Thucyd. l. 6. οὐδὲν ἄλογον ὅ, τι ξυμφέρον. Likewise, in the first Book, the Athenians being at that time in their pride, say thus to the Melians: Humane reason judgeth those things just which are necessary; and things possible to be done, are done by the mighty, and suffered by the weak.

wealth

wealth cannot be govern'd without injury. Adde hereunto, that Controversies arising between Nations or Kings, commonly have no arbitration, but are determined by force. Now, this is not onely the opinion of the Vulgar, that War is very far distant from all right and equity, but even learned and prudent men do often let fall words favourable to that opinion. For nothing is more frequent than Right † and Arms opposed one to another. Old *Antigonus* derided one that presented to him a Commentary of Justice, when he was assaulting Cities. And *Marius* said, *He could not hear † the Laws for the clashing of Armour.* That very *Pompey*, of so bashfull a Countenance, was bold to say, *What? would you have me*

† Ennius: *Non ex jure manu consertum, sed magè ferro Rem repetunt.* Horatius de Achille: *Jura negat sibi nata, nihil non arrogat armis.* Alius de alio: *Hic pacē temerataq; jura relinquo.*

† In *Plutarch*, *Lysander* shewing his sword, saith: He that hath this in his hand, best disputes of the bounds of his dominion. And *Cæsar* in the same Author: Laws have no place in the time of war. And *Seneca* saith, Princes, in war especially, give with their eyes shut; One man cannot satisfie so many armed lusts: nor can he at the same time act the good Man and the good General. *De ben. lib.* 4. *c.* 38.

think on Laws, now I am armed† In Christian Writers many sayings of the like sense occur: One of *Tertullians* may suffice instead of all: *Deceit, rigour, injustice, are the proper businesses of wars.* All that are of this mind, will (no doubt) object against us that in the Comedy*: *These uncertain things, if you seek to order by certain Reason, you do but endeavour to be mad with Reason.* Wherefore, seeing in vain is any Disputation of Right, if there be no such thing, it will pertain to the commendation and defence of our work, that this very great Errour should briefly be refelled.

Now, that we may not have to do with the Multitude, let us allow them an Advocate: and whom rather than *Carneades*, who had attained to that, which was the height of his Academy, that he could put forth the strength of his Eloquence for Errour no less than Truth. He there-

† *Plutarch* relates this saying of *Pompey* to the *Mamertines*, thus: *Will you never leave prating of the Laws to us that wear Sword?* Curtius, lib. 9. *So, doth war overthrow even the Laws of Nature.*

* Terent. *Incerta hæc, si tu postules Ratione certa facere, nihilo plus agas, Quam si des operam, ut cum ratione insanias.*

therefore, when he had undertaken to oppose Justice, that especially of which we treat, found no stronger Argument than this: *That Men had established for themselves various Laws (with respect to their Utility) according to their Customs; and among the same Men often changed with the times: That there is no natural Right or Law; But, that all Men, and other living Creatures, are carried by the guidance of Nature to things profitable for them: Wherefore, there is no Justice; or, if there be any, it is extreme Folly, because it hurteth it self, taking care for the benefit of others.*

But, what the Philosopher saith here, and the Poet followeth*, *That Nature cannot make any difference 'twixt right and wrong*, must not be admitted. For, Man indeed is an Animal, but excelling all the rest, and differing farther from them, than they do from one another: Which is confirmed by many Actions proper to Mankind. And, among these things that are proper to Man, is the Appetite of

* *Nec natura potest justo secernere iniquum.*

Society, that is, of Community, not of any sort, but Quiet, and (according to the measure of his understanding) Orderly, with those of his own kind: which the Stoicks call'd οἰκείωσιν †. What is objected then, that every living Creature is by nature carried onely to its own profit, so universally taken, ought not to be granted. For, even some of the meer Animals, in some sort, restrain * the desire of their own profit, with a respect, partly of their Issue, partly of others of their own kind. Which, in them truly, we think proceeds from some external intelligent principle; because, in other actions not more difficult than the former, they do not discover such intelligence in themselves. And the same is to be said of Infants: in whom, before all Discipline, there shews it self a certain propension to

† *Chrysostom* on the *Rom. Hom.* 30. saith, *We men have by nature society with men. What else? when even the Beasts have so too.* See the same Father in the 1. Ch. to the *Eph.* where he shews, that *we have given unto us by nature, the seeds of virtues.* *Marc. Antoninus.* That Philosopher in the Throne: *It hath appeared, that we are born for Society. Is it not plain, wo sir things are ordained for the Better, and the better for one another?*

* It is an old Proverb, *A Dog eats no Dogs-flesh.* Juven. *Tigris agit rabida cum Tigride pacem: Parcit cognatis maculis fera.* Philo hath an excellent passage upon the fift Command; *Be you Men imitators of the mute Creatures. They are taught to requite benefits, &c.* See *Porphyry* (*de non esu animal.* 3.) of the exceeding care of Doves about their young ones.

do

do good to others, prudently obſerv'd by *Plutarch:* as alſo, in that Age Compaſſion breaketh forth of its own accord. But, in a Man of perfect Age, knowing to do like things in the like manner, with an exceeding appetite † of Society, having Speech, the peculiar inſtrument thereof, as his priviledge above all other Creatures, we muſt conceive there is an Ability of Underſtanding and Working, according to general precepts; and the things agreeable thereto, belong not now to all living Creatures, but are peculiar to humane nature. Now, this cuſtody * of Society (which we have thus rudely expreſſed) convenient to humane Underſtanding, is the fountain of that Law, which is properly called by ſuch a name: to which pertains Abſtinence from that which

† *Mar. Antonin. l. 9.* ὁ ἄνθρωπος κοινωνικὸς πέφυκε. And he ſaith, *One may more eaſily find a thing of an earthly nature not inclining to the earth, than a man ſeparating from Mankind.* *Adde* Auguſt. de doct. Chriſt. l. 3. c. 14.

* *Nam quo alio tuti ſumus, quam quod mutuis juvamur officiis? hoc uno inſtructior vita, contraque incurſiones ſubitas mutitior eſt, beneficiorum commercio. Fac nos ſingulos, quid ſumus? præda animalium & victimæ, ac viliſſimus & facillimus ſanguis. quoniam cæteris animalibus in tutelam ſui ſatis virium eſt. quæcunque vaga naſcuntur, & actura vitam ſegregem, armata ſunt: hominem imbecillitas cingit: non unguium vis, non dentium, terribilem cæteris fecit. duas res dedit, quæ illum obnoxium cæteris validiſſimum facerent, rationem & ſecietatem. It que qui par eſſe nulli poſſet ſi diduceretur; rerum potitur, &c.* Seneca 4. de benefic. c. 18.

is Anothers; and if we have any thing of that ſort, or have gained by it, Reſtitution; Obligation to fulfill promiſes; Reparation of Damage unjuſtly done, and the Merit of Puniſhment amongſt Men.

From this ſignification of Law is derived another more large: for, becauſe Man above other Animals, hath not onely that ſocial virtue which we mention'd, but alſo judgement to diſcern what things delight or hurt, not preſent onely, but future; and what things can lead to either; it is convenient to humane nature, according to the meaſure of humane underſtanding, in theſe things alſo to follow a rectified judgement, and neither to be corrupted with fear, or the allurement of preſent pleaſure, nor to be tranſported with any impetuous raſhneſs: And that, which is plainly repugnant to ſuch a judgement, is alſo conceiv'd to be againſt the Law of Nature, to wit, humane.

What we have now ſaid, would have ſome place, though we ſhould grant, which cannot be granted

without

without the higheſt ſin, *That there is no God:* or, *That he hath no Care of humane Affairs:* the contrary whereof being implanted in us, partly by Reaſon, partly by perpetual Tradition, and confirmed by many Arguments and Miracles teſtified in all Ages, it follows, that we muſt without exception obey God, as our Maker, to whom we owe our ſelves, and all we have: eſpecially, ſeeing he hath many waies declared his infinite Goodneſs and Power; So that, he is able to give unto thoſe that obey him greateſt Rewards, and eternal, being himſelf eternal; and may be believed willing; and much the more, if he hath expreſly promis'd it: Which we Chriſtians, convinced by undoubted teſtimonies, do believe. This is now another fountain of Law, beſide that natural, coming from the free will of God *, to which, that we ought to be ſubject, our own underſtanding doth irrefragably dictate to us.

* Inde M. Antonino judice, lib. 9. ὁ ἀδικῶν ἀσεβεῖ. *He that is unjuſt, is irreligious*, in the judgement of that Philoſophick Emperour.

Moreover, that natural Law of which we have ſpoken, (whether it

be

be the Social, or that which is more largely so called) though it proceedeth from principles internal to man, yet it may deservedly be ascrib'd to God *, because it was his will that such principles should be in us: in which sense *Chrysippus* and the Stoicks said, *The Original of Law came from no other Head but* Jupiter †. Adde, that God, by Laws given, hath made the said principles more conspicuous, even to men of Weaker minds: and those *impetus* and passions regarding our selves and others, and drawing us several ways, He hath forbid to wander, regulating their vehemency, and keeping them in compass. And the sacred Historie, besides that which consists in precepts, doth not a little excite that social affection, by shewing that all men are descended from the same first Parents: so that, in this sense may be rightly said what *Florentinus* said in another, *Nature hath made us all Kinsmen*: Whence it follows, that 'tis impiety for one man to be treacherous to another *. Among men, Parents are as it were

* Chrysost. 1. ad Cor. 11. 3. *Cum naturam dico, Deum dico; ipse enim est naturæ opifex.*

† Jus à Jovis *nomine dictum, nisi forte veriùs per abscissionem, ut ex* ossum os, *ita ex* jussum, jus, jusis, *postea* juris, *ut ex* papisio, Papirii. *de quo vide* Cic. l.9. epist. 21. Chrysip. 3. de Diis: *Non potest inveniri principium aliud aut origo justitiæ, quàm ab Jove & communi natura. Inde enim initium duci debet, ubi de bonis malisq; disserendum est.*

* Leg. ut vim. D. de just. & ju.

were Gods †; to whom therefore, not an infinite, but a peculiar obſervance is due.

And further, being it is a point of the Law of Nature, *to ſtand to Covenants*, (for ſome way of binding themſelves was neceſſary among men, nor can any other natural way be imagined) from this very fountain *Civil Laws* have flowed. For, they that had joyned themſelves to any Aſſembly, or ſubjected themſelves to Man or Men, had either *expreſly* promis'd, or by the nature of the buſineſs ought to be underſtood to have promis'd *tacitly*, That they would follow what either the major part of the Aſſembly, or Thoſe to whom power was given, had conſtituted. Wherefore, what *Carneades* and others ſay *, *That Utility is even the Mother of Juſtice and Equity*, if we ſpeak accurately, is not true. For the mother of *Natural Law* is humane nature it ſelf,

† Θεοὶ ἐπίγειοι. Hier. ἐμφανεῖς Θεοί. Phil. *Secunda poſt Deum federatio.* Hieron. *Deorum ſimulacra.* Pla. *Honos parentibus ut diis debetur.* Ariſt.

* *utilitas juſti propè mater & æqui.* Ad quem locum Acron, aut quiſquis eſt vetus Horatii interpres: *Repugnat præceptis Stoicorum. oſtendere vult juſtitiam non eſſe naturalem, ſed natam ex utilitate.* Contra hanc ſententiam, vide quæ diſputat Auguſtinus, de doct. Chriſt. l. 3. c. 14.

which

which would carry us to a desire of mutual society, though we wanted nothing: but the mother of *Civil Law* is the very obligation by consent, which having its vertue from the Natural Law, Nature may be call'd the Grandmother of this Law also. But to *Natural Law* Utility is added: for the Author of Nature was pleased we should be weak *singly*, and stand in need of many things usefull to our life, that we might the more vigorously embrace Society: To the *Civil Law*, Utility gave occasion: for that consociation or subjection aforesaid, began to be ordained for some Utilities sake. And they that prescribe Laws to others, are wont, or ought, to respect some Utility therein.

But, as the Laws of every Common wealth respect the interest and profit of the same; so, between Common-wealths, either all, or most, some Laws may have arisen from Consent, (and it appears they have arisen) which might respect the Interest, not of several Societies, but of the Whole. And this is that which

which is call'd the *Law of Nations*, as oft as that name is diſtinguiſht from Natural Law. Which kind of Law *Carneades* omitted, diſtributing all Law into Natural Law, and the Civil Law of ſingle Nations: when yet, being to treat of that Law which is common to Nations one with another (for he added a diſcourſe of War, and things got by War) he ought by all means to have mentioned the ſame.

And it is another errour of *Carneades*, to traduce *Juſtice* by the name of *Folly*. For, as by his own confeſſion, the Citizen is not a fool, who follows the Civil Law in the Common-wealth, though for his reverence unto it he muſt omit ſome things profitable to himſelf: So, neither is that people fooliſh, that value not ſo much their own Intereſt, as to neglect therefore the Common Law of Nations. The reaſon is the ſame in both. For, as a Citizen †, who breaks the Civil

† *Antoninus* uſeth this ſimilitude appoſitely, lib. 9. *whatſoever action of thine hath not reſpect, either near or remote, to the Common Good, it makes a breach, and is againſt the peace, and ſeditious, like him that ſeparates himſelf from the people.* And as the ſame *Antoninus* ſaith, *what is good for the Hive, is good for the Bee.*

Law

Law for his present Commodity, breaks that wherein his own and his posterities perpetual benefit is contain'd: Even so a people violating the Laws of Nature and Nations, destroy the muniments of their own Tranquillity for the future.

Again, though no profit were expected out of the observation of Law, yet were it a point of Wisdome, not of Folly, to be carried unto that, to which we feel our selves directed and enclined by our nature. Wherefore, neither is that * which one hath in *Plato*, *Laws were found out through fear of receiving injury*, *and Men are forcibly drawn to advance justice*, universally true. For that pertains onely to those Institutes and Laws, which are invented for the more facile execution of Law: as, Many weak of themselves, that they might not be opprest of the stronger, conspir'd to institute, and by united force to maintain Courts of Justice, that all together might prevail against those they could not match single. And in this sense may that Saying be well taken,

* *Jura inventa metu injusti fateare necesse est.*

taken, *Law is that which pleaseth the Stronger*, conceiving Law to want its external end, unless it have Force to back it: as *Solon* did very great matters, **joyning Might and Right together*, as he said himself. Yet doth not Law, though destitute of Force, want Effect altogether; for Justice brings security to the Conscience, Injustice torments and tearings, such as *Plato* describes in the breasts of Tyrants. Besides, the consent of honest man approves of Justice, condemns Injustice. And, which is the greatest of all, this hath God for an Enemy, that for a Friend; who doth so reserve his judgements after this life, that he often too represents the power of them even in this life, as Histories do shew by many examples.

* ὁμοῦ βίην τε καὶ δίκην συναρμόσας.
Ovidius: *Valet causâ, causamq; tuentibus armis.*

Now, whereas Many require not that justice in a State or Governour, which they exact of private Men; the Cause of that errour is, first, in that they consider nothing in the Law, but the Profit arising thence: Which is evident in single Citizens, unable to defend themselves; but great

great Cities and States, ſeeming to contain all things in themſelves, which are needfull for the well ſupporting of life, ſeem not to have need of that virtue that looks abroad, and is called Juſtice. But (not to repeat what was ſaid, that Law was not onely provided for profits ſake) there is no Commonwealth ſo ſtrong, that may not ſometime ſtand in need of help from without; either for commerce, or alſo for repelling the Forces of many forein Nations united together againſt it: Whence we ſee the moſt potent States and Kings have deſired Leagues, all virtue whereof is taken away by thoſe that confine Law within the bounds of a City. It is moſt true, * *Take away Law, and all things are uncertain.* If there be no Community that can be conſerved without Law, (which *Ariſtotle* proved by a memorable example of Thieves †) certainly that

* *Omnia ſunt incerta, cum à jure diſceſſum eſt.* Cic. ep. 11.16. *Plutarch* blames that ſaying of *Pyrrhus*, That he ſhould be his Heir who had the ſharpeſt ſword, as a bloody ſpeech, adding, *So unſociable and ſavage is Ambition.* † *Thieves, if they be not true to one another* (ſaith *Polybius*, 4.) *and do not keep a Law among themſelves, cannot ſubſiſt.*

which

which binds Mankind and many Nations together, hath need of Law: as he perceiv'd who said, *Unhonest things are not to be done, no not for ones Countrey*. Greatly doth *Aristotle* * accuse them, who, when they would have no man govern among themselves, but he that hath right, have no regard of right or wrong toward Foreiners. That same *Pompey*, whom we named afore on the other part, corrected this Speech of a *Spartan* King, *That Commonwealth is most happy, whose bounds are terminated by the Spear and Sword*, saying, *That's truly blessed, which hath Justice for its bounds*: to which purpose he might have used the authority of another *Spartan* King, who preferred Justice before Military Valour †, upon this ground; because Valour must be govern'd by Justice; but if all men were just, there would be no need of Valour. Valour it self is defined by the Stoicks to be a virtue fighting for equity. *Themistius* elegantly shews, that Kings, such as the rule of Wisdome re-

* *Plutarch* in his *Agesilaus*, saith, *The Lacedemonians know no honesty but profit, nor law but that which makes for the advantage of* Sparta. The *Athenians* in *Thucydides*, *l.* 5. say of the same, *That they are civil to one another; but, in respect of others, that seems honest, which is pleasant; just, which is profitable.*

† *Agesilaus*, when he heard the *Persian* King stiled *Great*, *How*, saith he, *is he* Greater *than I am, unless he be* Juster?

requires, have not a tender eye onely to one Nation committed to their trust, but to all mankind, being, as he speaks, not * *Lovers of Macedonians*; or * *Lovers of Romans*, but * *Lovers of Men* †. * *Minos* his name was hated among Posterity, because he restrained equity to the bounds of his Empire.

* φιλομακεδόνες.
* φιλορρώμαιοι.
* φιλάνθρωποι.
†. Excellently *Antoninus*: *as I am* Antoninus, Rome *is my Country*; *as I am a Man*, *the world*.

But (so far is it from Truth, which some imagine, that all Laws cease in War) *War* ought neither to be undertaken, but for the obtaining of right, nor to be waged, being undertaken, but within the limits of Justice and Faith. Well said *Demosthenes*, War is against them, who cannot be ruled by Judgements; for Judgements prevail upon them, who feel themselves weaker: but against them, who make or think themselves equal, Arms are taken up, which truly, that they may be right, are to be exercised with no less religion, than Judgements are wont to be exercised. Let the Laws then be silent among Arms, that is, those *Civil Judiciary Laws* which are proper

* Vide Cyrillum adversus Julianum, l.6.

proper to peace, not those other Laws that are *perpetual*, and accommodate to all times. For it was excellently said by *Dion Prusæensis*, *Written Laws indeed, that is, the Civil, prevail not among Enemies, but the not-written Laws prevail* †, *that is, those that are dictated by Nature, and established by the Consent of Nations.* This appears by that old *Formula* of the *Romans*, *I judge those things are to be requir'd by a pure and pious War* *. The same antient *Romans*, as *Varro* noted, undertook Wars slowly, not licentiously, because they thought none but a pious War was to be waged. *Camillus* said, *Wars are to be waged justly, as well as valiantly*. Africanus: *That the People of* Rome *did both undertake Wars, and finish them with Justice.* In another you may read, *There are Laws of War also, as of Peace.* Another admires *Fabricius, a brave man, and (which is a rare thing) innocent in War, and one that believ'd an Enemy might be wrong'd.* What power the Conscience

† K. *Alfonsus* being asked, Whether he owed more to Books, or Arms, said, *He had learned out of Books, both Arms, and the Laws of Arms.* Plutarch saith, *There are among good men some Laws also of Arms: Nor is Victory so to be pursued, as not to refuse profit arising out of unjust and impious actions.*

* *Eas res puro pioque duello quærendas censeo.*

ſcience of Juſtice † hath in Wars, Hiſtorians frequently demonſtrate, often aſcribing Victory to this cauſe eſpecially. Thence thoſe common Sentences: *The Hearts of Souldiers riſe or fall at conſideration of the Cauſe: He ſeldome returns in ſafety, that fights unjuſtly: Hope waits upon a good Cauſe,* and the like. Nor ought any to be moved at the proſperous Succeſſes of unjuſt Attempts. For 'tis ſufficient, that the Equity of the Cauſe hath a certain peculiar, and that a great influence upon the Action, though that influence (as it hap-

† Benè apud Appianum Pompeius: *Conſidere oportet diis, & cauſæ belli, honeſto juſtoq; ſuſcepti ſtudio, ad tuendum patriæ ſtatum.* Caſſius apud eundem: *In bellis ſpes optima, & cauſæ jus.* Joſephus 15. antiquæ hiſtoriæ: *Abs quo ſtat jus, ab eo Deus.* Beliſarius apud Procopium: *Victoriam fortitudo datura non eſt, niſi juſtitiam habeat commilitem.* In Langobardorum ſermone ad Herulos, ſunt hæc, ſed correcta à nobis: *Teſtamur Deum; cujus potentiæ vel minima particula omnem humanam vim æquiparat; is, ut credibile eſt, belli cauſas intuens, dabit debitum utrisque prælii exitum:* quod dictum eventus mox admirabilis comprobat. Sic & apud eundem Procopium ad Gotthos Totilas: *Fieri nequit, Nequit (inquam) fieri, ut qui violentia & injuſtitia utitur, decus pugnando pariat; ſed prout vita cuique eſt, ita ei obtingit belli fortuna. Procopius* hath many paſſages to the ſame effect. And *Agathias, l. 2.* ſaith, *Injuſtice and neglect of God are to be eſchewed alwaies as hurtfull, but then moſt of all, when men go forth to Battel.* Which he proves in another place by the illuſtrious examples of *Darius*, *Xerxes*, and the *Athenians* in *Sicily. In* Thucydides, l.7. *The* Lacedemonians *confeſs they were juſtly overthrown for refuſing to ſubmit their quarrel to judgement; and renewed their hopes of better ſucceſs, when they ſaw the* Athenians *refuſed judgement after they had done many wicked acts.*

pens

pens in humane affairs) is oft hindred in its efficacy by the intervention and oppoſition of other cauſes. Alſo, for the procuring of Friends, which, as particular perſons, ſo States have need of to many purpoſes, much avails an Opinion and Fame of War not unwiſely nor unjuſtly undertaken, and piouſly managed. For, no man is deſirous to joyn himſelf, to ſuch, whom he ſuppoſeth to hold juſtice, piety, and faith in vile eſteem.

When, upon the grounds and reaſons aforeſaid, I ſaw moſt clearly, that there is among Nations a *Common Law*, which availeth both to Wars, and in Wars, I had many and weighty *cauſes to write* thereof. I ſaw, through the Chriſtian world, ſuch licence of going to War, as even barbarous Nations may be aſhamed of; that men take Arms greedily for light cauſes, or none at all: which being once put on, all reverence of divine and humane Right is put off, even as if the Furies had commiſſion given them to work all kind of mischief. In contemplation of which immanity, many good Men have gone so far, as to deny all Arms * to a Christian, whose Religion consisteth chiefly in Charity toward all the world: in which opinion seems to be sometimes, both *Johannes Ferus*, and my Countryman *Erasmus*, great Lovers of Peace both Ecclesiastical and Civil; but with that intent, as I suppose, wherewith we are wont to bend what is crooked to the other side, that it may return into straitness. Yet indeed, this endeavour of too much contradiction, is often times so far from being profitable, that it hurts, because it is easily found, that excess in some sayings takes away authority for other, even when they stand within the limits of truth. Wherefore both Parties had need of a Moderator, that it might appear, *Neither nothing, nor every thing is lawfull.*

* Tertullian. de resurrect. carnis: *Gladius benè de bello cruentus, & melior homicida.*

And withall, my Design was, by my private study and diligence, to advance the profession of the Laws, which

which heretofore in publick Offices I had exercised with as much integrity as I could: This comfort of my studies was left me, after I was unworthily cast out of my own Countrey, honour'd by so many Labours of mine. Many, before me, have purposed to bring this into a form of Art, but no man hath done it perfectly: Nor is it possible, unless (which hitherto hath not been done with care enough) the things which are by Constitution be rightly separated from Natural. For, Naturals, because they are alwaies the same, may easily be collected into Art: but the things that come from Constitution, because they are often changed, and are divers in divers places, are put without Art, as other precepts of singular things. Nevertheless, if the Priests of true Justice would undertake to handle the parts of natural and perpetual Jurisprudence (laying aside what hath its original from free will,) One of Laws, another of Tributes, another of the Judges Office, another of the conjecture of Wills, another of proving Facts, thereupon might be composed a Body of all parts collected. What course we thought fit to take, we have shewed in deed, rather than words: this work, containing that part of Juris-prudence, which is by far most noble. For in the *first Book*, having first spoken of the Original of Right and Law, we have examined that question, Whether any War be just and lawfull. After, to know the difference 'twixt publick and private War, we had to explain the nature of the Supreme Power; what States and Kings have it full, what in part; what with right of alienation, what otherwise. Last of all, we had to speak of the duty of Subjects towards their Superiours. The *second Book* expounds what are the Causes whence War may rise: And there we speak of Community and Propriety, Leagues, Oaths, Embassages, Punishments, &c. The *third Book* having expounded what is lawfull in the time of War, and distinguished

guiſhed what is done without fault, from what is done without puniſhment, ends with Arguments and Peace.

Now this Argument ſeemed the more worthy of our pains, becauſe, as I have ſaid, no man hath handled the whole; and, they that have handled the parts, have ſo handled them, that they have left much for anothers Induſtry. The old Philoſophers have nothing extant in this kind, neither the Greeks, among whom *Ariſtotle* made a Book, entituled, δικαιώματα πολέμων, nor They that gave their name to new Chriſtianiſm (which was much to be wiſhed:) And the Books of the old *Romans, De jure Feciali*, have tranſmitted to us nothing of themſelves, but the Title. I have ſeen alſo ſpecial Books *De Jure Belli*, partly by Divines, *viz. Franciſcus Victoria*, *Henricus Gorichemus*, *Wilhelmus Matthæi* *; partly by Doctors of Law, *viz. Jannes Lupus*, *Franciſcus Arius*, *Joannes de Lignano*, *Martinus Laudenſis*: But all theſe have

* Add to theſe *Joannes de Carthagena*, ſet forth at *Rome*, *An.* 1609.

perceived by our outward senses: which, if the organs be well formed, and other necessaries be present, do not deceive. Therefore *Euripides* in his *Phænissæ* makes *Polynice*, whose cause he will have to be manifestly just, speak thus:

* *Hæc sum profatus, mater, haud ambagibus*
Implicita, sed quæ regulis æqui & boni
Suffulta, rudibus pariter & doctis patent.

* *'Tis plain, and grounded on good right,*
*To th' * rude and learned clear as light.*

* Idem Euripides Andromachen Hermione dicenti: *Non barbarorum more in urbe hac vivitur*: respondentem facit: *Quæ turpia illis, hic quoque haut culpâ vacant.*

And presently he adds the judgement of the *Chorus* (which consisteth of Women, and those *Barbarians*) in approbation of her speech.

I have also used to the proof of this Law, the testimonies of *Philosophers* *, *Historians*, *Poets*, and lastly, *Oratours*: not that we must give credit to them without difference; for they are wont to serve their Sect, Argument, Cause; but that, where many in divers times and

* What else? when *Alexander Severus* continually read *Cicero's* Books, *De Rep.* & *De Officiis*.

and places affirm the ſame thing for certain, it ought to be referr'd to an univerſal Cauſe: which, in our queſtions, can be no other, than either right Illation proceeding from the principles of Nature, or ſome Common Conſent. That ſhews the Law of Nature, This the Law of Nations. The Difference of which Laws is to be conceived, not from the teſtimonies themſelves (for Writers do commonly uſe the words, *Law of Nature and of Nations*, promiſcuouſly:) but from the quality of the Matter. For, that which cannot, by ſure conſequence, be deduced out of ſure principles, and yet appears every where obſerved, muſt needs have its riſe from free will and conſent. Theſe two therefore, I have ſtill been very carefull to diſcern one from the other, and both from the Civil Law. Yea, in the Law of Nations alſo, I have diſtinguiſht what is truly and in every reſpect Right, and what onely brings forth a certain external effect, like unto that Primitive Right, *viz.* that

that it may not be refifted; or alfo, that every where, for fome Commodities fake, or the avoyding of great incommodities, it muft be defended. Which obfervation, how neceffary 'tis to many things, will appear in the contexture of the Work it felf.

Among Philofophers, *Ariftotle* defervedly obtains the principal place, whether you confider the order of his difcourfing, or the acuteneſs of his diftinguifhing, or the weight of his Reafons. Only I wifh, that Principality had not, for fome Ages, gone into Tyrannie; fo that Truth, to which *Ariftotle* was a faithfull fervant, is oppreft by nothing more, than by the name of *Ariftotle*. For my part, both here and elfwhere, I imitate the liberty of the Antient Chriftians, who were fworn to no Philofophers fect: not, that they did affent to them, who faid, *Nothing could be known*, than which nothing is more foolifh; but, that they judged no fect had feen all Truth, and not any but had fome.

Wherefore,

Wherefore, to gather up Truth dispersed among them all, and diffused into Sects, into a Body, This they thought was indeed to deliver Christian Institutions *. Our purpose is to magnifie *Aristotle*, but with that liberty, which He, in love of Truth, indulged to himself towards his own Masters. Histories have a two-fold use, as to our Argument: For they supply us with Examples, and with Sentences. The Examples have so much the more authority, as the times and Nations are more virtuous: therefore we have preferred the old Greek and Roman above the rest. Nor are the Sentences or Judgements of Historians to be contemned, especially when they are agreeing: for the Law of Nature, as we have said, is in some sort proved thence; and the Law of Nations cannot be proved otherwise. Sentences of the Poets and Orators have not so much solidity: and we

* Lactant. Instit. l. 6. c. 9. *Justin* in his former Apolog. saith, *The doctrins of* Plato *are not altogether different from those of Christ, nor altogether the same.* And so of the rest. *For every one saw and expressed in part what was planted in him by reason.* *Tertullian* cals *Seneca* *often, ours*: but saith, *the university of spiritual documents, no man ever had besides Christ.* Augustin. epist 202. *The good Manners, which* Cicero *and other Philosophers commend, are taught and learnt in Churches all the world over.* See the same *Austin* of the Platonists, *who, he saith, a few things being changed, are Christians.* epist. 56. & de vera relig. c. 3. & Confess. l. 7. c. 9. & l. 8. c. 2.

use

use them oft, not so much for proof as ornament.

I do often use the Authority of the Books either written or approved by Men inspir'd of God, making a difference 'twixt the old Law and the new. Some do urge the *Old Law* for the very Law of Nature: erroneously, no doubt: for many things in that proceed from the free will and pleasure of God, which yet never is contrary to the true Law of Nature: and so far is an argument rightly drawn thence, while we distinguish accurately the Right of God which God sometimes executes by Men, and the Right of Men among themselves. We have therefore, to our power, avoyded both this errour, and another opposite to it, that thinks there is no use of the Old Covenant, since the times of the New. Our judgement is otherwise, both upon that ground now mentioned, and because such is the nature of the *New Covenant*, that the things pertaining to virtue and good manners, commanded in the

Old,

Old, the ſame, or greater, are commanded in the New: And we ſee the Antient Christian Writers have uſed the teſtimonies of the old Covenant in the ſame way. But, to underſtand the meaning of the Books belonging to the Old Covenant, no little light may be borrowed from the *Hebrew Writers* *; thoſe eſpecially who throughly knew the Languages and the Manners of their own Countrey.

* Ita ſentit Caſſianus, Inſtit. divin. Scriptur.

The *New Covenant* I uſe to this end, that I may teach, what cannot be learned elſwhere, what is lawfull for Chriſtians: which yet, contrary to the opinion of many men, I have diſtinguiſht from the Law of Nature; being aſſured, greater Sanctimony is commanded us in that moſt Holy Law, than the Law of Nature exacteth by it ſelf alone. Yet have I not forgotten to obſerve, what is rather commended to us than commanded, that we may know, 'tis impious and penal to decline from the precepts; to aſpire unto the higheſt perfection, is the part of a generous

* * * mind,

mind, and ſhall not go without reward. *Synodical Canons*, which are right, are Collections out of the general ſentences of the Law Divine, fitted unto the preſent Occurrences. Theſe alſo either ſhew what the Divine Law commandeth, or exhort to that which God perſwades. And this is the office of the true Chriſtian Church, to deliver thoſe things which are delivered to Her from God, and after the ſame manner wherein they are deliver'd. Moreover, the *Cuſtoms* among thoſe old Chriſtians, who filled up the meaſure of ſo great a name, either received or praiſed, juſtly have the force of Canons. Next to theſe, is their Authority, who flouriſhed among the Chriſtians in ſeveral Ages, Men renowned for their Piety and Learning, and noted for no grievous Errour. For, what theſe men ſay with great aſſeveration, as certain, ought to have no ſmall moment for interpretation of things that ſeem obſcure in Holy Scriptures: and the more, by how much

greater

greater is their Consent, and nearer access to the times of the first purity, when neither domination as yet, nor any Faction, could adulterate the Primitive Truth. The *School-men*, that succeeded the *Fathers*, often shew what good Wits they had: but they fell into unhappy times, and ignorant of good Arts: the less cause we have to wonder, if, among many things to be praised, they have some things to be pardoned. Yet, when they agree in matter of morality, they seldome erre: having very clear eyes to perceive what was awry in the Sayings of other men. Neverthelesse, in this contentious study, they give us a commendable pattern of Modesty, opposing one another with Reasons, not (which is a fashion of late times risen up to the disgrace of Learning) with reproaches, the unhansome issue of an impotent and unruly mind.

The *Roman Lawyers* are of three sorts. *First* are they whose labours appear in the Pandect, the Codes of

Theodosius and *Justinian*, and in the Novel Constitutions. The *second* rank are they that succeeded *Irnrius*, viz. *Accursius*, *Bartolus*, and a number of names more, that a long time reigned in the Court. In the *third* place we have those, who joyned polite Learning with the study of Law. To the *first* I owe much: for they do both often afford excellent reasons, to demonstrate that which is of the Law of Nature; and often yield testimony to the same Law, and no less to the Law of Nations But thus, that they, as well as others, often confound these names; yea, and call that the Law of Nations, which is onely of some people; and that, not as on Agreement, but, which some have receiv'd by imitation of others, or by chance. Besides, they often handle what is truly of the Law of Nations, promiscuously and indistinctly, with those things which are of the Roman Law as appears by the Title, *De Captivis & postliminio*. That these thing therefore might be discerned, we

have

have taken ſome pains. The *ſecond* ſort, incurious of Divine Law, and of antient Hiſtorie, was pleaſed to define all the Controverſies of Kings and Nations out of the Roman Laws, aſſuming now and then the Canons. But theſe men alſo, by the infelicity of their times, were hindred from a right inſight into thoſe Laws, being otherwiſe ſubtil enough to ſearch into the nature of Right and Good: whence it comes, that they are often very good Authors of Law to be made, even when they are bad Interpreters of Law made before. But then chiefly are they to be heard, when they bear witneſs to ſuch a Cuſtom that makes the Law of Nations of our times. The Maſters of the *third* order, who confine themſelves to the Roman Laws, and expatiate, either never, or very lightly, into that which is Common, have ſcarce any uſe in our Argument. Two Spaniards, *Covarruvias* and *Vaſquius* (the latter with great liberty, the other more modeſtly, and not without exact judgement) have joyned Scholastical subtilty with their skill in the Laws and Canons, not abstaining from the Controversies of Nations and of Kings. The French have been more studious to insert Histories in the same profession of the Laws: amongst whom, *Bodin* and *Hottoman* are of great name, the former in a continued Work, the latter in scatter'd Questions: whose determinations and reasons will often furnish us with matter to examine.

In the whole Work I have proposed to my self three things; to make the reasons of defining most evident, to dispose in a certain order the matters to be handled, and to distinguish perspicuously the things which seemed to be the same, and were not. I have abstained from things that are not of this Treatise, as, those that shew what is usefull to be done: because they have their special consideration in the Politicks, which *Aristotle* handles so judiciously and distinctly, as to mingle nothing

nothing that is impertinent, otherwise than *Bodin* hath done, in whom this Art is confounded with the Art of our Law. Notwithstanding, in some places I have mention'd what is *profitable*, but on the by, and that I might distinguish it more plainly from the question of *just*. He will do me injury, that thinks I had an eye upon any Controversies of our Age, either already up, or like to rise. For I profess sincerely, as Mathematicians consider Figures abstract from Bodies, so have I in treating of Right, elevated my Meditations above all particular Actions. As to the stile and manner of speech, I was not willing, by adding a multitude of words to the multitude of matter, to cloy my Reader, whose Good I intended. I have therefore followed, as near as I could, a concise and plain way of expression convenient to a Teacher: that such as have a hand in publick Affairs may here behold, as in one view, both what Controversies are usually incident, and what are the

the Principles whereby they may be judged: which being known, it will not be difficult to accommodate that which is ſaid to the ſubject matter, and to extend it as much as you will. I have ſometimes alleged the very words of antient Writers, where they were ſuch, that they might ſeem ſpoken with authority, or with a ſingular grace: which I have done in the Greek too now and then, but eſpecially where either the ſentence was ſhort, or whoſe Elegancy I could not hope to equal by my tranſlation.

To conclude; the Liberty I have taken to my ſelf in judging the Sentences and Writing of other men, let All, I humbly intreat them, into whoſe hands this Book ſhall come, take the ſame to themſelves upon me. They ſhall not more readily admoniſh me of any errour, than I will obey their admonition. And at this inſtant, if here be any thing ſpoken by me diſſentaneous to piety, or good manners, or holy Scripture; if any thing againſt the

Conſent

Consent of the Christian Church, or against any Truth, with all my heart I wish it never spoken.

I. Of

I. Of the Lawfulneſs of War.

II. Of the Cauſes of War.

III. Of what is lawfull to be done in War.

THE CONTENTS.

I. PART.

The Contents.

XXV.

XXXIX.

LIV.

LXVI.

II. PART.

II. PART.

LXXII.

CVII.

CXVII.

CXLVII.

III. PART.

XI.

XXIII.

XXXVIII.

HVGO GROTIVS OF WARRE AND PEACE.

I. PART.

I. *What is War.*

W*AR is the State of those that contend by Force, as they are such.* Which generall Description comprehends all sorts of War that we shall speak of. For I exclude not here the Private, which indeed hath priority, and without question hath the same nature with the Publique; and therfore may properly be denoted by the

same

ſame word. But if the name of War be at any time given only to the Publique, it is as many other generall words are, often applied particularly to that * *Species* that is moſt excellent.

Philo. 2. de leg. ſpecial. *Hoſtes non ſoli exiſtimantur qui tam Navali aut Terreſtri prælio decertant, ſed pro talibus habendi et qui machinas admovent portubus aut mœnibus, etiamſi nondum pugnam incipiunt* Serv. ad illud primæ Æn. *Nec bello major et armis. Bellum et Conſilium habet : arma tantum in actu ipſo ſunt.*

II. *What is Law.*

LAW, taken in the largeſt ſenſe, is a Rule of Moral Actions, obliging to that which is Right. We ſay *Obliging*; For Counſells and other Precepts, though right, yet not obliging, are not called Laws; and Permiſſion properly is not the Action of Law, but the Negation of that Action, unleſs as it obligeth ſome other not to hinder him that is permitted. We ſaid, obliging to that which is *Right*, not ſimply to that which is juſt; becauſe it pertains not to Juſtice only, but to other vertues * . The beſt diviſion of Law is out of *Ariſtotle*, into Natural and Voluntary.

* For example, *Zaleucus* made a law inflicting puniſhment upon him, that againſt his Phyſicians Precept, drank Wine.

III. *Of Naturall Law.*

NAtural Law is the Dictate of right Reaſon * ſhewing moral turpitude, or

* Philo. *Lex mentiri neſcia eſt recta ratio, quæ lex, non ab*

or moral necessity to be in some act, by its convenience or disconvenience with the Rational Nature: and consequently that it is forbidden or commanded by the Author of Nature, God. The Acts, concerning which is extant such a dictate, are due, or unlawfull of themselves, and therefore are conceived necessarily to be commanded of God, or forbidden. By which note, this Law differs not from humane only, but from the Divine voluntary; which doth not command or forbid what is by it self and in its own nature, due or unlawful; but by forbidding makes the thing unlawfull, and by commanding makes it due. For the better understanding of Natural Law, we must observe, some things belong unto it not properly, but reductively, *viz.* the things whereto the Law Natural is not repugnant: So are things called just, which are without injustice. Somtimes also by abuse of the word, the things which Reason alloweth for honest and better than the opposite, although they be not due and necessary, are said to be of the Law Natural. Observe farther, this Law is not only conversant about things not subject to human pleasure, but about many things also which are consequent to the Acts of Mans Will: So the Will of Man introduc'd Dominion, such as is now in use: But, that being introduc'd, the law of * Nature tells me 'tis wickednes for me to take away, without thy con-

hoc aut illo mortali mortalis, non in Chartis aut columnis exanimis examima, sed corumpi nescia, quippe ab immortali natura insculpta in immortali intellectu. Tertul. *Quaeres igitur Legem Dei, habens communem illam in publico mundi, in naturalibus tabulis.* Vid. Chrysost. 12. et 13. de stat. Thom. sec. cund 57. 2. & Scot. 3. 37.

* *Furtum natura turpe* Ulpian. *Namque odit ipse vim Deus: nec*

divites nos esse rapto, sed prove partus cupit. Eurip. Hel.

consent, that which is under thy dominion. Moreover the Law of Nature is immutable: yet somtimes it comes to pass that in the Acts determined by that Law, a seeming mutation deceivs the unwary; when in truth the Law of Nature is the same, but the matter about which it is, is changed. For example, If my Creditor accounts the debt I owe him as received, I am not bound to pay: The reason is not, because the Law of Nature is become more indulgent, & requires me not to pay what I owe; But because by the indulgence of my Creditor the debt is forgiven me. So if God command a person to be slain, or his Goods to be taken away, it will not follow that Man-slaughter or Theft is lawfull; which words include a Vice; but the act is not Manslaughter or Theft which is done at his command who is supreme Lord of our Lives and Goods. Lastly, there are some things that do not simply, but in such a state of affairs, belong to Natural Law: as the common use of things was natural before Dominion was introduced; and before positive Laws, every man had right to get his own by force.

IV. *Of*

IV. *Of the Law of Nature and Nations.*

AS for that distinction extant in the Roman Law-Books, between the immutable Law, common to other Creatures with men, (call'd the Law of Nature;) And that which is proper to men alone, (usually called by them the Law of Nations,) it is of very little or no use. For no nature, that hath not the use of general precepts, is properly capable of a Law *. If at any time * Justice is attributed to the brute creatures, it is improperly, for that there is in them some shadow and print of reason. Whether the act it self, determined by the Law of Nature, be common to us with other creatures, as the breeding up of our Issue; or proper to us, as the worship of God, it is not in this respect material.

* *In equis, in leonibus justitiam non dicimus.* Cic. Offic. 1.

* *Pliny* notes a likeness of Justice in Elephants. *l.* 8. and he speaks of an Asp that kild her own young one, because that young one had kild the mans son that entertained her. *l.* 10. *c.* 74. Sen. *Muta animalia, ait, humanis affectibus carent; habent autem similes illis quosdam impulsus.*

V. *The proof of Natural Law.*

A Thing is proved to be of Natural Law two ways, *à priori*, or *à posteriori*. That way of proof is more subtil, this more popular. The proof is *à priori*, if we shew the necessary convenience

nience or disconvenience of any thing to the rational and social nature; *à posteriori*, if, though not with full certainty, yet very probably, we conclude that to be a point of Natural Law, which is receiv'd for such amongst all, or at least the most civil Nations. For an universal effect hath an universal cause; and of so generall an opinion, there can hardly be any other cause, but sense it self which is called common *. But I said, with good reason, the * *more civill* Nations; for as the Philosopher hath it, * *What is natural we must judge by those in whom nature is least corrupt, and not by the depraved.*

* *Argumentum veritatis est aliquid omnibus videri.* Sen. * *Non etenim penitus est vana est sententia, multi quam populi celebrant.* Hesiod. Tertul. *Quod apud multos unum invenitur, non est erratum sed traditum.* * Justin. coll cum Tryph. *Exceptis illis qui ab impuris spiritibus abrepti & per malam educationem, instituta prava & leges iniquas corrupti naturales notiones perdiderunt.* * Aristot. Polit. 1. 5.

VI. *Of Voluntary Humane Law.*

THe other kind of Law is Voluntary, which draws its original from the will. And this is either Divine, or Humane Law. We begin with Humane, because more known. And this is either Civil, or of larger extent, or of less extent than Civil. The Civil Law is that which proceeds from the Civil power. The Civil Power is that which rules the Common-wealth. And a Common-wealth

wealth is a ſociety of Freemen united for their common benefit. The Law of leſs extent, and that comes not from the Civil power, though ſubject to it, is various, conteining the precepts of Fathers, Maſters, and ſuch like. That of larger extent is the Law of Nations, *i. e.* which by the will of all, or of * many nations hath received force to oblige. I adde, *of many*, becauſe there is ſcarce found any Law, beſides the Natural, (which is alſo called the Law of Nations) common unto all. Yea, oft-times in one part of the world, there is not the ſame Law of Nations as in another: as we ſhall ſhew hereafter. This Law of Nations is proved in the ſame manner with the unwritten Civill Law, by continual uſe and the teſtimony of ſkilfull men. And to this purpoſe Hiſtorians are of ſingular profit.

* *Vaſqu. 2. controv. 54.4.*

VII. *Voluntary Divine Law.*

VOluntary Law Divine (as the words at firſt ſound inform us) is that which hath its riſe from the will of God; whereby it is diſtinguiſhed from Natural Law, that may be alſo, as we have ſaid, entituled Divine. Here hath place that indiſtinct * ſaying: *God wills it not, becauſe 'tis juſt; but 'tis juſt,* (i. e. due in Law) *becauſe God wills it.* This Law was given either to mankind, or

* *Anaxarchi apud Plut. in Alex.*

or to one people; thrice to mankind; presently after the creation, again in the restauration after the floud, lastly in that more sublime restauration by Christ. All these Laws doubtless oblige all men, after they have sufficient notice of them.

VIII. *That the Law given to the Hebrews obliged not other Nations.*

THe Hebrews were the only people in all the world, to whom God peculiarly gave his Laws, as *Moses*, and the Psalmist tell them. And certainly those Jews are out (one is *Trypho* in his disputation with *Justin*) who think all strangers, if they will be saved, must take upon them the yoke of the Hebrew-Law. No Law binds them to whom it was not given; To whom this Law was given, the Law it self speaketh, *Hear O Israel*! With them the Covenant is made; They are taken for a peculiar people of God, as *Maimonides* confesseth, and proves out of *Deut.*33.4. Amongst the Hebrews indeed there alwaies lived some strangers * that feared God, such as *Cornelius*, *Acts* 10. and the worshipping Greeks, *Acts* 17. These, as the Hebrew Masters say, were bound to observe the Laws given to *Adam*, and to *Noah*, namely to abstain from Idols and from blood: but to the proper Laws of the Israelites

Deut. 4.7. Psl.147.

* These pious men of the Gentiles, as *Maimonides* often saith, shall be partakers of future happiness.

Israelites they were not bound. The Prophets when they Preacht unto the Gentiles never imposed on them a necessity to submit to *Moses* Law. And the Jews in * *Josephus* said well, that God might be worshipt and his favour obteind without circumcision *. For, the reason why many strangers were circumcised, and by circumcision bound themselves to the Law (as *Paul* explains it) was to procure the Privileges of that Common-wealth (for such Proselytes * had the same right with native Israelites) and to partake of those promises which were not common to mankind, but peculiar to the Hebrew people. Yet I deny not, in after times it grew to an erronious opinion in some, as if without Judaism were no salvation. That we are bound by no part of the Hebrew Law, as it is properly Law, we collect hence, because all obligation, except by the Law of nature, comes from the will of the Law-giver: but, that it was the will of God, others besides the Israelites should be holden by that Law, we have not the least intimation. Wherefore, as to us, there is *no abrogation* of that Law; for how could it be abrogated in respect of them whom it never obliged? From the Israelites indeed is the bond taken off, as to Rituals, presently after the first publication of the Gospell (which was revealed to *Peter*, *Acts* 10.) and as to other

* *Antiqu.* 22. 2.

* Tryphon Justino sic ait. *Si in illa Philosophandi ratione mansisses erat tibi reliqua spes aliqua status melioris.*

Gal. 5. 3.

* Justin. coll. cum Tryph. *Proselytus qui circumcisus populo se aggregavit par est indigenæ.*

other points, after that people by the overthrow of their City and their utter desolation, without all hope of restitution, ceased to be a people. But, for us foreiners, we obteined not this by the comming of Christ, to be freed from *Moses* Law: but, we who before had only an obscure hope placed in the goodness of God, are now susteined with a perspicuous Covenant, and the Hebrews Law, the partition Wall between us, being taken away, we are incorporated with them into one Catholick Church.

IX. *What arguments Christians may deduce from* Moses *Law, and how.*

NOw, seeing the Law given by *Moses* cannot induce upon us a direct obligation, as we have shewed; let us see what other use it may have, both in this of War, and other the like questions. To know this is very usefull to many purposes. First then, the Hebrew Law doth manifest, that which is commanded in that Law not to be against the Law of Nature. For, the Law of Nature, as we have said, being perpetual and immutable, it consisteth not with the justice of God to command any thing contrary unto it. Moreover, the Law of *Moses* is called pure and
Ps. 19. right by the Psalmist; and, by the A-
Rom. 7. postle, holy, just and good. I mean the pre-

precepts ; for, of the permissions we must speak more distinctly. Legall permission (for that which is meerly of fact, and signifies removal of the impediment, is not pertinent here) either is plenary, which gives a right to do a thing lawfully ; or less than plenary, which only gives impunity among men, and a right that no other can lawfully hinder the doer, From the former permission, as from a precept, it follows, that the thing permitted is not against the Law of Nature : not, from the later. But this consequence seldom is of use : because, the permitting words being ambiguous, we must rather, by the Law of Nature, interpret what kind of permission is meant, than from such a kind of permission prove it to be the Law of Nature. Our second observation is, That it is now lawfull for Christian Governours to make Laws of the same sense, with the Laws given by *Moses:* unless the whole substance of any Law concern the time of Christ expected, and of the Gospel not yet revealed ; or, unless Christ himself, either in general or in special, hath ordained the contrary. For, no other reason can be imagined, why any of *Moses* constitutions can be now unlawfull. A third observation's this : Whatsoever pertaining to the vertues Christ requires of his Disciples, is given in precept by *Moses*, the

the same is now also, if not more, to be perform'd by Christians. The ground of this observation is, that the vertues requir'd of Christians, as Humility, Patience, Love, are requir'd in a greater degree * than they were in the State of the Hebrew Law. And justly, because also the heavenly promises are much more clearly proposed in the Gospel. Hence, in comparison of the Gospel, is the old Law said to have been neither perfect nor faultless; and Christ is call'd the end of the Law; and the Law a Schoolmaster to bring us unto Christ. So, that old Law of the Sabbath, and that other of Tithes * do shew, that Christians are oblig'd to separate no less than a seventh part of their time for Gods service; nor less than a tenth of their fruits, for the maintenance of his Ministers, and the like pious uses.

* Chrysost. de Virgin. 94. *Major nunc virtus ostendenda est, quia multa nunc spiritus effusa est gratia, & ingens donum est Christi adventus.* & v. Iren. l. 4. c. 26. Heb. 7. 19. & 7. Rom. 10. 5. Gal. 3. 25.

* *V. Iren. l. 4. c. 34. & Chrys. ad Eph. 11. 10.*

X. *That War is not against the Law of Nature.*

Ex. l. 1. c. 2.

We said afore, when the question is about the Law of Nature, the meaning is, whether a thing may be done, not unjustly; and, that is unjust which hath a necessary repugnance to the rational and social Nature. Now, among the first principles of Nature, there is nothing repugnant unto War; there is much in favour of it: For, both

both the end of War, the conſervation of life and members, and the keeping or acquiring of things uſefull unto life, is moſt agreeable unto thoſe principles: and, if need be, to uſe force to that purpoſe, is not diſagreeable, ſince every living thing hath, by the gift of Nature, * ſtrength, to the end it may be able to help and defend it ſelf. *Galen* * ſaith, that Man is by nature fitted for Peace and War; though comming into the world unarmed, yet he hath a hand fit to provide and to handle arms; which alſo Infants, we ſee, of their own accord without a teacher make uſe of for a weapon. So *Ariſtotle* * ſaith, the hand is to man inſtead of a ſpear, of a ſword, of any arms whatſoever; becauſe it can take and hold all. Moreover, Right reaſon and the nature of ſociety inhibites not all force, but that which is repugnant to ſociety, that is, which depriveth another of his right. For the end of ſociety is, that by mutual aid every one may enjoy his own. This were ſo, although the Dominion and propriety of poſſeſſions had not been introduced; for life, members, liberty would yet be proper to every one, and therefore cou'd not without injury be invaded by any other. And, to make uſe of what is common, and ſpend as much as may ſuffice nature would be the right of the occupant. Which right none could without

* *Dente lupus, cornu taurus petit; unde niſi intus monſtratum?* Hor.

* De uſu part. 1.

* De part. animal. 4. 10.

* Caſſiodor. de anima. *Et quoniam neque cornu, neque dente, neque fuga (ſicut alia animalia) corporis humani forma ſe prævalet vindicare, robuſtus illi thorax, brachiaque conceſſa ſunt: ut illatam injuriam manu defenderet, & objectu corporis quaſi quodam clipeo vindicaret.*

without injury take away. This is more plain, ſince by Law and uſe Dominion is eſtabliſhed: which I will expreſs in *Tullies* words: *If every member ſhould think to gather more ſtrength by drawing to it ſelf the ſtrength of the member next it, the whole body muſt needs be weakned and deſtroyed: So, if every one of us ſnatch unto himſelf the commodities of other men, and draw away from every one what he can to advantage himſelf, humane ſociety cannot ſtand. Nature gives leave to every man, in the acquiſition of things uſefull, to ſupply himſelf before another; but by the ſpoils of another to encreaſe his own ſtore, that nature doth not permit.* It is not then againſt ſociety to provide for one ſelf, ſo that anothers right be not diminiſhed: nor is that violence unjuſt, which doth not violate the right of another, as the ſame Author ſaith: *Of the two kinds of contention, by debate, and by force, the one agreeing to men, the other more becoming beaſts, we muſt fly unto the later, when the former will not ſerve.* And elſewhere: *What is there that can be done againſt force, but by force?* Ulpian ſaith: *Caſſius writes, that it is by nature lawfull to repell force by force; and arms by arms.* *

De offic. 3.

Epiſt. Fam. 12 3.

L. 1. Sect. Vim vi. D de vi & vi arma: a.

* *Armaque in armatos ſumere jura ſinunt.* Ovid. Caius Juriſcons. *Adverſus periculum naturalis ratio permittit ſe defendere.*

XI. Further

XI. *Further proof, out of the sacred History, that all War is not against the Law of Nature.*

THis is further proved out of the sacred History. For when *Abraham* having armed his servants and friends, pursued the four Kings that had spoiled *Sodom*, and returned with victory, God by his Priest *Melchizedeck* approv'd his action. *Blessed be the most high God*, said *Melchisedeck*, *who hath deliver'd thine enemies into thine hand.* Gen. 14. 20. *Abraham*, as appears by the story, had taken Arms without any special commission from God: therefore the Law of Nature was his warrant, whose wisdom was no less eminent than his sanctity, even by the report of aliens, namely of *Berosus* and *Orpheus*. The History of the seven Nations, whom God gave up to be destroyed by the hand of *Israel*, I shall not use: because there was a special mandate to execute Gods judgement upon people guilty of the greatest crimes; Whence, in the Scripture, these VVars are properly called the VVars of God, undertaken by his command not by humane Counsel. It is more pertinent, that the Hebrews, under the conduct of *Moses* and *Joshua*, when they were opposed by the *Amalekites*, repulsed them by Armies. The Action was Exod. 17. not

not set upon by Gods command,yet was it approved by him after it was done. Moreover, God hath prescribed to his people general and perpetual Laws of
Deut.20.10. waging VVar, thereby shewing, VVar
15. may be just even without his special mandate. For he doth plainly distinguish the cause of the seven Nations from the cause of other people : and prescribing nothing about the just causes of entring into VVar, thereby shews them to be manifest enough by the light of nature, as the cause of defending the frontiers in
Jud.11. the VVar of *Jephtha* against the *Ammonites*; and the cause of Embassadors
2 Sam.10. violated in the VVar of *David* against the same. It is also to be noted, which the divine writer to the Hebrews saith,
Heb.11. 33, that *Gedeon*, *Baruc*, *Sampson*, *Jephtha*,
34. *David*, *Samuel* and others, by Faith overthrew Kingdoms, prevailed in VVar, put to flight the Armies of Aliens. Where, in the name of *Faith*, as we learn by the *series* of that discourse, is included a perswasion whereby is believed that the thing done is pleasing unto God. So also the wise woman saith
1 Sam.25.28. of *David*, that he fought the *battails of God*, that is, pious and just.

XII. *That*

XII. *That War is not contrary to the voluntary Divine Law, before the time of the Gospell.*

THe greateſt difficulty lies in this point, concerning the poſitive Divine Law. Nor may any object, the Law of Nature is immutable, and therefore nothing could be conſtituted by God to the contrary; for this is true in things commanded or forbidden by the Law of Nature; not in things permitted only: which things, being not properly of the Law of Nature but without it, may be either forbidden or commanded. Firſt then, againſt VVar is brought by ſome that Law given to *Noah* and his poſterity: *And ſurely* (ſaith Gen. 9. 5, 6.
God) *Your blood of your lives will I require: at the hand of every beaſt will I require it; and at the hand of man, at the hand of every mans Brother will I require the life of man. Who ſo ſheddeth mans bloud, by man ſhall his blood be ſhed: for in the image of God made he man.* Here do ſome moſt generally underſtand that which is ſaid of *requiring blood:* and what is ſaid of *ſhedding blood for blood,* they will have to be a commination, not an approbation. I can allow of neither; for the prohibition, *not to ſhed blood,* is not of larger extent than that in the Law, *Thou ſhalt not kill:*

and

and this, 'tis manifeſt, hath neither taken away capitall puniſhments nor VVars. VVherefore, both this Law and that doth not ſo much conſtitute any new thing, as declare and repeat the old naturall Law obliterated and depraved by evill cuſtom. And the words are to be underſtood in a ſenſe which includes a crime: as in the word *homicide*, we underſtand not every killing of a man, but that which is on purpoſe and of an innocent perſon. That which follows, *of ſhedding blood for blood*, ſeems to me not to contain a naked act, but a Right. I explain it thus. By nature it is not unjuſt, that every one ſuffer as much evill as he hath done; out of a ſenſe of this naturall equity, *Cain* accus'd of paricide by his own conſcience ſaid, *Whoſoever findeth me ſhall ſlay me*. But, God in thoſe firſt times, either by reaſon of the paucity of men, or becauſe there being yet but few offenders, exemplary puniſhments were leſs neceſſary, repreſſed by his edict that which ſeemed naturally lawfull, and appointed the manſlayers company to be avoided, not his life taken away. The like was decreed by *Plato* in his Laws, and of old practized in *Greece* *. Pertinent is that of * *Thucydides*: *Antiently*

Quæ fecit ſi quiſque ferat, jus fiet & æquum.

Gen.4.14.

* Euripides. *Quam bene parentum provida ætas ſtatuerat: ut cogeretur de vita decedere Hominumque viſu cæde patrata nocens, Fugaq; lueret triſte non letho ſcelus.* * Hiſt.l.3.

great

great crimes had little punishments * : *but in progreß of time, those being contemned, death was inflicted.* From one notable act a conjecture being made of the divine pleasure went into a Law : so that *Lamech* also, upon the like crime committed *, promised to himself impunity from that example. Neverthcless, when before the floud, in the Gyants age, a promiscuous licence of shedding blood had prevailed, mankind being again restored after the floud, God, to restrain that licence, thought it meet to use more severity ; and laying aside the lenity of the former times, permitted now what nature did before dictate not to be unjust, that he should be guiltless who slew the man-slayer *. This, after Courts of Justice were established, was upon very great reasons restrained to the Judges only : yet so that some Print of the former custom was seen, even after *Mose:* Law, in his right. who was the next Kinsman to the person slain. We have no mean Author to countenance our interpretation. *Abraham*, who being not ignorant of the Law given to *Noah*, took arms against the four Kings, not doubting but his enterprize was very reconcilable with that Law. And *Moses* too gave order that the *Amalekites* violence should be withstood by Arms, using the right of nature : for it appears not that God was consulted

* Servius ad 1 Æn. *Luetis, persolvetis, Et hic sermo à pecunia descendit; antiquoriū enim pœnæ omnes pecuniariæ fuerunt.*

Adbuc enim videbatur nefas, quamvis malos, tamen homines, supplicio capitis affi ere. Lactant. l 2.

Gen. 4.24.

* Or rather [it he had committed the like : for the words bear this sense.

* Josephus. *Edico ut à cæde humana puræ habeantur manus ; quod si quis eadem commiserit, pœnam ferat.*

Exod. 17.9.

ted within this. Moreover, capitall punishments, it appears, were used not a-
Gen.38.24: gainst man-slayers only, but other Malefactors; and that as well among the holy people as other nations. By the aid of naturall reason, having some ground to make conjecture of the divine will, they proceeded from like to like, and collected, that the constitution against the man-slayer, might extend also to other notorious and great offenders. For, some things there are equall unto life, as reputation, virginall chastity, conjugall fidelity; or without which life cannot be secure, as reverence to authority, whereby society is preserved: Offenders against these seem no better than man-slayers. Hither pertains an old tradition extant among the Hebrews, that more Laws were given unto *Noah's* Sons by God, but *Moses* did not relate them all, because it was sufficient for his purpose, that they were after comprehended in the peculiar Law of the Hebrews; so, against incestuous Marriage, there was extant an old Law, though not remembred by *Moses* in its place, as appears *Levit.* 18. And among the Laws God gave to *Noah's* children, this also they say was decreed, that not only homicides, but adulteries, incests and rapes should be punished with death; which is confirmed by the words
Chap.31.2. of *Job*. Also, the Law given by *Moses*

ses addes unto the capitall sanctions, reasons, that are of no less value among others, then among the Hebrew people *: peculiarly it is said of homicide, that the earth cannot be purged but by the blood-shed of the man-slayer *. Besides, it is absurd to think, the Hebrew people were allowed to secure their Government, and the publick and private safety, by capitall punishments, and to bear Arms for their own defence, but other Kings and Nations at the same time were not allowed to do so; and yet were never admonisht by the Prophets for using capital punishments and making VVar, as they were oft reprov'd for other sins. Yea on the contrary, who would not believe, seeing *Moses* Judicial Law is an express of the divine pleasure, other Nations who would take a Copy thence, did well and wisely: as it is probable the Greeks, especially the Athenians did? whence there is so great similitude in the old Attick Law, and the of-spring thereof, the Roman of the 12. Tables, with the Hebrew Laws. This is enough to shew, that the Law given to *Noah* is not of such a sense as they would have it, who impugn all VVars by that Argument.

* As Levit. 18. 24, &c. Psal. 101. 5. Prov. 20. 8.

* Num. 35. 31, 33.

XIII. *Of the Goſpel-Law.*

THe objections againſt VVar taken out of the Goſpel have a greater ſhew; in the examination whereof, I will not ſay with many, that in the Goſpel, beſide the precepts of Faith and the Sacraments, nothing elſe is found but what is of Natural Law; for, as moſt underſtand this, it is not true. This I willingly acknowledge; in the Goſpel nothing is commanded us, which hath not a natural honeſty and comelineſs; but, that we are not further obliged by the Laws of Chriſt, than we are by natural Law, I cannot grant. It is marvellous to ſee what pains they take, who are in the other opinion, to proove the things forbidden by the Law of Nature, which by the Goſpel are made unlawfull, ſuch as are concubinacy, divorce, prolygamy *. Things indeed of ſuch a nature, that to abſtain from them, reaſon it ſelf tells us is more honeſt and becomming: Yet not ſuch, as contain in them (ſet the divine Law aſide) any apparent wickedneſs. And who can ſay, nature hath bound us to that which the Chriſtian Law gives in precept, to lay down our lives for the brethren? It is a ſaying of *Juſtin Martyr* *, *To live according to nature is his duty, who hath not yet attained to the Faith of Chriſt.*

* Spectat huc illud Hieronymi: *Aliæ ſunt leges Cæſaris, aliæ Chriſti; aliud Papinianus, aliud Paulus noſter præcipit.*

1 John 3.16.

* *ocus eſt, ad Zenam · idemque ſenſus apud Originem in excerptis illis, quæ Philocatia dicuntur.*

Chriſt. Neither will I follow their conjecture, who ſuppoſe Chriſt in his Sermon on the Mount, was only an Interpreter of *Moſes* Law. Theſe words Mat.5, &c.
of his ſo oft repeated have another ſound: *Ye have heard, that it hath been ſaid to them of old: but I ſay unto you.* Which oppoſition, and the *Syriack* and other verſions proove the truth of that reading, *to them* (not, *by them*) *of old.* Thoſe of old, or the antients, were no other than they that liv'd in *Moſes* time; for the commands rehearſed as ſpoken to the antients, are not the ſayings of the Lawyers, but of *Moſes*, either word for word, or at leſt in ſenſe. *Thou ſhalt* Ex.20.13.
not kill. Whoſoever ſhall kill ſhall be in Lev.21.21.
danger of judgement. Thou ſhalt not Ex.20.14.
commit adultry. Whoſoever ſhall put a- Deut.24.1.
way his Wife, let him give her a writing of divorcement. Thou ſhalt not Ex.20.7.
forſwear thy ſelf, but ſhalt perform unto the Lord thine oaths. An eye for an eye, Lev.24.20.
and a tooth for a tooth (underſtand *thou mayſt require in the Court of judgement.*) *Thou ſhalt love thy neighbour* Lev.19.18.
(i. e. the Iſraelite) *and hate thine enemy* (i. e. the ſeven Nations *, to whom they might not ſhew friendſhip nor pitty: to theſe the *Amalekits* are to be Deut.23.21.
added, againſt whom the Hebrews are Ex.34.11.
commanded to have VVar for ever.) Deut.7.1.
Ex.27.19
But, to underſtand the words of Chriſt we muſt note, that the Law given by

* *In hos odium lege permitti ait illuſtriſſimus Abarbaniel ad* Deut.23.21.

C 4 *Moſes*

Moses may be taken two ways: according to what it hath common with other Laws, made by men, reſtraining
Heb.2.2. the greater offences with fear of open puniſhments, and hereby containing the Hebrew people in the ſtate of civil ſociety; in which ſenſe it is called *the*
Heb.7.16. *Law of a carnal Commandement*, and *the*
Rom.3.27. *Law of Works*: Or, according to what is proper to the divine Law, as it requires alſo purity of mind, and ſome acts, which may be omitted without temporall puniſhment; in which ſenſe it is
Rom.7.14. called *a ſpiritual Law, rejoycing the*
Pſ.19. *heart*. Now the Lawyers and Phariſees, contenting themſelves with the former part, neglected the ſecond, which is the better part, nor did they inculcate it into the people. The truth of this appears not only in our Books, but in *Joſephus* alſo and the Hebrew Maſters. Moreover, as to this ſecond part, we muſt know, the vertues exacted at the hands of Chriſtians, are either commended or commanded to the Hebrews alſo, but ſurely not commanded in the ſame degree and latitude * as they are to Chriſtians. In both ſenſes Chriſt opposes his precepts to the old ones:

* Egregius imprimis Chryſostom. locus de Virgin. cap. 44. *Olim tanta nobis injuncta non erat virtutis menſura, ſed & vindictam ſumere de injuriam inferente*, &c *At poſt Chriſti adventum multo arctior facta eſt via.* Eud. l.3. c 83 *Non eadem virtutis menſura à nobis & ab illis exigitur.* Idem in orat filium Patri eſſe æqualem, ait, in Evangelio eſſe, *Præceptorum & intenſionem & adjectionem.*

whence

whence it is manifest, his words contain more than a naked Interpretation. The knowledge whereof conduces both to our present matter and to many other things, lest we strein the Authority of the Hebrew Law beyond its reach.

XIV. *That War is not against the Gospel-Law.*
The first Argument.

OMitting Arguments of less value in our judgement, our first and principal proof, that the Right of VVar is not wholy taken away by the Law of Christ, shall be that of *Paul,* to *Timothy*: *I exhort therefore, that first of all, supplications, prayers, intercessions, and giving of thanks be made for all men: For Kings, and for all that are in authority, that we may lead a quiet and a * peaceable life in all godliness and honesty. For this is good and acceptable in the sight of God our Saviour: who will have all men to be saved, and to come unto the knowledge of the truth.* Here we are taught three things; That it is pleasing to God, Kings should become Christians: That being made Christians, they should remain Kings; *Wee pray*

1 Tim. 2. 1, 2, 3.

* Sen. Ep. 73. Philosophiæ fideliter deditos, falso ait contemtores magistratuum ac regum existimari. *E contrario ait, nulli adversus illos gratiores sunt: nec immerito; nullus enim plus præstant, quam, quibus frui tranquillo otio licet.* Digna est, quæ legatur, Epistola, ubi & hoc: *Hujus pacis beneficium, ad omnes pertinens, altius ad eos pervenit qui illa bene utuntur.*

(faith

(saith *Justin Martyr*) *that Kings and Princes, together with their regal power, may also attain unto a right understanding*; and in the Book entitled *Clement's Constitutions*, the Church prays
* Nisi hic interpretari malis, *Christianum vitæ exitum.* Gr. χριστιανὰ τὰ τέλη. — * *for Christian Magistrates*: Lastly, that this is also pleasing to God, that Christian Kings should procure for other Christians a quiet life. How so? The Apostle sheweth in another place:
Rom. 13.4. — *He is the Minister of God to thee for good, but if thou do that which is evill, be afraid: for he beareth not the sword in vain.: for he is the Minister of God, a revenger to execute wrath upon him that doth evill.* By the right of the sword is understood all coercive power (as in the Lawyers sometimes) yet so, that the highest part of it, which is the true use of the sword, is not excluded. For the illustration of this place much light may be had from the second *Psalm*: which, although it were verified of *David*, yet
Acts 4.25. 13.33. Heb. 5.5. — more fully and perfectly pertains to Christ, as we learn out of the *Acts* and the Epistle to the *Hebrews*. Now this *Psalm* exhorts all Kings to receive the Son of God with reverence, *i. e.* to do service to him, as they are Kings, as *Augustin* explains it well: whose words
Contr. Crescon. Gram. l. 3 — are to this effect, *Herein do Kings, as they are commanded, serve God as Kings; if in their Kingdom they command good things, forbid evill things, not only pertaining*

taining to humane society, but also to divine Religion. And elsewhere: *How then shall Kings serve the Lord in fear, but by prohibiting with religious severity, and punishing offences against the commands of the Lord? For he serveth one way as a man, another way as a King.* Again: *Herein therefore doe Kings serve the Lord, as Kings, when they do him that service, which none can do but Kings.* Ad Bonifac. Epist. 50.

XV. *The second Argument.*

A Second Argument is deliver'd us by St. *Paul* in the place cited already in some part, out of the Epistle to the *Romans*: where the highest power, such as the regall is, is said to be of God, and is called the ordinance of God: whence it is inferr'd, that obedience and honour is to be given to it, and that from the heart: and he that resisteth it, resisteth God. If by *Ordinance* a thing were to be understood, which God only will not hinder, as in vicious acts, then would there follow thence no obligation either of honour or obedience, especially laid upon the conscience: nor would the Apostle say any thing, where he so much extols and commends this power, which might not agree to robbing and stealing. It follows therefore, that this power be conceiv'd to be ordained by the Rom. 13.

the will of God *approoving* it: whence it further follows, that, feeing God wills not contraries, this power is not repugnant to the will of God revealed by the Gofpel, and obliging all men. Nor is this Argument avoyded, becaufe the perfons that were in power when *Paul* wrote, are faid to have been enemies to Chriftian piety: For firft, that is not true of all. *Sergius Paulus* Propraetor of *Cyprus* had given his name to Chrift before this time: to fay nothing of the King of * *Edeffa*, of whom there is an old tradition, grounded (as it feems) on truth, though perhaps a little mixed with fables. Moreover, the queftion is not of the perfons, whether they were impious; but whether that function in them were impious: we fay, the Apoftle denys that, when he faith, the function, even for that time, was ordained of God, and therefore to be honoured, even within the receffes and fecrets of the heart where God alone hath Empire. Wherefore both *Nero* might, and that King *Agrippa* too, whom *Paul* fo feriously invites to his Religion, might fubject himfelf to Chrift, and retain, the one his regal, the other his imperial power: a power, which without the right of the Sword and of Arms cannot be underftood. As then of old, the Sacrifices according to the Law were pious, although adminiftred by impious

Acts 13.2.

* *Eft Edeffa in Ofroene. Nomen Abgari frequens illis locis. Apparet ex nummis, Tacito, Appiano, Dione, tum in pridem editis, tum in novis Excerptis, Capitolino.*

Acts 26.

impious Priests; so Empire is a pious thing *, although it be in the hand of an impious Prince.

* *Bene hoc exsequitur ad hunc locum Epist. ad Rom.* Chrysostomus.

XVI. *The third Argument.*

THe third Argument is from the words of *John* the Baptist, who being seriously asked by the Jewish Souldiers (many thousands of that Nation served the Romans in their Wars, as *Josephus* and other writers cleerly tell us :) what they should do, to avoid the wrath of God, He answered not, that they should forsake VVar (as he must have answered, if that be the will of God) but *abstain from violence and falshood, and be content with their wages.* Luke 3.14. To these words of the Baptist, containing an approbation of VVar plain enough, many answer, The Baptists prescripts are so different from the precepts of Christ, that we may conceive their Doctrine not to be the same. Which I cannot admit, for these reasons. *John* and Christ use the same beginning, and declare the sum of their doctrine in the same words, *Amend your lives, for the kingdom of Heaven is at hand.* Mat. 3.2. 4.17. Christ himself saith, the Kingdom of Heaven (*i. e.* the new Law, for the Hebrews use to stile the Law by the name of *Kingdom,*) began to be invaded *from the days of the Baptist.* Mat. 11.12. *John* is said to have preached the Baptism

Mar.1.4. tiſm of repentance *for the remiſſion of*
Acts 2.38. *ſins:* juſt as the Apoſtles are ſaid to
have done in the name of Chriſt. *John*
Mat.3.8.10. requires *fruits meet for repentance*, and
threatens deſtruction to them that bring
Luke 3.2. not forth ſuch fruit. He requires works
of Love above the Law. The Law is ſaid
Mat.11.13. to have *continued unto John:* as if, a
more perfect doctrine had from him be-
Mar.10.1. gun. And the *beginning of the Goſpell* is
Luke 1.77. deduc'd from *John. John* himſelf is there-
Mat 11.9. Luke 7.26. fore *greater than the Prophets:* being ſent
Luke 2.77. to give *ſaving knowledge* to the people,
Luke 3.18. and to Preach the *Goſpell.* Nor doth he
any where diſtinguiſh Jeſus from himſelf
by the difference of precepts (only the
things delivered by *John* more general-
ly, and confuſedly, and in the manner
of rudiments, are more plainly and ful-
ly declared by Chriſt, *the true light*:)
Acts 19.4. but by this, that Jeſus was that promi-
John 1.29. ſed *Meſſias:* the *King* of a heavenly
Mat.3 2. Kingdom, who ſhould give the power
Mar.1.8. of the *Holy Spirit* to them that believe
Luke 3.16. on him.

XVII. *The fourth Argument.*

THe fourth Argument ſeems to me of no ſmall weight. If the Right of capital puniſhments, and of defending the people by force of Arms againſt Robbers * and Spoilers, be taken away, thence will follow licence of wickedneſs and

* Chryſoſt. in Serm. ad pat. fidelem. *Propter hos ſunt*,

and a deluge as it were, and floud of evils: when as, although Justice be now executed, that stream is hardly kept within the banks. Wherefore, had it been the mind of Christ, to bring in such a state of things, as was never heard of, doubtless he would in most plain and express terms have commanded, that none should give sentence of death, that none should bear Arms: which command he hath no where promulged: for, the alleged places are very general, or very obscure. Now equity and common reason shews, not only general words must be restrained, and doubtfull words commodiously explained, but the propriety and received use of words somewhat declined, that a very incommodious and incoherent sense may be avoyded.

judicia & leges & supplicia totque pœnarum modi.

XVIII. *The Fift Argument.*

FIftly, it can be evinced by no Argument, that the Judicial Law of *Moses*, expired before the destruction of *Jerusalem*, wherewith fell both the form, and the hope of that Common-wealth; for, neither is any term prefixed to that Law in the Law it self, nor do Christ or his Apostles ever speak of the Cessation of it, but as it may seem comprehended in the destruction of the Common-wealth, as we have said: yea, on the contrary,

contrary, *Paul* ſaith, the High-Prieſt was ſet to give judgement *according to*
Acts 24.3. *the Law of* Moſes. Chriſt himſelf in the preface to his precepts ſaith, *He came*
Mat.5.17. *not to diſſolve the Law, but to fulfill it*; the ſenſe of which words, as to *Rituals*, is not obſcure: for the lineaments and ſhadowings are filled up and compleated, when the perfect *ſpecies* of a thing is preſented to our view; as to the *udicial* Laws, how can it be true, if Chriſt, as ſome do think, hath by his comming taken them away? But if the obligation of the Law remained, as long as the Common-wealth of the Hebrews ſtood, it follows, that even the Jews converted unto Chriſt, if they were called unto Magiſtracy, could not ſhun it, and that they ought to judge no otherwiſe than *Moſes* had preſcribed. Methinks, when I weigh all things, there is not the leaſt motive for any pious man, that heard Chriſt at that time ſpeaking, to underſtand his words in any other ſenſe; This I acknowledge, before the time of Chriſt ſome things were permitted, (whether in reſpect of outward impunity, or alſo of inward purity, I need not determine:) which Chriſt hath forbidden the Diſciples of his inſtitution, as, to put away ones wife for every cauſe, to ſeek reveng from the judg upon the injurious perſon: yet, between the precepts of Chriſt and thoſe permiſſions, there is a certain diverſity,

versity, no repugnance. For he that keeps his wife, and remits the injury, doth nothing against the Law, yea he doth that which the Law wills most. 'Tis otherwise with the Judge, whom the Law not permits, but commands to put the Murderer to death, himself becomming guilty of blood before God, unless in this case he shed it. If Christ forbid him thus to punish the murderer, his precept is plainly contrary to the law, he dissolveth the law.

XIX. *The Sixt, Seventh, and Eighth Arguments.*

THe sixth is from the example of *Cornelius* the Centurion, who received from Christ the Holy Spirit, an undoubted sign of his justification, and was Baptized in the name of Christ by the Apostle *Peter*: but, that he left his Office of War, or was advised by *Peter* to leave it, we do not read. Some answer, whereas he had instruction from *Peter* concerning Christian Religion, it is to be supposed that he was also instructed to desert his place. This were something, if it were certain and undoubted that Christ among the rest of his precepts had forbidden War. But, when that is no where else expressed, here at least was a fit place to say somewhat of it, that the age to come might not be ignorant of the rules of their duty. Nor is it the manner of *Luke*, where the quality of the perſons required a ſpecial change of life, to paſs it over with ſilence; as we may ſee elſewhere. (Acts 19.19.) The ſeventh Argument, like to this, is taken from that which we began afore to ſay of *Sergius Paulus*; for in the ſtory of his converſion, there is no intimation of his renouncing his office, nor of any admonition given him to do ſo. Now, that which is not related, (as even now we ſaid) when it is of moſt concernment, and the place requires it, is to be conceived not at all to be done. The eighth may be this, that * *Paul* the Apoſtle having underſtood the Jews plot againſt him, willed it to be revealed to the chief Captain: † and when the chief Captain gave him a guard of Souldiers to ſecure his journy, he accepted of it, making never a word to the Captain or the Souldiers, that God was not pleaſed with reſiſting of force by force. And yet *Paul* was a man, who would himſelf omit, nor ſuffer others to omit, no occaſion of teaching men their duty *.

* Utitur hujus loci autoritate Concil. Afric. *Quorum contra furorem poſſumus non inſolita nec à ſcripturis aliena impetrare præſidia, quando Apoſtolus Paulus, ſicut in Apoſtolorum Act. fidelibus notum eſt, factioſorum conſpirationem militari etiam ſubmovit auxilio.* Auguſtin. Epiſt. 154. ad Public. *Neque ſi in illa arma ſcelerati homines incidiſſent, Paulus in effuſione ſanguinis ſuum crimen agnoſceret.* † Acts 23. * 2 Tim. 4. 2.

XX. *The*

XX. *The ninth, tenth, and eleventh Arguments.*

NInthly, The proper end of a thing just and lawfull, cannot but be just lawfull. It is not only lawfull, but we have a precept obliging the conscience, to pay tribute; And the end of Tribute is, that the publick powers may have wherewith to defray the charge upon them, for the defence of good men, and the coercion of the bad. *Tacitus* speaks to our purpose, *The quiet of the world cannot be had without Arms, no Arms without Souldiers pay, nor pay without contribution.* Tenthly, * *Paul* speaks thus, *If I be an offender, or have committed any thing worthy of death, I refuse not to die* †. Whence I collect, that in *Paul*'s judgement, even since the publication of the Gospel, there are some crimes, which equity alloweth, yea and requireth, to be punished with death. Which also *Peter* sheweth in the first of his Epistles. Had the will of God been so now, that capital judgements should cease, *Paul* might indeed have made an Apology for himself, but he ought not to have left in the minds of his hearers such an opinion, as this, that it was no less lawfull now than heretofore, to put offenders to death. Now,

Rom. 13.

Hist. 4.

Augustin. contra Faust. l. 22. c. 74. Ad hoc tributa præstamus, ut propter necessaria militi stipendium præbeatur.

* Acts 25. 11. So also Acts 28. 18. For there was no cause of death in me.

C. 2. 19. 20.

† Justin Apol. 2. *Ut autem puniantur, qui non convenienter præceptis illis vivunt, & nomine solo sunt Christiani, & quidem à vobis, & nos optamus.*

Now, it being proved, that capital punishments are rightly used since the comming of Christ, it is withall proved, as I suppose, that some War may be lawfully waged, to wit, against a multitude of armed offenders, who must be overcome in battail, before they can be brought to judgement. For, the forces of offenders, and their boldness to resist, as in a prudent deliberation it hath some moment, so it diminisheth nothing of the right it self. Lastly, the Law of Christ hath taken away the Law of *Moses* only, which was the partition
Eph.2.14. wall between the Gentiles and the Hebrews. Things by nature honest, and by the consent of civil nations, it is so far from taking away, that it hath comprehended them all under the general
Phil.4.8. precept of *all honesty and virtue*. But,
2 Cor.11.13, 14. the punishment of crimes, and Arms to keep off injury are accounted laudable in their Nature, and are referred to the virtue of justice and beneficence. And here, on the by, we must note their error, who draw the Israelites right to War, from this alone, that God had granted to them the Canaanites Land. For this is not the only cause, though it be a just one. Before those times, men of piety, conducted by their reason, waged Wars: and the Israelites themselves afterward upon other grounds, as *David* for the violation of his Embassadors. Besides,

Besides, what any one possesseth by humane right, is no less his own, than if God had made an immediate grant thereof; which right is not taken away (but confirmed) by the Gospel.

XXI. *Objections answered.* *The first.*

LEt us now also see, by what Arguments the opposite opinion underprops it self, that the pious Reader may more easily judge, which of the two is more firm and weighty. The first is usually brought out of *Esay*'s prophecy *, who saith, it shall come to pass, *that the Nations shall beat their swords into plow-shares, and their spears into pruning-hooks: Nation shall not lift up sword against Nation, neither shall they learn War any more.* But this prophecy, either is to be understood (as many other) *conditionally*: Such shall be the state of things, if all people undertake and fulfil the Law of Christ; to which purpose God will suffer nothing to be wanting on his part: Sure enough it is, if all be Christians, and live Christian-

Es. 2. 4.

* Id de pace quæ orbi contigit beneficio Romani Imperii interpretatur Chrysost. oratione Christum esse Deum; *Neque vero prædictum tantum est, stabilem fore, immotam, atque inconcussam hanc religionem, sed cum ea adventuram orbi pacem, desituras illas in singulis civitatibus plurium potentias, regnaque ipsa, & unum fore super omnes imperium, ac ejus pleraque pacem habitura, contra quam ante fiebat*, &c. & vid. *Euseb. de præpar. l.* 1. *c.* 10.

ly, there will be no Wars *: Or, it is to be underſtood ſimply and purely; and thus, experience tells us, this prophecy is not yet fulfill'd, but the impletion thereof, as alſo of the general converſion of the Jews, is yet to be waited for. Which way ſoever you take it, nothing can be inferred hence againſt the juſtice of Wars, ſo long as there are who ſuffer not the lovers of peace to live at peace, but offer violence and uſe force againſt them.

* Lactant: *Quid fiet, ſi omnes in concordiam conſenſerint? Quod certe fieri poterit, ſi pernicioſo & impio furore projecto innocentes ac juſti eſſe velint.* Juſtin. de Chriſtianis. *Non pugnamus in hoſtes.* Planè ut de Eſſenis Philo in Orat. Omnem bonum eſſe liberum: *Nullum inter eos reperias qui aut jacula, aut ſagittas, aut gladium, aut galeam, aut loricam, aut ſcutum fabricet; Nullum qui aut arma conficiat aut machinas.* Simile eſt quod Chryſoſtomus ait ad 1 Cor. 13.3. *Si eſſet inter homines qualis oportet dilectio, nullas fore pœnas capitales.*

XXII. *The ſecond Objection anſwered.*

OUt of the fift of *Matthew* ſundry Arguments are deduced; which we cannot rightly judge of, unleſs we remember what was ſaid afore: If Chriſt had purpoſed to take away all capital judgements, and the right of Wars, he would have done it in words moſt expreſs and ſpecial, by reaſon of the greatneſs and newneſs of the matter: and the rather, becauſe no Jew could think otherwiſe, but that the Laws of *Moſes*, pertaining to judgements and the Common-wealth, ought to have their force upon the men of that Nation, ſo long

as

as their state endured. This being premised, let us weigh the places in their order. The second muniment of the adverse party is from these words, *Ye have* Mat.5.38,39.
heard that it hath been said, An eye for an eye, and a tooth for a tooth: But I say unto you, that ye resist not the injurious person (so the *Gr.* turns the original word, *Exod.* 21 *.) *But whosoever shall smite thee on the right cheek, turn to him the other also.* Hence do some infer, that no injury is to be repelled or revenged; neither privately, nor publikely. But this is not the meaning of the words; for Christ speaks not here to Magistrates, but to those that are injured; nor doth he speak of every injury, but of such as a blow on the cheek: the following words restrain the generality of the precedent. So likewise in the next immediate precept, *If any man will sue thee at the Law, and take away thy coat, let him have thy cloak also* *: Not every sute before the judge or arbitrator is forbidden (let *Paul* be the Interpreter, who denies not all sutes, but prohibites the Christians to contend in the Courts of Heathens; and that after the Jews example, whose common saying it was, *Whosoever brings the affairs of* Israel *before the stranger,*

* τῷ ἀδικοῦντι, *ut & Lucas in Stephani oratione*: ὁ ἀδικῶν τὸν πλησίον.

* Id ita exponit Cyprianus de patientia: *Ut tua oblata non repetas.* Irenæus l.4.c.27. *Tollenti tibi tunicam, remitte ei & pallium, sed non quasi nolentes fraudari contristemur; sed quasi volentes donaverimus, gaudeamus. Et si quis te, inquit, angariaverit mille passus, vade cum eo alia duo, ut non quasi servus sequaris, sed quasi liber præcedas.* Etiam Libanius, qui Evangelia legerat, laudat non litigantes de chlamyde & tunica, in orat. de custodia reorum.

 pollutes

pollutes the name of God :) but the will of Christ is, to exercise our patience; that we should not go to Law about things which may easily be repaired, as a Coat, or (if it so happen) the cloak also:- but that, although our cause be good, wee should omit the prosecution of our right.
Philostrat. 2. 15. *Apollonius Tyaneus* said, It was not the part of a Philosopher to contend about a little money.
L. Item. si S. 1. & D. de alien. jud. mur. causa facta. *The Prætor* (saith *Ulpian*) *approoves his doing, who would content himself and sit down with the loss of a thing, rather than be troubled with often sutes about it. For this mans disposition, that cannot endure contention, is in no wise to be dispraised.* What *Ulpian* here saith is approved by the best, the same doth Christ command, choosing the matter of his precepts from among the things that are most honest and most approved. But, you may not collect hence, that it is unlawfull for a Parent, or for a Tutor, to defend that before a Judge, without which the Children, without which the pupils cannot be maintained. For the coat and cloak is one thing, the Lively-hood another. In
L. 1. c. 45. *Clement*'s Constitutions it is said of a Christian man, if he hath a sute, *let him endeavour to end it, though he bear some damage.* As in matters of morality, so here we say, these things do not consist in a point, but have a certain latitude belonging to them. So in that which follows,

follows, *And whosoever shall compell thee to go a mile, go with him twain:* Our Lord said not, a hundred mile, a journey that would take a man off too far from his own occasions; but one mile, or, if need be, twain: a walk, not very irksom. The sense therefore is, in these things which import no great incommodity, we must not stand upon our own right, but yield, even more than another would require, that our patience * and our benignity may be known unto all men. It follows, *Give † to him that asketh thee: and from him that would borrow of thee, turn not thou away.* If you carry it on infinitely, and without measure, nothing is more hard. He that provideth not for those of his own house is worse than an infidel, saith *Paul.* Let us then follow the same *Paul,* the best interpreter of his Master's Law, who stirring up the *Corinthians* to exercise beneficence toward the poor of *Jerusalem: Not,* saith he, *that other men be eased, and you burthened: but by an equality: that your abundance may be a supply* * *for their want;* which sense is also in *Xenophon*'s *Cyrus; What I shall see superfluous in my own estate will*

* Justinus Apologet. 2. *Quæ dicit, huc pertinent, ut adversus omnes simus patientes, officiosi, minime iracundi.*
† Iust. Apol. eod. *De communicandis verò facultatibus nostris cum egentibus, & nequid ad gloriam aucupandam faciamus, hæc dixit: Omni petenti date,* &c. Alibi, *Communicantes nostra omni egenti.*
1 Tim. 5. 8.
2 Cor. 8. 13.
* Sen. de benefic. 2. *Dabo egenti, sed ut ipse non egeam.* Chrysost. in loc. *Deus pro facultate poscit, quatenus habet quis, non quatenus non habet.* Quod ut recte intelligatur accedant sequentia: *Laudat quidem quod facultates exsuperat* (nempe in Thessalonicensibus:) *sed hos* (Achæos sc.) *non cogit idem facere.*

serve

serve the necessities of my friends. The like equity must we use for the interpretation of that precept now in hand. The Hebrew Law, as it did indulge a liberty of divorce, to prevent the cruelty of Husbands toward their Wives; so also, for the restraint of private revenge, whereto that Nation was very prone, allowed the offended party a right, to exact, not by his own hand, but by the sentence of the Judge, a retaliation: a Law imitated in the 12. Tables. But Christ, a Teacher of more patience, is so far from approving that ardent desire of revenge in the person wronged, that he would not have some kind of injuries to be repelled, either by force, or Law. What injuries? Such as are tolerable; not, that patience is not laudable in the more * grievous, but he is content with a patience more limited. Therefore he puts the case in a stroke on the cheek, which endangereth not the life, maimeth not the body, but only signifies a certain contempt of us, which makes us nothing the worse. *Seneca* in his Book of a wise mans constancy distinguishes between an injury and a disgrace, *The former*, saith he, *is by nature the more grievous: this is lighter, and only grievous to the delicate, whereby they are not hurt, but offended.* Again, *Contumely is less than injury, which*

Si membrum rupit, talio esto.

* Vid. Chrysostomum dicto jam loco.

which we may rather complain of, than return: which the Laws also have thought worthy of no revenge. The same *Seneca* a little after saith, *The grief arising from disgrace, or an affront, is an affection comming from a meaneß and lowneß of the spirit, contracting it self for some word or deed against our reputation.* In such a case therefore, Christ commandeth patience: *to turn the other cheek*, is by an Hebraism, to bear patiently, as appears in * other places: and lest any one object that common sentence, *To suffer one injury is to invite another*, He addes, that we must rather bear * a new injury, than repel the former: because there is no evill to us thence, but that which consists in a foolish † persuasion.

* Es. 30. 6. Jer. 3. 3. *Præbere os contumeliis.* Tacit. & Terentius.

* Chrys 7. ad Rom. *Hæc egregia victoria, plus illi largiri quam velit, & fines improbæ in illo lubidinis liberalitate propria patientiæ transcendere.* † Idem de statuis 1. *Contumelia non ab inferentis animo, sed ex judicio eorum qui patiuntur aut fit aut perit.*

XXIII. *The third Objection answered.*

THe third Objection is taken from the words that follow in the same place of *Matthew* *: *Ye have heard, that it hath been said, Thou shalt love thy neighbour, and hate thine enemy. But I say unto you, Love your enemies, bleß them that curse you, do good to them that hate you, and pray for them which despitefully use*

* Mat. 5. 43, 44.

use you and persecute you. Some there be that hold, this love and beneficence towards enemies and persecutors cannot consist with capital judgements or Wars. But they are easily refuted, if we do but consult with that saying of the Hebrew Law. It was commanded the Hebrews to love their Neighbour, that is, their fellow-Hebrew *: for so the word *Neighbour* is taken there. Neverthelesss were the Magistrates commanded to put Murderers to death, and other capital offenders; neverthelesss was the Tribe of *Benjamin*, for an abominable transgression, prosecuted in a just War by all the other Tribes; neverthelesss did *David*, who fought the Lord's battails, rightly recover the Kingdom promised him, from *Isbosheth* by Arms. Be it so then, that the signification of *Neighbour* is larger now, and conteins every man; for all are now received into common grace, no people are by God devoted and given up to destruction: yet will that be lawfull towards all, which was then lawfull towards the Israelites, who were commanded to be lov'd as well, as all men now. But, if you would have a greater degree of love to be commanded in the Evangelical Law, let this be granted also, so that this be agreed on too, that all are not * equally to be loved, but a Father more than a foreiner. And so the good of

Levit. 19. 17, 18.
* Cui par proselytus.

* Tertul. adv. Marcion. 4. *Secundus gradus bonitatis est in extraneos: in proximos primus.* Hiero-

of an innocent person is to be prefer'd before the good of a nocent, the common good above the private, by the Law of regular charity. Now, from the love and care of the innocent, * both capital judgements and pious Wars have their original. Wherefore, the precepts of Christ, concerning love and charity to every one, ought so to be fulfill'd, unless a greater and more just and necessary point of charity will not suffer. That old saying is well known: *To pardon all is cruelty, as much as to pardon none* *: Adde, that we are enjoyned to love our enemies after the example of God, who makes his Sun to shine upon the bad. Yet the same God executeth punishment, even in this life, upon some bad ones, and hereafter will severely punish all. VVhereby is also answered whatsoever is wont to be alleged here out of the precepts of Christian lenity. For God is called gentle, merciful, and long suffering: Yet do the Holy Scriptures set forth in sundry places the anger of the same God against the obstinate *, and his will to punish the ungodly: And the Magistrate is

nym. adv. Pelag. dial. 1. *Praeceptum est mihi ut diligam inimicos & orem pro persecutoribus. Nunquid justum est ut ita diligam, quasi proximos & consanguineus; ut inter amulum & necessarium nulla distinctio fit.*
* Vid. Prov. 24.11.
* Sen. de Clem. 1. *Tam omnibus ignoscere, crudelitas est, quam nulli:* Chrys. 1. ad Cor. 3. 12. &c. de pœnis hum. agens: *Non ex saevitia, sed ex bonitate talia faciunt homines.* Augustin: *sicut est aliquando misericordia puniens, ita & crudelitas parcens.* Valentinianus, Theodosius & Arcadius, in lege tertia, Cod. Theod. de defensorib. Civit. *Removeantur patrocinia, quae favorē reis & auxiliū facinorosis impertinendo, maturari scelera faciunt.* Totilas apud Procop. Got. 2. *Peccare & prohibere pœnas peccantium in pari pono.* Joh. 4. 2. Exod. 34. 6. Num. 14. 18. Rom. 2. 8. * Vide hac de re Cyrillum lib. 5. cont. Julian.

ordained

Rom.13.4. ordained the Minifter of this wrath. *Mofes* is commended for his exceeding meeknefs: yet this fame *Mofes* punifhed the guilty, and that with death. We are often bid to imitate the meeknefs and patience of Chrift: yet Chrift is he, who did inflict moft heavy judgements, * upon the rebellious Jews, and will at the day of judgement condemn the wicked according to their deferts, Their Mafters lenity was followed by the Apoftles, who did neverthelefs make ufe of the power * given them from above for the chaftifement of ungodly men, as we read in feverall * places.

* Mat.21.44. 22.7. Luke 19.12, 14,27. Chryfoft. ad Rom.14. narratis malis ierofolymorum *Chriftū effe qui hac fecerit, audi ipfum praecidentem, tum per parabolas, tum apertè & exfertè.* * Chryfoft. 1 Cor.4.21. *Interficiam, mutilabo? Eft enim ut lenitatis, ita & feveritatis fpiritus.* Vide & Auguftin. de ferm. Dom. in monte lib.1. & alios quos citat Gratian.23.8. * 1 Cor.4.21. 1 Cor.5.5. 1 Tim.1.20.

XXIV. *The fourth Objection anfwered.*

Rom.12.17, 18,&c. THe fourth place, which is objected, is, *Recompence to no man evill for evill. Provide things honeft in the fight of all men. If it be poffible, as much as lyeth in you, live peaceably with all men. Dearly beloved, avenge * not your felves, but rather give place unto wrath, for it is written, Vengeance is mine, I will repay, faith the Lord. Therefore if thine enemy hunger, feed him: if he thirft, give*

* Tertul. de pat. *Quid mihi cum ultione, cujus modum regere non poffum per impatientiā doloris?*

give him drink; for in so doing thou shalt heap coals of fire on his head. Be not overcome of evil, but overcome evil with good. But here also the same Answer offers it self, which was given above. For at what time it was said by God, *Vengeance is mine, I will repay*, at the same time were capital judgements exercised, and Laws written concerning Wars. Moreover, benefits are commanded to be done (even then) to enemies, being their own Countrymen. These things notwithstanding, there were, as we have said, both capital punishments, and just VVars upon the Israelites themselves. Wherefore, the same words or the like precepts, though of larger extent, are not now neither to be forced to such a sense: the less, because the division of Chapters is not from the Apostles, nor their age, but of much later time, for the more distinct reading, and easy allegation of the text. So, the beginning of the 13. to the *Romans, Let every Soul be subject to the higher powers*, and that which follows, was continued with those foregoing precepts against revenge. Now, in this dissertation *Paul* saith, the publike powers are Ministers of God, to execute wrath (*i. e.* punishment) upon them that do evil: therein most plainly distinguishing between vengeance for the publike good (which is administred in

August. Epist. 154. *Hinc autem dictum est, non resistamus malo, ne nos vindicta delectet, quæ alieno malo animum pascit.*

Exod. 23. 4, 5.

in behalf of God, and is to be referred to the vengeance reserved to God;) and that revenge for private satisfaction, which he forbad in the former words. For, if you will have that vengeance also which is expected for the publike good, comprehended in that in-interdict, what will be more absurd, than for the Apostle, when he had said we must abstain from capital judgements, presently to adde, The publike powers are ordained of God for this end, to exact punishments in his stead?

XXV. *The fift, sixt and seventh Objections answered.*

THe fift place which some make use of is in the second Epistle to the *Corinthians*: *Though wee walk in the flesh, we do not War after the flesh: For the weapons of our warfare are not * carnal, but mighty, through God to the pulling down of strong-holds*, &c. But this place makes nothing to the matter. For both the antecedents and consequents do shew, that by the name of *flesh*, *Paul* understands here the weak constitution of body, which came under their eyes, and in respect of which he was contemned. Hereunto *Paul* opposeth his weapons, that is, the power given him, as an Apostle, to subdue the refractory, such as he used upon *Elymas*, upon

2 Cor. 10. 3, 4.

* Chrysostomus hoc loco intelligit, *opes, gloriam, potentiam, eloquentiam, solertiã, prensationes, assentationes, fallacias.*

upon the incestuous Corinthian, upon *Hymeneus* and *Alexander*. This power, he saith, is not carnal, that is, weak: yea on the contrary, he asserteth it to be most mighty. What is this to the right of capital punishments, or of War? Yea, on our side, because the Church at that time was destitute of ayd from the publick powers, Therfore had God raised up, for her defense, that prodigious power, which began afterward to fail about the time when Christian Emperours were given the Church, even as Manna ceased, when the Hebrew people were come into the fruitful Land. That which is alleged, Eph. 6. 11. sixtly, out of the Epistle to the Ephesians, *Put on the whole Armour of God, that yee may be able to stand against the wiles of the devil: for we wrestle not against flesh and bloud*, (supply, *only*, after the Hebrew phrase) *but against principalities*, &c. This place, I say, speaks of the fight which belongs to Christians, as they are Christians, not, which they may have common with other men, upon certain occasions. The place of *James* which is urged, seventhly, *From* Jam. 4. 1. *whence come Wars and fightings among you? come they not hence, even of your lusts that War in your members?* &c. This conteins nothing universal: only it saith, the Wars and fights, whereby the dispersed Hebrews were at that time miserably dashed to pieces, and beaten one by another

another (some part of which sad story is to be seen in * *Josephus*) had their rise from causes not commendable: a thing which comes to pass in our dayes also, as we see with grief †. As for that which was spoken to *Peter*, *They that take the sword shall perish by the sword*, seeing it properly pertains not to War considered in common, but to private War (for even Christ himself gives this reason, why he forbad or neglected the defence of himself, because his Kingdom was not of this world) it shall be more rightly handled in its own place.

* *Antiq. l.* 18. *cap.* 12. *& lib. seq.*

† *Divitis hoc vitium est auri, nec bella fuere, Faginus astabat cum scyphus ante dapes.* Tibul. Lucan —— *O prodigia rerum Luxuries, nunquam parvo contenta paratu*, &c. Cic. de fin. I. *Ex cupiditatibus odia, dissidia, discordiæ, seditiones, bella nascuntur.* Max. Tyrius. *Nunc omnia bellis plena: ubique enim oberrant cupiditates, & per omnes terras excitant appetitum rerum alienarum.* Diogenis' dictum huc pertinet: *Non enim ex his qui polentam edunt, aut fures existunt, aut bellorum auctores.* Hieronymus adversus Jovinianum 2. *Diogenes tyrannos & subversores urbium bellaque vel hostilia, vel civilia, non pro simplici victu olerum pomorumque, sed pro carnium & epularum deliciis asserit excitari.* Polybius: *Animus necessariis contentus, alio ad sapiendum Magistro non eget.*

XXVI *Of the opinion of the antient Fathers. The first Observation.*

WHen the question is about the sense of a writing, both the following practice, and the authority of wise men is wont to have much value. This is a good rule in the interpretation of holy Scripture. For it is not probable, that the Churches founded by the Apostles

postles, did either ſuddainly, or all of them depart from thoſe things, which the Apoſtles having briefly written, had explained more largely by word of mouth, or alſo introduced into the practice and uſe of Chriſtians. Now, our opponents that fight againſt Wars, uſually draw out unto their aid, ſome ſpeeches of the antient Chriſtians: to which I have three things to ſay. The firſt is this: No more can be collected out of thoſe ſpeeches, than the private opinion of the ſpeakers, not the publick judgement of the Churches. It is moreover to be noted, that the Authors of thoſe ſayings love to go ſingle, for the moſt part, and to teach ſomewhat of a higher ſtrain, than others; namely, *Origen* and *Tertullian*; who yet are not very conſtant to themſelves. For the ſame *Origen* ſaith, God hath given us a leſſon in the Bees, *That juſt and orderly Wars may be waged amongſt men, if neceſſity require.* And the ſame *Tertullian* ſaith, *That it is good when Offenders are puniſhed no man denies* †. And he is at a ſtand concerning Warfare; for in his *De Idolatria*, he propoſeth the queſtion, *Whether Chriſtians may turn*

† Idem Tertul. de anima. *Quis non præferat ſæculi juſtitiam, quam & Apoſtolus non fruſtra gladio accinctam conteſtatur, quæ pro homine ſæviendo religioſa eſt?* Et ad Proconſ. Scapula: *Non te terremus, qui nec timemus. Sed velim ut omnes ſalvos facere poſſimus, monendo μὴ θεομαχεῖν. Potes & officio juriſdictionis tuæ fungi, & humanitatis meminiſſe, vel quia & vos ſub gladio eſtis.*

Souldiers, and Souldiers Christians; Where he seems to incline to the opinion against War. But in his *De corona militis*, when he had disputed some things against warfare, presently he distinguishes those that were Souldiers before their Baptism, from others that after Baptism enter into Arms. *Plainly*, saith he, *their case is otherwise, whom Christian Religion found out after they were engag'd in the profession of Arms, as the Souldiers whom* John *admitted to his Baptism; as the most faithful Centurions, whom Christ commendeth, and whom* Peter *instructeth. Provided, that after their receiving of the faith* * *and signing it, they forsake the War, as many have done; or else, by all means beware, they commit no offence against God.* His opinion therefore was, that they continued Souldiers after Baptism: which certainly they would not have done, had they understood warfare to have been forbidden by Christ; no more than South-sayers, Magicians, and other professors of unlawfull † Arts, were permitted after Baptism to remain in their Art formerly professed. In the same Book, praising a certain Souldier, and one that was a Christian, he spareth not to exclame, and stile him, * *a Souldier glorious in God.*

* Distinctionem quam hic de militia affert, alibi ad nuptia applicat, tum lib. de Monogamia, tum exhortatione castitatis.

† Tertul. de idolatria. *Ad ecclesiam non admittuntur, qui artes exercent, quas Dei disciplina non recipit.* Aug. de fid. & op. *Meretrices & histriones & quilibet alii publicæ turpitudinis professores, nisi solutis aut diruptis talibus vinculis, ad Christi sacramenta non permittuntur accedere.* De histrione exemplum vide apud Cyprianum Ep. 65. * *O militem in Deo gloriosum!*

XXVI. *The*

XXVII. *The second Observation.*

OUr second Observation is, That the Christians have either disallowed or avoided serving in the Wars, by reason of circumstances and condition of the times, which would scarce permit Military orders to be executed without some acts repugnant to the Christian Law. In the Letters of *Dolabella* to the Ephesians, extant in *Josephus*, we see the Jews requested immunity from expeditions of War; because in such a mixture with strangers, they were not able to keep their legal rites with due observance: and because they were constreined to carry Arms, and make long marches upon the Sabbath dayes. For which causes, they obteined a dismission from *L. Lentulus*, as the same *Josephus* sheweth. He declares in another place, that when the Jews were commanded to depart the City of *Rome*, some of them were listed, others punished for their refusal out of a reverence toward their own Country-Laws; for those reasons which we have mentioned: unto which sometimes a third was added, because they had a necessity imposed on them to fight against their own Country men. But, *to take arms against those of their own Nation was great impiety*, to wit, when their Country-men try-men were perſecuted, for obſerving the Laws of their Fathers. Nevertheleſs, as often as the Jews could eſchew theſe incommodities, they bare arms, even under foreign Kings; but, * *perſiſting in their Fathers Ordinances, and living according to their preſcripts*: which they were wont to ſecure themſelves of, by agreement aforehand, as the ſame *Joſephus* teſtifieth. To theſe hazards are thoſe moſt like, which *Tertullian* objecteth againſt ſerving in the Wars in his time: *The enſign of Chriſt hath no agreement with the enſign of the devil, nor the oath of God with that of man*: for the Souldiers were made to ſwear by the Gods of the Gentiles, *Jove*, *Mars*, and the reſt. Again: *ſhall a Chriſtian keep watch for the Temples, which he hath renounced, and eat there where the Apoſtle will not permit him? ſhall he guard thoſe evil ſpirits by night, whom he hath exorciſed by day?* a little after: *How many other great offences may be viewed in the Camp-Offices, which muſt needs be interpreted tranſgreſſions of our Law?*

* Joſeph. 11. Hiſtoriæ antiquæ.

Lib. de Idol.

Lib. de cor. militis.

XXVIII. *The third Obſervation.*

THirdly we note, that the Chriſtians of the firſt times were enflam'd with ſo great ardour to undertake all things which were moſt excellent, that they oft

oft embraced divine Counsels for commands. The Christians (saith *Athenagoras*) *do not go to law with them that by violence take away their goods. Salvian* saith, it is the will of Christ, that we let go the things about which is any controversie, that we may be acquitted of the sute. But this, so generally taken, is perhaps a matter of Counsel, and of a more sublime and perfect way of life *, but not under any precise command. In like manner, very many of the antients disapprove all oaths, without exception; yet *Paul*, in a matter of great consequence, used an oath. *Tatian* speaks of a certain Christian that refused the prætorship: and saith *Tertullian, a Christian loves not to be made an Edile*. So *Lactantius* will not let a just man (such he would have every Christian) go to War: neither would he have him go to Sea. And how many of the old Doctors dehort Christians from Marriage? All which particulars, suppose they be laudable, excellent, very acceptable to God, yet are they not required at our hands by the necessity of any Law. And this is sufficient for the solution of objections.

* Concil. Carth. 4. *Episcopus nec provocatus de rebus transitoriis litiget.* Adde Ambros. l. 2. Off. c. 21. & Gregor. M. l. 2. Ind. 11. Epist. 58.

XXIX. *A Confirmation of the lawfulneſs of War, out of the Antients.*

NOw, that we may confirm our doctrine; firſt there are not wanting to us VVriters, and thoſe of the more antient ſort, who think both capital puniſhments, and VVars which depend thereon, may lawfully be us'd by Chriſtians. For *Clemens* of *Alexandria* ſaith, A Chriſtian, if he be call'd to govern, will be like *Moſes*, a living Law unto his ſubjects, and he will render to the good rewards, to the evil puniſhments. And elſewhere deſcribing the habit of a Chriſtian, he ſaith, it becomes him to go barefoot, unleſs perhaps

L.7. c.3. he be a Souldier. In the * Conſtitutions which bear the name of *Clemens Romanus* we read thus: *All killing is not unlawful, but only of the innocent: yet is that which is juſt reſerved only to the Magiſtrates.* But, private authorities being laid aſide, let us come to the publick authority of the Church, which ought to be of greateſt weight. I ſay then, that the Church never rejected, nor excommunicated any for ſerving in the Wars; Which yet ought to have been done, and would have been done, if War had been repugnant

L.8. C. 22. to the new Teſtament. In the Conſtitutions now cited, that writer ſpeaking

* Videtur ſcriptus is liber finiente ſæculo ſecundo.

king of such as antiently were wont to be admitted to Baptism, or rejected from it, saith: *Let a Souldier requiring Baptism be taught to abstein from injuries and oppressions: to be content with his wages. If he observe these things, let him be admitted.* *Tertullian* in his Apologetick speaking in the name of Christians; *We go to Sea, and to War in your Company.* C. 42. A little before he had said: *We are strangers, and yet we have filled all places, your Cities, Islands, Castles, Towns, Councils, yea your Camps also.* C. 37. In the same Book he had related, how by the prayers of the Christian Souldiers a shower of Rain was obteined from Heaven to refresh the Army of *Marcus* * *Aurelius* Emperour. In his *De corona* he saith, That Souldier, that threw away his Garland was more constant than his other Brethren; and sheweth, that he had many Christian fellow-Souldiers. Moreover, some Souldiers were not wanting, who having suffered torments for Christ, even to the death, received from the Church the same honour with the rest of Martyrs; Among whom are remembred the three Companions of *Paul* *; *Certalis* under *Decius*, *Marinus* under *Valerian*, fifty under *Aurelian*; *Victor*, *Maurus*, and *Valentinus* the Master of the Souldiers under *Maximianus*; *Marcellus* the Centurion about the same time; *Severian* under *Licinius*.

* Vide & Xiphilinum de hac historia.

* Adde militem quendam à Cornelio Baptizatum, cujus apud Adonē mentio.

Concer-

Concerning *Laurentinus* and *Ignatius Africans*, these are the words of *Cyprian*, *Being Souldiers in the secular warfare, but spiritual Souldiers too, whilst they get the victory over the Devil by the confession of Christ, they have obtained, by their passion, victorious palms and glorious Crowns of their Lord.*

XXX. *Further proof out of Ecclesiastical History.*

FRom the former testimonies it is evident, what opinion the community of Christians had of War, even before the Emperours were Christian. If, in those times, the Christians were not willingly present at capital punishments, it may not seem a wonder, when for the most part Christians were the persons condemned. Adde hereunto, that in other matters also, the Roman Laws were harder than Christian lenity would suffer, as appears sufficiently, though we instance only in the * *Silanian* Decree of Senate. But, after *Constantine* began both to approve and advance the Christian Religion, capital punishments did not therefore cease. Yea *Constantine* himself, among other Laws, made one about sowing up paricides in a sack: which Law is extant in the *Code* * : though otherwise in exacting punishments he was so gentle, that he is

* Cujus asperitatem mitigavit Adrianus Imp. ut apud Spartianum est. Asperis Romanorum legibus addi possunt quæ servum nisi tortum testimonium dicere vetant.

* Tit. de iis qui par. vel lib. occiderunt.

is accus'd of too much * lenity by some Historians. Besides, He had in his Army very many Christians, as the Histories do teach us, and inscribed on his Ensign the name of Christ. And from that time was the military oath changed into that form, extant in *Vegetius*: *By God and Christ, and the Holy Spirit, and by the Majesty of the Emperour, next after God to be lov'd and honour'd by mankind.* And at that time, among so many Bishops, of whom many had suffer'd very much for Religion, we do not read of any one, who deterred either *Constantine* wholy from capital punishments, and from War, or the Christians from serving in the War, by threatning them with the wrath of God for the same: when yet there were very many most rigid keepers of Discipline, and such as would not dissemble or pass by any thing that pertained either to the Office of the Emperours or of other men. Such a Prelate was *Ambrose* in the time of *Theodosius*, whose words are these: *It is no sin to be a Souldier; but, for a Souldier to fight for the spoil only, that's a sin.* And in another place: *Valour, which either in War defends our Country from Barbarians, or at home defends the weak, or our friends from robbers, is full of Justice.* This Argument is to me of so much weight, that I require no more. Yet am

* Zonaras: *Clementem se ostendebat iis qui pravam vitam deseruerant, quod diceret abscindendum membrum ægrotans ac putridum, ne sana contagio corrumpat, non id quod aut sanatum jam sit, aut sanescat.* Vide & Eusebium. Sicut de nimia Constantini Christianos, ita de Haraldi regis questos Danos apud Saxonem Historicum invenias.

Serm. 7.

De Offic. l. 1. c. 27.

am I not ignorant, that Bishops * often, and the Christian people, by their intercessions averted punishments, especially the capital ones: and, that a custom was introduced, that persons who had fled unto the Church † and taken Sanctuary, were not rendred without promise given to save their lives: and, that at *Easter* *, they should be deliver'd out of prison, whom their crimes had laid there: But, whosoever, shall advisedly consider these, and such like things, will find, they are indeed signs of Christian goodness, taking all occasion of shewing mercy, not arguments of a mind condemning all sentences of death upon capital offenders: wherefore, those benefits, and intercessions too, were tempered and limited by certain † exceptions both of times and places.

* Augustin. *Officium sacerdotis est intervenire pro reis.* In ejus Epistolis multa sunt hujus bonitatis specimina.

† Vide Chrysostomum 16. de Statuis. Concil. Aurelian c. 3. legem Wisigothorum l. 6. tit. 5. 16. 9. tit. 2 3.

* L. Nemo, C. de Episc. audientia.

† Quas vide apud Cassiadorum. 11. 40. &c. inter alia de immunitate Ecclesiastica in Decreto.

XXXI. *The twelfth Canon of the* Nicene *Council objected and answer'd.*

SOme do here object against us the twelth Canon of the *Nicene* Council, which is to this effect: *Such * as have been call'd by grace, that have shewed their first love and faith in throwing off their belt, and have afterward like Dogs returned to their vomit; some giving money*

* *Simeon Magister in ejus Canonis epitome: Qui vi adhibita visi sunt restitisse, sed ab impietate victi sunt, &*

money and bribes to return into their place; let them lye among the penitents ten years, after they have been three years among the Hearers. But in them all must be observed the sincerity and measure of their repentance. For, they that by fear, and tears, and patiance, and good works do shew their conversion to be without hyprocrisy, after they have fulfilled their appointed time of hearing, shall be admitted to the prayers of the Church, and afterward the Bishop may entertain some favourable thoughts concerning them. But, they that have indifferently and slightly taken their fall, and think it sufficient to their conversion, if they have but entred into the Church, shall without any dispensation fulfill the whole time appointed. The time it self of thirteen years is evidence enough, that no light or ambiguous fault, but some grievous and undoubted crime is here meant. And certainly 'tis no other than * Idolatry. For the times of *Licinius* mentioned afore in the eleventh Canon, ought to be understood in this: as it often happens, that the sense of the Canons subsequent depends upon the precedent; for example, see the eleventh Canon of the *Eliberin* Council. Now *Licinius*, as *Eusebius* relates, *cashier'd the Souldiers that would not sacrifice † to his Gods*: which also *Julian* after did: and therefore *Victricius* with

militiam resumere, decem per annos abstineantur. Eundem hujus Canonis sensum exprimunt Balsamo & Zonaras & Ruffinus l. 10. c. 6.

* *Quod principale crimen, summus saeculi reatus dicitur Tertulliano de Idolatria: Gravissimum & extremum delictum Cypriano, Ep. 12.*

† *Sulpitius Severus: Sane tum Licinius qui adversus*

Constantinum de Imperio certavit, milites suos litare præceperat: abeuntes militia rejiciebat. Ob hanc causam Valentinianus, qui Imperator postea factus est, & sub Juliano abjecit cingulum. Non dissimile est quod Victor Uticensis narrat, multos sub Hunericho R. militiam temporalem abjicisse quia cum Arianismo connexa.

with others are read to have cast off their Belts for Christ's sake. So, in former times, had one thousand one hundred and four likewise done in *Armenia*, who are remembred in the Martyrologies; and, in *Egypt*, *Menna* and *Hesychius*. And so, in the times of *Licinius*, many cast off their Belts, of whom were *Arsacius*, named among the Confessors; and *Auxentius*, afterward made Bishop of *Mopsvestia*. Wherefore they, who touched in conscience had once left the Army, had no access unto it again, under *Licinius*, but by denyal of the Christian Faith. Which denyal, because it was so much the more grievous, by how much their former act did testify their greater knowledge of the divine Law, therefore are these Apostates more grievously punished than those mentioned in the former Canon, who without peril either of life or fortunes had renounced Christianity. But, to interpret the alleged Canon of VVarfare in general, is against all reason: for the History plainly shews, They, that had forsaken the Army under *Licinius*, and returned not unto it during his reign, lest they should violate the Christian Faith, had their choice given them afterward by *Constantine*, whether they would be free from serving in the War, or else return again into their places: which, without question, many did.

XXXII. Leo's

XXXII. Leo's *Epistle objected and answered.*

SOme do also object an Epistle of *Leo*, which saith: *It is contrary to the Ecclesiastical rules, after repentance, to return unto the secular warfare.* But, we must know, in penitents, as well as in the Clerks and Monks, was required a Christian life, not of an ordinary strein, but of a singular kind of purity; that they might be as great examples * for correction of manners, as they had been afore of transgression. Likewise, in the most antient customs of the Church, commonly called the Apostolical Canons, that by this sacred name they might be the more reverently received, in the 82. Canon it is enjoyned: *That no Bishop, Presbyter or Deacon follow the War, and retein at once a Roman office and a sacerdotal Function. For let* Cæsar *have the things that are* Cesar's, *and God the things that are God's.* Whereby, it is manifest, VVarfare was not interdicted such Christians as did not aspire unto the honour of the Clergy. More than this, they also were † excluded from the Clergy, who after Baptism had medled either

* Leo Epist. 9. ad Rust. *Illicitorum veniam postulantem oportet etiā multis licitis abstinere. In Epistola Episcoporum ad Ludovicum Regem legimus: Quilibet tanto à se licita debet abscindere, quanto se meminit & illicita perpetrasse. In Capit. Calvi: Tanto quisque majora quærat bonorum operum lucra, quanto graviora sibi intulit damna per culpam.*

† *Eusebius demonstrationum l. 1. duplicem describit Christianorum vitam, aliam* ἐντελῆ, *aliam inferiorem, qui in hac sunt eos inter alia iis qui juste militant agendo indicare.*

with

with Magiſtracies, or Offices of War, as may be ſeen in the Epiſtles of *Syricius* and *Innocentius*, and in the Council of *Toledo*. The Clergy, we may be ſure, were choſen, not out of ordinary Chriſtians, but of thoſe that had given teſtimony of a moſt exact converſation. Adde, that the military, and ſome of the civil offices brought with them a perpetual obligation; but, it was not fit that the perſons devoted to the Holy Miniſtry, ſhould be diverted from it * by any other daily care and labour. Wherefore the 6. Canon too ordains, That no Biſhop, Presbyter or Deacon, adminiſter any ſecular charge: the 80. That he intrude not himſelf into publick adminiſtrations: and the 6. among the African Canons, That he undertake not the procuration * of other mens affairs, or the defence of cauſes: and Cyprian judgeth, it is unlawful ſuch perſons ſhould be appointed † Guardians.

* *Vide Canonem Concilii Moguntini apud Gratianum, titulo, Ne clerici vel monachi.*

* *Vide* Epiſt. *Hieronymi ad Nepotianum.*

† *In Epiſtola ad Presbyteros diaconos & plebem Furnis conſiſtentem. Adde l. Generaliter, C. de Epiſc. & Clericis.*

XXXIII. *The laſt proofs out of Church-ſtory.*

BUt for our opinion we have the expreſs judgement of the Church in the firſt Council of *Arles*, held under *Conſtantine*; the 3. Canon whereof determines thus: *It ſeemeth good unto us to keep them from Communion, who throw down their Arms in peace:* that

that is, who forsake the War in the times when the Church is free from persecution; for the Christians understood this by the name of *peace* *, as appears in *Cyprian* and others. Adde the example of the Souldiers under *Julian*, Christians of no mean proficiency, being ready to bear witness to Christ even to the death; of whom saith *Ambrose*, *The Emperour* Julian, *though an Apostate, had Christian Souldiers under his command. When he gave them the word, Draw out for the defense of the Common-wealth, they obeyed him: but when the word of command was, Draw out against the Christians, then they acknowledged the Emperour of Heaven.* And of the same resolution was the *Thebaan* Legion long before, which in the time of the Emperour *Diocletian* had receiv'd the Christian Religion from the hand of *Zabdas* the thirtieth Bishop of *Hierusalem*, and shewed forth an example of Christian constancy and patience memorable to all posterity, which we shall relate hereafter. Here it may suffice to set down that speech of theirs, which with solid brevity expresseth the Duty of a Christian Souldier: *We offer against any enemy in the world these our hands, which we*

* Tertullianus idolatria: *Imo quomodo etiam in pace militabit?* Idem de fuga persecutionum: *Nostræ paci quod est bellum quàm persecutio?* Cyprianus Epistola 10. *Quando ipsa ante mater nostra Ecclesia pacem de misericordia Domini prior sumserit.* Epist. 22. *Cum Dominus cœperit ipsi Ecclesiæ pacem dare.* Epist. 31. *Ecclesiæ pacem sustinendam*, i. e. exspectandam. De lapsis, *Disciplinam pax longa corruperat.* Sulpitius Severus: *Antonino Pio imperante pax Ecclesiis fuit.* Mox *Interjectus deinde annus 38 pax Christianis fuit.* Et in Constantini ætate: *Exinde tranquillis rebus pace perfruimur.* Et initio historiæ. *Vexationesque pop. Christiani & mox pacis tempora.*

 think

think impiety to embrue with the bloud of innocent men. These our hands are expert to fight against wicked men and enemies, they know not how to cut in pieces pious men and those of our own Country. We have not forgotten that we took up Arms for our Countrymen, not against them. We have alwaies fought for justice, for piety, for the safety of the innocent: these have been hitherto the price of our perils. We have fought for Faith; which, how shall we keep with you (they speak to the Emperour) *if we preserve it not with our God?* *Basil*, of the more antient Christians, thus, *The slaughters made in War, our Ancestors accounted not for slaughters, having them excused who draw the sword on behalf of piety and vertue.*

Ex. l. c. c. 3. XXXIV. *That all private War is not unlawful, by natural Law.*

THat some private War may be lawfully waged, as to the Law of Nature, appears sufficiently by what hath been said above, when we shewed, it is not repugnant to the Law of Nature to repel force by force, and defend ones self from injury. But haply some may think it now unlawful, since the constitution of publick Courts of Justice; for although these Courts be not from nature, but from humane Ordinance, yet

yet seeing it is much more honest and becomming, and more conducible to mans quietness, that the matter should be tryed before an indifferent Judge, than that the parties themselves interessed, who too often favour themselves overmuch, should execute what they think right, by force; equity and natural reason dictate to us, that it is our duty to observe so laudable an Institution. *Paulus* the Lawyer saith: *It is not to be granted to the parties to do that which may be done publickly by the Magistrate, lest it be an occasion of making a greater tumult.* And the King *Theodoricus* *: *Hence it is, that the reverence of the Laws was found out, that nothing might be done by force, nothing by ones own impulse. For what difference between the clamness of Peace and the confusion of War, if controversies be determined by force.* The Laws call it *force, as often as any man requireth that which he thinks due unto him, not by course of Law.* Certainly, it must be confessed, the licence permitted before the constitution of Courts of Justice, is much restrained since. And yet since, it sometimes taketh place, namely, where publick Justice is wanting: for the Law forbidding a man to seek his own otherwise than by course of Law, ought commodiously to be understood with this clause, where Law and judgement may

L. non est de R. I. Cass. l. 4. Var. Epist. 4.

* *Eundem vide in Edicto c. 10. & 124.*

L. Exstat. D. quod metus.

be had. Now, this is wanting either at the *instant*, or for *continuance*: at the * instant, as, where the Judge cannot be waited for, without certain peril and loss: for continuance, either *by right*, or *by fact*. By right, if one be in places unpossest, as on the Sea, in a desert, in void Islands, and if there be any other places wherein there is no Government: by fact, if the Subjects do not acknowledge the Judge, or the Judge openly hath rejected the tryal of such a cause. That we have said, all private War is not repugnant to natural right, even since the constitution of Courts of Justice, may also be made apparent from the Law given the Jews, where God speaks thus by *Moses*. *If a thief be found breaking up, and be smitten that he die, there shall no bloud be shed from him. If the Sun be risen upon him, there shall be bloud shed for him.* Truly, this Law, so accurately distinguishing, seems, not only to induce impunity, but withall to explain natural right: nor seemeth it to be grounded in any peculiar divine mandate, but in common equity: Whence we see other Nations also have followed the same. That of the 12. Tables is notable, drawn no doubt, from the old * *Attic* Law:

* Serv. ad 11. Æneid. *Injecere manum parcæ. Traxerunt debitum sibi. Et sermone usus est iuris, nam manus injectio dicitur, quoties nulla iudicis autoritate, rem nobis debitam vindicamus.*

Ex. 22. 2. 3. Molin. disp. 100. sect. dubium vero.

* Solonis verba: *Si quis de die quod plus quinquaginta drachmis valeat, furetur, cum jus sit ad undecim viros deduci; quod si quis noctu vel minimum quid furetur, etiam liceat vel occidere.*

If

If a thief steal by night, and be killed, he is justly killed. So, by the Laws of all Nations, whom we have known, is he judged guiltless, who hath by arms defended his life against a violent assault. This so manifest consent is testimony enough, that here is nothing contrary to natural right.

XXXV. *Nor by the Law Evangelical. Objections proposed.*

Concerning the more perfect, voluntary divine Law, that is, the Evangelical, there is more difficulty. That God, who hath more right over our lives than we have our selves, might have required of us so much patience, as to lay down our lives, and, when we are brought in danger by the assault of a private person, rather choose to be killed than to kill, I do not doubt. But, the question is, whether it hath pleased him to oblige us so far, or no. On the affirmative part, are usually brought two places, which we alleged afore upon the general question. *But I say unto you, resist not the injurious person: and Revenge not your selves, dearly beloved.* There is a third place in those words of Christ * to *Peter, Put up thy Sword into the sheath; for they that take the Sword, shall perish by the Sword.* Some adde unto these, the example of Christ who *dyed for his enemies*

Mat. 5.39. Rom. 12.19. *Ubi Latina versio habet,* Non vos defendentes.

* Mat. 26.52.

Rom. 5.8,10.

enemies. Nor are there wanting among the old Doctors, who although they disapproved not publick Wars, were nevertheless of opinion that private defense was forbidden. We have above set down some places of *Ambrose* for VVar; and more of *Austin*, and more clear, known to all. Yet hath the same *Ambrose* said: *And perhaps therfore the Lord said to* Peter, *shewing two Swords, It is enough, intimating it was lawful until the Gospel came, which instructeth us in the truth, as the Law did in Justice*. The same Father elsewhere: *A Christian if he fall upon an armed thief, cannot strike him again that striketh; lest while he defends his safety, he offend against piety*. And *Augustin* hath said: *I do not indeed reprehend the Law which permitteth such* (thieves and other violent assaulters) *to be slain, but how to defend those that slay them I do not find*. And elsewhere: *As to killing of men, lest one be killed, I do not like that course, unless perhaps one be a Souldier, or bound by publick Office, that he doth not this for himself but others, having received lawful power*. And that *Basil* was of the same mind, appears sufficiently out of his second Epistle to *Amphilochius* *.

Lib. 10. in Luc.

De offic. 3. 3.

Lib. 1. de Lib. arb. c. 5.

Epist. 154. ad Publicolum.

Cap. 43. & 55.

* *Adde Concil. Aurelianensis canonem citat. à Gratiano c. ult. caus. 13. q. 2.*

XXXV.

XXXV. *The lawfulness of private defense confirmed.*

BUt the opposite opinion, as it is more common, so it seemeth unto us more true, that an obligation is not laid upon us to be so patient. For we are commanded in the Gospel to love our neighbour as our selves, not above our selves: yea where equal evil is imminent, we are not forbidden to provide for our selves * rather than for others, as we shewed above by the authority of *Paul* explaining that rule of beneficence. Some perhaps urge against us thus: Although I may prefer my own good before my neighbour's, yet this hath not place in unequal goods: wherfore my temporal life is rather to be deserted than the invader permitted to fall into eternal damnation. But thus it may be answered: He that is invaded hath oftentimes himself also need of time to repent, or hath some reason to think so; and that the assailant too may possibly find some space for repentance before his death. Besides, in a moral judgement, that peril seemeth not fit to be regarded, into which a man casts himself, and from which he may free himself, if he will. Certainly, some of the Apostles, even to the last times, Christ himself seeing and knowing it, seem

* *Cassiodorus de Amic. Sane nullus aliquo præcepto, vel aliqua ratione tenetur, salutem animæ proximi perditione animæ suæ; aut corporis ejus liberationem, citra spem perpetuæ salutis, proprii corporis interitu procurare.*

ſeem to have made their journys armed with the ſword: and that other Galileans travelling out of their Country toward the City did the ſame, by reaſon of danger on the way from Robbers, we learn out of *Joſephus*; VVho hath alſo deliver'd the ſame of the Eſſenes, men moſt innocent and harmleſs.
Luke 22.36. Hence it was, that when Chriſt ſaid, *the time was at hand*, when he that wanted a Sword ſhould ſell his garment and buy one, preſently the Apoſtles anſwer'd (for there were none but Apoſtles in that Company:) they had among them two Swords. Moreover, that which Chriſt ſaid, although in truth it conteins not any precept, but is a proverb, ſignifying very great
Verſ. 35. dangers to be at hand, as appears plainly by the oppoſition of the firſt time, which was ſafe and proſperous; yet is it ſuch, as is manifeſtly taken from the uſual cuſtom, and which the Apoſtles eſteemed lawful. *And ſurely it were not lawful to have Swords* (they are the words of *Cicero*) *if it be not lawful in any wiſe to make uſe of them.*

XXXVI. *The Objections anſwered.*

THat precept of Chriſt, not to reſiſt him that doth injury, is not more univerſal, than that which follows, *Give to every one that asketh:* which yet admits

mits of an exception ; So that our selves be not too much burthened : yea, to that precept of *giving*, no restriction is added, but it is restrained only by the sense of equity, whereas the precept of *not resisting* hath its explication adjoyned by the example of *a blow on the cheek*; that we may understand our selves to be then precisely bound, in case the injury offer'd us be either a blow on the cheek, or equal to it; for otherwise it had been fitter to say, *Resist not the injurious, but rather lose your life, than use your arms.* In the words to the Romans, *Avenge not your selves :*
for so it is, (not *Defend not your selves :*) * ἐκδικεῖν.
as the * word is used in other places, 1 Judith 2.&
2.1.
and here the connexion manifestly Luke 18.7,8.
shews : The words are these, *Recom-* 21.22.
pense to no man evil for evil : a description 2 Thes. 1.8.
of revenge, not of defense, this. And 1 Pet. 2.14.
Rom. 13.4.
Paul supports his precept with a place 1 Thes. 4.6.
of *Deuteronomy*, *Vengeance is mine, I will repay :* where the word in Hebrew, translated *Vengeance*, hath properly that signification, and the sense of the place will admit no other. That speech of Christ to *Peter*, contains indeed a prohibition of using the Sword, but not in the case of defense : neither had he any need to defend *himself :* for Christ had spoken on behalf of his Disciples :
Suffer these to go away : that his saying
might be fulfilled ; Of those whom thou Jo. 18,8,9.
hast

hast given me, have I lost none : nor *Christ* ; for he would not be defended. Therefore he addes in *John*, this cause
Ver.11. of his prohibition, *Shall I not drink of the cup which my Father hath given me?* and in *Matthew* he saith, *How then should the Scriptures be fulfilled, which say these things ought to be done?* Wherefore, *Peter* a man of a hot Spirit, was transported, it seems, with a mind of revenging, not of defending his Master. Adde, that he took arms against those that came in the name of the publick powers; Whom, whether in any case it be lawful to resist, is a peculiar question, to be handled by us hereafter. That which the Lord saith after, *All they that take the sword, shall perish by the sword,* either is a proverb taken from vulgar use ; whereby is signified, that bloud draweth bloud, and so the use of arms is never without peril : or, it declares *, that we have no season to prevent God in taking revenge, which he in his time will duly exact : just as in the *Apocalyps, He that killeth with the sword, must be killed with the sword : Here is the patience and the faith of the Saints.* Wherewith agrees that of *Tertullian : So bounteous a rewarder of patience is God ; that if you commit*

* *Quæ Origenis, Theophylacti, Titi & Euthymii sententia est.*

Apocal.13. 10.

Adeo satis idoneus patientiæ sequester Deus : si injuriam deposueris penes eum ultor est ; si dolorem, medicus ; si mortem, resuscitator est : quantum patientiæ licet, ut Deum habent debitorem. Tertul.

your

your injury to him, he is a Revenger; if your grief, a Healer; if your death, a Reviver. How great is the power of patience, to have God himself a Debter to it? And withall, in these words of Christ, seems to be conteined a prophecy of the revenge, which was to be executed upon the bloudy Jews by the sword of the *Romans*. To the example of Christ, who is said to have dyed for his enemies, it may be answered, That it is true, all the actions of Christ are full of vertue, and such as (so far as may be) it is laudable to imitate, and 'twill not want a reward: yet are they not all of such a sort, that they either proceed from some Law, or impose a Law on us. For, that Christ dyed for his enemies and the wicked, was not determined by any Law, but by agreement as it were, and special Covenant made with his Father: who, upon that condition, promised him not only the highest glory, but a *seed* to endure for ever. Besides, *Paul* Es.43.10.
shews this to be a singular and unparalleld act of Christ: Rom.5.7. and Christ commands 1 Jo.3.16. us to expose our lives to danger, not for all sorts of men, but for those that are partakers of the same Discipline. As for the sayings produced out of Christian writers, they seem partly to contein Counsel rather and a commendation of a more excellent way, than any strict precept; and partly are their

their own private opinions, not of the whole Church. For in the oldest Canons *, which are call'd the Apostles, excommunication is not denounced but against him, who in a fray at the first stroke hath slain his enemy. * for his too much heat and forwardness. And *Austin*, whom we brought on the other side, seems to go into this opinion, *quæst.* 84. *in* Exod.

* Can. 45. c. *si vero*: & c. *signif.*

* *Ob nimium calorem.* Ambrос. l. 10. in Luc. *O domine, cur me emere jubes gladium, qui ferire me prohibes? Cur haberi præcipis, quem vetas promi? nisi forte ut sit parata defensio, non ultio necessaria.*

XXXVIII. *Publick War solemn, or less Solemn.*

PUblick VVar is either *Solemn* by the Law of Nations, or *less Solemn*. What I here call solemn is commonly called *just*, in the same sense as a just Testament is opposed to Codicils *: not that it is not lawful for him that pleaseth to make Codicils, but because a solemn Testament hath, by the Civil Law, some peculiar effects. This is worth our observation, seeing many misunderstanding the word *just*, conceive all VVars to be condemned as unjust and unlawful, whereunto this appellation of just is not agreeable. That VVar, according to the Law of Nations, may be solemn, two things are requisite: first, that it be waged on both sides by his

* *Ita inter cives erant quædam matrimonia non justa, non justi liberi. Paul. sent. l. 2. t. 19. Sic & libertas quædam non justa. Sen. de vit. bea. c. 24.*

his authority who hath the higheſt power in the Common-wealth: Secondly, that certain rites be uſed, of which we ſhall ſpeak in due place. One of theſe, becauſe they are both required, without the other, doth not ſuffice. Publick War leſs ſolemn, may want thoſe rites, and be waged againſt private perſons, and have for the author any Magiſtrate. And truly, if the matter be conſidered without civil Laws, it ſeemeth that every Magiſtrate hath right to wage War, as for defenſe of the people committed to his charge, ſo for the exercise of juriſdiction, if he be oppoſed by force. But becauſe by War the whole Common-wealth is endangered, therefore by the Laws of all people almoſt, it is provided, that War be not undertaken without the authority of him, whoſe power in the Common-wealth is higheſt. There is extant ſuch a Law of *Plato's* *; and in the Roman Law, it is called treaſon in him, who without the command of the Prince hath waged War, or liſted Souldiers and raiſed an Army. In the *Cornelian* Law brought in by L. *Cornelius Sylla* it was, *without the command of the people.* In *Juſtinians* Code is extant a Conſtitution of *Valentinian* and *Valens* : * *None have leave to take any arms without our knowledge and di-*

* *ult. de leg.*

L. 3. D. ad l. Jul. maj.

* *Nulli prorſus nobis inſciis atque inconſultis quorumlibet armorum movendorum copia tribuatur.*

rection

rection. Pertinent is that of *Augustin* * : *Natural order for preserving of peace among men requires this, that authority and counsel in undertaking War should remain in the Princes.* But, as all sayings how universal soever must be interpreted by equity, so must this Law. For first, there is no doubt, but that 'tis lawful for one having jurisdiction, by force of his Apparitors or Serjeants to constrain a few disobedient persons, as oft as there is no need of greater power to that purpose, and no danger imminent to the Commonwealth. Again, if it be so present a danger, that time will not admit of consultation with him, who hath supreme power, here also necessity affordeth an exception. By this right L. *Pinarius* * Governour of *Enna* a Garrison in *Sicily*, having certain information that the Townsmen were falling off to the *Carthaginians*, making a slaughter of them, kept the Town. Without such necessity, to revenge the injuries which the King neglecteth to persue, a right of warring is allowed to the Citizens by the bolder pen of * *Franciscus Victoria*: but his opinion is by others justly rejected.

* Citat Gratian. c.23. qu.1. ex Lib.22.c.74. cont. Faust. *Apud Hebraeos bellum omne quod speciali Dei jussu suscipitur, vocatur* Bellum potestatum.

* *Liv.l.*39.

* *Vict.de ju. belli, n.9. Molin.disp.*100 *sect. idem Vict.*

XXXIX. Of

XXXIX. *Of War waged by inferiour Magistrates.*

IN ſuch caſes, wherein the lower powers have right to make War, the Interpreters of Law do not agree, whether that War may be called publick. Some ſay, Yea * : ſome, No *. Certainly, ſuch VVars are publick, if by publick we mean that which is made by the right of the Magiſtrate ; and therefore, they that in ſuch a caſe oppoſe themſelves againſt the Magiſtrates fall into the puniſhments of perſons contumacious againſt Superiours. But if *publick* be taken in the more excellent ſignification for that which is *ſolemn* (as it is without controverſy oft taken) thoſe Wars are not publick, becauſe to the plenitude of that right, both the judgement of the higheſt power, and other things are requiſite. Nor am I mov'd with this, that in ſuch contention alſo they are wont to take the ſpoil of the reſiſters and give it to the Souldier † : for this is not ſo proper to ſolemn War, but it may have place elſewhere *. And it may alſo happen, that in an Empire of larger extent, the inferiour powers may have power granted them to begin a War : in which caſe, the VVar is ſuppoſed to be made by the higheſt Power ; becauſe, every one is judged author of that

* *Ajala de jur. bel. l. 1. c. 2.*
* *Innoc. c. olim de reſt. ſpol. n. 8.*
† *Livius D. loco.*
* *Vict. n. 29. Cajet. 2. 2. qu. 40. art. 1.*

that which he giveth another Commission to do. That is more controverted, whether a conjecture of the will of the highest, where there is no mandate, be sufficient. To me it seemeth not. For it sufficeth not to see, what would be the pleasure of him that hath the highest Power, if he were consulted with in this conjuncture of affairs; but this is rather to be considered, what he, where the matter admits delay, or is of doubtful deliberation, may desire should be done without consulting with him, if a Law were to be made about it. For, although in some particular fact the particular reason ceaseth, which moves the will of the Soveraign, yet the universal reason holdeth, which requires dangers to be withstood. VVhich cannot be, if every Magistrate draw unto himself the judgement thereof. Justly therefore was *C. Manlius* accused by his Legats *, because without command of the Roman people he had made VVar upon the Gallo-Grecians; for, albeit the Legions of the *Galli* had served in the Army of *Antiochus*, neverthe'ess after the peace agreed on with *Antiochus*, whether that injury were to be revenged upon the Gallo-Grecians, was not at the pleasure of *C. Manlius* but of the people of *Rome*. That *C. Cæsar* for carrying VVar against the Germans, should be yielded up to the Germans, was

Liv.l.48.

* Or, Lieutenants.

was the sentence of *Cato*; not so much (as I conceive) regarding justice, as desiring to acquit the City from the fear of an Usurper; for the Germans had given aid to the Gauls, enemies of the Roman people, and therefore had no reason to complain of injury done them, if the Romans had just cause of warring against the Gauls. And yet *Cæsar* ought to have been content with the expulsion of the Germans out of *Gallia*, the Province committed to him, and not to pursue the Germans with War within their own bounds, especially without any appearance of danger thence, unless he had advised first with the people of *Rome*. So then, the Germans had no right to require him to be given up into their hands, but the people of *Rome* had right to punish him: just as the Carthaginians answered the Romans, *Whether Saguntum was assaulted by private or publick Counsel, we conceive is not to be made the question; but this, whether it was assaulted justly, or unjustly: for to our selves is an account to be given by our Citizens, whether he did it of himself, or by Commission; With you this alone is disputable, whether it were a violation of the league or no.* *Cicero* defends the action both of *Octavius* and *Decimus Brutus*, who on their own heads took Arms against *Antonius*. But, suppose Liv. l. 31.

Antony deserved hostile opposition, yet was the judgement of the Senate and people of *Rome* to be waited for, whether it were for the good of the Commonwealth to dissemble what was done, or to revenge it; to come to conditions of peace, or go forth to War. For no man is compell'd to use his own right, which is often conjoind with hazard. Again,
App. c. 4. suppose *Antonius* be declar'd an enemy, yet the deliberation was to be left to the Senate and people of *Rome*, by whose conduct especially they would please to make the War. Thus the Rhodians answer'd *Cassius*, when he demanded aid according to the league, that they would send him aid if the Senate would command. Being admonisht by this example (and we may meet with more) let us remember not to approve of all things, though deliver'd by Authors of greatest name; for they often serve the times, or their affections, and bend the rule as occasion requires? wherefore we must take some pains in matters of this nature to clear the eye of our judgement, and examine things thorowly, and not rashly draw into example what may rather be accounted capable of excuse, than worthy of our praise and imitation: Wherein some fall into pernicious errours. Now whereas it hath been said, that publick War is not to be waged unless by his authority who hath the highest

highest power, to the understanding hereof, and of that question that is about solemn War, and so to many other purposes, it will be necessary to understand what is that highest Power, and who have it: and so much the more necessary, because in our age learned men, every one having pursued that Argument rather according to the exigence of present affairs, than according to the Truth, have rendred the matter much more difficult, which of it self is not very easy.

XI. *Wherein consisteth civil Power.*

THe moral faculty of Governing a City *, which is stiled by the name of civil Power, is described in *Dionysius Halicarnassensis* by three especial notes; a right of creating Magistrates, a right of making and abolishing Laws, a right of decreeing War and Peace; elsewhere he addes a fourth, Courts of justice; and elsewhere the care of Religion, and calling of assemblies. Others * express themselves otherwise. But if one will make an exact partition, he shall easily find all that pertains hither, so that nothing may be wanting or superfluous. For the Governour of a City governs it partly *by himself*, partly *by others*. By himself he is either conversant about *universals*, or about *singulars*:

* Or, Common wealth.

* *Servius ad* 1. Æn. Omni ditione. *Rectius* omni *quam* omnis: *ut significet omni potestate, pace, legibus, bello.*

Lib. 4.

Lib. 7.

Lib. 2.

* *Thucydides civitatem, quæ vere civitas est, vocat,* αὐτόνομον, αὐτόδικον, αὐτοτελῆ.

gulars. About Universals, by making and abolishing Laws, as well about sacred (so far as the care of them belongs unto the City) as about civil affairs. This art is call'd by *Aristotle architectal*. The singulars about which he is conversant, are either directly publick, or private, yet in order to the publick. *Directly publick* are Actions, as of Peace, War, Leagues; or Things, as Tributes and the like: Wherein is comprehended also that *eminent* Dominion, which the City hath over the Citizens and their estates for the publick use. The Art about these is exprest in *Aristotle* by the general name *political* or civil, and is also called the Art of consultation. *Private things* are such as are controverted between party and party, which it concerns the publick quiet to be determined by publick authority. And this Art is by *Aristotle* termed *judicial*. The things done *by another*, are dispatched either by Magistrates, or by other procurators, to which number Embassadors are to be referred. And in these particulars consisteth the civil power.

ἀρχιτεκτονική. πολιτική, βουλευτική. δικαστική.

XLI. *What Power is Highest.*

THat is call'd the Highest Power whose acts are not under the right of another, so as to be made void at the pleasure of another humane will. When

I

I say *of another*, I exclude him who enjoyeth the highest Power (who may change his own will) as also his Successor *, who enjoyeth the same right, and therefore hath the very same power. Let us now see, in what subject this highest power is. There is a *common* subject, and a *proper* subject: as the common subject of *sight* is the body, the proper is the eye; so the common subject of the highest Power is a *City*, that is, a perfect society. We exclude therefore people or Countries that have yielded up themselves, or fallen to the dominion of another people, such as were the Provinces of the Romans: for these are not by themselves a City, as now we take the word, but less worthy members of some great City, as servants are members of the family. Again it comes to pass, that several Nations or Countries have one and the same *head*, which do nevertheless every one make up a perfect society by themselves: for it is not in the *moral* body as in the *natural*; in the natural, *one* cannot be the head of several bodies; but in the moral, the same person, considered in a divers relation, may be the head of bodies many and distinct. Wherof this is a certain Argument, that the Royal Family being extinct, the Empire returns to every people severally. So also it may happen, that more Cities

* Cacheran Decis. pedem. 139. num. 6.

Vict. de ju. belli, n. 7.

ties may be confederated one with another by a most close league, and make a certain *System*, as *Strabo* uses to speak; and yet, not any one of them ceases to retain the State of a perfect City: which is noted both by others, and by *Aristotle* in more places than one. Well then, let a *City*, so understood as we have said, be the *common* subject of the highest Power: the *proper* subject is a *person*, one or more, according to the Laws and customs of every Nation *

* ἡ πρώτη ἀρχὴ *apud* Galenum lib. 6. de placit. Hip. & Plat.

XLII. *That the highest Power is not alwaies in the people.*

HEre is first to be rejected their opinion, who will have the highest Power every where, and without exception, to be in the people, so that they may restrain and punish Kings, as oft as they use their power amiss: which opinion, how many mischiefs it hath occasion'd, and may yet produce, if it be throughly entertain'd, every wise man sees. We oppose these Arguments against it. It is lawful for every man to addict and yield himself into private servitude to whom he pleaseth, as appears both out of the Hebrew Law and the Roman. Why then may not any people, being at their own dispose, give up themselves to one or more, so as to transcribe the right of governing

Ex. 21. 6. *Instit. de jure person. sect. Servi aut.* Gell. l. 2. c. 7.

ning them wholy to their Ruler, no part of that right retained or reserved to themselves? Nor may you say, that cannot be presumed: for we do not here enquire, what may be presumed in a doubtful case, but what may be done in point of right. In vain also are here alleged the incommodities that follow, or are possible; for what kind of Government soever you shall frame in your mind, you will never exclude all incommodities or hazards. You must be content, in every way, to take the good and evill * one among another. Now as there are many courses of life, one more excellent than another, and every man is at liberty among many to choose which he doth most affect; so may any people also make choice of what form of government they please: neither is the right to be measured by the excellency of this or that form (for divers men have divers judgements hereof) but by their * will. And indeed there may arise many causes, why the people may abdicate from themselves the whole right of commanding, and give it to another, *viz.* because being brought into danger of their life, they can find no other way to preserve themselves; or because being opprest with

Gail. de Arrest. s.6.22. & seq.

* *Aut haec cum illis sunt habenda, aut illa cum his mittenda sunt.* Com. *Est iniqua in omni re accusanda praetermissis bonis malorum enumeratio.* Cicero.

* At the same time the City *Augusta* petitioned *Charls* the Emperour, that the Decrees of their Senate might not be of force without the consent of the Masters of the *Curiae*; when *Norimberga* desired the plain contrary thing.

want, they can have no sustenance on other terms. For if the *Campanians* of old, being subdued by necessity, subjected themselves * to the Roman people in this form: *The people of* Campania, *and the City* Capua, *our Lands, the Temples of our Gods, all divine and humane things, we yield up into your hands, O ye Conscript Fathers:* and sundry people when they desired to subject themselves to the dominion of the Romans * were not accepted, as *Appian* saith: what hinders, but that a people after the same manner may yield up it self into the hand of one prepotent and over-mighty man * ? Moreover, it may happen, that some Father of a Family, possessing a large estate of Lands, may please to receive no inhabitant into his possession, but upon such condition: or, that some Master having a great number of servants may manumit and set them at liberty, on condition that they be subject to his Government, and pay him tribute. VVhich cases are not without their examples. *Tacitus*, concerning the servants of the Germans, saith, *Every one is Master of his own house and estate: The Lord imposeth and requireth of them (as his farmers) a rent of Corn, or Cattle, or cloths; and the servant so far is subject.* Adde, that as *Aristotle* hath said, some men are by nature servants, i. e. fit for servitude;

* Ut Falisci apud Liv. l. 5. Samnites. l. 8. *Sic Epidamnii à Corcyræis deserti Corinthiis se dediderunt, ut protegerentur.* Thucyd. l. 1. *Populum Campanum, urbemque Capuæ, agros, delubra Deûm, divina humanaque omnia, in vestram P. C. ditionem dedimus.*

* *Et Venetorum.* Bembus lib. 6.

* Apud Virgilium legimus, *Nec cum se sub leges pacis iniquæ Tradiderit regno.*

vitude; so also some Nations are of this disposition, that they know better how to be ruled, than how to rule: Which the *Cappadocians* seem to have thought of themselves, who preferred the life under a King before the Liberty offer'd them by the Romans, and affirmed, they could not live without a King. So *Philostratus*, in the life of *Apollonius*, saith, It is a folly to bestow Liberty upon the Thracians, Mysians, Getes, which they would not gladly accept. And moreover, some might be moved by the examples of those Nations, which for many ages lived happily enough under a Government plainly regal*. The Cities † under *Eumenes*, saith *Livy*, would not have changed their fortune with any free City whatsoever. L. 42. Sometimes also the State of the * City is such, that it cannot be safe, unless under the free Empire of † One: which conceipt many prudent men had of the Roman, as the case stood in the time of *Cæsar Augustus*. For these causes therefore, and the like, it may not only possibly, but

Strabo. 12. *Justin.* 38.

Lib. 6.

* Sen. de benef. l.2.c.20. de Bruto locutus: *Mihi, cum vir magnus fuerit in aliis, in hac re videtur vehementer errasse, nec ex institutione Stoica segessisse: qui aut Regis nomen extimuit, cum optimus civitatis status sub Rege iusto sit; aut ibi speravit libertatem futuram, ubi tam magnum præmium erat & imperandi & serviendi; aut existimavit civitatem in priorem formam posse revocari, amissis pristinis moribus; futuramque ibi æqualitatem civilis juris, & staturas suo loco leges, ubi viderat tot millia hominum pugnantia, non an servirent, sed utri.* Vide & Bizarrum hist. Genuensi. l.14. p.329. † Sic multos ex liberis Græciæ Civitatibus in Salamina Cypri, quod Evagoræ regnum erat, venisse narrat Isocrates. * Or, Common-wealth. † Dion apud Philostrat. 5.11. *Metus ne Romani longis dominatibus edomiti nullam jam ferre possint mutationem.*

doth

doth usually come to pass, that men subject themselves to the Empire and power of another: which also *Cicero* notes in the second of his offices.

XLIII. *The same further proved.*

FUrther yet, by a just War (as we have said afore) as private dominion may be acquired, so also civil dominion, or the right of reigning without dependence. Neither do I speak this only in behalf of the Empire of *One*, where that is receiv'd, I would not be so mistaken: but the same Arguments are of force for conserving the Empire of *many*, where many *nobles* or *states* have this same right of supreme power, and govern the City, the *Plebeians* being excluded. What, that no Commonwealth hath ever been found so popular, wherein some, such as are very poor or foreigners, and also Women and Youth are not kept from publick Counsels? Besides, some † States have other people under them, not less subject, than if they did obey Kings. Whence that question, *Is the Collatin*

† *Sic Samii multa in continente oppida tenuere, ut* Strabo *docet lib.14. Sex oppida Halicarnasso attributa per* Alexandrum *magnum, memorat Plinius Histor. nat.l.5.c.29. Idem lib.33. cap.4. Lindum insulam ait esse Rhodiorum. Tantundem de Cauno habes, lib.35. Testatur idem* Cicero Epist. *ad fratrem. Rhodiis iisdem, quod Romanos contra* Antiochum *juvissent, complures urbes dono datus ait* Eutropius *lib.3. nempe Carum & Lyciorum, quæ rursus eis ablatæ à senatu. utrumque est in exceptis* Polybii.

people

people in their own power? and the Campanians, when they had yielded up themselves to the Romans, are said to be under the power of others. Many are the examples to this purpose; and they are all of no value, if we once grant this, that the right of ruling is alwaies subject to the judgement and will of them who are ruled. But on the contrary, it is evident both by sacred and prophane history, that there are Kings that are not inferiour to the people, though taken all together. *If thou shalt say,* saith God speaking to the people of *Israel, I will set a King over me:* and to *Samuel, Shew unto them the right of the King that shall reign over them.* Hence is a King called, the Anointed *over* the people, *over* the inheritance of the Lord, *over Israel: Salomon* King *over all Israel.* So *David* giveth thanks to God, for subduing his people *under* him. *The Kings of the Nations,* saith Christ, *bear rule over them.* And that of *Horace* * is well known:

Deut. 17. 14. 1 Sam. 8. 4. 1 Sam. 9. 16. 10. 1. 15. 1. 2 Sam. 5. 2. 1 Reg. 4. 1. Ps. 144. 2. Luke 22. 25.

Commands of Kings their subjects move:
And Kings are subject unto Jove.

* *Regum timendorum in proprios greges; Reges in ipsos imperium est Jovis.*

Seneca thus describes the three forms of Government: *Sometimes the peo-* ple

Epist. 14: *Interdum populus est quem timere debeamus; interdum, si ea civitatis disciplina est, ut plurima per senatum transigantur, gratiosi in ea timentur viri; interdum singuli quibus potestas populi & in populum data est.*

ple are they whom we ought to fear; sometimes, if the Discipline of the Commonwealth be so, that most things be transacted by the Senate, the gracious men therein are feared; sometimes single persons to whom the power of the people and over the people is given. Such are they who, as *Plutarch* saith, have a command not only according to the Laws, but over the Laws also; and, in *Herodotus*, *Otanes* thus describes a single Empire: *to do what one pleaseth, so as not to be accomptable to any other;* and *Dio Prusaensis* defines a Kingdom; *to have command without controul.* *Pausanias* * opposes *a kingdom to such a power as must give account to a superiour.* *Aristotle* saith, there are some Kings with such a right, as elsewhere the Nation it self hath over it self, and that which is its own. So, after that the Roman Princes began to take upon them an Authority truly regal, the people is said to have conferred upon them all their Authority and power, and that over themselves, as *Theophilus* interprets. Hence is that saying of *M. Antonius* the Philosopher: *None but God alone can be judge of the Prince. Dion.* of such a Prince: *He is free, having power over himself and the Laws, that he may do what him pleaseth, and what likes him not, leave undone.* Such a kingdom was of old that of the *Inachidæ* at *Argos*;

3. Pol. 14.

* Messenicis.

Institut. de jure nat. sect. sed & quod.

Xiph. vita M. Ant. l. 4.

Lib. 53.

Argos *; far different from the Athenian Common-wealth, where *Theseus* †, as *Plutarch* tells us, acted only the part of a General, and Guardian of the Laws, in other respects not superiour * to the rest. Wherefore, Kings subject to the people are but improperly called Kings: as after *Lycurgus*, and more, after the *Ephori* were established, the Kings of the Lacedemonians are said † to have been Kings in name and title, not really and indeed. Which example was also followed by other States in *Greece*. *Pausanias Corinth*. *The Argives in love of equality and liberty have long since very much abated the regal power, so that they have left the Sons of* Cisus, *and his posterity, nothing beside the name of a Kingdom*. Such Kingdoms *Aristotle* saith, do not make any proper kind of Government, because they only are a part in an Optimacy or Populacy. Moreover, in Nations that are not perpetually subject unto Kings, we see examples as it were of a Kingdom temporary *, which is not subject to the people. Such was the power of the *Amymones* among the Cnidians, and of the *Dictators* among the Romans in the first

* In Argiva Trag. Supplicibus, sic populus regem affatur apud Æschylum: *Tu res populi, tuque urbs tota es, Non judicio subditus ullis, Regni solio fultus ut ara, Vnoque regens cuncta arburio.*

† Rex ipse Theseus apud Euripid. — *Hæc juris sui Parere domino civitas uni negat: Rex ipse populus annuas mandat vices Honoris huic illive.* —

* Thesei filius Demophon apud eund. *Nec enim potestas barbarum in morem mihi, Sed justa refero obsequia, dum juste impero.*

† Polyb. l. 4. Plut. in Cleom. Cornel. Nep. Verba ipsius aut quisquis is est qui vitas illustres scripsit, in Agesilao: *Vt duos haberent Reges nomine magis quam imperio.* Alibi: *Lacedæmoniorum autem Agesilaus nomine non potestate fuit Rex, sicut cæteri Spartani.* * Livius Salinator *in censura omnes tribus exceptâ unâ ærarias fecit, ac sic ostendit jus sibi esse in populum omnem.*

times,

times, when there was no appeal unto the people: whence the Dictators Edict, as *Livy* saith, was observed as an Oracle, and there was no help but in their care of obeying it: and the force of the regal power, was besieged with the Dictatorship, as *Cicero* speaketh.

XLIV. *Arguments to the contrary answered.*

THe Arguments brought on the contrary part are not hard to be solved. For first, that they affirm the *Constituent* to be superiour to the *constituted*, is true only in that constitution whose effect perpetually depends on the will of the Constituent; and not in that which at first proceeds from the will, but afterward hath the effect of necessity: even as a woman makes to her self a husband by consent, whom she must of necessity obey for ever. *Valentinian* the Emperour, to the Souldiers who had made him so, when they asked somewhat of him which he thought unreasonable, gave this answer *: *To elect me to rule over you, was in your power, O my Souldiers, but since you have elected me, the thing you ask is at my plea-*

* Sozom. hist. Eccl. lib. 16. Verba ejus sic refert Theodoretus l. 4. c. 5 *Vestrum fuit, milites, cum Imperator nullus esset, mihi tradere Imperii hujus habenas, eas ex quo adeptus sum, de caetero non vestrum sed meum dispicere quid reip. expediat.*

sure

ſure, not yours. You as ſubjects ought to obey, I muſt conſider what is fit to be done. Beſides, the Aſſumption is not true, that all Kings are conſtituted by the people: which may be ſufficiently underſtood by the examples of a Father of a family admitting Tenants on condition of obedience, and of Nations overcome in War, which above are mentioned. Another Argument they draw out of that ſentence of Philoſophers; *All Government is for the benefit of them that are govern'd, not of them that do govern:* Whence they think it follows from the Nobilitie of the end, that the Governed are ſuperiour to the Governour. But, neither is that univerſally true, *The good of the governed is the end of all Government:* for ſome Governments are by themſelves for the Rulers ſake, as that of a Maſter: for the ſervants profit is there extrinſecal and adventitious; even as the Phyſicians Fee pertains nothing to the Medicine it ſelf. Other Governments there are for mutual benefit, as the Husband's. So, certain Empires may have for their end the utility of the Kings; namely, ſuch as are gotten by conqueſt, and are not therefore to be called Tyrannical, ſeeing *Tyranny*, as the word is now taken, includes injuſtice. Some alſo may reſpect as well his utility that rules, as his that is ruled; *i.e.* when an impotent people ſet

set over themselves a potent King for their defense. Yet do I not deny, that in many Empires is properly respected the profit of the subjects; and true it is, which *Cicero* after *Herodotus*, *Herodotus* after *Hesiod* hath delivered, That Kings were constituted to the end justice may be had. And yet, it doth not follow thence, what they infer, that the people are superiour to the King; for tutelage also was found out for the Pupils good, yet is tuition a right and power over the Pupil. Nor is the objection of any moment, if one say, the Tutor may be put out of his charge upon mal-administration of the Pupils estate, and therefore the same must take place upon the King: for this holds in the Tutor, who hath a Superior; but in Empires, because a progress *in infinitum* is not granted, we must by all means make a stop in some person or persons, whose faults, because
Jer.25.12. they have no Superior Judge, *God* himself testifies that he takes into his peculiar cognizance. And he either doth justice upon them, if he judgeth it to be needfull, or else forbeareth them for a punishment or tryal of the people. Excellently saith *Tacitus*: *As drougth or excessive rain and other evils of na-*

Tacitus: *Quomodo sterilitatem aut nimios imbres, & cetera naturæ mala, ita luxum vel avaritiam dominantium tolerate. Vitia erunt donec homines; sed neque hæc continua, & meliorum interventu pensantur.*

ture;

ture, so bear ye patiently the luxury or avarice of Rulers. Vices will continue as long as there are men: but, neither are they continual, and they are recompensed by the intermixture of better things. And it was a good saying of *M. Aurelius: Magistrates judge of private persons, Princes of Magistrates, God of Princes* *. Notable is the place in *Gregorius Turonensis*, where that Bishop thus addresses himself to the King of *France: O King, if any one of us go beyond the bounds of justice, he may be corrected by you: but if you exceed, Who shall chastise you? For we speak unto you, and you hear us; if you will; but if you will not, who shall condemn you, but He who hath pronounced Himself to be JUSTICE?* Among the doctrines of the *Essens*,† *Porphyry* remembers this: That Empire falleth not to any man without Gods * especial care. *Ireneus* very well: *By whose appointment men are born, by his appointment also Kings are constituted, fit for the people, who in those times are go-*

* Xiphilin: *De summo principatu Deus solus potest judicare.* Vitigis rex apud Cassiodorum: *Causa regiae potestatis supernis est applicanda judiciis, quandoquidem illa è cœlo petita est, & soli cœlo debet innocentiam.* Apud eundem Cassiodorum rex: *Alteri subdi non possumus, quia judices non habemus.*
† Lib. 5.
* Homerus: Τιμὴ δ' ἐκ Διός ἐστι. *Ab Jove summus honos.* Diodorus Sic, l. 1. de Ægyptiis. *Existimant enim non sine divina quadam providentia pervenisse Reges ad summam de omnibus potestatem.* Augustin. l. 5 de Ci. D. *Qui Vespasiano vel patri vel filio, suavissimis Impp. ipse & Domitiano crudelissimo; & ne per singulos ire necesse sit, qui Constantino, ipse Apostatae Juliano:* nempe, majestatem dedit, quod præcesserat. Vitigis apud Cassiodorum: *Omnis provectus, maxime Regius, ad divinitatis munera referendus est.* Titi Imperatoris erat dictum, *Potestatem fato dari.*

govern'd by them. There is the ſame ſenſe in the Conſtitutions which are
Lib. 7. c. 17. call'd *Clement's*: Thou ſhalt fear the King, knowing that he is choſen by the Lord. Nor doth it overthrow theſe things which we have ſaid, that we
2 Sam. 24. 17. read the people puniſhed ſometimes for the ſins of their Kings: for this came not ſo to paſs, becauſe the people did not puniſh nor reſtrain the King, but becauſe they did, at leaſt tacitely, conſent to his faults. Neverthe leſs it is certain too, without that, God might uſe his ſupreme dominion, which he hath over the life and death of every one, for to puniſh the King; whoſe puniſhment indeed it is, to be deprived of his Subjects.

XLV. *Of mutual Subjection.*

OThers there are, who feign unto themſelves a certain mutual ſubjection, ſo that the whole people ought to obey the King governing well; and the King governing ill, ought to be ſubject to the people. Theſe men, if they did ſay, Things manifeſtly unjuſt are not to be done at the Kings command, would ſpeak a truth, which is acknowledged among all honeſt men: but this includes no coaction, or right to command the King. And, had it been the purpoſe of any people to divide the

power

power with the King (of which we shall say somewhat hereafter) such bounds surely ought to have been assigned to either power, which might easily be distinguisht by the difference of places, persons, or affairs. But, the goodness or illness of act, especially in civil matters which oft have an obscure disceptation, are not fit to distinguish parts. Whence very great confusion cannot but follow, whilst under pretence of a good or evill act, on the one side the King, on the other side the people draw unto themselves, according to their right of power, the cognizance of the same matter. Such a perturbation of things, so far as I can remember, never any people was so phantastick as to introduce.

XLVI. *Cautions for the understanding of the true Opinion. The first.*

FAlse opinions being removed, it remains that we set down some *cautions*, that may open a way to make a right judgement, to whom the right of supreme power in every Nation belongs. Our first caution is, *that we be not deceived with the ambiguous sound of a name, or the shew of external things.* For example, although among the Latins *principality* and *Kingdom* are wont to be opposed, as when *Cæsar* saith, the

Father of *Vercingetorix* held the principality of *Gallia*, but was ſlain for affecting the Kingdom; and when *Piſo* in *Tacitus* calls *Germanicus* the Son of a Prince of *Romans*, not of a King of *Parthians*; and when *Suetonius* ſaith *Caligula* wanted but a little of turning the principality into a Kingdom; and when *Maroboduus* is ſaid by *Velleius* to have embraced in his mind, not a principality conſiſting in the will of thoſe that obey, but a regal power: Nevertheleſs, we ſee theſe names are often times confounded; for, both the Lacedæmonian Leaders of *Hercules* poſterity, after they were ſubject to the *Ephori*, were yet ſtiled Kings, as we have ſaid afore; and the antient *Germans* had Kings, which, as *Tacitus* ſpeaketh,
Lib. 1. were Soveraign by the authority of *perſwading*, not by the power of *command-*
Lib. 15. Cap. 7. *ing*. And *Livy* ſaith of King *Evander*, that he ruled by authority rather than command: and *Ariſtotle* and *Polybius* call *Suffetes* King of the Cartha-
Lib. 13. ginians, and *Diodorus* too, as alſo *Hanno* is called King of the Carthaginians by *Solinus*. And of *Scepſis* in *Troas*

Sic qui vitam ſcripſit Annibalis: *Ut enim Romæ conſules, ſic Carthagine quotannis annui bini Reges creabantur*. To theſe improperly ſtiled Kings may be added the Sons of Kings, to whom that royal name was given by their Fathers, retaining the power in themſelves. Such was that *Darius*, whom his Father *Artaxerxes* cauſed to be judged and put to death. *Plutarch. Artax.*

Strabo

Strabo relates, when having joyned to them the *Milesians* into one Commonwealth, they began to use a popular Government, the posterity of the old Kings retained the royal name & somewhat of the honour. On the contrary, the Roman Emperors, after that openly and without any dissimulation they held a most free regality, yet were stiled *Princes*. Moreover, Princes in some free Cities have the Ensigns and marks of royal Majesty given unto them. Now, the Assembly of the States *, that is, of them that represent the people distributed into *classes*, in some places indeed serve only to this purpose, that they may be a greater Council of the King, whereby the complaints of the people, which are oft concealed in the Privie Council, may come unto the Kings ear: in other places have a right to call in question the actions of the Prince, and also to prescribe Laws, whereby the Prince himself is bound. Many there are, who think, the difference of the highest Empire, or of that less than the highest, is to be taken from the conveyance of Empire by way of *election* or *succession*. Empires devolved this way, they affirm to be highest, not those that come the other way. But it is most certain, this is not universally true; for succession is not the title of Empire, which gives it form,

* *Prælati, proceres, missisque potentibus urbes*, ut Guntherus loquitur.

but a continuation of what was before, The right begun from the election of the Family is continued by succession: wherefore, succession carries down just so much, as the first election did confer. Among the Lacedemonians, the Kingdom passed to the Heirs, even after the *Ephori* were ordained. And of such a Kingdom, that is, a principality, saith *Aristotle* *: *some of them go by right of bloud, some by election:* and in the Heroical times most Kingdoms in *Greece* were such, as besides him, *Thucydides* * notes. On the contrary, the Roman Empire, even after all the power both of Senate and people was taken away, was bestowed by election.

* *Pol.* 3, 14.

* *Lib.* 1; *Notatum id & Dionys. Halicarnass. l.* 2. & 5.

XLVII. *The second Caution.*

Let this be the second caution. '*Tis one thing to enquire of the thing, another of the manner of holding it:* which is appliable not only to corporal things, but incorporal also. For, as a Field is a thing possessed, so is a passage, an act, a way. But these things some hold by a full right of *propriety*, others by a right *usufructuary*, other by a *temporary* right; So the Roman Dictator, by a temporary * right, had the Highest power: and some Kings, both the first that are elected, and they that succeed them in a lawful order, by an usufructuary right; but

* *Vide cui vacat Car. Molinaeum ad consuetud. Paris. Tit.* 1. *sect.* 2. *gl.* 4. *num.* 16.

* You have an example of an Emperour made for a time, in *Gregoras, lib.* 4. *initio.*

but some Kings by a full right of propriety, as they that by a just War have gotten their Empire, or into whose power some people, to avoid a greater evill, have so given up themselves, that they excepted nothing. Neither do I assent to them, who say the Dictator had not the highest power, because it was not perpetual; for the nature of moral things is known by the operations: wherefore such faculties as have the same effects are to be called by the same name. Now, the Dictator, within his time, exerciseth all acts by the same right *, as a King of the best right; nor can his act be rendred void by any other. As for duration, that changeth not the nature of the thing: though if the question be of dignity, which is wont to be stiled *Majesty*, this is greater, no doubt, in him to whom perpetual right is given, than to whom temporary right; because the manner of the Tenure is of moment in respect of dignity. And I would have the same understood of these, that before Kings come to age, or whilst they are hindred by loss of reason or their liberty, are appointed Curators of the Kingdom, so, that they be not subject to the people, nor, their power revocable before the appointed time. Another judgement is to be made concerning those that have received a right revocable at any time, that is, a precarious right,

* So that the people, when they would save *Fab. Rutilian*, made Petition to the Dictator.

right, ſuch as of old was the Kingdom of the *Vandals* in *Africa*, and of the *Goths* in *Spain* *, when the people depoſed them, as oft as they were diſpleaſed †; for every act of ſuch Kings may be rendred void by theſe that have given them a power *revocably*; and therefore, here is not the ſame effect, nor the ſame right, as in other caſes.

Procopius. Vand. l. 1. Aimol 2. 20. & 4. 35.

* *Moris antiqui veſtigium in Behetriis, vide Marianam l. 16.*

† *Hoc de Herulis etiam prodidit Procopius Got. 2. de Longobardis Paulus Warnafredi l. 4. & 6. de Burgundis Ammianus lib. 28. de Moldavis Laonicus Chalcondylas, de rege Agalis apud Afros Joannes Leo lib. 7. de Norwagis ait Guil. Neubrigenſis regem ibi factum quiſquis regem occidiſſet. de Quadis & Jazygibus ſimilia habes in excerptis Dionis.*

XLVIII. *That ſome higheſt Empires are holden fully*, i. e. *alienably*.

That which I have ſaid, that ſome Empires are in full right of propriety, *i. e.* in the patrimony of the Ruler, is oppoſed by ſome learned men with this Argument, *That free-men are not in commerce*. But, as power is either *Lordly*, or *Regal*; ſo alſo Liberty is either *perſonal*, or *civil*; and again, either of *ſingle* perſons, or of *all* together: for the Stoicks too did ſay, there is a certain ſervitude conſiſting in * ſubjection; and in the holy Scriptures the Kings ſubjects are call'd his ſervants. As therefore perſonal liberty excludes Maſter-ſhip, ſo civil liberty oppoſes regality, and any other *dition* properly ſo called.

Hotom. cont. ill. qu. 1.

* ὑποταξει. *Diog. Laert.* 1 Sam. 22. 28. 2 Sam 10. 2. 1 Reg 9. 22.

called. So *Livy* opposeth them, saying, *The people of* Rome *are not in a kingdom, but in liberty:* and elsewhere he distinguisheth the people enjoying liberty * from those that lived under Kings. *Cicero* † said, *Either the Kings should not have been expell'd, or liberty should have been given to the people really, and not in words.* After these *Tacitus*, *The City of* Rome *from the beginning was under Kings:* L. Brutus *brought in Liberty and the Consulship.* *Strabo* saith of *Amisus*, it was sometime free, sometime under Kings. And frequently in the Roman * Laws, foreiners are divided into *Kings* and *free States*. Here then the question is not concerning the liberty of single men, but of a people. And further, as for private, so for this publick subjection some are said to be, not of their own right, not of their own power †. Yet properly, when a people is alienated, the men themselves are not alienated but the perpetual right of governing them, as they are a people. So, when the freed servant of a Patron is assigned to one of his children, it is not the alienation of a freeman, but he transcribes and makes away the right he had over another man. Nor is that more firm, which they say, If a King hath

Lib. 45.
* Thucydides: *Pars Thracum libera.* Seneca pater suasoria. *Non eadem modo in libera civitate dicendam esse sententiam, quo apud* Reges. Josephus antiq. hist. l. 13. *Ad Reges populosque liberos.* Cicero Epist. 15.4. *Populorum liberorum, regumque sociorum auxilia.* Plinius l.6.c. 20. de Indis: *Jam hi montium qui perpetuo tractu Oceani oram tenent, liberi & regum expertes.*
† *Lib.* 3. *de legib.*
Annal. 1.
Lib. 12.
* *De bello & de judiciis recuperatoriis.*
† Hinc illa: *Quæ urbes, qui agri, qui homines Ætolorum juris aliquando fuerunt.* Et, *Estne pop. Collatinus in sua potestate?* Liv. lib. 38. & lib. 5.

gotten

gotten any people by War, whereas he subdued them not without the bloud and sweat of his subjects, they are rather to be taken for the acquest of the Subjects than of the King. For haply, the King maintain'd his Army out of his own private * substance, or out of the profits of that Patrimony † which follows his principality; for suppose a King hath but the *usufruit* of that very Patrimony, as also of the right of governing the people which hath elected him, yet are those fruits his own. (As it is declared in the † civil Law, that the fruits of an inheritance, which is commanded to be restored, are not restored; because they arise not from the inheritance, but from the Thing.) Wherefore it may come to pass, that a King may have command over some people by a proper right *, so that he may also alienate them. *Strabo* † saith, the Island *Cythera* lying over against *Tanarus* was by his own private right pertaining to *Eurycles* Prince of the Lacedemonians. So, King *Salomon* gave to *Hirom* *, King of the Phenicians, twenty Cities; not

* *M. Antoninus ad bellum Marcomannicum cum ærario exhausto indicere populo nihil vellet, facto in foro Trajani sectione, distraxit vasa aurea, pocula Chrystallina & murrina, uxoris & suam sericam & auream vestem, multa ornamenta gemmarum.*

† *Ideo Ferdinandus Granatensis Regni partem alteram, ut stante matrimonio ex castellæ proventibus quæsitam, sibi vindicavit.* Docet Mariana lib. 28. Hist. Hispan. † *L. in fidei commissaria sect. plane. D. ad S. C. Trebellianum.* * *Balduino concessere, qui cum ipso in orientem belli causa venerant, ut urbium, provinciarum, vectigalium, rerum bello captarum dimidium ipsi cederet.* † *Lib. 8.* * *Ita enim eum Græce vocat Philo Biblius qui Sanchuniatonis historiam vertit.* 1 Reg. 12.

of

of the Cities of the Hebrews: for *Cabul* (which name is attributed to those Cities) is seated without the Hebrew bounds, *Jos.* 19. 27. but of those Cities, which the conquered Nations, enemies of the Hebrews, had retained till that day; and which partly the King of *Egypt*, *Salomon*'s Father-in-Law, had overcome, and given as a dowry to him, partly *Salomon* himself had taken in; for that they were not inhabited by the Israelites, at that time, is proved by this argument, because after *Hirom* restored them, then at last *Salomon* carried thither Colonies of the Hebrews. So *Hercules* * is read to have given to *Tyndareus* the Empire of *Sparta* taken in War, upon these terms, that if *Hercules* should leave any children, it should be returned to them. *Amphipolis* was given as a dowry to *Acamas* the Son of *Theseus*; And in *Homer* *Agamemnon* promiseth to give *Achilles* seven Cities. King *Anaxagoras* freely bestowed two parts of his Kingdom upon *Melampus* *. † *Justin* saith of *Darius*, *He gave by Testament* the Kingdom to *Artaxerxes*, to

1 Reg. 9. 5. ibid. 12. 1 Paralip. 8. 14.

Diod. l. 4.

* *Idem Hercules Dryopes, qui juxta Parnassum habitabant, à se victos donavit Apollini. Servius ad 4. Æneid. Herculem adversus Lapithas belli socium sibi sumsit Doriensium Rex, parte Regni in mercedem societatis data. Cychreus Salaminis Rex prole carens regnum testamento reliquit Teucro. Peleus ab Eurytione Phthiæ Rege tertiam Regni partem accepit in dotem; quæ habet Apollodorus. Apud Livium est libro* 1. Proca Numitori regnum legat. * *Lanassa nubens Pyrrho Epirotarum Regi in dotem ei attulit Corcyram urbem ab Agathocle patre suo bello captam.* Plutarchus Pyrrho. † *Lib.* 5.

Cyrus,

Cyrus certain Cities, whereof he was Governour. So the successors of *Alexander* are to be thought, every one for his part, to have succeeded into that full right and propriety of ruling over the Nations, which were subject to the * Persians, or else themselves to have acquired that power by the right of Victory. Wherefore it is no marvell if they assumed to themselves a right of alienation. So when King † *Attalus* the Son of *Eumenes* had by his testament made the people of *Rome* heir of his Goods, the people of *Rome* under the name of Goods comprehended his Kingdom too. And after when *Nicomedes* King of *Bithynia* dying had made the Roman people Heir, the Kingdom was reduced into the form of a * Province.

* Ammianus de Perside, non exacte tamen ad historiæ fidem: *Ex testamento nationem omnem in successoris unius jura translatam* Libro. 22.

† Valerius Maximus: *Attalus testamenti æquitate gratus Asiam pop. Romano legavit.*

Florus de ea re: *Addita igitur hæreditate provinciam pop. Romanus, non quidem bello nec armis, sed quod est æquius, testamenti jure retinebat. Flor. l. 2. Epit. Liv.* 58 Cic. secundum in Rullum: *Hæreditatem crevimus, regnum Bithyniæ.* Cic. de lege Agraria: *Qui ignorat Regnum Ægypti testamento Regis Alexandrini, populi Romani esse factum?* Ex Josepho discimus *Herodem, Augusto ei concedente ut Regnum cui è liberis vellet relinqueret, testamentum aliquoties mutasse.* Antiq. hist. l. 15. & 16. *Alfonsus Arragonius Neapoleos Regnum, ut armis partum, Ferdinando notho suo reliquit. In eodem Regno urbes quasdam Ferdinandus legavit nepoti.* Mariana lib. 30.

XLIX. *Some highest Empires are not holden fully.*

BUt in Kingdoms which are conferred by the will of the people, I grant * it is not to be presumed that it was the will of the people, that an *alienation* of his Empire should be permitted to the King. Wherefore, what *Crantzius* notes in *Unguinus* as a new thing, that he had bequeathed *Norway* by his testament, we have no reason to disapprove, if he respecteth the manners of the Germans, among whom Kingdoms were not held with so full a right. For, wheras *Charls* the Great and *Lewis* the pious and others after them even among the Vandals and Hungarians have disposed of Kingdoms in their testaments, that had rather the vertue of a *commendation* † among the people, than the force of a true *alienation*. And of *Charls*, *Ado* specifies the same, that he desired his testament should be confirmed by the chiefest of France. Whereunto that is like which we read in *Livie*, that *Philip* King of *Macedonia*, when he had a mind to keep *Perseus* from the Kingdom, and in his place to advance

* Imperium non debere regi, qui ut agros & servas dicit Vopiscus Tacito. Salvianus: *Non poterat populos quos regebat per testamentum egenis tradere.*

† *Vide Capitulum 12 conventus ad Carisiacum sub Carolo Calvo. Huc refer testamentum Pelagii quo Hispaniam reliquit Alfonso & Ofmisinda, & de Dania quædam apud Saxonem. Neque mirum igitur, quædam testamenta improbante populo fuisse irrita, ut Alfonsi Arragonii. Vide Marianam lib. 10. Et Alphonsi Legionensis, cum is filias filio prætulisset. Idem Mar. l. 12.*

Antigonus

Antigonus, his Brothers Son, visited the Cities of *Macedonia* to commend † *Antigonus* to the Princes. Nor is it material, that the forementioned *Lewis* is read to have rendred the City *Rome* to Pope *Paschal*, seeing the *Franks* might rightly render to the people of *Rome* that power over the City, which they had received from the same people: of which people he did sustein as it were the person, who was Prince of the first order.

† Vide rem similem apud Cassiodorum Lib. 8. Epist. 8. & seq. Ita pacta successionis mutuæ inter Sancium & Jacobum Arragonenses à proceribus firmata. Mariana lib. 12. & Henrici Navarræ Regis qua Joannem instituit hæredem. Id. l. 13. & Isabellæ Reginæ Castellæ. Id. lib. 28.

L. *A further manifestation of the second caution.*

THe truth of our foresaid note, about distinguishing the height of power from the fulness of having it, will appear in this, that as many highest Empires are not, so many not highest are held fully. Whence it is that * Marquessates and Earldoms are wont to be sold and disposed of by will more easily than Kingdoms. Moreover the same distinction shews it self in the Protectorship †, whilst a King, either by non-age or by disease, is unable to manage his own power. For, in Kingdoms that are not Patrimonial, the Protectorship belongs to them, to whom the Publick Law,

* *Vide de Vrgetii principatu Marianam lib. 12. c. 16.*

† *Vide Cothmannum Tomo 1. Cons. 41. num. 2.*

Law, or in defect thereof the consent of the people * doth commend it: in Patrimonial Kingdoms, to them who are chosen by the Father † or by the next of Kin. So we see in the Kingdom of the *Epirots*, which arose from the peoples consent, *Aribas* a Pupil-King had Tutors publikely appointed him: and so had the posthume Son of *Alexander* the Great by the Macedonian Peers. But in the lesser *Asia*, gotten by War, King *Eumenes* appointed his Brother to be Tutor to his Son *Attalus*. So *Hiero* the Father reigning in *Sicily* ordained by his testament whom he pleased to be Tutors to his Son *Hierom*. Now, whether a King be withall, in his private right, a Lord of Land, as the King of *Egypt* was after the time of *Joseph*, and the Indian Kings which *Diodorus* and *Strabo* speak of; or be not, this is extrinsecal to his Empire, and perteins not to the nature of it: wherefore, it neither maketh another kind of Empire, nor another manner of holding the same Empire.

* *Vide Marian. in Alphonso 5. Legionis Rege. At testamentum Regis Joannis de tutela & administratione Regni à proceribus improbatum. Mar. lib.* 18.

† *Ptolomæus Rex Ægypti Tutorem filio suo reliquit populum Romanum.* Val. Max. *l.* 6. *c.* 6. 1. *Justin. l.* 13. *Justin. l.* 67. *Plutarch. de am. frat. Lib.* 2. *Lib.* 15.

LI. *A third Observation.*

LEt this be observed in the third place, *An Empire ceaseth not to be supreme, although hee that is to rule promise certain things*

to

** to the subjects or to God, even such things as pertain to the way of ruling.* Nor do I now speak of keeping the natural and divine Law, adde also that of Nations, unto which all Kings are bound, though they promised nothing; but of certain rules, to which without a promise they were not bound. The truth of what I say appears by similitude of a Father of a Family: who, if he hath promised his Family to do somewhat which belongs unto their Government, shall not thereby cease to have, so far as may be in a Family, supreme right therein. Nor is the Husband deprived of marital power, because of some promise to the Wife. I confess, by this means the Empire is in some sort streightned, whether the obligation ly upon the exercise of the act only, or also directly upon the faculty it self. In the first way, the act done against promise will be unjust: because, as we shew elsewhere, a true promise gives him a right, to whom 'tis made: and in the other way, it will be null by want of faculty. Nor yet doth it thence follow, that he that makes the promise hath any superiour: for, in this case, the act is rendred null, not by superiour force but in Law. Amongst the Persians, the King was Supreme and absolute *; adored as the Image of God; and as *Justin* † saith, he was not chan-ged

* *Trajanus caput suum, dextram suam, si scienter fefellisset, Deorum iræ consecrabat.* Plin. Paneg. *Adrianus Imp. juravit nunquam se senatorem nisi ex senatus sententia punitu[r]um. Anastasius Imp. juravit servaturum se decreta Chalcedonensis Concilii. Meminere Zonaras, Cedrenus, alii. Seriores Imperatores Græci Ecclesiæ jurabant. Vide eundem Zonaram Michaele Raugabe & alibi. Vide & in Gothis Regibus exemplum apud Cassiodorum.* 10.16,17.

* αὐτοκρατὴς καὶ ἀνυπεύθυνος. *Plutarchus.*

† *Lib,* 10.

ged but by death. A King was he that to the Peers of *Persia* spake thus: *I have called you together, that I might not seem to use only my own Counsel: but remember it is your duty rather to obey than perswade.* Yet he took an oath at his entrance, as *Xenophon* and *Diodorus Siculus* have noted, and it was not lawful for him * to change certain Laws made after a particular form. The same is related of the Ethiopian Kings by † *Diodorus Siculus.* And by his relation the Egyptian Kings, who (no doubt) as well as other Kings of the East had Supreme power, were bound to the observation of many things: but, if they had done the contrary, could not be accused living; dead, their memory was accused *, and being condemned they wanted solemn burial: as also the bodies of the Hebrew Kings †, who had reigned ill, were not buried in the royal Sepulchers: an excellent temperament, whereby, both the highest power was kept sacred, and yet by fear of a future judgement, Kings were kept from breaking their trust. That the Kings also of *Epirus* were wont to swear, they would reign according to the Laws, we

Val. Max. lib. 9. 6, 5.

* Dan. 6. 8, 12. 15.

Plutarch. in Themistocle. Diodorus Siculus lib. 17. *& multo post tempore Procopius Persici belli lib.* 1. *Ubi insignis ad hanc rem historia exstat. Tamen idem de Lethe castello legem à Rege mutatam refert, sed non probat.*

† *Lib.* 3.

Lib. 1.

* *Leges tyrannorum corpora insepulta extra fines projici jubent.* Appianus Civilium tertio. *Andronicus Imp. Patrem suum Michaelem, quod fidem Latinam sequi cœpisset, mortuum sepultura privavit. Gregoras lib.* 6. † *Vide Josephum de Joramis duobus, altero Hierosolymorum, altero Israelis Rege, lib.* 8. *cap.* 3. *&* 5. *Item de Joaso Hierosolymorum Rege.*

I learn

learn of *Plutarch* * in the life of *Pyrrhus*. But suppose it be added, *If the King breaks his trust, he shall be deposed* †? Yet will not the power hereby cease to be the highest, but the manner of holding it weakned by this condition, and the Empire will be as it were temporary. It is said of the King of *Sabæans*, that he was absolute * and of a most free power, but that he might be stoned if he went out of his Palace †. In like manner, an estate of Land, that is held in trust, is an estate, as well as if it were possessed in full dominion, but it is holden for a time or at the pleasure of another. And such a Commissory Law or condition may be annexed not only in the bestowing of a Kingdom, but in other contracts; for some Leagues too with neighbours, we see, are entred with the like * sanction.

* Plutarchus: *Solebant Reges in Cassaiorum terra, quæ Molottidos pars est, Jovi Areo sacrificare ac juramentum præstare Epirotis. Jurabant autem Reges se imperaturos secundum leges. Epirotæ autem se imperium ejusdem conservaturos secundum easdem leges.*

† *Vide exemplum apud Crantzium lib. 9. Suedicorum.*

* ἀνυπεύθυνος. *Agatharchides apud Photium.*

† *Quod & Artemidoro auctore Strabo annotavit. lib. 16.*

* *Aut etiam ne subditi Regem pacta violantem juvent: aut ne ei pareant. Vide Crommerum Polonicis 19. & 21. Est & exemplum apud Scafnaburgensem in rebus Henrici an. 1074.*

LII. *The fourth Observation.*

FOurthly it must be noted, *Although the highest power be one and undivided by it self, consisting of the parts above set down, supremacy * being added; Yet may it sometimes happen to be divided *, either by parts, which they call potential, or by parts subjective.* So

* τῷ ἀνυπευθύνῳ.

* *Vide Zazium singularium responsorum lib. 2. c. 31.*

So when the Roman Empire was one, it often came to pass, that one Ruler had the East, another the West, or that three divided the world between them. And so it may be, that a people choosing a King may reserve some acts to themselves, and may commit others to the King with full right. Yet is not that done, as we have shewed already, whensoever the King is bound up with certain promises, but then we must conceive it to be done, if either a partition be made expressly †, of which we have spoken afore; or, if a people, yet free, lay upon their future Kings a charge by way of an abiding precept; or, if a clause be added to signifie that the King may be compeld or punisht. For a *precept* is from a superiour, superiour at least in that particular which is given in precept: and to *compell* is not alwaies the property of a superiour (for also naturally every one hath a right to compel his debtor) but is repugnant to the nature of an inferiour. Parity therefore at least follows from coaction, and so a division of the supremacy. Against such a State, as being double headed, many allege many incommodities: but (as we have also said above) in civil affairs there is nothing wholy without incommodities; and Right is to be measured, not by that which seems best to you or me, but by the will of him whence right ariseth.

† *Ita Probi tempore Senatus firmabat principum leges, de appellationibus cognoscebat, proconsules creabat, legatos consulibus dabat. Vide & Gail. lib. 2. observ. c. 57. num. 7. & Card. Manticam de tacitis & ambiguis conventionibus lib. 27. tit. 5. num. 4.*

An antient example is brought by *Plato* in his third *de legibus*: For when the House of *Hercules* had built *Argos*, *Messena* and *Lacedemon*, the Kings were bound to keep their Government within the bound of prescribed Laws; and whilst they did so, the people were obliged to leave the Kingdom to them and their posterity, and suffer none to take it from them. And to this, not only Kings and their own people have mutually covenanted, but Kings with other Kings*, and one people with another people, and Kings with neighbourig States, and States with neighbouring Kings, have entred into Covenant, and promis'd aid to each other respectively.

* *Exempla sunt eum plura in historia populorũ septentrionalium. Vide Joannem Magnum historia Suedica lib. 15. & 29. Crantzium Suedicorum 5. Pontanum Danicorum 8.*

LIII. *A further explication of the last note, about division of power and mixture.*

YEt are they much deceived, who think the power of Kings divided, when they will have some of their acts not accounted firm unless they be approved by the Senate, or some such Assembly. For the acts voided for want of such approbation, must be understood to be cancelled by the Kings own command, who ordained this by way of caution, lest any thing fallaciously gained from him, should pass under the notion of his true and deliberate will.

King

King *Antiochus* the third sent such a rescript to the Magistrates, that they should not obey him, in case he should command any thing against Law: and *Constantin* published the like, that Orphans and Widows be not constreined to come to the Emperours Court for Justice, no not if the Emperours rescript be shewed. Wherefore this case is like to that of testaments, which have a clause, that no later testament shall be of force: for this clause also makes it be presumed, that the later testament proceeds not from the true will of the maker. Neverthelesse, as this clause, so that other by the Kings expresse command and special signification of his later will may be annulled. Again, I do not here use the authority of *Polybius* neither, who refers the RomanCommonwealth to a mixt kind of Government; which, at that time, if we respect not the doings themselves but the right of doing, was meerly popular. For, both the authority of the Senate, which he refers to an Optimacy, and of the Consuls, whom he will have to be like Kings, was subject to the people. The same may be said concerning other writers of the Politicks, who conceive it more agreeable to their design, to behold rather the external appearance and daily administration of affairs, than to weigh the right it self of the highest power.

Boer. ad c. 1. de const. in Decret. Plut. Apoph. L. unica. c. quando Imperator. Addel. 1. c. de petitionibus bonorum sublatis.

LIV. *True examples of the ſupreme power divided.*

MOre pertinent is that which *Ariſtotle* hath written: Between a full Kingdom *, and a Laconical †, which is a meer principality, ſome other *ſpecies* are interjected. An example hereof, as I ſuppoſe, may be found in the Hebrew Kings; for, of theſe, that they ruled, in moſt things, by the higheſt right, I think it is impiety to doubt; for the people deſired ſuch a King as their neighbours * had: but the Nations of the Eaſt were ſubject to their Kings in the moſt humble way †. And above we have noted, that the *whole* Hebrew people was *under* the King. And *Samuel* deſcribing the right of Kings, ſufficiently ſhews that the people have no power left in themſelves againſt the Kings injuries. Which the Fathers do rightly gather from that of the *Pſalm: Againſt thee only have I ſinned*. Upon which

* *Quod* παμβασιλείαν *vocat*; *eadem eſt* παντελὴς μοναρχία *Sophocli Antigone, Plutarcho* αὐτοκρατὴς βασιλεία καὶ ἀνυπεύθυνος, *Straboni* ἐξουσία αὐτοτελής.

† Dionyſius Halicarnaſſenſis de Laconicis regibus: *Neque enim Lacedæmonii pleno jure Reges erant.*

* *Putabat populus nihil eſſe abſurdi ſi cum viciniregnarentur, ipſi eandem imperii formam acciperent.* Joſephus.

† Æſchylus' Perſis de Rege Perſarum ſic loquentem facit Atoſſam: — οὐχ ὑπεύθυνος πόλει. Notum illud Maronis: — *Regem non ſic Ægyptus, & ingens Lydia, nec populi Parthorum aut Medus Hydaſpes Obſervant.* — Apud Livium: *Syri & Aſiatici genera hominum ſervituti nata*; à quo non diſcrepat illud Apollonii apud Philoſtratum: *Aſſyrii & Medi dominationem etiam adorant.* Ariſt. 3. Polit. 14. *Aſiatici dominatum æquo animo ferunt.* Cicero de prov. conſular b. *Judæus & Syrus nationibus natis ſervituti.* Salluſt. de gentibus orientis: *Adeo illis ingenita eſt ſanctitas Regii nominis* Apud Tacitum Civilis Batavis ad Gallos: Hiſt. 4. *Servirent Syria Aſiaque & ſuetus regibus Oriens.* Nam & in Germania & in Gallia tum Reges erant, ſed ut idem Tacitus notat, precario jure regnandi, & autoritate ſuadendi, non jubendi poteſtate.

place

place *Hierom* * : *Because he was a King, and feared not another.* And *Ambrose : Being a King, he was in danger of no Laws, because Kings are free from such bonds ; neither do any Laws bind them over to punishment, being secured by their Soveraign power* † : *against man therefore he sinned not, to whose restraint he was not obnoxious.* I see there is consent among the Hebrews, that stripes were inflicted on the King offending against those written Laws exstant about the Kings office ; but those stripes among them had no infamy, and they were of his own accord received by the King in token of repentance, and therefore he was not beaten by an Officer, but by one whom he was pleased to make choice of, and at his own pleasure he was eased. As to coactive punishments, the Kings were so free from them, that even the Law of excalceation, as having in it something ignominious, was not of force upon them. The Hebrew *Barnachmon* hath a sentence exstant amongst the sayings of the Rabbins, in the title of Judges : * *No creature judgeth the King, but the blessed God.* These things being so, neverthelels I think some causes were exempted from the Kings judgement, and remained in the power of the Synedry of LXX. instituted by *Moses* at Gods command, and by perpetual succession continued to the times of *Herod.* Therefore, both *Moses* and *David* call Judges *Gods,*

* Idem Hieronymus Epist. ad Rust. de pænitentia: *Rex enim erat : alium non timebat, alium non habebat super se.*

† Paria habet ad eundem Psalmum Arnobius minor Virges apud Cassiodorum : *Causa Regiæ potestatis supernis est applicanda judiciis, quandoquidem illa à cœlo [illegible] est, ita soli [illegible] debet innocentiam.* *Idem legere est apud Isidorum Pelusiot. Epist. postremo editarum.* 383.

* *Nulla creatura judicat Regem, sed Deus benedictus.*

Ex. 32. 8. Deut. 1. 17. Psal. 72. 1. 2 Chron. 19. 6. 8. 1 Chron. 26. 32. 2 Chron. 19. 11.

Gods, and judgements are called *the judgements of God*, and Judges are ſaid to judge not in the place of man but of God. Yea the matters of God are plainly diſtinguiſht from the matters of the King: where, by the matters of God, the moſt learned of the Hebrews bid us underſtand judgements to be exerciſed according to Gods Law. The King of the Jews, I deny not, exerciſed by himſelf certain capital judgements (in which particular *Maimonides* prefers him before the King of *Iſrael*) which alſo is evinced by examples not a few, both in the ſacred Scripture and in the writings of the Hebrews: Yet certain kinds of cauſes ſeem not permitted to the Kings cognizance, *viz.* of the Tribe, of the high Prieſt, of the * Prophet. And hereof there is an argument in the hiſtory of the Prophet *Jeremy*, whom when the Princes required unto death, the King anſwered: *Behold, he is in your power, for the King can do nothing againſt you:* to wit, in this kind of matters. Yea, and the perſon that for any other cauſe was impeached before the Synedry, could not by the King be exempted from their judgement. Therefore *Hircanus*, when by power he could not hinder their judgement concerning *Herod*, eluded the ſame by Art. In *Macedonia*, they that deſcended from *Calanus*, as *Caliſthenes* in *Arrian* ſaith, *bare rule over that people not by force but by Law. The Macedonians*, ſaith *Curtius*, *are accuſtomed to*

* *Non capit Prophetam perire extra Jeruſalem.* Luke 13 33. Jer. 38. 5.

Joſeph. Antiqu. 14. 17.

Lib. 14.

to the Regal government, yet are in a greater shadow of liberty than other nations: For even the judgment of life and death was not in the Kings hand. *Of Capital matters*, saith the same *Curtius*, *by the old custome of the* Macedonians, *the Army did enquire, in time of Peace the Commons; the power of the Kings prevailed no further than their authority could move.* Lib. 6. There is in another place of the same Author another token of this mixture: *The Macedonians decreed according to the custome of their nation, that the King should not hunt on foot, without the attendance of his elect Princes or courtiers.* Lib. 8. Tacitus relates of the Gothones: *They are now in greater vassalage under their Kings, than other Germans: nor are they yet depriv'd of all liberty.* For he had afore describ'd the principality by the authority of perswading, not by the power of Commanding: and after he expresseth a full Royalty in these words: *One commandeth, without all exceptions, not by a precarious right of governing.* Eustathius upon the sixt of the *Odysses*, where the Commonwealth of the *Phaeaces* is described, saith it had *a mixture of Power, of the King, and of the States* †. Something like it I observe in the times of the

† *Laonicus Chalcocondylas talia ait esse regna Pannonum & Anglorum, l. 2. Arragonum, l. 5. & Navarræ eodem libro, ubi ait, nec magistratus à Rege creatos, nec præsidia imposita nisi volentibus, nec quicquam populo imperatum contra mores. Reges alios esse pleno cum jure, alios sub legibus, etiam Judæus Levi Gersonides notavit ad* 1 *Sam.* 8. 4.

Mira quæ de Taprobane scribit Plinius lib. 6. c. 22. Eligi regem à populo senecta clementiaq; liberos non habentem, & si postea gignat, abdicari, ne fiat hæreditarium regnum. Rectores ei à populo xxx. dari, nec nisi plurium sententia quenquam capite damnari.

damnari. Sic quoq; appellationem esse ad populum, lxx, judice dari. Si liberent ii reum, non amplius xxx. (*ita enim legi locus hic debet*) iis nullam esse dignitatem, gravissimo probro. Regi cultum liberi patris, cæteris Arabum. Regem si quid delinquat morte mulctari, nullo interimente, sed aversantibus cunctis & commercia etiam sermonis negantibus. *Servius ad illud* 4. *Æn.* populumq; patresque. Quidam hoc loco voluit tres partes politiæ comprehensas, populi, optimatum, regiæ potestatis. Cato enim ait de tribus istis partibus ordinatam fuisse Carthaginem.

Roman Kings; for then all matters almost went through the Royal hand. *Romulus reigned over us, as he pleased*, saith Tacitus. *It is manifest, at the beginning of the City Kings had all power*, saith *Pomponius*: yet *Halicarnassensis* will have something excepted by the people even at that time. But if we give more credit to the *Roman* Authors, in some causes there lay an appeal from the Kings to the people, as *Seneca* hath noted out of *Cicero*'s books *de Republica*, out of the Pontifical books also, and *Fenestella*; shortly after, *Servius Tullus* advanced to the Throne, not so much by right, as by the favourable breath of the people, yet more abated the regal power. For, as *Tacitus* speaketh, *he establisht Laws, which even the Kings themselves were to obey*. The less cause have we to wonder at that which *Livy* saith, The power of the first Consuls differd from the regal in little more than that 'twas annual. Such a mixture also of a Democracy and Optimacy was at *Rome* in the time of the *Interregnum*, and in the first times of the Consuls. For in

Epist. 100.

3. *Annal.*

certain

certain affairs, and those of the greatest moment, the will of the people was a law, if the Fathers would go before them with their authority*, and (as it were) prepare the bill; which authority afterward, the peoples power encreased, was onely for a shew, when the Fathers, as *Livy* and *Dionysius* note, began with their voices, but the Assembly did what they pleased. For all this, in after times there remained somewhat of a mixture, whilst, as the same *Livy* speaketh, the Government was in the hand if the *Patricians*, that is, of the Senate, but the *Tribunes*, that is, the *Plebeians*, had a share, to wit, a right of forbidding or interceding. And so *Isocrates* will have the *Athenian* Commonwealth, in *Solon*'s time, to have been * an Optimacy mixt with a Democracy.

* Plutarchus Coriolano: *Populus jus non habebat aut legem condendi, aut aliud quid jubendi nisi Senatus praecessisset auctoritas.*

Similem mixturam in Genuatium rep. suis temporibus observat Chalcocondylas l. 5.

Liv. lib. 6.

* δημοκρατίαν ἀριστοκρατίᾳ μεμιγμένην.

LV. *Whether He can have supreme power, that is comprehended in an unequal league.*

UPon these premises, let us examin some questions, which are of frequent use in the argument we have in hand. The first is, whether He may have supreme power, who is comprehended in an unequal league. By an *unequal League* I understand here, not that which is made between parties unequal in their forces, as the *Theban* City in the time of of *Pelopidas* had a league with the King of *Persians*, and the *Romans* of old with the *Massilians*, and afterward with King *Massanissa*; nor that which hath a transient act, as when an enemy is receiv'd to friendship, on condition he pay the cost of the war, or perform somewhat else: but, that which in the very nature of the agreement gives a certain permanent prelation to one side; that is, when the one is bound to conserve the Empire and Majesty of the other; as it was in the league of the *Etolians* with the *Romans*; that is, both to endeavour that the others Empire may be in safety, and that his dignity, which is signified by the name of Majesty, may be violat †. Unto which kinde are to be referr certain Rights of them which are now calld Rights of *Protection*, *Advocacy*, *Mundiburg*: also the Right of mother-cities amongst the *Grecians* over their Colonies. For the Colonies were as free, saith *Thucydides*, as the mother-Cities, but they ought to exhibit reverence to their *Metropolis*, and certain signes of honour. *Livy* saith of the old league between the *Romans*, who had received all the right of *Alba*, and the *Latins* of the *Alban* race: *In that league the Roman state was superiour.* Rightly speaks *Andronicus Rhodius* after *Aristotle*: *It is the property of friendship 'twixt unequals, that the stronger have more honour, and the weaker have more help.* We know

Justin. l. 43. *Val. Max. l. 7. cap. 1.*

† Imperii reverentiam dixit *Tacitus*, & sic explicat: *Sede finibusq; in sua ripa, mente animoq; nobiscum agunt.* Lib. 4. Florus: *Illi quoq; reliqui, qui immunes imperii erant, sentiebant tamen magnitudinem, & victorem gentium populum Romanum reverebantur.*

Lib. 1.

Lib. 1.

Nicom. l. 9. c. 18.

know what *Proculus* answerd to this question, to wit, *that the people is free which is subject to the power of no other, though it be contained in the league, that that people should fairly conserve the Majesty of the other people.* If then a people bound in such a league remain free, if they be not subject to anothers power, it followes that they retain the highest power. And the same is to be said of a King; For there is the same reason of a free people and of a King, who is truly so. *Proculus* addes, such a clause is in the league, to signify, the one people is superiour, not that the other is not free. *Superiour* here is meant, not in power (for before he had said, the one people is subject to the others power) but in authority and dignity; which the following words do express by a fit similitude: *As we understand our Clients to be free, though they be not equal to us, neither in authority, nor in dignity, nor in every right: So also are they to be conceived free, whose duty it is to have a fair respect to the conservation of our Majesty.* Clients are under the trust of their patrons, so are a people inferiour * in the league under the trust of that people which in dignity is superiour. They are *under patronage not under rule*, as *Sylla* speaks in *Appian* †. *Livy* * saith, *in parte, non in ditione*: and † *Cicero*, describing those more honest times of the *Romans*, tells us, they had *patrocinium*

L. non dubito D. de cap.

**Vide Cardinalem Tuschum PP. concl. 935. exemplum habes in Dilimnitis, qui αὐτόνομοι suiq; juris Persis militabant apud Agathiam lib. 3. Sic Irene consilium fuit inter mariti liberos ita partiri Imperium ut post natos faceret dignitate quidem minores, caeterum sui juris plenaeque potestatis. Vide Crantzium Saxonicorum 10. de urbibus quae se in Austriacorum protectionem dedere. Herodian. l. 5. Osroenorum & Armoniorum, quorum hi subditi erant, illi amici & socii.*

† *Appian. Mithr.*
* *Liv. lib. 38.*
† *Cic. Offic. 2.*

patrocinium sociorum, non imperium. With whom agrees well that saying of *Scipio Africanus* the elder: *The people of Rome had rather oblige men by favour than fear, and unite forein Nations to them by a faithfull association, than subdue them to a grievous servitude*: and that which *Strabo* relates of the *Lacedemonians* after the *Romans* came into *Greece*: *They remained free, conferring nothing, beside a friendly aide.* As private patronage taketh not away personal liberty, so publique patronage taketh not away Civil liberty, which without supremacy of power cannot be understood. Therefore we see these are opposed in *Livy*, *To be under protection*, and *To be under command*: And *Augustus*, in *Josephus*, threatens the *Arabian* King *Syllaus*, unless he would cease from doing his neighbours wrong, He would take order, that of a *friend* he should be made a subject: of which quality were the Kings of *Armenia*, who (as *Patus* wrote to *Vologeses*) were within the *Roman* dominion; and therefore were Kings, rather in the sound of the name than really: such as were the *Cyprian* and other Kings of old under the Kings of *Persia*: * *Subjects*, as *Diodorus* saith.

Liv. lib. 26.

* ὑποτεταγμένοι. *lib. 16.*

LVI. *An Objection Answered.*

PRoculus addeth somewhat which seemeth opposite to that we have said: *There are*

are accused before us some of the confederat Cities, & after sentence of condemnation we inflict upon them punishment. But, for the understanding hereof, we must know, that four kindes of Controversies may happen. First, if the subjects of a people or King, that is under the protection of another, be said to have done against the league: Secondly, if the people or the King himself be accused: Thirdly, if the Fellowes, which are under protection of the same people or King, contend with one another: Fourthly, if the subjects complain of the injuries of their own Rulers. In the first kinde, if a fault appear, the King or people is bound, either to punish the offendor, or to give him up to the party injured: which holds, not only 'twixt unequals, but between those that are equally confederat, yea and among them that are not at all confederate, as we shall shew elswhere. He is also bound to endeavour that dammages may be repaired: which at *Rome* was the Office of the *Recuperators* *. But one of the Associats in the league hath no direct right to apprehend or punish the subjects of his confederate. Wherefore *Decius Magius*, a Campanian, being put in bands by *Annibal*, and carried to *Cyrene*, and thence to *Alexandria*, shewed that he was bound by *Annibal* against the league, and so was freed. In the second way, the confederate hath a right to

* Gallus Ælius apud Festum: *Reciperatio est cum inter populum & Reges nationesq; ac civitates peregrinas lex convenit, quomodo per reciperatorem reddantur res, reciperenturq; resq; privatas inter se prosequantur. Liv. lib. 23.*

to compell his Confederate, to stand to the Articles of the league, and, if he will not, to punish him. But this also is not peculiar to the unequall league: it hath place too in that which is equall. For, that one may take revenge of him that hath offended, 'tis sufficient, that he be not subject to the offender (of which elsewhere:) wherefore the same thing comes to pass between Kings, or people not confederate. In the third kinde, as in an equal league, controversies are wont to be brought before an Assembly * of the Confederates, to wit, such as are not concerned in the question; as we read the Grecians, the ancient Latins, and the Germans of old have done; or else before Arbitrators, or before the Prince of the Association as a common Arbitrarot: So in a league unequal, it is agreed for the most part, that the controversies be debated before him who is superiour in the league. This therefore doth not prove any power of command: for Kings also do usually try their causes before judges of their own constitution. In the last kinde, the confederates have no right of cognizance. Therefore when *Herod* voluntarily carried to *Augustus* certain accusations against his sons; *You might*, said they, *punish us your self, both as a father, and as King*. And *Scipio* *, when *Annibal* was accus'd at *Rome* by certain *Carthaginians*, said, the Conscript Fathers ought not to interpose

* *Talis conventus vocatur συνέδριον.*

Joseph. l. 16. c. 7, 8.

* *Vide Polyb. in legationum excerpto 105.*

terpose in a business of the *Carthaginian* *Val. Max.l.* Commonwealth. And herein (as *Ari-* *4. c. 1.* *stotle* teacheth) a confederacy and a com- *Polit. 3. 9.* monwealth do differ, that Confederates take care no common injury be done unto them; not that the Citizens of a Confederate Commonwealth do no injury one against another.

LVII. *Another Objection answered.*

IT is objected also, that in histories he that is superior in the league is sometimes said to command; he that is inferior, to obey. But, neither ought this to move us. For, either it is treated of things pertaining to the common good of the Society, or of his private utility who is superior in the league. In common affairs, out of time of Assembly, even where the League is equal, the custome is for him who is chosen Chief of the league, to have command over his Confederates, as *Agamemnon* over the *Gracian* Kings, the *Lacedæmonians* over the *Gracians* afterward, and after them the *Athenians*. In the Speech of the *Corinthians* in *Thucydides* we read: *It becomes them that are Princes of the league, not to seek their own particular advantage, but content themselves with an eminency above the rest in taking care of the common Interest.* Isocrates relates, that the antient *Athenians* had the conduct of *Greece*, and *the charge of all*

K *their*

*their Fellowes, but ſo, that they left them all their liberty entire.** *This the Latins call, Imperare* to command, the *Greeks* more modeſtly τάσσειν to order. The *Athenians*, when the conduct of the war againſt the *Perſians* was committed to them, ἔταξαν, ſaith Thucidides, *they ordered* (ſo the Commiſſioners from *Rome* to *Greece* were ſaid to be ſent thither † for *ordering* the ſtate of the free Cities) *what towns ſhould contribute money againſt the Barbarians, what ſhould provide ſhips.* Now, if he doth this, who is only chief in a league, no marvell he doth the ſame who is ſuperior, in a league unequal. Wherefore Empire in this ſenſe, that is, the * conduct of affairs, takes not away the liberty of others †. But in thoſe things that concern the proper utility of the Superior, his Requeſts are uſually call'd Commands, not by right, but by likeneſs of the effect, as the Deſires of Kings are ſo called, and as Phyſicians are ſaid to *rule* their patients. Livy *: *Before this Conſul* (C. Poſthumius) *never was any one in any thing a charge or burthen to our Confederates: therefore the Magiſtrats were furniſht with Mules, tents, and all*

* Iſocrates alibi: *ita ut imperium habere belli, non dominari ſe debere cenſerent*: Item: *Socialiter non heriliter res eorum curantes.*

† *Plinius epiſt.* 8. 24.

* ἡγεμονία.

† Rhodii in oratione apud Senatum Romanum, quæ apud Livium exſtat l. 37. *Græci domeſticis quondam viribus etiam imperium amplectebantur: nunc imperium ubi eſt, ibi ut ſit perpetuum optant: libertatem veſtris tueri armis ſatis habent, quoniam ſuis non poſſunt.* Sic poſt Cadmeam à Thebanis receptam narrat Diodorus lib. 15. multas civitates Græcas conveniſſe: *Omnes ut liberæ eſſent, ſed Athenienſium ductu uterentur.* De ipſis Athenienſibus Philippi Macedonis tempore Dion. Pruſæenſis: *quo tempore ductu belli omiſſo libertatem ſolam retinebant.* Sic Cæſar, quos ſub imperio Suevorum fuiſſe dicit, eoſdem mox ſocios nominat. * *Lib.* 42.

other

other necessaries, that they might not command such things from our Fellows. Mean while tis true, it often comes to pass, that the Superior in a league, if he much excell in strength, by little & little, usurps an Empire properly so calld, especially if the league be perpetual, with a right of bringing in Garrisons into towns, as the *Athenians* did, when they sufferd an appeal to be made unto them from their Fellows; which the *Lacedemonians* never did. In which times *Isocrates* compares the Empire of the *Athenians* over their Confederates, to a Kingdom. So the Latins complaind, they endured servitude * under the shadow of a league with *Rome*: so the *Etolians*, of a vain shew and empty name of liberty; and the *Achaians* afterward, *that a league in appearance was now become a precarious servitude.* So in *Tacitus* † *Civilis* the *Batavian* complaineth of the same Romans: *We are not Associats, as heretofore, but are esteemed as slaves*: and in another place, *A miserable slavery is falsly named peace.* Eumenes also in * *Livy* saith, the Fellows of the *Rhodians* were Fellows in word, indeed subjects to their Empire, and obnoxious: And *Magnetes*, that in shew *Demetrias* was free, but indeed all things were done at pleasure * of the *Romans*. So *Polybius* notes, the *Thessalians* had a seeming liberty, but really were under command of the *Macedonians*. When these things are

* *Hal. l. 6. Liv. l. 34. Hist. 4.*

† *Hoc ipsum est quod Arato Plutarchus dicit* συμμαχίαν ὑποκορίζεσθαι. Molle servitium, *vocula apud Tacitum hist. 4. Festus Rufus de Rhodiis*: Primum liberè agebant, postea in consuetudinem parendi, Romanis clementer provocantibus, pervenerunt. *Vide Agathiam lib. 1. ubi monentur Gotthi quid à Francis cum tempore exspectandum habeant.*

* *Lib. 35. Lib. 37.*

* *Tales & Lazi Justiniani temporibus. Vide Procopium Pers. 2.*

done, and so done, that patience passeth into a right (of which elswhere) then either they which were Fellows become Subjects, or at least there is a partition of the supreme power, such as we have declared above to be possible.

LVIII. *That the highest power may consist with paying of Tribute.*

I See no cause to doubt, but they that * pay a certain Tribute † either for redeeming of injuries, or to gain safeguard (such as were the Hebrew * Kings, and of the neighbouring nations after the time of *Antonius*) may have the highest power; although this confession of their weakness diminish somewhat of their dignity.

LIX. *That the highest power may be holden in Fee.*

TO many it seems a more difficult question concerning feudal obligation, but it may easily be solved out of that which hath been said. For in this contract,

* *ξύμμαχοι φόρῳ ὑποτελεῖς, ut est apud Thucydid.*

† *Persæ pecuniam annuam ab Justiniano accipiebant, qua de re vide Procopium Persicorum 2. & Gothicorum 4. Id molli vocabulo vocabatur stipendium ad tutandas portas Caspias. Turcæ Arabas montanas pecunia placant.*

* *Joseph.* l. 15. Negabat Antonius rectum esse regem vocari ad rationes reddendas de iis quæ ut Rex fecisset: ita enim ne regem quidem eum fore. Par esse ut qui honorem ei dederint, etiam potestate quam liberrimè uti cum sinant.

Chrysostomus 2. de Eleemosyna: Judæi, ex quo retro ferri res eorum cœpere, Romano attributi imperio, neq; in plena, ut ante, erant libertate: neq; tamen ita ut nunc omnino servi, sed sociorum vocabulo honorabantur, regibus suis tributa pendentes & ab iis accipientes præfectos. Cæterum in plerisq; suis utebantur legibus, ita ut & popularium delinquentes ipsi punirent secundum mores patrios.

(which

(which is proper to the *German* Nations , nor is any where found but where the *Germans* have ſeated themſelves) two things are to be conſidered, Perſonal obligation , and Right over the thing. Perſonal obligation is the ſame, whether one by feudal right poſſeſs the right it ſelf of Governing, or any other thing alſo placed elſewhere. Now , ſuch an Obligation, as it would not take away from a private man the right of perſonal liberty , ſo neither doth it take away from a King or people the right of the higheſt power , which is civil liberty. Which is moſt apparently to be ſeen in the free feuds which they call *Franca* , which conſiſt not in any right over the thing , but in perſonal obligation onely. For theſe are nothing but a kind of unequal league , (whereof we have ſpoken) wherein the one party promiſeth aid and ſervice , the other ſafeguard & protection. Suppoſe alſo that aid was promiſed againſt All, which Feud they now call *Ligium* (for that word was of larger ſignification) this detracteth nothing from the right of the higheſt power over ſubjects : not to mention now that there is alwayes a tacit condition, while the war is juſt , of which elſwhere. But, as to the right over the thing, truly it is ſuch, that the right it ſelf of governing , if it be holden in Fee , may be loſt , either the family being extinct , or alſo for ſome ſort of crimes. Yet in the mean it ceaſeth not to be higheſt : for we must distinguish (as hath been said) between the thing it self, and the manner of having it. And by such a right I see many Kings constituted by the *Romans*, so, that the royal family exspiring, the Empire should return to themselves: which is noted by *Strabo* concerning *Paphlagonia* and some other.

Lib. 12.

LX. *The Right, and the Exercise of it distinguished.*

Moreover, both in Empire and Dominion, we must distinguish the Right from the Use of right, or the first act from the second. For as an Infant King hath right, but cannot exercise his power; so also one of an alienated mind, and in captivity, and that lives in the territory of another, so that freedome of action about his distant Empire is not permitted him: for in all these cases Curators or Vicegerents are to be given. Therfore * *Demetrius*, when being in the power of *Saleucus* he was under some restraint, forbad any credit to be had, either to his seal, or letters, but appointed all things to be administred, as if he had been dead.

* *Vide Plutarch. Demetrio.*

LXI.

LXI. *Of the war of Subjects against their Superiors. The question stated.*

L. 1. c. 4.

WAr may be waged, both by private men against private, as by a traveller against a robber; and by those that have the highest power against those that have it likewise, as by *David* against the King of the *Ammonites*; and by private men against those that have the highest power, but not over them, as by *Abraham* against the King of *Babylon* and his neighbors; and by those that have the highest power over private men, either subject to them, as by *David* upon the part of *Isboseth*; or not subject, as by the *Romans* against the pirats. Only the question is, whether it be lawfull for private or for publique persons to make war upon them, under whose power, whether supreme or subordinate, they are. And first, that is beyond all controversy, Armes may be taken against inferiors by those who are armed by authority of the Highest power: as *Nehemias* was armed by the Edict of *Artaxerxers* against the neighboring Governours. So the *Roman* Emperors grant leave to the Lord of the soil to force away the Camp-measurers. But it is inquir'd, what is lawful against the Highest Power, or the Lower Powers doing what they doe

L. volu m c. de Metatorib. l. 12.

doe by authority of the Higheſt. That's without controverſy amongſt all good men ; If they command any thing contrary to naturall right or to the divine precepts , what they command is not to be done. For the Apoſtles , when they ſaid , we muſt obey God rather than men, appealed to a moſt certain rule , written in all mens minds , which you may finde almoſt in the ſame words in *Plato* : but if for any ſuch cauſe, or otherwiſe becauſe it is the pleaſure of the Soveraign , injury be offerd us , it is to be ſufferd with patience , rather than reſiſted by force.

LXII. *By the law of Nature, war upon Superiors , as ſuch , is not ordinarily lawfull.*

ALl men indeed naturally (as we have ſaid above) have right to keep off injury from themſelves. But , Civil ſociety being ordained for the maintenance of tranquillity , thereupon ariſeth preſently to the Commonwealth a certain greater right over us and ours , ſo far as it is neceſſary to that end. The Commonwealth therefore *may* , for publicque peace and order, prohibite that promiſcuous right of reſiſting : and no doubt is to be made of the *will* thereof, when without that the end cannot be attained. For if that promiſcuous right of reſiſting continue, it wil not be now a Commonwealth, but a diſ-

ſolute

solute multitude, such as were the Cyclops, of whom *Euripides* saith, *Every one gives lawes to his wife and children*, and, *A confused company, where every one commands and none obeyes* †: And the *Aborigines*, who, as *Salust* relates, were a savage kind of people, without laws, without rule, disorderly and dissolute: and the *Getulians*, of whom he speaketh in another place, that they were not govern'd, neither by customes, nor by the Law or command of any Ruler. The manners of all Commonwealths are so, as I have said: *It is a general agreement of human society*, saith Augustin, *to obey Kings. To the Prince*; saith Tacitus, *have the Gods given supreme power; to the subjects is left the glory of obedience. Hic quoque,*

Indigna digna habenda sunt Rex quæ facit.

Æquum atq; iniquum Regii imperium feras. Seneca.

Add that which is in Salust *. *To doe what he will without punishment, that is to be King.* Hence it is, that every where the Majesty, that is the dignity, whether of a people, or of One that hath the highest power, is defended by so many Lawes, by so many punishments: which dignity cannot consist, if the licence of resisting do remain. A Soldier, who hath resisted his Captain willing to chastise him, if he hath laid hold on his rod, is cashierd; if he purposely break it, or laid violent hand upon his Captain, dyes. And

Euripid. Cyclope.

† De Bebriciis similia prodidit Valerius: *Non fœdera legum Ulla colunt placidas aut jura tenentia mentes.*

Rex est suo utens jure nulli obnoxius. Æschylus. *Nam Principes sunt: obsequendum. quippe ni?* Soph. *Imperia habentum perferenda inscitia est.* Euripid.

* *Impune quidvis facere, id est Regem esse.* Pertinent huc M. Antonii verba quæ ex Josepho modo adduximus. *L. Milites. §. irreverens. D. de re milit. Rufus legi. militaribus. cap. 15.*

And in Ariſtotle it is, *If one that beareth office beateth any man, he muſt not lift up his hand againſt him.*

LXIII. *Nor is it allowed by the Hebrew Law.*

Deut. 17. 12. Joſ. 1. 18.

IN the *Hebrew Law*, he is condemned to death, who is diſobedient, either to the High Prieſt, or to him who is extraordinarily appointed by God to be Ruler of the people. That which is in *Samuel* of the Kings right, plainly appeares to him that looks rightly on it, neither to be underſtood of true right, that is, of a faculty to do a thing honorably and juſtly (for a far other manner of life is preſcrib'd the King in that part of the Law, which declares his office) nor to ſignify a naked fact :(for there would be nothing peculiar in it, ſith alſo private men are wont to do injuries to private men:) but a fact which hath ſome effect of right, that is, an obligation of nonreſiſtence *. Wherefore it is added, that the people oppreſt with theſe injuries ſhould cry to God for help; to wit, becauſe no human remedies remained. So then is this called right, as the Pretor is ſaid *reddere jus*, to do right, even when he determineth unrightly.

1 Sam. 8. 11. Deut. 17. 14.

* Philo in Flaccum: *Quando enim defectionis ſuſpecti fuimus? quando non pacis amantes ab omnibus judicati ſumus? inſtituta vero, quibus utimur quotidie, nonne extra reprehenſionem ſunt? nonne ad concordiam bonumq; ſtatum civitatis conducunt?*

L. jus pluribus. D. de juſt. & jure.

LXIV.

LXIV. *Least of all, by the Evangelical Law. The first proof, out of S. Paul.*

IN the new Covenant Christ commanding to give to *Cæsar* the things that are *Cæsars*, would have the disciples of his institution understand, that no less, if not greater obedience, with patience (if need be) is due to the Highest Powers, than the Hebrews owed to the Hebrew Kings: which his best Interpreter *Paul* the Apostle explaining more at large, and describing the duties of subjects, amongst
other words hath these: *Whosoever resisteth the power, resisteth the ordinance of* Rom. 13. 2.
God: and they that resist shall receive to
themselves damnation. He addes: *For he* Vers. 4.
is the Minister of God to thee for good.
And again: *Wherefore ye must needs be*
subject, not onely for wrath, but also for Vers. 5.
conscience sake. In subjection he includeth a necessity of not resisting, nor that onely that springs from fear of a greater evill, but that flowes from the very sense of our duty, and obligeth us, not to men only, but to God. He addes two reasons: *First*, because God hath approved that order of ruling and obeying, both of old in the Hebrew Law, and now in the Gospell; wherefore the publique powers are to be so esteemed by us, as constituted by God himself. For we make those things ours, which we grace with our authority

ty. *Second*, becauſe this order ſerves to our good. But, one may ſay, to ſuffer injuries is nothing profitable. Here do ſome, more truly I think than appoſitely to the meaning of the Apoſtles, ſay, theſe injuries are profitable to us; becauſe the patience ſhall not go without reward. To me the Apoſtle ſeemeth to have conſidered the univerſal end propoſed to that order, which is the publique tranquillity*, wherein alſo is comprehended the peace of every one. And truly, 'tis not to be doubted, but that for the moſt part we attain unto this good by the publique powers: for no man wiſheth ill unto himſelf: now, the Rulers fecilitie conſiſteth in the felicitie of his ſubjects. **Let there be, whom thou mayſt rule*, ſaid One. The Hebrews have a proverb: *If there were no Government, one man would devour another alive.* Which ſenſe is in *Chryſoſtom* too: *Unleſs Cities had Rulers, we ſhould lead a life more wilde than the wilde beaſts, not biting only but eating us one the other* †. But if at any time Rulers are tranſported by too much fear, or anger, or other affections diverting them from the way that leadeth to tranquillity, that is to be accounted among accidents leſs frequent, and which, as *Tacitus* ſaith, are

* *Bene Chriſoſtomus*: συνεργός ἐστι σοι, συμπράττει σοι. *princeps nimirum Evangelium prædicanti. Dedolat ille quod tu deſcobinas*,

* Sint quibus *imperes. Dictum hoc Sullæ aiunt Plutarchus, Florus & alii, unde ſimſit Auguſtinus l. 3. c. 28. de Civ. Dei.*

† Eſt hoc de ſtatuis ſexto: ſed & hoc: *Tolle tribunalia, & omnem de vita tranquillitatem abſtuleris.* Deinde, *Nec mihi illos refer, qui male uſi ſunt honoribus, ſed ipſius inſtituti vide pulchritudinem, & ſapientiam ejus admirabilis qui primus ejus auctor fuit.* Idem ad Romanos; *Magiſtratus ſi abſtuleris, perierint omnia, non urbes ſtabunt, non agri, non forum, nec quicquam aliud. Evertentur omnia, & fortioris eſca fiet quilibet infirmior.* Idem ſenſus apud eundem ad Epheſ. 5.

recompenſed

recompensed by the intervenience of better things. Now, Lawes content themselves with bearing a respect to what falleth out for the most part, as *Theophrastus* said; whereto is pertinent that of Cato, *No Law is perfectly commodious; this onely is enquired, if it be profitable to the greater part and in the main.* But the things that happen more rarely, are notwithstanding to be bound up in common rules, because although the reason of the Law in this speciall fact especially hath not place, yet the reason abides in its generality, whereunto the specials are to be subject. For that is better than to live without rule, or that the rule be left to every ones pleasure. *Seneca* to the purpose: *Better it was, that even the just excuse of a few should not be accepted, than that all men should attempt to make some excuse.* Here also hath place that speech of *Pericles* *, never enough remembred: Thus *I conceive, that the Commonwealth which is well in the general is better for particular men, than where private estates are flourishing, and the publique is sick. For he that hath his domestique fortunes wel settled, his country being overthrown, must needs fall with it.* But he *whose private estate is decayed in a prosperous Commonwealth, is thereby much more easily repaired. Wherefore, when the publique may sustain losses of particular men,* But *particular men cannot make amends for the publique calamities,*

L. τὸ γὰρ. D. de Legib. l. 3. in fine. D. de pet. hæred.

Liv. lib. 34.

Sen. de ben. cap. 16.

* Thucydid. lib. 2. quicum bene convenit illud Ambrosii lib. 3. de Offic. *Eadem singulorum est utilitas quæ universorum.* Et illud in jure: *Semper non quod privatim interest uni ex sociis servari debet, sed quod communi societati expedit.* L. Actiones, sect. Labeo. D. pro Socio.

ties, why should we not all joyn together in maintaining the common Interest, not doing as you do, while you are astonisht at your private dammage, betraying the Commonwealth. The sense whereof is in brief expres's'd by *Livy thus: *The Commonwealth being safe, secures the private estates easily; in vain shall you keep your own, if you betray the publique* †. Now among things concerning the publique, the principal no doubt is that order, which we have said, of ruling and obeying: and that cannot consist with a private licence of resisting. I desire to explain this by a noble passage in *Dio Cassius*: *Truly I think it not becoming, that the Ruler of a City should give place to his subjects, nor is there hope of safety if they will command, whose duty is to obey. For consider, what order will be in a family if the elder be despised by the yonger; What method in a school, if the learners care not for the teachers; how can the sick recover their health, if they will not in all things be obedient to their Physicians; how can Seamen escape danger, if the Saylors will not hearken to the commands of their Masters. For by nature it is necessary and safe for men, that some should govern, and some be subject.*

* Lib. 26.

† Plato dixerat legum 4. *Quod commune est connectit civitates, quod singulorum dissipat; quare & publice & privatim utilius est, ut publica magis quam privata curentur.* Xenophon vero: *Qui in bello contra ducem seditiose se gerit, facit hoc cum suæ salutis periculo.* Eodem & illa Jamblichi pertinent: *Non disjuncta & privata utilitas à publica, imò in bono communi singulare etiam continetur: & ut in animalibus cæteraq; natura, ita in civitatibus, in totius salute salus est partium.*

LXV.

LXV. *The second proof, out of S. Peter.*

TO *Paul* let us add *Peter* as a fit companion: his words are these; *Honour the King: Servants be subject to your Masters with all fear, not only to the good and gentle, but also to the froward. For this is thankworthy, if a man for conscience toward God endure grief suffering wrongfully. For what glory is it, if when ye be buffeted for your faults, ye shall take it patiently? but if when ye do well, and suffer for it, ye take it patiently: this is acceptable* * *with God.* And when he confirmes this by the example of Christ. The same sense also is expressed in *Clement's* Constitutions in these words: *Let a Servant fearing God bear a good affection to his Master, though ungodly, though unjust.* Two things are to be noted here. *First*, that the subjection due to masters, even to the froward, is also to be referd to Kings: for that which followes, built on the same foundation, respects no less the office of subjects than of servants. *Second*, the subjection requir'd of us is such as carries with it patience of injuries. So is it usually said of parents:

* *A gentle parent's dear:*
Yet the ungentle bear.

And a youth that had long frequented *Zeno's* school being asked, What he had learned there, answerd, *To bear my Fathers*

1 Epist. 2. 18, 19, 20.

* Tertullian. de pœnitentia. *Timor hominis Dei honor est.*

* *Ames parentem, si æquus est: si non, feras.* Terentius Hec. *Nam matris ferre injurias me, Parmeno, pietas jubet.* Cic. pro Cluentio: *Non modo reticere homines parentum injurias, sed etiam æquo animo ferre oportet.* Habet ad hoc præceptum pulchra Chrysostomus tum 2. ad Timoth. cum libro 5. adversus Judæos. Pertinent huc & quæ Epictetus & post eum Simplicius habent de duabus ansis.

thers anger. Justin of Lysimachus: *With a good courage he receiv'd disgrace from the King, as from his father.* And it is in Livy; *As the hardness of parents, so is that of our Countrey to be mollified by patience and sufferance.* It is said in Tacitus, *The natures of Kings must be endured.* and again, *We must pray that we may have good Emperors, and tolerate the bad* *.

* Apud persas, laudante Claudiano, *Quamvis crudelibus æquè Paretur dominis.*

LXVI. *Further proof from the examples of the antient Christians.*

FRom this Law of our Lord, the practice † of the antient Christians, the best interpreter of the Law, departeth not. For although very ill men often possessed the Roman Empire, nor were there wanting who under colour of relieving the commonwealth oppos'd themselves against them, yet the Christians never adjoyned themselves to their enterprizes. In *Clements*'s Constitutions we read, *It is unlawfull to resist the Royal power.* Tertullian in his Apologetique saith: *Whence are those Cassii, Nigri and Albini? Whence are they that set upon* Cæsar *between the two laurels? whence are they that shew their palestric art in stopping his breath? whence are they that break into the palace armed, bolder than all those * Sigerii* (so the MS. plainly, in the library of the most worthy *Puteans*) *and bolder than the Parthenii? They were of the Romans, unless*

† *Ad quam pertinet Canon 18. Concilii Chalcedonensis, repetitus Canone 4. Concilii in Trullo: Concilium Toletanum 4. Capitulum 2. Caroli Calvi in villa Colonia. Synodus Suessionensis canone 5.*

* Xiphilinus Domitiano: *Insidias autem ei communicato inter se consilio struxere Parthenius præpositus cubiculariorum, & Sigerius, & ipse è cubiculariis.* Martial. l. 4. *Sigeriosq; meros, Partheniosq; sonas.* Corruptum id nomen non modo hic in Tertulliano fuerat, sed adhuc est in Suetonio, ubi *Saturius*, & in Victore vulgari ubi *Casperius* legitur.

unless I am deceiv'd, i. e. of such as were not Christians. That which he saith of the palestrick art pertains to the death of *Commodus*, wrought by the hand of a palestrite at the command of the Prefect *Ælius Lætus*: than which Emperour yet, scarce any was more wicked. *Parthenius*, whose fact likewise is detested by *Tertullian*, was he that had slain the Emperour *Domitian*. To these he compares *Plautianus* the Prætorian Prefect, who designed to kill *Septimius Severus*, a very sanguinary Emperour, in his palace: Against the same *Severus*, took armes, as on behalf of the Commonwealth, in *Syria Pescennius Niger*, in *Gallia* and *Britain Clodius Albinus*: But their enterprize also displeased the Christians, which *Tertullian* likewise boasteth of to *Scapula*: *We are defamed concerning the Emperours Majesty: yet could the Christians never be found, either Albinians, or Nigrians, or Cassians.* *Cassians* were they that followed *Avidius Cassius* an eminent man, who having taken up arms in *Syria*, pretended he would restore the Commonwealth, undone by the negligence of *M. Antonius*. *Ambrose*, when he thought injury was done, not to himself alone, but to his flock, and to Christ, by *Valentinus* the son of *Valentinian*, would not use the commotion of the people ready enough to make resistence. * *Violence*, saith he, † *being offerd, I have not*

* Idem Ambros. ep. 33. *Vultu in vincula rapere? voluntas est mihi. Non ego me vallabo circumfusione populorum.* Imitatus est magnus Gregorius lib. 6. epist. 1. *Si in morte Longobardorum me miscere voluissem, hodie Longobardorum gens nec Regem, nec Duces, nec Comites haberet, atq; in summa confusione esset divisa.*

† *lib. 5. Orat. in Auxent. Inseruit Gratianus caus. 23. quæst. 8.*

not learned to resist: I can grieve, I can weep, I can sigh: against armies and souldiers, even Goths, *my arms are my tears. For such are the muniments of Priests. In any other sort, neither ought I, nor can I resist.* After: *It was required of me, that I should restrain the people: I answerd, it was in me, not to raise them; in Gods hand, to quiet them.* The same *Ambrose* would not use the forces of *Maximus* against the Emperour, being both an *Arrian* and a persecutour of the Church. So was *Julian* the Apostat, when he plotted the Churches ruine, repressed by the tears of Christians, as *Nazianzen* saith, adding, *This was the only remedy against a persecutor.* And yet almost all his Army was made up of Christians. Adde hereunto, that, as the same *Nazianzen* observes, that persecution of *Julian*, was not onely injurious to the Christians, but had brought the Commonwealth also into extreme danger. We will close up this with a saying of *Augustin*, where he explaines the words of *Paul* to the Romans: *It is necessary for this life we should be subject, not resisting, if they* (the Governors) *shall please to take any thing from us.*

Theodoret. hist. Eccles. lib. 5. cap. 4.

Orat. 1. in Julian.

Prop. 74.

LXVII.

LXVII. *It is not lawfull for inferiour Magistrates to make war upon the Highest.*

OUr age hath brought forth men, learned indeed, but too observant of times and places, who perswaded themselves first (for so I believe) and then others, that the things above spoken have place among private persons, not also among inferiour Magistrates †: who (as these men thinke) have a right to resist the injuries of the Soveraign; yea they sin, unless they do resist. This is not to be admitted. For as in Logick the intermediate * *species*, if you respect the *genus*, is *species*; if the *species* below it, is *genus*: so these Magistrates, in regard of their inferiours are publique persons, but in relation to their superiours are private. For all faculty of governing, which is in Magistrates, is so subjected to the highest Power, that whatsoever they do against the will of the soveraign, is destitute of that faculty, and therefore to be accounted for a private act. For, that saying of the Philosophers hath place here also, * *There can be no order without relation unto somewhat which is first.* Who think otherwise, to me they seem to introduce such a state of things, as the Antients feign to have been in heaven before the the Rise of Majesty, when they say the minor

† *P. Martyr ad Judicum 3. Paræus ad 13. cap. ad Rom. Jun. Brutus. Danæus lib. 6. polit. & alii.*

* Genus speciale, *Sen. epist.* 58.

* Averroes 5. Metaph. tom. 6. *Ordinem non dari nisi cum relatione ad aliquid primum.*

minor Gods yeelded not to *Jove*. But the Order (which I have mentioned) and † subalternation is not onely known by common sense *, but proved also by divine authority. For the † Prince of the Apostles would have us to be subject otherwise to the King, otherwise to the Magistrates: to the King as supereminent, i. e. without any exception, beside those things which are directly commanded by God, who approves patience of injury, forbids it not: to the Magistrates, as sent by the King, i. e. deriving their power from him. And when *Paul* requires every soul to be subject to the highest powers, he included also the inferiour Magistrates. If we look back upon the Hebrew people, where so many Kings were contemners of divine and human Law, we shal never finde that the inferiour Magistrates, amongst whom were very many men pious and valiant, took so much upon them, as to oppose any force against the Kings, unless they had receiv'd from God, who is King of Kings, a speciall mandate. But on the contrary, what is the duty of Peers, * *Samuel* shews, when in the sight of the Peers, and people, with accustomed veneration he attended *Saul* now ruling perversly. Moreover, the state of publique Religion alwayes depended on the will of the King

† *Sic in familia paterfamilias primus, inde materfamilias, inde filii, mox ordinarii servi, postremo servi vicarii.* vide Chrysost. 1 Cor. 13.3. * Unde illud, *Omne sub regno graviore regnum est*: Et Papinii illud, *Vice cuncta reguntur, Alternisq; regunt*: Et Augustini dictum celebre, *Ipsos humanarum rerum gradus adverte, si aliquid jusserit Curator, faciendum: non tamen si contra Proconsul jubeat: aut si Consul aliquid jubeat, & aliud Imperator. Non utique contemnis potestatem, sed eligis majori servire: nec hinc debet minor irasci, si major prælatus est.* Et hoc ejusdem de Pilato, *Talem quippe Deus dederat illi potestatem, ut esset etiam ipse sub Cæsaris potestate.* † 1 *Ep.* 2. * 1 *Sam.* 15. 30.

and

and *Sanedrin*. For, that the Magistrates and people, after the King, promised their fidelity to God, this must be understood so far as it was in the power of every one. And more, the images of false Gods, publikly exstant, we never read to have been thrown down, unless by command either of the people in the free State, or of the Kings if they ruled. Howbeit, if at any time any thing was done by force against the Kings, it is related for testimony of divine providence permitting it, not for approbation of humane fact. The Authors of the contrary opinion are wont to object a saying of *Trajan*, when he gave a sword to the Prætorion Prefect; **Use it for me, if I govern well; if ill, against me.* But we must know that *Trajan*, as appears by *Plinie's* Panegyric, was very studious to shew nothing regal, but to act a † true Prince, subject to the judgment of Senate and people, whose decrees the Prefect's duty was to execute even upon the Prince himself. Like to this is that we read of M. *Antoninus*, who would not touch the publique money without the advice of the Senate.

* *Hoc pro me utere, si recte impero; si male, contra me.*

† *Quod postea imitati Pertinax & Macrinus, quorum orationes egregias apud Herodianum vide. Dion. lib. 6.*

LXVIII. *In case of extreme and inevitable necessity, what may be done.*

THis is a greater question, whether the Law of not resisting bind us in extreme and most certain danger. For even

 some

ſome Laws of God, although generally expreſt, have a tacit exception of extreme neceſſitie: which in the time of the *Haſmoneans* was defined by wiſe men concerning the Law of the Sabbath. Whence it is a common ſaying, *Peril of life drives away the Sabbath:* and a Jew in *Syneſius* gives this reaſon of neglecting the Law of the Sabbath, *We were brought into moſt certain danger of our life.* Which exception is approv'd by Chriſt himſelf; as alſo in another Law of not eating the ſhew-bread. And the Hebrew maſters, out of the old tradition, adde the ſame exception to the laws of forbidden meats, and to ſome other: And rightly; Not, that God may not bind us over to certain death, if he pleaſe; but, becauſe certain laws are of ſuch an argument, that it is not credible they were given out of ſo rigid a will. Which holds more ſtrongly in humane laws. I deny not, but even a humane law may command ſome acts of vertue under certain peril of death, as the law of not deſerting ones * Station: but we muſt not raſhly conclude, that was the will of the Law-maker; nor do men ſeem to have taken ſo much right over themſelves and others, but ſo far as extreme neceſſity requires it. For laws are wont (and ſo they ought) to be made by men with ſenſe of humane imbecillity. Now the law of which we ſpeak, ſeemes to depend upon their will, who firſt

Vide etiam verba Jonathan. 1 *Macc. c.* 9. 44.

* *Vide Joſephum ubi de cuſtodibus Saulis agit.* Polyb. παρὰ ῥωμαίοις θάνατός ἐστι πρόστιμον τοῖς ἐφεδρείας λιπόντι τὴν τάξιν.

first consociate themselves into civill society ; from whom thenceforth a right flowes and comes unto the Rulers. And these , if they were asked, whether their will was to impose upon all this burden , to dy rather than in any case to repell by force the force of their superiours , I know not whether they would answer , it was their will , unless perhaps with this additament ; if resistance cannot be made without very great perturbation of the Commonwealth, or the destruction of very many innocent persons. For, what in such a circumstance charity would commend , may be also , I doubt not , deduced into a humane Law. One may say , that rigid obligation, to dy rather than ever to repell any injury of superiours , proceedeth not from humane law, but from divine. But we must note, Men at first , not by divine precept , but drawn of their own accord upon experience of the infirmity of divided families to defend themselves against violence , closed together in the bond of civill society : whence civill power hath its spring, which therefore *Peter* calls *a humane ordinance**, though elsewhere too, it is called *a Divine ordinance*,because God approved this wholsome institution of man. But God, approving humane law, is supposed to approve it as humane , and in a humane manner. *Barclay* , the most stout defender of Regall Power , descendeth

1 Pet. 2. 13. Rom. 13.

Barclaius lib. 3. adv. Monarchom. cap. 8.

deth yet so farr, as to grant the people,
* Insigni parti. and an * eminent part thereof, a right of defending themselves against immane
Lib. 6. c. 23. & 24. cruelty; when yet the same Author acknowledgeth the whole people to be subject to the King. I do easily conceive, the more value that is of which is conserved, the more equity it is, which give us an exception against the words of of the Law: neverthelesse, indistinctly to condemn either single persons, or a less part of the people, which heretofore hath used the last safeguard of necessity, so, as to have respect in the mean time to the common good,* I scarce dare. For *David*,
* Vix ausim.
1 Sam. 22. 2. & 23. 13. who, except a few acts, hath testimony of a life exactly conformed to the laws, had about him armed men, first four hundred, and then a greater number; to what purpose, but to keep off violence, if it should be offered. But withall, this is to be noted, *David* did not this, till after he had found, both by *Jonathan*'s discovery, and by very many other most certain arguments, that *Saul* sought after his life; And then, neither invades he Cities, nor takes occasions of fighting, but retreats and hides himself, sometimes in the wildernesse, sometimes amongst other people, and hath a religious care never to hurt his own Country. Parallel to this may seem the action of the *Maccabees*. For, that some defend their arms upon this title, as if *Antiochus* had not been

King

King but an Invader, I think it vain; when the *Maccabees* and their followers, in all the history, never call *Antiochus* by any other but the name of King: and rightly, when long before the *Hebrewes* had acknowledged the *Macedonian* Power, into whose right *Antiochus* succeeded. As for that prohibition to set an alien over the people, that Law is to be understood of voluntary election, not of what the people was compeld to do, drawn by necessity of the times. And for that which others say, that the *Maccabees* used the right of a people, who had liberty * to live by their own laws, it is not firm neither: for the Jews, subdued first to *Nebuchodonosor* by the law of war, by the same law were subject to the successors of the *Chaldaans*, the *Medes* and *Persians*: all whose Empire devolved to the † *Macedonians*. Hence are the *Jewes* call'd by Tacitus, * *The most vile part of those that serve, while the East was in the power of the Assyrians, Medes and Persians.* Nor did they covenant for any thing with *Alexander* and his successors, but without any condition came under their dominion, as before they had been under *Darius*. But if the Jews were sometimes permitted to have open exercise of their Rites and Laws, this was a precarious right, arising from the favour of the Kings, not from any law or condition annexed to the Government. There

* αὐτονομία.

† Justin. lib. 36. *Primus Xerxes Rex Persarum Judaeos domuit, postea cum ipsis Persis in ditionem Alexandri magni venere, diuq; in potestate Macedonici Imperii fuere. A Demetrio cum descivissent, amicitia Romanorum petita, primi omnium ex Orientalibus libertatem recepe-runt, facile tunc Romanis de alieno largientibus.*

* *Vilissima pars servientium.* Tac. Hist. l. 5.

is nothing therefore that can clear the *Maccabees*, besides extreme and most certain danger: to wit, so long as they conteind themselves within termes of self-defense, so, as to retire into devious places, after *David's* example, to secure themselves; and not to enter into battail but when they were assaulted.

LXIX. *The King's Person Sacred.*

MEan while, this caution is to be observed, even in such a danger the person of the King must be spared: which they that think *David* did, not out of any necessity of duty, but out of some higher design, are much mistaken. For *David* himself plainly said, *No man can lay hands upon the King, and be innocent.* Well he knew, 'twas written in the law, *Thou shalt not revile the Gods* (that is, the highest Judges) *nor curse the Ruler of thy people.* In which law the speciall mention made of the eminent powers, evidently shewes something speciall to be commanded. (Wherefore *Optatus* speaking of this fact of *David* saith, *He was hindred by a full remembrance of the divine commands.*† And he puts these words into *Davids* mouth, *I was willing to orecome my enemy, but that I chose rather to keep the Command of my God.*) Now, for evill words that are false, it is not lawfull to cast them at a private person: against

1 Sam. 26.9. Exod. 22.28. Optat. l. 2.

† Josephus de Davide. *sed statim pœnitudine ductus, injustum facinus esse dixit, Dominum suum occidere.* Et post: *Horrendum, regem quamvis malum interficere, pœnam enim id facienti imminere ab eo qui regem dedit.*

against a King therefore we must not use them, when they are true. For, as the Writer of the Problems, which bear *Aristotles* name, affirmeth, *He that reproacheth the Ruler is injurious to the City* *. And if the Ruler must not be offended with the tongue, much less certainly with the hand: whence we also read, that *David*'s heart smote him for violating the garment of the King; so much did he apprehend the sanctitude of his person. And not without cause: For sith the highest power cannot but ly open to the hatred † of many, the Rulers person was with a peculiar sense to be secur'd. The *Romans* made a Constitution that the Tribunes of the common people should be inviolable. The *Essenes* had a saying, that Kings are to be accounted sacred *. It is in *Curtius*, that the nations which are under Kings, reverence their Kings as Gods. And *Artabanus* the *Persian* saith: * *Amongst our many good Laws, this is the best, that the King is to be reverenced and adored, as the Image of God the Saviour of all.*

Problem. sect. 40.

* Julianus Misopogone: *Sunt enim leges severæ pro principibus, ita ut qui in principem injuriosus fuerit, is ex animi libidine conculcaverit leges.*

† Quintil. Declamat. 348. *Hanc esse conditionem omnium, qui administrationem reipub. aggrediuntur, ut ea quæ maxime pertinent ad salutem communem, cum quadam sui invidia efficere cogantur.* Vide ea de re Liviæ verba ad Augustum apud Xiphil. ex Dione. * Plutarch. Agide: *Nec fas, nec licitum regis corpori manus inferre.* Insigne illud apud Homerum: —*Nam pro populi pastore timebat, Ne quid ei accideret.* Bene Chrysostomus 1 Tim. 1. *Si quis ovem juguiet ab eo gregem imminui: ut si quis pastorem de medio sustulerit ab eo totum gregem dissipari.* Seneca lib. priore de Clem. c. 3. *Somnum ejus nocturnis excubiis muniunt: latera objecti circumfusiq; defendunt: incurrentibus periculis se apponunt. Non hic est sine ratione populis urbibusq; consensus, &c.* * Apud Plutarch Themistocle.

LXX. *Of*

LXX. *Of Christian subjection.*

TIs a greater question, whether so much as was lawfull for *David*, and lawfull for the *Maccabees*, be allowed unto Christians; whose Master so often commanding his disciples to undertake the cross, seems to require a patience more exact. Certainly, where Superiours threaten Christians with death for religion sake, Christ gives them leave to fly; them I mean whom necessary office binds not to any place: beside flight he permits nothing. And *Peter* saith, Christ, when he suffered, left us an example to follow;
1 Pet. 2. 22, 23. *Who did no sin, neither was guile found in his mouth: Who when he was reviled, reviled not again; when he sufferd, he threatned not; but committed himself to him that judgeth righteously.* The same Apostle
1 Pet. 4. 13. &c. bids Christians give thanks to God, and rejoice, if they *suffer as Christians.* And surely, by this patience most of all, we finde Christian religion to have prevailed and spread it self. Wherefore, in my opinion, the antient Christians, who, coming fresh from the disciplin of the Apostles and Apostolical men, did more perfectly both understand and obey their prescriptions, are very much injur'd by them, who think the reason why they defended not themselves in most certain perill of death, was, because they wanted not

not will, but strength. Imprudent, no doubt, and impudent had *Tertullian* been, if, before the Emperours, who could not be ignorant of the truth, he had so confidently dared to tell a ly: *If we were willing* (saith he) *to use open hostility, should we want numbers and forces? We have fill'd your Cities, Ilands, Castles, Towns, Camps, Palace, Senate, all your places, but your Temples. And were our forces unequal to yours, we might easily make war upon you, when we are so willing to be slain, if our Religion did as well allow us to kill, as to be killed.* Here also * *Cyprian* followes his master, and openly proclames; *Hence it is, that none of us, when he is apprehended, resisteth: nor revengeth himself against your unjust violence, albeit our people is exceeding numerous. Our security of the future revenge makes us patient. The innocent yield unto the nocent* †. And Lactantius * *We put confidence in his Majesty, who can as well revenge the contempt of himself, as the labours and injuries of his servants. And therefore when we suffer such horrid things, we oppose not so much as a gainsaying word, but leave vengeance to God.* Nor did *Augustin* look upon any thing else when he saith: *Let not the just man especially have any other thoughts in these matters, but that he may undertake war to whom it is lawfull, for to all it is not lawfull.* And this is his: *As oft as*

Emperours

* Ad Demetrianum.

† Ejudem hæc libri primi epistola 1. *Intellexit* (adversarius) *Christi milites vigilare, jam sobrios & armatos ad prælium stare, vinci non posse, mori posse; & hoc ipso invictos esse, quia nec mori timent, nec repugnare contra impugnantes, cum occidere innocentibus nec nocentem liceat, sed prompte & animas & sanguinem tradere.*

* *Lib.* 5.

Lib. 6. *qu.* 10. *in Jos.*

Emperours are in errour, they make Laws to maintain errour against the truth, by which laws the righteous are examined and crowned. The same elswhere: *Princes are so to be borne with by the Commons, and Masters by their servants, that by the exercise of patience temporall things may be endured, and eternall things assured.* Which in another place he explains by the example of the antient Christians thus. *The City of Christ, though as yet travelling on earth, and having so great multitudes against ungodly persecutors, did not fight for temporall safety; but, to obtain eternall, refused to fight. They were bound, they were imprisoned, they were beaten, they were tormented, they were burn'd, torn in peeces, cruelly slain, and still they were multiplyed. They could not fight for salvation, unless for salvation they did contemn their safety.* And *Cyrills* words upon that of *John*, concerning the sword of *Peter*, are of like sense, and no lesse to the purpose.

Epist. 166.

De Civit. Dei. l. 22.

LXXI. *The famous example of the Thebean Legion.*

THe *Thebaan* Legion, as the acts do shew us, consisted if six thousand six hundred sixty six Soldiers, all Christians, Who, when *Maximianus Casar* at *Octodurum* compelld his Army to sacrifise to false Gods, marched away first to *Aganum*

num : and, when the Emperour had sent some thither to command them to come to sacrifise, upon their refusall, *Maximianus* commanded every tenth man to be slain, by his Serjeants. The command was executed easily without resistence of any one. *Mauritius* † the chief of that legion, from whom *Agaunum* was afterward call'd *Vicus Mauritii*, at that time spake thus to his fellow soldiers, as *Eucherius* Bishop of *Lions* hath related: *How afraid was I, lest any one by way of defense (which is easy for armed men) should attempt by violence to save those blessed men from death? For the resistance whereof I was preparing the example of our Christ, who by the word of his own Command put up the drawn sword of his Apostle again into the sheath: shewing, that the vertue of Christian confidence is greater than all arms; that none should oppose the mortal work with mortal hands, but faithfully accomplish his undertaken duty with a persevering religion.* After this decimation, when the Emperour gave the same command to the survivors, they all answer thus: *Cæsar, we are indeed thy soldiers, and have taken arms for defense of the Roman Commonwealth: nor have we ever been run-awayes or traytors; nor deserved any mark of dishonour for our cowardise. And willingly should we obey these your commands, unless the laws of our Christianity did forbid us the worship of Devils,*

† De hujus Martyris honoribus apud Helvetios vide Guillemanum in veteri scripto de translatione sancti Justini in novam Corbeiam: *Unde juxta fidem Chronicorum sub atrocissima & incomparabili illa decima post Neronem persecutione passum eum colligimus: qua & prioribus persecutionibus immanior, dum venerabilem multitudinem Martyrum cœlis mitteret, inter quos etiam præcipuum S. Mauritii Collegium, & innocentiæ speculum.* De Thebæis martyribus Brunsvicum translatis vide Crantzium Saxonicorum. 7. 16.

Devils, and their altars alwayes polluted with blood. We see, it was your will, either to pollute Christians with sacrileges, or to terrify us by slaying every tenth man. You need not make any long search after us. Know that we are all Christians. You shall have all our bodies subject to your power: but our souls look up to Christ their Lord, and you shall not lay hold on them. Then *Exuperius* the Ensign-bearer of the Legion, is related to have spoken to them in this manner: *My right valiant fellow-soldiers, you perceive I carry the ensign of secular war: but I provoke you not to these arms; I call not your vertue and courage forth to these wars: Another kind of fight is to be chosen by you. You cannot, by these swords, attain unto the heavenly Kingdom.* Afterward, he desires these words should be reported to the Emperour: *O Emperour, desperation, which is most valorous in dangers, hath not armed us against thee. Behold, † we have weapons in our hands, yet do we not resist: because we had rather dy, than overcome; and perish innocent, than live rebells.* And again; *We throw down our arms: thy officer shall finde our hands without weapons; but our heart armed with the Catholique faith.* After this follows the slaughter of them not resisting: in the narration whereof, these are the words of *Eucherius* *, *The multitude availed not to free the just from punishment: albeit the crime*

crime

† Similia sunt illa Judæorum Alexandrinorum ad Flaccum: *Inermes sumus, ut vides. Et tamen sunt qui nos tanquam hostes publicos hic criminantur. Etiam eas quas ad nostri tutelam partes dedit natura retrovertimus, ubi nihil habent quod agant. Corpora præbemus nuda ac patientia ad impetum earum qui nos volent occidere.*

* Ne justi punirentur multitudo non obtinuit: cum multum (male editur, multorum) esse soleat quod multitudo delinquit.

crime is wont td go unpunisht , when the multitude is the delinquent. In the old Martyrology the same thing is related on this wise. *They were promiscuously slain with swords; without contradiction: yea, their arms being laid down, they offered their throats to the persecutors, or their uncovered body; neither provoked by their own multitude, nor by the motion of arms, to endeavour to assert the cause of righteousness by the sword; but, mindfull of this alone, that they confessed him, who not reclaming was led to the slaughter, and as a lamb opened not his mouth; They also, as a flock of the Lords sheep, sufferd themselves to be torn in peeces, as it were by wolves running on them.* † *Valens* impiously and cruelly raged against them, who according to the holy Scripture and the tradition of the Fathers professed * τὸ ὁμούσιον, who, although a very great number, never defended themselves by force. Certainly, where patience is prescribed us, we see the example of Christ is oft brought in, and even now we heard it alleged by the *Thebaan* soldiers, as an example to be imitated by us; the example I say of Christ, whose patience extended it self even to the Death. And he that so loseth his life is truly pronounced by Christ to have sav'd it.

† *Vide excerpta ex Joanne Antiocheno, ex MS. lib. viri æterna memoria dignissimi* Nicolai Peiresii.

* *The identity of nature of the Father and Son.*

1 Pet. 2. 21.

Mat. 10.39. Lu. 9. 34.

LXXII. *In what cases force is lawfull against a Prince.*

WE have said, Resistence is not lawfull against the highest powers. Now, lest the Reader think, they offend against this rule, who indeed offend not, we must adde some advertisements. *First* then, Princes that are under the people, whether from the beginning they received such power, or afterward it was so agreed, as at *Lacedæmon*†, if they offend against the Laws, and the Commonwealth, may not only be repelled by force, but, if need require, punished with death: which befell *Pausanias* King of the *Lacedemonians*. And, sith the most antient Kingdoms through *Italy* were of this kinde, it is no wonder, if, after the relation of most cruell things done by *Mezentius*, *Virgil* addes:† *Then all Etruria flam'd with a just ire: And call for the Kings bloud to quench the fire.* *Secondly*, if a King, or any other hath abdicated his Empire, or manifestly accounts it as forsaken, after that time all things are lawfull against him, as against a private man. Yet is not he to be judged to desert his estate, who manageth it somewhat negligently. *Thirdly*, 'tis the opinion of * *Barclay*, if the King alienate his Kingdome, or subject it to another, he forfeits it. I stop here.

† Plutarchus Lysandro: *Spartiatæ regem ad capitis judicium vocarunt, quod ille declinans fugit Tegeam.* Idem Sulla: *Quibusdam regibus Spartiatæ regnum ademerunt, ut ineptis regno, quippe abjectis nihilq; hominibus.* De Agide injuste, sed damnato tamen, vide eundem Plutarchum. Mosynæci regem inedia puniebant. Mela lib. 2.

† Et aruspex Etruscus in Mezentium insurgentibus: *—Quos justus in hostem Fert dolor.*

* *Lib. 4. c. 16.*

For such an act, if a Kingdom be conveyed by election or by successory law, is null: and therefore can have no effect of right. Whence also, concerning an Usufructuary, to whom we have compared such a King, it seemes to me the truer opinion of Lawyers, that, if he yield his right to an extraneous person, his act is nothing. And, as to that, that the usufruit reverts to the Lord of the propriety, it is to be understood, *in due time*. But, if a King really attempt even to deliver up, or subject his Kingdom, I doubt not, he may be herein resisted. For, as we have distinguished afore, the Empire is different from the manner of holding it: which manner, the people may hinder from being changed; for that is not comprehended under the Empire. Hither you may fitly apply that of *Seneca* in a case not unlike: *Though a son must obey his father in all things, yet not in that, whereby he is made to be no father.* *Fourthly*, the same *Barclay* saith, a Kingdome is lost, if the King be caried with a truly hostile minde to the destruction of the whole people †, which I grant. For, the will of ruling, and the will of destroying cannot consist together. Wherefore, he that professeth himself an enemy of all the people, thereby abdicates the Kingdom; but this seemeth scarce possible to happen in a King, that is himself, that rules over one people. It may happen, if

Instit. de usuf. §. fruitur. L. Usufr. D. de jure dotium.

Lib. 2. contr. 9.

† *Pari causa tribunus plebis qui sit, ipso jure desinere esse talem, ingeniose defendit Gracchus, cujus verba digna lectu apud Plutarchum.*

if he rule over more than one, that in favour of one people, he may will the ruine of another, to make Colonies there. *Fiftly*, if a Kingdome be committed; whether by felony against him whose Fee it is, or by a clause put in the very grant of the Empire, that, if the King † do so or so, the subjects be loosed from all bond of obedience; in this case also, the King falls back into a private person. *Sixtly*, if a King hath one part of the supreme power, the People or Senate the other part †, against the King invading that part which is not his, a just force may be opposed, because so far he hath no power. Which, I think, hath place, notwithstanding it be said, the power of war is in the King. For that's to be understood of forein war: when otherwise, whosoever hath part of the supreme authority, cannot but have a right to defend that part. When this comes to pass, the King may also, by the Law of war, lose his part of the Empire. *Seventhly*, if in the conveyance of the Empire it be conditioned, that in a certain case * resistance may be made against the King, although it cannot be supposed, part of the Empire is thereby reteined, yet is there reteined some naturall liberty, and exempted from the Regall power. And, he that alienateth his right, may abate of that right by covenant.

LXXIII.

† *Vide de regno Arragoniæ Marianam l. 8.*

† *Exemplum habes in Genuat. repub. apud Bizarum lib. 18. in Bohemia tempore Wenceslai historiæ lib. 10. Adde Azorium instit. moral. l. 10. c. 8. & Lambertum Scafnaburgensem de Henr. 4.*

* *Exempla vide apud Thuanum hist. 131. in narratione anni 1604. & l. 133. in anno 1605. utrumq; de Hungaria: apud Meierum narratione anni 1339. in Brabantia & Flandria. narratione anni 1468. in fœdere inter Regem Galliæ & Carolum Burgundum. Adde de Polonia quæ habet Chytræus Saxonicorum 24. & de Hungaria Bonfinius Decadis 4. libro 9.*

LXXIII.. *How far we must obey an Invader of anothers Empire.*

WE have considered him which hath, or had the right of governing. It remaines that we speak of the Invader of Empire, not after by long possession or by covenant he hath gotten a right, but so long as there continues the cause of possessing it unjustly. And truly, whilst he is in possession, the acts of empire which he exerciseth, may have power to oblige, not out of his right, which is none, but from this, that it is most probable, He that hath the right of governing, whether people, King or Senate, had rather the Invaders commands should prevail and be of force, than utter confusion be brought in, the Laws and judgments taken away. *Cicero* condemnes *Sylla*'s Laws of cruelty to the sons of the proscribed, that they could not seek for honours: Neverthelesse, he thought they were to be observ'd, affirming (as *Quintilian* tells us) the state of the City so to be contained in these Laws, that it could not stand if they were dissolv'd. *Florus* of the same *Sylla*'s acts: Lepidus *went about to rescind the acts of so great a man, deservedly, if yet he could without great damage to the Commonwealth.* And a little after: *It was expedient for the sick and wounded Commonwealth to take some rest at any hand, lest* the

Vict. de potest. Civ. n. 23 Suarez de Legib. lib. 3. c. 10. num. 9. Lessius de just. & jure l. 2. c. 29. dub. 5. n. 73.

Lib. 2. c. 1.

the ſores ſhould be opened and bleed too much in the cure. Howbeit, in things not ſo neceſſary, and which pertain to the eſtabliſhing of the Invader in his unjuſt poſſeſſion, if without great danger obedience may be denied, it muſt not be given.

LXXIV. *Whether it be lawfull to kill an Invader, or expell him by force? and in what Caſes.*

TO this queſtion we frame this anſwer: Firſt, if the Invador, by unjuſt war, and ſuch as hath not the requiſits according to the Law of Nations, hath ſeiſed on the government; nor hath there followed any agreement, or faith given him, but his poſſeſſion is kept onely by force; in this caſe. the right of war ſeemeth to remain, and therefore it is lawfull to act againſt him as againſt an enemy, that may lawfully be ſlain by any, even by a private man. *Againſt Traitors,* ſaid Tertullian, *and publick enemies, every man's a ſouldier.* So alſo, againſt deſertors of the war that run from their colours, all perſons, for the common quiet, have a right indulged to them to execute publick revenge. And I am of *Plutarch's* * opinion, that the ſame is lawfull, if, before the invaſion, a publick Law were extant, giving power to every one to kill him, that ſhall adventure to do this or that, which

Apolog. 9. c. quando liceat. lib. 2. *In reos Maieſtatis & publicos hoſtes omnis homo miles.*

* *Qui ita ſentit lib. de fato ad Piſonem.*

which falls under sight; as, that being a private man shall get a guard about him, or shall invade the Fort; that shall slay a Citizen uncondemned, or not by lawfull judgment; that shall create magistrats without just suffrages. Many such Laws were extant in the Cities of *Greece*, in which therefore the killing of such Tyrants was to be esteemed Lawfull. Such was at *Athens* the Law of *Solon* revived after the return out of the *Piraeum*, against the overthrowers of the popular State, and such as had born offices after the overthrow of it. As also at *Rome* the *Valerian* * Law, if any one without the peoples will should take the authority of a Magistrate: and the *Consular* Law after the *Decemvirate*, that none should create a Magistrate without appeal; whosoever had done so, it should be lawfull to kill him. Moreover, it will be lawfull to kill the Invader, by the express authority of the rightfull Governour, whether King, Senate or People: As also, of the Protectors of Children that are Kings, such as *Jojada* was to *Joas*, when he dethroned *Athalia*. Unless in these cases, I cannot yield it lawfull for a private person by force to expell or kill an Invader of the highest power. The reason is, because it may be, the rightfull Governour had rather the Invader should be left in possession, than occasion given to dangerous and bloody Commotions, that do

* Plutarchus Publicola. *Ut injudicatum occidere eum liceret qui dominatum concupisceret.* Mox addit: *Solon ei qui dominatum invadit deprehenso diem dici vult. at Publicola etiam ante judicium talem permittit interfici.*

2 Chron. 23.

do usually follow upon the violating or slaying of those men, who have a strong faction among the people, or forein confederates also. Surely it is uncertain, whether a King or people be willing the State should be so endangered: and, without knowlege of their will, the force cannot be just. *Favonius* said: *Civil war is worse than unlawfull and usurped Goverment.* And Cicero. † *To me any peace with our Countrey-men seemeth more profitable than Civil war.* Better it had been, said *Titus Quintius*, the Tyrant *Nabis* had been let alone at *Lacedemon* *, when he could not otherwise be thrown down, but with the grievous ruine of the Commonwealth, likely to perish in the vindication of her liberty. To the same purpose is that of *Aristophanes*, *A Lyon is not to be bred in a City; but if he be brought up, he must be kept.* Verily, seeing it is a most weighty deliberation, whether peace or liberty be to be preferd, as *Tacitus* speaks; and, in *Cicero's* opinion, it is a politick question of greatest difficulty, *Whether, when our Country is oppressed by an Usurper, all endeavour is to be used against him, although the Commonwealth be thereby extremely endangered*; Single persons ought not to arrogate unto themselves that judgment which belongs to the people in common. Nor can that saying be approv'd,

† *Mibi pax omni cum civibus bello civili utilior videtur.* Cic.

Liv. l. 34.

*Quod Plutarchus in T. Quintii vita sic explicat: *Cum videret sine gravi aliorum Laconum malo non posse tyrannum destrui.* Non alienum est ab hac re quod Plutarchus refert, Laconem quendam cum legisset, *Hos, dum Marte parant dominatum extinguere, saevus Ante Selinuntis moenia Mars rapuit:* Respondisse, *Merito viri illi periere. Exspectare enim debuerant ut ipse per se dominatus conflagraret.*

* Wee

*Wee pull the proud Usurpers down,
That Lord it o'r the willing Town†.*

So did *Sylla* answer, being asked why he troubled his Country with taking arms: *That I may free it from tyrants.* Better is the advice of *Plato*, * in an Epistle of his to *Perdicca*; *In the Commonwealth, contend so far as thou canst approve thy doings to thy Citizens; it is not fit to offer violence, neither to thy parent, nor to thy country.* The sense whereof is extant in *Salust* * too: *For* *to over-rule thy country or thy parents, although thou art able, and canst reform what is amiss, yet is it uncivill; especially, seeing all changes in affairs of state portend slaughter, flight, and other hostilities.* *Thomas** saith, The destruction, though of a tyrannical Government, is sometimes seditious †. The fact of *Ehud* upon *Eglon* King of *Moab* ought not to bring us over to the contrary side: for the sacred Scripture plainly witnesseth, He was raised by God himself, and sent as an Avenger, to wit, by special command. And besides, it is not manifest, that this King of *Moab* had not some right of Government conditionall. Against other Kings also God

* *Detrahimus Dominos urbi servire paratae.*

† Plutarch Catone Maj de Antiocho Magno. *Bello praetextum sumebat, liberare Graecos, libertatis non egentes.*

* *Appian.civ.* 1.

*Cujus verba Latine sic posuit Cic. ep. fam. l. 1. *Tantum contendere in rep. quantum probare tuis civibus possis; vim neq; parenti, neq; patriae offerri oportere.*

* *Bell. Jugurth.*

* 2.2. *Qu.* 42. *art.* 2.

† Huc & Ambrosii illud non male referas: *Adjuvat hoc quoq; ad profectum bonae existimationis si de potentis manibus eripias inopem, de morte damnatum eruas, quantum sine confusione fieri potest; ne videamur jactantiae magis facere causa, quam misericordiae; & graviora inferre vulnera, dum minoribus mederi desideramus.* De offic. 2. c. 2. Non longe abit illud Stallii apud Plutarchum in vita Bruti: *Aequum non esse ut vir prudens ac sapiens improborum & desipientium causa in pericula & turbas se conjiciat. Jud.* 3. 15. *Nehem.* 9. 27.

executed

executed his judgments by what hand he pleased, as by *Jehu* upon *Joram*. Lastly, it is to be noted, in a controverted case, a private man by no means ought to take upon himself to judge, but follow the possession. So did Christ command tribute to be paid to *Cæsar*, because the Money bare his Image; that is, because he was in possession of the Empire.

2. Reg. 9.

Mat. 22. 20.

LXXV. *Who may lawfully wage war.*

AS in other things, so in voluntary actions there are wont to be three kinds of efficient causes, principal, adjuvant, and instrumental. In war, the principal is he, whose work is done; in private, a private person; in publick, the publick power, especially the highest. Whether, for those that stirr not themselves, war may be raised by another, we shall see elsewhere. Mean while, this we take for certain, naturally every one may vindicate his own right; Therefore were our hands given us. But, to profit another in what we can, is not only lawfull but commendable. The writers of Offices truly say, *Nothing is more serviceable to man, than another man*. Now, there are divers bonds between men, which engage them to mutual aid: For kinsmen assemble to bring help, and neighbors are calld upon, and fellow-citizens*. *Aristotle* said*, It behoveth every one, either to take

l. servus. D. de serv. export. Cic. l. 2. Offic. ex Panetio. DD. ad leg. si quis in servitutem. D. de fur. l. probib. c. de jure fisci.

* Unde illud, *Porro Quirites, & quiritari.*

* *Rhet. ad Alex. c. 3.*

take arms for himself, if he hath received injury, or for his kindred, or for his benefactors, or to help his fellows, if they be wronged. And *Solon* taught, that the Commonwealths would be happy, wherein every one would think anothers injuries to be his †. But, suppose other obligations be wanting, the communion of humane nature is sufficient. No man is unconcerned in that which is humane. * It is a saying of *Democritus*: *Our duty is, to defend the opprest with injury, and not neglect them: for that is just and good.* Which is thus explained by *Lactantius*: *God, who hath not given wisedom to other living creatures, hath secured them by natural muniments from assault and peril: But to man, because he formed him naked and frail, that he might rather furnish him with wisedom, he hath given, beside other things, this pious affection, whereby one is inclined to defend, love, cherish another, and afford mutual aid against all dangers.* When we speak of Instruments, we do not here understand arms, and such like things, but those persons, who act so by their own will, that their

Bart. in l. Ut vim. D. de justit. & jure n. 7. & 8. Jason ibid. n. 29. Panor. n. 18. Sylvest. in verb. Bellum. q. 8.

† Plutarchus refert: *Civitatum illa felicissimè colitur, in qua qui injuriam non sensere, & qui sensere se opponant, & injuriam captantes puniunt.*

* Menandri dictum est:

Injuriarum si improbis auctoribus
Reponeremus ultionem singuli,
Nobis putantes fieri quod fit alteri,
Inter nos junctis conspiratis viribus;
Non prævaleret innocentiæ impetus
Audax malorum, qui custoditi undique,
Jussique pænas quas merentur pendere,
Aut nulli penitus essent, aut pauci admodum.

Lib. 6.

L. cum sumus. C. de agricolis, lib. 11.

their will depends upon another will. Such an instrument is the son to the father, being naturally a part of him: such also is a servant, as it were a part legally. *Democritus*: *Use servants as parts of the body, some for one thing, some for another.* Now, as a servant is in the family, so is a subject in the Commonwealth; and therefore an instrument of the Ruler. And, no doubt, all subjects naturally may be used for war, but some are exempted by special Law: as of old servants * at *Rome*, now in most places Clerks †: which Law yet, as all of that kind, is to be understood with exception of extreme necessity. And so much be spoken generally concerning Adjutors and subjects: the specials shall be considered in their proper places.

The end of the first Part.

Arist. l. 5. de moribus. cap. 10. L. Gracch. cap. de adul. Sen. 1. cont. 4. Thom. 2, 2. 40. art. 2. Sylvest. de bello p. 3.

* *Servius ad 9. Æn.*

† *Ac Levitæ olim extra belli munia, ut notatum Josepho. De Clericis vide Nicetam Chroniatem lib. 6. Caroli Calvi capitulum in Sparnaco 37. in Gratiano c. clericum. dist. 5. & causa 23. qu. 8. Et Canones quidem sic habent: sed quanto illi servati à Græcis quam à Latinis diligentiùs, vide Annam Comnenam.*

HUGO GROTIUS OF WARRE AND PEACE.

II. PART.

I. *What are call'd justifick causes of War.* Ex l. 2. c. 1.

LEt us come to the *Causes* of Wars; I mean *justifick*: for there are also other which move under the notion of *profitable*, distinct sometimes from those that move under the notion of *just*: which *Polybius* accuratly distinguisheth one from the 3. Hist.

the other, and both from the *Beginnings* * of war, such as the Stagg in the war of *Turnus* and *Æneas*. But although the difference 'twixt these is manifest, yet the words are wont to be confounded. For, the causes which we call justifick,* *Livy* in the *Rhodians* speech hath also called Beginnings :* *Certainly ye are the Romans, who pretend that your wars are therefore prosperous, because they are just; nor do ye so much glory in the event of them, that you overcome, as in the beginnings, that you undertake them not without cause* *. Those justifick causes properly belong to our argument: whereto is pertinent that of *Coriolanus* in *Halicarnassensis* : *I suppose, it ought to be your first care, that you take a pious and just cause of war* †. And this of *Demosthenes* ; *As in houses, ships, and other buildings, the lowest parts ought to be most firm: so in actions, the causes and foundations* * *must be true and just*. To the same purpose is that of *Dio Cassius* †; *We ought to have greatest regard of Justice; if this be present, the war is hopefull; if not, there is nothing certain to any one, though he have successe at first according to his minde*. And that of *Cicero** ;

* Exordia pugnæ, *dixit Virgilius*.

* *Lib.* 45.

* Certè vix ulla gens tam diu constans mansit in spectandis belli causis. Polybius apud Suidam, voce ἐμβαίνειν, *Romani summopere id curarunt, ne priores ipsi finitimis inferrent violentas manus. Sed ut semper crederentur in hostem ire ad arcendas injurias.* Ostendit id Dion egregia comparatione Romanorum cum Philippo Macedone & Antiocho in excerptis Peiresianis. In quibus est, *Valde id student Romani justa ut bella suscipiant, nihilq; tale decernant sine causa ac temere.* * Eodem sensu ἀρχὰς πολέμων dixit Ælianus: & Diodorus Siculus, *l.* 14. easdem vocat προφάσεις & ἀρχὰς. δικαιώματα dixit Procopius Gotth. 3. † *Dion. Halic. l.* 8. *Olynth.* 2. * ὑποθέσεις. *Sic &* ὑπόθεσιν *belli dixit Julianus* 2. *de laudibus Constantii* † *Lib.* 12.

cero *; *Those wars are unjust, which are undertaken without cause*: who elsewhere reprehends *Crassus* for passing o'r *Euphrates*, when there was no † cause of war. Which is no less true of publique, than of private wars. Hence is that complaint of *Seneca: Do we restrain homicides and single slaughters? Why doe we not restrain wars, and that glorious wickedness of slaughtering Nations? Avarice and cruelty know no bounds. By the Decrees of Senate and people outrages are done, and things privately forbidden are † publiquely commanded.* Wars, I grant, undertaken by publick authority, have some effects of Law, as also Sentences: of which hereafter: but they are not therefore the less blamable, if there be no cause. So that *Alexander*, if without cause he warred upon the *Persians* and other nations, is, by the *Scythians* in *Curtius*, and by *Seneca* too, deservedly call'd a *Robber* †, by *Lucan* a *Spoyler*, and by the *Indian* wisemen *unjust* *, and by a certain pirate was drawn into the society of his crime. And likewise *Justin* relates, that two Kings of *Thrace* were spoyled of their Kingdom by his Father *Philip*, by the fraud and wickedness of a Robber. That of *Augustin* * is to the same

* *De Repub. l. 3.*

† Appianus eidem Crasso à Tribunis denunciatum dicit; *ne bellum Parthis inferret nulla injuria cognitis.* Plutarchus de eodem: *Coibant multi indignantes esse aliquem qui bellatum iret in homines non modo nullius injuriæ compertos, sed & pace defensos.*

* *Epist. 96.*

† Idem Seneca de ira 2. c. 8. *Pro gloria habita, quæ, quamdiu opprimi possunt, scelera sunt.*

† Locus est de Benef. 1. c. 13. Non male Just. Martyr Apolog. 2. *Tantum possunt Principes qui opiniones vero præferunt, quantum in solitudine latrones.* Philo: *Qui magna furta committunt, qui honesto principatus nomine obumbrant ea quæ reipsa nihil nisi latrocinia sunt.* * ἀπίσϑαλος. *Arrian. lib. 7.* * De Civ. Dei. l. 4. c. 4. *Remota justitiâ, quid sunt regna nisi magna latrocinia.*

same purpose, *Take away Justice, and what are Kingdomes but great Robberies?* To such agrees that of Lanctantius: *Deceived with the shew of vain glory, they colour their wickedness with the name of virtue* †. Just cause of taking Arms can be no other, than injury. *The iniquity of the adverse party brings in just wars*, saith the same *Augustin*; where by iniquity * he means injury *. So in the form of words used by the Roman Herald; *I call you to witness, that people is unjust, and doth not performe what is right* *.

† *Lib. 1. de fal. sa relig.* *De Civit. 4.* * *αδικία.* * *αδίκημα.* *Sylv. de bel. c. 1. n. 2.* **Ego Vos testor, populum illum injustum esse, neq; jus persolvere.*

II. *Three just causes of Wars.*

THere are, according to most Authors, these three just causes of wars, *Defense, Recovery, Revenge* †. In which enumeration, unless the word *Recovery* be taken more largely, is omitted the prosecution of that which is due to us: which *Plato* * omitted not, when he said, Wars are waged, not onely if one be opprest by force, or robbed, but also if one by deceived. With whom agrees that of Seneca *, *It is a most eqnal word, and conformable to the Law of Nations, Render what thou owest.* And in the Herald's *formula* it was: *They have not given, nor paid, nor done the things they should.* And in Salust, *By the law of Nations I demand those things. Augustin,* when

† Camillus ad Gallos, Liv. l. 5. *Omnia quæ defendi, repetiq; & ulcisci fas sit.* * *Alcibiade.* * Lib. 3. de benef. c. 14. Liv. lib. 1. In Historiis.

when he said, *Just wars* * *are those, that revenge injuries*, tooke the word *revenge* more generally for *to take away* : as the following words do shew, wherein is not an enumeration of parts, but an addition of examples : *So is a nation or common-wealth to be opposed, which hath either neglected to avenge what was done wickedly by their men, or to render what was injuriously taken.* Upon this naturall knowledge the *Indian* King, as *Diodorus* relates, accus'd Semiramis ; *that she began a war, having received no injury.* And so do the *Romans* † require of the *Senones*, not to fight against them, that had done them no wrong. *Aristotle* saith : *Men war upon such as have provoked them by injury* : and * *Curtius* of certain *Scythians*, *They were manifestly the most just of all the Barbarians : they took not armes, unless they were provoked*†.

Lib. 6. q. 10. super Josue. * Servius ad 9. Æn. de Romanis : *Cum volebant bellum indicere, Pater patratus, h. e. Princeps Fecialium, proficiscebatur ad hostium fines, & præfatus quædam solemnia, clara voce dicebat, se bellum indicere propter certas causas : aut quia socios læserant, aut quia nec abrepta animalia, nec obnoxios redderent.* † *Liv. l. 5. Apodict. 2. c. 2.* * *Lib. 12.*

† Plutarchus Nicia : *Herculem etiam cuncta subegisse, dum lacessitus se defendit.* Josephus 17. antiquæ hist. *Quin id veniunt ut in nihil hostile cogitantes violentas inferant manus, hi sunt, qui invitos cogunt ad arma semet tutatura confugere.*

III. *War is lawfull in defense of life; onely against an assailant : and in present certain danger.*

THe first cause of just war is Injury not yet done, but offer'd either against *Body* or *Goods*. If the Body be assaulted by present force, with perill of life, not

 otherwise

otherwiſe avoidable *, in this caſe war is lawfull, even with the ſlaying of him that brings the danger; as we have ſaid afore, when by this inſtance, as moſt approved, we ſhewed that ſome private war may be juſt. Tis to be noted, this right of defenſe, by it ſelf and primarily, ſprings from hence, that nature commends every one unto himſelf, not from the injuſtice or ſin of the other, from whom the danger is*. Wherefore although he be without fault, as one that warreth faithfully, or thinketh me other than I am, or is beſide himſelf, or affrighted, as to ſome hath happened, hereby is not taken away the right of ſelf-defenſe: it ſufficeth, that I am not bound to ſuffer what he offereth, no more than if another mans beaſt did threaten me with the danger. Whether alſo innocent perſons, who being interpoſed hinder my defenſe or flight, without which death cannot be eſcaped, may be ſlain, is queſtion'd. Some, even Divines, there are, that think it lawfull. And ſurely, if we reſpect nature alone, with her the reſpect of ſociety is much leſs, than the care of proper ſafety. But the law of Charity, eſpecially the Evangelicall, which equals another to our ſelves, plainly permits it not. That ſaying of *Thomas*, if it be rightly taken, is true: In a true defenſe a man is not ſlain on purpoſe: not that it is not lawfull ſometimes, if there be no other means

* *Sylv. in verbo Bellum, p. 1. n. 3. & p. 2. P. 1. n. 36.*

* *Bartol. ad leg. ut vim. D. de juſt. & jure. Bal. in rep. l. 1. c. unde vi.*

Cajet. 2. 2. art. 6 7. q. 2.

2. 2. q. 64. art. 8.

meanes of safety, to do that on purpose whence the death of the assailant wil follow, but that in this case that death is not chosen as a thing primarily intended, as in judiciall punishment, but as the only thing remaining at that time; when he that is assaulted, even at that time, ought to desire rather to do somewhat whereby the other may be terrified or weakened, than destroyed. Present * danger is here requir'd, and as it were in a point. I confess, if the assailant draw his sword, and so that it appears he doth it with a mind to kill, it is lawfull to prevent him: For in morals, as in naturals, a point is not found without some latitude. Neverthelesse are they deceived and do deceive, who admit of any fear whatsoever, as a just occasion of such preventing. For it is well observed by † *Cicero*, Very many injuries proceed from fear, when he that thinks to hurt another feareth, unlesse he do it, himself shall receive hurt. *Clearchus* in *Xenophon*: *Many have I known, drawn either by calumny or suspicion, whilst they fear others, and had rather prevent than suffer, to have done much evill to those, that attempted not, nor so much as thought any such thing against them.* *Cato* in his Oration for the *Rhodians*: *What*, saith he, *shall we first execute, that which we say they designed?* *Cicero* * again: *Who ever made this*

* Hujus distinctionis usum egregium vide apud Agathium lib. 4. Apud Thucyd. 8. Phrynichus: *Caviturum invidia si ipse jam in vitæ per ipsos adductus periculum, & hoc & aliud quidvis aggrediatur potius, quam ab hominibus inimicissimis perdi se sinat.*

† *Offic.* 1.

* *Citat Quintil. lib.* 5. Insignis est illa apud Gellium sententia: *Gladiatori composito ad pugnandum, pugnæ hæc proposita sors est, aut occidere si occupaverit, aut occumbere si cessaverit. Hominum autem vita non tam iniquis neq; tam indomitis necessitatibus circumscripta est, ut idcirco prior injuriam facere debeas, quam nisi feceris, pati possis.* Locum hic habet illud Euripidis.

Te si, ut ais, interficere vir voluit tuus,
Voluisse sat erat & tibi, ubi tempus foret.

Statute, or to whom may it be granted without extreme hazard of all, that one might lawfully kill him first, of whom he saith he was afraid, lest himself should afterward be killed? Pertinent is that of Thucydides: *The future is yet uncertain: nor ought any one therefore to make a quarrell present and certain.* The same Author, where he declareth the hurt of Sedition among the *Grecian* Cities, sets down this for one fault: *He was praised, that first did, what another was about to commit* †. To such agrees that saying of *Vibius Crispus* cited by *Quintilian,* * *Who permitted thee to be so fearfull?* And *Livia* in *Dio* * saith, They escape not infamy, that by way of prevention do the evill which they fear. Now, if any one offer not present force, but be found to have conspired or lyen in wait, if to prepare poyson, if to plot a false accusation, to suborn witnesses, to corrupt judgment, such a one, I say, cannot be justly slain: if either the danger may be otherwise avoided; or it be not certain enough, it cannot be otherwise avoided. For, for the most part, the delay of time interposed affords many remedies, and many accidents for our rescue; according to the Proverb, † *Between the cup and the lip.* Yet there are not wanting both Divines and Lawyers that extend their indulgence farther. But the other also, which is the better and safer way, wanteth not the consent of Authors.

IV.

Lib. 1.
Lib. 3.
† Livius lib. 3. *Cavendo ne metuant homines, metuendos ultro se efficiunt, & injuriam à nobis repulsam, tanquam aut facere aut pati necesse sit, injungimus aliis.* As Cæsar, who when he seised on the Common-wealth, said he was forc'd to it by fear of his adversaries. See an excellent passage in Appian, *Civilium 3.*
* *Quis tibi sic timere permisit?*
* *Lib. 55.*
† *Inter os & offam.*
Bann. q. 64. art. 7. Lab. 4. Bald. in l. mult. C. de lib. caus.
Less. lib. 2. c. 9. dub. 8.
Covaruv. p. 3. §. 1. n. 2.

IV. *Of the loss of a member, and the defense of chastity.*

WHat shall we say of the danger of mutilation, and loss of some part of the body? Certainly, the loss of a member, especially one very needfull, being very grievous, and as it were equiparable to life; besides, it being hard to know, whether it draw not after it perill of death; if there be no other way to come off, I may suppose the author of such a perill forefeits his own life, and may be justly slain by the defendant. In defense of Chastity, it can scarce be doubted but the same is lawfull: when both common estimation, and the divine law too, equals chastity to life †. Therefore *Paulus* the Lawyer said such a defense is right. We have an example in *Cicero* * and *Quintilian*, of a *Tribune* of *Marius* slaine by a Soldier. Yea, and women have often slain the invaders of their modesty, as histories relate. *Chariclea* in *Heliodorus* calls such an act, *a just revenge on behalf of injur'd chastity.*

† Seneca de benef. 1. c. 11. *Proxima ab his sunt sine quibus possumus quidem vivere, sed ut mors potior sit, tanquam libertas & pudicitia & mens bona.* Paulus sententiarum 5. t. 23. *Qui latronem cædem sibi inferentem, vel alium quemlibet stuprum inferentem occiderit, puniri non placuit. Alius enim vitam, alius pudorem publico facinore defendit.* Augustin. l. 1. de lib. arbit. *Lex dat potestatem vel viatori ut latronem, ne ab eo ipse occidatur, occidat; vel cuipiam viro aut feminæ, ut violenter sibi stupratorem irruentem, aut post illatum stuprum, si possit, interimet.* * Vide & Plutarchum Mario. Mars quoq; deorum judicio absolutus dicitur interfecto eo qui filiæ ipsius stuprum inferebar. Testis Apollodorus biblioth. 3. Adde insignem historiam apud Greg. Turonensem lib. 9.

V. Defense may lawfully be omitted.

WHat we have ſaid afore, although it be lawfull to kill him that attempts to kill, yet he doth more commendably who had rather be killed than kill; ſome do grant, ſo, that they except a perſon profitable to many: But, to me it ſeemeth unſafe, to impoſe this Law contrary to Patience upon all, in whoſe life others are concernd. Wherefore I may conceive it is to be reſtrained to them whoſe office 'tis to keep off force from others; ſuch as are the companions in a journey undertaken on thoſe termes, and publick Rulers, to whom that of *Lucan* may be applyed:

* *Twas cruelty to yeeld himſelf to death,*
So many thouſands living by his breath.

* Cum tot ab hac anima populorum vita ſaluſq;
Pendeat, & tantus caput hoc ſibi fecerit orbis,
Sævitia eſt voluiſſe mori.——

Curtius lib. 10. *Sed cum tam avidè manifeſtis periculis offeras corpus, oblitus tot civium animas trahere te in caſum.*

VI. *Defenſe*

VI. *Defenſe is unlawfull ſometimes againſt a perſon very profitable to the Publick.*

ON the contrary it may happen, that, becauſe the Invader's life is profitable to many, he cannot be ſlain without ſin: nor that onely by force of Divine Law, whether old or new (of which afore, when we ſhewed the Kings perſon to be ſacred) but by the very Law of Nature. For the Right of nature, as it ſignifies a Law, doth not onely reſpect thoſe things which are dictated by that Juſtice that is calld *Expletrix* *, but conteineth in it ſelf the acts of other vertues alſo, as of *Temperance*, *Fortitude*, *Prudence*; as being, in certain circumſtances, not onely honeſt, but due. Now, to that which we have ſpoken *Charity* obligeth us. Nor doth *Vaſquez* remove me from this opinion, when he ſaith, a Prince who aſſaulteth an innocent perſon, ceaſeth to be a Prince in that very act: than which, ſcarce any thing could be ſpoken, either leſs truly, or more dangerouſly. For, as dominions, ſo alſo Empires are not loſt by delinquency, unleſs the Law ordain it. But, no where is found a Law ordaining this concerning Empires, that they ſhould be loſt by an offence againſt a private man; nor will ever ſuch a Law be found, as I believe; for it would bring in

* συναλλακτικὴ *Ariſtoteli, nimis arcto vocabulo: itaque* ἐπανορθωτικὴν *idem feliciùs dixit.*

Lib. 1. controv. illuſt. 18.

in very great confuſion of things. As to that foundation which *Vaſquez* lays for this and many other Concluſions, That al Empires regard the utility of thoſe that obey, not of thoſe that governe; grant it were univerſally true, it would not ſerve the turne: for the thing doth not preſently fail, whoſe utility in ſome part faileth. And whereas he adds, that the ſafety of the Commonwealth is deſired by every one for his own ſake, and therefore every one ought to prefer his own ſafety even before the whole; this doth not ſufficiently cohere. Tis true indeed, for our own ſake we would have the Commonwealth be ſafe: but not onely for our own ſake; others are alſo to be regarded. For, it is a falſe opinion, and rejected by the ſounder Philoſophers, to think that Friendſhip is born of indigence alone †, ſith of our own accord and by nature we are carryed to it. Now, that I ſhould prefer the good of a great many before my own proper good, *Charity* adviſeth often, ſometimes commandeth. Here is pertinent that of *Seneca* *: *Princes and Kings, and whoſoever by any other name are Tutors of the publick State, no wonder They are beloved, even above all private Relations. For, if to men of ſound judgment publick things are dearer than private, it followes, that he be dearer alſo, on whom the publick affairs depend.* Ambroſe *: *Every one thinks it better to keep*

† *Refutat perniti oſam hanc opinionem* Seneca *lib.* 1. *de Beneſic. c.* 1. & *lib.* 4. *c.* 16.

* *Lib.* 1. *de Clem. c.* 1.

* *De Offic. l.* 3. *cap.* 3.

keep off destruction from his Country, than danger from himself. The foresaid *Seneca* *: Calistratus *and* Rutilius, *the one at* Athens, *the other at* Rome, *would not be restored to their home, at peril of the Commonwealth: because it was better these two should endure one private loss, than all suffer a common evill.*

Lib. 6. de Benef. c. 37.

† Plutarchus Pelopidæ initio: *Primum virtutis opus servare servantem cætera.* Cassiodorus de Amicitia: *Si manus oculorum obsequio vibratum in aliud membrum senserit gladium imminentem, ipsa suum minimè discrimen attendens, plus alii quam sibi timens, gladium excipit.* Post: *Proinde qui morte propria dominos suos à morte redimunt, rectè quidem hoc faciunt, si potius salutem animæ suæ quam liberationem alieni corporis in causa constituunt. Cum enim eis conscientia dictet, quod fidem dominis suis debeant exhibere, videtur etiam consonum rationi, quod suæ vitæ corporali vitam dominorum debeant anteferre.* Deinde rursus: *Dilectione itaq;, & maximè pro salute multorum, potest quis salubriter morti suum corpus exponere.*

VII. *It is not lawfull to kill another for to avoid a box on the ear, or the like disgrace.*

IF one be in danger to receive a blow on the cheek, or the like, * some are of opinion, he also hath a right to defend it by the slaughter of his enemy. I dissent not, if we respect onely expletory justice. For, although death and a blow are unequall, yet he which prepares to do me an injury, thereby gives me a right, *i. e.* a certain morall faculty † against himself *in infinitum*, in so much as otherwise

Navar. c. 15. n. 3. Soto lib. 5. q. 1. Sylvest. in verbo homicidium *1. qu. 5.*

† Apollodorus lib. 2. de Lino agens: *Ad Thebas cum venisset, civisq; Thebanus factus esset, ibi interiit ab Hercule percussus cithara. Nam cum Linus feriisset Herculem, iratus Hercules mortem ei intulit, reusq; à nonnullis factus patratæ cædis, legit in judicio legem Rhadamanthi, qua insons pronuntiatur, si quis nocuerit ei qui vim prior intulerit.*

otherwise I cannot keep off that evill from me. Charity also, by it self, seems not to bind us here, in favour of the offender. But the Evangelicall Law hath clearly made such a deed unlawfull. For, Christ commands a blow to be received rather than any hurt be done the adversary; how much more forbids he him to be slain for to avoid a blow? By which example we are admonished to beware of that saying of *Covarruvias*, Humane understanding, not ignorant of naturall right, allows not any thing to be permitted by naturall reason, which very thing is not also permitted by God, who is Nature it self. For, God who is the Author of Nature, so, that he can also work freely above nature, hath a right of prescribing us Laws even of those things, which by their own nature are free and indefinite: and much more, that a thing may be due, which is by nature honest, though not due. But it is strange, seeing the will of God appears so manifestly in the Gospel, that there are found Divines, and those Christian Divines, who do not only think slaughter to be rightly admitted, that a blow may be avoided; but also after a blow received, if he that gave it fly; for a reparation of honour, as they say. Which to me seemeth very contrary to Reason and Religion. For, Honour is an opinion of excellency. But, he that beareth such an injury, shewes himself excellently

Covar. p. 3. sect. 1. de Homicid.

Navar. cap. 15. 4. Henr. de irregul. c. 11. Victor de jure belli n. 5.

excellently patient: and therefore hath encrease of honour rather than diminution. Nor is it materiall, if some men of a corrupt judgment traduce this vertue with names made for disgrace: for those perverse judgments neither change the thing, nor the estimation of it. Neither did the antient Christians onely see this, but the Philosophers too, who said, It is a token of a weak spirit not to be able to bear contumely, as we have shewed elsewhere. Hence also it is apparent, how unsound that is, which very many Authors * say, That Defense with slaughter is lawfull, to wit, by divine Law (for I contend not about the right of nature:) although one may fly without perill; because flight forsooth is dishonourable, especially for a Gentleman. But, here is indeed no dishonour; onely a certain false opinion of dishonour, to be despised by all the Followers of vertue and wisedome. Wherein, I rejoice that I have, among the Lawyers, *Carolus Molinæus* * of the same mind with me. What I have said of a blow and of flight, I desire should be understood of other things by which true honour and existimation is not lessened. And what if one should report that of us, which being believed among good men would touch our Name? He also may be kill'd, say some †: very falsly, and against the Law, even of nature too. For that is no fit way to defend our Reputation. VIII.

* *Dd. in l. ut vim. D. de just. & jure Sylv. in verbo* Bellum, *p. 2, n. 4.*

* *In addit. ad Alex. cons.* 119.

† *Petr. Navar. l. 2. c. 3. n.* 376.

VIII. *In defense of Goods, to kill a man is not unlawfull by the Right of nature,*

COme we now to the injuries whereby our goods are invaded. If we respect expletory of Justice, I will not deny, but for the conservation of our goods, the Invader, if need be, may be slain: For, the inequality between these things and life, is made up by favour to the innocent, and by hatred to the injurious. Whence it follows, if we regard onely that right, that a Thief running away with stoln goods, if they cannot otherwise be recover'd, may be overtaken with a Gun, or other weapon. *Demosthenes* * said: *It is very hard and unjust, and contrary both to the written Laws, and the common rules amongst men, not to be sufferd to use force against him, who in hostile manner hath taken away my Goods.* Nor doth Charity hinder by way of precept, the Law divine and humane set aside, unless the thing be of very small value, and therefore contemptible: which exception some do rightly adde.

* *Oratione in Aristocratem.*

IX. *How far the same is permitted by the Law of Moses.*

LEt us see what is the meaning of the Hebrew Law, wherewith agrees also that

that old Law of *Solon*, which *Demosthenes* * mentioneth, and the Law of the XII. Tables * taken thence, and *Plato*'s decree in the ninth of his Laws. For all those Laws meet in this, that they distinguish a Theif by night from a Theif by day. About the reason of the Law, there is the question. Some † think this is it, that by night he cannot be discerned who comes, whether he be a Thief or a Murderer: and therefore may be killed as a Murderer. Others * conceive the difference lyes here, that in the night, because the Theif is unknown, there is less possibility to recover the Goods. To me the Law-giver seems to have properly respected, neither this, nor that; but to have meant thus rather, that no man, for Goods, ought *directly* to be slain: (which would be done, if, for ex-example, I should with a weapon knock him down as he runs away, that after he is slain I might recover my Goods:) but if my self be brought into danger of life, then it is lawful for me to avert the danger, even with the peril of another mans life. Nor is it against me, that I brought my self into that hazard, whilst I desire to keep or to recover my Goods, or to take the Theif: for herein no blame can be laid on me, who am about a lawful act, and do no injury to any one, but use my own right. The difference then 'twixt a Theif by day and by night lyes here,

* *Adversus Timocratem.*

* *Addi potest lex Wisigotthorum l. 7. t. 1. c. 15. Et Capitulare Caroli M. l. 5. c. 191. Lege Longobarda, qui noctu alienam cortem ingreditur, nisi ligandum se praebeat, occidi potest.*

† *Lessius dub. 11. num. 68.*

* *Covarruv. d. loco.*

here, that by night there is ſcarce any poſſibility of calling witneſſes: and therfore if the Theif be found ſlain, more eaſy credit is given to him, who ſaith hee was neceſſitated in defenſe of his own life to kill the Theif, being armed with ſome weapon, wherewith he might do hurt. For, that is required in the *Hebrew* Law, ſpeaking of a Theif found *breaking up*, as ſome tranſlate; others perhaps better, * *with an inſtrument to break up*, as the word is rendred elſwhere by the moſt learned of the *Hebrews*. To this interpretation we are led by the Law of the XII. Tables, which forbids a Theif by day to be ſlain, this exception added, unleſs he defend himſelf with a weapon. Therefore, againſt a Theif by night it is preſumed, that with a weapon he defended himſelf. And, by a weapon is underſtood a ſword, a club, a ſtone, as *Caius* noteth upon this very Law. But *Ulpian* hath declared, that what is ſaid of the Theif by night, If one kil him he ſhal go unpuniſhed, is to be conceived to have place, if he could not ſpare his life without peril of his own, to wit, in ſaving of his goods. There is then, as I have ſaid, a preſumption on his ſide who hath ſlain a theif by night: but if haply witneſſes were preſent, by whom it is evident, the ſlayer of the theif was not brought into danger of his life, then will that preſumption ceaſe, and ſo the ſlayer will be guilty of Homicides.

Exod. 22. 2.

* Cum perfoſſorio inſtrumento.

L. ſi pignore Sect. furem. D. *de furtis.*

L. furtum. D. *ad legem Corn. de ſicar.*

Homicide. Add, that as well by day as by night the Law of the XII. Tables requir'd, that he that found the theif should testify so much by an out-cry (as we learn out of *Caius*) to the end, if it might be, the officers or neighbours might run thither to bring help, and to bear witness. Now because such a concourse is more easily made by day than by night, (as *Ulpian* notes upon the forecited place of *Demosthenes*) therefore is more easy credit given to him, that affirms, he was in danger in the night time. In like manner, the *Hebrew* Law allowes a maid credit concerning a rape in the field †, and not in the town, because here she might and ought to have cryed out, and called aid. Moreover, although in other respects there were no difference, yet this is considerable, that the things that happen in the night are more obscure, and cannot be so well known what and how great they are; and therefore are more terrible. The Law therefore, both *Hebrew* and *Roman*, gave in precept to the people that which Charity perswades, that they kill no man for this reason onely because he stealeth goods, but in case he that desires to save them, comes himself into danger. *Moses Maimonides* hath noted, that the killing of another is not permitted to any man on other terms, than to preserve that which is irreparable, as life and Chastity.

L. Itaque. D. ad legem Aquiliam.

† Philo *explains it well: that the place is set for more frequent example sake, not that thereby always the controversy may be determined. For it may come to pass, as he discourses in his book of special Laws, that a maid may be ravished in a city, her mouth being stopt, and in the field one may consent to the act.*

X.

X. *Whether, and how far it is permitted by the Evangelicall Law.*

AND what shall we say now of the Evangelicall Law: that the same is permitted by it, which is permitted by the Law of *Moses*; or that, as in other things it is more perfect than the Law of *Moses*, so here also it requireth of us more? I doubt not, but it requireth more. For, if Christ commandeth to lose a coat or cloak, and *Paul* would have us suffer damage rather than go to law, which is a contention without bloud: how much more would he, that even things of greater moment be lost, rather than we should kill a man, the image of God, and of the same flesh and bloud with us? Wherfore if our things may be saved, so that there seem not to be any danger of making slaughter, well; otherwise, we must suffer losse, unless haply it be such a thing, upon which our life and of our family depends, and which cannot be recoverd in judgment, haply because the Theif is unknown, and there is some hope to carry the matter without slaughter. And although almost all, as well Lawyers as Divines, do now teach, that a man may be rightly slain by us, in defense of our goods, even beyond those bounds, wherein the Law of *Moses* and the *Roman* permit;

Soto d. art. 8. Less. dub. 11. n. 74. Sylv. in verbo Bellum, 2. n. 3.

permit;as,if a thief having taken the thing fly; yet do not we doubt, but that which we have set down, was the judgment of the antient Christians: nor did *Austin* doubt, whose words are these, *How are they free from sin before God, who, for these things which are contemptible, are polluted with human blood?* No wonder if in this matter, as in many other, Discipline became looser † with the time, and by degrees the Interpretation of the Evangelical Law began to be accommodated to the manners of the Age. Of old, the form of the primitive Institution was wont to be retained among the Clergy; at length, to these also censure was remitted upon the same ground.

Lib. 1. de lib. arb.

† Hieronymus in vita Malchi: *Postquam Ecclesia cœpit habere Christianos Magistratus facta est quidem opibus major, sed virtutibus minor.* Vide c. suscepimus, de homicidio voluntario, & c. de his, distinct. 1. *Pan. c. 2. de Homicid. Less. d. loco.*

XI. *Whether the Civil Law permitting one to kill another in his own defense, give a right, or only impunity.*

A Question is here propos'd by some, Whether the Law, at least the Civil, as having right of life and death, in what case it permitteth a thief to be killed by a private person, doth also exempt the person from all fault. I conceive that is not to be granted: For first, the Law hath not right of death over all the Citizens upon every tranſgreſſion, but upon a tranſgreſſion ſo grievous that it deſerves death. And it is a very probable opinion of *Scotus*, that 'tis not juſt to condemn any one to death, unleſs it be for thoſe tranſgreſſions, which were puniſhed with death † by the Law given by *Moſes*; this onely added; or which are equal to thoſe in a right eſtimation. And indeed, knowledge of divine will, which alone quiets the mind, ſeems not poſſible to be had elſwhere in this buſineſs, but out of that law; which ſurely appointeth not pain of death for a thief. Moreover alſo, the Law neither ought, nor is wont to give a right, privately to kill, even thoſe that have deſerved death, except in crimes very hainous: otherwiſe, in vain were the Authority of Courts of judgment ordained. Wherefore, if at any time the law ſaith, a thief may be killd without danger of puniſhment, it is to be ſuppoſed to take away the *penalty*, not to grant a *right*.

† Contra leges quæ venantes ruſticos morte puniunt, vide Gregorium Turonenſem libro 10.c.10. Joan.Sarisbur. policratici 1. cap.4.Pet.Bleſenſem epiſt. 129.

XII. *When a ſingle combat may be lawfull.*

IT appears by what we have ſaid, that two ways it may come to paſs, that a ſingle combat may be undertaken by private perſons without ſin. Firſt, if the Invader grant the other licenſe to fight, and and will kill him unleſs he will fight: Secondly,

condly, if a King or Magistrat oppose two, that have both deserved death, one against the other: in which case, it will be lawful for them to lay hold on some hope of life; but he that appoints the Duel will seem to have not so well done his duty, sith it were better, if the punishment of one seem to be sufficient, to choose by Lot the party that should dy.

XIII. *Of defense in publick War.*

WHat hath been said by us hitherto concerning the right of defending ones self and his goods, perteineth most to *privat* War; yet so, that it may be applyed to *publick* *, regard being had to the diversity. For, in private war the right is as it were momentaneous, and ceaseth, so soon as the matter admits of an access unto the Judge: but publick, because it ariseth not, but where Courts of Justice either are not, or not exercised, hath a continued tract, and is perpetually cherished by addition of new damages and injuries. Farther, in private war mere defence, for the most part, is considered: but publick powers, together with defense, have also a right of revenging. Whence it is, that they may lawfully prevent force, that is not present, but seems impending afar off; not directly, (that we have shewed above to be injust,) but indirectly, by revenging a wrong

* Ammianus lib. 23. *Cùm irruentibus armis externis lex una sit & perpetua salutem omni ratione defendere, nihil renitente vi morus.* Alexauder Imp. oratione ad milites apud Herodian. 5. *Injurias qui prior infert nihil habet probabilis coloris: at qui sibi molestos arcet ex bona conscientia sumit fiduciam, bonaq; ei spes adest, inue quod injuriam non inferat, sed auferat.*

wrong begun already, but not consummate: Of which elswhere.

XIV. *It is not lawful to take arms to diminish a Neighbor's power.*

THat is in no wise to be allowed, which some have deliver'd, that by the Law of Nations, arms may be rightly taken to abate a growing power, which being encreased might be able to do hurt. I confess; in consultation about war this is wont also to come in, not under the respect of just, but of profitable: that if the war be just upon some other ground, upon this it may be judged prudently undertaken. Nor do the Authors cited here say any more. But, that a possibility of suffering force should give a right of offring force, this is far from all equity. So is the life of man, that full security is never in our hand. Against uncertain fears, we must guard our selves by meditation of divine providence, and by harmless caution, not by doing violence to our neighbours.

Bald. lib. 3. de rer. divis.

XV. *Defensive war also is unjust on his part, who gave just cause of War.*

Alb. Gent. l. 1. c. 13.
Cast. lib. 5. de Justit.

AS little are we pleasd with this, which they teach, that also their defense is just, who have deserved the war; because forsooth, few are content to re-

turn

turn only so much revenge, as they have received injury. For, that fear of an uncertain thing cannot give a right to use force: whence, neither hath a person accused of a crime, any right to resist by force the publick officers willing to apprehend him, for fear lest he may be punisht more than he deserves. But, he that hath offended another, ought first to offer the offended party satisfaction, according to the arbitration of an upright man: and then afterward his arms will be lawfull. So *Ezechias*, when he had not kept the league, which his Ancestors had made with the King of *Assyria*, being set upon by a war, confesseth the fault, and submits himself to a mulct at the Kings pleasure. Having done that, and being after that again provoked by war, encouraged by a good conscience he withstood the enemies force, and his cause was supported by the favour of God. *Pontius Samnis*, after restitution made to the *Romans*, and the Author of the breach yeelded up; *we have*, saith he, *expiated our fault, and pacified the wrath of heaven, that was against us for our violation of the league. I know full well, what Gods soever were pleas'd we should be subdued to a necessity of restitution, the same Gods are displeas'd with the* Romans *for their proud contempt of our expiation of the breach.* A little after: * *What more do I owe to thee, O Roman! What to the league, what to the*

2 Reg. 18. 7. & c. 19.

* *Quid ultra tibi Romane, quid fœderi, quid Diis arbitris fœderis debeo? Quem tibi tuarum irarum, quem meorum suppliciorum judicem feram? Neminem neq; populum, neq; privatum fugio.*

the Gods the Judges of the league? Whom shall I bring unto thee to be judge of thy anger, and of my punishment? I refuse no people, nor private man. So, when the *Thebans* had offerd all right to the *Lacedemonians*, and they required more, the good cause passed over from these to them: saith * *Aristides* †.

* Leuctricâ primâ.
† De Principe Chalepi, qui pacem & residua tributorum obtulerat Romano Argyropolo Imperatori, vide Zonaram: simile de Cruciferis in Cromero lib. 17. De Helvetiis qui Carolo Burgundo, de curru ovium pellibus onusto, ademptoq; mercatoribus, satisfactionem obtulerant, vide Philippum Comminæum, lib. 7.

Cap. 2.

XVI. *The rise and progress of propriety.*

There follows among the Causes of war, *Injury done*, and first against that which is *ours*. A thing is *ours* either by a *common*, or by a *proper* right. For the better understanding whereof we must know the Rise and beginning of *propriety*, which the Lawyers call *dominion*. God bestowed on mankind in general a right over the things of this inferiour nature presently after the creation, and again upon the reparation of the world after the floud. *All things*, as Justin speaks, *were undivided & common** *to all, as if all had one patrimony.* Hence it was, that presently every man might take unto his uses what he pleased, and spend what might be spent. Which use of the universal right was then instead of propriety. For, what any one had so taken, another

Gen. 1. 29. 30. & 9. 2.

Lib. 43.
* Ejus vestigium mansit in Saturnalibus.

another could not, without injury, take away from him. This may be understood by that similitude which is in *Cicero*, *A theater is common* *, *yet the place possessed by any one, may be rightly call'd his own.* Nor was it impossible for that state to have continued, if either men had persisted in a certain great simplicity, or had liv'd together in a certain mutual excellent charity. One of these, to wit, Communion by reason of an exceeding simplicity †, may be observed in some people of *America*; who, through many Ages, without any incommodity, have persisted in that custome: The other, to wit, communion of Charity, the *Essens* * practised of old, and then the Christians, who were first at *Hierusalem*, and now also not a few that lead an ascetick life. The simplicity, wherein the first parents † of mandkind were created, was demonstrated by their nakedness. There was

Campestres melius Scythæ,
Quorum plaustra vagos rite trahunt domos,
Vivunt, & rigidi Getæ;
Immetata quibus jugera liberas
Fruges & Cererem ferunt;
Nec cultura placet longior annua,
Defunctumq; laboribus
Æquali recreat sorte vicarius.

De finibus, 3.
* Seneca de Benef. 7. 12. *Equestria omnium Equitum Romanorum sunt: in illis tamen locus meus fit proprius, quem occupavi.*

† Horatius:

* Et ab his orti Pythagoristæ. Vide Porphyrium, Diogenem Laertium, Gellium, 1. 9.

† Adam typus humani generis. Vide Originem contra Celsum: neq; nihil huc pertinet quod Tertullianus dixit libro de anima. *Naturale enim rationale credendum est, quod animæ à primordio sit ingenitum, à rationali videlicet auctore. Quid enim non rationale quod Deus jussu quoq; ediderit, nedum id quod proprie afflatu suo emiserit? Irrationale autem posterius intelligendum est, ut quod acciderit ex serpentis instinctu, ipsum illud transgressionis admissum, atq; exinde inoleverit, & coadoleverit in anima ad instar jam naturalitatis, quia statim in primordio naturæ accidit.*

was in them rather an ignorance of vice, than the knowledge of vertue, as *Trogus* saith of the *Scythians*. *The most antient of mortals*, saith *Tacitus*, *lived without any evill lust* *, *without dishonesty and wickedness, and so without punishment and coercion*. And in *Macrobius* *, *First, there was amongst men simplicity, ignorant of evil, and as yet void of craft*. This simplicity seemes to be called ἀφθαρσία † by the Hebrew wise man, by the Apostle *Paul* ἁπλότης, which he opposeth τῇ πανουργίᾳ to craftiness. Their only busines was the worship of God, whereof the Symbole was the tree of life *, as the antient *Hebrews* do expound, and the Apocalyps assenteth †. And they lived easily of those things which the earth of her own accord brought forth without labour *. But in this simple and innocent way of life Men persisted not, but applyed their minds to various arts, whereof the Symbole was the tree of the knowledge of good and evill †, that is, of those things which may be used

Just. l. 2.
* Seneca de iisdem epist. 90. *Ignorantia rerum innocentes erant.* Deinde locutus de justitia, prudentia, temperantia, fortitudine, addit: *Omnibus his virtutibus habebat similia quædam rudis vita.* Josephus: μυδρμοῖς ξενιζόμενοι ψυχῶν φροντίδι.
* 2. *Ad Somn. Scip.*
Sap. 3. 24.
† *Sic & Paulus Eph. 6. 24. qui & ἀδιαφθορίαν dixit, Tit. 2. 17.*
* Sanctitas superior, Rabbinis. ἰδίᾳ σοφία, Arethæ ad Apoc. De paradiso vide Eccl. 40. 17. Et de fluminibus paradisi eundem librum 24. 35. & seq. † Prov. 3. 18. Philo de mundi creat. Apocalyps. 22. 2. * Vide egregium hac de re locum lib. 2. Varronis de Re rustica, ex Dicæarcho: & confer quæ ex eodem Dicæarcho habet Porphyrius de non esu animalium libro 4. † Josephus: *Quæ arbor erat solertiæ & intelligentiæ.* Telemachus apud Homerum. —*Omnia novi Quæ bona, quæ mala sunt, nec sum jam parvus ut ante*, Zenoni Cittiensi prudentia, scientia bonorum & malorum & mediorum. Est id apud Diogenem Laertium. Plutarchus de Communibus notitiis: *Quid nocebit, si ablatis malis nulla erit prudentia, pro eo autem aliam habeamus virtutem, quæ non bonorum ac malorum, sed solorum bonorum sit scientiâ?*

both

both well and ill *. In regard of this Solomon * saith, *God created man right*, that is, *simple, but they have found out many inventions* †. *Dion. Prusaensis*, in his 6. Oration; *To the posterity of the first men, their craftiness and various * inventions were not very conducible: for they used their wit, not so much for valour and justice, as for pleasure*, The most antient Arts, Agriculture and Pasture, appeared in the first Brothers; not without some distribution of estates; From the diversity of their courses arose emulation, and then slaughter: and at length, when the good were infected by the conversation of the bad, a gigantick * kind of life, that is, violent, such as theirs whom the Greeks call χειροδίκας. The world being washed by the floud, in stead of that fierce life, succeeded the desire of pleasure †; whereunto wine was subservient; and thence arose unlawfull loves *. But concord was chiefly broken by that more generous vice, Ambition; whose sign was the Tower of *Babel*: after which, men parted asunder, and severally possessed severall parts of the earth. Yet afterward also, there remained among Neighbours a Communion, not of cattell, but of pastures. Because, in the small number of men, so great was the latitude of the Land, that without any incommodity it might suffice to the uses of many †: untill, the number, as of men, so of cattell, being

encreased,

* φρόνησιν μέσην vocat, Philo.

* Eccles. 8.30.

† ὅρρεπον εἰς πανουργίαν, ut dicto loco Philo loquitur.

* Late hoc explicat Seneca epist. 90. quem lege: & Dicæarchum apud dictos jam scriptores.

* Seneca naturalium 3. in fine: *Extinctis pariter feris in quarum homines ingenia transierant.*

† Seneca dicto loco: *Illis quoque innocentia non durabit, nisi dum novi sunt.*

* *Præmiumque summum ebrietatis libido portentosa ac jucundum nefas.* Seneca ibidem.

Gen. 10. 11.

† *Ne signare quidem aut partiri limite campum, Fas erat.* Virg. Georg. 1.

encreased, Lands every where began to be divided, not among nations as before, but among families too. But Wells *, a thing in a thirsty Country very necessary, & not sufficing many, every one made his own by seisure. These are the things, we are taught out of sacred history, agreeing well with what the Philosophers and Poets have said of the first state of things common, and the distribution of things which followed: whose testimonies are produced by us in another * book. Hence we learn, what was the cause, for which men departed from the primitive communion of things, first of movables, and then of immovables also: to wit, because when, not content to feed upon that which grew of it self, to dwell in caves, to go naked, or clad with rindes of trees, or skins of beasts †, they had chosen a more exquisite kind of life, there was need of industry, which every one should use in every matter. And the reason, why fruits were not brought together for common use, was, because of the distance of places, whereby men were separated; and moreover, the defect of Justice and love; whereby it came to pass, that neither in labour, nor in spending of the fruits, was observed due equality. Withall we learn, how things went into propriety: not only by act of the mind (for they could not know the thoughts of one another, what every one would have to be his own, that they

Gen. 13. & 21.

* De puteis ad Oasim inter multos communibus, vide Olympiodorum apud Photium.

* *Mari libero*, c. 15.

† Qualem vitam Scritefinnorum nobis accurate describit Procopius Gotthicorum 2. Adde Plinium 12. 1. Vitruvium 2. 1.

they might abstain from it, and many might desire the same thing:) but by a certain *covenant*, either *express*, as by division; or *tacit*, as by occupation*. For so soon as communion did not please them, and division was not made, it ought to be supposed an agreement amongst all, that every one should have proper to himself, what he seised on †. *It is granted*, saith *Cicero*, *that every one may prefer himself before another, in getting things usefull for his life, nature being not repugnant hereunto* *. To which is to be added that of *Quintilian* *: *On this condition, that what is come into a mans possession is his own, certainly whatsoever is possessed by right, is taken away by wrong*. And the antients, when they called *Ceres* * *Legiferam*, and her rites *Thesmophoria*, signified this, that by the division of lands came up the original of a certain new right †.

*Vide quæ hac de re ex Gemara & Alcorano nobis protulit honos Britanniæ Seldenus in Thalassocratico.
† Cicero: *Ex quo, quia suum cujusq; fit eorum quæ natura fuerunt communia, quod cuiq; obtigit id quisq; teneat.* Quod similitudine illustrat à Chrysippo reperta de stadio, ubi currendo licet vincere adversarium, non cum detrudendo. Scholiastes ad Artem poet. Horatii: *Quemadmodum domus aut ager sine domino communis est, occupatus vero jam proprius fit.* Varro in Age modo: *Terra culturæ causa attributa olim particulatim, ut Etruria Thuscis, Samnium Sabellis.*
* Cicero Offic. 3. Solon: *Divitias habuisse velim, sed non bene partas non cupiam.* Cicero Offic. 1. *Nec vero rei amplificatio nemini nocens vituperanda est, sed fugienda semper injuria.* * Declam. 13.
* Macrob. Saturn. lib. 3. c. 12. † *Postquam ex agrorum discretione nata sunt jura.* Ita Servius ad illud 4. Æn. *Legiferæ Cereri.*

XVII. *Some*

XVII. *Some things cannot be made proper, as the Sea, taken for the whole or principal parts: and why?*

UPon these premises we say, that the Sea taken either in regard of the whole, or in regard of the principal parts, cannot go into proper right. Which, because some do grant it, of private persons, not of nations, we prove, first by *moral* reason. For, the cause, for which men departed from communion, here ceaseth, the Sea being so great, that it can suffice all nations for every use, for watering, for fishing, for sailing. The same were to be spoken of the aire, if any use might be made thereof, to which the use of the earth were not necessary, as it is to Hawking *: whence it receiveth law from him, who hath command over the Land. In the same manner we judge of the *Syrtes*, where is nothing that can admit of culture, and the onely use of fetching sand thence can never be exhausted. There is also a *natural* reason, which forbids the Sea considered as we have said, to become proper: because occupation proceeds not, but in a thing * terminated: and liquid things, because they have no * bounds of their own, cannot be occupied, but as they are containd in some other thing: as lakes and ponds, and rivers, because they are contain'd with banks. Now

* Et ad habitandi jus. Tam soli quam cœli mensura facienda est, ait Pomponius, l. si opus. D. quod vi aut clam.

* Ideo jugera quæ possessorem non habent immetata dixit Horatius.

* τὸ ὑγρὸν ἀόριστον οἰκείῳ ὅρῳ, Inquit Aristoteles, De Gener. l. 2. c. 2.

Now the Sea is not contained by the earth, being equal to the earth or greater *; whence the antients say, the earth is contained by the Sea †. Nor may we feign a division: for when first the earth was divided, the Sea, most part, was unknown: and so no way can be imagined for nations so far distant to agree upon the division. Wherefore the things which were common to all, and in the first division were not divided, they do not now pass into proper right by division, but by occupation; nor are they divided, unless after they have begun to be proper.

* Ita de Oceano sensit Jarchas apud Philostratum, 3. 11.

† τὸν ὠκεανὸν [illegible] Apollonii verba apud Philostrat. Sulpitius Apollinaris apud Gell. *Quid potest dici circa Oceanum esse, cum undiq; Oceanus circumscribat omnes terras, & ambiat?* Marcus Acilius apud Livium: *Oceano*, inquit, *qui orbem terrarum amplexu finit*. In Senecæ Suasoriis dicitur Oceanus totius orbis vinculum terrarumq; custodia: Lucano, Unda mundum coercens.

XVIII. *Of things that may be made proper.*

Let us now come to things which may be made proper, but are not yet made so. Such are many incult places †, Ilands in the Sea *, wild beasts, fishes, birds. But two things are to be noted, First, there is a twofold *occupation*, one by the *whole*, another by the *parts*: the former usually by the people, or by their Ruler: the other afterward by several persons; yet rather by *assignation*, than free *occupation*. But if any thing, seised on in general, be not divided among several Lords, it

† Vide Bembum, Historiæ 6.

* ut Echinades, *quas occupando suas fecit Alcmæon.* Thucyd. lib. 2. in fine.

it is not therefore to be eſteemed void. For it remains in the dominion of the firſt occupator, to wit, the people or King. Such are wont to be rivers, lakes, ponds, woods, wild mountains. Next, concerning wild beaſts, fiſhes, birds, it is to be noted, that he who hath command over the lands and waters, may by his Law hinder others from catching and acquiring the beaſts, fiſhes, and birds: and by that Law are foreiners alſo bound. The Reaſon is; becauſe to the goverment of a people it is morally neceſſary, that they who mingle with them but for a time (which is done by entring the territory) render themſelves conformable to the Inſtitution of that people. Nor is that againſt us, that we read often in the *Roman* Law, ſaying, by the Law of nature, or nations, it is free to hunt and take ſuch creatures. For, this is true, ſo long as no Civil Law intercedes; (as the *Roman* Law left many things in that primitive ſtate, concerning which things other nations made other conſtitutions) But when the Civil Law ordaineth otherwiſe, the very Law of nature dictates, that it ought to be obſerved. For, the Civil Law, though it can command nothing which the Law of nature forbids, nor forbid what it commands, nevertheleſs may it circumſcribe natural liberty, and prohibit what was naturally lawfull, and alſo by its force antevert that very dominion, which naturally is to be acquired.

Covarr. c. peccatum. par. 2. Sect. 8.

Dd. in l. cunctos populos. l. de ſum. Trin. Covar. d. loco.

XIX.

XIX. *Over things made proper, men have a right to use them, in time of necessity: and whence it comes.*

NOw let us see, what common right is competent to men over those things, which are made proper unto some. Which question, perhaps some may wonder at, seeing propriety may seem to have swallowed up all that right, which arose from the common state of things. But it is not so. For, it must be considered, what was the mind of them, who first introduced singular dominions: which is to be believed such, as hath receded as little as might be from natural equity. For, if also written Laws are to be drawn, as far as they may, into that sense; much more are Customs, that are not bound up in writing. First then, it follows hence, that, in extreme necessity, that old right of using things revives, as if the things had remained common: because, in all human constitutions, and therefore in the Law of Dominion too, that extreme necessity seems excepted. Hence it is, that in navigation, if at any time victuals faile, what every one hath ought to be brought forth for the common use. And so, in a fire, I may pull down my neighbours house to save mine: and cut in pieces the tackling or nets upon which my ship is driven,

L. 2. Sect. cum in eadem. D. ad l. Rhodiam. l. quo naufragium. S. quod ait. D. de incend. L. Quemadmodū. Sect. Item. D. ad L. Aquiliam. Thom. 2.2.66. 7. Covarr. c. peccat. 2. sect. 1. Soto l. 5. q. 3. art. 4.

driven, if it cannot be disintangled † by other means. All which are not introduced by the Civil Law, but expounded. For among Divines also, it is a received opinion, in such necessity, if one take from another what is necessary to save his life, he doth not commit theft. Of which determination this is not the cause, that some alleage, that the owners of the thing are bound by the rule of charity to give it to the necessitous; but, that all things seem divided amongst the owners, with a certain benign reception of the primitive right. For, if the first dividers had been asked their opinion thereof, they would have return'd our answer. *Necessity*, saith *Seneca* the father, *the defense of human imbecillity, breaks every Law* †, understand *human*, or made after the manner of human.

† Talia non procedunt nisi ex magna & satis necessaria causa. *Ulp. l. Si alius. D. quod vi aut clam.* Ubi sequitur exemplum illud de ædibus intercisis arcendi incendii causa.

† *Quicquid coegit defendit.* l. 4. controv. 27. Exemplis idem Seneca illustrat in excerptis controversiæ 4. *Necessitas est, quæ navigia jactu exonerat: necessitas est, quæ ruinis incendia opprimit: necessitas est lex temporis.* Cicero Philippica 11. *Cassius in Syriam profectus est, alienam provinciam, si homines legibus scriptis uterentur: his vero oppressis, suam lege naturæ.* Apud Curtium est: *In communi calamitate, suam quemq; habere fortunam.* Theodorus Priscianus vetus medicus: *Expedit prægnantibus in vitæ discrimine constitutis sub unius partis sæpe jactura salutem mercari certissimam; sicut arboribus crescentium ramorum accommodatur salutaris abscissio, & naves pressæ onere, cum gravi tempestate jactantur, solum habent ex damno remedium.* Prima illa verba ad ἐμβρυοθλάστην pertinent, cujus instrumenti descriptio apud Galenum & Celsum: ac proinde eadem vix restituenda apud Tertul. de anima.

XX. *Three*

XX. *Three Cautions to be applyed to this case of necessity.*

BUt Cautions are to be used, that this licence be not extravagant. *First*, By all means tryall must be made first, whether the necessity may be evaded some other way, as by an address unto the Magistrat, or by endeavouring to obtain the use of the thing from the Owner by intreaty. *Plato* permits one to fetch water out of his neighbours Well, so that he hath digged in his own ground, as far as the chalk, to find water: if he hath digged forty cubits deep, saith *Solon*: where *Plutarch* adds*, *He thought necessity was was to be succoured, idleness not to be maintained. Xenophon** in his answer to the *Sinopenses*: *Where we are not permitted to buy, be it among Barbarians or Græcians, there do we take what we want, not out of wantonness, but necessity.* Our *second* Caution is, This is not to be allowed, if the Possessor be pressed with an equall necessity. For in a like case the * Possessor hath the advantage. *He is not a fool*, saith Lactantius, *who thrusteth not a shipwrackt man from his plank, nor a wounded man from his horse, to save himself: because he hath kept himself from doing hurt, which is a sin; and to avoid this sin is wisdom.* Cicero had said: *Will not then a wise man, if himself be almost famisht,*

Less. lib. 2. cap. 12. dub. 12. num. 70.

* *Subveniendum necessitati non instruendam pigritiam.*

* Expedit. Cyri, 5.

* *Possidentis melior est conditio.*

L. 5. c. 16.

Offic. 3.

might, force another mans food from him, being a man whose life is worth nothing? No sure. For my life is not more deer to me, than that disposition of mind, to violate no man that I may profit my self. We read in *Curtius* *: *Better is the cause of him that delivers not up his own, than of him that requires what belongeth to another.* The *third* is this: Where it may be, restitution is to be made. Some think otherwise upon this ground, that he who hath used his own right is not bound to restitution. But it is more true, that the right here was not full, but restrained with a condition of restoring, when the necessity should be over. For such a right sufficeth to keep up natural equity against the rigour of dominion.

* *Melior est causa suum non tradentis, quam poscentis alienum.* Q. Curtius.
Adrian. quod. lib. 1. *art.* 2. *c.* 3. *Covarr. d. loco.*

XXI. *An example of this right in Wars.*

Hence we may collect, how it may be lawful for him, that wageth a pious war, to seise upon a place situate in a peaceable Country; to wit, if there be, not an imaginary, but a certain danger, lest the enemy invade that place, and thence do irreparable damage: moreover, if nothing be taken, but what is necessary for caution, *i. e.* the bare custody of the place, the jurisdiction and profits being left to the Lord thereof: Lastly, if it be with a mind to restore the custody

so

so soon as the necessity is over. Enna, *was reteined either by an evil, or by a necessary enterprize*, saith *Livy*: because it is *evil* here, whatsoever is different, even in the least degree, from *necessary*. The *Grecians* that were with *Xenophon*, having extreme need of ships, by the advice of *Xenophon* himself, took up such as passed by; yet so, that they kept the lading safe for the Merchants, and to the Mariners gave both food and wages. *Lib. 24.* *De exped. Cyri. 5.*

XXII. *Another right of men over things proper, for their benefit, without damage to the owner.*

BEsides that right of *necessity*, there is another relique of old communion, namely, the right of *harmeless utility*. *For why should not one*, saith Cicero, *when without his own detriment he may, communicate to another, in those things, which are profitable to the Receiver, and to the Giver not chargeable?* Therefore *Seneca* saith, it cannot be call'd a benefit, to give leave to another to light his fire by yours. We read in *Plutarch*, It is not lawful to spoil our victuals, when we have more than enough; nor to stop or hide a fountain, when we have drank our fill; nor to abolish the way-marks either by Sea or Land, which have been useful for us. So a River, as a River, is *De Offic. 1.* *De benef. 4.* *Sympos. 7.*

 proper

proper to that people, or that Prince, within whose dominion it runs, and they may make a mill on it, and take what fish the River yields: But the same River, as a running water, remained common, as to drinking or drawing of it. Ovid * therefore calls the use of water common, and *Virgil* saith, it is open to all.

L. Quadam. D. de rerum divis.

**Quis vetet apposito lumen de lumine sumi;*
Atq; cavum vastas in mare servet aquas?
Ovidius: apud quem & Lycios Latona sic alloquitur.
Quid prohibetis aquas? Usus communis aquarum est?

XXIII. *The right of passages explaned, by Land and Water.*

SO also Lands, and rivers, and if any part of the Sea be come into the propriety of any people, it ought to be open to those that have need of passage for just causes: namely, because being expelld out of their own Country they seek void places, or because they desire commerce with a remote Nation, or also because they contend for their own in a just war. The reason here is the same which hath been set down above, because dominion might be introduced, with a reception of such use †, which profits these, hurts not those: and therefore the Authors of Dominion are to be supposed willing rather to have it so. We have an eminent example in the history of *Moses*: who, when he had to pass thorow the countryes of other

Bald. 3. cons. 293.

† Serv. ad 7. Æn. *Littusq: rogamus innocuum. Cujus vindicatio, ait, nulli possit nocere.*

Numb. 20. & 21.

other Princes, made this offer, firſt to the *Edomite*, then to the *Amorite*; that he would go in the High-way, and not divert to private poſſeſſions: if he had need of any thing of theirs, he would pay them the juſt price. Which conditions when they were refuſed, he waged a juſt * war, upon that ſcore, againſt the *Amorite*. *For harmleſs paſſage was denyed*, ſaith * Auſtin, *which by the moſt equal right of humane ſociety ſhould be open.* The *Gracians* that were with *Clearchus*: *We will go home, if no man trouble us: if any one do us wrong, by the Gods help we will endeavour to keep it off.* Not much unlike is that ſaying of *Ageſilaus*, when returning out of *Aſia* he was come to *Troas*, he asked, whether they would have him paſs as a friend, or as an enemy: And *Lyſander* asked the *Bœotions*, whether they would have him paſs with ſpears charged, or inclined. The *Batavians* in † *Tacitus* declare to the *Bonnenſes*, *If none oppoſed them, they would march quietly; if they met with force, they would cut their way with the ſword.* *Cimon* going to aide the *Lacedemonians*, led his army through the territory of *Corinth*: being reprehended by the *Corinthians* for not asking leave of the City; for even he that knocks at anothers door, enters not without the permiſſion of the Maſters; anſwerd, *But you did not knock at the doors of the* Cleonæi *and* Megarenſes, *but broke*

* *Juſta bella gerebantur à filiis Iſrael contra* Amorræas, ait Auguſtinus. *Sic* Amyntorem Orchomeni regem ob negatum tranſitum interfecit Hercules, notante id Apollodoro. Adde legem Longobardicam lib. 2. tit. 54. c. 2.

* *Lib. q. 4. ſuper Num. ad ca.* 20.

Plut. Apoph. & in vita Ageſilai.

Plutarch in Lyſand.

† *Hiſt.* 4.

Plutarch. in Cim.

broke them open, thinking that all things ought to give place to the stranger. The truth is in the middle sentence, that passage is first to be requested †, and, if it be denyed, it may be forced. So *Agesilaus* * returning out of *Asia*, when he had required passage of the *Macedonian* King, and he had answered, that he would consult: *Let him consult*, saith he, *We in the mean time will march on*. Nor may any rightly except, and say, he fears the multitude of those that pass. For my right is not taken away by thy fear: and so much the less, because there are ways of security; as, if the army pass in divided companies; if † unarmed, (which they of *Agrippina* said to the *Germans*, and *Strabo* notes that custome antiently observed in the Countrey of the *Eleans*:) if, at the charge of him that passeth, he that grants the pass, provide himself sufficient Guards; if Hostages * be given, which *Seleucus* demanded of *Demetrius*, that he might suffer him to quarter within the bounds of his Empire. So also, fear of him, against whom, he that passeth makes a just war, is no sufficient reason to deny passage. Nor is it more to be admitted, if you say, he may pass some way els: for

† *Veneti & Germanis & Gallis de Marano certantibus iter præbuere.* Paruta 11. *Iidem Germanis conquerentibus de transitu hostibus dato, ostendunt id nisi armis impediri non potuisse: quibus uti non mos sibi, nisi in hostes manifestos.* eod. lib. *Sic & pontifex se excusat*, lib. 12.
* *Plutarch. in vita ejus.*
† *Exemplum in excerpto legationum* 12. apud Bembum 7. Hist. Ital. *Vide & notabilia pacta de transitu inter Fredericum Barbarossam & Isacium Angelum* apud Nicetam l. 2. de vita ejusdem Isacii aliquot locis. *In Imperio Germanico transitum postulans de damno resarciendo cavet.* Vide & Cranzium Saxon. c. 10. & Mendosam in Belgicis. *Cæsar Helvetiis iter per provinciam noluit concedere, quod homines inquo animo existimabat non temperaturos ab injuriis & maleficio.* De bello Gallico lib. 1. * *Exemplum habes* Procopii Persicorum. 2.

any

any one may say as much, and by that means the right of passing world come to nothing: but it is enough, if, without deceit, passage be demanded, where it is next and most commodious. Indeed, if he makes unjust war, who would pass; if he lead my enemies † with him, I may deny him passage: and more than so, I may meet him on his own ground and lawfully hinder his expedition.

† *Hoc dicebant Franci, qui in Venetia erant, Narseti Longobardos secum ducenti*, Gothicorum 4. *Alia negati itineris exempla habes* apud Bembum lib. 7. Italicorum. apud Parutam. l. hist. Venet. 5. & 6.

XXIV. *Of passage for Merchandise, and of Impost.*

NOr is passage onely due to persons, but to Merchandise also; for no man hath right to obstruct the way of Commerce to any Nation with any other that is remote; because the permission of Trade is for the interest of human society, and is not discommodious to any one. For, although some hoped gain, but not due, departs from any, that is not to be reputed as a loss. *Philo* * speaks to our purpose: *On the Sea, all Ships of burden safely pass, according to that right of Commerce* †, *which is between all Nations*

* *In legat. ad Caium.*

† Apud Florum est l. 3. *Sublato Commercio, rupto foedere generis humani.* Servius ad Georgic. 1. *significat necessitate quarendarum rerum homines navigandi peritiam ac studium reperisse. commune bonum erat patere Commercium maris.* Ambrosius in opere de Creatione: *Bonum mare tanquam hospitium fluviorum, invectio commeatuum, quo sibi distantes populi copulantur*; quæ ex Basilio sumta Hexemeri 4. Mare forum mundi, insulas stationes in mari, eleganter dixit de provid.

Provid. 2. Theodoret. Adjungam his Chrysostomi ad Stebechium verba: *Quomodo autem satis digne quis explicet facilitatem ad mutua commercia nobis datam? Ne enim itineris longitudo impedimentum aliorum ad alios commeatibus adferret, breviorem viam, mare scilicet, ubiq; terrarum disposuit Deus, ut mundum tanquam unum domum communiter inhabitantes, crebro nos invicem viserimus; & apud se nata quisq; alteri communicans vicissim, commode acciperet res apud illum abundantes; ac sic exiguam tenens terræ partem, ita tanquam si teneret universam, frueretur ejus quæ ubivis sunt bonis. Licet itaq; nunc, tanquam in communi mensa convivarum, unicuiq; ea quæ sibi apposita dare alteri longius accumbenti, ac contra quæ apud ipsum sunt accipere manu tantum extenta.*

arising from the desire of natural society; while they supply one another mutually, with that, which the one wanteth, and the other can spare. For envy hath never invaded either the whole world, or the great parts thereof. Another testimony we have from *Plutarch*, speaking thus of the Sea: *This element hath made our life sociable and perfect, that would otherwise be wild and without correspondence; it supplies our wants with mutuall aide, and by exchange of things needful procures fellowship and friendship.* Wherewith agrees that of *Libanius*: *God hath not granted all things to every land, but hath distributed his gifts to several Countrys, that men having need of one another might maintain society for their common good, Therefore hath he made the Merchant, to convey to all, what any place affords. Euripides* * also brings in *Theseus*, accounting Navigation among the Inventions, which human reason hath found out for the general benefit, thus:

* *Supplicib.*

What

What nature any land deny'd
By Navigation is supply'd.

But it is a question, whether Tribute may be impos'd, by him that rules the Land, upon merchandise passing by Land, or by river, or by part of the Sea, which may be call'd an accession of the Land. Certainly, whatsoever burdens have no relation to the merchandise, no equity suffers such to be imposed on the same. Neither can Head-money, put on the inhabitants to sustein the charge of the Commonwealth, be exacted of passengers. Nevertheless, if either to secure the goods, or if, among other reasons, for this also, the publick be charged, some Taxe, by way of compensation, may be layd upon the Commodities, so that the measure of the cause be not exceeded. For upon this depends the justness of Tributes & Toll*. So, *Strabo** relates, that the *Corinthians* even from the most antient times, received Tribute † of the Commodities, which to avoid the compassing of *Malea*, were carried by land from Sea to Sea. So, the *Romans* received a price for the passage of the *Rhene**: and the Lawyers† books are ful of the like. But oft-times an equal measure is not kept; whereof the *Arabian Phylarchs* are accus'd by †*Strabo*, adding, *It is a hard matter, amongst powerful and fierce people, to compound upon termes not grievous to the Merchant.*

* *Vide legem Longobardicam tit.* 31. *c.* 33. *& epistolam Episcoporum ad Ludovicum Regem quæ inter capitula legitur Caroli Calvi, c.* 14.

* *Libro octavo.*

† De thure Plinius, 12. 14. *Evehi non potest, nisi per Gebanitas: itaq; & horum regi penditur vectigal.*

* *Etiam in pontibus pro transitu datur*, inquit Seneca.

† *Pereg. l.* 1. *de jure Fisci cap.* 1. *num.* 22. *Ang. cons.* 199. *Zabar. cons.* 38.

† *Lib.* 16.

XXV.

XXV. *The right of staying for a time, of inhabiting, of having desert places.*

Vict. de Ind. rel. 2. n. 1.

* Servius ad eum loc. *Occupantis enim est possessio littoris, unde ostenduntur crudeles, qui etiam à communibus prohibeant.* Loomedon ab Hercule occisus, quod eum Trojæ portu pelleret, Servio ibidem narrante.

† *Plutarch. Pericle.* παρὰ τὰ κοινὰ δίκαια. *Diod. l. 12. Thucyd. 1.*

TO stay sometime, for health sake, or for any other just cause, ought also to be permitted passengers. For this too is among the innoxious utilities. Wherefore *Ilioneus* in *Virgil* *, when the *Trojans* were prohibited to stay on the shore of *Afric*, is bold to invoke the Gods as Judges: and the complaint of the *Megarenses* against the *Athenians*, who drave them from their havens †, *against common right*, was approv'd by the *Greeks*: so that the *Lacedemonians* esteemed no cause of war more just. Consequent hereto is this, that is is lawfull to build a Cottage on the shore, to shelter them for a season, though we grant the shore to be possest by the Inhabitants. For, what *Pomponius* said, of having the *Pretor's* decree, that it may be lawfull to build on the common shore or in the Sea, perteins to buildings * that are permanent. Moreover, perpetuall habitation is not to be denied these foreiners, who being expulsed from their own seats, seek entertainment abroad; on condition, they submit to the government in being, and to other things needfull for the avoiding of seditions. Which equity is well observed by

* Quo & illud Poetæ: *Contracta pisces æquora sentiunt, Jactis in altum molibus.*

by the divine Poet, when he brings in *Æneas* yielding to *Latinus* the *Militia*, and soveraign power. And in *Halicarnessensis*, *Latinus* himself saith, the cause of *Æneas* was just, if compelld by want of roome he came thither. It is the part of *Barbarians* to repell strangers, saith *Strabo* out of *Eratosthenes* : nor were the *Spartans* in this respect commended : and in the judgment of *Ambrose* also, they that prohibit strangers to dwell among them, are in no wise to be approved. *The Eolians* admitted the *Colophonians*, the *Rhodians Phorbas* and his Fellows, the the *Carians* the *Melians*, the *Lacedemonians* the *Minyans*, the *Cumeans* others that came unto them. But, of the same *Minyans*, requiring a part of the Empire after they were admitted, *Herodotus* rightly saith, *They were injurious, and did what was not lawfull to do.* And *Valerius Maximus* saith, *They turned a benefit into an injury.* Lastly, if within the territory of a people, there be some desert and barren ground, that also is to be granted to strangers upon their request, yea it is also rightly seised on by them; because, that ought not to be esteemed occupied, which is not cultivated, but only as to the Empire, which remains entire to the first people. To the *Trojans* were granted by the *Latin Aborigines*, seven hundred Acres of hard and rough Ground, as *Servius* noteth. In *Dion Prusaensis* we

Virgil: *Socer arma Latinus habeto, Imperium solemne Socer.*
Lib. 1.
Lib. 17.
De Offic. l. 3. *c.* 7.
Herod. l. 1. & 4.
Paus. l. 7.
Oros. 7.
Diod. l. 5.
Lib. 4. *cap.* 6.
Ad 11. *Æn.*

Orat. 7. we read, *They do no offence, who inhabit and manure a part of the land, that lyes*
Tac. Annal. 13. *neglected.* The *Ansibarians* in *Tacitus* cry out: *As the Heaven to the Gods, so is the Earth granted to mortals, and what is void is publick: looking up to the Sun and Stars, they did openly as it were enquire of them, whether they were pleased in beholding any ground empty and without inhabitants: They should rather call forth the sea, and overwhelm the spoilers of the Earth.* But these men did ill apply these generall sayings to that particular business. For those lands were not altogether void, but served to feed the cattell and heards belonging to the Army; which was a just cause for the *Romans* to deny them. And no less justly did the *Romans* of old ask of the *Galli Senones*,
Liv. lib. 5. *What right they had to require lands from the possessors, or to threaten them with War.*

XXVI. Of Oaths. *How great their vertue is, even in the opinion of Pagans.*

† Sophocles Hippodamia:

Mens excitari jurejurando solet,
Ut bina diligenter evitet mala,
Culpari amicis, & Deos offendere.

AMong all people, and from all time, about promises and contracts, very great hath been the vertue of an oath †. *Our Ancestors*, saith Cicero, *esteemed no bond of faith stronger than this.* Hence it hath been alwaysbelieved,

lieved, that some heavy punishment hangs over the head of perjur'd persons *: So that posterity † also paid for the sins of their forefathers: (which was not believ'd, but of most grievous crimes:) and even the will without the deed drew punishment upon it: both which *Herodotus* confirms by the narration of *Glaucus Epicydides*, who only deliberated, whether he should break his oath concerning a thing commited to his trust.

* Ut Hesiodus dixit de Juramento:
——*clades Mortalib. unde Adveniunt, quoties fallaci pectore jurant.*

†Vide Servium in excerptis Fuldensibus ad 1. Æneid.

Lib. 2. ubi hoc carmen Pythiæ adfert idem Herodotus:

Ad juramento quædam est sine nomine proles,
Trunca manus, & trunca pedes: tamen impete magno
Advenit, atq; omnem vastat stirpemq; domumq;

And *Juvenal* rehearsing the same story so concludes:

——*Such is the pain,*
The bare intent of perjury doth gain.

V. Zachar. 5. 1, 2, 3. & interpret. ejus loci Chrysostomum de Statuis 15.

Well said Cicero: *An oath is a religious affirmation: and what you have firmly promised, as in the presence of God, is to be made good.* But, that he adds; *For now it belongs not to the wrath of the Gods, which is none, but to justice and fidelity*; if by the name of wrath he understand a perturbation, it is not to be rejected; if any kind of affection or will to punish, it is not to be received, as *Lactantius* rightly proves.

Offic. 3. *Est Jusjurandum affirmatio religiosa: quod autem affirmate quasi Deo teste promiseris, id tenendum est.*

Lib. de ira Dei.

XXVII.

XXVII. *In an Oath is required a deliberate minde.*

LEt us now consider, whence ariseth the vertue of an oath, and how far it reacheth. First, what is said of promises and contracts hath place here also: that a mind having use of reason, and deliberate is required. Wherefore, if any one, not conceiving that he swears, utter swearing words, as is related of *Cydippe*, that may be said, which *Ovid* ascribeth to her, taken out of Euripides, *I have not sworn; because my mind went not with my tongue* *. But if one, willing to swear, is not willing to oblige himself, he is never the less obliged; because obligation is inseparable from an oath, and a necessary effect thereof †.

* Ovid epist. *Quæ jurat mens est; nil conjuravimus illa.*
Eurip. Hippol. *Jurata lingua est: mente juravi nihil.* quia de re honesta tacenda, nutricis verba intellexerat Hippolitus, non de adulterio & incestu.
Ovid. ibidem: *Consilium prudensq; animi sententia jurat,*
Et nisi judicii vincula nulla tenent. mox:
Sed si nil dedimus præter sine pectore vocem,
Verba suis frustra viribus orba tenes.
Non ego juravi; legi jurantia verba: &c.
† Soto lib. 8. qu. 1. art. 7. Covarr. ad c. quamvis. p. 1. §. 5.

XXVIII. *In what sense the words of an Oath bind.*

But, if one deliberately pronounce swearing words, yet without a minde of swearing, some say, he is not bound, yet sins in swearing rashly. More truly, he is bound to make good his words, whereto he hath called God a witness. For, that act, which by it self is obligatory, proceeded from a deliberate minde. Consequent to this it is, that although that of *Tully* be true, *What thou hast sworn according to thy minde, not to do is perjury* †; Yet hath it this exception, unless he that swears know, or probably believe, the words are taken otherwise by him, with whom he dealeth. For calling God to witness his words, he ought to make the words true, as he thinks they are understood *. And this is that which the same *Cicero* saith: *What is so sworn, as the minde of the giver of the oath conceives it must be done, it must be kept.* In

† Tullius: *Quod ex animi tui sententia jurasti, id non facere perjurium est.* Quo & illud pertinet quod apud Homerum jurans Ulyssi Calypso ait: ἀλλὰ τὰ μὲν νοέω, καὶ φράσομαι.

* Augustinus epist. 224. de illo locutus qui è Punicis castris egressus in castra redierat; inde Romam venerat: *Ita non attenderunt qui illum Senatu moverunt, quid ipse jurando cogitasset, sed quid ab illo quibus juraverat exspectarent.* Vide & sequentia. Vide ad hanc rem pulcre dicta Concilio Tridentino Tom. 3. Concil editionis Sirmondianæ, & apud Hincmarum in opusculo de divortio Lotharii & Tethbergæ ad interrogationem 6. ubi in hanc sententiam recte de Deo dicitur: *Qui non ut juras, sed ut is jurasse putavit cui juras, audit: Sic est utrique reus.* In professione jurata Hebræorum per Hispaniam: *Si non ea intentione perfeceris, sicut à nobis me profitente audita atque intellecta sunt.*

Tacitus

Histor. 4.

Epist. 224.

Lib. 2. de sum. bono. cap. 31. 1. citatur causa 22. quæst. 5. c. quacunq,.

* Donatus ad illud in Andria: Quia si forte opus ad berum jurejurandum mihi, Non opposuisse, ut liquido possim. Liquido, pure, & manifeste.

Nicetas in Alexio fraudem Andronici Comneni culpans: Oportuit non quæsita locutione verba adulterare, sed ut concepta ea fuerant, eloqui. qui & alibi de Alexio contra sensum verba captante: ita verbis illis insidebat, ut musca vibici. Graviter in hanc regulam peccavit aula Arcadiana, quæ effecit ut Chalcedone occideretur, is qui Constantinopolim, salute ipsi per jusjurandum promissa, venerat. Zozomen. lib. 5. Appian. de bello civili lib. 1. Pan. in c. clericus de jurejur. Sil. in verbo jurament. 4. qu. 23. 6. 17. ibi. Thom. Heb. 6. 17, 18. * Ita recte verti puto illud ψεύσασθαι, sicut aperta locutio vocatur veritas, Dan. 7. 16. & 8. 26. & 10. 1.

Tacitus we read, *Trembling and changing the words of the Oath by various arts, conscious of their own wickedness.* Augustin: *They are forsworn, who, the words being salved, have deceived their expectation to whom they have sworn.* And Isidore: *with whatsoever art of words one swears, God notwithstanding who is a witness of the conscience, takes it so as he doth to whom it is sworn.* And this is that which is meant by the phrase *Liquido jurare* *. Therefore did *Metellus* rightly refuse to swear to the *Apuleian* Law, albeit there were some that said, the Law, by fault in the preferring of it, was void; and that the oath to the Law was so to be understood, if the Law were rightly preferd and made. For, albeit in other promises is easily understood some tacit condition, which may exsolve the promiser, yet is not that to be admitted in an oath. Pertinent here is that noble place of the Apostle to the Hebrews: *God willing most abundantly to shew unto the heirs of promise the immutability of his counsell, confirmed it by an oath: That by two immutable things, in which it was impossible for God to * deceive, we might have a strong*

consolation.

consolation. For the understanding of which words, we must know, the holy Writers often speak of God ἀνθρωποπαθῶς, and rather according to that which seems to us, than that which is. For, God doth not truly change his Decrees; yet is he said to change and to repent *, as oft as he doth otherwise than the words seemed to sound; to wit, by reason of a condition tacitly understood *, that ceaseth, *Jer.* 18. 8. Examples are frequent to be * seen. In which sense also God may *improperly* be said to deceive us: and the word ψεύδεσθαι, that appears in the said place to the Hebrews, is wont to have the signification of an event frustrating hope, as we may see in sundry * places. And this proceeds most easily in comminations, because they do not confer a right on any; in promises sometimes, to wit, where a certain condition is secretly couched. Therefore doth the Apostle name two things, that note immutability, the promise, because it gives a right; and the oath, because it repels tacit, and in some sort latent conditions; as we may see, † *Psal.* 89. For, 'tis another thing if the very nature of the business openly declare some conditions. Whereunto some refer that which is read, *Numb*, 14. 30. But it is more true, that the promised land is by oath appointed to them, not the *persons*, but the *people*, that is, to the posterity of them, to whom God had sworn,

Jona. 4. 1.

* Concil. Tolet. 8. c. 2. *Jurare namq; Dei est à seipso ordinata nullatenus convellere: pænitere verò, eadem ordinata, cũ voluerit, convellere.* Retulit Gratianus in causam 22. q. 4. explicata vero ut in textu nostro.

* Senec. vide Nat. Quæst. 2. 37.

* Gen. 20. 3. Exod. 32. 14. 1 Reg. 21. 29. 2 Reg. 20. 1. Es. 38. 1. Jonæ 3. 5, 11.

* Levit. 6. 2. Jos. 24. 27. Es. 58. 2. Ose. 1. 2. Abac. 3. 17. Job 41. 6. Ose. 9. 2.

† Psal. 89. 30, 31, 32, 33, 34, 35, 36.

v. 23. And ſuch a promiſe may be fulfild at any time, nor is limited to certain perſons.

XXIX. *An oath deceitfully procured, when binding. Of Joſhuah's oath.*

BY that which is ſaid, may be underſtood what is to be judged of an oath procured by deceit. For, if it be certain, that he who ſweareth ſuppoſeth ſome-
Navar. c. 12. *n.* 13. thing done, which indeed is not ſo *; and
* Ut Hippolytus, de quo modo diximus. that, unleſs he had believed it, he would not have ſworn, the oath will not binde: But if it be doubtfull, whether he would not, even without that, have ſworn the ſame, he muſt ſtand to his word, becauſe the greateſt ſimplicity, that can be, agrees unto an oath. And hither do I refer the
Joſh. 9. oath, which *Joſhua* and the Princes of the people of *Iſrael* ſware to the *Gibeonites*. They were indeed deceived by the *Gibeonites*, feigning that they came from a far Country. Yet did it not follow thence, that *Joſhua* and the Princes, had they known their vicinity, would not have ſpar'd them. For, what they ſaid to the *Gibeonites*, *Peradventure ye dwell among us, and how ſhall we make a league with you?* may have this ſenſe, that the *Gibeonites* may be asked, what league they deſire, whether *Social*, or of *dedition*: or alſo, that the *Hebrews* may ſhew, it was not lawfull for them, with certain people,

people, to enter into a social league: and not, that they may deny, life might be given to those that yield themselves. For, the divine Law, which devoted those nations to destruction, by comparison † with another law, was so to be understood, that it had place, except in them, that being summond were ready to obey. Which is proved, as by other arguments, so by the history of *Rahab* *, who was spared for her good deserts; and of *Solomon*, who received the reliques of the *Canaanites* under Empire and tribute. And to this purpose is that we read in the Book of *Joshua* *; That there was not one City of the seven Nations, which made their peace: for they were hardened, that mercy might not be shewed them. Wherefore, sith it was credible, if the *Gibeonites* had told the plain truth, which for fear they did not, they should neverthelesse have obtained their lives, and saved themselves on condition of obedience, the Oath was of force, in so much that afterward most grievous revenge was taken by the hand of God for the violation of it. *Ambrose* treating upon this story: *Joshua* (saith he) *thought not fit to recall the peace which he had granted them, because it was confirmed by the Religion of an oath, lest while he condemned their fraud, he should lose his own credit.* Notwithstanding, the *Gibeonites*, being now by their dedition become subjects of the

Deut. 20. 10.

† Imo & ex causa Legi de internecione addita, Ex. 24. 33, Deut. 7. 4. cessat enim ea causa in illis, qui præcepta filiorum Noæ suscipiunt, & tributa pendunt. Ita Maimonides, & Samson Micosi, & Moses de Kotzi in præcepto jubente 15, & 108.

* Et Gazere habitantium, Jos. 16. 10. Gergesæos ad Christi usq; tempora superstites fuisse ex Evangelio apparet, Matt. 8. 28. nam hi ab initio se dediderant; Ideo omittuntur in hostium enumeratione. Deut. 20. 17. Jos. 9. 1.

* Jos. 11. 19, 20.

2 Sam. 21. 6.

De Officiis l. 3. c. 10.

Hebrews, sufteined some punishment for their craft; For, they were put under a certain personal servitude †, when, if they had dealt openly, they might have been received into a tributary condition.

† *ut Brutiani olim à Romanis. Gellius* 10. 3. *Festus verbo Brutiani.*

XXX. *The words of an oath not to be extended too far.*

YEt is not the signification of an oath to be extended beyond the received custome of speech. Therefore they were not perjurd, who, when they had sworn they would not give their daughters in marriage to the *Benjamites*, permitted the ravished to live with the raptors. For, 'tis one thing to give; another thing not to require that which is taken away†. *Ambrose*, of this deed: *Which indulgence seemeth to carry with it a congruous revenge upon their intemperance, when they were permitted only to enjoy whom they had ravished, without the solemnity of marriage* *. Whereto is not unlike, that the *Achaians*, when the *Romans* allowed not of some things done by them, and confirmed by oath, requested them to alter what themselves pleased; and not bind the *Achaians* with religion to make the things void, which by oath they had established.

† *Nec hortabantur Israelitæ, nec prohibebant*, ait in hac historia Josephus. Seneca excerptorum 6. 2. *Lex eum tenet, qui juvat exulem, non qui patiatur juvari.*
* *De Officiis lib.* 2. *c.* 14.
Livius lib. 39.

XXXI. *Or*

XXXI. *An oath binds not, being made of unlawfull matter.*

THat an oath may be of force, it is requiſite the obligation be * lawfull. Wherefore a ſworn promiſe of a thing unlawfull, either naturally, or by divine interdict, or by human alſo (of which hereafter) will have no force at all. Well ſaith *Philo* the Jew *: *Whoſoever, for his oaths ſake, goes about any injuſt action, let him know, he is not an obſerver, but an everſor of an oath; which is worthy of great care and religion, and wherewith honeſt and righteous things are wont to be confirmed. For he adds one fault to another; to an oath not rightly made, and from which it had been better to abſtain, he adds an act unlawfull. Wherefore, abſtaining from the unjuſt action, let him pray to God, whoſe property is to have mercy, that he may obtain his pardon. For to chooſe a double evill, when one may be eaſed of the one half, is extreme folly and madneſs.* An example hereof may be given in *David*, who ſpared *Nabal*, whom he ſware he would kill. *Cicero* mentions a like example in the vow of *Agamemnom*; *Dionyſius Halicarneſſenſis* in the conjuration of the *Decemviri* about oppreſſing the Commonwealth. † Ambroſe *: *It is ſometimes againſt duty to perform a promiſe, to keep an oath.* Auguſtin: *If ones faith*

* *Tractat hoc bene Ambroſius de offic.* 1. *& alii relati in cauſæ* 22. *quæſtionem* 4. *Pertinet huc Canon* 7. *Concil. Hilerdenſis relati in Tom.* 3. *Conciliorum Galliæ, & in Hincmari opuſculis non pauca.*

* *Philo de ſpecial. Leg.*

1 Sam. 25.

Lib. 2.

† Seneca: *Præſtare fateor poſſe me tacitam fidem, ſi ſcelere careat: interim ſcelus eſt fides.* Ubi *interim* valet *interdum.*

* *Offic.* 1. *c. ult.*

faith be pawned to commit a sin, it is strange to call it faith. *Basil* saith the same, in his second to *Amphilochius.*

XXXII. *Or, which hinders a greater morall Good.*

YEa, although what is promis'd be not unlawfull, but hinders a greater morall good †, in this case also the oath will not be of value. The reason is, because we owe to God proficiency in good, so that we may not take away from our selves the liberty thereof. Hither pertains a remarkable passage of the forecited *Philo*, worthy to be read here: *Some are of so hard and unsociable a nature, either haters of mankind, or enslav'd by that cruel mistress anger, that they grow more obstinate in their ferity of manners by swearing, they will not admit such a one to their Table or within their doors, they will never do him any good, they will never receive any thing from him till death.* That he saith, some swar never to do good to such or such*, the *Hebrews* called this *A vow concerning beneficence.* The form whereof, as the *Hebrew* Masters have it, is agreeable to that *Korban* in the Gospel, of this sense: *Be it a gift dedicated to God, whatsoever good thou mightest ever receive from me.* The vow, the penalty of consecration being added, was judged very valid by the *Hebrew* Masters (the worst

† *Quale Honorii de pace nunquam facienda cum Alarico, Zozimo narrante. Vide Concil. Hilerd. d. loco. Hincmarum quoq; dicto opusculo ad interrogationem 14.*

* *Vide Baba Kama c. 9 sect. 10. & ibi notata à doctissimo Constantino. Levit. 5. 6. Mat. 15. 5.*

worst interpreters in this part of divine Law) though 'twere made against one's parents: which, in that place, is refuted by Christ, in whose words *to honour* is *to benefit*, as appears by comparing the place in *Mark*, and 1 *Tim*. 5. 3, 17. and *Numb*. 23. 11. But against whomsoever it is conceived, we shall rightly pronounce the oath not obligatory, because, as we have said, it is against proficiency. τιμᾶν.

XXXIII. *Of oaths about things impossible.*

WE need not speak of things altogether impossible: for it is manifest enough that no man is obliged unto such. But, for that which is impossible for the time, or upon supposition, the obligation is pendent, so that he who hath sworn upon a supposition, is bound to do his best endeavour, to render that possible which he hath sworn. Ad impossibile neminem obligari.

XXXIV. *In oaths God is named, and in what sense.*

THe form of swearing differs in words, agrees in deed. For it ought to have this sense, that God may be invoked, to wit, in this manner, *God be witness*, or *God be Avenger*, which two are coincident. For, when a Superiour having right of punishing is call'd to witness, there

there is withall asked of him a revenge of perfidiousness †: and he that knows all things is a revenger, because a witnes. Plutarch *: *Every oath ends in imprecation, if one shall be perjurd.* Hither pertein the old forms of leagus, wherein it was the custom to use sacrifices, as appears, *Gen.* 15. 9, &c. As that *Roman* form in Livy †: *Thou O* Jupiter *so smite him, as I do this Hogg.* And elswhere; *Praying the Gods, they would so slay him, as he had slain the Lamb.* And in *Polybius* and *Festus*; *If wittingly I deceive, so let* Diespiter *cast me away, as I cast away this stone.*

† Ambrosius ad Valentinianum imp *Quid est jurare, nisi ejus quem testaris fidei tuæ præsulem divinam potentiam confiteri?* Vide formulam insignem Chagani Avarorum apud Menandrum excerptis Legationum.

* *Quæst. Roman.*

† *Tu Jupiter ita illum ferito, ut ego hunc porcũ.* *Liv. lib.* 1. *Lib.* 21. *Deos precatus ita se mactarent, ut ipse agnum mactasset. Si sciens fallo ita me Diespiter ejiciat, ut ego hunc lapidem.*

XXXV. *In oaths also other things are named, with respect to God.*

Moreover, it is an antient custom to swear by other things named, & by other persons; either because they wished those to be hurtfull to them, as the Sun, the earth, the heaven, the Prince; or because they desired to be punisht in the same, as in their head, in their children, in their Country, in their Prince. Nor was this the custom of prophane nations onely, but of the Jews, as *Philo* * sheweth. For he saith, men that are about to swear, ought not for every matter presently *to have recourse to the maker and father of all things*, but to swear by their parents, by heaven, earth, the universe. Where-

* *De special. Legibus.*

Wherewith agrees, what the Interpreters of *Homer* note, that those old *Greeks* were not wont *hastily to swear by the Gods, but by other * things present*, as, *by this Scepter*: and that the same was constituted by the most righteous King *Rhadamanthus*, is deliverd by *Porphyry* and the *Scholiast* upon *Aristophanes*. So we read, that *Joseph* swore by the life of *Pharaoh*, according to the manner of the *Ægyptians*, noted there by *Abenesdras*; *Elisha*, by the life of *Elija*. And truly Christ, in the 5. of *Matthew*, doth not, as some think, pronounce these oaths less lawfull, than the other made by the express name of God: but, whereas the *Hebrews* less regarded these, out of an opinion like to his who said, *He did not think the scepter to be God*, He shews that these also are truly oaths. For *Ulpian* too hath very well said; *He that swears by his life, seems to swear by God; for he swears with respect of the Deity*. So saith Christ, *He that sweareth by the Temple, sweareth by him that dwelleth therein*: *and, he that sweareth by heaven, sweareth by him that sitteth thereon*. But the *Hebrew* Masters of those times were of opinion, that men were not bound by the oaths made by Creatures, except a penalty being added, as, if the thing of which the oath was made, were consecrated to God. For, this is the oath *Korban*, or *of the gift*, whereof, not only in the said place of *Matthew*, but

* De Socrate Apollonius apud Philostratum 6. *Jurabat per ista, non ut per Deos, sed ne per Deos juraret.*

Gen. 42. 15.
2 Reg. 2. 2. *Adde* 2 Reg. 4. 30.
Cant. 2. 7.

L. Qui per D. de jurejur. Ita & Grat. causa. 22. quæst. 1.

Matth. 23. 21.

but in the Laws also of the *Tyrians*, mention was extant, as we learn out of *Josephus* 's disputation against *Appion**. This errour therefore, in that place, Christ opposeth. *Tertullian* saith, the antient Christians sware *by the life of the Prince* more sacred than all *Genii*. In *Vegetius* there is a form, above mentioned, wherein the Christian soldier swear, not by God only, but also by the Majesty of the Emperour, which is next to God to be lov'd and honour'd.

* *Nec aliunde arbitrer Orientis populos dictos Græcis καρβάνας, quæ vox apud Æschylum & Euripidem exstat. καρβάνα δ' αὐδάς, apud eundem Æschylum.*

XXXVI. *Of swearing by false Gods.*

AND, if one swear by false Gods, he shall be bound †; because, though under false notes, yet in a generall notion, he looks upon the Deity: wherefore the true God, if one swear falsly, interprets it to be done to his dishonour. And we see that holy men, though they never gave an oath under that form, much less did they ever swear so; which I wonder is permitted by *Duarenus*; yet, if the persons with whom they dealt, could not be drawn to swear otherwise, they contracted with them, themselves truly swearing as they ought, but receiving from them such an oath as could be had. Wee have an example hereof in *Jacob* and *Laban*, *Gen.* 31. 53. This is that which * *Austin* saith: Even he that swears *by a stone, if he swear false, is* † *perjur'd*. After:

† Liber Sap. c. 14. ut vertit Latinus: *Non enim juratorum virtus, sed peccantium pœna perambulat semper injustorum prævaricationem.* *Aug. epist. ad Pub.* 154.

* *Serm.* 28. *de verb. Apostoli. citatur c. ecce dico, causa* 22. *qu.* 5.

† *Et qui per lapidem jurat, si falsum jurat, perjurus est. Non te audit lapis loquentem, sed punit Deus fallentem.* Augustin.

ter: *The stone hears not thy words, but God punishes thy fraud.*

XXXVII. *The effect of an oath.*

THe principal effect of an oath, is *to end controversies*, as the divine writer to the *Hebrews* saith: and likewise Philo, *An oath is Gods testimony of a thing in question*: and Halicarnassensis, *The last* * *confirmation among men, both Greeks and Barbarians, which no time will abolish, is that which by oath calleth the Gods to be Sureties of their Covenants.* So, to the *Egyptians* was an oath *the greatest assurance among men.* Wherefore he that swears is under a double tye, first that the words agree unto his meaning, which *Chrysippus* calls ἀληθορκεῖν, next that the deed agree unto his words, which he calls εὐορκεῖν. He that offends in the former, is said by the same *Chrysippus* *, ψευδορκεῖν, in the later ἐπιορκεῖν, very distinctly, though the terms are wont sometimes to be confounded.

* Procopius Persicor. 2. *Jusjurandum quod ab hominibus habetur omnibus ultimum atq; firmissimum & fidei mutuæ & veracitatis pignus.*

Diod. Sic. μεγίστη παρ' ἀνθρώποις πίστις.

* *Hoc* ψευδορκεῖν *vetatur* Exod. 20. ἐπιορκεῖν Levit. 19. *ut Hebræi volunt præcepto jubente* 240.

XXXVIII. *When an oath gives a right to God and man, when to God alone.*

ANd verily, if the matter be such, and the words so conceived, that they be referred not to God alone, but to man, a right doubtless will be acquir'd by man out of the oath, as out of a promise or contract, which ought to be understood most simply

simply and plainly. But, if either the words do not respect man, by conferring upon him a right; or, if they do respect him, but there is somewhat which may be oppos'd against him; then, such will be the force of the oath, that indeed he can attain no right, yet neverthelefs he that hath sworn is bound to God to stand to his oath. An example hereof is in him, who by unjust fear gave cause to a sworn promise †. For he attains no right, or such as he ought to render, upon this ground that he gave cause to the loss. So we see the *Hebrew* Kings, both reproved by the Prophets, and punished by God, because they kept not their faith sworn to the *Babylonian* Kings. *Cicero* commends the *Tribune Pomponius*, who performed what being compell'd by terrour he had sworn. *So much*, saith he, *in those times did an oath prevail.* Wherefore it was not only the duty of *Regulus* to return to prison, how unjust soe'r it was; but of those ten also, whom *Cicero* mentions, to return to *Annibal:* for they were obliged by their oath.

† *Austin teacheth, that an oath extorted by force is also to be kept for the reverence of God.* Epist. 124, 125.

Ezech. 17.12. 13. 15.

Jerem. 29. 7.

Tantum temporibus illis juramentum valebat. Cic. Offic. 3.

Tolet. l. 4. c. 22.

Offic. 3.

Tho. 2. 2. 89. art. 7. & ibi Cajet. Alex. Imol. in c. verum de jurejur. Soto lib. 8. q. 1. art. 7.

XXXIX. *Of an oath to a Pirate, or to a Tyrant.*

NOr is it thus only among publick enemies, but among all: For, the person alone to whom we swear, is not respected; but He by whom we swear *, God,

* Gregoras: *Perjurium Deo culpam impingit negligentiæ.*

God, who sufficeth to create an obligation. *Cicero* therefore is to be rejected, when he saith, it is no perjury, if the price promised for life be not brought unto Robbers: because a Pirate is not a determinate but a common enemy of all, with whom we ought to have no society either of faith or oath. Which is also said by him elsewhere of a tyrant; and by *Brutus*, in *Appian*, *With a tyrant, the Romans have no faith, no Religion of an oath*. But, as in the constituted Law of Nations it is true, and shall be shewed hereafter, that an enemy differs from a Pirate; so cannot that difference have place here, where, though the right of the person is deficient, God is concernd†: for which reason an oath is called by the name of a *vow*. Besides, it is not true which *Cicero* assumes, that there is no society of right with a Robber. For 'twas well answerd by *Tryphoninus*, that a thing deposited is to restored to a thief*, by the very Law of Nations, if the owner thereof appear not. Wherefore I cannot allow that which is deliverd by some, that he who hath promised some thing to a Robber, may satisfy his conscience with a momentaneous payment, so that it may be lawfull for him to recover what he hath payd. For the words, in an oath, as to God, are to be understood most simply and with effect. And therefore he that returned secretly to the enemy, and again

Civil. 2.

† Plutarchus Lysandro: *Qui juramento hostem circumvenit, is ostendit à se hostem metui, Deum contemni.*

* Et ei qui regnum sine jure invasit: quomodo Orosferni depositum redditum à Prienensibus. *Polybius & Diodorus Siculus in excerptis Peiresianis.*

gain departed, made not good his oath concerning his return, as it was rightly judged by the *Roman Senate*.

XL. *Of an oath to one that is perfidious.*

* ——T. *Fregisti fidem.* A. *Quam neq; dedi, neq; do infideli cuipiam.*

BUt that of *Accius**, T. *Thou hast broken thy faith.* A. *Which I neither gave, nor give to any one that is unfaithfull*, may be allowed of in this sense, if the sworn promise had openly respect unto another promise, which was as it were an implicit condition to it; not, if the promises be of divers kind, and without mutuall respect; For then must every one keep that which himself hath sworn. And upon this ground *Regulus* is praised by this compellation of the Poet:

L. sicut in fine. de jurejurando c. pervenit quod est 3. de jurejur. Adde L. Lege fun. in fine D. de lege Commiss.

Silius.

Thy Memory is lasting, thy Fame grow'th:
'Cause to th' unfaithful thou hast kept thy oath.

The Psalmist, where he enumerates the vertues of a good man, addes this: *Having sworn to his own hurt, he changeth not.*

Psal. 15.

XLI. *Of the Heirs obligation.*

HEre is to be noted, whensoever the person hath no right, by reason of some such defect which we have said, but the

the obligation is to God, in this case the Heir of him that hath sworn is not bound. Because, as goods pass to the Heir, that is, such goods as are in the commerce of men, so do the burdens accompanying the goods pass with them; and not other things, which one oweth out of the duty of piety, favour, or faith. For these do not pertein to that which is strictly called right among men.

XLII. *Two cases wherein the obligation ceaseth.*

BUt also where the person hath a right, if yet the oath regard the utility of any one, and he refuseth † it, he that hath sworn shall not be bound. Neither shall he be bound, if the quality * ceaseth under which he hath sworn to any: as, if a Magistrate cease to be a magistrate. *Curio* in *Cæsar*†, to those that had been the soldiers of *Domitius*, speaks thus: *How could he hold you bound by oath, when having cast away his authority and left his command, being a private man and a captive, himself was come under the power of another?* And after he saith, the oath was voided by * the loss of his place.

† Plautus Rudente: *Jurisjurandi rogo gratiam facias.*

* *Similia vide in L. si duas. Sect. Gentium. D. de excus. tut. & apud Gailium 2. observ. 144. num. 8. & de Arrest. 10. 9. & apud Azor. Instit. mor. 5. 22. q. 6. p. 1.*

* *Lib. 2. de bello civ.*

* *Capitis diminutione.*

XLIII. *Of*

XLIII. *Of that which is done against ones oath.*

C. dilecto. de præben. Covar. in d. c. quamvis p. 2. sect. 2. n. 10.

IT is a queſtion, whether that which is done againſt ones oath be unlawfull only, or alſo void. Of which I think we muſt diſtinguiſh thus: that if ones faith be onely engag'd, the act done againſt oath is valid, namely a teſtament, or ſale; not valid, if the oath be ſo conceiv'd, that withall it conteins a full abdication of power to that act.

XLIV. *What Superiours can do about the oaths of their ſubjects.*

Auguſt. epiſt. 240, 241.

THe acts of Superiours cannot ſo far prevail, that an oath, ſo far as it was truly obligatory, is not to be performed: for that is of naturall and divine right.

Tho. 2. 1. qu. 89. art. 9.

But becauſe our acts are not fully in our own power, but ſo that they depend upon our Superiours, therefore may there be a twofold act of Superiours about that which is ſworn, the one directed upon the perſon of him that ſwears, the other upon the perſon to whom he ſwears. Upon the perſon of him that ſwears it may be directed, either before the oath is taken, by making ſuch oath void, in as much as the right of the inferiour is conteind under the power of the ſuperiour; or after the oath is taken, by forbidding it to be fulfill'd.

fill'd. For, an Inferiour, as Inferiour, could not bind himſelf, but ſo far as it ſhould pleaſe his Superiour: for he had not more ample power. Thus, by the Hebrew Law, Husbands made void the Oaths of their Wives, Fathers of their Children, which were not yet in their own power. *Seneca* † propoſes this queſtion: *What if a Law be made, that none ſhall do, that which I have promiſed my Friend I will do?* and anſwers, *The ſame Law defends me, which forbids me.* But, the act alſo may be mixt of both, as, if the Superiour ordain, what the Inferiour ſhall ſwear in this or that caſe, namely, out of fear, or weakneſs of judgement, ſhall be of force, if it be approved by him. And upon this ground may be defended thoſe abſolutions of oaths, which of old * were exercis'd by Princes, and are now, by the will of Princes, exercis'd by the Prelates of the Church, for the better ſecuring of piety. Upon the perſon of him to whom one ſwears, the act may be directed by taking away from him the right which he hath gotten, or alſo, if he have no right, by forbidding his emolument out of ſuch an oath; and that two ways, either for his puniſhment, or for the publick good, by vertue of ſupereminent dominion. Hence alſo may be underſtood, if the party ſwearing be not of the ſame country with him to whom the oath is made, what his

C. Venientes de jurejur. c. 1. de probibit. feud. alien. per Fed.

† *Lib. 4. de Beneſic. 35.*

* *Sueton. Tib. 35. ſic & in Hiſpania diu uſurpatum notat Ferdinand. Vaſquez de ſucceſſ. creat. l. 2. ſect. 18. L. ult. ad mun. Molin diſp. 149. c. ſi vero: de jurejur.*

or the others Rulers may do concerning it. But, he that hath sworn and promised something to a nocent person as such, namely, to a pirate, cannot therefore take away from him, in the way of punishment, the right which he hath gotten by the promise: because then the words would have no effect, which by all means is to be avoided.

XLV. *What oaths are properly meant in the charge of Christ against swearing.*

HEre it is observable by the way, that the words of Christ and of *James* against swearing, do not properly belong to an *assertory* oath, whereof are some examples in the Apostle *Paul*, but to the *promissory* of a future uncertain thing. This evidemtly appears by the opposition in the words of Christ: *Ye have heard, it hath been said to them of old, Thou shalt not forswear thy self, but shalt render to God thy oath. But I say unto you, swear not at all*; and the reason given by *James* is this, * *Lest ye be found deceitfull* †: for that is the meaning there. The same is proved by the words of Christ; *But let your Communication be yea, yea; nay, nay*: which is exprest by *S. James* thus; *But let your yea be yea; and your nay, nay* ‡. Where the first *yea*, and *nay*, signifies the promise, the later its performance. For *yea* is a word of promising: whence it is explain'd

* *μὴ εἰς ὑπόκρισιν πέσητε.*

† *Eum sensum vox ὑποκρίσεως apud Hellenistas habet, ut apparet Job* 34. 30. *Matt.* 24. 51. *& alibi.*

‡ *ubi manifeste est figura quam πλοκὴν Rhetores vocant, ut in illo,* ex illo Corydon Corydon est tempore nobis. *Et in altero simili*: Ad illum diem Memmius erat Memmius.

explain'd by *Amen*, Apoc. 1. 7. and of the same signification among the *Roman* Lawyers are the words μάλιστα and *quidni*, in answer to a stipulation. For the implement-ion of a promise, it is taken in that place of *Paul*, where he saith, All the promises of God in Christ are *Yea* and *Amen*. Hence the old saying of the *Hebrews*, *A just mans yea is yea, and his nay is nay*. On the contrary, whose deeds differ from their words, with them is said to be *yea* and *nay*: that is, their *yea* is *nay*, and their *nay* is *yea*. So the Apostle himself expounds it: for when he had denyed himself to have used lightness, he addeth, his speech was not *yea* and nay †. Now, if *yea* and *nay* signify lightness, it follows, that *yea yea*, *nay nay*, signify constancy. Christ therefore saith the same with *Philo* *, *It is best and most profitable, and to the rational nature most convenient, to abstein from swearing, and so to accustom ones self to veracity, that ones word may be taken for an oath* †. Josephus of the Essens: *Whatsoever they say is firmer than an oath: and to swear is accounted, among them, a thing superfluous*. From the *Essens*, or those *Hebrews* whom the *Essens* followed, this seems received † by *Pythagoras*, whose sentence 'tis, *Let no man swear by the Gods, but every one take care of his credit, that he may be believed*

2 Cor. 1. 20.

2 Cor. 1. 18, 19.

† *Festus varias, referens sententias de significatione vocis* naucum, *sic scribit*: Quidam aiunt ex Græco ναὶ καὶ οὐχὶ levem hominem significari. *Recte in hoc Festi loco scripseris* ἂν καὶ, *ut sæpe apud Homerum: id enim ad vocem* nauci *propius accedit.*

*De Decalogo.

† Idem Philo de special. leg. *Viri boni oratio pro juramento sit firmo, immutabili, fallere nescio*,

† *Nam & Hermippus Pythagoricus Pythagoræ Philosophiam ab Hebræis ductam dicebat, teste Origene contra Celsum. Idem & Josephus Hebræus prodidit, & Jamblichus Pythagoricus.*

without an oath *. The *Scythians* say of themselves to *Alexander*, as *Curtius* relateth, *Think not that the Scythians confirm their friendship by oath : * they swear by keeping their word.* † *Cicero* relates in his Oration for L. *Cornelius Balbus*, When one at *Athens*, who had lived amongst them in great repute for his gravity and sanctity, had publickly given his testimony, and approched to the Altars to make his oath, all the Judges with one voyce reclamed, and would not let him swear; because they would not have it thought, that truth depended more upon the religion of an oath, than upon the word of an honest man. With the saying of Christ well agrees that of *Hierocles* upon the golden verses : *He that in the beginning said, Reverence an oath, therein gave a precept to abstain from swearing about such things, which may be done and not done* *, *and are of an uncertain issue. For such things are little to be regarded,*

* Philo : *Jam enim is à quo jusjurandum exigitur, perfidiæ est suspectus.* Sophoclis Oedipode Coloneæ dixerat Oedipus: *Nolo te adigere jurejurando ut malum. Respondet Theseus : Nec plus haberes inde quam vocis sonum.* Marcus Antoninus in viri boni descriptione : *Nec opus habens jurejurando.* Chrysost. de statuis 15. *Si credis veracem esse eum quicum tibi negotium est, noli ei jurejurandi imponere necessitatem; quod si scis fore ut mentiatur, ne coge eum & pejerare.* * *Colendo fidem jurant.*

† Cicero pro Roscio Comœdo : *Quæ pœna à Diis immortalibus perjuro, hæc eadem mendaci constituta est: Non enim ex pactione verborum quibus jusjurandum comprehenditur, sed ex perfidia & malitia per quam insidiæ tenduntur alicui, Dii immortales hominibus irasci & succensere consuerunt.* Solonis dictum celebratur : *Ea esto probitate, ut ei magis quam juramento credatur.* Clemens quoq; Alexandrinus dixit viri boni esse, *Fidem promissi ostendere in Verborum ac vitæ stabilitate & constantia.* Alexis Comicus : *Nutus mei pro Jurejurando valent.* * Bene hoc animadvertit Chrysostomus de statuis 12. *Periculosum est de suo actu jurare. multa enim nobis eripit ipsa rerum natura, subjecta casibus.*

and

and are mutable, and therefore neither are they worthy of an oath, nor is it safe. And *Libanius* accounts it among the praises of a Christian Emperour, *He is so far from perjury, that he is even afraid to swear the truth* †.

† Eustachius ad illud Odysseæ ξ. ἀλλ' ἤτοι ὅρκον μὲν ἐάσομεν, sic ait: *In rebus incertis non ad asseverationem Juramentum adhibendum, sed preces pro bono exitu.*

XLVI. *Of faith given without an Oath.*

THerefore in many places, in stead of swearing, it was invented, that faith should be bound by giving the right hand (which was * *the firmest bond of faith among the Persians*) or by some other sign: which was of that force, that if the promise were not fulfilled, the promiser was accounted no less detestable, than if he had forsworn himself. Principally of Kings and Princes it is a most usual saying, *Their word is as strong as an Oath.* For, they ought to be such, that they may say with *Augustus*, *Bonæ fidei sum*, My credit's good; and with *Eumenes*, *I will lose my life sooner than my credit* †. *Cæsars* right hand is praised by *Cicero* for firmness in keeping pro-

* πίστις βεβαιοτάτη. *Diod. lib.* 16.

Pan. in c. ad Aurel. De his quæ vi vel metus causa. Jas. in lib. 3. ¶. *jurari. D. de jurejur. Mynf. obs.* 17. *Cent.* 1.

† Guntherus Ligurinus: *Nudo jus & reverentia verbo Regis inesse solet, quovis juramine major.* De Evagora Salaminis rege Isocrates: ὁμοίως τοῖς ἐν τοῖς λόγοις ὁμολογίαις, ὥσπερ τοῖς ἐν τοῖς ὅρκοις διαφυλάττων. Symmach. 10. 19. *Nunquam major spes, quam in bonorum Principum sponsione.* Nicetas de Alexio Isaci fratre lib. 3. *Regibus jurisjurandi fides ante omnia alia ponenda est.*

mises, no less than valour in wars and battails: and in the Heroical times the Scepter lifted up went for the Oath of Kings, as *Aristotle* hath noted, 3. *Polit.* 14.

XLVII. OF LEAGUES. *They are lawfull with aliens from true Religion, by the Law of Nature.*

LEagues are Covenants or Agreements made by command of the highest powers: wherein the parties are bound over to the divine wrath, in case they break their faith. It is a famous question, Whether they may be enterd into with those that are aliens from true Religion: which in the Law of Nature hath no doubt or difficulty; for that Law is so cōmon to all men, that it admitteth not any difference of Religion. But the question is about the Law Divine: out of which it is discussed, not by * Divines only, but by some Lawyers too, and amongst them by *Oldradus* and *Decianus*.

* *Antoninus*, *Cajet. Tolet. Molina*, *Valdesius*, *Malderus*.
Tho. 2.2.*qu.*10. *art.* 10. *Oldr. consf.* 71. *Decian.* 3. *consf.* 20.

XLVIII. *They are not universally forbidden by the Hebrew Law.*

FIrst let us consider of the old Divine Law, and after of the new. It was lawful, before the Law of *Moses*, to contract a League with aliens from Religion, for

for an offensive and harmless behaviour. We have an example in the League of *Jacob* with *Laban* : to say nothing now of *Abimelech*, seeing it is not certain he was an Idolater. Nor did the Law given by *Moses* make any change. The *Egyptians* may be an example: who were then (no doubt) Idolaters; yet are the *Hebrews* forbidden to be averse from them. The seven Nations are to be excepted, condemnd by divine sentence, whereof the *Israelites* were delegated to be the executioners. For these persisting in their Idolatry, and refusing to submit, might not be spared; to whom, by divine decree, were added the *Amalekites*. Leagues of commerce also, and such like perteining to the utility of both or of either party, are by the Law permitted with the prophane: for nothing is found to hinder them. And we have the examples of Leagues which *David* and *Solomon* made with *Hiram* King of *Tyrians* : and it is observable, that in the sacred history the league made by *Solomon* is said to be made according to the wisedom which God had given him. Indeed, the Law of *Moses* specially commands, *to do good unto their Countrymen*; Moreover, the peculiar diet and course of life, prescribed to the Jews, did scarce admit any familiar conversation with other people. Yet doth it not follow hence, either that it was not lawfull to do good to foreiners,

Gen. 31. 44.

Deut. 23. 7.

Deut. 7. 1.

Deut. 25. 17.

Levit. 19. 8.

Deut. 23. 1.

ἀγαπᾷν τὸν πλησίον.

reiners, or that it was not alſo laudable, which the ill Interpretation of later Maſters, not rightly, hath collected thence. And therefore *Juvenal* ſaith of the Jews, *That they would not ſhew the way to any differing from them in Religion.* Where, by the example of ſhewing the way, are ſignified eaſy courteſies and benefits that may be done without any trouble or

Offic. 1.
De benef. 6. 9.

charge; ſuch as *Cicero* and *Seneca* ſay are to be done to ſtrangers, whom we never

Hiſtor. 5.

ſaw before. To the ſame purpoſe is that of *Tacitus* of the ſame Jews; *Among themſelves they are of obſtinate faith, and very mercifull; to all others they bear an hoſtile hatred.* So, in the New Teſtament we often read, that the Jews have no dealing with other Nations; and *Apollonius Molo* objected to them, *that they admitted not thoſe, that had different opinions of God, nor had any thing to do with men of another inſtitution* †. But, that this is not the ſenſe of the Law, Chriſt hath taught us by his own example, when, being every where moſt obſervant of the Law, he refuſed not water from the *Samaritan* woman. And *David* long before ſought for refuge among ir-

† Amici Antiochi apud Diodorum Judæos accuſant, *Solos ex omnibus populis inſociabiles eſſe ex traneis, ita ut cæteros pro hoſtibus ducant.* Sequitur de iiſdem: *cum nulla gente alia menſam habere communem, neq; bene eos aliis velle.* Mox eis tribuitur, *odium humani generis.* Et apud Philoſtratum Tyanenſis de Judæis, *vitæ genus adeo ſecretum ab humano commercio reperērunt, ut ne menſam quidem cum aliis communem habeant. Sicut & p ſſi n Judæis apud* Joſephum *objicitur*, τὸ ἄμικτον, τὸ ἀσύμφυλον, ἐ[illegible]

religious

religious people, no where reprehended for it. *Solomon* in *Josephus*, dedicating the Temple, and praying, that God in that place would hear also the prayers of strangers, saith, *We are not of an inhuman disposition, nor ill affected to those that are not of our own Nation.* From this rule are to be excepted not only the Nations before mentiond, but the *Ammonites* too, and *Moabites*; of whom it is written, *Thou shalt not seek their prosperity* (so we turn it rather than *their peace*) *nor their good all thy days.* In which words beneficent leagues with them are forbidden, and not a right of War allowed; or to be sure (which is the judgment of some *Hebrews*) peace is forbidden to be asked of them, not, to be accepted when tis offerd. Certainly, a right of War upon the *Ammonites* is denyed the *Hebrews*, *Deut.* 2. 19. Nor did *Jephtha* carry arms against them, but after he had tryed the ways of an equal Peace; nor *David*, till he was provoked by cruel injuries. It remains, that we enquire about society in War. That this also, before the Law, was not unlawfull with prophane Nations, appears by the example of *Abraham* *, aiding the wicked *Sodomites* with his arms. Nor do we find any thing in this matter generally changed by the Law of *Moses*. And this we see to have been the opinion of the *Asmonaans* †, being both skilful of the Law and very reverent, as

tis

Antiq. 8. 2. Deut. 23. 6. Jud. 11. 16. 2 Sam. 10.

* Idem cum Escole & Anero fœdus fecit. Sic & David cum Achi & Naaso: Solomon cum Ægyptiis: Asa cum Benadado.

† Laus eorum est in Thargume Chaldaico, in libris Maccabaicis, in epistola ad Hebræos. Horum exemplum secuti Impp. & Reges Christiani fœdera aut cum non Christianis, aut cum non sanè Christianis fecere, Constantinus cum Gotthis & Vandalis, Justinianus cũ Longobardis, &c. Adi Johan. de Carthag. l. 3. *De jure Belli Rom. Pontificis*, c. 1. *Julius* 2. *Pontifex Turcis usus.*

tis evident by their Religious obſervation of the Sabbath, no other uſe of arms being permitted, but only for ſelf-defenſe. And theſe yet made a league with the *Lacedemonians* and *Romans*, by the aſſent of the Prieſts and people : yea and publickly offerd Sacrifice for their ſafety. Inſtances to the contrary have peculiar cauſes. For if, beſide thoſe that were expreſſed in the Law, God had ſignified by his Prophets, any Kings or Nations to be odious to him, and condemned to an overthrow ; to undertake the defenſe of them, or to joyn forces with them, was, without doubt, impiety. Hither perteins that of the Prophet to *Jehoſaphat* touching the King of *Iſrael : ſhouldeſt thou help the ungodly, and love them that hate* † *the Lord ? therefore is wrath upon thee from before the Lord*. For *Michaia* the Prophet had already foretold an unhappy iſſue of the War. And that of another Prophet to *Amaziah, O King, let not the Army of Iſrael go with thee : for the Lord is not with Iſrael, to wit, with any of the Children of Ephraim*. Now, that this comes not from the nature of the League, but from ſome peculiar quality of the perſon, is evinc'd even hence; becauſe *Jehoſaphat* was heavily rebuked, a curſe alſo being added, for this, that for commerce ſake he had joyned himſelf with *Ahaziah* King of *Iſrael*, and had entred into ſuch a ſociety, as *David* and *Solomon*

2 Paralip. 19. 2.

† Gratianus Valenti patruo contra Scythas opem petenti ſcripſit, *Fas non eſſe ſocialia arma jungere cum eo qui Dei ſit hoſtis*. Zonaras.

2 Paralip. 25. 7.

2 Paralip. 20. 37.

Solomon had made with *Hiram*: whom we have said to have been, for that reason, partly not reprehended, partly commended. For, what is added, that *Ahaziah* did wickedly, ought to be referred to his whole life: for which God was offended with him, and with all his enterprizes, as this history is explained in the book entitled *Clement*'s Constitutions. Moreover, this is to be noted, that their cause, who being sprung from *Jacob* had forsaken God well known unto them, was worse than the cause of strangers. For against those Revolters the rest of their Countrymen were armed * by a Law extant. Sometimes also Leagues are blamed for some vice of the mind whence they did proceed: so was *Asa* reprehended by the Prophet, for betaking himself to the society of the *Syrian*, upon distrust of God; which he had shewed in sending to the *Syrian* things consecrated. But the same King was reproved too, because he had plac'd his hope, not in God, but in Physicians. Wherefore, it doth not, from this history, more follow that it is evil, by it self, or generally, to contract society with such as the *Syrians* were, than to consult with Physicians. For, many things not unlawfull are vitiated by the mind, as *David*'s muster, and *Ezechia*'s shewing of his treasure. So elswhere, confidence put in *Egypt* is reprehended, when it was lawful neverthelefs for *Solomon* to contract

2 Paralip. 16. 2, 7. Es. 8. 6.

Lib. 6. cap. 18.

Deut. 13. 13.
* Adde exemplum Josue cap. 22.

2 Paralip. 16. 12.
Ambros. ad Roman. c. 3.
Auct. imperf. ad Matth. c. 16.

2 Sam. 24.

2 Reg. 20. 13.
Esa. 31. 1.
1 Reg. 3. 1.

tract affinity with the *Egyptian*. To all which, this is to be added, that the *Hebrews*, under the state of the old Law, had express promises of victory, if they kept
Deut. 28. 7. the Law; the less need had they to have recourse unto human aids. Lastly, there
Prov. 1. 15. 13. 20. 22. 24. 24. 1. are indeed extant in *Solomons* Proverbs, Sentences not a few, of shunning the society of wicked men: But these are the *Advisos* of prudence, not Precepts of Law; and those very Admonitions, as most moral sayings, are capable of very many exceptions.

XLIX. *Nor are they forbidden by the Evangelical Law.*

Vict. de Indis relect. 1. n. 15. & 17. *Fra. Arias de bello n. 192.* *Cajet. 2. 2. qu. 40. art. 1.* *Molin. tract. 2. disp. 112.* Matth. 5. 45. Gal. 6. 10.

NOw, the Law of the Gospel hath changed nothing in this business; yea, it hath a more favorable aspect upon leagues, whereby aliens from Religion, on just cause, are relieved; because, it hath not left beneficence to all sorts of men, upon occasion given, only free and laudable, but hath put it under precept. For, by Gods example, who maketh his Sun to arise upon the good and evil, and sendeth rain to refresh them both, we are commanded to exclude no kind of men
Lib. 7. c. 3. from our benefits. *Tertullian* said well: *So long as Israel only was his people, God did justly command mercy toward their brethren alone: But after that he gave unto Christ the Nations for his inheritance,*

tance, and the ends of the earth for his possession, and that began to be paid which was promised in Hoseah, *They that were not my people shalbe my people, and the Nation that had not obtained mercy shall obtain mercy; from that time Christ hath extended unto all the Law of fraternal benignity, excluding none from our compassion, no more than from his vocation.* Which words are to be understood, with differenee of degree, that we must be good to all, but especially to the professors of the same Religion. In *Clement*'s Constitutions we read, *It is our duty to communicate of our goods to all; yet so, that we have a speciall eye to the poor Saints* †. Familiar conversation also with aliens from Religion is not prohibited: no not with them whose cause is worse, and who fall away from the rule of Christian Disciplin, is all commerce interdicted, but familiar without necessity, not also that which affords any hope for their amendment. And that which is in *Paul, Be yee not unequally yoked together with unbelievers: for what fellowship hath righteousness with unrighteousness? and what communion hath light with darkness? And what concord hath Christ with* Belial? *or what part hath he that believeth with an Infidel?* pertains to those that feasted in the Idol-Temples, and so either committed Idolatry, or at least made a shew thereof. This is manifest by the following

† *Perfecta liberalitas*, inquit Ambrosius offic. 1. 3. *fide, causa, loco, tempore commendatur, ut primum operis circa domesticos fidei.* Simile est illud Aristotelis; *Neq; enim par est aequalem curam subiri pro externis & pro amicis.* Nic.

2 Thess. 3. 15.

2 Cor, 6. 14, 15.

following words, *What agreement hath the Temple of God with Idols?* parallel to the words in the former Epistle to the
1 Cor. 10. 21. same, *Ye cannot be partakers of the Table of the Lord, and the table of the Devills.* Nor will the argument proceed rightly from this, that of our own accord we are not to submit to the Government of the prophane, nor contract mariage with them: For in both these cases appears greater hazard, or certainly greater difficulty, to the use of true Religion. Add, that these bonds are more lasting, and in matrimony there is a free choice; when leagues are to be made according to the exigence of times and places. And as it is no evill to do good to the prophane, so neither is it unlawfull to implore their help, as *Paul* invoked the aid of *Cæsar* and the Chief Captain.

L. *Cautions about such Leagues.*

Sylv. verbo bellum. 1. 9. 3. *Pan. in cap. quod super de voto.* † Vide Oration. Phartazæ ad Lazos apud Agathiam 3. Saxo lib. 9. in verbis Ludovici Regis Francor. ad Heraldum: *Nullam posse animorum intervenire concordiam dissona sacra complexis. Quamobrem petitorem opis primum religionis contubernio opus habere, neq; magnorum operum consortes existere posse, quos superna venerationis formula disparasset.*

Here then is no intrinsecal or universal pravity, but to be esteemed by the circumstances †. For, heed must be taken, lest too much commixture bring contagion to the infirm: to which end it will be profitable, their seats should be distinct, as the *Israelits* dwelt asunder

from

from the *Egyptians* *. Hither pertains, what we have elsewhere alleged, concerning the Religion of Jews and Christians in their fellow-souldiership with the Pagans. Again, if by such society the prophane State be like to receive great encrease, there will be no joyning with them, except in point of extreme necessity. Wherein hath place, what *Thucydides* said in a like matter: *They that are treacherously assaulted, as we are by the Athenians, are not to be blamed, if they seek for safety, and secure themselves, by the aid, not of Greeks only, but Barbarians.* For it is not every right, that is sufficient for the doing of that, which may be esteemed indirectly, if not directly, hurtfull to Religion. Because, in the first place we must seek the Kingdom of Heaven, that is, the propagation of the Gospel. It were to be wisht, that many Princes and people at this day would take into their consideration that free and pious speech of *Fulco* Archbishop once of *Rhemes*, admonishing *Charles* the simple thus: *Who may not be afraid, seeing you covet amity with the enemies of God* †, *and to the overthrow and ruine of the Christian name take unto you Pagan arms, and enter into leagues detestable? For there is little difference*

* Neq; enim ratione caret illud Alexandridæ:
Ego esse vester non queam commilito,
Quando nec Leges, nec mores consentiunt,
Sed multis inter se intervallis discrepant.

Lib. 1.

Matth. 6. 33.

Fred. lib. 4. hist. Remens. cap. 6.

† *Exemplum in Mancasa apud Nicetam rebus Isaaci Angeli l.* 2. Welfare the piety of *Emanuel* Duke of *Savoy*, who when he was able to take *Cyprus* by the aid of the *Turk*, refus'd it.

ference between associating with Pagans, and worshipping of Idols, God being deny'd. In *Arrianus* is extant a saying of *Alexander: They are great Offendors, who serve the Barbarians against the Greeks, contrary to the Laws of Gracia.*

LI. *All Christians are oblig'd to joyn in League against the enemies of Christianism.*

1 Cor. 12. 18, 26.

HEre is to be added, sith all Christians are members of one body, and are commanded to be sensible of one anothers pain, as this pertains to single persons, so doth it also concern Commonwealths as they are Commonwealths, and Kings as they are Kings. Nor ought every one, in his own particular only, but according to the power committed to him, to do service unto Christ. Now Kings and Commonwealths are not able to do thus, while an impious enemy overruns all with arms, except they mutually aid and assist each other †, which cannot commodiously be effected without entring a League to that purpose. Which League hath been long since entred, and the *Roman* Emperour, by common consent, chosen Prince thereof; Wherefore it is the duty of all Christians, according to their power, to contribute men or moneys to this common cause: and I do not see how any can be excused for not doing so, unless they

† Ad hanc rem vide Marianam lib. 30. Parutam l. 4. Bezarum 7. & 12.

they be engaged at home, and deteined by some inevitable war, or other the like unhappy hindrances.

LII. *If divers Confederates wage War, which is to be aided.*

THis question also is often incident, If divers wage war, to which of them he ought to give assistance, who is confederate to Both. Here first we must remember, that there is no obligation to unjust wars. He then is to be preferr'd who hath a just † cause of war, if he hath to do with one without; yea, if with one within the league. So * *Demosthenes* shews, the *Athenians* ought to assist their fellows the *Messenians*, against their other fellows the *Lacedæmonians*, if the injury begin from these. But this is true, so, unless it were agreed, that no aid should be sent against such a confederate. In the agreement of *Hannibal* with the *Macedonians*, it was an article, † *We will be enemies to your enemies, except the Kings, and Cities, and havens, wherewith we have league and friendship.* Moreover, if the confederates quarrel upon causes unjust on both sides (which may happen) neither part is to be taken. So it is said in *Aristides*: *Did they crave aid against aliens, 'twere easy to answer: but, when one confederate opposes another, they would not mix in the business.* But if

† In fidelitate Feudali dicitur: *Et si scivero velle te aliquem juste offendere, & inde generaliter vel specialiter fuero requisitus, meum tibi, sicut potero, præstabo auxilium.*

* *Orat. de Megalopoli.*

† *Polyb. l. 6.*

Leuctricâ 5.

confederates make war upon others, each upon just ground, if aids can be sent to both, *viz.* men or money, they are to be sent, as it is done about personall creditors: but, if his presence, who hath promised, be requir'd; seeing he cannot be present with both, reason determines him to prefer that side, wherewith his League is more * antient: which the *Acarnans* tell the *Spartans* in *Polybius*: and to the same effect is the answer of the *Roman Consul* to the *Campanians*, *It is meet, our relations should so be orderd, that no elder friendship and society be violated* †. Yet is this exception to be added: unless the yonger league have, beyond the promise, some thing that conteins in it, as it were, a translation of dominion *, that is, something of subjection. For so also, in *vendition* †; we say the former is to be preferr'd, except the later hath translated a dominion. So the *Nepesins* in *Livy* * held the faith of *dedition* more sacred than that of society. Some distinguish of these things more subtilly, but what I have said, as it is more simple and plain, so I suppose it is more true.

*Vide de Feudis lib. 4. c. 31. Libro 9.

† *Amicis auxilia ferenda contra hostes, non contra amicos*, dicit Ptolomæus Atheniensibus apud Appianum in Legationum excerptis. *Sylvest. in verb. bellum*, 1. 7.

* *Vide Radevicum* 2. 7.

† *Edicto Theoderici c.* 138.

* Lib. 6.

LIII. *Of the dissolution of a League.*

Dec. Cons. 407.

THe time being expir'd, the League is not to be conceiv'd tacitly renew'd, unless by such acts, which do admit no other

-ther interpretation; For a new obligation is not easily presumed. If one part hath violated the league, the other may depart from it. For the several heads of the League have every one the force of a condition. For example may be that in *Thucydides: They bear the blame of breaking the League, not, who being deserted betake themselves to others; but they, who perform not really that assistance which they had promised upon oath.* Elswhere in the same Historian: *If either part transgress their Articles never so little, the Agreement's broken.* But this is thus true, except it were otherwise condition'd; which is wont sometimes to be, that for every offense it may not be lawfull to depart from the League.

Dec. Cons. 260.

Lib. 1.

LIV. *Of Interpretation.*

IF we look upon him alone, who hath promised, he is bound of his own accord to perform that to which he meant to bind himself. *In a promise must be considered, what you thought, not what you said*, as *Cicero* hath it. But, because internal acts are not visible by themselves, and somewhat certain must be determined, lest there be no obligation at all, if every one might free himself by affixing on his own words what sense he please; by the dictate of natural reason, he to whom any thing is promis'd, hath

In fide quid senseris non quid dixeris cogitandum. De off. 1.

a right to compell the promiser to that, which right interpretation suggesteth. For otherwise the matter would have no end, which in morals is accounted for impossible. In this sense, it may be, *Isocrates*, when he had discoursed of Covenants in the prescription against *Callimachus* (as the most eminently learned *Petrus Faber* hath rightly amended the place) saith: *This Common Law we men perpetually use among our selves*; nor *Grecians* only, but *Barbarians* too, as he had said a little afore. Pertinent is that in the old form of Leagues in *Livy*, *Without evil deceit, as those words here are most rightly* † *understood at this day*. The measure of right interpretation is, a collection of the meaning out of signes most probable. If there be no conjecture drawing another way, the words are to be understood according to their propriety, not Grammatical, which is from their original, but from popular * use. Wherefore the *Locrians* used a foolish refuge for their perfidiousness, when, having promised they would stand to their agreement, so long as they stood upon the earth, and caried heads upon their shoulders, they cast out the earth put into their shoos, and threw away the heads of other men placed on their shoulders, as if by that means

Liv. lib. 1. *Sine dolo malo, utiq; ea hic hodie rectissime intellecta sunt.*
† Vota interpretanda ut communiter sumuntur, notant Hebræi ad Num. 30.
* *Quem penes arbitrium est, & jus & norma loquendi.*
Bene Procopius Vandalicorum 1. ubi de voce agit Fœderatorum. *Longa dies non solet servare voces in quibus primum dicta sunt; sensu vertuntur enim res ipsæ qua volunt homines, vocabula illa primitus imposita rebus nihil curantes.*

they

they could acquit themselves; The history is extant in *Polybius* †; and some other examples of like falsness in *Polyænus*, which need not be transcribed, because they have no controversy. By such frauds, *Cicero* * said honestly, perjury is bound faster, not dissolved.

† Polyb. 12. Simile quod *Bœoti* urbem polliciti reddere, non stantem, sed eversam reddidere. *Thucyd.* 5. Et quod *Mahumetes Sultanus*, *Eubœa Capta*, eum dissecuit, cui caput incolume fore promiserat. * *De Offic. l.* 3.

LV. *How words of Art are to be interpreted.*

TO Words of Art *, which the people hardly understand, is to be applyed the definition of men skilful in every Art: as, what is *Majesty*, what is *Paricide*: which the Masters of Oratory refer *ad statum finitivum*. For *Cicero* * said truly, *Logicians have no vulgar terms, they use their own: and so do almost all other arts*. So, if in an Agreement an *Army* be spoken of, we shall define an Army to be such a number of Soldiers, which openly dares invade the territories of an enemy. For Historians usually do oppose that which is dome privily, or after the manner of robbers, and that which is done by a just Army. Wherefore in proportion to the enemies strength, it is to be judged of what forces an Army doth consist. *Cicero* makes it to consist of six legions and the Auxiliaries, *Polybius* saith, the *Roman*

* Augustin. in Rhetor. *ut m[illegible] à tec[illegible] & Mathematicis quàm à Philosophis cognominantur, accipere debemus, non tam pro solito usu consuetudinis, quam pro conditione præcepti.* * Acad. I.

Paradox 6.

Roman Army for the most part did contain sixteen thousand of *Romans*, twenty of aids. But a less number also may fill up the greatness of that name. For *Ulpian* saith, he is leader of an Army, who commands but one Legion with the aids: that is, as *Vegetius* expounds it, ten thousand foot, two thousand horse. And *Livy* sets down a kind of just army of eight thousand. In like sort must we judge of a Navy. So, a Fort † is a place which can keep off the hostile forces for a time.

L. 2. D. de hu qui not. infamia.

Lib. 3. c. 1.

† Servius ad 1. Æn. *Arces dictæ ab eo quod est arceo: quod inde hostes arceantur, hoc est, prohibentur.*

LVI. *Interpretation by Conjecture.*

Conjectures are usually taken from the matter, and the effect. From the matter: as the word *day*, if thirty days truce be agreed on, ought not to be understood of natural days, but of Civil: for that is congruous to the matter. So the word *donare, to give*, is taken for *to transact*, according to the quality of the business. So the word *arms*, which sometimes signifies instruments of war, sometimes armed Soldiers, with respect to the matter, is to be interpreted for this, or that. So he that hath promised to render men, ought to render them alive, not dead; contrary to the cavill of the *Plataeans*. And they that are commanded *ferrum deponere*, satisfy the command in putting off their swords, though not their steel

L. si uno. D. loc. conduct. § ver. in loco à subjecta materia.

steel buttons; upon which *Pericles* jested. And *to march away* freely out of Town, must be understood so, that the way also may be secured: contrary to what was done by *Alexander*. And *half the ships* in the division, must be understood of whole ships, not cut asunder: contrary to what the *Romans* did to *Antiochus*. Of the like matters we may make the same judgment. From the effect we make conjecture, if the word taken in the more received use draw after it any thing against reason. For, in an ambiguous word, that interpretation is rather to be received, which hath no hurt in't. Wherefore that cavillation of *Brasidas* is not to be admitted: who having promised he would depart out of the *Bœotian* fields, denyed the fields he possessed with his Army, to belong to the *Bœotians*: as if the word were meant, not of their ancient bounds, but of warly possession; in which sense 'twere a vain agreement.

Everh. in loco ab absurdo.

L. in ambig. D. de Legib.

Thucyd. 4.

LVII. *Some distinctions and rules for interpretation.*

MAny words have several significations, one *more strict*, another *more large*: which proceeds from many reasons; either because the general name adheres to one of the *species*, as in words of cognation and adoption; also in *Nouns masculin*, which are taken for

for the common too, where common are wanting; or becaufe the ufe of art is wider than popular ufe; as *death* * in the Civil Law is enlarged to fignify *deportation*, when among the people it fignifies otherwife. Moreover, we muft note, that things *promifed*, fome are *favorable*, fome *odious*, fome *mixt*, or of a middle nature. *Favorable* are thofe which have in themfelves equality, and which regard common utility; the greater this is, and more extended, fo much greater is the *favour* of the promife; as of things which make for peace, than of thofe which make for War; and of War Defenfive, than upon other caufes. *Odious* are fuch as burden one part only, or one more than the other, and fuch as contein in them punifhment, and make acts void, and bring in a change of what was before. That which is *mixt*, as bringing a change, but for peace fake, proportionally to the good, or the change will be efteemed fometime favourable, fometime odious, yet, fo that *cateris paribus* favour is to be preferred. Upon thefe grounds thefe *Rules* are to be kept. In things *not odius*, the words are to be taken according to the full propriety of popular ufe, and if there be more fignifications, the largeft is beft; *viz.* the Mafculin is to be taken for the Common Gender, and an indefinit fpeech for an univerfal. So thefe words, *unde quis dejectus eft*, *whence one is difpoffeft*, will pertain

* Vide Guicc. l. 16. ubi de pactis Car. 5. ad Mediolanenfem Ducatum pertinentibus fermo. Alc. 5. refp. 17.

Gl. in l. non poffunt. D. de Legibus.

pertain alſo to the reſtoring of him, who by force is prohibited to come into his own. For the word taken more largely bears that ſignification, as *Cicero* diſputes for *A. Cæcina.* In the *more favorable*, if the ſpeaker underſtand the Law, or uſe the Counſel of Lawyers, the words are to be taken more largely, that they may alſo include the ſignification of Art, or which the Law hath given. But we muſt not recur † to ſignifications plainly improper, unleſs otherwiſe ſome abſurdity or inutility of the Agreement would follow. On the other ſide, words are to be taken, even more ſtrictly, than propriety ſuffers, if it be neceſſary for the avoiding of iniquity or abſurdity: but, if there be not ſuch neceſſity, but manifeſt equity or utility in the reſtriction, we muſt ſtay within the narroweſt bounds of propriety, unleſs the circumſtances diſſwade. But in *odious* things, even a figurative ſpeech is admitted, whereby the *odium* or burthen may be ſhunned. Therefore in donation and remiſſion of ones right, words, though general, are wont to be reſtrained unto thoſe things which were probably thought upon. And in this kind of things, that will be ſometime underſtood to be *occupied*, which, it is hoped, may be reteined. So, aids promiſed from one part only, will be underſtood to be due at the charges of him who ſhal require them.

Bart. in lib. ſi is qui pro emptore. D. de uſuc.

† Vide exemplum in l. cum virum c. de fidei com.

Covar. 3. Var. c.3. n. 5. Tiraq. in leg. connub. Gl. 5. n. 115.

Barb. 4. conſ. 62.

LVIII. *Whether in the name of Confederates are conteined those that shall be so.*

IT is an illustrious question, Whether in name of the Confederates are meant only those that were so in the time of making the league; or also those that become so afterward: as in the league made between the people of *Rome* and *Carthage* after the war about *Sicily*; *The Confederates of either people shall be secured from them both.* Hence the *Romans* inferred, although the Agreement made with *Asdrubal*, of not passing the river *Iberus*, profited them nothing, because the *Carthaginians* had not confirmed it; yet, if the *Carthaginians* did approve the fact of *Annibal* setting upon the *Saguntines*, whom the *Romans*, after the league, had taken to them as Confederates, that then war might be proclam'd against them, as Violators of the League. *Livy* thus declares the Reasons: *The* Saguntines *were sufficiently provided for, the Confederates of both parties being excepted: For it was not added, Confederates that then were, nor that none afterward should * be assumed. Now, sith it was lawfull to assume new Confederates, who would think it equity, either that any should be receiv'd into friendship upon no desert, or being receiv'd should not be defended?*

Utriusq; populi socii ab utroque populo tuti sunto.

Lib. 21.

* Which was added in the *Peloponnesian* peace between the *Lacedæmonians* and *Athenians*. Thucyd. lib. 5.

ded: Only it was provided, that the fellows of the Carthaginians *should neither be tempted to revolt, nor be entertained revolting of their own accord.* Which words are almost all translated out of *Polybius*. What shall we say in this case? It cannot be denyed, but the word *Confederates*, without any violence, may receive both the *strict* signification of them who were so in the time of the League, and the other more *large* which includes the future too. Wherefore we must see, by the former rules, which interpretation is to be preferr'd: according to which rules we say, the future are not comprehended; because the question is about rupture of the league, which is an odious matter; and about depriving the *Carthaginians* of their Liberty, to use force of arms against such as were believed to have done them injury: which liberty is natural, nor is it suppos'd easily quitted †. Was it not lawfull then, for the *Romans* to take the *Saguntines* into society, or to defend them being admitted? Surely it was, not by vertue of the League, but by natural right, which by the League was not renounced: so that the *Saguntines* were, in respect of Both, in the same condition, as if nothing had been agreed concerning

Histor. lib. 3.

† Romani Samnitibus, Sidicinos bello petere volentibus, petentibusq; ut id per Romanos fieri liceret, responderunt: *Nihil intercedi, quo minus Samniti populo pacis belliq; liberum arbitrium sit.* Liv. lib. 8. In Antiochi fœdere est: *Si qui sociorum populi Romani ultro bellum inferrent Antiocho, vim ei arcendi jus esto: dum ne quam urbem aut belli jure teneat, aut in amicitiam recipiat.* Liv. 38. Polybius in excerptis Legationum, 35.

their

their Confederates. In which case,neither were the *Carthaginians* violators of the League, if they did war upon the *Saguntines*, when they judged it to be just; nor the *Romans*, if they did defend them. Plainly, as in the time *Pyrrhus*, it was
Polyb. Hist. 3. agreed 'twixt the *Carthaginian* and the *Roman*, that if either of them entred League with *Pyrrhus*, he should so do it, saving the right of sending aids to him, whom *Pyrrhus* should invade. I do not say, that war could have been just on both sides; but I say this perteined not to the violation of the League †. So doth *Polybius*, in the question touching aid sent by the *Romans* to the *Mamertins*, distinguish the Querees, Whether it were just, and, Whether it were lawfull by the League.

† Procop. Persic. 2. *Dicebat Alamundarus Rex Saracenorum, non violari à se quæ inter Persas Romanosq; convenerant, quandoquidem ipse à neutra parte conventis inscriptus esset.*

LIX. *One shall not wage war without leave of the other, How understood. And, That Carthage shall be free.*

THe former example was in an equal League, we will set down another in an unequal: if it were agreed, that one should not wage war without consent of the other Confederate. This was an article in the League of the *Romans* and *Carthaginians*, after the second *Punic* war:
Liv. lib. 42.
and

and likewiſe in that of the *Macedonians,* with the *Romans*, before the reign of *Perſeus*. Whereas the word *Warring*, may both ſignify *all* war, and peculiarly that which is *offenſive*; here we ſhal take the narrower ſignification, that liberty may not be too much reſtrained. Of the ſame kind it is, that the *Romans* promiſed, *That Carthage ſhall be free* †: Which, although, by the nature of the act, it could not be underſtood of the fulleſt power (for they had afore let go the right of undertaking war and ſome other things) yet did it leave them ſome liberty, and at leaſt ſo much, that they were not bound, at anothers command, to change the ſeat of their City. In vain therefore did the *Romans* urge the word *Carthage*, ſaying the multitude of Citizens, not the City, were thereby ſignified (which, though improper, may be granted, by reaſon of the attribute, which is more meet for the Citizens than the City:) For, in the word, *free* (αὐτόνομον, as *Appian* ſpeaks) there was a manifeſt fallacy.

† Diodorus Siculus ſic refert excerpto legationum 27, *manſura illis Leges, regionem, ſacra, ſepulcra, libertatem.*

LX. *Of Agreements perſonal and real.*

IT is alſo a frequent queſtion, pertinent here, concerning Agreements perſonal and real. And truly, if the Treaty was with a free people, no doubt but what was, is promiſed them, is in its own nature

ture real, becaufe the fubject is a permanent matter. Yea, though the ftate of a Commonwealth be chang'd into a Kingdom, the League will remain, becaufe the body remains the fame, though the head being chang'd: and, as we have faid above, the Empire which is exercis'd by a King, ceafeth not to be the empire of the people. An exception it will be, if the caufe appear to have been proper to that ftate, as, if free Cities contract a League to maintain their liberty. But if it be contracted with a King, the League will not prefently be efteemed perfonal: for, as it is rightly faid by *Pedius* and *Ulpianus*, the perfon is for the moft part inferted into the Agreement, not that the Agreement may be perfonal, but to fhew with whom 'tis made. But if it be added to the League, that it fhall be perpetual, or that it is made for the good of the Kingdom, or with himfelf and his fucceffors (fuch an addition ἐν τοῖς ἐκγόνοις is ufual, faith *Libanius* in his Oration for *Demofthenes*:) or for a time defined, now it appears plainly to be real. Such, it feems, was the league of the *Romans* with *Philip* King of *Macedon*, which when *Perfeus* his fon denyed to concern him, a war followed upon that ground. Moreover, other words, and the matter it felf fometimes, will afford a conjecture not improbable. But if the conjectures be equal on both fides, it will remain, that the favourable

L. jure gentium fect. pactum. D. de pactis.

Livius lib. 42. vide Parut. lib. 5. & 7.

vourable be accounted real, the odious personal. Leagues made for peace, or for commerce are favourable: those made for war, are not all odious, as some think; but the * defensive have more of favour, the * offensive of burthen. Add hereunto, that in a league for any war, it is presumed, that regard is had to the prudence and piety of him who is treated with, as one who seemed not likely to undertake a war, neither unjustly, nor yet rashly. As to that saying, *Societies are broken off by death*, I do not allege it here: for it perteins to private societies, and to the Civil Law. Therefore, whether by right or wrong, the *Fidenates* *, *Latins* †, *Etruscians*, *Sabins* departed from their league upon the death of *Romulus*, *Tullus*, *Ancus*, *Prisci*; *Servius*, cannot be rightly judged by us, because the words of the League are not extant. Whereunto that controversy in *Justin* is not unlike, Whether Cities which were tributary to the *Medes*, the Empire being changed, had changed their condition. For, it is to be considered, whether in the agreement they had committed them-

* ἐπιμαχίας.
* συμμαχίας.

Societates morte finiri. *Dec. l. 1. cons.* 22.

*Vide Dionys. Hal. lib. 3.
† De Appulis & Latinis idem eod. lib. De Turno & Hordeanio & Latinis idem lib. 4. Ammianus lib. 26. *Persarum Rex manus Armeniis injectabat, eos ad suam ditionem ex integro vocari vi nimia properans, sed injuste; causando quod post Joviani excessum, cum quo fœdus firmaverat & pacem, nihil obstare debeat, quominus ea recuperaret, quæ ante ad majores suos pertinuisse monstrabat.* Similia de Justiniani pactis cum Saracenis vide apud Menandrum Protectorem. Adde quæ Helvetii causantur post mortem Henrici 3. apud Thuanum l. 97. in an 89. Vide & insignem locum apud Camdenum in an. 71. ubi de fœdere antiquo Gallorum cum Scotis.

selves

ſelves to the truſt of the *Medes.* But
* Lib. 5. c.ult. *Bodin's* * argument is in no wiſe to be allowed, that leagues do not paſs to the ſucceſſors of Kings, becauſe the vertue of an oath goes not beyond the perſon. For, the obligation of an oath may bind the perſon only, and yet the promiſe it ſelf may oblige the heir. Neither is it true, which he aſſumes, that leagues depend upon the oath as their *firmament*, when for the moſt part there is efficacy enough in the promiſe it ſelf, to which, for Religion ſake, the oath is added. The commons of *Rome*, in the Conſulſhip of *P. Valerius*, had ſworn, they would come together at command of the Conſul. *L. Quintius Cincinnatus* ſucceeds him being dead; Some Tribunes cavill, as if the people were not bound by their oath. *Livie's* Judgment follows:
Lib. 3. *That neglect of the Gods, which this age is guilty of, was not yet: nor did every one, by interpreting for himſelf, make his oath and the Laws comply with his affections, but rather accommodated his own manners unto them.*

LXI. *A League made with a King, is extended to him being expelled, not to the Invader.*

CErtainly, a League made with a King remains, although the ſame King, or his

his succor, be driven out of his Kingdom by his Subjects. For, the right of the Kingdom remains with him, however he hath lost the possession †. On the contrary, if the Invader of anothers Kingdom, the rightfull King being willing; or the Oppressor of a Free-people, before he hath gotten sufficient consent of the people, be assalted by war; nothing will thereby be done against the league: because those have possession, they have not right *. And this is that which *T. Quintius* said to *Nabis*: *We have made no friendship nor society with thee, but with* † Pelops *the just and lawfull King of the Lacedemonians.* These qualities of King, successor, and the like, in leagues, do properly signify a right; and the Invaders cause is odious.

† Lucanus de Senatu Romano: *Non unquam perdidit Ordo Mutato sua jura loco.*

LXII. *To whom a promise, made to the first, is due, when more have performed a thing together.*

CHrysippus, of old, had handled this question, whether the reward promised to him, who came first to the mark, be due to both, if they came together, or to neither of them. And truly, the word *first* is ambiguous *, for it signifies, either

* So Valens received not the excuse of the King of the *Goths*: who said, he had sent aid to *Procopius* an Invader. *Ammianus* saith, it was a most vain excuse, l. 27. There is the same history in the Greek writers, but under the name of *Scythians*. For so they called the *Goths*. So *Justinian* said, he would not break the League made with *Gizerichus*, if he warred against *Gelimer*, who had taken away both his Kingdom and liberty from *Ilderichus* the lawful King. *Vide Cardinalem Tuschum PP. verbo Tyrannus, concl. 309. num. 6. Cacheranum decis. 79. n. 35.* † *Liv. lib. 34.* * *Vide Albericum de Rosato de Statutis q. 106, & 107.*

him who goes before all, or him whom no man goes before. But becauſe the rewards of vertues are favourable, it is the truer anſwer, that Both concur to the reward: though * Scipio, *Cæſar*, *Julian*, dealt more liberally, and gave full rewards to them that aſcended the walls together.

* At the taking of New Carthage in Spain.

LXIII. *How far States are accountable for damages done by their Subjects.*

Kings and Magiſtrats are reſponſible for their neglect, who do not uſe the remedies, which they can and ought, for the reſtraint of robbery and piracy: upon which ſcore the *Scyrians* were antiently condemnd by the *Amphyctiones*. I remember a queſtion was propos'd upon the fact, when the Rulers of our Country had, by their letters, given very many power of taking prizes from the enemy at Sea, and ſome of them had ſpoyled our friends, and their countrey being forſaken wandred about, and would not return when they were recalled; whether the Rulers were faulty upon that account, either becauſe they uſed the ſervice of naughty men, or becauſe they had not required of them caution. I gave my opinion, that they were bound no farther, than to puniſh, or yield the offenders if they could be found; and to take care, that legal reparation might be made out of the goods of the Robbers. For, they were not

Plut.

the

the cause of the unjust spoil that was made, nor were partakers of it in any wise: yea, they forbad, by their Laws, any hurt to be done their friends. That they should require caution, they were obliged by no Law, seeing they might, even without letters give all their subjects power to spoil the enemy: which was also done of old. Nor was such a permission any cause, why damage was done to their friends, when even private men might without such permission send forth ships of war. Moreover, it could not be foreseen, whether they would prove evill men: and besides, it cannot be avoided, but we must imploy such, otherwise no Army can be raised. Neither are Kings to be accused, if their soldiers, either by land or sea, wrong their confederates contrary to their command, as appears by the testimonies of *France* and *England*. Now, that any one, without any fault of his own, should be engaged by the fact of his Ministers, is not a point of the Law of Nations (by which this controversy is to be judged) but of the Civil Law, nor this general, but introduc'd upon peculiar reasons against seafaring men and some others. And on this side, sentence was given, by the Judges of the supreme Auditory, against certain *Pomeranians*, and that after the example of things judged, in a case not unlike, two Ages before.

Const. Galliæ Tom. 3. tit. 3. constitutione anni 1583. cap. 44. vide etiam tomo constit. 3. tit. 2. constit. anni 1543. cap. 44.

LXIV. *Of the right of Embaſſages.*

AMong the Obligations which that Law of Nations, which we call voluntary, hath by it ſelf introduced, a principal head is of the right of Embaſſages. For we frequently read of the ſacred privileges of Embaſſages, the ſanctimony of Embaſſadors, the right of Nations, right divine and human due unto them, and many ſuch like expreſſions. † *Cicero de Haruſpicum reſponſis* : *My judgment is, that the right of Embaſſadors is ſecured both by the ſafeguard of men, and alſo by the protection of Law divine.* Therefore to violate this, is not only unjuſt, but impious too, by the confeſſion of all, ſaith *Philip* in his epiſtle to the *Athenians.*

† *Sanctum populis per ſecula nomen* : Papinius. *Sancti habentur Legati* : Pompon. l. ſi quis D. de Legationib. *Itaq; eum qui Legatum pulſaſſit, dedi hoſtibus quorum erant Legati, Q. Mucius reſpondit.* ib. *Sancta ſunt corpora Legatorum*: *Var. l.3. de l.l.* *Tutiq; regreſſus Legato* : Papin. Totilas apud Procopium Got. 3. *Barbaris omnibus mos, Legatos venerari.* Aimonius : *Exuit hoſtem, qui Legatione fungitur. Vide & Radevicum in Append. De Polonis vide Cromerum l.20. De Turcis Leunclavium l.8. & l. 17. De Mauris Marianam lib. 12.*

L XV. *Among whom the right of Embaſſages hath place.*

HEre we muſt know, whatever this right of Nations be, it pertains to thoſe Legats, which are ſent from ſupreme Rulers, by one to another. For, beſides them, Provincial Legats, and Municipal, and

and others are directed, not by the Law of Nations, which is between one Nation and another, but by the Civil Law. An Embassador in *Livy* calls himself the publike messenger of the *Roman* people. Lib. 1. In the same *Livy* elswhere the *Roman* Senat saith, The right of Legation was provided for a foreiner, not a Citizen. Lib. 6. And *Cicero*, that he may shew, Legats are not to be sent to *Antonius*, saith, *For we have not to do with Annibal an enemy of the Commonwealth, but with one of our own Country.* Who are to be accounted foreiners *Virgil* hath so expressed, that none of the Lawyers can more clearly:

> *That I suppose a forein Land,*
> *Which is not under our Command.*

They then that are joind in an unequal league, because they cease not to be in their own power, have a right of Legation: Cromerus 30. and these also, who are partly subject, partly not, for that part wherein they are not subject. But Kings, conquerd in a solemn war, and deprived of their Kingdom, with other Royalties, have lost also the right of Legation. Therefore did *P. Æmilius* detein the Heralds of *Perseus* whom he had conquer'd. Yet, in Civil wars, necessity sometimes, maketh place for this right, beside the rule; as, when the people is so divided * into equal parts, that it is doubtfull on which side the right of Empire

* *Vide de Legatis Civitatis Toleti ad Regem Jo. Marianam l. 22. 8. de Flandris Crantzium Saxonicis 12. 33.*

Empyre lyeth: or, when the right being much controverted, two contend about succession into the Throne. For in this case, one Nation is for the time reckoned as two. So, *Tacitus* † charged the *Flavians*, that, in the Civil rage, they had violated, in respect of the *Vitellians*, that right of Legats, which is sacred even amongst forein Nations. Pirats and Robbers, that make not a Society, cannot have any succour from the Law of Nations. *Tiberius*, when *Tacfarinas* had sent Legats to him, was displeas'd that a traitour and plunderer us'd the manner of an enemy, as **Tacitus* hath it. Neverthelesss sometimes such men, faith being given them, obtain the right of Legation, as once the Fugitives in the *Pyrenean* Forest.

† Hist. 3. & Magnentium Zosimus lib. 2. *Magnentius apud animum suum volvebat deberetne Philippum irritum dimittere, an apud se retinere calcato jure Legationum.* Is Philippus à Constantio venerat.
*Annal. 3.
Cæsar. l. 3. de bello Civili.

LXVI. *Whether an Embassage be alwayes to be admitted.*

TWo things there are concerning Embassadors, which we see commonly referrd to the Law of Nations: first, that they be admitted †; next, that they be not violated. Of the former is a place in *Livy*, where *Hanno* a *Carthaginian* Senator inveighs against *Annibal* thus: *Embassadors coming from our Confederates, and on their behalf, our good General admitted not into his camp: but took away the right of Nations.* Which yet is not to be

† Donat. ad prol. Hecyra: *Oratorem audire oportere jus gentium est.*

be understood too crudely : for the Law of Nations commandeth not * that all be admitted, but forbiddeth them to be rejected without cause. There may be cause from him that sendeth, from him that is sent, from that for which he is sent. *Melesippus* Embassador of the *Lacedemonians*, by the Counsel of *Pericles*, was dismist out of the bounds of *Attica*, because he came from an armed enemy. So the *Roman* Senate † said they could not admit the Embassage of the *Carthaginians* whose Army was in *Italy*. The *Achaians* admitted not the Embassadors of *Perseus* raising war against the *Romans*. So *Justinian* rejected the Embassy of *Totilas*, and the *Goths* at *Urbin* the Orators of *Belisarius*, And *Polybius* relates how the messengers of the *Cynethenses* being a wicked people were every where repulsed. An example of the second we have in *Theodorus* call'd the *Atheist*, to whom, when he was sent unto him from *Ptolomaeus*, *Lisimachus* would not give audience: and the like hath befallen others, because of some peculiar hatred. The third hath place where the cause of sending, either is suspected *, as that of *Rabshake* the *Assyrian* to disturb the people was justly suspected by *Hezekia*; or not honourable, or unseasonable. So the *Etolians* were warned by the *Romans*, that they should send no Embassy without permission of the General : *Perseus*, that he should not send

* *Vide Camdenum An.* 1571. *quaestionum ibi propositarum* 4.

Thucyd. lib. 2.

Zonaras.

† *De hoc Romanorum more vide Servium ad* 7. *Aeneidos.*

Liv. l. 41.

Procop. l. 2. & 3.

Lib. 4.

* *Sic Andr. Burgus Caesaris Legatus in Hispaniam non admissus.* Mar. l. 24.

2 Reg. 18.

Liv. l. 27.

Lib. 32.

Salluft.
† *Carolus Quintus Imp. Legatos Galliæ, Venetorum & Florentinorum ad bellum sibi indicendum missos deduci jussit in locum, qui à comitatu suo abesset triginta millaria. Guicc. l. 18. Bellaius lib. 3.*

ſend to *Rome*, but to *Licinius*: and the Meſſenges of *Iugurtha* were commanded to depart *Italy* † within ten days, except their comming were to deliver up the *Kingdom*, and the King. As for thoſe aſſiduous Legations which are now it uſe, they may with very good right be rejected; for the no-ceſſity of them appears by the ancient cuſtom, whereto they are unknown.

LXVII. *Of not violating Embaſſadors.*

* Menander Protector de Juſtino 2. Imp. *Ille Avarorum Legatos contra jus Legationum in vinculis habuit.* vide *Ern. Cothmannum resp. 32. n. 29. & seq. vol. 5.*

OF not violating * Embaſſadors, is a more difficult queſtion, and variouſly handled by the moſt excellent wits of this Age. And firſt we muſt conſider of the perſons of Embaſſadors, then of their Train and their Goods. Of their perſons ſome think thus, that, by the Law of Nations, onely *unjuſt* force is kept from the bodyes of Embaſſadors; for they conceive priviledges are to be underſtood by Common right. Others think, force may not be offerd to an Embaſſador, for *every* cauſe, but on this ground, if the Law of Nations be broken by him; which is a very large ground: for, in the Law of Nations the Law of Nature is included, ſo that the Embaſſador may now be puniſht for all faults, except thoſe which ariſe meerly out of the Civil Law. Others, reſtrain this to thoſe Crimes which are done

done againſt the State of the Commonwealth, or his Dignity, to whom the Embaſſador is ſent. Which alſo ſome hold perillous, and would have complaint made to him that ſent him, and the Embaſſador left to his Maſter's judgment. There are ſome too that ſay, the Kings or Nations *unconcerned* are to be conſulted with: which indeed may be a point of prudence, cannot be of right. The reaſons which every one brings for his opinion conclude nothing definitely; becauſe this right, not, like *natural* right, certainly ariſeth out of certain reaſon, but is determined by the *will* of Nations. Now, it was in the power of Nations, either *abſolutely* to provide for the ſafety of Embaſſadors, or with certain *exceptions*; for on this ſide may be alleged the utility of puniſhing great offenders, and on the other ſide the utility of Embaſſages, the facility whereof is beſt promoted by ſecuring them as much as may be. We muſt therefore ſee, how far Nations have conſented; which cannot be evinced by examples only; for many are extant on both ſides. Wherefore we muſt have recourſe both unto the judgments of wiſe men, and unto conjectures. Two judgments I have moſt illuſtrious; one of *Livy*, another of *Salluſt*. *Livy*, if the Embaſſadors of *Tarquin*, who had raiſed treaſon at *Rome*, ſaith: *Although they ſeemed to have committed that, for which they*

Quanquam viſi ſunt commiſiſſe ut hoſtium loco eſſent, jus tamen gentium valuit. Liv.

they ought to be in the place of enemies, yet the right of Nations prevailed. We see here the right of nations extended even to them that do hostility. The saying of *Sallust* pertains to the Embassadors train, of whom we shall speak anon, not to the Embassadors themselves: but the Argument will proceed rightly *à majori ad minus*, that is, from a thing less credible to that which is more. He saith: *Bomilcar the Companion of him, who came to Rome on the publick faith, is made guilty rather according to rules of equity, than by the Law of Nations.* Equity, that is, the meer Law of Nature suffers punishment to be exacted, where is found a delinquent; but the Law of Nations excepteth Embassadors and such like, who come upon publick faith. Wherefore, that Embassadors be made guilty, is against the Law of *Nations*, whereby many things are wont to be prohibited, which, by the Law of *Nature*, are permitted. Conjecture also goes on this side; for it is more true, that *privileges* should be so understood, that they may give somewhat beyond *Common* right. Now, if Embassadors be only secur'd from *unjust* violence, therein were no great matter, nothing of preeminence. Add, that the security of Embassadors outweighs the utility arising from punishment. For punishment may be taken by him, that sent the Embassador, being *willing*: and if he

Fit reus magis ex æquo bonoq; quam ex jure gentium, Bomilcar Comes ejus qui Romam fide publica venerat. Sal. Jug.

he be *unwilling*, it may by man be exacted of him, as an approver of the crime. Some object, better one be punisht than many involv'd in war. But, if he that sent the Embassador approve his deed, the Embassadors punishment will not free us from the war. Now on the other side, the safety of Embassadors is in a slippry place, if they ought to render a reason of their actions to any other, but him by whom they are sent. For, when the Counsells of them that send and receive Embassadors are for the most part divers, often contrary, it can scarce happen but always somewhat may be said against an Embassador, that may bear a *shew* of a crime. And though some are so manifest, that they have no doubt, yet is a general danger sufficient for the equity and utility of a general Law. Wherefore my opinion clearly is, that it pleas'd the Nations, that the Common custom, which subjecteth every one being in a strange land to the Law of that land, should admit an exception in Embassadors, 1. That, as they are accounted, by a certain fiction, for the persons of their Masters (*He brought with him a face of the Senate, the authority of the Commonwealth*, saith *Tully* of an Embassador:) so also, by the like fiction, they should be set as it were without the compass of the land: whereupon, they are not bound by the Civil Law of that people amongst whom they live.

[illegible] faciem secum attulerat, auctoritatem Reipub. Tull. Philip. 7.

live. Wherefore if the offenſe be ſuch a one as may ſeem poſſible to be contemned, it is either to be diſſembled, or elſe the Embaſſador is to be commanded to depart † the Country. Which, *Polybius* ſaith, was done to him, who had given cauſe to the Hoſtages at *Rome* to eſcape away. And hence, on the by, we may learn the reaſon, why, at another time, the Embaſſador of the *Tarentines*, for the ſame offenſe, was beaten with rods; namely, becauſe the *Tarentines* being conquerd begun to be under * the *Romans*. If the crime be cruel, and publickly miſchievous, the Embaſſador muſt be ſent † to his Maſter, with a requeſt, that he would puniſh him, or give him up, as we read, the *Galls* required, the *Fabii* ſhould be deliverd to them. But, that which we have ſaid afore, that all human Laws are ſo temperd, that they bind not in extreme neceſſity, hath place alſo here, about the Precept of the ſanctimony of Embaſſadors. Indeed, that hight of neceſſity is not in the taking of puniſhment, which alſo in other caſes is taken away by the Law of Nations, as we ſhall ſhew hereafter: much leſs in the place, time and manner of taking puniſhment, but in the precaution of a great miſchief, eſpecially publick. Wherefore that an imminent danger may be withſtood, if there be no other remedy, Embaſſadors may be both apprehended and examined. So the *Ro-man*

† *Fecit id. Steph. Poloniæ Rex Moſcu. Thuan. l. 73. An. 1581. Elizabetha Scoto & Hiſpano Camd. Anno 71. & 84.*

* *Sic Carolus 5. Legato Ducis Mediolanenſis ut ſubditi ſui, imperavit ne à Comitatu ſuo abſcederet.* Guicciard. indicat. jam loc.

† Dion. Excerpt. Legationum: *Cum juvenes quidam Legati à Carthagine Romam veniſſent ibiq; contumelioſe quædam feciſſent, miſſi ſunt Carthaginem, traditiq; Carthaginienſibus: ab his verò nihil illis nocitum eſt, ſed dimiſſi ſunt incolumes.*

man Consuls apprehended * the Embassadors of *Tarquin*, especiall care being had of their † letters, as *Livy* speaks, that they might not be lost. But, if an Embassador use force of Arms, he may be slain, no doubt: not by way of *punishment*, but by way of Naturall *defense*. So might the *Galls* kill the *Fabii*, whom *Livy* stiles *violaters of human Law*. Therefore in *Euripides*, *Demophon*, when the *Herald* sent by *Euristheus* endeavour'd to cary away the suppliants by force, opposeth him by force, and when he said,

> *Dare you strike me a Herald sent?*
> *Answers, Yes, if you be violent.*

His name was * *Copreus*, and because he proceeded † violently and used force, he was slain by the *Athenians*, as *Philostratus* relates in the life of *Herod*. By a distinction not unlike to this, *Cicero* resolves that question, *Whether the son ought to accuse the father being a traytor to his Countrey*. For he will have it to be his duty *, to avert an imminent danger, but not for punishment of the fact, when the danger is past.

* *Pelopidas in vincula conjectus ab Alexandro Phereo, quod Legatus cum esset Thessalos ad libertatem concitaret. Plutarch. & lat. Scriptor vitæ Pelopidæ.*

† Vide Serranum in Henrico. 4.

* *Vide Iliados O.*

† Sic interpretandum quod Theodahatus Gotthus, Justiniani Legatis dicit apud Procopium Gotthicorum, 1. *Sanctum apud homines Legatorum nomen, plenumq; honoris. Sed hoc jus Legati sibi interdum servant, quandiu sua modestia Legationis dignitatem tuentur. Ita enim existimant homines fas esse vel interficere Legatum, si is in Principem ad quem mittitur, sit injuriosus, aut alienum matrimonium violet.* Legati verò, cum ostendissent longissime se abesse ab adulterii suspicione, quorum ne exitus quidem sine custode essent, addunt prudenter: *Si Legatus ea dixerit, quæ audivit à Principe qui ipsum misit, ea si non sunt commoda, præstare non ipse debet culpam, sed qui eum misit: Ipsi quippe nihil aliud concessum est, quam Ministerio mandato fungi.* Vide & Camdenum indicato jam loco an. 1571. * Offic. 3.

LXVIII.

LXVIII. *The Law in favour of Embassadors binds not him to whom he is not sent.*

THat Law, which I have mentiond, of not offring force to Embassadors, is to be conceiv'd obligatory to him, unto whom the Embassy is sent; and so too, if he hath admitted it: there being after that time, as it were, a tacit Covenant between them. Nevertheless, it may, and is wont to be denounced, that Embassadors be not sent; if they be, they shall be taken for enemies: as it was denounced to the *Etolians* by the *Romans*, and of old by the *Romans* to the *Veientes* it was proclamed, unless they would get them out of the City they should give what *Lars Tolumnius* gave: and to the *Romans* by the *Samnites*, if they did come to any Council in *Samnium*, they should not go away inviolate. Wherefore this Law doth not pertain to them through whose bounds Embassadors pass without leave; for, if they go to their enemies *, or come from their enemies, or otherwise make any hostile attempt, they may even

Liv. l. 27.

Idem l. 4.

Lib. 10.

* *Siculi Atheniensium socii Legatos Syracusanorum missos ad Civitates alias cepere.* Thucyd. lib. 7. *De Gallorum ad Turcam Legatis quos in Pado Hispani cepere & occiderunt, vide judicia Perutæ lib.* 11. *Bezari l.* 21. *De Flandriæ Civitatum Legatis ad Gallum captis à Maximiliano, Crantzium Saxonic.* 12. *Laudatur Belisarii Clementia, quod Gelimeris Legatis in Hispaniam missis, & ab Hispania reversis Carthaginem, quæ jam facta erat Romanorum, pepercerit. Procop. Vandal.* 1.

be

be slain: which the *Athenians* did to the Embassadors between the *Persians* and *Spartans*; the *Illyrians* to the Embassadors between the *Essians* and *Romans* †; and much more may they be bound, which *Xenophon* * orderd against some, *Alexander* against them that were sent to *Darius* from *Thebes* and *Lacedemon*, the *Romans* against the Embassadors of *Philip* † to *Annibal*, and the *Latins*, against the Embassadors of the *Volsci*. If there be no such provocation, and Embassadors be ill used, not that law of Nations †, whereof we treat, but the friendship, and the Honour, either of him that sent, or of him to whom they go, will be judged violate. *Justin* of the latter *Philip* King of *Macedon*: *Afterward he sent his Embassador with letters to Annibal, to join in league with him: The Embassador being taken and brought to the (Roman) Senate was sent away safe, not in honour to the King, but lest he should be made a certain enemy, that hitherto was dubious.*

† *Thucyd. l. 2. Appian. de bello Illyrico.*

* *Xenoph. lib. 4. de exped. Cyri. Arrian. lib. 2.*

† Liv. lib. 23.

† *Vide Appian. in excerptis Legationum n.* 19.

† *Aliud fit si quis extra fines suos insidias ponat Legatis alienis, eo enim jus gentium violatur. Et hoc continetur in Thessalorum oratione contra Philippum apud Livium.* Justin. lib. 29.

LXIX.

LXIX. *An enemy, to whom an Embassador is sent, is bound.*

BUt an Embassy admitted, even with enemies † in Arms, much more with enemyes not in actuall hostility, hath the safeguard of the Law of Nations. *Diodorus Siculus* said, Heralds have peace in the time of War. The *Lacedemonians*, who had slain the Heralds of the *Persians*, are said thereby *to have confounded the rights of all men.* Livy saith, *Embassadors being brought into danger, there was not left so much as the Law of War.* Curtius: *He sent Messengers to compell them unto peace, whom the Tyrians, against the Law of Nations, killed, and threw into the Sea.* Justly is it said: for in war also many things fall out, which cannot be transacted but by Embassadors, and peace it self can hardly be made, and differences reconciled, but by their Mediation.

† Pomponius l. ult. D. de Legatis. *Si quis Legatum hostium pulsasset, contra jus gentium id commissum esse existimatur, quia sancti habentur legati.* Et Tacit. hoc jus vocat. *Hostium jus & sacra legationis & fas gentium.* An. 1. Cic. 1. Verrina: *Nonne Legati inter hostes incolumes esse debent?* Sen. de Ira. *Violavit legationes rupto gentium jure.* Livio, *cædes ruptura jus gentium, scelus, causa nefanda, cædes impia* dicitur, in historia Legatorum quos Fidenates occiderunt. Donatus ad illud Eunuchi: convenire & colloqui. *Sic pronunciandum est, ut quasi dicat, liceat per te, miles, quod etiam inter hostes & in bello licet.* vide loca producta LXV.

LXXI.

LXX. *Embassadors may not be wronged by way of retaliation.*

THis is a question too, Whether by the right of rendring like for like an Embassador may be slain, or ill used, coming from him that hath done so. And truly there are in Histories examples enough of such revenge; but histories, we know, relate not only things done justly, but those things also that are done unjustly, angrily, impotently. The Law of Nations provides not only for the dignity of him that sends, but for the security of him that is sent: Wherefore there is a tacit contract with him also; and wrong is done to him, though none is done to his Master. Wherefore *Scipio* did not only magnanimously, but according to the Law of Nations, who, after the Embassadors of the *Romans* were ill entreated by *Carthaginians*, the Embassadors of the *Carthaginians* being brought unto him, and being asked what ought to be done, answered, *not as the Carthaginians have done* †. *Livy* * addes, he said, *He would do*

† Diodorus Sic. in excerptis Peiresianis: *Dixit Scipio non esse id faciendum quod ipsi in Carthaginiensibus accusarent.* Et Romani ipsi Legatos jam comperto Carthaginiensium facto, dimiserunt. Vide Appian. Constantius Titianum à Magnentio ad se missum remisit, quanquam Philippum à Constantio missum ad se retinebat Magnentius. Zosim. l. 2. Vide & historias apud Cromerum lib. 19. & 21. & Parutam de Legatis Venetis in itinere in Galliâ retentis l. 7. * *Appian de bello Pun. Liv. l. 30. Val. M. l. 6. c. 7.*

V *nothing*

nothing unworthy of the manners of the Roman people. Valerius Maximus puts the like words, but more antient, into the mouth of the *Roman* Consuls on a like occasion: *Hanno, the integrity of our City quits thee of that fear*; For then too, against the right of Legation, *Cornelius Asina* was cast into chaines by the *Carthaginians*.

LXXI. *The companions also of Embassadors, and their Goods, are inviolable.*

THe Companions also and the Goods of Embassadors have in their proportion a kind of sanctimony. Whence it was in the old form of the Heralds; *O King, do you make me a Royall messenger of the Roman people? do you privilege my companions and my Goods?* And by the *Julian* Law *de vi publica* they are pronounced guilty, not only that have wronged Embassadors, but their attendants too. But these are sacred *accessorily*, and so far as it seems good to the Embassador. Wherfore if his Attendants have greatly offended, they may be demanded of him, that he may yield them: For they are not to be drawn from him by force. When this was done by the *Achaians* against some *Lacedemonians*, that were with the *Roman* Embassadors, the *Romans* cryed out, the Law of Nations was broken. Whither may

Rex, facisne me tu regium nuntium populi Romani Quiritiū? vasa comitesq; meos?

Vide Fraxini Canæi Epistolas p. 75. & 279.

Serranus Henrico 4.

may be also referred the judgment of *Sallust* concerning *Bomilcar*, which we made use of above. But if the Embassador will not yield them, the same course is to be taken, which before we said about the Embassadors own offense. Now, whether an Embassador hath jurisdiction over his own family; and whether his house be a sanctuary * for all that fly unto it; depends upon the concession of him with whom he resides. For this belongs not to the Law of Nations. That the movable Goods also of the Embassador, which are accounted an accession to his person, cannot be seised on, neither as a pledge, nor for payment of a debt, nor by order of judgment, nor (which some allow) by the Kings hand, is the truer opinion. For all coaction ought to be far from an Embassador, as well that which toucheth his necessaries, as his person, that he may have full security. If therefore he hath contracted any debt, and (as it is) possess no immovables in that place, He is to be calld upon kindly, and if he refuse, his Master; so that at last that course may be taken with him, which is usual against debters in another territory. Nor is it to be feared, which some think, lest, if this be so, none will be found to contract or deal with an Embassador: For even Kings, who cannot be compell'd, want not creditors; and among some Nations it was a custome, saith *Nicolaus Damas-*

* *Distingui fermè hac in re solent crimina. Vide Parutam lib. 10. ubi Rex Galliæ hanc ob causam iratus pacatur. Vide eund. lib. 11.*

cenas, that contracts which were gone into trust should bear no action, no more than ingratitude: so that men were constrained either to fulfill the contract presently, or be content with the naked faith of the debter. And *Seneca* wisheth all the world were in this condition:

De benef. 3. 15.

Would we could perswade men to receive mony lent, only from those that pay it willingly; would no stipulation did bind the buyer to the seller, nor sealed bonds and indentures were laid up. Faith should rather keep those agreements, and a mind studious of right.

Civil. 1. τὸ ὀφείλειν χρέος. Τὸ ἀφείλειν χρέος pro eodem dixit Herodotus Clio.

Appian also saith, it displeased the *Persians, to owe money, being a thing obnoxious to deceit and lying. Ælian* † saith the same of the *Indians.* With whom *Strabo* * agrees in these words:

† Lib. 4.
* Lib. 15.

They have no judgments but about slaughter and injury; because a man cannot help it, but he may fall into these: But contracts are in every ones power; wherefore one must bear with it, if a man break his word, and consider afore hand whom one trusts, and not fill the Commonwealth with Law-suits.

Stob. de Legibus.

And it was a constitution of *Charondas*, that none should commence an action, who had trusted another with the price of his commodity: which also pleased *Plato.*

De Legib. 8. Mor. Nic. 8. 15. Mor. 9. lib. 1.

And it is noted by *Aristotle, that some have no tryalls about these matter: for they think men ought to be content with the faith which they have taken.* And elsewhere, *In some*

some places the Laws permit no action for what is trusted, as if he were onely to be dealt with privately, with whom one hath contracted, and taken his word. The objections brought against this opinion out of the *Roman* Law, concern not our Embassadors, but those that are provincial or municipal.

LXXII. *The right of Embassadors vindicated by War.*

PRophane Histories † are full of wars undertaken because of wrong done to Embassadors. And in the sacred * story is exstant the memory of the war which *David* upon that ground waged against the *Ammonites.* Nor doth *Cicero* esteem any cause more just against *Mithridates.*

† *Romani ob id bellum suscepere in Senonas. Appianus excerpto Legationum 4. & 10. in Illyrios & Ligures: Polybius excerpto Legationum 125. & 134. in Issios: Dion. exc. leg. 2. in Corinthios: Livius lib. 2. in Tarentinos: Dionys. Hal. exc. Leg. 4. Francorum & Germanorum exempla habes apud Aimonium lib. 3. c. 61. & 88. & Withikindum l. 3.* * *2 Sam. 10. Vide Chrysost. ad Stagirium lib. 3.*

LXXIII. Of the right of Burial. *The right of burial springs from the same Law of Nations.*

BY the Law of Nations, which hath its rise from their *will*, sepulture is also due to the bodies of the dead. *Dion Chrysostom*, amongst manners or customs, which he opposeth to written Law, after the rights of Embassadors, mentions, *not to forbid* *dead men to be buried.* And *Seneca* the father, among unwritten Laws, but more certain than all written ones, sets down this, to beſtow earth upon the dead. The *Hebrews*, *Philo* and *Joſephus*, call this the Law of nature †; as it is uſual, under the Name of *Nature*, to comprehend common cuſtomes agreeable to natural reaſon. He that hinders burial, puts off man, ſaith *Claudian*; gives an affront to nature, ſaith *Leo* the Emperor; is an enemy to piety, ſaith *Iſidore Peluſiot*. And becauſe theſe rights common to Civil men, that they might ſeem the more ſacred, were by the Antients referd unto the Gods, we ſee this right as well as that of Legation frequently aſcribed to them. Therfore you ſhal find it in *Sophocles* called νόμον δαιμόνων, a Law of the Gods. *Iſocrates** ſpeaking of the war of *Theſeus* againſt *Creon*, ſaith, *Who knows not what ill ſucceſs Adraſtus had before Thebes, where attempting to reſtore the ſon of Oedipus, his ſon-in-Law, he loſt very many Argives, and ſaw their leaders ſlain: And himſelf ſurviving with diſhonour, when he could not obtain leave to bury the ſlain, went to Athens with a petition to Theſeus the King, that he would not ſuffer ſuch men to lye unburied, nor the old cuſtome to be deſpiſed, and the right of all men violated, being eſtabliſhed not ſo much by human nature as by divine power: Theſeus hearing this, decrees to ſend to Thebes without delay;*

† φύσεως θεσμὸς Iſidorus Peluſiota. Apud Ælianum eſt, *Cum mortuum condi ipſa imperet communis natura.* Idem alibi vocat γῆν καὶ ταφὴν, *terram & ſepulturam, hominibus cunctis communia & ex æquo debita.* νόμους βροτῶν dixit Euripides, κοινὸν νόμον Ariſtides, Lucanus *hominum ritus, terrarum Leges & mundi fœdera* Papinius, *ſortis humanæ commercium* Tacitus, *ſpem communem* Orator Lyſias.

Sophocles Ajace. idem θεῶν νόμους *dixit in Antigone.*

* *Panathenaico.*

delay? A little after the same Author reprehends the *Thebans* *, that they preferred the Statutes of their own City before Lawes Divine: and he mentions the same history in other places †. So do others. And frequently in good Authors we see eminent titles of vertue ascribed to this office. For *Cicero* and *Lactantius* call it humanity, *Valerius Maximus* humanity and mildness, *Quintilian* mercy and and Religion, *Seneca* mercy and humanity, *Philo* compassion of human nature, *Ulpian* mercy and piety. *Modestinus* the memory of human frailty, *Capitolinus Clemency*, *Euripides* and *Lactantius* justice, *Prudentius* a gracious work. On the contrary, the *Donatists*, who forbad the bodies of the Catholicks to be buried, are accus'd of impiety by *Optatus*: *Spartianus* saith, such are without reverence of humanity; *Livius* calls it cruelty beyond belief of human anger; and *Lactantius* saith, it is wicked wit in them that made sepulture to be a vain and superfluous thing †.

* Pacto non prælio obtentum à Thebanis jus sepeliendi vult Plutarch. Theseo; at prælio, Pausanias Atticis.

† *Panegeryco, Helenæ encomio, Plataica oratione: Herodotus quoq; Calliope. Diodorus Siculus historiarum 4. Xenophon hist. Græcæ 6. & Lysias ea quæ est in honorem sepultorum: postremo Aristides in Panathenaico, qui bellum hoc susceptum ait pro communi natura hominum.*

† Apud Papinium, —*bello cogendus & armis, in mores hominemq; Creon*. Homerus dixerat ἀεικέα ἔργα. Idem Iliados ω, Jovem & Deos Achilli iratos fuisse dicit ob malè tractatum corpus Hectoris. Eandum ob causam impius Eteocles, Papinio.

LXXIV. *What was the first cause of this custome.*

WHat was the first cause of this custome of interring bodies, whether enbalmed before, as among the *Egyptians*, or burnt, as among most of the *Grecians*, or so as they are, which *Cicero* notes to be most the antient way, and after him *Pliny* *, of this all have not the same opinion. For *Moschion* thinks the occasion was given from the gigantick ferity in eating men, the abolition whereof is signified by Sepulture †.

* Plin. Histor. natur. 7. 54. ubi & hoc: *Sepultus intelligitur quoquo modo conditus: humatus vero, humo contectus.*

† *Tunc morte raptos Imperatum Legibus*
Mandare terræ, pulveremq; inspargere
Necdum sepultis, ne darentur conspici
Abominanda signa pastus pristini.

Others think, men didin this manner, as it were of their own accord, pay the debt, which otherwise nature requireth of them even against their will. For, that the body of man made of earth is due to the earth †, not only God declared to

† *Job* 10. 9. Philo in Flaccum: *Proprium hominibus locum natura terram tribuit, nec vivis tantum, sed & mortuis, ut eadem quæ primos suscepit natales, suscipiat & ex hac vita exitum.* Attamen, sicut nullum est in homine factum laudabile, cujus non vestigium in alio aliquo animantium genere Deus posuerit, ita & in hac re evenit. De formicis Plinius lib. 11. 30. *Sepeliuntur inter se viventium solæ, præter hominem.* At ipse de Delphinis l. 9. 8. *conspectiq; jam defunctum portantes, ne laceraretur à belluis.* Et de apibus Virg. *Tum corpora luce carentum Exportant tectis & tristia funera ducunt.* Servius: *cum exsequiali scilicet pompa.*

Adam

Adam, but also the *Greeks* & *Latins* frequently acknowledge. *Cicero* out of *Euripides*: *Earth is to be rendred to the earth.* And the same *Euripides* hath elswhere more fully exprest what we read in *Solomon* *, *The body returns to the earth, from whence it came, and the soul to God that gave it.* *Pliny* hath also written, that the earth entertains us at our birth, feeds us being born, and all along our life susteins us, and last of all, when we are abdicated by the rest of nature, she like a gentle mother embraces us in her lap and covers us. There are some that hold, the hope of resurrection, as it were by this monument, was consignd to posterity by the first parents of mankind. For, that *Democritus* also taught, Bodies are to be conserved because of a promise of returning to life, *Pliny* witnesseth. And Christians oft refer the rite of decent burial to this hope, *Prudentius* *.

* *Eccles.* 12. 7. Euripides ex persona Thesei in supplicibus.

Jam sinite terra mortuos gremio tegi:
Res unde quæq; sumserat primordium
Eo recipitur: spiritus cælo redit
Corpusq; terræ: jure nec enim mancupi,
Sed brevis ad ævi tempus utendum datur:
Mox terra repetit ipsa quod nutriverat.

Lucretius similiter de terra:

Omniparens eadem rerum est commune sepulcrum.

Cicero de Legibus 2. ex Xenophonte: *Redditur terræ corpus, & ita locatum ac situm, quasi operimento matris obducitur.*

* *Quidnam sibi saxa cavata,*	Why do Marbles cover dust,
Quid pulcra volunt monumēta?	And Monuments our bodies keep?
Nisi quod res creditur illis,	Because the thing they have in trust,
Non mortua, sed data somno.	Is not dead, but laid to sleep.

The

The more plain and simple opinion is, whereas man excells other living creatures, it seemed an unworthy thing, that other animals should be fed with his body: for the preventing whereof, as much as might be, sepulture was invented. By the pity of men bodies are kept from the invasion of fouls and wild beasts †, said *Quintilian*. And *Cicero*, *Vexed by wild beasts*, *he wanted the common honour in his death.*

† Vide Vaticinium de Jeroboami posteritate in pœnam peccatorum ejus. 1 Reg. 14. 11. & Tertullianum de resurrectione. De Ægistho Homerus Odyss. γ'.

Ergo nec leviter Glebam injecere peremto,
Illius volucres lacerarent ossa canesq;. De Ægistho loquitur, quem, ut adulterum & regni invasorem, Argivi insepultum abjecerant; cujus tamen reliquias humanior terræ dedit Orestes, ut mox dicetur. Menelaus de Ajace in Sophocle:

Sed ille arenis jactus in pallentibus,
Gratum marinis pabulum alitibus dabit.

Sed hoc quoq; ibi prohibet Ulysses, prudentiæ exemplar. Sophocles Antigone in ipsius Antigones laudem:

Illa obsitum cruore germanum suum,
Non insepultum sivit, alitibus feris
Canibusq; fieri pabulum mordacibus.

Appianus Civilium primo, de interfectis jussu Marii: *Nec cuiquam licebat quenquam interfectorum sepelire, sed viros tam egregios lacerabant aves & canes.* Ammianus Marcell. l. 17. de Juliano: *Sollicitusq; ne diræ volucres consumerent corpora peremptorum sine discretione cunctos humari mandavit.* Apud Virgilium legimus:

——— Non te optima mater
Condet humo, patriove onerabit membra sepulcro;
Alitibus linquere feris. ———

God

God in the Prophets, threatneth the Kings he hates, that they should have the burial of an Asse, that dogs should lick their blood. Nor doth *Lactantius* consider any thing els in burial, when he saith, *We will not suffer the Image and work of God to ly a prey for beasts and birds*; And *Ambrose* his words are these, *You can do no better office for him, who is now past requiting of you: save him from the fouls of the air, save from the beasts a partaker of the same nature.* But, though such injuries were not, yet for the body of man to be trod under foot, and broken, seems very unbecoming the dignity of his kind. That in *Sopater*'s controversies is to our purpose: *It is a comely thing to bury the dead, and by nature it self appointed unto bodies, lest they be vilified after death if they putrify naked. All the Gods are pleased to indulge this honour to bodies deprived of life. For, because it is unreasonable, the secrets of human nature should be exposed after death to the sight of all, we have received a custome of old, to Inter human bodies, that being laid up in their sepulchers they may conceal their rottenes.* To the same purpose is that of *Gregory Nyssen, That the Sun may not see what is shamefull* † *to human nature.* Hence it is,

† Simili modo Agathias dicit moris esse, *Obtegere puerperii pudorem.* Ita quam nihil natura simus, apparet in ortu & interitu. Quod ut significarent sapientes Hebræi, vetuere ne Plebeiæ aut summæ fortunæ qui essent, aliusmodi fasciis involverentur, aut modo nati aut mortui.

that

that the office of burying is ſaid to be performed, *not ſo much to the perſon, as the nature,* [*Non tam homini, quam humanitati:*] whence *Seneca* and *Quintilian* called it publick humanity, *Petronius tralatitious.* Whereunto this is Conſequent, that Burial muſt not be envyed, neither to our own, nor our Countreyes enemies. Of private enemies, excellent is that diſſertation of *Ulyſſes* in *Sophocles* for the burial of *Ajax*, where we have this among the reſt to *Menelaus*;

After ſo many wiſe words ſaid,
Beware you do not wrong the dead.

Euripides † gives the reaſon in his Antigone,

Mens quarels dy with their laſt breath:
For what revenge is after death?

And *Optatus Milevitanus* renders the ſame cauſe: *If you had any difference living, let the other's death kill your hatred. He is now ſilent, with whom you quarrell'd.*

† Idem Supplicib. *Fecere vobis ſi quid Argivi malè, Cecidere: in hoſtes iſta vindicta eſt ſatis.* Et Virg. *Nullum cum victis certamen & æthere caſſis.* Quam ſententiam citans ſcriptor ad Herennium addit: *Nam quod malorum eſt extremum accidit illis jam.* Papinius,

——— ———bellavimus: eſto:
Sed cecidere odia & triſtes mors obruit iras.

LXXV. *Burial is also due to publick enemies.*

WHerefore also to publick enemies, all men think Burial to be due †. Enemies do not envy burial, saith *Tacitus*: and *Dio Chrysostomus* having said, this is a Law observ'd among enemies in war, addeth, *although their hate hath proceeded to the highest degree. Sopater* above cited: *What war hath deprived mankind of this last honour? What enmity hath so far extended the memory of evil deeds, as to dare violate this Law? Dio Chrysostom* cited a little afore, in his Oration of Law: *By this, no man judgeth dead men enemies, nor is anger and disgrace extended to their bodyes.* And examples are every where * extant. So *Hercules* sought his enemies, *Alexander* those slain at *Issus*, *Hannibal* sought *C. Flaminius, P. Æmilius, Tib. Gracchus, Marcellus* †, *Romans*, to bury them. The same was done by the *Romans* for *Hanno*, for *Mithridates* by *Pompey*, by *Demetrius* for many, for King *Archelaus* by *Antonius*. It was in the oath of the Greeks warring against the *Persians*: *I will bury all my fellows, being victorious, I will bury the Barba-*

† Belli hoc jus κοινὸν ἐν τοῖς πολέμοις vocat Appianus: *Belli Commercia* Philo. Idem in Flaccum: *Etiam qui in bello occubuerunt, eos homines solent ad sepulturam dare, illi quidem quibus bonitatis & humanitatis plus est, suopte impendio: alii vero, qui odia & in mortuos extendunt, sub pactis dantes corpora, ne careant eorum quæ mos imperat honore ultimo.* De eadem re agens Lucanus hominum ritus in hoste servandos dixit.

* Josephus in legib. *Sepeliantur & hostes.* Agamemnon Trojanos sepelit Iliad. η. Antigonus Pyrrhum apud Plutarchum. Vide eundem in vita Thesei. † Plutarchus Marcello. *Credas*, inquit Silius Italicus, *Sidonium cecidisse ducem.*

rians

rians too : and frequently in histories you may read of leave obtained to carry off the dead. We have an example in *Pausanias : The Athenians say , they had buried the Medes, because it was their Religion to Interr all the dead , whatsoever they were.* Wherefore, by the interpretation of the antient *Hebrews* , the High Priest, when otherwise he was forbidden to be present at any funeral , was commanded neverthelesss to put into the earth a man found unburied. But Christians so much esteemed sepulture, that for this, as well as to feed the poor , or to redeem captives, they thought even the consecrated Vessels of the Church might be lawfully coined or sold. There are indeed examples also to the contrary, but condemned by common judgment †.

Atticis.

Idem ex jure Pontificio Romano Servius notat.

† *Hunc oro defende furorem*, est apud Virgilium. Interpretatur Servius, *Inimicorum iram & post fata saevire cupientem.*
Apud Claudianum : —— *hominemq; cruentus Exit, & tenuem caesis invidit arenam.*
Diodorus Siculus : *Ferinum est bellum gerere cum mortuis , qui ejusdem naturae fuerint.*

L X X V I. *Whether Burial be due to notorious malefactors.*

Concerning these, I see there are causes of doubting. The divine Law given to the *Hebrews* , the mistress, as of every vertue , so of humanity too , commands that

that they which were hanged on a tree (which was esteemed very * ignominious) should be buried the same day. * Numb. 25.4. Deut. 21. 23. 2 Sam. 21.16.
Hence *Josephus* saith, The Jews have such care of sepulture, that they take down the bodies condemned to publick execution, before Sun-set, and commit them to the earth: and other *Hebrew* interpreters adde, This reverence was given to the divine image, after which man was made. *Ægisthus*, who had seconded his adultery with the murder of the King, was buried by *Orestes* the son of the murdered King, as *Homer* relates. Odyss. 3.
And among the *Romans*, *Ulpian* saith, the L.1.de cap.punit.
bodies of them that are condemnd to dy are not to be denyed their kindred: yea *Paulus* his opinion is, they are to be granted to any, whoever they be, that ask them. And *Diocletian* and *Maximian* Emperours answered thus: *We do not* *L.2.c. de Relig.*
forbid, that offenders, after execution worthy of their crimes, be deliverd to the grave. Hujus Romanorum moris mentio est apud Philonem contra Flaccum.
Indeed, we read in histories examples of them that have been cast out * unburied, more frequent in Civil than Forein wars: and at this day we see the bodies of some condemned persons to be left a long time in publick view: which manner yet, whether it be commendable, is disputed not by Politicks only, but Divines. On the contrary, we find, they are praysed, who gave burial to the bodies of such as had not permitted the same

* Id ἀταφιᾳ ὑβρίζειν τὸν νεκρὸν dixit Josephus in morte Judæorum Regis Alexandri. Adde Quintil. declam. 4.

ſame to others, namely *Pauſanias* King of the *Lacedemonians*, who being provoked by the *Æginetæ* to revenge the deed of the *Perſians* upon *Leonides*, with the like deed, rejected the advice as unworthy of the *Græcian* name †. And the *Phariſees* buried *Alexander Jannæus*, who had been very contumelious againſt his dead Countreymen *. But if God ſometimes hath puniſhed ſome with the loſs of burial, he hath done this above the conſtituted Laws; and, that *David* kept the head of *Goliah* to be ſhewed, was done againſt an Alien, a Contemner of God, and under that Law, which extended the name of *Neighbour* to the *Hebrews* only.

† Apud Papin. Theſeus Creontem ſic alloquitur: —*Vade atradaturus Supplicia, extremiq; tamen ſecure Sepulchri.*

* Joſ. Antiq. l. 13. c. 13. & Gorion.

LXXVI. *Whether it be due to thoſe that have kill'd themſelves? to the ſacrilegious and traiterous?*

IT is here worthy to be noted, concerning burial of the dead, that the rule among the *Hebrews* themſelves had an exception of them that had layd violent hands upom themſelues, as *Joſephus* tells us: Nor is it any wonder, when no other puniſhment can be appointed them that eſteem not death for a puniſhment. So the *Mileſian* maids were frighted from voluntary death, and likewiſe the † *Plebs* of

Lib. 3. de Bel. Jud. cap. 25. Hegeſ. l. 3. c. 17. Gell. l. 15. c. 10.

† Servius ad 12. Æn. *Sane ſciendum quod cautum fuerat in Pontificalibus libris, ut qui laqueo vitam finiiſſet inſepultus abjiceretur. unde merito ait* informis Lethi, *quaſi mortis infamiſſimæ. Ergo cum nihil*

nihil sit hac morte deformius, poetam etiam pro Reginæ dignitate dixisse accipiamus. Cassius autem Hemina ait Tarquinium Superbum, cum cloacas facere populum coegisset, & ob hanc injuriam multi se suspendio necarent, jussisse corpora eorum cruci affigi. Tunc primum turpe habitum est, mortem sibi consciscere.

Rome sometime, though *Pliny* * approve it not. So the body of *Cleomenes*, who had slain himself, *Ptolomy* commanded to be hang'd up. And saith *Aristotle*, it is commonly receiv'd †, that some disgrace be done to them, who have been the Authors of their own death: which *Andronicus Rhodius* expounding saith, their bodyes were forbidden to be buried. And this among other Decrees of *Demonassa* Queen of *Cyprus* is commended by *Dion Chrysostomus*. Nor is that any great objection against this custome, that *Homer*, *Æschylus*, *Sophocles*, *Moschio* and others say, That the dead feel nothing: and therefore can neither be affected with loss nor shame. For it is sufficient, that that which is inflicted on the dead be feared by the living, and they by this means be deterd from sin. Excellently do the *Platonists* maintain against the Stoicks, and whoever els admit the avoiding of servitude and diseases, yea and the hope of glory, for a just cause of voluntary death, That the soul is to be retained in the custody of the body, and that we must not depart out of this life without his command who gave it to us. To which point, much may be seen in *Plotinus*, *Olympiodorus*,

* Plin. lib. 36. cap. 15.

Nic. 5. 5.

† Athenis Æschinis tempore ejus qui se interfecisset manus seorsim à corpore sepeliebatur. Æschin. in Ctesiph. Adde Hegesippum lib. 3. cap. 17.

Orat. 65. Vide Stob. tit. 126. & Sophoc. Ajace.

dorus, and *Macrobius* upon *Scipio*'s dream. *Brutus* was at firſt of this judgment, and condemned † the fact of *Cato*, which afterward he imitated: *For he thought it neither pious nor manly to yield to fortune, and fly away from imminent adverſities, which are couragiouſly to be undergone.* And *Megaſthenes* noted the fact of *Calanus* to be reprehended by the *Indian* wiſe-men, whoſe doctrines did not ſuite with ſuch an end of men impatient of life. The *Perſians* *, it ſeems, were of the ſame opinion: whoſe King *Darius* ſaith in the Hiſtorian *, *I had rather dy by anothers crime, than by my own.* Upon this ground, the *Hebrews* ſaid to *dy* was to be* *diſmiſt*: as we may ſee, not only *Lu.* 20. 29. but alſo in the Greek verſion, *Gen.* 25. 2. & *Numb.* 20. *in fine.* A phraſe us'd by the *Grecians* too. *Themiſtius*, *de anima*, *They ſay, a man that dyes is diſmiſt, and death they cal a departure or diſmiſſion.* In *Plutarch*'s conſolation the word is uſed in the ſame ſenſe: *Until God himſelf diſmiſs us.* Yet ſome † of the *Hebrews*, concerning the Law of not Killing himſelf, except one caſe, as an honorable *exit*, if one ſee he is like

† Et Philoſophorum non pauci extra Stoicos. Seneca Epiſtola 70. *Invenies etiam profeſſos ſapientiam, qui vim afferendam vitæ ſuæ negent, & nefas judicent ipſum interemptorem ſui fieri. Expectandum eſſe exitum quem natura decrevit.* Procopius Gotthicorum. 4. *Violentus vitæ exitus res inutilis & plena inſipientis impetus, & illa in mortem ferens audacia, conſilio cum careat, prudentibus judicatur immerito ſibi fortitudinis nomen uſurpare. Tum vero & illud cogitandum, ne in Deum ſitis ingrati.*

* Idem Arabibus viſum non minus quam Indis & Perſis, è Jobo diſcas c. 3. 21. * Curt. l. 5. * ἀπολύεσθαι. † Variaſſe Hebræorum ſuper hac quæſtione ſententias cognoſcas ex Joſepho, ubi de morte Phaſaëlis & de deliberatione Herodis agitur. Judæi ad Petronium, Philone recitante: *Miſcebimus inter nos ſanguinem, morte ſponte ſumta; tum mortuis iſta imperentur. Ne Deus quidem nos culpet in duo intentos,*

lentos, ut & Imperatorem revereamur, & sacratas Leges custodiamus. Id autem ita demum efficere dabitur, si abeamus hinc contemta vita minime vitali.

to live to the reproch of God himself. For, because they hold, not we our selves but God hath power over our life (as *Josephus* rightly instructed his soldiers:) they think, a presumtion of the will of God is that alone, which may perfect the resolution of anticipating death. And to this they refer *Samson*'s example, who saw true Religion exposed to contempt in the sport made with him; and *Saul*'s, who fell upon his sword, that he might not be mocked by God's and his enemies. For they suppose he repented, after *Samuel*'s ghost foretold him of his death; which, though he knew would come to pass, if he did fight, he neverthelesss declined not the battail for his Country and the Law of God, and thence got eternal honour, even by *David*'s Elogy: who also gave to them that honorably buried *Saul*'s body, a testimony of their wel doing. There is a third example of *Razes* a *Jerusalem* Senator in the history of the *Maccabees*. Moreover, in the Christian history, we read like examples, of them that dyed by their own hands, lest by the force of torments they should be compeld to forswear the Christian Religion; and of Virgins, who that they might not lose their virginity,

1 Sam. 31. 4.

2 Macc. 14. 37.

Vide Euseb.

† cast themselves into the river; whom also the Church hath listed in the noble Army of Martyrs. But yet, of these, it is worth our paines to see what *Austins* * opinion is. Another exception also, I see, obtained among the *Greeks*, opposed by the *Locri* to the *Phocenses*: † *That it is a common custom among all the Greeks, to cast away sacrilegious persons unburied:* And so *Dion Prusaensis* saith, the *impious and prophane* are denyed burial. The

† Narrat Cicero nobilissimas Virgines se in puteos abjecisse, & morte voluntaria nefariam turpitudinem depulisse, Oratione de Provinciis Consularibus. Tale est & quod de Milesiis virginibus memorat Hieronymus adversus Jovinianum; & epigramma vetus Anthologiæ l. 3. Tit. de Juvenibus incipiens ᾠχόμεθ' ὦ Μίλητε. Narrant & Judæi fæminam in navi ad stuprum expetitam, cum à marito quæsiisset, an & mari mersa corpora essent resurrectura, isq; id affirmasset, jecisse se in mare. Christianarum autem mulierum plurima sanè habemus exempla. Feminarum Antiochenarum sub Dioclesiano; Sophroniæ sub Maxentio, in martyrologiis, Zonara, Sexto Aurelio. Alias Antiochenas sub Chosroe addit Procopius Persicorum 2. Laudat Virgines, quæ morte pudorem servarant, Ambrosius. Hieronymus in Commentariis ad finem capitis primi Jonæ: *Unde & in persecutionibus non licet mihi propria perire manu, absq; eo ubi castitas periclitatur.*

* Lib. de Civit. Dei c. 26. epist. 61. ad Dulc. & lib. 2. c. 23. contra 2. Gaudent. epist. Cui addere licet Chrysostomum, Gal. 1. 4. & Concilium Aurelianense 3. *Oblationes defunctorum qui in aliquo crimine fuerint interempti, recipi debere censemus, si tamen non ipsi sibi mortem probentur propriis manibus intulisse.* Et tamen is ipse August. l. 1. de Civit. Dei cap. 16. *Ac per hoc & quæ se occiderunt, ne quicquam hujusmodi paterentur, quis humanus affectus eis nollet ignosci?* Capitulare autem Francic. lib. 6. 70. *De eo qui semetipsum occidit, aut laqueo se suspendit, consideratum est, ut si quis compatiens velit elecmosynam dare, tribuat, & orationes in Psalmodiis faciat: Oblationibus tamen & Missis ipsi careant; quia incomprehensibilia sunt judicia Dei & profunditatem Consilii ejus nemo potest investigare.*

† Diod. lib. 16. Rhodiaca.

same

same, at *Athens*, was constituted against Traitors, as *Plutarch* relates †. But, to return to my purpose, for sepulture denyed, the antients with great consent have judged, war may justly be undertaken, as appears by the forementión'd history of *Theseus*, handled by *Euripides* in his *supplices*, and by *Isocrates* in the place alleged.

Antiphonte.

† At Nicetas l. 3. vitæ Alexii fratris Isaaci, cum narrasset mortem Joannis Comneni Crassi, qui per seditionem imperium affectaverat, sic loquitur: *Post corpus inde ablatum, canibus & avibus esca ponitur: quod ab humanitate alienum ac penè ferinum omnibus videbatur.*

LXXVIII. Of Punishments.

The Definition of punishment, and the original.

FActs, which are the causes of war, are considerd two ways; as they are to be *repair'd*, or as they are to be *punish'd*. This later part, which is of punishments, is the more diligently to be handled by us, because the original and nature thereof not well understood hath given occasion to many errors. *Punishment*, in general, *is the evil of passion, which is inflicted for the evil of action.* For, though certain works are wont to be imposed upon some by way of punishment, yet those works are to be consider'd only as troublesome, and therefore are to be referrd to passions. And the incommodities sufferd by some by reason of a contagious disease, or a maimed body, or other impurities, such as are many in the *Hebrew* Law, to wit, to be kept from assemblies or functions, are not *properly* punishments, although for a certain similitude, and *abusively*, they are called so. Now, among the things which nature it self dictates to be lawful and not unjust, this is one, *that he who hath done evil should suffer evil:* which the Philosophers call a most ancient and *Rhadamanthean* Law. Pertinent is that saying of *Plutarch*, *Justice accompanieth God, to punish them that transgress the Law Divine: which all we men by nature use against all men as fellows.* *Plato* said, *Neither God nor man will say, that an offender ought not be punisht.* And *Hierax*, by this as the noblest part, defined Justice, *an exacting* † *of punishment from offenders.* What we have said, that punishment properly so named, must be renderd to some offense, this is also noted by *Augustin*; *All punishment*, saith he, *if it be just, is the punishment of sin.* Which is to be understood of those punishments too, that God inflicteth, though in them sometimes, by reason of human ignorance, as the same Father speaketh †, *the sin is secret, where the punishment is not secret.*

Lib. de exilio
† Et Hierocles ἰατρείαν πονηρίας. Lactantii dictum est, de ira Dei c. 17. *Non exiguo falluntur errore, qui censuram sive humanam sive divinam acerbitatis & malitiæ nomine infamant, putantes nocentem dici oportere, qui nocentes afficit pœna.* Convenit huc & illud Belisarii apud Procopium Vandal. 1. *Primum justitiæ documentum erit pœna exacta de injustis interfectoribus.* Adde Agath. l. 5. ubi de Anatolio.
† Augustin: *Latet culpa, ubi non latet pœna.*

LXXX.

LXXI. *Who should punish an Evil-doer.*

REason dictates, that an evil-doer * may be punished, not who should punish him: but that nature sufficiently sheweth, it is most convenient to be done by him that is superior: yet doth it not demonstrate this to be necessary, except *superior* be taken in that sense, that the evil-doer be thought to have made himself thereby inferior to any other, and to have as it were degraded himself from the order of men into the number of beasts subject to man, as some Divines have determined. *Democritus: By nature it is ordaind, that the better command the worse.* And *Aristotle* saith, the worse are provided for the use of the better, as well in naturals as artificials. It follows hence, that at least a guilty person ought not to be punisht by another equally guilty: to which purpose is that sentence of Christ, *Whosoever of you is without sin* (such a sin) *let him throw the first stone.* Which he therefore spake, because in that age the manners of the Jews were most corrupt, so that they who would seem most pure were in the mire of Adultery and such like crimes, as we may perceive *Ro.* 2. 22. The same that Christ had said, the Apostle said also: *Therefore thou art inexcusable, O man, whosoever thou art* that

* August. *Si non reddit faciendo quod debet, reddet patiendo quod debet.* Philo: *Peccare dum festinatis, ad pœnas ferendas festinatis.*

Tho. 2. 2. *qu.* 64. *art.* 1. & Ib. *Cajet. Sic & Moses Maimon ad Deut.* 33.

7. *Pol.* 14.

Jo. 8. 7.

that judgest: for, wherein thou judgest another, thou condemnest thy self: for thou that judgest dost the same things. That of *Seneca* is pertinent; *The sentence can have no authority, where he that judgeth is to be condemned.* And elswhere, *The respect of our selves will make us more moderate, if we consult our selves, whether we also have not committed the like*†. *Ambrose* in the Apology of *David*: *Whosoever will judge of another, let him judge of himself first; neither let him condemn lesser faults in another, when himself hath committed greater.*

† *Pertinet huc & Ambrosi locus serm. 20. in Psal. Beati immac. item Cassiodori 6.21.*

LXXX. *Of the end of punishment*

NOcent persons are not injurd if they are punished: yet doth it not thence follow that always they must be punished. Nor is it true. For, both God and and men forgive many things to many nocent ones, and are praised for it. Famous is that saying of *Plato*, which *Seneca* turnes, to this effect: *No wise man inflicteth punishment, because a fault is done, but that it may be done no more. For things past cannot be revoked: the future are prohibited.* Again, *We will not hurt a man, because he hath offended, but that he may not offend; nor shal punishment ever be referred to what is past, but what is to come: for it is not anger but caution.*

Plato de Leg. Sen. de clem.

caution. Diodotus in *Thucydides* speaking of the *Mitileneans* to the *Athenians*, saith, *Although I grant them to have dealt very unjustly, yet I will not yield they should be slain, except it be expedient.* This is true of men punishing: for one man is so bound unto another by consanguinity, that he ought not hurt him, without it be for the obtaining of some good †. In God 'tis otherwise, to whom *Plato* * ill extends his sayings. For the actions of God may be grounded on the right of his supreme dominion, especially where the special merit of man is also found, though they propose unto themselves no end beside themselves: and so some *Hebrews* expound that apposite place of *Salomon*, in this sense, *God hath made all things for themselves, even the wicked for the evil day*: that is, even then when he punisheth the wicked, he doth it for no other end, but that he may punish. Yet, if we follow the more received interpretation, 'twill be all one: that God may be said *to have made all things for himself*: that is, by the right of his soveraignty and perfection seeking or respecting nothing beside himself: as God is said *to be of himself*, because he is not of any. Certainly, that the punishments of some very wretched persons are exacted by God, not for any thing els, the holy writ testifies, where we read, that he taketh pleasure in their calamity, that he

† Cassiodor. de Amicit. *Quod si manus una casu aliquo forte lædat alteram, illa quæ læsa est non repercutit, nec se erigit in vindictam.*

* Gorgia.

Moses Maim. in directore dubitantium l. 2. c. 13. & Rab. Iram. ad Prov. 16. 4.

αὐτοφυής.

Deut. 28. 63. Es. 1. 24. Prov. 1. 26.

he laugheth and mocketh at wicked men. And moreover, the laſt Judgment, after which no Amendment is expected, and alſo ſome ſecret puniſhments in this life, as obduration, evince it to be true, that we ſay againſt *Plato*. Nevertheleſs man, when he puniſheth man, that is by nature equal to him, ought to propoſe ſomewhat to himſelf. And this is that which the Schoolmen ſay, the mind of the puniſher ought not acquieſce in the evil of any one. Yea, before them *Plato* in his *Gorgias* ſaith, They that puniſh any one with death, or exile, or mulct, do will it, *not ſimply*, but for ſome good end. And *Seneca: We muſt come to vengeance, not as if it were ſweet to revenge, but profitable.* And *Ariſtotle* ſaith, Some things are honeſt *ſimply*, ſome *upon neceſſity*, and gives an example of the later in the exaction of puniſhment.

Th. 2.2.q.108. Silv. in verb. vindicta.

Sen. lib. 2. de ira. c. 32. Idem, c. 22. *Exſequar quia oportet, non quia dolet.* Ariſt. 7. de repub. c. 13.

LXXXI. *In what ſenſe Revenge is naturally unlawfull.*

WHerefore that which is ſaid, that the pain † of the injurd perſon is eas'd by revenge or puniſhment of the offender, agrees indeed with that nature which man hath common with beaſts *. For, anger is, as in beaſts, ſo in

† Mimus: *Læſo doloris remedium inimici dolor.* Cicero *Dolorem ait pœna mitigari.* Idem dicit Plutarchus ex Simonide.

* Inde iſta Homerica:
——*illum fera prenderat ira*, item:
Efferat ipſe animum magnum ſibi pectore in alto.

in man, as *Eustathius* rightly defines it, *a fervour* † *of the bloud about the heart from an appetite of revenge*: which appetite is of it self so void of reason, that it is often carried against those things that did no hurt, as, against the yong ones of the beast thath hath offended, or, against things senseless *, as against a stone thrown at a dog. But such an appetite considered in it self agrees not to the rational part, whose office 'tis to command the affections †: and therefore not to the Law of Nature, because that is the dictate of the rational and social Nature, as such. Now, reason dictates, man must do nothing to hurt another man, unless it have some good end. And in the pain of the enemy alone, so nakedly consider'd, there is no good but false and imaginary: as in superfluous riches, and many other things of like sort. In this sense, not only Christian Doctors, but Philosophers too *, condemn revenge in men. *Seneca* †: *Revenge is an inhuman word, received indeed for just, but differs from contumely in order only: He that returneth pain, offends, only he hath some excuse.* Yea, if we believe *Maximus Tyrius*, *He is more unjust, who revengeth himself, than he, who gave the first hurt.* *Musonius* saith, *To devise how one may bite him that bites, and hurt him that hurts, is the part of a beast, non of a man.* In *Plutarch* *Dion*, he that turned *Plato*'s wisedom to civil

† *Inde* σβέσαι χόλον bilem extinguere,

* Sen. de ira l. 2. c. 26. *Hu irasci quam stultum est, quæ iram nostram nec meruerunt, nec sentiunt.* Brasiliani, feri homines, de ferro, ita ut de homine, se vindicant.

† *Vide quæ in hanc rem Seneca de ira l. 1. cap. 5.*

* *Plato Gorgia. vide de eo Theodoretum lib. 20. curationis.*

† *Lib. 2. de ira. cap. 32.*

civil acts: *Revenge, by the judgment of Law, is esteemed more just than the offerd injury: but if Nature judge, it springs out of the same disease of minde.* Wherefore it is repugnant to the nature of man, dealing with man, to be satiated with anothers pain, as it is pain. And by consequence, the less rational any man is, the more revengeful. *Juvenal. Sat.* 13.

Sir R. S.

Revenge than life it self's a greater good.
Thus fools † *at no cause, or at toyes, take fire;*
The least occasion serves to blow up ire.
Chrysippus his opinion was not such,
Mild natur'd Thales would not say thus much;
The good old man, that did a neighbour live
To sweet Hymettus, *would not fetter'd, give*
Part of that hemlock in his cup infus'd,
Even to the slave by whom he was accus'd.
Happy Philosophy! that by degrees
Kills vices first, then souls from errour frees.
For to rejoice, when those we hate do smart,
Argues a feeble and a narrow heart:
Which instantly you may from hence collect,
That women * *most of all Revenge affect.*

† Seneca de ira l. 1. 3. *Atqui iracundissimi infantes senesq; & ægri sunt, & invalidum omne natura querulum est.*

* Terent. Hecyra.
Pueri inter sese quam pro levibus noxiis iras gerunt.
Quapropter? quia enim qui eos gubernat animus infirmum gerunt.
Itidem mulieres sunt ferme ut pueri, levi sententia.

In

In the ſame ſenſe *Lactantius* : ***Unlearned and unwiſe men , if at any time they receive injury, are drawn by a blind and unreaſonable fury , and labour to repay the like to thoſe that offend them.*** It is plain then, that man is not rightly puniſht by man,only for the puniſhment ſake.What utilities make the puniſhment right,let us now ſee.

LXXXII. *The utility of puniſhment is threefold.*

HEre is pertinent that partition of puniſhments , which *Plato* hath in his *Gorgias,* and *Taurus* the Philoſopher upon that place, whoſe words are rehearſed by *Gellius.* For thoſe partitions are taken from the end, but that , when *Plato* had ſet down two ends *Amendment* and *Example* , *Taurus* adds a third τιμωρίαν*, which *Clemens* of *Alexandria* defines , *a retribution of evil , which is referred to the profit of the exactor. Ariſtotle* *,who omitting exemplary puniſhments , puts down this *ſpecies* † only , with *amendment* , ſaith it is uſed , *for the exactors ſake , that he may be ſatisfyed.* And this is properly that which the ſame *Ariſtotle* referrs to the juſtice, which he calls *Commutative.* But theſe things are to be examined more narrowly. We will therefore ſay , that in puniſhments is reſpected either the utility of him that hath offended, or

* Tria hæc νουθεσίαν, τιμωρίαν, κόλασιν, emendationem, ſatisfactionem, exemplum , etiam Chryſoſt. ponit in 1. ad Cor. 11.

* *Rhet.* 1.c.10.

† Plutarchus quoq; eam non omiſit , cum dixit : *Quæ facinus ſtatim ſubſequuntur pœnæ non modo in poſterum inhibent delinquendi audaciam , ſed & injuria affectos maximè conſolantur.*

or of him against whose interest the offense was, or of any other indistinctly. To the first of these ends belongs the punishment called by Philosophers, sometime νουθέτησις, sometime κόλασις, sometime παραίνεσις: *Paulus* the *Lawyer* calls it punishment *for emendation*, *Plato to make one wise*, *Plutarch a medicine of the mind*, having this effect to make one better by way of Physick, which works by Contraries. For because all *action*, expecially deliberate and frequent, begets a certain proclivity to the like, which after growth is call'd a *habit*; therefore with all speed vices are to be deprived of their allurement: and this cannot be better done, than by embittering their sweetness with some pain * following. The *Platonists* in *Apuleius*: *It is worse than any punishment, if the guilty scape unpunished*: and in *Tacitus* we read, *The corrupted and corrupting minde, sick and inflam'd, is to be restrained and cooled with remedies as vehement, as the lusts wherewith it burneth.*

* Sen. de ira l. 1. *Quemadmodum quædam hostilia detorta, ut corrigamus, adurimus, & adactis cuneis, non ut frangamus, sed ut explicemus elidimus: sic ingenia vitia prava, dolore corporis animiq; corrigimus.*

Annal. 3.

LXXXIII. *Of punishing a delinquent for his own benefit.*

Punishment for this end is by nature lawful for any one that is of good judgment and not obnoxious to the same or equal vices, as appears by that castigation which is by words †. but in stripes

† Plautus Trin. *Amicum castigare ob meritam noxiam, Immune est facinus, verum in ætate utile.*

ſtripes and other puniſhments that contein ſomewhat of coaction, the difference between perſons that may, or may not, is not made *by nature* (nor could it be made, only reaſon peculiarly commends to parents the uſe of that right over their Children by the neerneſs of affection) but *by Laws*, which for the avoiding of contention, have reſtrained that common propinquity of mankind to the next Relations, as may be ſeen, both elſwhere, and in *Juſtinians Code* (*tit. de emendatione propinquorum.*) Whither perteins alſo that of *Xenophon* to his Soldiers: *If I have beaten any one for his good, I confeſs I owe ſuch a puniſhment, as parents do to their Children, Maſters to their Scholars; And Phyſicians too, for their patients recovery, ſear and cut.* Lactantius lib. 6. *Jubet Deus &c. God commands us always to have our hand over our inferiours, to chaſtiſe them daily for their offences, leſt by our unprofitable love and too much indulgence, they be ill bred and nouriſhed for vice.* But this kind of puniſhment cannot extend unto death, except *reductively*, as negations are reduc'd to the oppoſite things. For as Chriſt ſaid, it had been *better* for ſome, that is, not ſo bad, if they had never been, ſo to incurable natures it is better, that is, leſs evil, to die than to live, when it is certain, they will become worſe by living. *Seneca* ſpeaks of ſuch, when he ſaith, *To periſh is ſome-*

Vide Auguſt. Enchir. c. 72.

Mar. 14. 21.

De ira.

time

* Jambl. *Quomodo suppurato melius est uri quam sic manere, ita improbo mori quam vivere.*

time for the good of those that perish *; Such a one *Plutarch* saith, *is hurtful indeed to others, but most of all to himself.* And *Galen*, when he had said men are punished with death, first that living they may not hurt, next that others by fear of punishment may be deterred, adds, *And thirdly, it is expedient for themselves to dye, being so sick and corrupted in their mind, that they cannot be restored to health.* Some think, these are they whom *John* the Apostle saith *do sin to death*: but because the arguments hereof are fallacious, we are taught by charity to have no man for deplored, and past hope; so that punishment for this end can have place but very seldome.

1 John 5. 16.

LXXXV. *Of punishment for his profit who was offended. And of revenge by the Law of Nations.*

* Etiam hujus rei in feris imago quædam. *Leo in adulteræ pœnam consurgit.* Plin. Hist. nat. 8. 16.

THe * utility of him, against whose interest the fault was made, is herein placed, that he suffer the like no more, neither from the same nor others. *Gellius* out of *Taurus* describes it thus: *When the dignity or authority of him that is wronged is to be maintaind, lest pretermission of the penalty breed contempt of him, and diminish his respect.* What is here said of authority wronged, is to be understood of every ones liberty or other right, wherein he he is injured. In *Tacitus* we read, *He should provide for his security by a just revenge.* That the injur'd party may not suffer wrong from the same hand, three ways may be taken: first, by destroying the person that hath offended; secondly, by weaking his force that he may not be able to do hurt; and lastly, if he be taught by his own evil to do so no more, which is the same with emendation, whereof we spake even now. That the injur'd party may not be hurt by others, is effected, not by every punishment, but that which is open, conspicuous and exemplary. If then, to these ends, and within the bounds of equity, vindication be directed, though private, if we respect the bare Law of Nature, abstract from Laws Divine and Human, and from all not necessary accidents to the thing, it is not unlawfull; whether it be made by him that is wronged, or by another, seeing it is consentaneous to nature that man should receive aid from man. And in this sense may be admitted, that *Cicero*, having said, the Law of Nature is that which comes not from opinion but innate vertue, among the examples of it placeth Vindication, which he opposeth to Favour: and that none might doubt how much he would have to be understood by that name, he defines Vindication, *Whereby by defending or revenging we keep off force and contumely from us, and ours, who ought to be dear unto* *De Invent.* 2.

to us; and whereby we punish offences †. By this natural right *Samson* defending himself against the *Philistins*, saith, He should be guiltless, if he did return evil for evil to them; and after a slaughter made, He defends his doing by the same reason, saying, he had served them, as they would have served him. The *Plataeans* in *Thucydides*; *Justly have we taken revenge upon them, by the Law received among all men, allowing recompence to enemies.* It is a common Law among men, saith* *Demosthenes*, that we may be reveng'd of him that takes our goods by violence. And *Iugurtha* in *Sallust*, when he had said, *Adherbal* lay in wait against his life, adds, the people of Rome *would do that which is neither good nor right, if they hindred him from the right of Nations*, that is, from revenge.† *Aristides* the Orator saith, Poets, and Authors of Lawes, and Proverbs, and Orators, and all men do approve of this; *That revenge should be taken of those that have offerd injury.* The *Maccabees* are prais'd by* *Ambrose* for revenging the death of their innocent brethren, even on the Sabbath. The same Father disputing against the Jews making grievous complaint that their Church was fir'd by the Christians, saith, *should I plead the Law of Nations*,

† Mithridates apud Justinum lib. 38 *Adversus latronem, si nequeant pro salute, pro ultione tamen sua, omnes ferrum stringere.* Hoc ipsum ἀμύνης νόμον vocat in vita Arati Plutarchus. Apud eundem Romulus de Tatio occiso à Laurentibus: *Cædem cæde pensatam.* Idem Plut. de Mantinensibus male tractatis ab Achæis: *Et hæc quidem ultionis æquitatem in se habebant.* Belisarius apud Procopium Vandalic. 1. *Naturalis enim est læsi hominis in eum qui vim intulit inimicitia.*

* *Orat. cont. Aristocrat.*

† *Orat. pro quatuor.*

* *De offic. l. 1. c.* 40. *Epist.* 29. *Eundem vide orat. contra Symmachum. Vide Joseph. Antiqu.* 13. 1. *de vindicata Johannis morte.*

I

I might shew how many Churches the Jews set on fire in the time of Julian's *Empire* ; where he calls it the Law of Nations, to render like for like †. But because in our and our friends affairs we are corrupted by affection, therefore many families came together into one place, judges were appointed, and power was given to these alone to avenge the injurd, the liberty which nature had indulged being taken away from others *. *Demosthenes : It was decreed, justice should be done, in all these injuries, according to the Laws, and not according to every ones lust † and pleasure.* Quintilian: *The compensation of injury is not only against Law, but peace. For there is the Law, the Court, the judge, unless one be ashamed to seek a remedy by Law.* The Emperours *Honorius* and *Theodosius : Therefore are judgments in force, and the publick Laws ordained for the protection of men, that none may take the liberty to revenge himself.* King Theodoricus : *Hence was the sacred reverence of Laws found out, that nothing might be done by violent hands, nothing* by

† Sic & Liv. lib. 1. *Cum Laurentes jure gentium agerent.* Nec aliter apud Tacitum Civilis : *Egregium pretium laboris cepi necem fratris & vincula mea, & sævissimas hujus exercitus voces, quibus ad supplicium petitas jure gentium pœnas reposco.* Hist. 4.

* Lucretius :
Acrius ex ira quod enim se quisq; parabat
ulcisci, quam nunc concessum est legibus æquis,
Hanc ob rem est homines pertæsum vi colere æquum.

† Tindareus adversus Orest. apud Eurip. *Irata si uxor conjugem occidet suum, Hanc ultor ipse filius tradet neci, Et rursus illo genitus hanc cædem nova Cæde expiabit, fine quo stabunt mala ?* Aristid. orat. de pace. *Quis enim Græcorum erit reliquus si propter eos qui jam periere, superstites alii perpetuo idem malorum ferent. L. nulli C. de Jud. Cassiod. ep. 1. l. 4.*

by the impulse of a private spirit. Howbeit, the old natural liberty remains, first in places where are no judgments, as on the Sea. Whither perhaps may be referrd that act of *C. Cæsar*: who being yet a private man pursued the Pirats, by whom he had been taken, with such a navy as he could provide in hast, and partly chased, partly sunke their ships: and, when the Proconsul neglected to do justice upon the captives, himself returning to Sea hanged them up. The same will have place in deserts, or where they live like the *Nomades*. So among the *Umbrici* †,* *Nicolaus Damascenus* relates, every one was his own Avenger: which also is done done at this day among the *Moschi*, some time after an addresś to the judge. Nor had *Duels* and single *Combats* any other original, which before Christianity were used by the *German* Nations *, and in some places are not yet enough disused. Therefore the *Germans*, in *Velleius Paterculus*, wonder, when they beheld the form of the *Roman* Jurisdiction that they ended injuries by justice, that things wont to be decided by arms were determined by Law. The *Hebrew* Law permits the Kinsman of one slain to kill the manslayer without the places of refuge: and the *Hebrew* interpreters do rightly note, that such a recompence, for the dead, may be required by force; for one self, as in a wound, not unless by the judge; because moderation

Vell. Pat. lib. 2. & Plut. in Cæs.

† An umbros in Italia significatos volunt? Apud Afrorum multos idem moris fuisse testis Leo Afer lib. 2.

**Apud Stob. de Legibus.*

* Gotthos suos corrigens Rex Theodericus apud Cassiodorum 3. 23. *Remove consuetudines abominanter inolitas, verbis ibi potius non armis res tractetur.* & 24. *Cur ad monomachiam recurritis? quid opus est homini lingua, si causam manus agit armata?* Trachonitis in Oriente: *Mos omnibus modus ultionem sumere de propinquorum homicidis.* Sen. 1. de Clementia. 203.

on is more difficult where a mans own pain is urgent. A like custom of privately revenging slaughter was among the most antient Greeks, as appears by *Theoclymenes* words in *Homer*. Odiss. ό. But most frequent are the examples hereof amongst them that have not any common judge. Hence are *just wars defined to be those that revenge injuries*, as *Austin* saith; L.2.q.10. super Job. and *Plato* approves of force of arms, *until they that are in fault be compelled to give satisfaction to the innocent and wronged party*. L. de rep. 12.

LXXXVI. *The end of punishment is also the profit of All.*

THe utility of all sorts, which was the third end, hath the same parts with that which perteins to the wronged person. For, either this is the intent, that he who hath wronged one, may not wrong others (which is brought to pass by destroying him, or by weakning him, or by binding him so that he may not be able to hurt, or by amending him:) or, lest others encouraged by his impunity be troublesome† to any other persons, which end is obtained by conspicuous punishments; which the Greeks call παραδείγματα, the Latins *exempla*: which are therefore used, that the punishment of one may be the fear of many: that by the kind of punishment

† Plin. l. 8. c. 16. *Polybius Leones ob hominum appetitum crucifixos vidit, quia cæteri metu pœnæ similis absterrerentur eadem noxa.*

 others

others may be deterred, as the * Lawes ſpeak: *that others may beware and fear*, as *Demoſthenes*. The power alſo of this Law is in every mans hand *naturally*. So *Plutarch* † ſaith, a good man is by nature deſignd a Magiſtrate, and that perpetuall: For by the very Law of Nature he is Prince that doth juſt things. So *Tully* proves by the example of *Naſica*, that a wiſe man never is a private man; and *Horace* calls *Lollius* Conſul not of one year; Which ſayings are nevertheleſs to be underſtood in a Commonwealth, ſo far as the Laws thereof do bear. Of this natural right Democritus; *He that kills a Theef or a Robber any way, either by his own ſtrength, or by command, or by ſuffrage, is innocent*. And † Seneca: *When I ſhall command a malefactors head to be cut off, I will be of the ſame mind and countenance, as when I ſmite Serpents*

* *Quoniam C. ad L. Flaviam. l. 1. C. ad L. Jul. rep.*

† Præc. pol. Idem Pelopida; *Prima eademq; antiquiſſima lex eum qui ſervare poteſt ei qui ſalute opus habet naturaliter magiſtratum deſignat.* Et Philopœmene: *Suſceperunt cives ſuos, qui neq; legum neq; ſuffragiorum tempus expectaverant: ſed ipſum ſequebantur naturæ lege, quæ ſemper potiorem vult imperare deterioribus.* Similia apud eum habes fine vitæ F. Flaminii. Scriptor de cauſis corruptæ eloqu. de oratoribus agens: *Hi ne privati quietem ſine poteſtate erant, cum & populum & Senatum conſilio & auctoritate regerent.* Chryſoſt. 2. ad Cor. 7. 13 de Moſe: *Etiam antequam manu populum educeret, dux erat ipſis factis. Valde igitur ſtul è Hebræus ille ei dixit, Quis te conſtituit nobis principem ac judicem? quid dicis? Facta vides, & de nomine facis controverſiam? velut ſi quis medicum videat optimè ſecantem ac ſic opitulantem ægro corporis membro, deinde ei dicat, Quis te conſtituit medicum, quis ſecare præcepit? Ars, mi bone vir, & morbus tuus: ſic & Moſem ſua peritia talem fecit. Nam & imperare non dignitas tantum eſt, ſed & ars, & quidem omnium artium ſublimiſſima.* Tractat idem ſcriptor hoc ipſum argumentum ad Eph. 3. in fine. *Tua*, inquit, *injuſtitia, tua feritas me conſtituit Principem & Judicem.* Euripides Iphigenia in Aulide: *Mente qui prudente pollet, is magiſtratum gerit.* * *Lib. 2. de ira.*

and

and venemous creatures †. But, whereas both the inquisition of the fact often requires great diligence, and the estimation of the penalty, much of wisedom and equity, lest, while every one presumed too much of himself, others not giving place, contentions should arise, therefore it pleased the just communities of men to make choice of the best and wisest; such as they esteemed so, or hoped would prove so. The same Democritus: *The Laws would not have hindred every one to live after his own pleasure, unless one had gone about to offend another. For envy lays a ground for sedition.* But, as above we said of revenge, so in this exemplary punishment, some footsteps and reliques of the old right do yet remain, in those places, and among those persons, which are not under certain Jurisdictions; and moreover in some excepted cases. So, by the customs of the *Hebrews*, an *Hebrew* falling away from God and his Law, or misleading any to false worship, might presently be slain by any man. The *Hebrews* call it the judgment of zeal, which, they say, was exercised first by *Phineas* †, and thence grew into a custom. So *Mattathias* killed a certain Jew, polluting himself with *Greekish* rites. So three hundred other Jews were slain by their Countrey-men, as is related in the book commonly call'd the third of the *Maccabees*. Nor was *Stephen* stoned upon other pretence, or conspiracy

† Cl. Neap. apud Porphyrium l. 1. de non esu anim. *Serpentem & Scorpium, etiam si ipsi ab iis non impetamur, occidimus, ne cui noceant alii, & vindictam hanc praestamus humano generi.* Pythagoras apud Ovidium Metam. 15. *—Nostrumq; petentia Lethum corpora Missa neci salva pietate fatemur.*

Deut. 13. 9. *Adde locum Joseph.* 12. 8. *Mosem Maim. ad* 13. *artic. & directoris lib.* 3. *c.* 41.

† Numb. 25. vid. 1. Macc. 2. 24, 26. Macc. 2.

Act. 6. 57.

Act. 23. 13.

cy made against *Paul*: and many other examples of like sort are extant both in *Philo* †, and in *Josephus*. Moreover; among many people, both to Masters over their servants, and Parents over their children, remained a full right of punishing them, even to death. So at *Sparta*, the *Ephori* might put a Citizen to death without judgment. Thus by what we have said, may be understood what the right of Nature is touching punishments, and how far it hath remained.

† Cujus & hoc in libro de sacrificantibus: *Puniendus talis ut hostis publicus omnium, spreta qualis cunq; cum eo necessitudine, ejusq; suasiones vulgandæ omnibus pietatem amantibus, ut sine mora accurrant undiq; ad expetendum de viro improbo supplicium, firmè credentes sanctam esse rem ejusmodi hominis interficiendi appetitum.* Et alter locus non minus insignis circa finem de Monarchia.

LXXXVII. *What the Evangelical Law hath constituted about this matter.*

NOw must we consider, whether the Evangelical Law hath more narrowly circumscribed that Liberty. Surely, as we have elswhere spoken, it is no wonder, that some things, which by nature and the Civil Laws are Lawful, are forbidden by Divine Law, and that most perfect, and promising a reward above human nature; to the attaining whereof, not undeservedly are requir'd vertues that exceed the meer precepts of Nature. Castigations *, which do leave neither infamy nor permanent loss, and are necessary in respect

* *Servorum filiorumq; peccata non coërcere, peccatum est.* Lactant. de ira Dei cap. 18. ubi plura ad hanc rem.

respect of age or other quality, if they come from those hands, which are permitted by human Laws to inflict them, (namely, Parents, Tutors, Masters and Teachers) have nothing repugnant to the Evangelical Precepts, as we may sufficiently conceive by the nature of the thing it self. For these are remedies for the mind, not less innocent than medicines ungrateful to the sense. Of revenge we must have another opinion. For, as it only exsatiats the mind of the offended person, it is so far from agreement with the Gospel, that, as we have shew'd afore, it is even naturally unlawfull. But the *Hebrew* Law not only forbids hatred to be kept against the *neighbour*, that is, Levit. 19. 17.
one of the same nation, but also commands certain common benefits to be conferrd upon such enemies. Exod. 23. 4, 5. Wherefore, the name of *neighbour* being extended by the Gospel to all men, it is manifest here is required of us, not onely that we hurt not our enemies, but that we do them good: which is also plainly commanded *Matth.* 5. 44. Yet the Law permitted the *Hebrews* to revenge greater injuries, not with the hand, but by address unto the Judge. But Christ doth not permit the same to us, as appears by that opposition, *Ye have heard it hath been said, An eye for an eye:* and after: *But I say unto you.* For although the words that follow, properly speak of repelling injury, (and re-
strain

ſtrain this licence too, at leaſt in ſome meaſure) yet are they to be conceived much more to diſallow of revenge, becauſe they reject the old permiſſion as agreeing to a more * imperfect time; *not, that juſt revenge is unlawfull, but becauſe patience is preferd before it*, as it is in the Conſtitutions of *Clement, l. 7. c. 23.* Whereof *Tertullian* † ſaith, *Chriſt plainly teacheth a new kind of patience, forbidding even that recompence of injury, which was permitted by the Creator, requiring an eye for an eye, and a tooth for a tooth: on the contrary He will have the other cheek alſo to be offer'd, and the cloak to be yielded after the coat. Plainly hath Chriſt added theſe as meet ſupplements to the diſciplin of the Creator, &c. Tertullian* was of opinion, that retaliation of injuries was forbidden, not Chriſtians only, but that even to the *Hebrews* it was not permitted, as a thing without fault, but for the avoiding of a greater evil. Which is true, no doubt, of ſuch a retaliation that proceeds from hatred, as appears by our former diſcourſe. For, that this is diſallow'd even by them who among the *Hebrews* excell'd in wiſedom, and regarded not the words only but the purpoſe of the Law, is manifeſt out of *Philo*; in whom the *Alexandrian* Jews, upon the calamity of *Flaccus*, the Jews oppreſſor, ſpeak thus: *We are not delighted, Sir, with the revenge upon our enemy; for we have learned*

* *Oculum pro oculo, quæ, ſi dici poteſt, injuſtorum juſtitia eſt*. Auguſtin. in expoſ. Pſal. 108. citatus C. ſed differentiæ 23. quæſt. 3.

† Adverſ. Marcion. 4. Idem lib. de patient. *Chriſtus gratiam legi ſuperducens ampliandæ adimplendæq; legi adjutricem ſuam patientiam præfecit, quod ea ſola ad juſtitiæ doctrinam retro defuiſſet.*

ned out of our holy Laws * *to take pity on men.* And hither it perteins, that Christ exacteth of us indistinctly, to forgive *all* that have trespassed against us; that is, neither to procure nor to wish evil to them upon sense of our evil; for, to speak with *Claudian*,

* Vide Origenem adversus Cellum. Matth. 6. 14, 15.

Who rights himself doth wrong, in that he draws
Unto himself the office of the Laws.

Claud.—*ferus est, Legumq; videtur Vindictam præstare sibi.*

For which reason *Lactantius* mentioning that saying of Cicero; *It is the first part of Justice to hurt none, except provoked by injury*, saith, A good sentence is spoil'd by adding two words: and *Ambrose* saith, the same sentence of *Cicero* is without the authority of the Gospel. But what shall we say of revenge, not as it respecteth the time past, but as it provideth for the future? Surely this also Christ would have to be remitted: first, if he that hath trespassed against us give probable testimonies of a penitent mind †. In which places a certain more plenary remission is spoken of, such as restores the offender to the right of former friendship: whence it follows, that nothing ought to be exacted of him in the name of a punishment. Moreover, though signs of such repentance be wanting, that a damage, not too grievous, is to be sleighted, Christ hath taught by the Precept of

Cicero de offic. *Justitiæ primum munus est, ne cui noceat, nisi lacessitus injuria.*

Vide Mosem Maim. citatum ab eruditissimo Constantino lib. de damno dato, cap. 3. s. 7.

† Eph. 4. 12. Col. 3. 13. Lu. 17. 3.

letting

letting go the coat. Yea and *Plato* said, evil is not to be returned, *Albeit some greater evil be imminent, and must be sufferd*; and *Maximus Tyrius* hath words of the like sense. *Musonius* said, He would not have an action against any one for contumely received (such as Christ signifies by a blow on the cheek) nor would he perswade any other to contend about it: for such things are much better passed by, and forgiven. But if the putting it up draws much danger with it, we ought to be content with that caution which hath least incommodity. For, as *Josephus* and other *Hebrew* Doctors note, the *Hebrews* themselves had not common use of retaliation, but the offended party, beside his charges, of which a distinct Law is extant *Exod.* 21. 19. (this is simple * restitution conteining nothing penal) was wont to receive, for retaliation, a pecuniary * mulct: which was also done at *Rome*, as *Favorinus* notes in *Gellius*. So *Joseph* the foster-father of our Lord Jesus, when he believed his wife had been unchast, chose rather to free himself by * divorce, than to make her an example: and he is said to have done it, because he was a just man, that is, honest and gentle. Upon which place *Ambrose* saith, the person of a just man is not only abhorrent from the atrocity of revenge, but averse, also from the severity † of accusation. So *Lactantius* had said before: *Neither*

Lex Wingotth. *6.* 13.
* Vide Constantinum d.c. 8. l. 1.
Lib. 20. c. 1.
* Aug. l. 2. de adulterinis conjug. *Si autem (quod verius dicitur) non licet homini Christiano adulteram conjugem occidere, sed tantum dimittere.*
† Gail. de pace pub. 8. 3.
Lib. *6.* c. 10.

Neither may a just man accuse any one of a capital crime. Justin, of the accusers of Christians, saith; *We would not have them punished, who cast calumnies upon us. Sufficient to them is their own wickedness, and their ignorance of good things.* There remain those punishments which provide not for private but publick good; partly by taking out of the way or restraining the nocent person, that he may not hurt; partly by deterring others with the severity of the example: That such punishments are not taken away by Christ we have proved elswhere by a most certain argument: because, when he gave his precepts, he testified that he destroyed not any tittle of the Law. Now, the Law of *Moses*, which ought to stand in these things, as long as the Commonwealth, rigidly commanded magistrats, to punish homicides and certain other crimes. But, if Christ's Precepts might consist with the Law of *Moses*, as it did inflict even capital † punishments, they may also consist with human Laws *, which, in this part, do imitate the Divine?

Justinus, *Noluimus*, ait, *eos puniri qui in nos calumniantur. Sufficit illis sua pravitas, & verum bonarum ignorantia.*

Ejusdem est: *Ne minimum quidem ulcisci quemquam volentes, ut novus legis conditor praecipit.*

Exod. 21. 14. Num. 35. 14, 37. Deut. 19. 13.

† Pharisæorum circa pœnas ἐπιείκειαν prædicat Josephus. Hinc tot Legum ad publicas pænas pertinentium exceptiones, & illud, ut ubi omnino mors inferenda est, inferatur quam levissimè; quod est in Talmude titulo Ketuboth. * *Augustinus quæst. Evangel. lib. 1. qu. 10.*

LXXXVIII. *An Objection taken from Gods mercy in the Gospel, anſwered.*

SOme, to defend the contrary opinion, allege the very great lenity of God in the new Covenant, which is therefore to be imitated by men, even Magiſtrats too, as the Vicars of God. This we yield in ſome ſort true, but not ſo far as they would extend it. For, the great mercy of God manifeſted in the new Covenant, eſpecially regardeth ſins againſt the Primitive Law, or alſo committed againſt the Law of *Moſes*, before the knowledge of the Goſpel was received. For, the ſins committed after, eſpecially if accompanied with contumacy, have a commination of judgment far more ſevere †, than that which was ordained by *Moſes*. Nor only in the life to come, but in this life too, doth God often ſhew his wrath againſt ſuch offences, 1 *Cor.* 11. 30. And pardon of theſe crimes is not uſually obtaind, unleſs man himſelf do as it were exact puniſhment of himſelf †, 1 *Cor.* 11. 3. by a certain grievous ſorrow and afflicting of his ſoul, 2 *Cor.* 2. 27. The ſame objectors urge, that at leaſt to the penitent is to be granted impunity. But, to omit, that men can hardly be certain when repentance is ſincere; and, that every one would ſcape unpuniſhed, if it were ſufficient

Act. 17. 36. Rom. 2. 25. Act. 13. 38.

† Heb. 2. 23. 4. 10. 29. Matth. 5. 21, 22, 28. Chryſoſtomus idem dicit tum in oratione ad Patrem fidelem, tum ſecunda de jejunio.

† *Peccator ante veniam deflere ſe debet.* Tertull. de pœnit. Ambr. in Pſal. 37. Chryſoſt. in 1. Cor. hom. 28. Adde 2. Cor. 7. 9, & 10.

cient in any manner to make profession of repentance; God himself doth not always remit all punishment to the penitent, as appears even by *Davids* example. Wherefore, as God might remit the penalty of the Law, that is, violent or otherwise immature death, and yet inflict no small evils upon the offender: so now also may he remit the punishment of eternal death, and in the mean time, either himself punish the sinner with immature death, or be willing he should be so punished by the magistrat. Hieronym. in c. 1. in Naum. Agath. l. 5. ex Platone. Synes. ep. 44.

LXXXIX. *Another objection answerd, about precision of repentance.*

AGain, others find fault, that together with life, space of repentance is also cut off. But these men are not ignorant, that pious Magistrats have great care hereof, and appoint not any one to to be executed, without some time allowed, wherein he may acknowledge his sins, and seriously detest them. Which kind of repentance *, though works, intercluded by death, follow not, may be accepted by God, as is proved by the example of the Thief crucified with Christ. If it be said, a longer life might be profitable to a more serious repentance and amendment; it may be answer'd, Men are found sometimes such, to whom that of *Seneca* †

* Hieronym. ad Damas. cit. in c. importuna De pænit. Dist. 1.

† Cujus & hoc est de Benef. 7. 10. *Ingeniis talibus vitæ exitus remedium est; optimumq; est abire ei, qui ad se nunquam rediturus est.*

* *Lib. 1. de ira c. 16. c. 15.*

ea † may be spoken justly: *We will do you, all the good that can now be done you, and put you to death* *. And that also of the same Author; *There is but one way for them to cease to be evil, that is, to cease to be*. Likewise said *Eusebius* the Philosopher. This then, beside what hath been said in the beginning of our work, be answer'd to them, who would have either all, or capital punishments, without any exception, forbidden Christians: contrary to the Apostles doctrin, who having included in the regall office the use of the sword, as the exercise of Divine revenge, in another place exhorteth to pray, that Kings may be made Christians, and, as Kings, be a protection to the innocent. This cannot be obtain'd (such is the improbity of a great part of men, even after the propagation of the Gospel;) unless the boldness of some be repressed by the death of others: and thus too, among so many punishments and executions of the guilty, innocency is hardly enough secured. Nevertheless, it is not amiss, to propose to the imitation of Christian Rulers, at least in some part, the example of *Sabacon* † King of *Egypt*, for his piety very famous, by whom Capital punishments, with most happy success, were commuted for tasks, and malefactors condemned to work, as *Diodorus* relates: and *Strabo* saith, there are some Nations neer Caucasus, *among whom the greatest offenders*

† Yea, and of the Romans, great part, of whom no man, after the *Porcian* Law, could be put to death or beaten, except a Traitor, or one condemned by the people.

ders received not the sentence of death. Lib. 1
Nor is that of *Quintilian* to be despised, Lib. 11.
No man will doubt, but if wicked men may Lib. 12. 1.
by any means be recalled unto a right mind, as sometimes it is known they may, it is better for the Commonwealth to save, than to destroy them. Balsamon notes, that the *Roman* Laws, which imposed penalty of death, were most of them changed, by the later Emperours being Christian †; into other punishments *; to the end, a deeper impression of repentance might be made upon condemned persons, and the continuance of the punishment might serve the more for example.

† Vide apud Nicætum lib. 1. juramentum Isaaci Angeli Idem Joannis Comneni Imperium sine morte cujusquam fuisse ait. Vide de Zenone Malchum; & Augustini epist. 158. & 159. ad Marcellinum Comitem. Et Chrysost. 5. adv. Judæos, ubi de Caini pæna. * Ad opera maxime. Augustin. epist. 160. *Alicui utili operi integra eorum membra inserviant.* Vide & Nectarii epist. ad Augustin. quæ est 201.

XC. *Three Inferences from the former Doctrine.*

OUt of these things last spoken, it may be collected how unsafe it is for a private Christian, whether for his own, or for the publick good, to take punishment of any wicked man, especially capital, though we have said it is sometimes permitted by the Law of Nations. Whence the manner of those people is to be commended, amongst whom such as go to Sea have commission from the publick Power, to purſue Pyrats, if they find any; that they may uſe the occaſion given, not as by their own adventure, but publickly commanded. Not unlike to this, is another cuſtom receiv'd in many places, that unto criminal accuſations † are admitted, not all that pleaſe, but certain men, upon whom, by publick authority, that office is impoſed: that no man may do any thing at all tending to the ſhedding of anothers blood, but by the neceſſity of his office. Hither perteins the canon of the *Eliberan* Synod: *If any believer turn informer, and by his accuſation any be proſcribed or put to death, Our decree is, that he ſhall not, no not at the end, receive Communion.* Laſtly, this alſo is underſtood by what hath been ſaid, that a man truly Chriſtian is not well adviſed, nor doth it become him, to affect and thruſt himſelf into publick Offices † that have judgment of blood, and think and profeſs it fit, that power of life and death over his fellows ſhould be committed to him, as moſt excellent of all, and as it were a God among men. For certainly, what Chriſt admoniſheth, that it is dangerous to judge of others, becauſe ſuch judgment as we give, muſt we in like caſes expect from God, is not impertinent in this place.

† Chryſoſt. de Pænitentia 8. *Optimum itaq;, ut dixi, etiam privatas lites antervertere benignis tranſactionibus, ut amicum dirigas ad id quod lites ſibi propoſitum habent: publicorum autem judiciorum accuſationes, non dicam tranſigendo abrumpere, ſed nunquam eas incipere.*

† An ſapienti capeſſenda ſit reſpublica, vide Senecam de otio Sapientis.

Matth. 7. 1, 2.

XCII.

XCI. *Whether human Laws that permit the killing of some men, give the killers a true right before God, or only impunity among men.*

THis is a noble question, and *Covarruvias* and *Fortunius* answer, that such Laws give only impunity: whose opinion is so displeasing to *Ferdinandus Vasquius*, that he calls it an ungodly opinion. No doubt, as we have said elswhere, the Law *may* do both, in certain cases; but, whether it *will* or no, is to be understood partly by the words, partly by the matter of the Law. For, if the Law give indulgence to passion, it takes away human punishment, not the fault, as in case a husband kill his Adulterous Wife, or the Adulterer *. But if the Law respect the danger of future evill by delay of punishment, it is to be conceived to grant right and publick power to a private man, so that now he is not private. Of this kind is that Law in *Justinians Code*, under the rubric, *quando liceat unicuiq; &c.* Where every man hath licence given him to oppose force against plundering and pillaging Soldiers, this reason being added: *For it is better to meet with them it time, than to seek redress after the injury done. We therefore permit you to defend & avenge your selves,* and

Covar. 4. decr. 12. c. 7. n. 8. Fort. tract. de ult. fine legum, illat. 11. Vasq. lib. 4. contr. illust. cap. 8.

* *Vide August. de Civitate Dei citatum C. quicunq;, causa 23. quæst. 8.*

and what is too late punished by judgment, we suppress by edict; that none spare a Soldier, but use his weapon against him as a thief. And the subsequent Law, about desertors, saith, *Let all men know, they have power given them against publick robbers, and desertors, that run from their colours, and all are ministers of publick revenge for the quiet of all.* To this purpose is that of Tertullian: *Against Traitors and publick enemies every man is a Soldier* †. And herein differs the right of killing exiles, whom they call *Bannitos*, from this kind of Laws, because there precedes a special sentence, here a general Edict, the fact being evident *, obteins the force of a sentence pronounced.

† Agathias l. 4. *Non solùs ducibus aliisq; potentibus innasci solet atq; immorari bene agendi propositum, sed cuiq; volenti & licet & honestum est ejus in qua vivit Reipublicæ malis commoveri, & publicas utilitates pro suis viribus promovere.* vide suprà LXXXVII.

* *Quædam sunt reipub. læsæ ad quorum pronuntiationem oculi sufficiunt.* Quintil. declamat. 260.

XCII. *What acts are not punishable by men.*

NOw let us see, whether all vicious acts are such, that they may be punished by men. Certainly, all are not such. For first, acts meerly *internal*, though by some chance, to wit, by confession afterward, they may come to knowledge of others, cannot by men be punisht; because, as elswhere we have said,

said, it is not agreeable to human nature, that from acts meerly internal, any right among men, or obligation should arise. And in this sense is to be taken, that in the *Roman* Laws: *No man is punishable for his thought*. Neverthe- less, internal acts, as they have influence into external *, come under estimation, not of themselves properly, but of the acts external, which do thence receive the quality of their merit. Secondly, men cannot punish acts inevitable to human nature. For, although it cannot be sin, which is not done freely; yet, from all sin, altogether, and always, to abstain, is above human condition. Whence, among the Philosophers, *Sopater*, *Hierocles*, *Seneca*; among the Jews, *Philo* †; among the Historians, *Thucydides*; many among the Christians have delivered, That it is natural to man, to sin. *If he must be punished*, saith *Seneca* *, *whosoever is of an evil and malefice nt nature, every one must be punished.* And *Sopater*; *If one punish men, as those that may be void of all sin, he exceeds the measure of that correction which is according to nature:* which *Diodorus Siculus* †

Cogitationis pœnam neminem mereri.

* Ita Sayrus l. 3. Thesauri c. 6.

† *De Mose lib. 3. addi potest Aben-Esdras ad Jobum 5.7. & Rabbinus Israel c. 8.*

* De ira l. 2. c. 31. Ejusdem est eodem de ira l. c. 14. *Nemo invenitur, qui se possit absolvere.* cap. 9. dixerat; *Inter cætera mortalitatis incommoda, & hæc est caligo mentium, nec tantum necessitas errandi, sed errorum amor.* Lib. 3. & 20. *Omnes mali sumus.* De clem. 1. 8. *Peccavimus omnes: alii gravia, alii leviora, &c.* Procopius Gotth. 3. in orat. Belisarii; *Nihil plane delinquere neq; hominis est, neq; id rerum fert natura.* Adde Basilium Imp. c. 50. † L. 11. Idem in fragmentis; *Non oportet per calumnias traducere infirmitatem humanæ naturæ.*

ſaith, is *to be injurious to the common imbecillity of mankind:* elſewhere, *to be unmindful of human infirmity.* The forementiond *Sopater* ſaith, *Smal faults, and of daily incurſion, are to be diſſembled.* Yea, it may be doubted, whether theſe may rightly and properly be called ſins, when the liberty which *in ſpecie* they ſeem to have, conſiderd in their generality they have not. *Plutarch* in his *Solon*; *A Law muſt be framed according to that which is poſſible if one will puniſh a few profitably, not many to no purpoſe.* Some things alſo are inevitable, not to human nature ſimply, but to this perſon at this time, by reaſon of the body's temper † paſſing into the mind, or of an old cuſtom, which yet is wont to be puniſht, not ſo much for it ſelf, as for a precedent fault *, becauſe either remedies were neglected, or diſeaſes in the mind voluntarily contracted. Thirdly, ſins are not to be puniſht, which do neither directly nor indirectly reſpect human ſociety, or another man. The reaſon is, becauſe there is no reaſon why theſe ſins ſhould not be left to be puniſhed by God, who is moſt wiſe to know them, and moſt righteous to weigh them, and moſt powerfull to avenge them. Wherefore ſuch puniſhment would be executed by men without any utility, and ſo not rightly. Here are to be excepted puniſhments emendatory, which have this for their cauſe, that the offender may

† Seneca de ira l. 2. c. 18. *Morum varietates, mixtura elementorum facit, & proinde in aliquos magis incumbunt ingenia, prout alicujus elementi major vis abundavit.* Alibi hæc ea vocat, quæ attribuit conditio naſcendi & corporis temperatura. epiſt. 11.

* *Vide c. inebriaverunt, cauſa 15. qu. 1.*

may be bettered, though haply it concern not other men. Moreover, punishable are not, acts opposed to vertues, whose nature refuseth all coaction; in which kind are mercy, liberality, gratitude. *Seneca* handles this question, Whether the vice of an ungrateful man ought to be unpunished: and brings many things to the purpose, but this especially, which may be extended to other like qualities; *When as it is a most commendable thing, to make requital of a benefit, it ceaseth to be commendable, if it be necessary*: that is, it loseth that excellent degree of praise, as the following words do shew; *for one will not more praise a gratefull man, than him that restores a thing committed to his trust, or payes what he owed without a sute.* A little after; *Tis no glory to be gratefull, were it not safe † to have been ungratefull.* That of *Seneca* the father, in his controversies, may be applyed to vices of this kind; *I desire not the accused person should be praised, but absolved* †.

Lib. 3. de benef. c. 6. & 7.

† Idem Sen. de ben. l. 1. c. 1. *Ita demum turpe est non reddere* (beneficia nempe) *si & licet.* Pater Sen. contr. 5. 34. *Dicis mihi: Hoc facere non oportet. Huic rei æstimatio immensa est; itaq; nulla vindicta est.* August. l. 2. c. 83. cont. Petil. *Sic igitur quod adversus vos Leges constitutæ sunt, non eis benefacere cogimini, sed male facere prohibemini.* † Est hoc 4. Contr. simile eodem libro contr. 24. *Non speramus ut probet, sed ut dimittat.* Et in Excerptis, 6. 8. *Multum interest objurges an punias.* Sunt enim quædam, ut Cimone ait Plutarchus; *deliquia magis virtutis alicujus, quam ex vitio crimina.*

XCIII.

XCIII. *That it is lawful to pardon, both before and after the Penal Law.*

IT follows that we consider, whether sometimes it be lawfull to grant a pardon. For the *Stoicks* † deny, but upon a light ground: *Pardon*, say they, *is a remission of due punishment: but a wise man gives every one his due*. Here the fallacy lyes in the word *due*. For, if you understand punishment to be due to him who hath done a fault, so that he may be punished without injury, it will not hence follow, if one punish him not, he doth wrong. But, if you conceive punishment so to be due from a wise man, that it is his duty to exact it, we say, that is not always so, and therefore in this sense, punishment may be, not *due*, but onely *lawfull*. And that may be true, both before the constitution of a penal Law, and after. Before a penal Law ordained, there is yet no doubt but punishment may have place: because naturally he that is a delinquent is in that state, that he may lawfully be punished: but it doth not therefore follow, that the punishment *ought* † to be exacted; because this depends upon the connexion of the ends, for which punishment was ordained, with the punishment it self. Wherefore if those ends by themselves, in a moral estimation, be not necessary;

† Ut videre est in fragmento apud Stobæum titulo de Magistratu, in oratione Tullii pro Muræna, & in fine librorum Sen. de Clementia. *Contra eos bene Diodorus Sic. in fragmentis, Venia melior pœnæ exactione.* Pro Christianis sententiam dicet Cypr. ep. 52. *Alia est Philosophorum & Stoicorum ratio, qui dicunt omnia peccata paria esse, & virum gravem non facile flecti oportere. Inter Christianos autem & Philosophos Plurimum distat.*

† Julian. de Eusebia: *Non enim si qui sunt meriti male tractari, puniriq;, hos perire utique necesse est.*

necessary; or, if other ends, on the opposit part, occur; not less profitable or necessary; or, if the ends proposed to the punishment may be attained another way; now it appears, there is nothing which precisely obligeth to the exacting of the punishment. An example of the first may be in a sin known to very few: the publick traduction whereof may therfore not be necessary, yea it may be hurtfull; to which that of *Cicero* is pertinent, concerning one *Xerxes*: *It was not fit perhaps to dismiss him being brought to judgment; but that he should be enquired after and brought to judgment, was not necessary.* An example of the second, in him, who opposeth to the fault either his own or his parents good deeds worthy of recompence; for, saith *Seneca*, *a benefit supervenient suffers not the injury to appear.* Of the third, in him, who is amended with words, or with words hath satisfi'd the wronged party, so that there is now no need of punishment to those ends. And this is one part of clemency freeing from punishment; which the *Hebrew* wise man respecting saith; *It becometh a just man to be mercifull.* For, because all punishment, expecially the more grievous, hath somewhat, which by it self considered, is repugnant, not indeed to Justice, but to Charity, Reason easily permits to abstein from it, unless greater and juster Charity do as it were irrefragably

Ad Quintum frat. 1. 21.

δεῖ τὸν δίκαιον εἶναι φιλάνθρωπον. 12. 19.

gably hinder. *Sopater* hath a place appofite to this matter, where he faith, *That part of juftice, which reduceth contracts to equality, wholly refufeth all kind of favour; but that part which is converfant about offences doth not difdain the kind and amiable countenance of the Graces* †. Now thefe three things may occur, either that punifhment is by all means to be exacted, as in wickedneffes of the worft example †; or, that it is by no means to be exacted, as when the publick good requires it to be omitted; or, that it is lawfull either to omit to exact it; whither pertains that of *Seneca*, *Clemency hath free choice.* A wife man then, fay the Stoicks, *parcit non ignofcit*; fpareth, doth not pardon. As if forfooth it were not lawfull for us, with the common people the mafters of fpeech, to call that *to pardon*, which they call *to fpare*. Truly, both here and elfwhere, as *Cicero*, *Galen*, and others have noted, a great part of Stoical difputations is fpent about words; which a Philofopher fhould principally take heed of *. After a penal Law, the difficulty feems greater; becaufe the author of a Law is in fome fort bound by his own Laws; but this is true, fo far as the Author of a Law is confidered as a part

† Cujus fenfus partem priorem fic expreffit Cicero, ad Q. fr. 1. 2. *Via juris ejufmodi eft quibufdam in rebus ut nihil fit loci gratiæ*: Pofteriorem fic Dion Prufæenfis oratione ad Alexandrinos; *Boni præfidis eft, ignofcere.* Favorino *ea quæ dicitur Clementia apud homines eft tempeftiva relaxatio de fummo jure.*

† Jofeph: *Parricidium & naturam & vitam humanam violat, ita ut qui id non punit & ipfe in naturam peccat.*

Clementiam liberum habere arbitrium. Sen. * Veriffime dixit fcriptor ad Herennium; *Vitiofum eft controverfiam intendere propter nominum mutationem.* L. 2. quod Ariftoteles dixerat: εὐλαβητέον τὸ [illegible]· τὸ [illegible] διαλέγεσθαι. *Top.* 24.

of

of the Commonwealth, not as he susteins the person and authority thereof. For in this later respect, he may take away even a whole Law; because the nature of a human Law is, to depend upon the will of man, not in its original only, but also in duration. Howbeit, the Author of the Law ought not to take away a Law, except upon some approvable cause: otherwise, he will transgress the rules of just Goverment. Now, as he may totally take away a Law, so may he unty the bond thereof, as to a person or singular fact, the Law remaining firm in other respects; and this after the example of God himself, *who* as *Lactantius* saith, *when he gave the Law, deprived not himself of all power, but hath reserved a liberty to pardon.* And *Austin* saith, *The Emperour may revoke his sentence* †, *and absolve a man guilty of death, and pardon him:* he expresseth a reason for it: *because He is not subject to the Laws, who hath it in his power to make Laws. Seneca* would have *Nero* think this: *No man at all can put any one to death against Law; and no man, beside my self, can save any.* But this also is not to be done, unless there be good reason for it. And what are good reasons, though it cannot be precisely defined, yet this is certain, they ought to be greater after the Law, than those that were considerd before the Law: because the authority of the Law, which to be kept is profi-

† Symmachus lib. 3. epist. 63. *Alia enim est cōditio magistratuum, quorum corruptæ videntur esse sententiæ, si sint legibus mitiores; alia divorum Principum potestas, quos decet acrimoniam severi juris instectere.* Idem discrimen inter Regem & Judicem est apud Themistium orat. 5.

profitable, is now added to the causes of punishing.

XCIV. *Causes of freeing one from punishment of Law.*

THe Causes of freeing one from punishment of Law are wont to be either intrinsecal, or extrinsecal. *Intrinsecal*, when the punishment, if not unjust, yet is hard, being compared with the fact. *Extrinsecal*, from some merit or other thing commending the person; or also, from good hope of him for the future; which kind of cause will be then most sufficient, if the reason of a Law, at least particularly, cease in the present fact. For although, to sustein the efficacy of the Law, the universal reason be enough, where no contrary reason is; yet, even the particular reason ceasing, the Law may more easily and with less diminution of authority be dispensed with †. This is most usual in those offences, which are committed through ignorance, though not without all fault, or vincible; but by reason of the minds infirmity, not easily vincible. Upon which offences a Christian Ruler of men ought to look with a gentle eye, in imitation of God, who in the old Covenant indeed required many such to be expiated with certain Sacrifices: but in the new, by words and by examples hath testified, that he is ready to

† Multa ad hanc rem utilia congessit Gratian. causa. 1. qu. 7.

Levit. 4. & 5.

Luc. 23. 34. Heb. 4. 15. 5. 2.

to grant pardon of such to those that repent. And truly, that *Theodosius* * was induc'd by those words of Christ, *Father forgive them, they know not what they do*, to forgive the *Antiochians*, is noted by *Joannes Chrysostomus*. And hence appears how ill *Ferdinandus Vasquius* said, a just cause of dispensing, that is, of loosing one from the Law, is only that of which the Author of the Law being consulted would have said, it was beside his meaning, that it should be observed. For he distinguisheth not between the equitable * interpretation of the Law, and the relaxation of it. Whence in another place he reprehendeth *Thomas* and *Sotus* for saying, The Law bindeth, although the cause particularly ceaseth: as if they had thought the Law to be the letter alone; which never came into their minde. All Relaxation of the Law, which may oft be given and omitted freely, is so far from *equity* properly so call'd; that neither that relaxation which is due either out of charity or justice, can be referred thither. For to take away the Law either on probable or urgent cause, is one thing; another, to declare the fact not to have been comprehended in the mind of the Law from the beginning.

1 Tim. 1. 13.
* Historiam vide apud Zonaram.

Lib. 1. c. 46.

* ἐπιείκεια.

Lib. 1. c. 26. & cap. 46.

XCV.

XCV. *Of War for punishment; and whether war be just for offences begun.*

IT is manifest, that wars are not to be undertaken for every offence: for, neither do the Laws bestow that their revenge, which is safe and hurts only the nocent, upon all faults. Rightly saith the forecited *Sopater*, That less and common transgressions are to be winked at, not revenged. Now, that which *Cato* said in his Oration for the *Rhodians*, that it is not equal any one should be punisht for an intent of doing evil, was indeed well set in that case; because no decree of the *Rhodians* could be alleged, but only conjectures of their fluctuating minde: yet is not this to be received universally. For, an intent or will, that hath proceeded to external acts (for the internal are not punished by men, as we have said afore) is wont to be lyable to punishment†. So the *Romans* decree a war against *Perseus*, unless he give satisfaction for

Gell. l. 7. c. 3.

† Seneca pater in Controversiis: *Scelera quoq;, quamvis citra exitum subsederunt, puniuntur. Injuriam qui facturus est, jam facit*, ait alter Seneca. *Non exitus rerum sed consilia Legibus vindicari*, Cicero dixit pro Milone. *Periandri dictum erat*; μὴ μόνον τοὺς ἁμαρτάνοντας, ἀλλὰ καὶ τοὺς μέλλοντας κόλαζε. Val. Max. de Cn. Sergio Silo damnato: *Non factum tunc, sed animus in quaestionem deductus est: plusq; voluisse peccare nocuit, quam non peccasse profuit.* Sen. de benef. l. 5. c. 14. *Latro est etiam antequam manus inquinet: quia ad occidendum jam armatus est, & habet spoliandi atq; interficiendi voluntatem.* Liv. lib. 42.

holding

holding consultation, and preparing war against the *Roman* people: for indeed he had provided arms, soldiers, ships. And this is well noted in the orations of the *Rhodians*, which *Livy* hath recorded; *It agrees neither with the customs nor Laws of any Commonwealth, that if one desire the destruction of his enemy, and have done nothing to effect it, he should lose his life.* Neither doth all ill will, though declared by some deed, make room for punishment. For, if sins finished are not all avenged, much less are they that are purposed and begun. In many, that saying of *Cicero* may take place: *Perhaps it may suffice, that the offender repent of his injury.* The Law given to the *Hebrews*, against very many sins inchoated against piety, or even against a man's life except judgment, constituteth nothing special: because, both in things divine, as being hard to be discerned by us, it is easy to erre; and the violence of anger is capable of pardon. But, when so many wives were easy to be had, to injure anothers bed; or, when possessions were so equally divided, by fraud to enrich himself with anothers loss, was not to be endured. For that, *Thou shalt not covet*, which is in the Decalogue, though, if you consider the scope of the Law (that is *the spirituality*) it be of larger extent (for the Law would have all to be most pure † in minde also:) yet, as to the external

† Chrysostomus ad Rom. 3. 13. & ad c. 7. multa habet in hanc rem.

ternal precept, (or *carnal commandment*) it pertaineth to the motions of the minde that are discovered by some fact : which plainly appears by *S. Mark* the *Evangelist*, who hath expressed that command thus, *Defraud not :* when he had set down a little before, *Do not steal.* And in that sense the *Hebrew* word and the *Greek* answering it are found, *Mich.* 2. 2. and elsewhere. Wherefore offences inchoate are not to be avenged with arms, unless both the matter be of great concernment, and it be gone so far, that either some certain mischief (though not yet that which was intended) hath already followed from such an act, or at least some great danger : so that the revenge either may be joined with caution of future harm (of which above, when we spake of defense) or maintain injur'd honour, or withstand a pernicious example.

Mar. 10. 19.

XCVI. *War for violation of Natures Law.*

Moreover, we must know, that Kings, and such as have equal power with Kings, have a right to require punishment not only for injuries committed against themselves or their subjects, but for them also that do not peculiarly touch themselves, whatsoever the persons are that do immanely violate the Law of Nature or Nations. For the liberty, by punishments

nishments, to provide for human society, which at first, as we have said, was in the hand of every man; after Commonwealths and Courts of justice were ordained, resided in the hand of the highest Powers: not properly as they are over others, but as they are under none. For, subjection to others hath taken away that right. Yea, so much more honest is it to vindicate other mens injuries than ones own, by how much more it is to be feared, that a man in his own, by too deep a resentment, may either exceed a measure, or at least infect his mind. And upon this score, *Hercules* was praised by the antients, for setting Countryes at liberty from *Antaus*, *Busyris*, *Diomedes*, and the like tyrants: travelling o'r the world, as *Seneca* speaks of him, not to please his humor, but execute justice: being the Author of very much good to mankind, as *Lysias* declares, by punishing the unjust †. *Theseus* is likewise praised for cutting off those Robbers, *Sciron*, *Sinis* and *Procrustes*: whom *Euripides* in his *Supplices* brings in speaking thus of himself:

† Diodorus Sicul. de eo sic loquitur: *Homines injustos & Reges insolentes tollendo beatas reddebat civitates.* Alibi dixit: *Orbem obiit pœnas de iniquis expetens.* Dio Prusæensis de eodem: *Homines malos puniebat, & superborum regna destruebat, aut in alios transferebat.* Aristides in Panathenaico ait *eum suscepta communi humani generis cura meruisse in Deos referri.* Philo de Legatione: *Hercules purgavit terras & maria, certamina subiens hominibus omnibus partim necessaria, partim perutilia, ut tolleret hominum animantiumq; aliorum ea quæ exitialia aut noxia essent.*

My Deeds have ſtil'd me through all
Greece ,
*The Puniſher * of wickedneſs.*

So we doubt not,but wars are juſt upon them , that are impious toward their parents (as the *Sogdians* were , before *Alexander* * beat them out of this barbarity :) upon them that eat † mans fleſh (from which cuſtom *Hercules* * compelld the old *Galls* to deſiſt , as *Diodorus* relates:) upon them, that exerciſe piracy †. For , of ſuch barbarians , and wild beaſts rather than men,it may be rightly ſpoken, which *Ariſtides* ſaid perverſly of the *Perſians* , who were nothing worſe than the Grecians; *War upon them is natural:* and, which *Iſocrates* in his Panathenaick ſaid, *The moſt juſt war is againſt the wild beaſts, the next againſt men like unto thoſe beaſts.*

* Ibidem dicenti Feciali : *Ten' ergo ſevit omnibus genitor parem?* Reſpondet Theſeus : *Injurioſis. Nam bonos non tangimus.* Valer. Max. de eodem : *Quicquid ubiq; monſtri aut ſceleris fuit, virtute animi ac robore dextræ comminuit.* Lib. 5. cap. 3. Plutarch. in ejus vitæ: *Peſſimis tyrannis Græciam liberavit.* Item: *Nihil ipſe paſſus injuriæ,pro aliis in homines malos impetum ſumebat.* * *Plutarch. de fortuna Alex.* † Hoc quoq; Scythas Alexander dedocuit, * Vide Dionyſ. Hal. narrantem ut Hercules hunc morem aliaq; multa abſtulerit, in beneficiis ſuis Græcos à barbaris non diſtinguens. Romanorum non minora in genus humanum merita prædicat Plinius, 30. 1. *Non ſatis æſtimari poteſt , quantum Romanis debeatur , qui ſuſtulere monſtra ; in quibus hominem occidere religioſiſſimum erat , mandi vero etiam ſaluberrimum.* Sic Juſtinianus principibus Abaſgorum edixit ne ſubditorum pueros caſtrarent. Procopius meminit Gotthicorum 4. & Zonaras , Leone Iſauro. Et Inchæ in Peruana Reges vicinos populos , qui moniti non parerent , vi coegere abſiſtere ab inceſtis , à marium cum maribus concubitu , à comiſtione hominum, aliiſq; id genus facinoribus: atq; eo modo imperium ſibi pararunt omnium quæ uſquam legimus,

mus, excepta religione, justissimum. † Seneca 7. de Benef. *Si non patriam meam impugnat, sed suæ gravis est, & sepositus à mea gente suam exagitat, abscidit nihilominus illum tanta pravitas animi.* Augustinus l. 5. de Civitate Dei; *Opinantur scelera facienda decerni, qualia si aliqua terræ Civitas decerneret, decrevissetve, genere humano decernente fuerat evertenda.*

And so far we follow the opinion of *Innocentius* * and others, who hold that war may be made against them that offend against nature *: contrary to the opinion of *Victoria*, *Vasquius* and others; who seem to require to the justice of war, that the undertaker be harmed in himself or his republick, or els that he have jurisdiction over the other party that is assailed. For their position is, that the power of punishing is a proper effect of Civil Jurisdiction, when we judge it may proceed even from natural right. And truly, if their opinion, from whom we dissent, be admitted, no enemy now shall have the power of punishment against another enemy; no not after war undertaken, from a cause not punitive: which right neverthelesse very many grant, and the use of all Nations confirmeth; not only after the war is done, but even while it endures; not out of any Civil Jurisdiction, but out of that natural right, which was before the institution of Commonwealths, and now also prevaileth, where men live distributed into families and not into Cities.

* *Innocent. c. quod super his. de voto Arch. Flor. 3. p. tit. 22. sect. 5.*

* Vide Josephum Acostam de procuranda Indorum salute l. 2. c. 4. *Sylv. in verbo Papa. sect. 7. Vict. Rel. 1. de Indis n. 40. Vasq. contr. ill. lib. 1. cap. 25.*

XCVII. *Three cautions to be observed.*

BUt here are to be used some Cautions: First, that civil customs, though received among many people not without reason, be not taken for the Law of Nature: such as those were, whereby the *Gracians* were distinguisht from the *Persians*: whereunto you may rightly refer that of *Plutarch* *; *To reduce the barbarous nations to more civility of manners, is a pretence to colour an unlawful desire of that which is anothers.* Second, that we do not rashly account among things forbidden by nature, those things which are not manifestly so, and which are forbidden rather by Divine Law: in which rank haply you may put copulations without marriage †, and some reputed incests, and usury. Third, that we diligently distinguish between general principles, *viz.* We must live honestly, *i. e.* according to reason, and some next to these, but so manifest, that they admit no doubt; *viz.* We must not take from another that which is his; and between illations, whereof some are easily known, as, Matrimony being supposed, we must not commit Adultery; others more hardly, as, that revenge which delighteth in the pain of another is vitious. It is here almost as in the Mathematicks, where some

* πρόφασις πλεονεξίας ἡμερῶσαι τὸ βαρβαρικόν. Plutarch.

† Asterius Amaseæ Episcopus: *Qui hujus tantum seculi leges condentibus obtemperant, impunitam relinquunt meretricii licentiam.* Adde locum Hieronymi ad Oceanum. *L. si Adulterium. sect. fratres. D. ad L. Jul. de adult.*

some are first notions, or next unto the first; some demonstrations, which are presently both understood, and assented to; some, true indeed, but not manifest to all. Wherefore, as about Civil Laws we excuse them that have not had notice or understanding of the Laws; so about the Laws of nature also it is fit they should be excused, whom either the imbecillity of their reason, or evil education keeps in ignorance †. For, ignorance of the Law, as, when it is inevitable, it takes away the sin; so, even when it is joynd with some negligence, doth lessen the offense. And therefore *Aristotle* compares barbarians, that are ill bred, and offend in such matters, to them, who have their palats corrupted by some disease. *Plutarch* saith, *There are diseases of the mind, which cast men down from their natural state.* Lastly, that is to be added, which I set down once for all, Wars undertaken for the exacting of punishment, are suspected of injustice, unless the acts be most heinous and most manifest, or else some other cause withall concur. That saying of *Mithridates*, concerning the *Romans*, was not perhaps beside the truth: *They do not punish the offenses of Kings, but seek to abate their power and majesty.*

† *unaquaeq; gens hoc legem naturae putat, quod didicit.* Hieron. 2. adv. Jovin.

Matth. 10. 15. Luc. 12. 47, 48. Nicom. 7.

Justin. 38. *Non delicta regum illos, sed vires ac majestatem insequi.*

XCVIII. *Whether war may be undertaken for offenses against God.*

NExt we come to those offenses which are committed against God: for it is enquired, whether, for the vindicating of them, war may be undertaken: which is largely handled by *Covarruvias*. But he, following others, thinks there is no punitive power without jurisdiction properly so called: which opinion we have before rejected. Whence it follows, as in Church-affairs Bishops are said in some sort, * *to have received the charge of the universal Church*; so also Kings, beside the peculiar care of their own states, have lying upon them the care of human society. The chief reason for the negative opinion, that such wars are not just, is this: Because God is sufficient to revenge offenses done against himself; whence it is said, *The Gods take care of their own injuries*; and, *Tis enough that perjury hath God for an Avenger*. But, we must know, that the same may be said of other offenses too. For, God, no doubt, is sufficient for the punishing of them also; and yet are they rightly punished by men, no man contradicting. Some will

C. peccatum. p. 2. sect. 10.

* τῆς καθολικῆς ... πεπιςευκώς. Est id in constit. præferentibus nomen Clementis. Cyprianus epist. 30. *Omnes enim nos decet pro corpore totius Ecclesiæ, cujus per varias quasq; provincias, membra digesta sunt, excubare.* Et de Unitate Ecclesiæ: *Episcopatus unus est, cujus à singulis in solidum pars tenetur.* Exempla hujus curæ universalis passim apud Cyprianum. Illustre imprimis epist. 67. Adde Chrysostom. in laudibus S. Eustachii.

reply

reply and say, other offenses are punished by men, as other men are thereby harmed or endangered. But on the other side we must note, not only those offenses are punished by men, which *directly* hurt other men, but those also that do so *by consequence*, as killing one self, bestiality, and some others. Now, though Religion by it self prevailes singularly to procure God's favour, yet hath it also, in human society, very great effects. And it is not without good reason, that *Plato* calls religion *the fortress of power, and the bond of Laws and vertuous disciplin* †. Irreligion, on the contrary is the cause of all iniquity *. *Jamblichus* hath a saying of *Pythagoras*: *To know God is vertue, and wisedom; and perfect happiness*. Hence *Chrysippus* said, The Law is the Queen of Divine and human things; and *Aristotle* accounts, among publick cares, that about things divine † to be the chiefest *: and the *Romans* defined skil in Law to be the knowledge of things divine and human; And *Philo* * describes the art of government, the ordering of things private, pub-

† Plutarchus similiter, *coagulum omnis societatis, & fundamentum legislationis.* Philoni quoq; est, *Efficacissimum amatorium & vinculum indissolubile benevolæ amicitiæ, unius Dei cultus.* Idem de fortitudine: *Summa ac maxima concordiæ causa, de uno Deo sensus: ex quo velut fonte procedit insolubilis & animos inter se vinciens amicitia.* Josephus autem contra Appionem libro: *Eandem de Deo habere sententiam, nihilq; vita & institutis inter se discrepare pulcherrimam in animis hominum concordiam excitat.* * Silius Italicus: *Heu primæ scelerum causæ mortalibus ægris, Naturam nescire Dei.*— So Josephus against Appian rendring the reasons why many Commonwealths were ill established, saith, It was because their Founders did not at first see the true nature of God, and through ignorance of him, and of true Religion, were not

not able to ſettle good Orders in the State.† To the knowledge whereof Juſtin Martyr inviting the Emperours, ſaith, *βασιλικὸν ἂν τοῦτο ἔργον εἴη*, This will be a work truly royal. *Adde quæ habet Covarr. in c. poſſeſſor. ſect.* 10. * *Ariſt. pol.* 7. * *Philo de creat. Magiſtr.*

lick and ſacred. All which things are not to be conſiderd only in ſome one State, (as when *Cyrus* in *Xenophon* ſaith, his

Cyri inſtit. Lib. 8.

ſubjects would be ſo much more obedient to him, by how much more they feared God:) but alſo in the common ſociety of mankind. *Take away Piety*, ſaith* *Cicero, and you take away faith alſo, and fellowſhip of mankind, and that moſt excellent of all vertues, Juſtice.* And hereof we have an evident argument in *Epicurus*; who, when he had taken away Divine providence, left nothing of juſtice neither, but an empty name †, ſaying, It had its birth from agreement alone, and endured no longer than common utility laſted, and that we muſt abſtein from things hurtfull to another, only for fear of puniſhment. His own words to this purpoſe very notable are extant in *Diogenes Laertius*. *Ariſtotle* * alſo ſaw this connexion, who ſpeaks thus of a King; *The people will the leſs fear any unjuſt uſage from their Prince, whom they believe to be religious.* And *Galen*, where he had ſaid, many queſtions are made about the world and the Divine Nature, without any benefit to mens manners; acknowledgeth the queſtion concerning Providence to be of very great uſe both for private

* Cic. lib. 1. de natura Deorum. Idem de finib. 4. *Juſtitiam adfert, cum cognitum habeas quod ſit ſummi rectoris & Domini numen, quod conſilium, quæ voluntas.*

† Seneca epiſt. 97. *Illic diſſentiamus cum Epicuro, ubi dicit nihil juſtum eſſe natura, & crimina vitanda eſſe, quia vitari metus non poſſit.*

* Ariſt. 5. de repub. cap. 11.

L. 9. de placitis Hipp. & Plat.

vate and publick vertues. *Homer* also saw this, who opposeth to men *fierce and unjust*, those that are *of a religious mind*. So *Justin* out of *Trogus* praiseth the antient Jews for their *Justice mixt with Religion* *; and *Strabo* commendeth them for being *really just and pious* †. Furthermore, Religion hath *greater* use in that greater society, than in the Civil: because in the Civil State, part of it is supplyed by Laws, and an easy execution of the Laws; when, on the contrary, in that great Community, the execution of Law is most difficult, not to be done without arms, and the Laws are very few: and these too have their sanctimony chiefly from the fear of a divine power; whence offenders against the Law of Nations are usually said to violate the Divine. Rightly therefore have the Emperors said; that the pollution of Religion perteined to all mens injury, as that wherein all mankind is concerned.

Odyss. 6. & 9.

* Philo vita Abrahami: *Ejusdem est naturæ Religiosum esse & hominum amantem: apud eundem spectantur pietas in Deum, & in homines justitia.*

† Lactantius: *Si ergo pietas est cognoscere Deum, cujus cognitionis hæc summa est ut eum colas, ignorat utiq; justitiam, qui religionem Dei non tenet. Quomodo enim potest eam nosse, qui unde oritur ignorat?* Inst. lib. 5. Idem, De ira Dei; *Religioni est propria Justitia. Lib. 4. C. de Hæreticis.*

XCIX. Four

XCIX. *Four most common principles of Religion.*

THat we may take a more perfect view of the whole matter, we must note, True Religion, which is common to all Ages, depends especially upon four principles. 1. There is a God, and He is One. 2. God is not any of the things visible, but of a nature more sublime. 3. All human affairs are under Gods providence, and governed by his most righteous Judgment. 4. The same God is Maker of all things without Himself. These four are expressed in so many Precepts of the Decalogue. For in the first is plainly deliverd the Unity of God: in the second, His invisible Nature: therefore to make an Image of him is forbidden, *Deut.* 4. 12. As *Antisthenes* † also said: *He is not seen with eyes, he is not like to any thing, neither can be known by an Image:* and *Philo* *, *It is profane to exhibite an Image, by picture or sculpture, of Him that is invisible;* † and *Plutarch* renders this cause, why *Numa* * took away

† Laudatus Clementi Alexandrino. Ex illo videtur hoc promsisse Seneca l. 7. c. 30. nat. qu. *Ipse qui ea tractat, qui condidit, qui totum hoc fundavit, deditq; circa se, majorq; est pars operis sui ac melior, effugit oculos, cogitatione visendus est.* * Dicit hæc apud Philonem Rex Agrippa. † Diodorus Siculus de Mose: *Simulacrum non constituit, eo quod Deum non crederet humana forma esse.* Tacitus; *Judæi mente sola unumq; numen intelligunt: profanos qui Deûm Imagines mortalibus materiis in speciem hominum effingunt.* * De hoc Numæ instituto vide & Dionys. Halicarn.

Images

Images from the Temples, *Because God cannot be conceiv'd but by the mind alone.* In the third precept is understood the knowledge and care of human actions, and thoughts too: for this is the foundation of an oath. For, God is call'd a witness, even of the heart, and, if one deceive, a revenger too: whereby both the Justice of God is signified, and his power. In the fourth is acknowledged the beginning of the world by God's Creation: for the remembrance whereof, the Sabbath † was instituted of old, and that with a singular kind of sanctimony above other rites. For, if one had sinned against other rites, the punishment of the Law was arbitrary, as about forbidden meats; if against this, 'twas capital: because the violation of the Sabbath, by the institution, conteined a denyal of the world's Creation by God. And the world's being created by God tacitly declares his goodness, and wisedom, and eternity, and power. Now, from these contemplative notions follow the active, *viz.* That God is to be honour'd, lov'd, worshipped and obeyed. Wherefore *Aristotle* said, he that denyeth, *God is to be honour'd*, or *Parents to be loved*, is not to be refuted with arguments, but with stripes. And elswhere. That it is the duty of an honest man, every where to honour God. Moreover, the verity of these notions, which we call contemplative, doubtless may be demonstra-

† Scriptor responf. ad Orthodoxos, ad quæst. 69. *ut ergo memoria mundi conditi inter homines servaretur, ideo voluit Deus septenarium numerum in sacris literis eminere cæteris honoratiorem.* Vide & quæ præcedunt.

Topic. 1. 9.

Topic. 2. 4.

demonſtrated, even by arguments fetcht from the nature of things: amongſt which, that is of moſt force, that ſenſe aſſures us ſome things were made; and the things made plainly lead us to ſomething that was not made. But becauſe this reaſon, and other the like, are not apprehended by all men, it is ſufficient, that, from the beginning to this preſent, in all parts of the world, all men (a very few excepted) both of the ſimpler ſort that would not deceive, and of the wiſer ſort that would not be deceived, have conſented to theſe notions: which conſent *, in ſo great variety both of Laws and other opinions, evidently ſhews the tradition propagated from the firſt men to us, and never ſolidly refuted; and this alone is enough to procure belief. What we have ſet down afore, concerning God, agrees with *Dion Pruſaenſis*, where he ſaith, our perſwaſion of God is either connate to us and drawn from arguments, or e's acquired by tradition. *Plutarch* calls it, *An antient perſwaſion, than which no argument can be more ſure, being the common foundation, upon which is built all pie-*

* Tertull. adv. Marc. *Animæ à primordio, conſcientia Dei, dos eſt. Pietas naturalis*, Diodoro Siculo in Fragmentis. Philo de Unius Imperio: *Nihil artem præferens caſu oritur. Maximam autem artem mundus præfert, teſtaturq; à ſummo perito ſummeq; perfecto ſe fabricatum. Notitia, qua Deum eſſe credimus, hinc ortum habet.* Tertull. adv. Marcion. 1. *Nos defendimus Deum primum natura cognoſcendum, deinde doctrina recognoſcendum: Natura ex operibus: doctrina ex prædicationibus.* Cyprian. de Idol. van. *Hæc eſt ſumma delicti, nolle agnoſcere quem ignorare non poſſis.* Julianus ad Heraclitum: *Omnes ante doctrinam numen aliquod eſſe perſuaſi ſumus: eo reſpiciendum, ad eum properandum: credoq; ſic animos noſtros ſe habere ad Deum, ut viſu prædita ad Lucem.*

ty. Aristotle * , All men have a perswasion concerning the Gods : and *Plato* * speaketh also to the same purpose.

* De cælo l. 3.

* De legib. 10.

C. *The first violators of these may be punished.*

WHerefore they are not without fault , who , though they be of duller wit than either to find out or to comprehend certain arguments for these notions, do reject them, seeing they guide to vertue , and the contrary opinion hath no arguments to support it. But , because we treat of punishments , and those human, a difference is here to be made 'twixt the *notions* themselves , and 'twixt the *manner* of departing from them. These notions , *That there is a God* (one or more , I say not :) and , *That he hath care of human affairs* , are most universal , and absolutely necessary to the constitution of Religion , whether true or false. *He that cometh unto God,* (that is, He that hath any Religion : for Religion is call'd by the *Hebrews* an access unto God :) *must believe that God is , and that he is a Rewarder of them that seek him* †. Epictetus : *This is the principal*

Heb. 11. 6.

† Similiter Cicero, de nat. deorum. l. 1. *Sunt Philosophi , & fuerunt , qui nullam habere censerent humanarum rerum procurationem deos. Quorum si vera sententia est, quæ potest esse pietas, quæ sanctitas, quæ religio ? Hæc enim omnia pure & caste tribuenda Deorum ita numini sunt , si animadvertuntur ab his , & si est aliquid à Diis immortalibus humano generi tributum.*

part

part of Religion to have a right opinion of the Gods, both that they are, and that they do justly order all things. Ælian saith, none of the *Barbarians* fell to *Atheism*, but all affirmed, there is a God, and such a one as careth for us *. *Plutarch* in his book of common Notions saith, the notion of God is none, if you deny a Providence: *For God must be conceived, not only immortal and blessed, but a lover of men, one that takes care of them, and doth them good. Neither can any honour* (saith *Lactantius*) *be due to God, if he favour not the godly; nor fear, if he be not angry with the ungodly*. And truly, to deny the *Being* of God, and to deny his *Providence*, if we respect the moral consequence, is all one. Wherefore, upon necessity, these two notions, through so many Ages, have been preserved, even amongst all Nations whom we have known. Hence religion toward God is ascribed by *Pomponius* to the Law of nations: and *Socrates* in *Xenophon* saith, *To worship God is a Law, which hath force amongst all men*. Which also *Cicero* * affirms. *Xenophon*, in his *Convivium*, averreth, that both *Greeks* and *Barbarians* think all things, present and future, to be known unto the Gods †. These notions

* Seneca epist. 95. *Primus est Deorum cultus, Deos credere: deinde reddere illis majestatem suam, reddere bonitatem, sine qua nulla majestas est.*

L. veluti. de justit. & jure.

* *De nat. Deor. lib. 1. & 2. de Invent.*

† Dion Prusæensis orat. 41. vocat, *persuasionem quæ misit hominibus communiter omnibus, non minus Barbaris quam Græcis necessariam, ac naturalem cunctis ratione utentibus.* Et paulo post: *Persuasionem valde robustam ac sempiternam, apud omnes gentes & cœptam & permanentem.* Seneca epist. 117.

Tanquam

Tanquam Deos esse inter alia sic colligimus, quod omnibus de Diis opinio insita est: nec ulla gens usquam est adeo contra leges moresq; projecta, ut non aliquos Deos credat. Idem de Benef. 4. 4. *Nec in hunc furorem omnes mortales consensissent alloquendi surda numina & inefficaces Deos.* Adde Platonem Protagora, & 10. de leg. & pulchra quæ habet Jamblichus post principium de mysteriis Ægyptiorum, ubi Deum nosse ita homini ait proprium, ut hinnitum equo.

therefore, whosoever first begin to take away, as they are wont to be restrain'd in well governd Cities (as *Diagoras Melius* was, and the *Epicures*, who were ejected out of good towns:) so, my judgment is, they may be restrain'd † in the name of human society, which without probable cause they violate. *Himerius* the Sophister in his action against *Epicurus*: *Do you then punish me for an opinion? No, but for impiety. It is permitted to deliver opinions; not, to oppose piety too.* The other notions are not so evident: *viz. That there are not more Gods than one: That none of the things we see, is God: not the world, not the heaven, not the earth, not the air: That the world is not from all eternity no nor the matter of it, but was made by God.* Wherefore, we find the knowledge of these, in process of time, obliterated among many people, and as it were extinct: and so much the more easily, for that the Laws took less care of this part; without which also some religion might after a sort subsist. The Law of God it self (given to that people, whom the Prophets, and prodigies, partly seen

Ælian. lib. 9.

† *Moxus Lydus Crambi urbis inhabitatores obsidione captos mersit, omnes ὅσιον ἀθέως, ut qui Deum nullum nossent colerentve.* Nicolaus Damascenus in excerptis Peiresianis.

ſeen with their eyes, partly deliverd to them by undoubted fame, had inſtructed with knowledge of theſe things, neither obſcure, nor uncertain) though it moſt deteſteth the worſhip of falſe Gods, yet doth it not puniſh with death all that are convicted of that crime; but them alone, whoſe facts are aggravated by ſome ſingular circumſtance: as, him, who hath firſt ſeduced others; the City, which hath begun to worſhip Gods formerly unknown; him that worſhippeth the ſtars, that he may forſake the whole Law, and withall the ſervice of the true Gods (which is, in *S. Paul's* phraſe, *to ſerve the creature, not the Creator* *; for παρὰ there and elſwhere often hath an excluſive ſignification:) which thing, even amongſt *Eſau's* poſterity ſome time was liable to puniſhment, as we may ſee, *Job* 31. 26, 27. him alſo, who offerd his children to *Moloch*, that is, to *Saturn*, *Levit.* 20. 2. But, the *Cananites* and the neighboring Nations, that had aforetime fallen to evil ſuperſtitions, God did not preſently judge fit to be puniſhed, but then at laſt when they had filled up the meaſure of their iniquities, *Geneſ.* 15. 16. So alſo in other Nations he winked at the times of ignorance about the worſhipping of falſe Gods, *Act.* 17. 38. *Philo* indeed hath rightly ſaid, *Every mans own Religion ſeems beſt to himſelf*, as that which for the moſt part is not judged

Deut. 13. 16.
Deut. 13. 23.
Deut. 17. 2.

* Philo ad Decalogum de tabulis: *Sunt autem alii quorum ulterius impietas procedit, qui ne paria quidem Deo & operibus ejus tribuunt, ſed quicquid honoris excogitari poteſt his exhibent, illud communiſſimum bonum nulli memoratione dignantes, id prætereunt quod ſoli meminiſſe debuerant, ſponte miſeri ſibi accerſentes quæſitam oblivionem.* Sic locum Deuteronomii interpretatur Maimonides Directore 3. 41.

Legat. ad Caium.

judged of by reason but affection: wherewith agrees that of *Cicero*, *No man approves any course of Philosophy, but that which himself followeth*. He addes, *Most men are engaged to a sect, before they are able to judge which is best*. Now, as they are excusable, and at least not to be punisht by men, who having receiv'd no Law delivered from God, worship either the vertues of the starrs, or of other natural things, or spirits, whether in images, or in living creatures, or somewhat else; or also the souls of such as have excelled in vertue and benefits done to mankind, or certain incorporeal intelligences; especially if they neither have devised such worships themselves, nor do therfore forsake the worship of the most High God†; So are they to be numbred among the injurious rather than erroneous, who either to *Cacodemons*, whom they know to be such or to the names of vices, or to men whose life hath been very vitious, do appoint and exhibite divine honours. And so are they, who worship the Gods with the blood of innocent men; from which custom, that he compeld the *Carthaginians* to abstein, is the praise of * *Darius* the *Persian* King, and of *Gelo* the *Syracusian* Tyrant. *Plutarch* also relates, that certain *Barbarians*, that worshipped their Gods with human sacrifices, were about to be punished by the *Romans*: but when they excused themselves by antiquity of the

Academ. 4.

† Sacrifices sent by the Kings of Egypt, by Augustus, by Tiberius, were admitted into their Temple by the Jews: as Josephus and Philo tell us.

* The son of Hystaspes, father of Xerxes. *Justin, lib.* 19.

Plutarch. Apophth. & de sera num. vind. Idem quæst. Roman. 12.

custom, they sufferd nothing, but only were forbidden to do so any more.

C I. *Wars are not justly made against them that will not embrace Christian Religion.*

WHat shall we say of those Arms which are carried against any people for this cause, that they will not entertain Christian Religion proposed to them? I will not now enquire, whether it be proposed in such a quality, and in such a manner, as it ought. Suppose it be: two things we say are to be noted. The first is this; that the truth of Christian Religion (to wit, so far as it superaddes to natural and primitive Religion things not a few) cannot be perswaded by arguments meerly natural, but depends upon the history both of Christ's Resurrection, and of the miracles wrought by himself and his Apostles: which is a matter of fact, of old indeed confirmed by irrefragable testimonies; but, of old; so that this is a question of fact, and that now very antient. Whence it happens, that this doctrin cannot throughly sink in into the minds of such as, now first, hear it, unless it be seconded by the secret assistances of God; and these, as they are not given to them that have them for a reward of any work, so if they be denyed to any or

any,

any,or granted more ſparingly,this comes to paſs for cauſes,not unjuſt indeed,but for the moſt part unknown to us,and therefore by human judgment not puniſhable. Pertinent here is the Canon of the *Toletan* Council : *The precept of the Holy Synod is , that henceforth none be * compelled to believe. For God will have mercy on whom he will , and whom he will he hardeneth.* For it is the manner of Scripture , when the cauſes of things are ſecret to us, to aſſign the will of God for the cauſe of them †. The next thing to be noted is , that Chriſt the Author of the new law his will and pleaſure is , that no man ſhould be drawn to receive his Law by the puniſhments of this life, or fear of them * ; in which ſenſe that of *Tertullian* is moſt true , *The new law doth not vindicate it ſelf by the revenging ſword.* In that antient book , entitled the Conſtitutions of *Clement* , it is ſaid of Chriſt : *He hath left unto men the freedom of their own choice , not puniſhing them with temporal death , but calling them to account in the world to come. Athanaſius* * ; *The Lord*

Cap. de Judæis diſt. 45.

* Joſephus ita cenſet : *Debere quemq; libero animi propoſito Deum colere, non vi coactum.*

† Servius ad initium 3. Æn. *Quotieſcumq; ratio vel judicium non apparet* , ſic viſum *interponitur*. Sic & Donatus ad act. 5. ſc. 2. Eun. atq; in eum ſenſum poni Hebræum חפץ notat Abarbaniel.

* Rom. 8. 15. Heb. 2. 15. Jo. 6. 67. Lu. 9. 54. Matth. 13. 24. Tractat hoc Gregorius Naz. orat. Cum aſſumtus eſt à patre ; & Beda lib. 26. Iſidorus de Siſebuto Rege ; *Qui in initio regni ſui Judæos ad fidem Chriſtianam permovens , æmulationem quidem Dei habuit, ſed non ſecundum ſcientiam ; poteſtate enim compulit, quos provocare oportuit fidei ratione.* Tranſcripſit hoc in hiſtoriam Rodericus 2. 13. Poſteriores in Hiſpania Reges eodem nomine culpant Oſorius & Mariana, quem vide 26, 14, 27, 5. * Epiſt. ad ſolitarios.

not compelling, but permitting to the will its own liberty, said unto all, If any one will come after me; and to the Apostles, Will ye also go away †? *Chrysostom* on the same place of *John*: *He asketh, whether they also will go away: which are the words of one laying aside all force and necessity.* Nor is that in the Parable of the Marriage any objection, that the servants are commanded to compel some to come in, *Lu.* 14. 23. For as in the parable it self, that word *compel* signifies the instance † of the Messenger, so also in the moral of it: in which sense a word of the same signification is taken *Lu.* 24. 29. and no otherwise *Matth.* 14. 22. *Mark.* 6. 45. *Gal.* 2. 14. *Procopius* in the secret part of his history saith, *Justinian's* * order was blam'd by wise men, that he compell'd the *Samaritans* by force and threats to profess the Christian Religion: he addes also the incommodities ensuing thence, which may be read in the Author himself.

† Cyprianus epist. 55. *Conversus ad Apostolos suos dixit, Nunquid & vos vultis ire? servans sc. Legem, qua homo libertati suae relictus & in arbitrio proprio constitutus, sibimet ipse vel mortem appetit, vel salutem.*

† Cyprianus de idolorum vanitate hunc locum respiciens: *Per orbem vero discipuli, magistro & Deo monente diffusi, praecepta Dei in salutem darent, ab errore tenebrarum ad viam lucis adducerent, caecos & ignaros ad agnitionem veritatis ocularent. Ac, ne esset probatio minus solida & de Christo delicata confessio, per tormenta, per cruces, per multa poenarum genera tentantur.*

* Ad eundem Justinianum Epistolam Theodaljadi vide in Cassiodoro 10. 26.

CIII.

CII. *Justly against them that deal cruelly with Christians only for Religion sake.*

BUt they that subject to punishments, the Teachers or Professors of Christianism for that cause, certainly do that which is contrary to reason it self. For, there is nothing in the Christian disciplin (I consider it here by it self, not as it is mixt with any corruption) which is hurtfull to human society, yea, there is nothing which is not profitable to it. The matter is apparent, and the Aliens are constreined to acknowledge this truth. *Pliny* saith, the Christians bound themselves by Sacrament, not to commit theft, nor robbery, nor break their trust. *Ammianus* † saith, nothing is taught in that Religion, but what is just and gentle. And it was a By-word among the people, *Caius Seius is a good man, but that he is a Christian* *. Nor is this excuse to be admitted, All innovations are to be feared, es-

† The same Author truly calls Christian Religion absolute & simple. And Zozimus a Pagan too saith, the design of it is to free men from all wickedness and impiety.

And frequently it was acknowledged by the Infidels to be a Sect injurious and offensive to none. *Tertull. Scorpiaco. Justin. Apol. 2.* We do you much service, and help you to keep your Empire quiet, teaching, that no man can conceal himself from God, whether he do good or evil; and that according to his deeds every man shall enter into life or death eternal. Arnobius lib. 2. speaking of the Christian Assemblies, saith, nothing was heard in them, but what may make men meek and modest, and charitable to all their Brethren. * *Bonus vir Caius Seius, tantum quod Christianus. Tertull. Apol. cap. 3. & 1. adv. Nat. cap. 4.*

pecially Assemblies: for, neither are doctrins to be feared, though new, if they lead to all honesty, and to obedience toward superiors; nor ought Assemblies of honest men to be suspected, and of such who seek not hiding places, unless they be compell'd. Rightly may be applied here, what Philo † relates *Augustus* said of the Jewish Synagogues: *They are not Bacchanals, or Conventicles to disturb the peace, but schools of vertue.* They that rage against such, are themselves in such a condition, that they may be justly punished: which is also the opinion of *Aquinas*. And for that cause did *Constantin* * war against *Licinius*, other Emperors against the *Persians* *; though these wars pertein rather to the Defense of the Innocent, of which hereafter, than to the exaction of punishment.

† *In legatione. Similiter & libro de Sacrificantibus facunde ostendit quantum Synagogæ distent à Paganicis mysteriis. Locus uterq; dignus inspici. Simile habet libro altero contra Appionem Josephus.*
Tho. 2.2.108.
* Vide Zonaram. Simile illud apud Augustinum epist. 50. *Maximianus Episcopus Vagiensis auxilium petiit ab Imperatore Christiano contra hostes Ecclesiæ, non tam sui ulciscendi causa, quam tuendæ Ecclesiæ sibi creditæ.* Relatum est in causam 23. qu. 3. * Vide Menandrum protectorem.

CIV.

CIII. *Not against them who are mistaken in the sense of Scripture.*

AS to them that embrace the Law of Christ for true, but doubt or mistake in some things, which either are beside the Law, or in the Law seem to have an ambiguous sense, and have been expounded by the antient Christians not after one manner, they that persecute such do very unjustly: as appears both by what we have said afore, and by the old example of the Jews. For these having a Law established by punishments of this life, did yet never punish the *Sadduces*, who rejected the article of the resurrection, a point indeed most true, but in that Law not deliverd but obscurely, and under a veil of words or things. And what if it be a more grievous error, and such as before equal Judges may easily be revinced by authority of Scripture or consent of Fathers? Here also is to be considered, how great is the force of a settled opinion, and how much every man's judgment is darkned by Affection to his own Sect, an evil, as *Galen* saith, incurable. *Origen* speaketh appositely: *More easy 'tis for a man to put off any other customs, how much soever he is affixed to them, than to lay aside his accustomed opinion* †. Adde, that the estimation of this fault depends upon the measure of illumination, and other

† Sequitur hoc Chrysostom. in 1 Cor. 2. *ubi vero consuetudo in dogmate inciderit, multo fit immobilior. Nihil enim est quod non facilius homo mutet quam ea quae religionis sunt.*

other dispositions of the mind, which are not in the compass of mans knowledge. He at last is an Heretick in *Austins** judgment, who, for some temporal profit, and especially for glory and principality, either is the Father, or the follower of new doctrins †. Let us hear *Salvian* discoursing of the *Arians : They are Hereticks, but know it not : Hereticks in our judgment, not in their own; for they do so much think themselves to be Catholicks, that they asperse us with the stain of heresy. Wherefore we are the same to them, that they are to us. We are sure they do injury to the divine generation, because they make the Son less than the Father. They think us injurious to the Father, because we believe them to be equal. The truth is with us, but they presume it is with them. The honor of God is with us, but they suppose what they believe is for the honour of the Deity. They are inofficious, but this is to them the chiefest office of Religion. They are impious, but this they think to be true piety. They err then, but they err with a good mind *, not out of hatred but love of God, believing that they honour and affect the Lord. Although they have not a right faith, yet they esteem this to be*

* *Lib. de util. credendi. Locus refertur in caus. 24 qu. 3.* Austin adds, that he that believs hereticks seemeth not to him the same thing with an heretick. Heresy is the madness of a more obstinate mind. *Vide eundem epist. 162.*

† Scriptor responsorum ad orthodoxos quæst. 4. *Apertum est ex cupiditate gloriæ aut ex æmulatu qui primos repertores agitaverit, sectas omnes existendi originem cepisse.* Chrysostom ad Gal. 45. τῶν αἱρέσεων μήτηρ, ἡ τῆς φιλαρχίας ἐπιθυμία The desire of dominion is the mother of heresy.

* Agathias in the first of his histories, where he had spoken of the absurd superstitions of the Almans, addeth, They are more worthy of pity than hatred, for their errors. For they do not stumble and wander willingly, but being desirous of good & deceived in judging, what they have approved they hold fast, whatsoever it is.

perfect

perfect charity: and how they are to be punisht, for this error of their opinion, at the day of Judgment, none can know but the Judge †. *In the mean therefore, as I conceive, God lends them patience, because he sees them, though not right believers, yet erring through affection of a pious opinion.* Concerning the *Manichees*, let us hear him who stuck long in their mire, *Augustin*; *Let them rage against you, who know not with what labour Truth is found, and how hard it is to avoid errors. Let them rage against you, who know not how rare and difficult it is to overcome carnal phantasms by serenity of a pious mind. Let them rage against you, who know not with what groanes and sighs it is effected, that in any sort God may be understood. Lastly, let them rage against you, who are deceived with no such error, as they see you are deceived with. For my part, indeed I cannot rage against you, with whom, as once with my self, I ought now to bear, and treat you with as much patience, as my friends shewed to me, when I went astray in your opinion, mad and blind. Athanasius* * sharply inveighs against the *Arian* heresy †, because it first

† Chrysostom in his Homily against Anathematiz[illegible]s: That which is secret let him alone securely judge, who is Judge of the whole world; to whom alone is known the measure of mens knowledge, and the quantity of their faith. For tel me, whence can we know, with what words a man will accuse or excuse himself in that day, when God shall judge the secrets of men? His Judgments are inscrutable and his ways past finding out.

* Epist. ad solit. † Deservedly do we hate the Authors of so ill an example among Christians. See their cruelties in Eusebius of the life of Constantin, lib. 1. 5. 38. Socrates lib 4. 29. Procopius Vandal. 1. & Gotth. 1. and Victor Uticensis. Epiphanius of the Semi-arians; They vex the Teachers of truth, and confute them not with words but swords, and have destroyed, not one, but many Towns and Countries. Of such Gregory Bishop of Rome

Rome to the Bishop of Constantinople; It is a new and unheard of way of preaching, which beats men into belief.

used the power of the Judges against Dissenters, and endeavoured to draw unto it self by stripes and imprisonment, whom it could not prevail with by perswasion; *and so*, saith he, *it manifesteth it self, how far it is from piety, and from the worship of God*, respecting, as I take it, that which is read, *Gal.* 4. 29*. *Hilary* hath a like passage in his Oration to *Constantin.* In *Gallia* long since, were condemned by the judgment of the Church, the Bishops, who took order, that the *Priscillianists* might be convicted with the sword: and in the East the Synod was condemn'd, which had consented to the burning of *Bogomilas*, Wisely said *Plato*; *It is the fittest punishment for one in error, to be made to learn* †.

* *Ad quem locum vide Hieronymum citatum c. qui secundum causa 23. quest. 4.*

Errantis pœnam esse doceri.

† Seneca in Tragœdia:
Quis nomen unquam sceleris errori dedit?
Et de ira, 14. *Non est prudentis errantes odisse; alioquin ipse sibi odio erit.* M. Antoninus l. 9. *Si potes, meliora doce: si non potes, memento in hoc tibi lenitatem datam. Ipsi dii lenes sunt talibus.* Chrysost. ad Eph. 4. 17. *Eum qui ignorat neq; malo affici, neq; accusari oportet; sed æquum est, ut discat quæ ignorat.* Valentinianus, laudante Ammiano Marcellino l. 30. *Nec quenquam inquietavit, neq; ut hoc coleretur imperavit, aut illud: nec interdictis minacibus subjectorum cervicem ad id quod ipse coluit inclinabat, sed intemeratas reliquit has partes, ut reperit.*

CV.

CIV. *Justly are they punisht, that are irreverent to the Gods they own.*

MOre justly shall they be punished, who are irreverent and irreligious toward those whom they think to be Gods†. And this was alleged among other causes of the *Peloponnesian* war* between the *Athenians* and *Lacedemonians*, and by *Philip* of *Macedon** against the *Phocenses*; of whose sacrilege *Justin* * thus; *It was a thing that ought to be expiated by the forces of all the world. Hierom* on the sixt of *Daniel*: *So long as the vessels were in the Idol-temple of Babylon, the Lord was not angry (for they seemed to have consecrated the things of God to divine worship, though by an erroneous opinion they mistook the Deity:) but after that they pollute the divine things by human uses, presently punishment waits upon the sacrilege.* And truly *Austin* is of opinion, that God advanced the Empire of the *Romans*, because, though in a false way, they were so studious of religion; and, as *Lactantius* speaks, performed the chiefest business of man, though not in truth, yet with a good intention. And we have said above, that perjuries, even by false Gods, are revenged by the true God. *He is punished*, said *Seneca*, *because he did it as to God: his opinion makes*

† *Vide de hac re Egregia apud Cyrillum libro contra Julianum 5. & 6.* Solon, as Plutarch in his life relates, prevailed with the Amphictyones to make war upon the Cyrrhæans, because they had robbed the Temple of Delphi. And so are they rightly punisht who falsly take upon them the name of Prophets. *Consule Agathiam l. 5.*

* Thucid. l. 1.

* Diodor. l. 16.

* Justin. l. 8.

7. de benef. 7.

makes him liable to punishment. So also do I take that other saying of *Seneca : In divers places the violators of Religion are punisht diversly ; but every where they are punisht :* and that of *Plato* likewise, where he condemnes them as capitall offenders.

3. De Benef. 6.

De Leg. 10.

CVI. Of Communication of punishment. *How it passeth to partakers of the fault.*

WHen the question is about Communication of punishment, either we mean partakers † of the fault, or others. They that are partakers of the fault, are punished not so much for anothers as for their own offense. They then, that command a vicious act, that give consent required *, that aid †, or entertain *, or any other way partake in the crime : that give counsel †, that praise and encourage †; that when by right properly so called they are bound to forbid, do not forbid * ; or,

† Tertull. de resurr. carnis; *Docent enim ministros & socios habere arbitrium ministrandi atq; sociandi, & potestatem suæ voluntatis in utrumq; homines sc. & ipsos, idcirco cum auctoribus merita communicare, quibus operam sponte accommodant.* * *Saulus manibus omnium lapidabat.* Aug. serm. 5. de sanctis cap. 4. similia, serm. 1. & 14. † Institut. de furt. sect. interdum. Edicto Theuderici, c. 120. * Hieronym. super parab. *Non fur solum, sed ille reus tenetur, qui furti conscius, quærente possessore, non indicat.* Chrysost. de statuis 14 *Non enim perjuri, sed & qui conscii cum sint, celant perjuria, criminius tenentur.* † Vide Instit. & edict. Theud. d. l. Androcides ex lege Attica, *Qui consilium dedit eum non minus pœna teneri, quam qui manu rem effecerit. Neq; enim sine consilio res facta fuisset,* ait Arist. de Poet. c. 17. † Chrysost. 1. ad Rom. circa fin. *Pejor peccante qui peccantem Laudat.* Qui facinorosum adstans hortatur, pro faciente habetur lege Longogobardica l. 1. c. 9. sect. 25. * Chrysost. 1. adversus Judæos : *Sic non*

non ii modo qui furtum fecere, sed & qui prohibere cum possent non prohibuere, puniuntur, & quidem pari uterq; pœna. Sic eum qui sanari ægrotum prohibet, teneri quasi vulnerasset, ait idem Chrysostomus 2. ad Cor. cap. 7.

when they are bound by like right to help the sufferer of injury, do not help; that do not disswade, when they ought to disswade; that conceal the fact, which they were bound by some Law to make known: all these may be punisht, if there be found in them such malice as may suffice to the merit of punishment, according to the rules set down afore.

CVI. *The Community or Rulers are engaged by their subjects fault, if they know and do not forbid it, when they can and ought.*

THis point will be more cleered by examples. As another Community so also the Civil is not to answer for the fact of particular men without committing or omitting somewhat themselves. S. *Augustin* saith well; *We must make a difference between the proper sin of every one, and the common sin of the people, which is committed by a multitude disposed to it with one heart, and one will.* Hence it was in the form of leagues; *If there be a failing by publick Counsel* †. The *Locrians* in *Livy* make remonstrance to the *Roman* Senate, that the

† Chrysost. de stat. 3. *Non commune fuisse delictum Civitatis, sed extraneorum & advenarum, qui cuncta temeritate ac legum ignorantia quàm ratione facerent. Neq; vero æquum, ut ob paucorum imperitiam tanta urbs everteretur, & pœnam ferrent culpæ exortes.* Ammian. l. 30 de Quadis: *Nihil ex communi mente procerum gentis delictum asseverantes in nostros.*

the defection did not proceed from any publick determination. In the same Author *Zeno* interceding for the *Magnetes* to *T. Quintus* and the Legats with him, besought them with tears, *That the madness of one might not be imputed to the City, but that the Doer might run the peril of his own actions.* And the *Rhodians* before the Senate separate the publick cause from the private, saying, *There is no City which hath not sometimes wicked Citizens, and a rude multitude alwayes.* So, neither is a Father bound by the fault of his children, nor the Master of his servants, nor other Governours, except somewhat that is vitious adhere to them. Now, among the wayes whereby Governours of other men become guilty, there are two of especiall use, and require our diligent consideration: *Sufferance* and *Receipt*. Of sufferance we determine thus; He that *knows* a fault to be done, that is *able* and *bound* to forbid it, and doth not, is guilty. *Cicero* against *Piso*: *Nor is the difference much, especially in a Consul, whether himself by pernicious Laws and wicked speeches vex the Commonwealth, or suffer others to vex it.* *Brutus* to *Cicero*: *You will say then, Do you make me guilty of anothers fault? Yes truly, if it were in you to hinder it* †. So, in the Army of

† *Par est delinquere, & delinquentes non prohibere*, ait Agapetus ad Justinian. *Quisquis patitur peccare peccantem, is vires subministrat audaciæ*, ait Arnobius. *Qui desinit obviare cum potest, consentit*: Augustinus. Egregie Proclus ad illud Hesiodi,

Sæpe

Sæpe luit populus pænas unius iniqui: ait, *ut qui cum prohibere possit, non prohibet unius malitiam.*

the *Grecians*, where *Agamemnon* himself and the rest were under the Common Council, it is right, that the *Grecians were punisht for the offences of their Princes*; because it was in their power to compel *Agamemnon* to render the Priest his daughter. It is in *Livy*, *The Kinsmen of King Tatius beat the Embassadors of the Laurentes: and when the Laurentes pleaded the Law of Nations, Affection to his friends prevailed more with Tatius: thus he drew upon himself the punishment due to them*. Here is proper that of * *Salvian* concerning Kings. *The Highest power which can restrain the highest sin, doth seem to approve it, if knowingly it be permitted*†. The *Veientes* and *Latins* excuse themselves in *Livy*, that their subjects helped the enemies of *Rome* without their knowledge. But the excuse of *Teuca* Queen of the *Illyrians* is not accepted, saying, Piracy was not exercised by herself, but by her subjects; For she did not forbid them. So, of old, were the *Scyrians* condemned by the *Amphictyones* *, for suffering some of their men to exercise Piracy. Now, tis easily presumed, the things are known, which are conspicuous, which are frequent. *That which is* done

* So is this explained by Cyril in his 5. book gainst Julian. Chrysostom in his first homily to the Antiochians involves them all in the crime: The act, saith he, was done by a few, the guilt is laid upon all. We are all in fear and expect punishment for their offense: which if we had prevented, and driven them out of the City, we had been now in safety. Liv. lib. 1.

* Lib. 1.

† *Thucyd. l.* 1. & 6. δυνάμενος παῦσαι, ἀληθέστερον δρᾷ. Dion saith in the life of Galba, It is sufficient for private men not to offend, but Rulers must take care that no other do transgress. * Plutareh. Cimone.

done by many, can be unknown to none, ſaith
Rhodiacâ. *Dion Pruſienſis*. The *Ætolians* are grave-
Polyb. lib. 2. ly reprehended by *Polybius*, that, when they pretended to be the friends of *Philip*, they did nevertheleſs ſuffer their men openly to act hoſtility, and preferred unto honours the principal actors of it.

CVII. *Likewiſe if they receive them that have offended elſwhere, unleſs they puniſh them or yield them up.*

NExt, let us conſider of *Receipt*. Puniſhments, as we have ſaid, may be required *naturally* by any one, to whom no like offenſe can be objected. Commonwealths being inſtituted, it was agreed, that the faults of particulars, which do properly belong to their own ſociety, ſhould be left to themſelves and their Rulers, to be puniſht or diſſembled at their pleaſure. Howbeit, ſo full a right they have not, in offenſes which in ſome ſort belong to the Society of mankind; which other Commonwealths and their Rulers have a right to proſecute; juſt as in every Commonwealth, any one in ſome caſes, may commence an action: much leſs have they that full power in thoſe offenſes, whereby another ſtate, or the Governour of it is peculiarly wronged; and for which therefore He or She, for their dignity or ſecurity, have right to require puniſhment; according

according to what we have said above. This right then, the Commonwealth in which the delinquent lives, nor the Ruler thereof, can justly hinder. But, seeing Commonwealths are not wont to permit another State to come armed within their bounds to exact punishment, nor is that expedient, it follows, that the Commonwealth, wherein he lives that is found † guilty, ought to do one of the two, either punish him according to his desert, being called upon; or leave him to the judgment of the offended State. For, this is that which is meant by * *delivering up*, so often mentioned in histories †. So the other *Israelites* require of the *Benjamits* to deliver up the wicked men, *Jud.* 20. The *Philistins* of the *Hebrews* to deliver up *Samson* to them as an Evil-doer, *Jud.* 15. So the *Lacedemonians* waged war against the *Messenians*, because they deliverd not up a certain man that had slain some *Lacedemonians*: and at another time for not delivering them that had ravished the Virgins sent to offer sacrifice. So *Cato* gave his vote, that *Cæsar* should be deliverd to the *Germans*, for warring against them without just cause. So the *Galls* required the *Fabii* should be deliverd to them *, for fighting against them. The *Romans* demanded of the *Hernici* the spoilers of their fields, and of the *Carthaginians*, *Amilcar*, not that Noble Captain, but another that stirred

† For the knowledge of the cause ought to precede the dedition. It is not meet to give up men untry'd, saith Plutarch in his Romulus. The King of Scotland in Camden An. 85. saith to Q. Elizabeth, that he would transmit Fernihust and the Chancellor too, if they were convicted by a fair tryal.

* Dedere.

† Lucullus requir'd Mithridates of Tigranes, and for denyal made war upon him. Appian & Plut.

* Plutarchus Camillo. Livius lib. 28.

up the *Galls* : and afterward they demanded *Annibal* : and *Ingurtha* of *Bocchus*, in these words in *Sallust*; *So shalt thou at once free us from the sad necessity of prosecuting thee for thy error, and him for his villany.* By the *Romans* themselves were given up those that had done violence to the *Carthaginian* Embassadors, and those that had done the like to the Embassadors of the *Apolloniatæ*. The *Achaians* required of the *Lacedæmonians*, that they should be yielded, who had assalted *Lanvic*, adding, except they were yielded, the League seemed to be violate. So the *Athenians* by their Herald proclamed, if any one had lyen in wait for *Philip*, and had fled to *Athens*, he was to be yielded up. The *Bœotions* exacted of the *Hippotenses*, that they should be yielded up that had killed *Phocus*. All which examples yet, are so to be understood, that the people or King be not strictly bound to deliver up the party, but, as we have said, either to deliver him up, or to punish him. For, so we read the *Eleans* to have waged war upon the *Lacedæmonians*, because they did nothing to them that had done the *Eleans* injury : that is, they did neither punish, nor deliver up the guilty persons: for, it is a disjunctive obligation. Sometimes, choice † is left to them, for their

Diodor. l. 16. Val. Max. l. 6. c. 6.

† Vide fœdus inder reges Anglæ & Daniæ, memoratum Pontano de Mari. Cærites apud Livium Romanis significant lib. 7. *Transeuntes agmine infesto per agrum suum Tarquinienses cum præter viam nihil petiissent, quosdam traxisse agrestis*

populationis

populationis ejus quæ sibi crimini detur, Comites: Eos, seu dedi placeat, dedere se paratos esse, seu supplicio affici, daturos pœnas. Quintil. declam. 255. *Proximos existimo eos transfugis, à quibus transfugæ recipiuntur.*

better satisfaction, that demand the offenders.

CVIII. *Whether the persons yielded up, and not receiv'd, remain Citizens.*

P. *Mutius Scævola*'s opinion was for the negative: because, whom the people had given up, they seemed to have expell'd him out of their City, as when they interdicted him fire and water. *Brutus* is for the affirmative, and *Cicero* after him: which opinion is the truer, yet not properly for that Argument which *Cicero* brings, because, as donation, so dedition cannot be understood without acception. For, the act of donation hath not perfection, but by consent of two parties: but *to deliver up*, of which we speak here, is nothing els but to permit a Citizen to be under the power of another people, to do with him what they please. Now, this permission, neither gives, nor takes away any right; it only takes away the impediment of execution. Wherefore, if the other people use not the right granted, He who is given up will be in that condition that he may be punisht by his own people (which was done upon *Clodius* yiel- ded

L. ult. D. de Legat.

L. 1. & 2. de Orat. Top. & pro A. Cæcina.

Val. l. 6. c. 3.

ded to the *Corsi*, and not received by them ;) or not punisht, as there are many faults, wherein either way may be taken. The right of the City (as also other rights and goods) is not lost, by the fact it self, but by some decree or judgment, unless some Law will have the fact esteemed for a judged thing; which cannot here be said. (And after this manner goods also, if they be deliver'd up and not accepted, will remain whose they were.) But if the dedition be accepted, and afterward, by some chance the party return, he will not be a Citizen, except by a new favour: in which sense, true is the answer of *Modestinus*.

L. eos qui D.r de captiv.

C I X. *That the rights of suppliants belong to the miserable, not to the guilty; with the exceptions.*

WHat we have said of punishing, or giving up guilty persons, pertains not only to those that have always been the subjects of him with whom they are found; but to them also who after the crime committed have fled any whither. Nor do those so much-spoken-of rights * of *suppliants*, or examples of places of *refuge* hinder. For these profit such as are oppress'd with causeless hatred, not such as have committed that which is injurious to human society, or to other men. *Gylippus*

* κοινοὶ ἱκεσίας νόμοι, Polybio & Malcho in excerpt. Leg.

Gylyppus the *Laconian* in *Diodorus Siculus*, speaking of that right of suppliants, saith, *They that introduced these rights at first, meant the unfortunate should expect mercy; the injurious, punishment.* After: *These men, if by the unjust desire of that which is anothers, they have fallen into these evils, must not accuse fortune; nor impose on themselves the name of suppliants. For that, by right, belongs to them that have an innocent minde, & adverse fortune* †. *But the life of those men full of wicked acts, shuts up against them all places of refuge, and leaves no room for compassion.* *Cicero* hath a saying out of *Demosthenes*: *We must shew compassion to those, whom fortune, not their own evil deeds have made miserable.* So, in the most wise Law, when any one had been slain by an Axe slipping out of anothers hand, the Cities of refuge were open; but the most holy Altar it self was no protection for them that had slain an inno- L.13.biblioth.

Deut. 19. 1.
23. 15.
Exod. 21. 14.
1 Reg. 2. 29.
2 Reg. 11. 13.

† Oraculum vetus:

Carum occidisti, dum vis succurrere: nullum
Crimen habes; manus est tibi purior, ac fuit ante.

Duo illa fortunam & injuriam Menander optime distinxit:

Ἀτύχημα καὶ ἀδίκημα διαφορὰν ἔχει.
Τὸ γὰρ διὰ τύχην γίγνεται, τὸ δ' αἱρέσει.

Philo de Judice: *Misericordia infortuniis debetur: at qui deliberata scientia male agit, non infelix est, sed injustus.* Sic M. Antoninus mentem vult inspici, *ut noris ignorantia in aliquo an consilium fuerit.* Sic τὰ ἐξ ἀγνοίας ἢ λήθης, *quæ ex ignorantia aut oblivione veniunt;* & τὰ ἐκ προνοίας *quæ ex consulto fiunt*, distinguit Totilas apud Procop. Got. 3.

 cent

cent man deliberately, or had troubled the Commonwealth. Which Law *Philo* explaining saith: *Unholy men have no entertainment in the Holy place.* And no otherwise the more antient Greeks. It is related, that the *Chalcidenses* refus'd † to yield *Nauplius* to the *Achivi*: but the cause is added; for he had cleared himself from their objections. There was among the *Athenians* an Altar of mercy, mentioned by *Cicero* and others; but for whom? Only for the miserable and distressed. *Aristides* saith, it was the proper praise * of the *Athenians*, *that they were a refuge and comfort to all afflicted men every where* †. *Lycurgus* * the Orator relates, that one *Callistratus*, who had done a capital fault, advising with the Oracle received answer, *that if he went to Athens, he should have right*, and that, in hope of impunity, he fled to the most holy Altar there; and notwithstanding, was put to death by the City, most observant of her Religion; and so the Oracle was fulfill'd. *Tacitus* * disallows the custom in his time received through the

De spec. leg.

Plutarch. qu. Gr. 32.

† Pipin received and would not deliver those that fled to him out of Newstria opprest by tyranny. *Fredegarius in reb. Pipini* 1188. And Ludovicus Pius the Emperor received those that fled to him from the Roman Church, as appears by his Decree, Anno 817.

* Which Mariana ascribes to the Arragonians. l. 20. 13. The Gepidæ in Procopius had rather all perish than give up Ildigisales to the Romans. Got. 4. † Aristid. Panathen. Idem alibi. *His qui ubivis locorum infelices sunt, communis eis una est felicitas, bonitas Civitatis Atheniensis, per quam salutis compotes fiunt.* Apud Xenophontem Patrocles Phliasius in orat. quam Athenis habuit: *Laudabam hanc urbem quod omnes aut injuria affectos, aut sibi præmetuentes, si huc perfugissent, auxilii compotes fieri intellexeram.* Idem sensus est in Epistola Demosthenis pro Lycurgi liberis. Et vide Sophoc. Ædip. Col. * Advers. Leocr. * Annal. 3.

Grecian

Grecian Cities, to protect the wickedness of men, in reverence to the Gods. *Princes indeed* (saith the same Author) *are like Gods : but neither do the Gods hear the prayers of suppliants , except they be just**. Such then are either to be punisht, or yielded , or removed at least. So the *Cymæi* in *Herodotus* † , when they neither would deliver *Pactyes* the *Persian*, nor durst retein him , permitted him to depart to *Mitylene*. *Demetrius Pharius* , who being conquerd in war had fled to *Philip* King of *Macedon* , was requir'd of that King by the *Romans*. *Perseus* King of *Macedon*, in his defense to *Martius*, speaking of those that were said to have conspired against *Eumenes : So soon as, being admonisht by you, I found the men in Macedonia , I commanded them away, and charged them never to return into my dominion* †. The *Samothracians* declare to *Evander* , who had lyen in wait for *Eumenes* , that he should quit the Temple. But this right of requiring to punishment, them that had fled their Countrey, in these last ages, in most parts of *Europe* , is used only in those crimes which do touch the publick State , or are of a very hainous nature.

* Sophocles Ione; —*Non enim tangi decet, Manu nocente numina ; at justum fuit Piis patere Templa contra injurias.*

In Lusitania Ferdinand Lord Chamberlain, was taken by force out of the Church, and burnt, for forcing a noble Virgin. *Mariana lib.* 21. *Vide & de Asylis librum Viri magni Pauli Veneti , Societatis servorum quæ dicitur.* † Herod. lib. 1.

Livius lib. 22. lib. 37.

† So Rudolphus 2. Emperour remov'd from him Christopher Sbovius. *Thuan. A.* 1585.

Q. Elizabeth answers the Scots, that she would either render Bothwell, or send him out of England. *Camden. A.* 1593.

nature. Lesser faults are wont to be past by with mutuall dissimulation, unless † in the conditions of the League, it were otherwise provided, and a more close agreement made. This is also to be known, that Robbers and Pirats, who are grown so strong that they have made themselves formidable, are rightly received and defended, as to punishment; because it concerns mankind, that, if they cannot otherwise, they may be recalled from their evil course by being assur'd of impunity; and any people or Governour of people may, if they be able, effect so good a work. This is to be noted too, that suppliants are defended til their cause be tryed *; and if that whereof they are accused be not forbidden by the Law of Nature or Nations, the cause must be judged out of the Civil Law of the people whence they come.

† As Simler relates in the League of the *Helvetii* with the *Mediolanenses*. The Leagues of the English with the French, appointed rebells and fugitives to be yielded; with the Burgundians, to be expelled. *Camden Anno 1600*.

* Sic Demophon ad Legatum Euristheos apud Sophoclem; *Si crimen istic aliquot hospitibus struis, Jus impetrabis: vi quidem hinc non abstrahes.*

CX. *How subjects are partakers of the faults of their Rulers, or parts of the whole; and how their punishments differ.*

WE have seen how the fault passeth upon the Rulers from the Subjects, either antient or newly come: the fault will likewise pass upon the

the subjects from the highest Power, if the subjects consent to the crime, or do any thing by the command or perswasion of the highest power, which they cannot do without transgression; of which we shall more fitly speak below, where we shall examin the duty of subjects. Moreover, between the whole and the parts, the Community and single persons, the fault is communicated; because, as *S. Augustin* saith, *The Community and the particulars go together, that being made of these; and the whole being nothing else but the parts, in one.* Howbeit, the fault perteins to the severals that have consented, not to them that were overcome by the votes of others. For, the punishments of the whole, and of the parts, are distinct. As the punishment of particular men sometime is death, so it is the death of a Commonwealth to be overthrown: which is, when the Civil body is dissolved. Single persons are by way of punishment brought under slavery (as the *Thebans* by *Alexander* the Great, those excepted, who contradicted the decree of deserting his society;) So also a City undergoes Civil slavery, being reduced into a province. Single persons lose their goods by confiscation; so, from a City are taken away things common, as walls, shipping, ammunition and the like. But, that particular men for the offence of the Community, without their consent, should

† Eidem dicit & Chrysostomus de hac re, in 17. de statuis. In eosdem Antiochenos paria olim constituerat M. Antoninus Philosophus ut testis est Capitolinus:& in Byzantinos Severus, demto Theatro, thermis, honore, ornamentisq; omnibus; sed & ipsa urbs Perinthiis data; vide Herodian. 2.

should lose the things that are proper to them, is injust, as *Libanius* rightly shews in his Oration concerning the sedition of *Antioch*. The same Authour approves the doing of *Theodosius* †, who had punished a common fault by the interdiction of the Theater, Baths, and title of Metropolitan.

CXI. *How long the right of punishment lasts against a Community.*

HEre occurres an eminent question, Whether punishment for the fault of a Community may always be exacted. So long as the Community lasteth, it seems it may: because the same body remains, the parts succeeding one another. But, on the other side, is to be noted, that some things are attributed to a Community first and by it self, as, to have a treasury, Laws, and the like: some things, by derivation from the particulars. For so we call a Community learned, and valiant, which hath most such. Of this sort is *Merit* or Desert; for, primarily it agrees to the particulars, as having understanding, which the Community by it self hath not. Those then being extinct, by whom Merit was derived to the Community, the Merit

Aristot. 7. pol. cap. 13.

Merit it self also is extinguished, and therefore the debt of punishment, which we have said cannot consist without Merit. *It seemeth to me*, saith *Libanius*, *you may account it a sufficient punishment, that none of the offenders are now alive.* And the judgment of *Arrian*'s good, condemning *Alexander*'s † revenge upon the *Persians*, those being long since dead, who had offended *Greece*. Concerning the destruction of the *Branchidæ* by the same *Alexander*, this is the judgment of *Curtius*: *Had these things been done against the Authors of the treason, it would not seem cruelty, but a just revenge: Now, the Children pay for the fault of their forefathers, when as they were so far from betraying Miletum to Xerxes, that they never saw the place.* Like unto this is the judgment of *Arrian* in another place about the burning of *Persepolis* in revenge of what the *Persians* had done at *Athens*: *To me Alexander seemeth to have done unwisely: for this was no true revenge upon those Persians, who were dead before.* That of *Agathocles* is ridiculous to every man, who answererd the *Ithacenses* complaining of their damages, and told them, that the *Sicilians* had once sufferd more from *Ulysses*. And *Plutarch* in his book against *Herodotus* saith, it is not probable, the *Corinthians* would revenge the injury received from the *Samians*, *after three generations*. Nor is it a sufficient defense

Orat. de seditione Antioch.

† Wherefore Julian in the praise of Constantius attributes to him another cause of war, and saith, No war, accounted just, was ever waged for such cause, not by the Grecians against the Trojans, nor by the Macedonians against the Persians. For they pursued not old crimes with late punishment of the children; but set upon those that injured the posterity of men wel-deserving, τῶν εὐεργετῶν.

defenſe of ſuch deeds, which we read in *Plutarch*, of the late revenge of God. For the right of God is one thing, and the right of men another, as we ſhall ſhew preſently. Neither, if it be juſt that children ſhould receive honours and rewards for their Fathers good deeds, is it therefore juſt that they ſhould be puniſht for their evil. For, ſuch is the matter of a benefit, that it may be without injury conferr'd on any; not ſo, of puniſhment.

CXII. *Whether the puniſhment may paß without Communication of the fault. Two diſtincti- ons here needfull.*

WE have ſpoken of the ways whereby community of puniſhment happens from community of fault. It remains that we ſee, whether, the fault being not communicated, the puniſhment may. For the right underſtanding whereof, and that things really diſtinct may not be confounded by likeneſs of words, we muſt note, *firſt*, that the loſs *directly* given, and *by conſequence*, are to be diſtinguiſhed. Directly given I call that, whereby ſomewhat is taken away from one, to which he hath a proper right; By conſequence, that, whereby it comes to paſs that one hath not, what otherwiſe he ſhould have had: to wit, the condition ceaſing without which he had

not

not right. An example is in *Ulpian*: *If I have opened a Well in my ground, whereby it hath happened that the veins coming to you are cut off*: He saith, my work hath not done damage to you, in that wherein I have used my own right. And elswhere he saith, there is much difference 'twixt bearing damage, and being depriv'd of the gain which hitherto one hath received. And *Paulus* the Lawyer saith *: *It is preposterous to be said masters of riches, before we have gotten them.* So, the parents goods being confiscate, the children truly feel the incommodity, but it is not properly punishment; because those goods were not to be theirs, unless preserved by the parents to their last breath. Which is rightly noted by *Alphenus*, when he saith, By the Fathers punishment, the children lose that which should descend from him to them; but those things remain entire, which were given, not By the Father, but by nature, or some other way. So *Cicero* writeth, that the children of *Themistocles* were in want, nor thinks he it unjust, that the children of *Lepidus* should bear the same calamity. And that, he saith, is old, and of all Cities. To which custom yet, the later *Roman* Laws added much temperament. So, when by the fault of the major part, which, as we have said, susteins the person of the whole, the whole is in the fault, and for the same loseth Civil

L. Flumina sect. ult. de dam. inf.

* *Præposterum esse, ante nos locupletes dici, quàm acquisierimus.* L. pretia D. ad l. Falc.

Lib. 2. epist. 11. & 19.

L. cum ratio. D. de bonis dam.

Civil liberty, walls, and other things, the particulars who are innocent do alſo bear the loſs ; but in that thing, which perteined not to them but by the whole. *Secondly*, we muſt note, ſome evil is ſometimes impoſd upon one, or ſome good is taken away, by *occaſion* indeed of ſome fault, yet not ſo that the fault is the immediate *cauſe* of that action, as to the right of doing. So he, who by occaſion of anothers debt hath engaged himſelf, ſuffers evil * ; but the immediate cauſe of his obligation is his promiſe. For, as he who is become ſurety for a Buyer, is not properly bound by the bargain, but by his promiſe : ſo alſo he who is bound for a delinquent, is not held by the delinquency, but by his engagement. And hence it is, that the evil to be born by him receives its meaſure, not from the fault of the other, but from the power which himſelf had in promiſing. Conſequent whereunto is this, that (according to the opinion which we believe to be the truer) no man can, by his becoming ſurety, loſe his life : becauſe we determine, No man hath ſuch right over his own life, that he can take it from himſelf, or engage it to be taken away by another: though the antient *Romans* and *Greeks* were of another mind in this matter: and therefore thought ſureties were bound * over to capital judg-

* Sponde, noxa præſto eſt.

* This is plain by the words of Ruben to Jacob, Gen. 42. 37. and in Joſephus 2. Antiq. c. 3. *Hos vades* ἀντιψύχους *animæ vicarios vocat Eutropius Caligulâ.* ἐγγυητὰς θανάτου, *mortis*

mortis sponsores Diodorus Siculus in excerp. Peircsianis. Chrysost. ad Gal. 2. *Sicut homine aliquo ad mortem damnato, innocens alter pro illo se morti devovens illum supplicio liberat.* Augustin. epist. 54. ad Macedonium: *Et aliquando qui causa fuit mortis potius in culpa est, quam ille qui occidit. Velut si quispiam decipiat fidejussorem suum, atq; ille pro isto legitimum supplicium luat.*

ment, (as it is in a verse of *Ausonius*, and appears by the famous history of *Damon* and *Pythias*;) and also often put Hostages to death, as we will relate elswhere. What we have said of life, ought to be understood of members too; for, a man hath not right over them, but for preservation of the body. Now, if exile, if loss of money were in the promise, and by the others fault the forfeiture was made, the surety shall bear the loss, which yet in him, to speak exactly, will not be a *punishment*. The like is also in that right which one hath depending upon the will of another, as the right of that which is *precarious*, respect being had to the dominion of the things; and the right of private men, respect being had to the eminent dominion, which the Common-wealth hath for the publick good. For, if some such be taken from one by occasion of anothers fault, punishment is not properly therein, but execution of an antecedent right in the Taker. So, because Beasts are not properly guilty of a fault, when a beast is put to death (as in the Law * of *Moses*, for copulation with man) that is not truly punishment, but the use of mans dominion over the beast.

* *De qua vide Maimonidem directore dubitantium* 3. 40.

CXIII.

CXII. *None is justly punisht (in propriety of speech) for anothers fault.*

THese distinctions premis'd, we shall say, None free from the fault can be punisht for the fault of another. The true reason whereof is not, that alleged by *Paulus* the Lawyer, that punishments are constituted for the amendment of men (for, it seems, an example may be given, without the person of the offender, yet in that person that is neer him, as shall be said presently;) but because obligation to punishment ariseth from merit; and merit is personal, having its original from the will, than which nothing is more ours, whence it is called
Epist. 3. in morte Nepot. αὐτεξούσιον. *Hierom* saith, *Neither are the vertues, nor the vices of parents imputed to their children.*
Epist. 105. *Augustin: God himself should be unjust, if he should condemn any one guiltless. Dion Chrysostom*, when he had said, the posterity of Transgressors were accursed by the *Athenian* sanction added to *Solon*'s Laws, concerning God's Law addeth; This doth not, like that, punish the children and posterity of offenders: but every one is the author of his own calamity. Pertinent is the Proverb, *Noxa caput sequitur*: and that saying of the Christian Emperors, *Punish-*
L. Sancimus. c. de pœnis. *ment must remain there, where the fault is*; and, *Let sins light only upon their authors,*

*authors, and the fear go no farther than the offense. Philo** saith, *It is just, that the punishments should rest, where the sins do*, reprehending the custom of some Nations, that put to death the innocent Children of Tyrants or Traytors †. Which custom *Dionysius Halicarnassensis* reprehendeth also, and shews the iniquity of the reason pretended, *viz.* That children will be like their parents: for that is uncertain, and an uncertain fear ought not to be sufficient for the death of any. There was one so bold as to dictate this to *Arcadius* a Christian Emperor, that the children, in whom the examples of their Fathers crime are feared, should be involved in the fathers punishment; and * *Ammianus* relates how the Issue was slain, being but very young, *lest it should grow up after the parents pattern*. Neither is fear of revenge * a more just cause. *Nothing is more unjust*, saith *Seneca* †, *than that one should inherit his fathers hatred. Pausanias*, the Generall of the *Greeks*, touched not the children of *Attaginus* *, author of the *Thebans* defection to the *Medes*; *These*, saith he, *had no finger in the plot. M. Antonius* in a letter to the senate: *Ye shall pardon the son in law and wife of Avidius Cassius* (he had conspir'd against him:) *And why do I say pardon, when they have done nothing?* God indeed, in

*Lib. 2. de leg. special. Idem lib. de piet. *Haud scio an possit ullum pejus induci institutum, quam si nec malos è bonis genitos sequetur pœna, nec bonos habebitur bonis qui ex malis parentibus nati sunt. Aliter lex quæ de suis actionibus quemq; judicat, non ex cognatorum virtutibus laudat, aut ex eorundem vitiis punit.*

† Josephus cals such a fact of Alexander King of the Jews, exaction of punishment more than belongs to man. ὑπὲρ ἄνθρωπον δίκην.

L. quisquis. C. ad L. Jul. Majest.

* Lib. 2. 8. Victoria de jure bel. n. 38.

* *Græc. Prov.* He's a fool that kils the father, and spares the child. † Sen. lib. 9. de ira. c. 4. * Herod. Call.

the Law given to the *Hebrews*, threatens, *he will punish the iniquity of the fathers upon the children*; But He hath a most full right of dominion, as over our goods, so over our lives too, being his gift, which without any cause, and at any time, he can take away from any one at his pleasure. Wherefore if, by an immature and violent death, he cut off the children of *Achan*, *Saul*, *Jeroboam*, *Ahab*; upon them he uses the right of dominion, not of punishment *; and, by the same act, punisheth the parents in a more grievous manner. For, whether they survive (which the Divine Law had very much respect unto, and therefore extendeth not those threats beyond the children of the third and fourth Generation, *Exod.* 20. because a mans Age may be lengthened to a sight of them; and it is certain, the parents are punisht with such a spectacle; yea, it is more grievous to them, * than what they bear in their own persons:) or whether they do not live so long, yet to die in that fear is no small punishment. *The hardness of the people*, saith *Tertullian*, *brought in a necessity of such remedies, that in contemplation of their posterity † they might frame themselves unto obedience.* But withall we must note, God doth not use this more heavy vengeance, except against offences committed properly to his own dishonour, as false worships, perjurie, sacrilege. Nor did the Greeks

2 Sam. 21. 1 Reg. 14. 2 Reg. 8.

* So Rabbi Simeon Barsema, very truly.

* So Chrysostom obseves, and with him consenteth Plutarch, saying, There is no sorer punishment, than to see those, which had their beeing from us, to be miserable by our fault.

† Alexander apud Curtium. l. 7. *Non oportebat vos scire quid de his statuissem, quo tristiores periretis.*

Greeks think otherwise; For, the crimes which were supposed to make their posterity obnoxious (which they call ἄγη *) are all of that sort; upon which argument, *Plutarch* discourseth eloquently, in his book of the late Revenge of God. *Ælian* * hath an Oracle of *Delphi* to this effect:

Inevitable Vengeance from above
Falls on the wicked, though ally'd to Jove;
Stil imminent it is o'r them and theirs,
Successively entail'd upon their Heirs.

It is spoken there of sacrilege †; and it is confirmed by the history of the *Tholosane* gold in *Strabo* and *Gellius*. Like sentences we had afore of perjury. But to proceed, though God hath threatned thus, yet doth he not always use that right, especially if some eminent vertue * shine forth in the Children, as we may see, *Ezech.* 18. and is proved by some examples in the now-cited place of *Plutarch*. And, sith in the new Covenant more openly than in the old, are declared the punishments, which remain for the wicked after this life; therefore in that Covenant is there no commination † extant exceeding the persons of the Transgressors; to which purpose, though less plainly, is that foresaid passage of *Ezechiel*. Now for Men, they may not imi-

* Vide Plutarchum Pericle.

* Lib. 3. 43.

† As libanius also saith, some of them had been punisht, others not yet, but they shall not escape, neither themselves, nor their children. He saith the like in another Oration set forth by Gothofred.

* And a publick detestation of the fathers crime, like that of Andronicus Palæologus the Emperour, in Gregoras, lib. 5. c 81.

† Tertull. de Men: *Desivit uva acerba à patribus manducata dentes filiorum obstupefacere: unusquisq; enim in suo delicto morietur.*

tate that vengeance of God: nor is the reason alike: because, as we have said, God, without intuition of the fault hath right over the life; men have not, but upsome great crime, and such as is the persons own. Wherefore, that same Divine Law, as it forbids parents to be put to death for their children, so forbids children to be put to death for the deeds of their parents. Which Law pious * Kings, as we read, have followed, even in the case of Treason; and the same Law is very much praysed by *Josephus* and *Philo*, as a like *Egyptian* Law by *Isocrates*, and a *Roman* Law by *Dionysius Halicarnassensis* †. *Plato* hath a saying, which *Callistratus* the Lawyer expresseth in this sense, † *The crime or punishment of the father can inflict no blot upon the son.* He addes the cause. *For every one bears that lot, which his own doings have drawn for him; nor is he made successor of another's crime. Cicero* saith *; *Would any Commonwealth endure that Law-giver, by whose Ordinance the son or grandchild is condemned, if the Father or Grandfather be a Delinquent?* Hence it is, that, to put to death a woman with child, was accounted a wicked thing, in the Laws of the *Egyptians*, *Greeks*, and *Romans* †. Moreover, if those human Laws be unjust, which do slay the children for the parents offenses, more unjust surely was the Law of the *Persians* and *Macedonians*;

Deut. 24. 16.
* Amaziah for example.
Joseph. lib. 2. Philo de leg. sp. lib. 2. Isoc. Busir. Dionys. lib. 8.
† Who saith, that custom was proper to the Romans, to free the children from al punishment, whose parents were delinquents. The same is in a Law of the Wisigoths l. 6. tit. 1. c. 8.
† *L. Crimen. D. de pœnis.*
* *Lib. 4. de nat. Deorum.*
† Philo commends these Laws in his book of Humanity. *L. Imperator Adrianus. D. de statu hominum. L. pragnantis. D. de pœnis.*

ans, devoting also and destroying the lives of kinsmen *, to the end the offenders against the King *might fall the more sadly*, as *Curtius* speaks: a Law, saith *Ammianus Macellinus* *, that excelled all the Laws in the world, in cruelty. Notwithstanding all this, it is to be noted, if children of traitors have any thing, or can expect any thing, to which they have no proper right, but the right is in the people or King, that may be taken from them by a certain right of dominion, the use whereof, yet, may redound to the punishment of those that have offended. Hither is to be referd that of *Plutarch*, touching the Children of *Antiphanes* a traitor, *that they were kept back from honours* *, as at *Rome* the children of those that were proscrib'd by *Sulla*. So, in the foresaid Law of *Arcadius*, that is tolerable for the children; *Let them not be advanced to any honour, nor to any offices.* What we have said of punishing children for their parents faults, may be applyed also to a people truly subject (for a people not subject, through their own fault, that is, for their negligence may be punisht, as we have said:) if it be enquir'd, whether that people may suffer for the evil deed of their King, or Governour. We do not mean, if the peoples consent be added †, or any deed of theirs by it self wor-

* Philo said, it was the manner of tyrants, together with the condemned, to destroy five families of neerest relation. See Herodian. *lib.* 3. and the example at Milain, when Galeatius was slain, in Bezarus, *lib.* 14.

*He calls it an abominable Law. *Vide & Concil. Tolet.* 4.

* *Simile reperies in C. in quibusdam de pœnis.*

† Philo of the subjects of the King of Egypt in Abrahams time, saith, All his family were partakers of the pain, because none was displeas'd at the unjust act, but all by approbation were partakers of it. Josephus, where he relates the prophecy uttered against Jeroboam, addeth, The people shall be punisht too, and be expeld out of that happy land, and

and exiled beyond Euphrates, for accompanying the King in his impiety.

thy of punishment, but we speak of that contract, which springeth from the nature of that Body, whose Head is the King, and members were the rest. God indeed, for *David*'s sin, destroyed the people with pestilence, and truly (as *David* thought) being innocent; but, it was God, who had most full and absolute right over their lives. Mean while, the punishment was not the peoples, but *David*'s; for, as a Christian writer saith, *It is the most bitter punishment to Kings that do amiss, to see their people suffer.* This is all one, saith the same Author, as if he, that hath done ill with the hand, should be Beaten on the back. So *Plutarch*, in the like argument, compares it to a physicians method, in curing one part, to open a vein in another. Why men may not do so, we have said afore. The same is to be concluded of punishing particulars (in things proper to them) that have not consented, for the offence of the Society. And lastly, the cause why an Heir being liable to other debts, is not liable to the punishment † of the deceased, is, for that the Heir bears the person of the deceased, not in respect of merits which are merely personal, but of goods*,

Quæst. ad orth. 133.

† Paul. IC. L. si pœna. D. de pœnis. *Si pœna alicui irrogatur, receptum est commentitio jure, ne ad hæredes transeat.*

* Cic. 2. de legib. *Nulla est persona quæ ad vicem ejus qui è vita emigraverit propius accedat quam hæres.*

which

which are engaged. *Dion Prusæensis*: *What the Ancestors owed, their posterity must pay: for they have not refused the Inheritance.*

V. OF UNJUST CAUSES. Causes of War, some are justifick, others suasory.

POlybius, who first noted the difference, calls the former προφάσεις, *Pretences*, because they are wont openly to be shewed (*Livy* several times useth the word *Title*;) the later he stileth by the general name αἰτίας, *Causes* †. So, in the war of *Alexander* against *Darius*, the *Pretence* was Revenge of Injuries which the *Persians* had done the *Grecians*, the *Cause* was desire of Glory, Empire, and Riches: whereto was added great Hope of facility conceived from the expeditions of *Xenophon* and *Agesilaus*. So,

Cap. 22. Lib. 2. cap. 1. Vide supra num. I. hujus part.

† *Sic & Plutarchus distinguit in Galba, & Dion in rebus Cæsaris & Pompeii: & Polybius, ubi de Romanorum bello in Illyrios agit, excerpto legationum 126. Cum Suetonio, recte illas prætextum, has causas dixeris: Ita enim ille de Julio Cæsare*: Et prætextum quidem illi civilium armorum hoc fuit: causas autem alias fuisse opinantur. *Thucydides alibi distinguit* πρόφασιν *&* τὸ ἀληθές*, ut in Atheniensium motu adversus Siciliam, prætextum fuit opitulari Egestanis, res ipsa cupiditas Siciliæ sibi acquirendæ. Hermocrates in oratione, de Atheniensibus loquens, illud* πρόφασιν *prætextum vocat, hoc* διάνοιαν *propositum. utrumq; est in libro Thucydidis 6. Appianus etiam* προφάσεων *vocem usurpat in Mithridatico. Idem Civilium 5. ubi de rupta pace inter Octavium & Sextum Pompeium agit, dicit* αἰτίας *causas alias intus fuisse, alias quæ præferebantur. Agathias libro 5. id quod alii* πρόφασιν*, vocat* σκῆψιν καὶ προκάλυμμα*, figmentum & obtentum, cui opponit* αἰτίαν *in historia Hunni Zanurganis. Procopius Persic. 2. dicit stultum esse non libere loqui, ubi dux est justitia, comes utilitas.*

the

the *pretence* of the ſecond *Punick* war was the Controverſy about *Saguntum*, the cauſe was the indignation of the *Carthaginians* for the Agreements, which the *Romans* in unequal times had extorted from them, and their courage raiſed by the proſperity of their affairs in *Spain*, noted by *Polybius*. Likewiſe, *Thucydides* judgeth the true *cauſe* of the *Peloponneſian* war to have been the *Athenians* growing Greatneſs, which brought them into ſuſpicion with the *Lacedemonians*; but the *pretence* was the controverſy of the *Corcyreans*, *Politeans* and other things: where yet, he promiſcuouſly uſeth the termes,* *pretence* and *cauſe*. There is the ſame difference in the Oration of the *Campanians* to the *Romans*, when they ſay they fought againſt the *Samnites*, in word for the *Sidicines*, in deed for themſelves; becauſe they perceived, when the *Sidicines* were conſumed, the fire would paſs on to them. And *Livy* relateth, how *Antiochus* took arms againſt the *Romans*, *in ſhew*, for the death of *Brcilla*, and ſome other matters; *in truth*, becauſe he had great hope of ſucceſs by reaſon of the decayed diſciplin of the *Romans*. So *Plutarch* obſerveth, it was not truly objected to *Antony* by *Cicero*, that He was the cauſe of the Civil war, when *Cæſar*, reſolved upon a war, had only taken the pretext from *Antony* †.

Lib. 1.

* *Sic & libro 5. de Argivis contra Epidaurios agens, quam prius vocaverat* πρόφασιν, *mox vocat* αἰτίαν. *Quomodo & Græcum* ἀρχῶν, *Latinum* Principiorum *vocem, aliasq; ejus generis, eſſe ſenſus ambigui notavimus. Scriptores Conſtantinopolitani Imperii id quod alii* πρόφασιν, *ſæpe* παῖτεσμα *vocant, nimirum ex Achillis hiſtoria, qui ad reſumenda arma ex Patroclo ſumſit materiam.*

Livius lib. 7.

Lib. 36.

† Hæc quidem prætexto opus habent; ſpeciem aliquam & decorum titulum bellandi dedere. *Verba ſunt in hac hiſtoria Plutarchi. Lucani autem:*

——— Cunctaſq; Pudoris
Rumpunt fata moras. Juſtos Fortuna laborat
Eſſe ducis motus, & cauſas invenit armis.

CVI.

CVI. *Wars without any cause are wild and brutish.*

SOme, upon neither of these causes, are carried into wars, *greedy of dangers*, as *Tacitus* speaks, *for dangers sake.* The faults of these men exceed every human name, and is by *Aristotle* termed θηριότης, *ferity*. Of these, *Seneca*: *I may say, it is not cruelty but ferity, which takes pleasure in blood: we may call it madness; whereof there be sundry sorts, and none more evident than that which runneth to the slaughter of men, and cutting them to pieces.* To which sentence, very like are those words of * *Aristotle*: *Very cruel indeed is he to be accounted, who makes his friends his enemies, out of greediness to fight and shed blood.* Dion Prusæensis: *Without cause to be carried into wars and fights, is meer madness, that seeks mischief to it self.* And the forecited *Seneca* saith, *No man is so inhuman, as to wast human blood, or very few.*

Tacit. Periculorum, propter ipsa avidi. *De Alanis Ammianus, lib.* 31. Ut hominibus quietis & placidis otium est voluptabile, ita illos pericula juvant & bella. *Lib.* 2. *de Clem. cap.* 7. *Idem l.* 2. *de Ira c.* 5. *de Apollodoro locutus & Phalaride*: Hæc non est ira, feritas est. * *ultimo Nichomach. Orat.* 37. *Epist.* 4.

CVII. *Against wars, which have not justifick causes, or not truly such.*

BUt the greatest part of those that go to war have *suasory* causes, and those, either without justifick causes, or with them. Some care not at all for *justifick* causes:

causes: of whom that may be said, which is in the *Roman* Lawyers, *He is a Robber* *, *who being asked of the cause of possessing, brings no other, but that he doth possess.* *Aristotle*, of those that perswade to war: *Men, that oftentimes regard not at all, whether it be just or no, to subdue their harmless neighbours.* Such a one † was *Brennus*, who said, *Let the strongest* * *take all.* Such a one was *Annibal* in *Silius*, *Whose right was his sword.* Such also was *Attila*; and such are all, that use these words:

> *No matter how the war begins,*
> *If we can bring it to our ends.*

To these men, you may fitly apply that of *Augustin*: *To wage war against the neerest, and thence march on to others, and out of a desire of rule to conquer Nations that provoke you not, what is it to be named, but Great Robbery?* In *Cicero* * we read: *The height of mind, which is discoverd in dangers and labours, if it want justice, is so far from vertue, that 'tis rather immanity* †, *and an enemy to all humanity.* Andronicus Rhodius; *Who, for to gain much, receive whence they ought not, these are call'd evil, impious and unjust*;

* *L. pro haerede. sect. ult. & seq. leg. D. de haered. petit Talis Herulorum in Longobardos*, πόλεμος ἀπροφάσιστος, bellum sine praetextu. † *Talis Silio Annibal, cui* — pro faedere, proq; Justitia est ensis. *Talis Attila, & quibus illud in ore est*, Quaeritur belli exitus, Non causa. *Et*: Haec acies victum factura nocentem est. *Et*: In summa fortuna, id aequius quod validius. * Galli apud Livium 5. in armis se jus ferre, & omnia fortium virorum est. *Lib. 4. de Civit. Dei c. 6.* *De talib. bellis Velleius*: Bella non causis inita, sed prout eorum merces fuit. * Offic. 1. † *Agathias lib. 2.* Qui vero aut lucri causa aut caeco odio, nullam habentes justam querelam, alienas terras invadunt, innoxiis noxii, hi homines sunt & superbi & improbi. *Exemplum nobis dat illustre Menander Protector*: Baja-

nus

nus Avarorum Chaganus, nulla occasione aut obtentu, ne conatus quidem causam vel falsam contra Romanos Comminisci, invercunde planeq; barbarum in morem exuit pacta.

*such as are tyrants**, *and the Plunderers of Cities*. Others do allege causes, as it were, justifick; which being weighed in the scale of right reason are found unjust: and it appears, as *Livy* speaks, not a contention about right, but an offer of violence. Many Kings, saith * *Plutarch*, use the two names of Peace and war, not to that which is just, but to that which is expedient.

* Bene Philo ad Decalogum: *Qui vero furum vires nacti sunt, hi totas prædantur urbes, pœnarum securi, quod supra leges eminere videantur. Tales sunt homines ingenio minime civili, dominatuum' & potentatus avidi, magna furta committentes, qui pulcris nominibus magistratuum & imperiorum id obtegunt quod verius latrocinium appelletur.* * *Pyrrho.*

CVIII. *Fear of an uncertain danger no just cause of war.*

AMong the unjust causes of war is fear taken from neighboring power. Which fear, we have said above, is not sufficient. For, that Defense may be just, it ought to be necessary: it is not so, unless we be sure, not only of the power of a neighbour, but of his *will*: sure, by that certainty, which hath place in matter of morality. Wherefore, their opinion is not to be allowd, who make it a just cause of war, if a neighbour, hindred by no agreement, build a Castle on his own ground, or some other fortification, which may sometime

ſometime do us hurt. For, againſt ſuch fears, contrary fortifications in our land, and the like remedies, not warly forces, are to be provided. Unjuſt therefore were the wars of the *Romans* upon *Philip* of *Macedonia*, of *Lyſimachus* upon *Demetrius*, unleſs there were ſome other cauſe. I am very much pleaſed with that in *Tacitus*, of the *Cauchi*: *A people among the Germans moſt noble, who maintain their Greatneſs by their Juſtice; without covetouſneſs, without impotency; quiet and ſecret: They never provoke their neighbors to war, never make inrodes upon others, or depopulations: And this is a principal argument of their valour and might, that they attain not their ſuperiority by being injurious: yet are they all ready for war, and, if need be, they have an Army preſent: Great ſtore of Foot and Horſe: and famous, even in times of peace* †.

Zonaras Pauſan. lib. 1.

† Tacitus de Cauchis: *Populus inter Germanos nobiliſſimus, quiq; magnitudinem ſuam malit juſtitia tueri, ſine cupiditate, ſine impotentia: quieti, ſecretiq; nulla provocant bella; nullis raptibus aut latrociniis populantur: idq; præcipuum virtutis ac virium argumentum eſt, quod, ut ſuperiores agant, non per injurias aſſequuntur; promta tamen omnibus arma, ac, ſi res poſcat, exercitus; plurimum virorum equorumq;, & quieſcentibus eadem fama.*

CIX.

C IX. *Of some other unjust causes.*

NEither doth Utility make equal right with necessity. So, where other wives enow are to be had, the denyall of some Match cannot give cause of war; which yet *Hercules* took against *Euritus*, *Darius* against the *Scythians* †. Nor is the Desire of a people to change their seat, a just cause of war, that leaving moorish & desert Land, they may possesse a more fruitfull soil: which was the case of the old *Germans*, as *Tacitus* relates. No less unjust it is, to challenge by the title of a new found Land, what is held by another; though he that holds it be wicked, think amiss of God, or be of a dull wit. For, *Invention* is of those things that belong to none; neither is moral virtue, or religious, or perfection of understanding required to dominion. This indeed seemeth probable, if there be any people altogether destitute of the use of reason, such have no dominion, but out of charity only is due unto them what is necessary for life. For, what is said of the support of Dominion in behalf of infants and mad-men by the Law of Nations, pertains to those nations, with whom there is commerce of Covenants. Such are not they that are wholly mad, if there be any such, of which I do justly doubt. Unjustly therefore did the *Grecians* call the *Barbarians*

† Et Antonius Caracalla in Artabanum Parthorum Regem. Vide Xiphilinum. Hist. 4.

Vict. de Ind. rel. 1. n. 31.

Vict. de bello. n. 5, 6, 7, 8. Idem. l. 2. n. 18. Plato de respub. l. 2. c. 3. Euripid. Hecuba. Liv. l. 31. Isocrat. Panath.

Barbarians enemies to themſelves, as it were naturally, by reaſon of their diverſity of manners, and haply becauſe they ſeem'd inferiour in wit. Yet, for ſome grievous ſins, and ſuch as oppugn nature and human ſociety, we deny not but dominion may be taken away. Moreover, Liberty *, whether of ſingle perſons, or of Commonwealths, as if it did naturally and always agree to all, cannot yield a right to war †. For, when liberty is ſaid to agree by nature to a man or people, that is to be underſtood of the right of Nature preceding all human fact, in this ſenſe *, that one is not a ſervant by nature, not that he hath a right never to become a ſervant; for in this ſenſe no man is free. Here is pertinent that of *Albutius: No man is born free, no man is born a ſervant: theſe names were impos'd afterward upon every one by fortune.* And that of * *Ariſtotle: It is the effect of Law, that one is free, another ſerves.* Wherefore they that upon lawful cauſe are come into ſervitude, whether perſonal or civil, ought to be content with their condition, as alſo *Paul* the Apoſtle teacheth, *Art thou*

* αὐτονομία.

† Vide Concil. 4. Toletanum. Agrippa rex apud Joſephum in oratione ad Judæos, qui ex præpoſtero repetitæ libertatis ſtudio Zelotæ dicti ſunt, ſic ait: *Intempeſtivum eſt nunc libertatem concupiſcere. Olim ne ea amitteretur certatum oportuit. Nam ſervitutis periculum facere durum eſt, & ne id ſubeatur honeſta certatio. At qui ſemel ſubactus deficit, non libertatis amans dicendus eſt, ſed ſervus contumax.* Atq; ipſe Joſephus ad eoſdem: *Honeſtum quidem eſt pugnare pro libertate, ſed id olim factum oportuit. At qui victi ſemel ſunt, & longo tempore paruerint, ſi jugum excutiant, faciunt quod deſperatorum hominum eſt, non quod libertatem amantium.* Eadem ferme verba reperies in oratione Comitis Blanderatenſis ad Mediolanenſes apud Radevicum 1. cap. 40.
* *Intelligendum de libertate κατὰ στέρησιν, non de ea quæ eſt κατ' ἐναντίωσιν.* Seneca, 3. Contr. 21. * 1 Polit,

call'd

call'd to servitude? Let it not vex thee. 1 Cor. 7. 21. Farther, it is unjust, to subdue by arms any, as if they were worthy to serve, whom Philosophers sometimes call naturally servants. For, suppose a thing be profitable for one, it doth not therefore presently follow, that 'tis lawfull for me to force it on him. For, they that have the use of reason, ought to have a free election of things profitable and unprofitable, unless another have gotten some right over them. The case of Infants is quite otherwise, whose government, seeing they have not power * to moderate their own actions, nature committeth to the occupant, or some fit person.

* Jus exercendæ αὐτοκρατείας. *Vict. de Ind. n.* 24. *Ayala de ju. belli. lib.* 1. *Covar. c. peccatum p.* 2. *sect.* 9. *n.* 5. *&c. Ad leg. Hostes D. de capt. l.* ἀξίωσις. *ad l. Rhod.*

† *ut in conc. Chalcedon. Act.* 11. *&* 12.

* Ut & Athasius ad Solitarios. Id vix sexta pars erat mundi tunc cogniti.

† Philo de legatione; *De pluribus utilissimisq; orbis partibus loquor, quas & eminenter aliquis orbem appellet, definitum amnibus duobus Euphrate & Rheno,*

CX. *Of the Title of universal Emperour.*

I Would scarce adde, that it is an unwise title which some attribute to the *Roman* Emperour, as if he had a right of commanding over nations most remote and hitherto unknown; unless *Bartolus*, long accounted the Prince of Lawyers, had ventured to pronounce him an heretick that denyes it; forsooth, because the Emperour sometime stiles himself Lord of the world †; and because, in Scripture, that Empire, which later Writers call *Romania* *, is call'd by name of the word, † τῆς οἰκουμένης. So is that of the Poet, *The Roman Conquerour held all the world*, and

many

many like sayings, spoken by way of excess or excellence. And in the same Holy Scripture, *Judæa* alone comes oft under the title of the world * : in which sense is to be taken that old saying of the Jews, that the City of *Jerusalem* is seated in the midst of the earth, *i. e.* of † *Judæa*: as in the midst of *Græcia Delphi*, likewise call'd the navil of the world. Nor ought any one be mov'd with *Dante's* arguments whereby he endeavours to prove, the Emperour hath such a right, because it is expedient for mankind. For the commodities hereof are equalld with incommodities. And as a ship may be made of such a greatness which cannot be governd; so may the number of men and distance of places be so great, that it cannot admit the government of one. But, grant it is expedient, there follows not a right of Empire, which ariseth not but but either from consent, or punishment. Nay, the *Roman* Emperour now hath not right over all that of old perteined to the people of *Rome*. For, many things, as gotten by war, so were lost by war; some by covenant, and some by dereliction passed into the right of other nations or Kings †. Again, some Cities fully subdued once, afterward became subject only in part, or only confederate unequally. All these ways, either of losing or changing right, are or force, no less against the *Roman* Emperour, than any other.

* Hieronym. *Nomen terræ etiam cum additur particula omnis, restringi debet ad eam regionem de qua sermo est.*

† Discas hoc ex Jos. lib. 3. de bello Jud. Luc. 2. 1. Arist. 7. Polit. 4.

Silv. verbo Bellum. p. 1. n. 21. Covar. loco citato n. 9.

† *Exemplum sume in Hispania, de qua vide Gomerium in sect. fuerat num. 5. de actionib.*

CIX.

CXI. *Of the Empire of the Church.*

THere have been alſo, who would aſſert, the Church hath right over the Nations of the hitherto unknown part of the earth: when yet the Apoſtle *Paul* himſelf hath openly pronounced, He had no power to judge thoſe that are without. And whatſoever right of judging belonged to the Apoſtles, though it pertained alſo, in its way, to earthly things, yet was it of a heavenly (that I may ſo ſpeak) not of an earthly quality; to be exerciſed, not by the ſword and ſcourge, but by the Word of God generally propoſed, and applied to peculiar circumſtances, by the exhibition of the ſeals of divine grace, or the denyal of them, as it was for the good of every one: and laſtly by vengeance, not natural, but above nature, and therfore proceeding from God; ſuch as appeared in *Ananias*, *Elymas*, *Hymenæus* and others. Chriſt himſelf, the ſpring of all Eccleſiaſtical power, and whoſe life is the exemplar propoſed to the Church, as ſuch, ſaid, his Kingdom was not of this world, that is, not of ſuch a nature as other Kingdomes: adding, otherwiſe after the manner of other Kings he would uſe the ſervice of ſoldiers. But now, although he had deſired Legions, he would have called for, not thoſe of men, but of Angels.

Vict. de Ind. rel. 21. & ſeq. Ayala l. 1. n. 29.

1 Cor. 5. 12.

Jo. 18. 36. Matth. 26. 53. Vid. Petr. Dam. l. 4. epiſt. 9. & Bern. ep. 221.

gels. And whatsoever he did by right of his power, he did it not by human but divine vertue, even then when he cast the buyers and sellers out of the Temple. For, the scourge was not an instrument, but a sign of divine anger; as at other time spittle and oil a sign healing *, not a medicine. *Augustin* upon that place of *John*: *Hearken yee Jews and Gentiles, Circumcision and uncircumcision; Herken all ye Kingdoms of the earth: I hinder not your domination in this world* †. *My Kingdomn is not of this world: Do not ye fear most vainly, as Herod the Great feared, when he heard of the birth of Christ, and slew so many Infants, hoping to destroy him, being more cruel in his fear than in his anger. My Kingdom, saith he, is not of this world. What would you more? Come unto the Kingdom, which is not of this world. Come by believing, and do not rage by fearing.* *Paul*, among other things, forbids a Bishop to be a striker. *To rule by a necessity imposed, i. e.* which proceedeth from human force, is the part of Kings not of Bishops, said *Chrysostom* †. And elsewhere †: Christians are not permited to chastise, by force, the faults of the guilty. Secular Judges, awing evil-doers by their Laws, exercise power over them, and constrain them to obedience even against their will: But we must endeavour to reform men, not by compulsion but perswasion. Neither do the Laws allow us power of coercion; and if they did, how should we use it, seeing God doth not crown those that abstein from evil necessarily, but willingly? Wherefore, we must take pains to perswade sick soules to yield themselves of their own accord to be cured by us.

* Abulensis on Matth. 9. well explains this.

† *Hilarius Arelatensis*. For Christ came not to invade anothers glory, but to impart his own: not to take an earthly Kingdom, but to bestow an heavenly.

1. Tim. 3. 2.

† Act. Apost. hom. 3. epist. ad Tit. hom. 1. ep. 1. ad Thess. hom. 4.

† De sacerdot. lib. 2.

us. *A little after.* He that erreth from the faith, cannot be drawn unto it by force, nor compeld by fear. *And upon Ephes. 4.* We are appointed to teach men, not to command, not to exercise a coercive power. We are like Counselers, who advise the hearer, not force him, but leave him his free choice. *Ambros. l. 2. de Cain, & Abel. 4. Sacerdos quidem officium suum exhibet, at nullius potestatis jura exercet.* Citatur c. verbum. de pœnit. dist. 1.

where, *We have not power granted us to restrain men from offences by authority of our sentence: i.e.* such as conteins in it a powerful execution by a ruling or military hand, or a deprivation of any human right whatsover *. Hence it sufficient appears, that Bishops, as such, have no right to reign over men after a human way. *Hierom* †, comparing a King and Bishop together, saith, *The one rules the unwilling, the other the willing.* But, whether Kings themselves may wage war, in the way of punishment, against those that reject Christian Religion, is above inquired.

* *Ad reges enim, non ad Ecclesiam pertinet judicare de feudis, c. novit. de judiciis: de feudis: de possessionibus, c. causam quæ inter. qui filii sint legitime. Reges enim superiorem in temporalibus minime recognoscunt, c. per venerabilem. eod. tit.* Christus voluit ut Christiani Impp. pro vita æterna pontificib. indigerent, & Pontifices pro cursu temporalium rerum Imperialibus legibus uterentur; quatenus spiritalis actio à carnalibus distaret incursibus, & Deo militans minime secularibus negotiis se implicaret. *C. quoniam distinct 10. &c.*

† Hieron. in epitaph. Nepotiani. *Minus licet Episcopo quam Regi. Ille enim nolentibus præest, hic volentibus. Ille terrori subjicit, hic servituti donatur.* Cassiod. lib. 11. in epist. ad Episcopos: *Episcopus doceat, ne Judex possit invenire quod puniat.* Fredericus primus apud Guntherum Ligurino de pontifice:

Ecclesiam regat ille suam, divinaq; jura
Temperet: imperium nobis fascesq; relinquat.

Suennonem Daniæ regem excommunicatum cum Roschildensis

Episcopus Wilhelmus ab ingressu Ecclesiæ oppositu baculi pastoralis arceret, & regii capulis admoverent manum, fecit quod Episcopi erat, & cervicem porrexit.

CXII. *Of a desire to fulfill Prophecies.*

THis also I will add (not in vain, but because comparing new occurrences with old, I foresee much mischief, except care be taken:) that war is not justly grounded upon a hope conceiv'd out of some exposition of Divine Prophecies †. For, beside that Oracles not yet fulfill'd can hardly be interpreted with any certainty without a prophetical spirit *, the times even of things certain may be hid from us. And moreover, a prediction, without express command of God, giveth no right: for, by wicked men, or unjust actions, God doth oft-times permit the things he hath foretold to come to pass.

† *Vide de Theodoro quodam Gratiani tempore Zozimum & Ammianum Marcellinum: de Joanne Capadoce Procopium Persicorum 2. & Leunclavium Hist. Turc. l.* 18.

* For the Prophetical books are shut and sealed up til the appointed time, so that they cannot be understood, Dan. 12. 4, 8, 9. *Hierom upon Daniel*; If a Prophet heard and did not understand, what will they do, who, by presumption of mind, interpret a book sealed and very obscure until the time of consummation. *Procopius in the 2. of his Gotthicks*; I think it impossible for man to find out the sense of the Sibylline Oracles before they are fulfilled. *Gregoras in his 5. book*; As other predictions are most hard to be interpreted, because they have many perplexities, and admit serveral explications: so also this Oracle deceived all, even the Emperor himself, as long as he liv'd. But after his death, the Oracle explaned it self. Take heed to your selves, yee over-bold Divines: Take heed of overbold divines, yee Statesmen. Worthy is that place to be seen in Thuanus. lib. 79. in An. 1583. concerning Jacobus Brocardus.

CXIII.

CXIII. *Of that which is due, not by strict justice, but otherwise.*

AND this is also to be known, if one owe a thing, not by proper justice, but by another vertue, as liberality, favour, mercy, charity; that, as it cannot be required in the Court, so neither can it be demanded by arms. For to both of these ways it is not sufficient, that the thing required ought to be done by some moral reason, but moreover it is needfull there be in us a certain right unto it: which right sometimes divine and human Laws do give also about the dues of other vertues, and then a new kind of debt ariseth perteining unto Justice. But when that is wanting, war upon this cause is unjust; as, that of the *Romans* upon the King of *Cyprus* for his ingratitude. For, he that hath given a benefit, hath no right to exact a recompence; otherwise, it were not a benefit, but a contract.

CXIV. *A distinction of war, unjust in respect of the cause, or of some accident.*

ONe thing more is to be noted, It often falls out, that a war may have a just cause, and yet the action receive some stain from the minde of the doer: either for that some other thing, not unlawful by Vict. de jure belli n. 2.

by it self, doth more the mind than the right; (to wit, desire of honour *, or some profit, whether private or publick, which is expected from the war considerd apart from its justifick-cause:) or else, for that an affection plainly unlawfull is with him, as the joy of one pleasing himself in anothers evil without respect of good. So *Aristides* in his second *De societate* saith, the *Phocenses* perished deservedly, but *Philip* did not well when he destroyed them, not being studious of religion which he pretended, but ambitious to enlarge his Empire. *Profound ambition and avarice*, as *Sallust* speaks, *is one cause of war, and that an old one.* And *Tacitus* saith, *Gold and Power are the principal causes of wars* *. Whither you may also refer that of S. *Augustin* †; *Desire of hurting, Cruelty of revenging, an unpeaceable and unplacable mind, fierceness of rebelling, lust of domineering, and the like, these are the things that in wars are justly blamed.* But these, where a just cause is not wanting, do indeed argue a crime, yet do they not make the war properly unjust; whereupon, neither is restitution due for the same.

* Which vice especially flatters us with a shew of vertue; but S. Augustin well adviseth, saying, It is better undergo the shame of any cowardise, than seek the glory of such arms: *Lib.3. de Civit. Dei c.14.*

* *Rupere fœdus impius lucri furor, Et ira præceps.* Sen. Hippol.

† *Contra Faust. l.22. c. 74.*

Tho. 2.2.74. 66. 8.

XCV.

CXV. Of doubtfull causes. *Whence Doubts do arise in moral matters.*

IT is most true, which *Aristotle* hath written, that there is not so much certitude in moralls, as in the Mathematicks: because, the Mathematicks separate forms from all matters, and the forms, most part, are such, that they have nothing* interposed, as between straight and crooked there is no *medium*; But in moralls, even the least circumstances varie the matter, and the forms here are wont to have something † between them, with such latitude, that the access is neerer sometimes to this extreme, sometimes to that. For so, twixt that which ought to be done, and that which ought not to be done, is interposed that which *may* be done, but is neerer, now to this, now to the other part: whence ambiguity ariseth often, as in the dusk air, or in warm water. And this is that which *Aristotle* saith, *Oftentimes it is hard to judge, which is to be preferd.* *Andronicus Rhodius* saith; *It is to discern that which is truly just, from that which seemeth so.*

1 Eth. N c. 1.

* *In his mutatio fit* εἰς τὸ ἀντικείμενον, *in aliis* εἰς τὸ μεταξύ.

† *Vide Chrysostomum ad 4. eph. 2. Morali.*

3. Nicom.

CXVI. *Nothing is to be done against ones own judgment, though erring.*

THis is principally to be observed; that, although a thing be just in it self, but done by one, who having weighed all, thinks it unjust, the act in vitious. For, this is that which the Apostle *S. Paul* saith, * *Whatsoever is not of faith is sin.* Where *faith* signifies the mindes judgment about any matter. For, God hath given unto men a judging faculty, as a guide unto their actions, by contempt whereof the minde becomes brutish. Now, it often comes to pass, that the Judgment shews no certainty, but sticks; and if this hesitation cannot be cleared by attent consideration, that if *Cicero* must be followed: *Their precept is good, that forbid to do any thing, which you doubt* *, *whether it be right or wrong.* The *Hebrew* Masters say, *Abstein from a doubtfull matter.* But this cannot have place, where one must do one thing of the two, and it is doubted of both, whether it be right; for then a man may chuse that which seemeth to him the least evil. For that always, where the choice is inevitable, puts on the appearance of good. Of

* Rom. 14.23. To the same purpose are these words in the same ch. Let every one be fully perswaded in his own mind. And, Happy is he who condemneth not himself in that which he alloweth. Ambrose saith, 'Tis sin to do otherwise than ones judgment leadeth: *and so Augustin*: both cited by Gratian c. 28. q. 1. That of Plutarch in his Timoleon is of like sense: It is requir'd, saith he, not only that the thing done be honest and just, but that it be done with a firm perswasion, and with judgment. De Offic. lib. 1. * *Plin. lib.* 1. *epist* 19 Quod dubitas, non feceris. *Covar. tom.* 1. *de Matrim. p.* 2. *c.* 7. *sect.* 2. *n.* 9.

evils

evils take the least, saith *Aristotle*: and *Cicero* likewise: and *Quintilian*, *The lighter evil obteins the place of good, when several evils are compar'd together.* *Nicom.* 2. c. 9. *Cic. Offic.* 3. *De malis minima.*

CXVI. *How the Judgment in drawn either way.*

But, for the most part, in doubtfull matters after some examination the mind sticks not in the midst, but is drawn this way, or that, by Arguments * taken from the matter it self, or from the opinion a man hath of other men pronouncing sentence about it. For, here also is true that of *Hesiod*, *It is most excellent to be able to direct oneself: next, to follow the good direction of another* †. Arguments from the matter are deduced from the causes, effects, and other adjuncts. But to the right discerning of these, there is need of some experience and skill; they that have not this, to conform their active judgment rightly, must hear the Counsils of wise men. For, those things, saith *Aristotle*, are probable, which seem so to all, or to most, or at least to wise men: and to these again, either all, or most, or the more excellent. And this way of judging is most used by Kings, who have not leisure

* Augustin in his third *de Ordine*, saith, There are two ways, which lead us through the dark, when things are obscure, the one of reason, the other of authority. *Vasquez disput.* 62. c. 3. n. 10.

† Minutius in Livy lib. 22. borrowed this of Hesiod, saying, He is the first man, who can give Counsil, and shew what is good; next is he, that obeys the good Counsil of another; He that can do neither is a man of an extreme bad temper. Cicero hath words of the same meaning in his Oration for A. Cluentius. Victor. de Ind. rel. 1. n. 12. & de jure bell. 21. & 24. Arist. 1. Top. c. 1.

sure themselves to enter into the depth of learning;

* σοφοὶ τύραννοι τῶν σοφῶν συνουσίᾳ.

> * *The company of wise men brings*
> *Learning and Wisedom unto Kings.*

Aristides saith, As in questions of fact that is accounted for truth, which is supported by most and most sufficient witnesses; so those sentences are to be followed, which are grounded upon most and most worthy authorities. Thus the old *Romans* entred into war, not without consulting the College of the *Feciales* instituted for that end; nor the Christian Emperours, scarce ever, without advising with the Bishops, that if any thing did hinder in point of Religion, they might be admonisht of it.

CXVIII. *In doubtfnl cases, the safer way is to be taken. Three ways to avoid a doubtfull war.*

NOw, it may fall out in many Controversies, that on either side probable arguments may shew themselves, whether intrinsecal to the matter, or from authority. In this case, if the matter be of smal moment, the choice, which way soever it be, seemeth to be free from fault. But, if it be a weighty question, as concerning the life and death of a man, here, because of the great difference between the

the things to be chosen, the safer way is to be preferred *. Therefore, it is better to acquit the guilty than condemn the innocent. The writer of the problems that bear the name of *Aristotle* saith so *, and addes the reason which we have already given: *For, where one doubts, he must chuse that part, wherein the offense is less.* War is a thing of the greatest consequence, from which very many evils are wont to follow even upon the innocent: wherefore, when judgments differ, we must incline to † peace. And, three ways there be to keep Controversies from breaking forth into war. The first is *Conference. Being there are two kinds of disceptation,* saith *Cicero, one by conference, the other by force; and that is proper to man, this to beasts: we must fly to the later, if we cannot use the former* *. *Phaneas* in *Livy* saith; *To avoid a necessity of war, men do willingly remit many things, which cannot be forced from them by arms* †. *Mar-*

* *In istam partem potius peccato tamen.* Ammianus: *Lenitas acerbitati anteponenda.* lib. 28.
* *Prob. sect.* 29. *ubi pro* ἀδικοῦντος, *vulgo legitur* μὴ ἀδικοῦντα, *& contra.* Antiphon. *Si errandum est, sine jure absolvere, quam per injuriam condemnare est sanctius. Nam in illo error est, in damnatione insontis facinus.*

† Laudator Silio Italico Fabius:

——Cauta speculator mente futuri,
Nec lætus dubiis parvisq; lacessere Martem.

* De Offic. 1. Victor. de jure bel. n. 28. Terentius:
Omnia prius experiri quam armis sapientem decet:
Qui scis, an quæ jubeam sine vi faciat?
Euripides. *Verbi id impetrabo; sui nequeo, manu.*
Dionys. Halicarn. in excerptis legationum; *Non ante ad res veniendum est, quam tentata sit verborum via.* Menelaus apud Libanium: *Homini convenientius, prius verborum experimentum facere, quàm statim ad arma prosilire.* † Donatus ad Eunuchum: *Pervulgatum est enim, quod summa vi defenderis quum extorquetur, hoc idem postmodum remitti remittentis*

donius

donius in *Herodotus* blames the *Grecians* in this respect: *Who being of one language should have determined their Controversies by Commissioners, and not by battell. Coriolanus* in *Halicarnessensis*: *If one desire not anothers, but seek his own, and upon denial make war, all men confess it to be just.* In the same *Halicarnessensis* King *Tullus*: *Arms must decide, what words are not able to compose. Vologeses* in *Tacitus*: *I had rather preserve my Ancestors possessions, by equity than blood, by a fair tryall than by force.* And King *Theodoricus*: *Then only is it profitable to go to war, when Justice can find no place among our Adversaries.* Another way to avoid war, among them that have no common Judge, is *Compromise*. *It is not lawful*, saith *Thucydides*, *to invade him as injurious, who is ready to submit to an Arbitrator.* So, concerning the Kingdom of *Argos*, *Adrastus* and *Amphiaraus* made *Eriphyles* their Judge, as *Diodorus* relates. Concerning *Salamis*, three *Lacedæmonians* were chosen judges between the *Athenians* and *Megareans*. In the now-cited *Thucydides*, the *Corcyreans* signify to the *Corinthians* their readiness to debate their quarels before the cities of *Peloponnesus*, which they should agree upon. And *Pericles* is commended by *Aristides*, for his willingness *to have differences arbitrated*, that war might be avoided. And *Philip of Macedon* is praised by *Isocrates*, for that he

Cass. 3. Var. 17.

Orat. advers. Ctesiphont.

he was ready to permit the Controversies he had with the *Athenians* to the arbitration of any impartial City. *Plutarch* saith, this was the principal office of the *Feciales* among the *Romans*, *not to suffer things to come to a war, till all hope of obteining a quiet end was lost*. *Strabo* of the *Druids* of *Gallia*: *They were, of old, arbitrators between enemies, and often pacified them when they were entring into battell*. The Priests in *Iberia* performed the same office, as the same Author testifies. Now, *Christian Kings* and *Commonwealths* † are most of all bound to take this course to avoid war: for, if to avoid the sentences of Judges that were aliens from true Religion, certain Arbitrators were constituted both by Jews and Christians; and that is given in precept by *Paul*; how much more is the same to be done, that war, which is a far greater incommodity, may be avoided? So *Tertullian* somewhere argues, that a Christian must not follow the wars, to whom it is not lawful, so much as to go to Law. Which yet must be understood, (according to what we have said elswhere) with some temperament. And, both for this and for other causes, it were profitable, yea in some sort necesary to be done, that some Assemblies of Christian powers were held, where the controversies of others might be determined by Judges that are unconcerned; yea, and a course taken to compell the

Victor. de jure bell. num. 28.
† *Gregoras lib.* 10. *de Alex. Bulgaro*: It is uncomely for Christians to make such bitter wars against one another, when they may find a way of peace, and turn their arms against the Infidels.
Molin. disput. 103. *sect. quando inter.*

parties

parties * to entertain peace upon equal termes; which use also was made of the *Druids* † among the *Galls*, as *Diodorus* and *Strabo* have delivered. And we read, the *French* Kings, about division of the Realm, permitted the judgment to their peers. The third way is by *Lot* *; which is to this purpose, commended by *Dion Chrysostom* in his second Oration against Fortune, and long before him by *Salomon Prov.* 18. 18. Somewhat neer to *Lot* is *Single Combat*; the use whereof seems not altogether to be refused, if two, whose Controversies otherwise would involve whole multitudes in very great mischiefs, † be ready to fight one with the other. For, it seems, if not rightly to be done by them, neverthelels acceptable to the people on both sides, as a less evil. *Metius* in *Livy* speaks to *Tullus* after this manner; *Let us take some way, whereby, without much slaughter and blood of both parts, it may be determined, which people shal be superiour. Strabo* † saith, this was the old custom of the *Grecians*; and *Æneas* in *Virgil* * saith, it was meet, that the matter should be ended on this wise 'twixt him and *Turnus*. Certainly, among other customs of the ancient *Franks*, * this is at large commended by *Agathias*

* *Vide exemplum apud Cassiodorum* 3.1, 2, 3, 4. *& Gailium de pace pub.* 2. *c.* 18. *n.* 12.

† To the Druids, in this respect, and with better right, have succeeded Bishops: See the epistle of the Bishops to King Lewis. *In capitulis Caroli Calvi. vide & Roderic. Tolet.* 7. 3.

* *Vide August. de doct. Christ. lib.* 1. *c.* 28.

† Scriptor Tragœdiæ Thebaidos: *Rex sit è vobis uter, Manente regno quærite.* Dion Othone: *Multo enim satius justiusq; est unum pro omnibus, quam multos unius causa perire.*

† *Libro* 5.

* Æn. 11. *Æquius huic Turno fuerat se opponere morti.* Upon like cause Antonius challenged Octavius to a Duell. *Plutarch. Antonia.* * *Vide Caroli Calvi Capitulum apud S. Arnulphum, & pactionem Aquisgranensem. Æquitas eadem apud Langobardos. vid. Paul. Warnafred. l.* 1. *c.* 12. 4. *c.* 17. 5. *c.* 40.

in his first book: whose words are worthy to be added; *If any Controversies happen to arise between the Kings, they all muster their forces, as it were to determine the matter by battell, and they march forth into the field. But, so soon as the Armies have faced each other, they lay aside anger and embrace concord, perswading their Kings, to put their differences to triall of Law; or, if they will not do that, to enter into single combat, and bring the matter to an end, only with their own danger. Because, it is neither agreeable to equity, nor the orders of their Countrey, that they, for their proper hatreds, should weaken or overthrow the common good. Wherefore presently they disband, and the causes of their quarels being taken away peace is reestablished, and muttal security assured. So great care of Justice and love of their Country is in the Subjects: so gentle and yielding a disposition is in the Kings.* Now, although, in a doubtfull case, both parts are bound to seek condition, whereby war may be avoided, yet is he more bound, who requireth *, than he who possesseth. For, * *Vide Herreram tom.* 2. that in an equal case, the condition of the possessor is the better, is a point not only of the Civil but of the Natural Law. And here is further to be noted, that War cannot lawfully be undertaken by him, who knoweth he hath a just cause, but hath not sufficient proofs, whereby he may convince

vince the poſſeſſor of the injuſtice of his poſſeſſion: The reaſon is, becauſe he hath no right to compell the other to depart out of his poſſeſſion. And laſtly, where both the right is ambiguous, and neither poſſeſſeth, or Both equally, there he is to be thought unjuſt, who rejecteth the offered diviſion of the thing in controverſy.

CXIX. *Whether war may be juſt on both ſides.*

OUt of the premiſes may be determined that Queſtion agitated by many, whether War, reſpect being had of them that are the principal Movers of it, may on both ſides be juſt. For, the various acceptions of the word *juſt* are to be diſtinguiſhed †. A thing is called juſt, either from the *cauſe*, or according to the *effects*. From the cauſe again, either in a *ſpecial* acception of juſtice, or in that *general* uſe of the word, as all rectitude is ſo called. The ſpecial acception is again divided into that which perteineth to the *work*, and that which perteineth to the *worker*. For the worker himſelf ſometime may be ſaid to do juſtly, as oft as he doth not unjuſtly, though that which he doth be not juſt: So *Ariſtotle* rightly diſtinguiſheth *to do unjuſtly*, and *to do that which is unjuſt*. War cannot be on both ſides juſt, in the acception ſpecial and related

† *Sic Gratianus cauſa* 11. *q.* 3. *poſt C. Epiſc. diſtinguit juſtitiam cauſæ, ordinis, animi.*

Τὸ ἀδικεῖν τὸ ἄδικον πράττειν. *Lib.* 5. *Eth. c.* 10. & 11. *Rhet.* 1. 13. *Auguſt. lib.* 15. *de C. D. c.* 5. *Covarr.* &c.

lated to the thing it self, as a sute in Law neither; because a moral facultie to contraries, to wit, both to act and to hinder, is not granted by nature. But, that neither of the parties warring may do *unjustly*, is possible; for no man doth unjustly, but he that also knows he doth an unjust thing: and many are ignorant of that. So may a sute be followed justly, that is, with an honest mind, on both sides. For, many things, both in point of right and fact, whence right ariseth, are wont to escape men. In a general acception, just is wont to be called that which is without all fault of the Doer. And many things without right are done without fault through ignorance inevitable. An example whereof is in them, who observe not the Law, which without their fault they are ignorant of, after the law it self is promulged, and time sufficient by it self for knowledge hath passed. So also in Law-sutes it may happen, that both parties may be free from injustice and all other blame, especially where both parties, or either, goeth to law not in his own but anothers name, to wit, by the office of a Tutor or Guardian, whose duty is not to desert any right though uncertain. So *Aristotle* saith, *in contentions* 3. Rhetor. c. 17. *of controverted right, neither is any wicked.* With whom *Quintilian* agrees, when Lib. 2. 8. he saith it may come to pass, that *an Orator*, that is, a Good man *may plead on*

Top. 1. 13. *both sides*. Yea, *Aristotle* also saith, a Judge may be said *to judge justly* two wayes, either when he judgeth plainly *as he ought*: or, when he judgeth *according to his*
Nic. 5. 12. *judgment & conscience*. And in another place: *If one hath judged through ignorance, he hath not done unjustly*. Neverthelesse, in war, it can hardly fall out, but there will be at least some temerity and defect of love, by reason of the weight of this businesse, which in very deed is so great, that, not content with probable causes, it requireth grounds most evident. But, if we take *just* according to some effects of right, it is certain, war on both sides may be just in this sense, as will appear by what we shall say of publick solemn war in the next part. And in like manner a Sentence not given according to right, and Possession without right, have some effects of right.

CXX. ADMONITIONS.

For the eschewing of War, Right is often to be remitted.

THough it seemeth not properly a part of our work, our Title being of the Right of war, to declare what other vertues give in charge concerning it, neverthelesse, on the By, we must meet with this errour of such as think, where the Right is manifest enough, war presently either

either must, or alwayes may lawfully be undertaken. For, the contrary is true, that for the most part it is more pious and *Victor. de jur. bel. n.* 14. & 33. honest to depart from ones right. That we may honestly forsake the care even of our own life, that we may provide, as much as lies in us, for the eternal life and salvation of another, hath been shewed afore. Which is especially the duty of Christians, therein imitating the most perfect example of Christ, who dyed Rom. 5. 6. for us, while we were his enemies. This doth much more excite us, not to pursue our worldly interests with so much hurt of other men, as Wars do carry with them. That for every such cause war is not to be waged, even *Aristotle* and *Polybius* do *Arist. Polit.* 4. *Rhet. ad Alex. cap.* 3. advise. Nor was *Hercules* commended by the Antiens for commencing war against *Pausan. lib.* 5. *Laomedon* and *Augias*, because they paid him not for his labour. *Dion Prusaensis* in that Oration which is of War and Peace, saith, it is not only enquir'd, whether They, against whom we intend war, have done us injury, but whether the injury be of such moment that it may deserve a war †.

† Senec. *Suasor.* 5. Gallio said, war is to be undertaken, for liberty, for our wives, for our children: but for things that may be spared, and of small damage, it is not to be undertaken. Apollonius said somewhat more to the King of Babylon, in Philostrat. lib. 23. You ought not dispute with the Romans about Villages, which are less than private mens possessions: nor make war, no not for great causes. Josephus in his 2. against Appian saith of his Countrymen; That they shew not their valaur, to get riches, but to preserve their Laws: Other losses they bear patiently; but when they

they are forced to depart from their Laws, then they fight, even beyond their strength, and endure all extremities of war.

CXXI. *Punitive right especially is to be remitted.*

TO omit punishments, many things do exhort us. Consider how many faults Fathers connive at in their Children. Whereof *Cicero* hath a dissertation in *Dion Cassius*. *A Father*, saith *Seneca* *, *except many and great offenses have overcome his patience, except he hath more to fear than to condemn, will not proceed to extreme severity.* Not much different is that saying of *Phineus* in *Diodorus Siculus*; *No Father willingly takes revenge of his sons, unless the greatness of their wickedness exceed the natural affection of parents toward their children.* And that of *Andronicus Rhodius*: *No Father casteth off his son, that is not beyond measure wicked.* Now, whosoever will punish another, takes upon himself as it were the person of a Governor, that is, of a Father. † In this respect *Austin* saith to *Marcellinus*: *Fulfill the of-*

* *De clementia* l. c. 14. Augustus said to a certain Father consulting what he should do to his son guilty of paricide; He must be sent away whither his father would. He decreed not prison or torment: mindful of him to whom he gave advise, and saying, that a Father should be content with the softest kind of punishment. *Seneca eod. lib. c.* 15. Terent. Andria: *Pro peccato magno paululum supplicii satis est patri.* Philo: *Patres abdicationis tristia verba pronunciant, filiosq; à domo sua & omni cognatione abrumpunt, ita demum, ubi amorem illum, quem ingentem ac supra omnia eximium natura parentibus indidit, filiorum improbitas vicit.* Cicero pro Ligario: *Ignoscite, Judices, erravit: Lapsus est: non putavit: si unquam posthac; ad parentem sic agi solet.*
† Seneca epist. 87. *Clementia alieno sanguini tanquam suo parcit, & scit homini non esse homine prodigè utendum.* Diodorus Siculus in Fragmentis:

fragmentis: *Non omnes omnino qui deliquere puniendi sunt, sed ii quos malefactorum nihil pœnitet.* Chrysost. de statuis 6. *Discant omnes qui à fide nostra sunt extranei reverentiam quæ Christo exhibetur tantam esse, ut cuilibet potestati injiciat frænos. Honora Dominum tuum: condona peccata conservis tuis, ut & ipse multo magis te honoret, ut in illo judicii die vultum tibi ostendat serenum atq; clementem, hujus tuæ lenitatis memor.* Citat Gratianus cauf. 23. qu. 4. ex Augustino: *Duo ista nomina cum dicimus, homo & peccator, non utiq; frustra dicuntur: quia peccator est, corripe: quia homo, miserere.* Vide & quæ sequuntur.

fice of a pious Father, You that are a Christian Judge. Julian the Emperour commendeth the saying of *Pittacus, Who preferred pardon before punishment. Libanius* in his oration of the sedition at *Antioch* saith, *He that will be like unto God, must not so much rejoice in punishment, as in pardon.* Sometimes such are the circumstances of things, that it is not only laudable to abstain from ones right, but due, in respect of that dilection which we owe even to our enemies, whether considered in it self, or as the most holy Gospel-Law requires it. So, we have said, there are some, for whose safety, though they assalt us, we ought to desire death, in as much as we know them either necessary or very profitable for the common good of men. If Christ will have some things neglected, that sutes may be avoided, much more may we believe he would have greater things neglected, for the avoiding of war, by how much more hurtfull war is than a sute at Law. *It is not only liberal,* saith S. *Ambrose,* * *but for the most part commo-*

* *Ambr. Offic. l.* 2. *c.* 2. *vide Molin. tr.* 2. *de Just. disp.* 103. *Lorca dis.* 153. *n.* 11.

 dious

dious for a good man to remit somewhat of his right. *Aristides* perswades the Cities to a concession in things of less moment. He addes the reason: *For it is laudable, you know, even in private men, to be of a facile nature, and bear some loss rather than contend.* *Xenophon* in the sixt of his *Greek* history; *It is the part of wise men, not to go to war, no not for Causes of great importance.* And *Apollonius* in *Philostratus* is of the same mind.

CXXII. *Again, of the remission of punishment.*

CONcerning Punishments, it is our Duty, if not as Men, surely as Christians †, easily and willingly to forgive trespasses done against us, as God forgives us in Christ, *Ephes.* 4. 32. *Not to be angry*, saith *Josephus* *, *for the mortal offenses of the guilty, approacheth neer to the divine nature.* *Seneca* of a Prince *; *Let him be far more exorable in his own than other mens wrongs: For as he is not of a noble mind, who is bountiful out of anothers stock, but he that out of his own store giveth to another: so will I call him Gratious, not, that is gentle in anothers injury, but, who being spurred to revenge his own wrongs, restraineth himself; who thinks it Noblenesss to suffer injuries, being in the highest power, and that nothing is more glorious than a Prince pardoning his Offender* †.

† Theodosius was moved to pardon the crime of the Antiochians by those words of Christ pressed by the Bishop Flavianus: Father Forgive them: for they know not what they do. *Chrysost:* 20. *de statuis.*

* *Jos. antiq. lib.* 2. 3.

* *Sen. de Clem. lib.* 1. *c.* 20.

Offender †. *Quintilian: We will perswade a Prince to desire more the praise of Humanity, than the pleasure of Revenge.* *Cicero* sets it as the fairest flower in *Cæsar's* Garland, that he used *to forget nothing but injuries.* *Livia* in a speech to *Augustus* in *Dio: Most are of opinion, that Rulers ought to punish offenses against the Common weal, but dissemble and connive at those against themselves.* *Antoninus* the Philosopher in his Oration to the Senate *, *Revenge of his own wrong is never pleasing in an Emperor, which, though very just, seemeth very sharp.* *Ambrose* in his Epistle to *Theodosius: You have forgiven the Antiochians the wrong they did your Majestie.* And *Themistius* in the praises of the same *Theodosius* to the Senate; *It is the part of a good Prince, to overcome the injurious, not by revenge, but beneficence.* The magnanimous man, according to *Aristotle*, is not μνησίκακος, mindfull of injuries. Which is thus in *Cicero: Nothing is more worthy of a Brave man, than placability and clemency.* Eminent examples of this excellent vertue are proposed to us in the Holy Scripture, *Moses, Num.* 11. 12. and *David*, 2 *Sam.* 16. 7. And this hath place, then especially, when either we also are conscious to our selves of some offense, or that which is done against us proceedeth from some human and excusable infirmity, or it sufficiently appears, that he is penitent who

† Chrysostom saith, Clemency is an ornament to all men, most of all to a Ruler. For, to rule himself, and obey the Divine Law, is most honourable to the highest Governour. *In laude Clementiæ.*

* *Apud Vulcatium Gallicanum vita Avidii Cassidii.*

August. in epist. 104. *ad Bonifac. Comitem:* Remember to give a speedy pardon, if one hath trespassed against thee, and cryeth mercy.

De Offic. 1. *Nihil magno & præclaro viro dignius placabilitate & Clementia.*

who hath done amiss. *There is a mean* (saith *Cicero*) *to be observed in revenge and punishment : and I cannot tell, whether it be not enough, that he repent of his fault who hath provoked us* †. *A wise man* (saith *Seneca*) *will remit many things : many delinquents, unsound, yet not uncurable, he will peserve.*

† *Procopius Vandal.* 2. The Offenders timely Repentance is wont to prevail with the offended party, and obtain his pardon.

CXXIII. *War is to be declined, in favour of our selves and our own party.*

WE have shewed cause to abstein from war out of that love and pity which we either owe to our very enemies, or rightly bestow upon them : We are now to consider what reason there is from that care we owe to our selves and ours †. *Plutarch* in the life of *Numa* saith, After the *Feciales* had determined, that the war might be undertaken justly, it was consulted by the Senate, whether it were for their good. In a certain Parable of Christ's it is said, If one King intendeth war against another, he will first sit down (which is the posture of those that seriously advise about a mat-

† Procopius in his second book of the Gotthics, saith the Goths spake thus to Belisarius; It concerns the Commanders of both Nations, not to purchase their own glory at so great a price as the undoing of their people, but to prefer and chuse things just and safe, as well for themselves as for their enemies. Diodotus in Thucydides saith, Although they are very guilty, yet would I not have them slain, except it be expedient for us. *lib.* 3.

ter)

ter) and consider with himself whether he with his ten thousand be able to enter battell with his enemy that leadeth twenty thousand. And, if he find himself too weak, before the enemy enter his territories, he will send Messengers of Peace. So did the *Tusculans* *, by enduring all things, and refusing nothing, obtain their peace of the *Romans*. In *Tacitus* we read, *In vain did they seek a cause of war against the Æduans: Being commanded, to bring money and arms, they also brought provision freely.* So *Q. Amalasuntha* * protested to the Embassadors of *Justinian*, she would by no means make war. A temperament also, or mid-way may be used, as *Strabo* relates was done by *Syrmus* King of the *Triballians*, who denyed *Alexander* the *Macedonian* entrance into the Iland *Peuce*, and withall honoured him with Gifts: that he might shew his denyall to proceed from a just fear, and not from hatred or contempt of his Greatness. What *Euripides* said of the *Grecian* Cities may be fitly applyed to any other. *When they give their votes for war, no man thinks how imminent death is to himself; but every one destines ruine to another. But if, in the Council, Their own Funerals had been presented to their eys, Grecia had not been so mad to destroy it selfe with war* †. It is in *Livy*:

* *Vide Plutarch. Camill.* So did the King of Armenia in the time of Severus. *Herodian. l.* 3.

* *Vide Procop. Vandal.* 2. & *Gotthic.* 1. *Liv. lib.* 6. *Lib.* 7.

† *De*

Propose to thy meditation, and consider thy own strength, and the power of fortune, and the various chances of war. And in *Thucydides ; The unexpected Accidents in war must be thought upon, before thou dost engage.*

† *De Marte quoties itur in suffragia,*
Nemo imminere cogitat mortem sibi ;
Sed quisq; cladem destinamus alteri.
Quod si in Comitiis funera ante oculos forent,
Furiata bello non perisset Græcia.

† Of their own danger most men are,
Unmindfull, when they vote for war ;
They think not, death hangs o'r their head,
But wish that other men were dead.
The undone Grecians had not been
So mad, if this they had fore-seen.

CXXIV. *Rules of Prudence about the election of Good.*

THey that deliberate ; deliberate partly about the ends, not the last but the intermediate, partly about those things which lead thither. The end is ever some Good, or at least the Avoidance of some evil, which may be in the stead of good. The things that lead to the one or other, are not desired by themselves, but as they lead thither. Wherefore in Debates, are to be compared, both the ends among themselves, and the effective faculty of those things that lead to the end, to produce the same. (For, as *Aristotle* hath rightly noted, *propositions which bring forth action are of two sorts, from that which is good, and from that which is possible,*) Which comparison hath three Rules. The first is, If the thing under debate, seemeth to have, in

Arist. de animal. mot.

in a moral estimation, equal efficacy to Good and to Evil, it is so to be chosen, if the Good hath somewhat more of good, than the Evil hath of evil. Whence *Andronicus Rhodius*, where he describes the magnanimous man, saith, He will undergo dangers, not for every cause, but for the greatest. Another Rule is, If the Good and Evil seem equal, which may proceed from the thing in question, that thing is eligible, if the efficacy to Good be greater than to evil. The third, If both the Good and the Evil seem to be unequal, and the efficacy of the things no less unequal, that thing will be eligible, so that the efficacy to good be greater, being compar'd which the efficacy to evil, than the Evil it self is, being compar'd to the Good *. This have we set down after a more exact manner. But *Cicero* discourseth to the same purpose in a plainer way, when he saith, We must take heed we do not offer our selves to perils without cause, than which nothing can be more foolish: wherefore in running hazards, the custome of Physicians is worthy of our imitation: They apply gentle remedies to light diseases, but in the more grievous are compelld to use more perillous and doubtful Medicines: Wherefore, he saith, it is a wise mans part to take the opportunity, and the rather, if he may obtain more good by success of the matter, than he can fear evil upon the miscarriage.

* Narses in Procopius makes a prudent use of this rule. *Gotthic.* 2.

De Offic. 1.

Epist. ad Att. l. 13. 27.

carriage. In another place, *Where no great emolument is possible, and a little mischance will be hurtfull, what need is there to run the hazard.* Dion Prusæensis: *Be it unjust and unworthy, which is sufferd, Yet must we not therefore, in a contentious humour, expose our selves to greater incommodities.* And again: *We seek to rid our selves of burthens that do sorely pinch us; but if they be portable, and we fear we shall change them for heavier loads, we compose our selves to patience.* Aristides also, *Where our fear is greater, than our hope, have we not great reason to be cautious?*

Tarsensi alterâ.

Siculâ 2.

C XXV. *An Example of a Debate about Liberty and Peace.*

LEt us take an example from that which *Tacitus* saith was of old consulted of among the Cities of *Gallia*, *Whether they should prefer Liberty or Peace*: understand *Civil* Liberty, that is, a right of governing the Commonwealth by themselves; Which right is *full* in a popular state, *tempered* in an optimacy, especially such wherein none of the Citizens is excluded from honours: Understand also such a peace, whereby is avoided a *destructive* war; that is, as *Cicero* expresses it, wherein all is in danger to be lost: or, where a right estimation of the future seemeth

Lib. 9. epist. ad Attic. epist. 112.

seemeth to portend nothing els, but even the destruction of the whole people: Which was the case of the people of *Jerusalem* besieged by *Titus*. No man is ignorant, what *Cato* would say here, who chose rather to dy than to submit to One: to which purpose is that sentence, *It is none of the hardest vertues to embrace death, to avoid slavery*; and many the like. But right reason dictates otherwise, to wit, That life, which is the foundation of all good things temporal and eternal, is of more worth than Liberty; whether you take both in one man, or in a whole people. Wherfore God himself imputes it as a benefit, that he doth not destroy men, but deliver them up to servitude. And elswhere he perswadeth the *Hebrews* by the Prophet, to give up themselves to serve the *Babylonians*, that they may not perish by famin and pestilence. That then, which was praised by the Antients, *that Saguntum did being besieg'd by the Carthaginian*, is not to be praised, nor the things that lead thither. For the *internecion* of a people in this kind of things, is to be accounted as the greatest Evil. *Cicero* in his second *De Inventione*, setteth down this example of necessity; It was necessary the *Casilinians* shou'd yield themselves to *Annibal*: though that necessity had this adjunct, Except they would rather perish with hunger. Of the *Thebans*, who lived in

—Quam not sit ardua virtus Servitium fugisse manu.

2. Paral. 12. 78.

Jer. 27. 13.

Aug. de Civit. Dei. l. 22. c. 6.

in the times of *Alexander* the *Macedonian*, is extant this opinion of *Diodorus Siculus*: *Being more valiant than wise they brought ruine upon their Country.* Of that foresaid *Cato* and *Scipio*, who after the *Pharsalick* Victory would not submit to *Cæsar*, *Plutarch* passeth his judgment thus: *They are to be blamed, as they that lost many and gallant men in Africa, to no purpose.* † That which I have said of liberty, I mean of other things desirable, if there be a more just or an equal expectation of a greater evil opposite. For, as *Aristides* saith well, It is the manner to save the ship, by casting forth the lading, not the passengers.

Lib. 18.

† Guido Blandratensis ad Mediolanenses apud Guntherum:

Omnia securi pro libertate feremus:
Sed libertatem contemta nemo salute
Sanus amat; neq; enim certæ susceptio cladis
Quam vitare queas, nisi cum ratione salutis,
Libertatis amor, sed gloria vana putanda est.

Anaxilaus, whom the Famine constreined to yield Bizantium, made this defense, saying, Men were to fight against men, not against the nature of things. So Xenophon. Procopius Gott. 4. saith, Men do not praise voluntary death, so long as any hope prevailes over the danger. Diodorus Siculus having opened the Counsells of the war undertaken by the Sithonians after Alexanders death, saith, In the judgment of wiser men, they attempted a thing rather glorious than profitable, making hast into danger unnecessary, and not taking warning from the notable overthrow of Thebes.

CXXVI.

CXXVI. *He that is not much the Stronger ought to remit punishment.*

MOreover, in the exacting of punishments, it is most observable, that war should never be entred into, upon that ground, against him who hath equal forces. For as a Civil Judge must, so he that will avenge wicked acts by war, must be much stronger than the offender. Nor doth prudence only, or Love of his people require, that One abstein from a perillous war, but Justice too, that is, *governing* Justice, which by the very nature of government obligeth the superiour no less to care for inferiours, than the inferiours to obedience. Whereto is consequent, what is rightly delivered by Divines, that a King, who for light causes, or for to exact punishments not necessary, and drawing after them great danger, undertaketh a war, is bound to his subjects to repair the damages arising thence. For, though not to the enemies, yet to his own people, injury is done by him, who upon such causes involves them in so great an evil. *Livy* saith, *War is just, to whom it is necessary: and their arms are pious, who have no hope left them but in arms.* *Ovid*, thus:

Cajet. 2. 2. q. 95. art. 8. Molina tract. 1. de just. cap. 102.

Lib. 10.

> *Let not the soldier armed be,*
> *But to disarm the Enemie.**

* Ovid. Fast. 1. *Sola gerat miles, quibus arma coërceat, arma.*

CXXVII.

CXXVII. *War not to be undertaken, but upon necessity, or upon greatest cause, with greatest opportunity.*

* Servius ad illud in 10. Æn. *Iram miserantur inanem Amborum, & tantos mortalibus esse labores.* Quia nulla causa tam justa est, ut propterea bellum geri debeat.

There is then seldom * cause of taking arms, which either cannot, or ought not to be omitted: to wit, *when Laws are* (as *Florus* speaks) *worse than war. Seneca* bids us *venture upon dangers; when we fear no less dangers if we sit still*; or greater: so *Aristides, when it appears, our estate will be worse if we be quiet, then we ought to hazard our selves. Tacitus* saith, *A miserable peace is well exchang'd for war*: that is, when (as the same Author saith) either being victorious you shall be free; or being conquer'd, as you were: or where (as *Livy* * speaks) peace is more grievous to those that serve than war is to the free. Not if (as 'tis in *Cicero* *) this appears to be the event; If you be conquer'd, you shall be proscrib'd; if you conquer, you shall be never the less a slave. It will be also a time to take arms, if, in a true judgment, where most *Right* is, and that of greatest moment, there is most *strength*. This is that which *Augustus* † said, War is not to be undertaken, except there be greater hope of benefit, than fear of loss. And, what *Scipio Africanus*, and *L. Æmilius Paulus*, were wont to say of injoyning battell, may fitly

* Liv. l. 10.

* Cic. ad Att. 7. 7.

† Sueton. c. 24.

Gel. 13. c. 3. Val. Max. l. 7. 2.

fitly be applied here, *Fight not, without great necessity* *, *or great opportunity*. This will then chiefly have place, when it is hoped the business may be done, by terrour † and fame, with none or very little danger: such was *Dion's* counsell for delivering *Syracuse* †. *Pliny* in one of his Epistles hath an expression to our purpose: *He subdued the enemy (which is the fairest kind of victory) by the terrour of his name.*

* Plutarch. Gracchis: *Extra summam necessitatem ferrum inferre, nec boni medici est, nec boni praesidis.* Marciani dictum apud Zonaram: *Non debere Regem arma movere, quamdiu pace frui liceat.*

Aug. 50. epist. ad Bonifacium, *Pacem habere voluntatis est: Bellum autem debet esse necessitatis, ut liberet Deus à necessitate, & conservet in pace.* † The Lion despising weapons a good while defendeth himself by terrour alone, and sheweth that he is compelld. *Plin. Hist. Nat.* 8. 16. † Diod. l. 16.

CXXVIII. *The Evils of War.*

WAr is a cruell thing, saith *Plutarch*, and draws with it a train of injuries and insolence: And *S. Augustin* wisely: *Should I go about to declare the manifold Calamities, and extreme necessities, which attend upon war, (which I am not able sufficiently to express) when should I make an end? But they say, a wise man will wage war. Rather, if he remember himself to be a man, he will be sorry to find a necessity thereof* *. *It is the iniquity of the adverse part, which enforces a wise man to take arms, which iniquity of men, though war did not follow, were to be lamented. Wherefore the mischiefs of war,* whosoever

De civit. Dei lib. 19. *c.* 7.

* The Lacedemonians in Diodorus Siculus l. 13. Seeing the many enmities and sad effects of war, we think it our duty to testify before God and man, that we are not the causes of them.

See a notable place in Guiciard. lib. 16.

whosoever affectionately considers, must needs acknowledge it a misery; and if any one can pass them over without grief, he is the more miserable, in that he hath lost all sense of his misery. The same Father in another place; *It seems a felicity to evil men, to wage war, to good men, necessity.* And *Maximus Tyrius: Although you take out of war injustice, the very necessity is it self miserable.* The same: *It is plain, that just men take arms only upon necessity; the unjust, of their own accord.* Whereto may be added that of *Seneca: Man must not use man prodigally.* *Philiscus* admonisht *Alexander* to seek for glory, but on those terms, that he might not make himself a plague to the world: meaning the slaughter of people, and desolation of Cities, to be the effects of a plague: and that nothing is more Kingly, than to take care of all mens safety, which depends on Peace. If, by the *Hebrew* law, even he that had kill'd a man against his will, was to fly for refuge: If God denyed *David*, who fought the Lord's own battells, the honour of building his Temple, because he had shed much blood †: If, among the old *Greeks*, they had need of expiation, who even

Lib. 4. de Civitate Dei. c. 15. *Belligerare malis videtur felicitas, bonis necessitas.*

Ælian. lib. 14. 11.

† *Non permisit templum struere ei qui multa bella bellasset, pollutusq; esset, hostili quidem, attamen sanguine.* Joseph. lib. 7. cap 4. ubi & plura in hanc sententiam. *Plinius lib. 7. cap.* 25. after he had related the battells of Cæsar the Dictator, Truly (saith he) I will not account it Glory, to have done so much hurt to mankind, however urged. Philo de vita Mosis: *Quamvis enim legibus permissæ sunt hostium occidiones, attamen quisquis*

quis hominem interfecerit, quamvis justè, quamvis ad sui tutelam, quamvis coactus, aliquid labis contraxisse creditur, propter illam communem à summa causa venientem cognationem Quapropter & purgatione quadam opus habebant tales interfectores, ad eluendum quod commissum videbatur piaculum.

without fault had steined their hand with blood: Who seeth not, especially if he be a Christian, how unhappy a thing War is, and of an ill *omen*, and with how great endeavour it is to be avoided, though not unjust? Surely, among the *Greeks* that professed Christianity, that Canon was long observed, whereby they were kept for a time * from the sacred mysteries, who had killed an enemy in any war whatsoever.

* For three years. *Zonaras. Basil. ad Amphil.* 10, 13.

CXXIX. OF WAR FOR OTHERS:
And first, for Subjects. And whether an Innocent person may be yielded up.

WE have said afore, that Every man naturally may execute, not only his own, but anothers Right. Wherfore the same causes, that are just for him whose business is in hand, are also just for them that bring aid unto others. Now, the first and most necessary care is for subjects †, whether in the family, or in the Commonwealth; For they are as it were a part of the Governour, as there we have said. So, for the *Gibeonites*, who had subjected themselves to the *Hebrew*

† Procopius Pers. 2. saith, He is not just who doth no man wrong, except he defend from wrong those that are committed to him. *Navar.* 24.18.

Jos. 10. 6. people, that people took up arms under the command of *Joshua*. *Our Ancestors*

Ad Quirites. (saith *Cicero*) *have often waged war for injuries done to our Merchants and Seamen.* Elswhere: *How many wars have*

Verrin. 2. *our Ancestors undertaken, because our Citizens were said to be injur'd, our Saylors retein'd, our Merchants spoiled?* The same *Romans* thought it necessary to take arms for the same people being become their subjects, for whom being confederates they would not stir. The *Campanians* to the *Romans*; *Seeing you will not, by just force, defend our estate against violence and injury, you will certainly defend your own.* *Florus* saith, the *Campanians* made the league they had before, more

Lib. 7. *Fides agi visa, deditos non prodi.* holy, by the dedition of all they had: *It concern'd the Faith of the Romans*, as *Livy* speaks, *that a people which had yielded themselves, should not be deserted.* Howbeit, not always are Governors bound to take arms for the just cause of a subject, but so, if, without incommodity of all or most of the subjects, it may be done. For, the Governors office is rather conversant

Soto de just. & jure. lib. 5. q. 1. art. 7. about the whole than about the parts: and the greater the part is, the neerer it approcheth to the nature of the whole.

† *Satius judicemus esse, paucos aliquos mala ferre, quam immensam multitudinem*, Zonaras. Wherefore, if one Citizen, though innocent, be demanded by the enemy, he may (no doubt) be deserted †, if it appear that the Commonwealth is far inferious to the enemies power. Against this opinion

nion disputes *Ferdinandus* * *Vasquius*: but if we mark his meaning rather than his words, he seemeth to contend, that such a Citizen be not rashly forsaken, when there is a possibility and hope of defense. For he brings also an example of the *Italian Foot* who forsook *Pompey*, before all was lost, being assur'd of quarter by *Cæsar*; which act he deservedly reproveth. But, whether an innocent Citizen may be given into the hands of the enemy, for the avoiding of destruction otherwise imminent to the Commonwealth, Learned men dispute: And it was of old disputed, as, when *Demosthenes* produced that renowned Fable of the Doggs, whom the Wolves, treating with the Sheep about a peace, demanded of them. Not onely *Vasquius* denies it to be lawfull, but He, whose opinion is accus'd by *Vasquius* as perfidious, *Sotus*. Yet *Sotus* affirms, such a Citizen is bound to deliver up himself to the enemies: and this too *Vasquius* denies, because the nature of Civill society, which every one hath enterd into for his own benefit, doth not require it. But hence it follows only, that the Citizen is not bound to this by *right* properly so called; it doth not follow, that in *Charity* he is not bound to do it. For, there be many offices, not of proper justice, but of Love, which are not only performed with praise (which *Vasquius* grants) but also cannot be omitted without

* Lib. 1. cont. ill. c. 13.

without blame. And such in very deed seemeth this to be; that one prefer the life of a great innocent multitude before his own †. And therefore *Phocion* exhorted * *Demosthenes* and others, after the example of the daughters of *Leus* and the * *Hyacinthides*, rather to undergo death themselves, than suffer an irreparable mischief to be done to their Country. *Cicero* for *P. Sextius*: *If this had happened to me sailing with my friends in some ship, that Pirates surrounding us should threaten to sink us all, except they would deliver me; I would rather have cast my self into the Sea, to preserve the rest, than bring my friends either to certain death, or into great danger of their life.* The same in his third *de Finibus*: *A good man, wise and obedient to the Laws, and not ignorant of Civil duties, careth more for the interest of all, than of any one, or his own.* In *Livy* we read it spoken of certain *Molossians*: *Often have I heard of men that dyed for their Country: but these men are the first, that thought it fit, their Country should perish for them.* But, this being granted, a doubt remains, whether the innocent Citizen may be *compell'd* to do that which he is bound to do. *Sotus* denyes this, using the example of a rich man, who is bound by the precept of Mercy to give Almes to the poor, yet cannot be compell'd to give. But, we must note, tis one thing when the parts are compared among themselves, another

† Praxithea apud Euripidem. *Si namq; numeros, quidq; sit plus aut minus percipimus animo, non malo unius domus Commune vinci, sed nec aequari potest.* Philo: *Iniquum est totum fieri accessionem partis.* V. l. 2. de vit. Mos.

* Diodor. l. 17.

* Vide Apollod. in bibliotheca.

Lib. 45.

another when Superiours are compared to their subjects. For, an *equal* cannot compell his equal, but unto that which is due by right strictly taken: yet may a *Superiour* compell his inferiour to other things also which any vertue commands†, because this is comprehended in the proper right of a superiour, as he is superiour. * So, in great scarcity of corn, subjects may be forc'd to bring out what they have laid up. And therefore, in our controversy, it seemeth more true that the Citizen may be compeld to do that which *Charity* requires. So that *Phocion* whom whom we have mentioned, pointing at his most dear friend *Nicocles*, said, Things were come to that extremity, that if *Alexander* should demand him, he should think he were to be delivered.

† So, among the Lucanians, a punishment was appointed for the prodigal: among the Macedonians, for the ungratefull: for the idle, among the same Lucanians, and the Athenians.

* Less. lib. 2. c. 9. dub. 7. Plutarch. Phoc.

CXXX. *War may also be undertaken justly for Confederates; for friends, yea for all men.*

NExt to subjects (yea qual in this, that they ought to be defended) are Confederates in whose Agreement this was comprehended: that is, whether they have yielded up themselves to the safeguard and trust of others, or have covenanted for mutuall succours. *He that repelleth not injury from his Fellow, if he be able, is in fault, as he that offers it,* saith *Ambrose*. As for Agreements to war, when Offic. 1. 36.
there

when there is no juſt cauſe †, they hold not, as we have laid above. And this is the reaſon, why the *Lacedemonians*, before they enterd into the war againſt the *Athenians*, permitted all their Confederates to judge of the juſtice of the cauſe: and the *Romans* permitted the *Greeks* to judge of the war againſt* *Nabis*. Nay further we adde, the Fellow is not then bound to aid, if there be no hope of a good iſſue. For, Society is contracted for good and not for evil. Moreover, a Confederate is to be defended, even againſt another Confederate, unleſs in the former league there was ſome more ſpecial agreement. So the *Athenians* might defend the *Corcyreans*, if their cauſe were juſt, even againſt the *Corinthians* their more antient Confederates. Another cauſe there is, on behalf of friends, to whom though no promiſe of aid was made, yet in reſpect of friendſhip it is due, if it may be given eaſily and without incommodity. So *Abraham* took arms for his Kinſman *Lot*: The *Romans* charged the *Antiates* not to uſe Piracy upon the *Grecians* being the Couſins of the *Italians*: The ſame *Romans* oft undertook, (or threatned) wars, not for their Confederates only, as they were obliged by Covenants; but for their friends †. The laſt and largeſt relation of men to one another is, as they are men. Which alone ſufficeth to call for

† *Vide Simlerum de repub. Helvetiorum.* The Lord making war againſt any, if it be known, that he doth it juſtly, or if it be a doubful caſe, the Vaſſall is bound to aid him. But when it is manifeſt, that He doth unreaſonably, Let him help to defend him, not to offend another. *lib. 2. de Feud. c. 28.* [*Hic finitur.*]

* Liv. lib. 34. *Vict. de Ind. p. 2. n. 17. Cajet. 2.2. q. 4. art. 1.*

† Oraculum vetus:
Non ope juviſti præſens in morte ſodalem;
Effabor tibi nil, niſi Templi finibus exi.

for help. *Men were born to help one another*, saith *Seneca* *. And again, *A wise man will, as oft as he can, relieve the unfortunate* †. *Fortitude which defends infirmity*, saith S. *Ambrose* *, *is full of Justice*. Of this above.

Cic. de fin. 3. de Offic. 2. L. ut vim. D. de just. & jure. * De ira. l. 1. c. 7. de clem. 2. 5. † Euripides in supplicibus:

——Praebent saxa perfugium feris,
Araeq; famulis: urbibus pressis malo
Tutamen urbes.—— * Offic. 1. 5.

CXXXI. *Whether man is bound to defend man, and one people another.*

HEre it is a question, whether any obligation lyes upon one man; or one people to defend another from injury. *Plato*'s judgment is, that he deserves punishment, who doth not keep off force offerd to another: which also was provided for in the Laws of the *Egyptians*. But first, if there be manifest danger, it is certain he is not bound; for, he may preferr his own life and goods before another man's. And in this sense I understand that of *Tully*: *He that defends not, nor resists injurie, if he can, is in no less fault, than if he forsake his parents, or Country, or Companions*. If he can: that is, *Without his own hurt*. For the same Author saith in another place: *Men may perhaps be left undefended without any blame*. It is in *Sallust*'s Histories: *All that in their prosperity are intreated to society*

De legib. 4. Et Hebraei ita censent. Moses de Kotzi praecept. jubente 77, 80. Diodor. l. 1.

ciety of war, ought to consider, whether they may be permitted then to live in peace: and, whether that which is requested be pious, safe, glorious, or dishonourable. This of *Seneca* † too is not to be despised: *I will succour one that is about to perish, but so, that I my self may not perish; unless I shall redeem some great person, or great matter.* But then neither, he will not be bound, if the oppressed can no other way be freed, but by the death of the oppressor. For, if he that is invaded may preferr the life of the Invader before his own (as we have said elswhere) he will not sin who believes or desires that the oppressed should be of that mind: especially when, on the part of the oppressor or invader, the danger of an irreparable and eternal loss is greater.

† *De ben.* 2.15. And elswhere he saith, I will defend a worthy man at the cost of my own blood, and partake in his danger: And if I can deliver an unworthy man from theeves by raising a cry, I will not refuse to spend my voice to save a man. *De benef. lib.* 1. *c.* 10

Less. Lib. 3. *c.* 4. *dub.* 15

CXXXII. *Whether War be just to releeve the Subjects of Another.*

THis is also in Controversy; whether it be a just cause of War, for the Subjects of Another, that they may be deliverd from the injury of their Ruler. Verily, since civil Societies were instituted, it is certain the Rulers of every one have attained a special right over their own Subjects. And *Thucydides*, among the signes of Soveraignty hath put *the supreme power*

Power of Judgments *, no less than a right of making Laws and Magistrates.

* Euripides Heraclidis:

Nos quotquot hujus colimus urbis mœnia,
Sufficimus ipsi nostra judicia exsequi.
Nec alio illud pertinet; *Spartam tibi quæ contigit orna:*
Nobis fuerit cura Mycenæ.
Et huic non dissimile illud Poeticum: *Rescindere nunquam Diis licet acta Deûm.* Ovid. Met. 14. Et Virgil. Æn. 1.
Non illi Imperium pelagi sævumq; tridentem,
Sed mihi sorte datum.———

Ambrose gives the reason; *Lest one usurping the charge of another they should raise war among themselves.* The *Corinthians*, in the same *Thucydides*, think it Equity, *that every one should himself punish those that belong unto him* †. And *Perseus*, in his oration to *Martius*, saith, he would not excuse what he had done to the *Dolopis*: *I have done it* (saith he) *by my own right, seeing they were of my Kingdom, under my dominion.* But, all this hath place, where Subjects do truly offend, or where the case is doubtfull. For, to this purpose was ordained that distribution of Empires. Notwithstanding, where the injury is manifest, where any *Busiris*, *Phalaris*, *Thracian Diomedes* executeth such things upon his Subjects, that no good man can allow of, there the right of human society is not præcluded. So *Constantin* against *Maxentius* and against *Licinius*, other *Roman* Emperors against the *Persians* *, took arms, or threatned to take them, unless they would abstein from persecuting

Amb. l. 1. de Offic.

Thucy. lib. 5.

† Augustin in his second *de lib. arbitr.* saith, Although it be a part of goodness to do good to strangers, yet is it no point of Justice to punish them. *Procop. Vand.* 1. It is good for every one to govern well his own charge, and to appropriate to himself the cares of other men.

Vict. de Ind. rel. n. 15.

Vict. de Ind. rel. p. 2. n. 13.

* Exemplum simile habes in rebus Pipini apud Fredegarium in fine.

secuting the Christians for their Religion. Yea, supposing arms cannot, no not in extreme necessity, be taken rightly by Subjects (whereof we have seen those to doubt whose purpose was to defend the regal power:) nevertheless will it not therefore follow, that arms may not be taken by others on their behalf. For, as oft as a personal, not real, impediment is put against any action, so oft may that be lawfull for one for anothers good, which was not lawfull for that other; if the matter be of such a nature, wherein one may procure the good of another. So, for a Pupil, whose person is uncapable of judgment, the Tutor goes to Law or some other; for one absent, even without a mandate, his Defendor. Now, the Impediment, which prohibites a subject to resist, comes not from a cause which is the same in a subject and no-subject, but from the quality of his person which passeth not into others. So *Seneca* thinks, I may war upon him, who being divided from my Countrey troubleth his own; (as we have said when we spake of exacting punishment;) which thing is often joined with defense of the innocent. We are not ignorant, by reading of histories old and new, that Avarice and Ambition hideth it self under these pretences; but it doth noth not therefore presently cease to be a Right, which is abused by evil men. Pirates also go to Sea; and Robbers use the sword.

CXXXIII.

CXXXIII. *Concerning Soldiers of Fortune.*

Moreover, as warly Societies enterd into with such a mind, that aids are promised in every war * without any difference of the cause, are unlawfull; so is no kind of life more wicked than theirs, who without respect unto the cause are hired to kill men, thinking *, *There is most right, where is most pay.* Which *Plato* proves out of *Tyrtaus*. This is that which the *Ætolians* were upbraided with by *Philip*, and the *Arcadians* by † *Dionysius Milesius*, in these words; *Mercats are made of War, and the calamities of* Greece *are a gain to the* Arcadians, *and without regard of the causes arms are carried to and fro.* A miserable thing indeed, as *Antiphanes* speaks, *That men should get their living, by exposing themselves to death**. *What is more necessary to us* (saith *Dion Prusaensis*) *or what is more worth than life? and yet many men are prodigal of this, while they are greedy of money.* But, this is a small matter, * to sell their own blood, unless they did also sell the blood of other men that are oft-times innocent; So much worse than the Hangman, by how much worse 'tis to kill without cause †, than with cause: As *Antisthenes* said,

* *Iterum Simlerum vide de hac re. Soto in verb. bellum p.* 1. §. 10. *circa fin.*

* *Ibi fas ubi plurima merces.*

† Livy l. 32.

* *Suam qui auro vitam venditant.* Plaut. Bacch. Guntherus: *Ære dato conducta cohors, & bellica miles Dona sequens, pretioq; suum mutare favorem Suetus, & accepto pariter cum munere bello Hunc habuisse, dator pretii quem jusserit, hostem.*

* *Bellinus de re mil.* 2. *p. t.* 2. *n.* 4.

† *Seneca nat.* 5. 18. Who can stile it other than madness, to carry danger about with him and to run upon men unknown, angry without injury, wasting all in his way, and making slaughter (like wild beasts) of men that one hateth not.

ſaid, Hangmen are better than Tyrants, becauſe they execute the guilty, theſe the guiltleſs. *Philip of Macedon* the Elder
*Diod. lib. 18. ſaid *, Theſe men that get their living by making a trade of war, eſteem war to be their Peace, and Peace their war. War is not to be turned into an Art or profeſſion, being a thing ſo horrid, that nothing can make it honeſt, but the higheſt neceſſity, or true charity: as may be underſtood by what we have ſaid afore. *It is not indeed*
De verb. Dom. *in it ſelf a ſin* (ſaith S. *Auguſtin*) *to go to war, but to go to war for the ſpoil is a ſin.* Yea, and for the ſtipend or pay, if that alone be regarded, or that chiefly: when as otherwiſe it is very lawfull to receive
1 Cor. 9. 7. pay; for, *who goeth to war at his own charge?* ſaith *S. Paul* the Apoſtle.

Cap. 26.

CXXXIV. Of juſt Cauſes, that war may be waged by thoſe that are under others command. *Who they are, and what they ſhould do, where they are left free.*

WE have done with them that are in their own power: there are others in a condition of obeying, as ſons of families, ſervants, ſubjects, and ſingle Citizens if they be compar'd with the Body
Ægid. reg. de act. ſupern. diſp. 31. n. 80. of their Commonwealth. And theſe, if they be called to debate, or a free choice be given them to go to the war, or to ſtay at home, ought to follow the ſame rules with

with them that at their own pleasure undertake wars for themselves or others.

CXXXV. *What they should do, when they are commanded to war, and believe the cause of the war to be unjust.*

But, if it be commanded them to bear arms, (as it usually comes to pass;) What then? Why, truly if it be manifest to them that the cause of the war is unjust, they ought by all means to abstein. That we must obey God rather than men, is not only a sentence of the Apostles, but of *Socrates* too †; and the *Hebrew*-Masters have a saying *, That the King must not be obeyed, when he commands any thing contrary to the Law of God. *Polycarpus* said just before his death, *We have learned to give meet honour to the Empires and powers ordained of God, so far as may consist with our salvation.* And S. *Paul* the Apostle; *Children be obedient to your Parents in the Lord*; *for*

Victor. de jure bel. n. 22.

Act. 5. 9.

† Plato tells us so in his Apology. And Apollonius opposed against the edict of Nero that of Sophocles, Jupiter hath given me other Order.

* Which also Josephus ascribeth to them, Antiq. 17. No wonder, if we more observe those we have received of God by Moses, than your Commands. *Adde Rab. Tanchumam citante Drusio ad locum Actorum.* * i. e. *In quibus Deum offensurus non es.* Ita Chrysostomus. Sic accipe illud Hieronymi, *Per calcatum perge patrem*, declamator è dictum, sumptumq; à Latrone declamatore apud Senecam. *Subditos esse oportet, sed intra limites disciplinæ.* Tertull. *Jccirco Romanas leges contemnimus, ut jussa divina servemus.* Silvanus Martyr. Apud Euripidem dicenti Creonti:

Nonne exsequi mandata fas ipsum jubet?

Respondet Antigone:

Non

Non imperata jure nec jus exsequi. Musonius ita ait; *Si quis aut patri, aut magistratui, aut Domino turpia aut iniqua factu imperanti non paret, is nec inobediens est, nec injuriam facit, nec peccat.* Stob. t.t. lib. parent. honorand.

this is right. Upon which place *Hierom: It is a sin for children not to obey their parents; yet because parents might perhaps command somewhat amiss, he added, In the Lord.* And he annexed this of servants, *When the Lord of the flesh enjoineth a thing divers from the Lord of the Spirit, Obedience is not due.* And elswhere, *In those things only ought men to be subject to their Masters and Parents, which are not against the Commands of God.* For the same Apostle also saith, Every man shall receive a reward of his own worke, whether he be bond or free. *Seneca**; *Neither can we command all things, nor our servants perform. They must not obey us against the Commonwealth: They must not lend their hand to any wickedness.* Sopater: *Obey thy Father. If according to right, well: if otherwise, not so. Stratocles* was irrided, of old, who propounded a Law at *Athens*, that whatsoever pleased King *Demetrius*, might be accounted pious toward God, and just toward men. *Pliny* * saith he laboured somewhere to make it evident, That it is a crime to serve another † in doing evil. The Civil Laws

* De benefic. lib. 3. 20.

* *Lib. 3. epist. ad Minut.*

† Examples illustrious both of punishment and praise, See 1 Sam. 22. 18, 19. 1 Reg. 18. 4. 13. 2 Reg. 1. 10, 12, 14. Among the Christians Manuel and Georgius refused the service of killing the Empress. *Nicetas.* Among the Pagans are

are two noble examples of thoſe that would not obey the unjuſt commands of Princes, that of Papinian ſo famous, and another of Helpidius in Ammianus lib. 21. Severus would not have them ſcape unpuniſhed, who obeyed an Emperour in killing a Senator. *Vide Xiphilin.* Tertull. de Anima: *Plus cæditur qui jubet, quando nec qui obſequitur excuſatur. Vide Gail. de pace pub. lib. 1. cap. 4. num. 14.*

themſelves, which do eaſily give pardon to excuſable faults, favour thoſe that muſt needs obey, but not in all things: for they except things which have atrocity, which are heinous and wicked in their own nature, as *Tully* ſpeaks, and not by the interpretation of Lawyers. *Joſephus* relates out of *Hecatæus*, that the Jews which ſerved under *Alexander* the Great, could not be compell'd, either by words nor blows, to carry earth, with the other ſoldiers, to the repairing of *Belus*'s Temple at *Babylon*. But we have a more proper example in the *Thebæan* Legion (of which above) and in *Julian*'s ſoldiers, of whom *Ambroſe* thus: *Julian* * *the Emperour, though an Apoſtate, had under him Chriſtian ſoldiers: whom when he Commanded to Draw out in defenſe of the Commonwealth, they obeyed him. But, when he ſaid, Uſe your arms* † *againſt the Chri-*

* Auguſtin. epiſt. 50 ad Bonifac. *Julianus exſtitit infidelis Imperator. Nonne exſtitit Apoſtata iniquus & Idololatra? Milites Chriſtiani ſervierunt Imp. infideli: ubi veniebant ad cauſam Chriſti, non agnoſcebant niſi illum qui in cœlo erat: quando volebat ut idola colerent & thurificarent, præponebant illi Deum.* † For. Julian abſteined not from all violence againſt the Chriſtians, then eſpecially when he had gotten any colour for it, as he thought. Jerom to Nepotian calls him, The Cut-throat of the Chriſtian Army. *Aug. de Civit. Dei l. 1. c. 52.* tells of a perſecution begun at Antioch

tioch in his reign, and a certain yong man tormented. In the Martyrologies is celebrated the memory of S. Eliphius a Scot and his fellows, whom Julian caus'd to be beheaded. *Vide & Joan. Antiochenum in excerptis ex MS. Peiresiano.*

ſtians, then did they acknowledge the Emperour of Heaven. So we read of certain Spearmen converted unto Chriſt, that they choſe rather to dy, than to execute the Edicts & judgments againſt the Chriſtians. 'Twill be all one *, if a man be perſwaded, it is unjuſt which is commanded. For, that thing is to him unlawfull, ſo long as he cannot put off that opinion: as appeares by what we have ſaid already.

* *Victor de jure bell. n. 23.*

CXXXVI. *What they ſhould do, when they are in doubt.*

But, if a man doubt, whether the thing be lawfull or no, muſt he then obey, or not? Moſt Authors are of opinion, that he muſt obey: nor doth that hinder, *Do not, what you doubt of*: becauſe (ſay they) he that doubts contemplatively, may in his active judgment be out of doubt; For he may believe, that in a doubtfull matter he ought to obey his ſuperiour. And truly it cannot be denyed, but this diſtinction of a twofold judgment hath place in many actions. The Civil Laws, not of the *Romans* only but of other Nations, in ſuch a circumſtance, do not only grant

Quod dubitas, ne feceris.

L. damnum. de R. J. L. Liber homo. D. ad L. Aquil. L. non videtur. §. qui juſſu de R. I. Paul. l. 5. ſen. tit. 22. § 1. Leges Long. tit. 96. de tom. effoſs. Leges wiſigot. l. 2. tit. 2. c. 2. L. 8. tit. 1. c. 1.

impunity †

impunity † to those that obey, but also deny any Civil action against them. He doth the damage, say they, who commands it to be done: and he, who must needs obey, is in no fault. Necessity of the power excuseth, & the like. *Arist tle* himself in the fift his Ethicks, among those that do something unjust, but not *unjustly*, annumerates the servant of a Master commanding; and he saith, He doth unjustly, from whom the action takes beginning; upon this ground, because the faculty deliberative is not full, according to that verse *;

† *Chrysostom, de providentia*, 3. Many magistrates accus'd for unjust slaughter have been punisht oft: but never was any Executioner call'd in question, for they are excus'd by the necessity layd upon them, proceeding from the d g-nity of the Commander, and the fear of the Obeyer. Ulpian out of Celsus saith, a servant hath not offended, who hath obeyed his Masters command. Mithridates dismist the servants of Artilius, being conscious of the plot against hi life, u punished; and the children likewise of one that had revolted fro n him: *Appian*. Tiberius Gracchus was acquitted from the fau't of the Numantin league, because he had offended at the command of another. *In v lente necessitas non est.* Seneca. * *Et illud quo Philo utitur*: Δῦλ@ πέφυκας, ὁ μέτεσί σοι λόγυ.

> *Those men enjoy but one half of their soul,*
> *Whom their imp r ous Masters words controul.*

And that of *Tacitus*: *The Gods have given the Prince supreme judgment of things: to sub ects is left the glory of obedience.* *Piso's* son (in the same writer) was by *Tiberius* absolv'd from the crime of the Civil war; *Because the son was not able to reject the commands of the Father.*

Annal. 3. Themistius in his 9. oration, saith, Princes are like to reason, souldiers to wrath.

Controv. 3. 9.

Seneca: *A servant is not a Censurer, but a minister of his Masters will.* And specially in this question of warfare *Augustin* thought so; for so he speaketh: *A just man, if perhaps he serveth under a sacrilegious King, may rightly fight at his command, if keeping civil order, he be either sure what is commanded him is not against the Command of God, or be not sure that it is: so that perhaps the King may be guilty of iniquity in his command, but the soldier innocent in his obedience.*

Lib. 22. *c.* 74. *cont. Faustum.*

* *De Civit. Dei, lib.* 1. *c.* 26. & *de lib. arbit. l.* 1.

† *Sil. in verb. bell.* 1. *n.* 9. *concl.* 4. *Cast. in l.* 5. *D. de Instit. Soto l.* 5. *q.* 1. *art.* 7. *Covar. in c. pecc. p.* 2. §. 10. Quis justius induat arma, Scire nefas.

* *Adr. quæst. quod. l.* 2. See an example of those that followed this opinion in Scafnaburgensis.

The like he saith * in other places. And hence it is a common received opinion, that, as to subjects, a war may be on both sides *just*, that is, without injustice †; Yet this is not without its difficulty. And our Countryman *Adrian* *, who was the last Bishop of *Rome* of the *Cisalpins*, defends the contrary opinion: which may be confirmed, not by that reason precisely that he brings, but by this which is more urgent: Because he that doubts contemplatively, ought by his active judgment to chuse the safer part: And it is the safer part to abstein from war. The *Essens* are commended, for swearing, among other things, *That they would never do any one harm, no not if they were commanded:* And their Imitators the *Pythagoreans*, who as *Jamblicus* testifies, absteined from war, adding this for the reason, *because it is so bloody.* Nor is it any material objection, that on the other side there is dan-

φόνων χορηγέτης καὶ νομοθέτης ὁ πόλεμος. *Jamb.*

ger

ger of inobedience. For, when Both are uncertain (for if the war is unjust, then in avoiding thereof is no inobedience) that is faultless, which of the two is less. Now, inobedience, in such matters, is of its own nature less evill than homicide and slaughter, especially of many Innocents. The Antients tell how *Mercury*, being accus'd for killing *Argus* at the command of *Jupiter*, defended himself, and yet the Gods durst not absolve him †. Nor is it of great weight, which some bring on the contrary; That it will come to pass, if that be admitted, that the Commonwealth will be oft undone; because it is not expedient (for the most part) the reasons of Counsels shou'd be published and made known to the people. For, grant this to be true concerning the *suasory* causes of war, it is not true of the *justifick*; which must be clear and evident, and therefore such as may and ought to be openly declared †. And thus do some learned men interpret that in *Genesis* 14. 14. to this sense, that *Abrahams* servants, before the battell, were fully instructed by him concerning the

Baldus 2. *Cons.* 385. *Sotus de Det. secr. memb.* 3. *q.* 2. *in resp. ad* 1. *Vict. de jure bell. n.* 25.

† Nec Pothinum Ptolomæi satellitem Martialis, cum ait: *Antoni tamen est pejor, quam causa Pothini; Hic facinus domino præstitit, ille sibi.*

† Tertull. *Cæterum suspecta lex est, quæ probari se non vult: improba autem, si non probata dominetur.* Achilles apud Papinium Ulyssi: —— *Quæ Danaus tanti primordia belli. Ede: libet justas hinc sumere protinus iras.* Apud eundem Theseus: *Ite alacres, tantæq; precor confidite causæ.* Propert. dixerat. *Frangit & attollit vires in milite causa: Quæ nisi justa subest, excutit arma pudor.* Cui par illud panegyristæ: *Tantum inter arma bona conscientia sibi vindicat, ut jam cæperit non virtutis magis quam integritatis esse victoria.*

the Justice of his arms *. Certainly, denuntiations, as we shall shew hereafter, were wont to be made openly, and the cause exprest, that all mankind, as it were, might examin and know the justice of it. Prudence indeed is a vertue (as it seemed to *Aristotle*) proper to Governors; but Justice to man, as he is man. Now, in my judgment, that opinion of *Adrian* is clearly to be followed, if the subject not only be in doubt, but is induc'd by probable Arguments, and inclined rather to believe that the war is unjust: especially, if it be not defensive, but offensive. And so it is probable, that the Executioner of a man condemned, either by his presence at the Tryall, or by the confession of the party, ought so far to understand the case, that he may be assur'd he hath deserved death †: which, in some places, is the custome: and the *Hebrew* Law * looks this way, when, in the stoning of one condemned, it requires the witnesses to go before the people.

* Herod in Josephus tells the Jews after an overthrow in Arabia: I am willing to shew you, how justly we undertook this war, being compeld by the affronts of our enemies. For by the knowledge hereof, you will be greatly stirred up to shew your courage. *Ægid. Regius de act. supern. disp.* 31. *dub.* 5. *n.* 85. *Bannes* 2. 2. *q.* 40. *art.* 1. *Molina tract.* 2. *disp.* 113.

† Wherefore the servants of Saul, more honest than Doeg, would not slay the Priests of Nob, their cause being unheard, 1 Sam. 22. 17. And Ahabs third Captain of fifty would not hurt Elijah, 2 Reg. 1. 13. And some Executioners, converted to Christ, afterward usd not this office, as unsafe. *Vide Martyrol. & Bedam l.* 1. *c.* 7. * Deut. 17.

CXXXVII.

CXXXVII. *Such are to be dispensed with, upon payment of extraordinary Tribute.*

MOreover, if the mindes of the Subjects cannot be satisfyed by Declaration of the cause, it will certainly be the office of a good Magistrat, rather to impose upon them *double Contribution*, than military service; especially when there are not wanting enow *Voluntiers* to serve. Whose will, not only good, but evil too, a just King may use, as God doth use the ready service of the Devil and wicked men: and as he is without fault, who being in need of money takes it up at hard rates from an oppressing Usurer. Yea further, if there can be no doubt made about the Cause of the war, nevertheless it seemeth to be much against equity, that Christians against their wills should be compell'd and *prest Souldiers*, seeing, to abstein from war, even when it is lawfull to wage it, is a point of greater sanctity; which was *exacted* both of Clergy-men and Penitents, and to all other persons many wayes *commended*. *Origen* to *Celsus* objecting against the Christians, that they declined war, shapes this Answer: *To Infidels, who would have us go to war for the Commonwealth, and kill men, we will answer thus, They that are Priests of your Idols, and Flamens*

Silv. in verb. Bellum. p. 1. n. 7. circa fin.

Origen. cont. Celsum.

mens of your reputed Gods , keep their hands pure for sacrifices , that they may offer them to your supposed Gods , with hands unbloody, and defiled with no slaughter : nor are your Priests listed soldiers in any war. Now, if that be not without reason , how much more than other soldiers, are our men in their way to be accounted militant , as the Priests and worshippers of the true God , who indeed keep their hands pure, but strive with Godly prayers, on behalf of those that fight in just wars , and of him that is the just Commander? In which place he stileth all Christians *Priests* , after the example of the holy writers , *Apoc*. 1. 6. 1 *Pet*. 2. 5.

CXXXVIII. *When the arms of Subjects are just in an unjust War.*

AND I am of opinion , it is possible, that , in a war not only doubtfull but manifestly unjust , there may be some defense just on the *subjects* part. For, seeing an Enemy , through waging a just war , hath not true and internal right (except for necessary defense, or by consequence and beyond his purpose) to kill subjects *innocent* , and far remote from all blame of the war; (and such are not obnoxious to *punishment* ;) it followeth, that , if it certainly appear , the enemy comes with such a mind, that he will in no no wise (though he be able) spare the life of his enemies subjects; it followeth, I say, that these subjects may stand in their own defense by the *right of Nature*, whereof they are not deprived by the law of Nations. Neither shall we say (upon this) that the war is just on both sides: for our question now is not concerning the *War*, but concerning a particular and determinate *action*; which action, though of one otherwise having right to war, is unjust, and therefore is justly repelled.

The End of the Second Part.

Τῷ Θεῷ χάρις καὶ δόξα.

HVGO GROTIVS OF WARRE AND PEACE.

III. PART.

I. How much is lawful in War. *General Rules. First, Things are lawful in War, which are necessary to the end.* Cap. 1.

WHO may wage war, and for what causes, we have seen. It follows that we weigh what and how much † is lawful in war, and in what manner. Which is either *nakedly* considered,

† *Aug. epist.* 70. *ad Bonifac. com.* That you may be faithful in wars (if you must needs be engaged in them) seek peace. *Epist.* 205. Even in war be peaceable. Belisarius in Procopius Vand. 1. hath an excellent speech to his Soldiers, of

of Justice in waging War. Orosius saith of Theodosius, that his war was begun by a pious necessity, ended by a divine felicity, and neither his fights bloody, nor his victory insolent and revengefull.

or *upon promise* antecedent. *Nakedly*, First, by the Law of *Nature*; Secondly by that of *Nations*. What is by nature lawfull let us consider thus. *First*, as we have said afore, the things that lead to any end in moral matter receive their intrinsic estimation from the end it self*; wherefore we are understood to have a right to those things, which are necessary to the end of Right to be attained; *necessary* I mean, by a necessity taken not according to Physical subtilty, but *morally*: and *right* I mean, that which is *strictly* so called, and signifies a faculty of Doing in sole respect of Society. Wherefore, if I cannot otherwise save my life, it is lawful for me, by any kind of force, to keep off him that assaults it, though haply he may be without fault, as we have noted elswhere: because this right ariseth not properly from anothers sin, but from the right which nature granteth me in my own Defense. And further, I may invade that which is another man's, without consideration of any fault of his, if any certain danger be imminent to me from that thing: Yet may I not become Lord thereof; (for this is not accommodate to that end;) but keep it until I may be secured; which hath been also said * above. So, I have naturally a right to take away from

* *Vict. de ju. bell. n.* 15.

Vict. de jur. bel. n. 18. & 39. & 55.

* 2. Part. 21.

from another that thing of mine which he deteineth: and, if I cannot the same, something equivalent; as also, to obtain a debt. Upon which causes Dominion follows too, because equality impair'd cannot be repair'd otherwise. So, where punition is just, just also is all force, without which it cannot be exercised; and just is every thing which is a part of punishment, as the wast made by fire or other way, being within fit measure, and such as is answerable to the fault. Syl. in v. bell. p. 1. n. 10. v. pr.

II. *The second Rule, Right is consider'd, not only in respect of the first, but after-causes.*

SEcondly, we must know, that our right is not to be consider'd onely by the beginning of the war, but by causes arising after; as also in Trials of Law, after the sute commenced, a new right oft ariseth to a party. So, they that gather to my Assailant, whether Associats or Subjects, yield me a right of defending my self against them also. So, they that mixe themselves in a war which is unjust, especially if they may and ought to know it to be unjust, oblige themselves to repair the charge and damage, because by their fault they do it. So, whosoever engage in a war undertaken without probable ground, do also make themselves obnoxious to punishment,

nishment,by reason of the iujustice inheherent in their act. And thus *Plato* approves of war, *until they that are guilty, be compeld to make satisfaction to the innocent, whom they have wronged.*

III. *The third Rule. Some things follow without injury, which could not be lawfully intended.*

THirdly, we must observe,Many things follow upon the righr of Doing, indirectly, and without the purpose of the Doer †, to which there was no right directly and by it self.How this hath place in self-defence we have explained elswhere. In like manner, that we may recover our own, if just so much cannot be taken,we have a right to take more; yet under this obligation, of restoring the price of that which redounds. So may a ship fill'd with Pirats, or a house with Theeves, be battered with guns, though in the same ship or house are a few Infants, women or other innocent persons thereby endangered †. But, as we have noted often, that is not perfectly lawful always, which agreeth with right strictly taken. For, ofttimes Charity to our neighbour will not permit us to use strict and extreme right. Wherefore, those things which happen beside our purpose, and are foreseen that they may happen, must also be within

† *Vide Th. 1.2. q. 73. art. 8. Molinam tr. 2. disput. 121.*

† *Nec reus est mortis alienæ,* inquit Augustinus, *qui suæ possessioni murorum ambitum circumduxit, si aliquis ex ipsorum usu percussus intereat,* Ad Publ. epist. 154.

within our Caution, unless the good to which our action tendeth, be much greater than the evil which is feared: or, unless, when the good and evil are equal, the hope of good be much greater than the fear of evil; which is left to be determined by Prudence: yet so, that always in a doubful case we must incline to that part as the safer, which provides for Another more than for our selves. *Suffer the tares to grow*, saith the best Master, *lest while you would pluck them up, you pluck up the wheat too.* And *Seneca* saith, *It is the power of Fire and Ruine to kill many without making difference.* Histories teach us, with what serious repentance *Theodosius*, by *Ambrose's* direction, expiated such immodesty of revenge. Neither is it to be drawn by us into example, if God at any time doth such a thing, by reason of that most full right of Dominion he hath over us, which right he hath not granted us to have one over another, as we have before noted. Notwithstanding, the same God, Lord of men by his own right, for the sake of a very few good men, is wont to spare, even a great multitude of the bad; and thereby testifies his equity, as he is a Judge, as the Conference of *Abraham* with God concerning *Sodom* clearly shews us. And by these general rules it may be known, how much is lawful against an enemy *Naturally*.

Matth. 13.29. Th. 2. 2. q. 64. art. 2. Sen. in fine l. 2. de Clem. Gen. 18. 23. & seq.

IV.

IV. *What is lawful againſt them, that ſend things to the Enemies.*

IT is alſo enquir'd, what is lawfull againſt them, who are not enemies, or would not ſo be called, but furniſh the enemies with ſome things. For, both of old and of late, we know there hath been ſharp contention about it, ſome defending the rigour of war, others the Freedome of Trade. Firſt, we muſt diſtinguiſh of the things themſelves. For ſome things there are that have uſe onely in war, as arms; ſome, that have no uſe in war, as thoſe that ſerve for pleaſure; ſome, that have uſe, both in war, and out of war, as mony, victuals, ſhips and things belonging thereto *. In the firſt kind, true is that ſaying of *Amalaſuintha* to *Juſtinian* *, *They are on the enemies party, that ſupply the enemy with Neceſſaries for the war.* The ſecond kind hath no cauſe of complaint. So *Seneca* ſaith, he will make requital to a Tyrant, if the benefit will neither give any new ſtrength unto him to do publick miſchief, nor confirm the ſtrength he hath. That is, which may be rendred him without the hurt of the Commonwealth: for explication whereof he addeth, *I will not help him to Mony to pay his Guard; but if he ſhal deſire Marbles and Robes, ſuch things*

* *Athenis ἀπόῤῥητα, i. e. evehi vetita, lina, utres, lignum, cera, pix.* Scholiaſtes ad Ariſtophanis Nubes & Equites.

* *Procopius Goth.* 1. *Vide Parutam lib.* 7.

hurt not others, only they minister to his Luxury; Soldiers and arms I will not supply him with; if he shall seek for Players and Recreations to soften his fierceness, I will gladly offer them. Ships of war I would not send him, but such as are for pleasure and ostentation of Princes sporting in the Sea I will not deny. And in the judgment of S. *Ambrose*, to give to one that conspires against his Country, is a liberality not to be allowed. In that third kind of doubtful use, the state of the war is to be distinguished. For, if I cannot defend my self, unless I intercept the things sent, Necessity then, as we have elswhere said, will give a right, but with the burthen of restitution, except some other cause accede. But, if the apportation of those things hinder the execution of my right, and he could know so much who brought them; as, if I had streitned a town with siedge, or shut up havens, and were now in expectation of their yielding or compounding; He shal be liable for the damage by his fault done me; like one that hath taken my debtor out of prison, or hath helped him to escape, whereby I am injur'd; And according to the measure of my loss, his Goods also may be seised, and brought under my command, to the end I may obtain my Due. If he hath not yet done any damage, but hath been willing to do it, there will be a right, by retention of the things, to com-

Lib. 1. c. 30. De Offic.

Can. in c. Ita quorund. ad liberand. de Judæis.

Silv. in verb. Restitutio. p. 3. §. 12.

pell him to give Caution for the future, by hostages, pledges, or some other way. But, if moreover my enemie's injustice toward me be most evident, and He confirm him in that most unjust war, in this case He will not only *Civilly* be liable, but *Criminally*, as one that rescues a person manifestly guilty from the Judge at hand; and, for that cause, it will be lawful to determine against him that which is meet for his offense, according to what we have said of punishments: wherefore within that measure He may also be spoiled. And, for these reasons, They that wage war, are accustomed to give publick notice † thereof to other nations, to the end that both the right of their Cause, and the probable hope they have to execute the same, may appear to all. Now, for this question, we have therefore referr'd it to the right of nature, because out of Histories we could find nothing constituted thereof † by the voluntary Law of Nations. The * *Romans*, who had brought victuals to the enemies of *Carthage*, were taken by the *Carthaginians*, and again rendred upon request.

† See an example hereof in Camden, 1591. 1598. Yet were not such significations always regarded, but with difference of times, causes, places. The Hollanders in the heat of the war between Suedia and the King of Polonia never sufferd themselves to be interdicted the Commerce with either Nation. The same, having war with Spain, intercepted the French ships passing to or from Spain, but restored them. The same Hollanders having a Navy before Dunkerk, suffer'd not the English Merchants to enter there. † Many things perteining to this question are in the Danish History of the learned Meursius l. 1. & 2. *Camdenum vide an.* 1589. 1595. * Polyb. 1.

Demetrius,

Demetrius *, when he possessed *Attica* with his Army, and had taken the neighboring Towns *Eleusis* and *Rhamnus*, intending to famish *Athens*, hanged up both the Master and Governour † of a ship about to bring in corn, and by that means deterring others got the City.

* Plutarch. Demetrio.

† Not much unlike is that which Plutarch relates of Pompey, in the history of the Mithridatic war: He set a guard on Bosphorus, to observe if any Merchants sailed in thither. Whosoever were taken were put to death.

V. *Whether it be lawful to use Guile in War.*

As to the manner of acting, force and terrour is most proper to wars: whether it be lawful also to use guile, is a question. For *Homer*, and *Pindar*, and *Virgil*, do all concur in this sentence †:

† Homer: *sive dolo, seu vi manifesta, clamve palamve.* Pindarus: *Quidvis agendo scilicet hostica Delenda vis est.* Virgil: *Dolus an virtus quis in hoste requirat?* Sequitur ipse *Ripheus justissimus unus Qui fuit in Teucris & servantissimus aequi.*

Your Enemy, you lawfully may spoile,
Whether by open force, or secret guile.

And *Solon*, so famous for his wisedom, followed this Rule, and *Fabius Maximus* in *Silius* * helpeth his valour with cunning. *Ulysses*, in *Homer*, the exemplar of wisedom, is every where full of subtle devices against the enemy: whence

* Silius: *Exin virtuti placuit dolus.*

 Lucian

Lucian concludes, They are worthy of praiſe that deceive him. *Xenophon* ſaid, Nothing is more profitable in War than Deceits; and *Braſidas* in *Thucydides* holds it to be a ſingular commendation to over-reach * the enemy; and *Ageſilaus* in *Plutarch* thinks it very juſt and lawfull. *Polybius* is of opinion, that things done by ſtrength in war are inferiour to thoſe done by wit: and out of him *Silius* brings in *Corvinus* ſpeaking thus *;

> ——*Leſs praiſe I gain*
> *By my ſtrong hand: I war by a ſtrong brain.*

And *Plutarch* notes, that thoſe ſevere *Laconians* were of the ſame judgment, and that He offered a greater ſacrifice, who had effected his work by ſtratagem, than by plain battell. The ſame Author magnifies *Lyſander* † for his various ſleights of war, and reckons it amongſt the praiſes of *Philopemen*, that being inſtituted in the *Cretian* diſciplin, he had allayed that blunt and hardy manner of warring with deceits and ſtealths. *Ammianus* ſaith, *All proſperous events of war are to be praiſed, without making difference between Valour and Craft.* The *Roman* Lawyers call it an honeſt craft, if one deviſed it againſt an enemy, and ſay, it matters not, whether one eſcape the enemies power by force or fraud. Among Divines, *Auguſtin*: *When a juſt war is undertaken, it*

Lucian. Phil.

Xenoph. de Cyri Juſtit. lib. 1.

Thucyd. lib. 5.

* Belli furta *vocantur & apud Virgilium Æn.* 11.

Plutarch. Apoph.

Polyb. lib. 9.

* Sil. l. 5. *Bellandum eſt aſtu: Levior laus in duce dextra.* Muhammedis dictum ſimile: *Elharbu hudiatum. i.e. Pugnæ fraudem requirunt.* Apud Virgilium in Comitatu Martis, *Iræ Inſidiæq;.* Ubi Servius: *Non tantum virtute, ſed inſidiis comitatum ſe oſtendit.*

† Plutarch compares with him, Sylla, who had in him, as Carbo ſaid, as much of the Fox as the Lion.

D. lib. 1. *de dolo L. nihil. de capt.*

Euſtach. ad Iliad. 6. δόλος ἢ ψεκτὸς, ἢ ἐπαινετός. *Quæſt.* 10. *ſuper Joſue.*

is

is no difference in point of right, whether one fight with open force, or ly in wait. And Chrysostom; *Generals are most praisworthy, that have got the victory by stratagem.* Howbeit, there are not wanting Opinions that seem to perswade the contrary: some of which we will allege anon. The determination of this Question depends on that, whether Guilt or Deceit in general be of the number of Evils, concerning which it is said, Evil is not to be done, that Good may come of it; or of such as are not evil universally, and in their own nature, but may haply and in some cases be good. 1. De Sacerdot.

VI. *Guile in the negative act is not unlawfull.*

IT is therefore to be noted, that *Guile* either consists in a *negative* act, or in a *positive.* I extend the word to those things that consist in a negative act, upon the authority of *Labeo*, who refers it to Guile, but not evil, when one doth defend his own or another man's by dissimulation. Doubtless, it was too crudely spoken by *Cicero*: *Our whole Conversation ought to be free from simulation and dissimulation altogether.* For, when as you are not bound to discover unto others all things that you know, or intend, it follows, that to dissemble certain things before certain persons, that is, to hide and conceal them is

L. 1. §. Dolum malum. D. de dolo malo.

De offic. 1.

Lib. contra mend. cap. 10. Tho. 2. 2. q. 40. art. 3. in resp. & q. 71. art. 7. Silv. in v. bell. p. 1. n. 9.

is very lawful. *It is lawful*, saith S. *Austin* *, *to cast the veil of dissimulation sometimes over the face of Truth.* And *Cicero* himself, in more places † than one, confesseth it to be necessary and inevitable *, especially to men of place in the Commonwealth. A notable example to this purpose, we have in the history of *Jeremy*, *ch.* 38. For, that Prophet being questiond by the King about the event of the Siedge, upon the Kings request prudently conceals the same before the Princes, alleging another cause of their Conference, and that a true one too. Hither also may be referr'd, that *Abraham* * calls *Sara* his *Sister*, that is, according to the manner of speech used then, his neer kinswoman, not revealing his marriage.

* *Idem in 5. Psal.* It is one thing to ly, another thing to conceal the Truth.
† *Pro Milone. & l. 7. epist. 9. & pro Cn. Planc.*
* *Vide Chrysost. 1. de Sacerdotio.*
Gen. 20.
* *Veritatem voluit celari, non mendacium dici.* Aug. qu. 26. in Genes.

VII. *Guile in the Positive act, when lawfull.*

Guile which consists in a positive act, if in things, is called Simulation; if in words, a ly. Some do thus distinguish between these two, saying, Words are naturally signes of the mind, things not so. But on the contrary 'tis true, that Words, by nature it self and without the will of men, do signify nothing, unless perhaps it be a confused voice and inarticulate, as in grief; which yet comes rather under the appellation of a thing, than of a word or speech. Now, if this be said, that

Tho. 2. 2. q. 110. a. 3. in resp.

that this is the peculiar nature of man above other creatures, that he can expreſs unto others the conceptions of his mind, and that words were found out to that end, they do indeed ſay what's true; but 'tis to be added, that ſuch an expreſſion is not made by words alone, but alſo by nods † and ſignes; as to mutes, whether thoſe nods have by nature ſomewhat common with the thing ſignifyed, or els do ſignify only by inſtitution. To which are like thoſe Notes, which do ſignify, not words figured by the tongue, (as *Paul* * the Lawyer ſpeaks) but things themſelves, either by ſome convenience and agreement with them, as hieroglyphicks, or by meer will, as among the people of *China*. Wherefore, another diſtinction muſt be here given, ſuch as is uſed to take away the ambiguity in the Word, *Law of Nations*. For this law is either that which hath pleaſed every nation without mutual tye, or that which doth mutually oblige. Thus, Words, and nods, and notes, which we have ſaid, were found out to ſignify with mutual obligation *: other things not ſo. Hence it comes to paſs, that it is lawful to uſe other things, though we foreſee, that Another may thereupon conceive a falſe opinion †. I ſpeak of that which is intrinſecal, not of that which is accidental. Therefore an Example is to be put, where no nocument * follows thence, or where the nocument it ſelf, the conſidera-

L. Labeo. §. *ult. D. de ſup. Legata.*

† Plinius de Æthiopum gente lib. 6. 30. *Quibuſdam pro ſermone nutus, motuſq; membrorum eſt.* V. c. tuæ fratern. de ſponſal.

* *Non figura*, inquit, *literarum, ſed oratione quam exprimunt literæ obligamur, quatenus placuit non minus valere quod ſcriptura quàm quod vocibus lingua figuratis ſignificaretur.* Valde Philoſophice dixit *placuit*, ut oſtenderet hæc valere ἐν συνθήκῃ. *L. non figura. D. de obl. & act.*

* κατὰ συνθήκην. *Ariſtot. de Interp.* c. 4.

† *Vide Aug. de doct. Chriſt. lib.* 2. c. 24.

* As in the fact of Michol, 1 Sam. 19. 16.

confideration of the guile fet afide, is lawful. An example of the former is in Chrift, who to his companions going to *Emmaus*,
Luk. 24. 28. *made as though he would have gone farther*; unlefs we had rather underftand, he had really an intent to go farther, Except they conftrained him to ftay; as God alfo is faid to will many things which are not
Mar. 6. 48. done, and elfwhere Chrift himfelf is faid to have been willing to pafs by the Apoftles *rowing*, to wit, except he were earneftly entreated *to come up into the fhip*.
Act. 16. 3. Another example may be given in *Paul*, who circumcifed *Timothy*, when he well knew the Jews would take it fo, as if the precept of Circumcifion, which was indeed abolifhed, did ftill oblige the *Ifraelites*, and as if *Paul* and *Timothy* were of that opinion: when yet *Paul* meant not this, but only to procure unto himfelf and *Timothy* a more familiar way of Converfation with the Jews. Nor did Circumcifion any more, the Law Divine taken away, purpofely fignify fuch neceffity, nor was the confequent Evill of the prefent errour, after to be corrected, of fo great value, as that good which *Paul* had his eye upon, namely, the infinuation of Evangelical Truth. This fimulation the Greek Fathers often call οἰκονομίαν †. Of which is extant an excellent fentence

† So it is to be called, not ἀπάτη, frauds, faith Chryfoftom in his firft *De Sacerdotio*. The fame in his upon 1 Cor. 4. 6. This was not fraud, but a kind of compliance and difpenfation. Hither may be referred David's counterfeit madnefs.

of

of *Clemens Alexandrinus* ſpeaking of a good man thus : *For the good of his Neighbour he will do ſome things, which otherwiſe of his own accord, and by a primary intention he would not do.* Of this ſort is that in the war of the *Romans*, who threw loaves from the Capitol into the guards of the enemies, to poſſeſs them with a belief, that they were not ſtreitned with hunger. An example of the later is in a feigned flight, ſuch as *Joſhua* gave in command to his men, that they might conquer *Ai*; and other Captains often. For here, the nocument that follows we prove to be lawfull from the juſtice of war; and the flight it ſelf, by appointment, ſignifies nothing, although the enemy take it as a ſign of fear, which miſtake the other is not bound to acquit him of, uſing his liberty to go hither or thither, and with more or leſs ſpeed, and in this or that poſture or habit. Hither alſo is to be referred their act who are frequently read to have uſed the arms, enſigns, apparel, ſails of their enemies. For all theſe things are of that kind, that they may be uſed of any at his pleaſure, even contrary to cuſtom; becauſe the cuſtom it ſelf is introduced at pleaſure of every one, not as by common conſent, and ſuch a cuſtome obligeth no man

Liv. l. 5.

Joſ. 8.

Silv. in verbo bell. p. 1. n. 9.

VIII.

VIII. *Whether Guile by acts signifying by agreement be lawful? The difficulty of the question.*

IT is a harder question concerning those notes, which ; as I may say, are conversant in the commerce of men , of which sort properly is a ly. For , there are many places in Scripture against lying. *A righteous* (i. e. a good) *man hateth lying*. *Remove far from me vanitie and lies. Thou shalt destroy them that speak lyes. Ly not one to another*. And this part is rigidly maintaind by *Augustin* : and there are among the Philosophers and Poets †, that have the same opinion. That of *Homer* is famous ;

Prov. 13. 5. Prov. 30. 8. Psal. 5. 7. Col. 3. 9.

† *Aliena vero prologui nunquam decet*. Sophocles. *Mendacium odit quisquis animitus sapit*. Cleobulus.

> *Whose mind thinks one thing , and his*
> *Tongue doth tell*
> *Another , I hate like the pit of Hell :*

Aristotle said , *A ly is of it self foul and vituperable , Truth fair and laudable*. Yet, on the other side is not wanting Authority neither; first, Scripture-examples * of men approved without any note of reprehension ; next , the sayings of the antient Christians , *Origen* ; *Clement*, *Tertullian* , *Lactantius* , *S. Chrysostom* , *S. Hierom* , *Cassian* , yea almost all , as *S. Augustin* himself confesseth , so dissenting , that he doth nevertheless acknowledge

* Irenæus learned of an old Priest, and taught , Things, of which the Scripture passes no censure, but setteth them down simply , are not to be condemned by us. *l. 4. c. 50.*

knowledg it to be *a great question, dark, and subject to various disputation of learned men.* Among the Philosophers, plainly stand on this side, *Socrates* and his Scholars, *Plato*, *Xenophon*, and *Cicero* somewhere; and, if we believe *Plutarch* and *Quintilian*, the *Stoicks*: who, among the gifts of a wise man, mention a dexterity to ly, *when, and as one ought.* Nor doth *Aristotle* seem to dissent in some places: whose καθ' αὑτὸ, *by it self*, in the saying afore, may be expounded *commonly*, or the thing being considerd without circumstances. And his Interpreter *Andronicus Rhodius* saith of a Physician lying to his Patient, *He deceives indeed, yet is he not a Deceiver:* He addes the reason: *For his purpose is not to deceive, but to preserve the diseased. Quintilian* pleading on this side, saith, There are very many things, which are honest or dishonest, not so much in the doing, as in the causes of them. † And in the same Orator I read, *It is sometimes granted to a wise man to tell a ly. Eustathius Metropolitan* of *Thessalonica*, upon the second of the *Odysses*: *A wise man will ly*,

Plato 1. & 2. & 5. *de repub. Xenoph.* 4. *Socrat. Plut. de Stoic. contract. Quintil.* 12. 1.

Nic. 7. 3. 4. *Nic.* 8. ἀπατᾷ μὲν, ἀπατεὼν δ' οὐκ ἔστι.

† Diphilus:
Quod pro salute dicitur mendacium
Me judice habere nil potest incommodi
Quærenti apud Sophoclem Neoptolemo,
Non tibi videtur turpe falsiloquentia?
Respondet Ulysses,
Non, si salus nascatur ex mendacio.
Cui similia ex Pisandro & Euripide adferuntur.

upon

upon urgent occasion †: Where he also alledgeth testimonies out of *Heredotus* and *Isocrates*.

† κατὰ καιρὸν, *In tempore, ut Donatus loquitur ad Adelphos* 4. 3. Et ipsum fallere in tempore, quidam de Officiis scribentes rectum putant. *Cicero pro Q. Ligario, aliquod mendacium* honestum *&* misericors *vocat.*

IX. *Not all use of speech, which may be known will be taken in another sense, is unlawful.*

HAply some Reconciliation of so disagreeing sentences may be found out from the larger or stricter acception of a ly. Neither do we here take a ly, as it falls from a man unwittingly *; as, *to ly*, and *to tell a ly*, are distinguisht in *Gellius* †: but we speak of that, which is knowingly uttered with a signification that agrees not with the conception of the mind, whether in understanding, or in willing. For, that which is first and immediatly shewed by words and the like notes, are the conceptions of the mind: Therefore, he doth not ly, who speaketh a false thing, that he thinketh to be true; but, who speaketh a thing true indeed, which yet he thinketh false, He lyeth. It is then the falsity of signification, which we require to the common nature of a ly. Whence it follows; when any word or sentence is equivocal and admitteth more significations than one, (whether from vulgar use, or custom of art, or some

* The Tongue is not made guilty, but by a guilty mind. *And*, No man is to be censur'd for lying, who speaketh false, which he thinketh true; because, as for his part he deceiveth not, but is deceived. *August. de verb. Apost. Serm.* 28. *& Enchir. c.* 22.

† Gellius l. 11. c. 11. *Mentiri & Mendacium dicere.*

some intelligible figure) then, if the minds Conception agreeth to one of those significations, a ly is not made though it may be thought the hearer will take it another way †. True indeed it is, such a speech rashly used is not to be approv'd; but it may be honested by the causes annexed to it; *viz.* If it pertein to the instruction of him that is committed to our care, or to the avoyding an injurious question. Christ himself hath given us an example of the former sort, when he said, *Our friend Lazarus sleepeth*, which the Apostles received as if 'twere spoken of taking his rest in sleep. Jo. 11. 11. And, what he had said about restoring the Temple, meaning it of his Body, he knew the Jews understood of the Temple properly called so. Jo. 2. 20, 21. So, when he promised to the Apostles twelve seats of honour and next unto the King, after the manner of the Princes of Tribes among the *Hebrews* (and elswhere, the drinking of new wine in his Fathers Kingdom) he seems to have known well enough, that this would not otherwise be taken by them, than of some Kingdom of this life; with hope whereof they were full, to the very moment of Christ's Ascension into Heaven. The same our Lord, by the *Ambages* of Parables speaks unto the people, that hearing they might not understand him; that is, unless they did bring such attention and docility, as was meet. An example of the later sort may be given out of

† So Abraham spoke captiously with his servants, as Ambrose takes it and approves it: whom Gratian follows, *post. c. si qualibet. causa* 22. *q.* 2.

Luc. 22. 30.

Matth. 26. 25.

Act. 1. 6.

Tacit. Annal. 6.

of profane hiſtory in *L.Vitellius*, with who *Narciſſus* was inſtant, that he ſhould ſpeak openly, and tell him the plain truth, yet he did not ſo prevail, but that he gave anſwers doubtfull, and inclining whither they were drawn †. The ſaying of the *Hebrews* * is pertinent here: *If one knows to uſe the perplexed ſpeech, well; if not, let him hold his peace.* On the contrary, it may happen, that to uſe ſuch a kind of ſpeaking may be not only illaudable, but wicked, as, when the honour of God †, or Love due to our Neighbour *, or reverence to our Superiour, or the nature of the thing in hand, exact, that the thoughts of the heart be made apparent clearly in the words; as in contracts we have ſaid, that is to be opened, which the nature of the contract is conceived to require; in which ſenſe that of *Cicero* may be fitly taken: *All lying is to be baniſhed out of contracts and bargains*; taken from an old *Attick* Law †. Where the word, *Lying*, ſeems to be underſtood ſo large, that it includes alſo an obſcure ſpeech. But, ſpeaking properly, we have now excluded it from the notion of a ly.

† Idem Tacitus Hiſtor. 3. *Incerta diſſeruit, tracturus interpretationem, prout conduxiſſet.*

* Quorum & hoc eſt: *Licet perplexe loqui boni cauſa.* Citat doctiſſimus Manaſſes Ben Iſrael in ſuo Conciliatore quæſt. 37.

† Philo de vita Moſis: *De factis loquor, quæ ad Dei honorem pertinent, in quibus ſolus veracem eſſe oportuit, etiamſi quis cæterùm ingenio eſſet mendace. Veritas enim Dei Comes.*

* Æſchylus Prometheo:

Dicam diſerte quicquid audire expetis,
Sermone nudo, non per implicitos modos,
Quo more amicos alloqui verum ac bonum eſt.

† Lex Attica, κατὰ τὴν ἀγορὰν ἀψευδεῖν. Demoſth. in Leptinem.

X.

X. *The form of a ly, as it is unlawful, consists in its repugnance to the right of Another.*

IT is then requir'd to the common notion of a Ly, that what is said, written, noted, intimated, cannot otherwise be understood, than in that sense, which is different from the mind of the Author. And to this larger notion, the stricter signification of a ly, as it is naturally unlawful, must needs add some proper difference: which, if the matter be rightly examined, at least according to the common estimation of Nations, no other seems possible to be given beside the repugnance with the existing and remaining right of him to whom the speech or note is directed. For, that no man lyes to himself, how false soever he speaketh, is plain enough. Right I understand here, not of every sort, and extrinsecal to the thing, but, which is proper and connate to this business. And this is nothing els but the liberty of judging †, which Men speaking together are, as 'twere by a certain tacit agreement, understood to owe unto them whom they speak. For this and no other is that mutual obligation, which men had consented to introduce, so soon as they instituted the use of words and the like notes: without which obligation, such an Invention, had been in vain. And we require, that, at

† Hence the Hebrews say, He steals away the heart, who takes away the means of knowing, Gen. 31. 20, 26, 27. and Onkelos and the LXX. there. *Rabbi David lib. radicum. & Rab. Salomo in Comment. & Abenesd.*

at the time of ſpeaking, that right ſubſiſt and remain: for, it may fall out, that the right that was may be taken away by another right ſupervenient; as a debt, by acceptilation, or ceſſation of the condition. It is required further, that the right which is impaired be his with whom we ſpeak, not anothers; as alſo in contracts, injuſtice is not, but from the impaired right of the contractors. Hither perchance you may not amiſs refer, that *Plato* after *Simonides* reduces Truth of ſpeech to Juſtice; and, that the holy Scriptures oftentimes deſcribe that forbidden ly, by a teſtimony or ſpeech againſt ones neighbour; and, that S. *Auguſtin* himſelf, in conſtituting the nature of a ly, puts the intent of deceiving †. And *Cicero* will have the queſtion of ſpeaking truth referred to the fundamentals of Juſtice. Now, the right of which we have ſpoken, it ſeems, may be taken away, as by the expreſs conſent of him with whom we deal (as, if one hath foretold, he will ſpeak falſe, and the other hath given leave :) ſo alſo by his tacit conſent, or preſumed upon good reaſon, or by oppoſition of another right, which, by the Common judgment of all men, is of much more value. Three things being well underſtood, will furniſh us with many illations, conducing much to reconcile the different opinions above mention'd.

Lib. 1. de Repub.

† Lactant. inſtit. 6. 18. *ut non mentiatur unquam decipiendi aut nocendi cauſa.*

XI.

XI. *Five illations thence, about the Lawfulneſs of ſpeaking falſe.*

FIrſt, although ſomething be ſpoken to an Infant, or one beſide himſelf, that hath a falſe ſignification, therein is not the crime of a ly. For it ſeems to be permitted by the common ſenſe of all men, *that the ſimple age of Children be pleas'd with fictions.* Lucret. And *Quintilian* ſpeaking of Children, ſaith, *We ſeign many things for their benefit.* The next reaſon is, ſeeing Infants and mad men have not liberty of judgment, there can be no injury done them, as to that liberty. *Secondly*, as oft as the ſpeech is directed to him who is not deceived, though a Third draw from thence a falſe perſwaſion, it is no ly: Not in reſpect of him, to whom the ſpeech is; becauſe his liberty remains entire, even as theirs to whom a Tale is told which they underſtand to be a Tale; or to whom is uttered a figurative ſpeech, ironicall or hyperbolicall (which figure, as *Seneca* * ſaith, by a ly arrives at truth, and is called by *Quintilian* a lying ſuperjection.) Nor in reſpect of him who hears it on the by; becauſe the ſpeaker hath nothing to do with him, and ſo to him there is no obligation. Yea, if himſelf create to himſelf an opinion of that which is not ſaid to him, but to another, he hath ſomewhat to impute, not to another, but to himſelf.

* 7. *De benef.* 2. Senec. ibid. *Incredibilia affirmat, ut ad credibilia perveniat.*

For, if we will judge rightly, in respect of him, the speech is no speech, but a thing of an uncertain signification. Wherefore, neither was *Cato Censorius* in any fault, who falsly promis'd aid to the Confederates; nor *Flaccus*, who told others, that the enemies City was taken by *Æmilius*, though the enemies were deceived thereby; the like whereof *Plutarch* relates of *Agesilaus*. For, nothing was here spoken to the enemies; and the nocument that followed thence, is a thing extrinsecal, and by it self not unlawful to be wished or procured. To this kind *Chrysostom* & *Hierom* * have referred the speech of *Paul*, wherewith he reprehended *Peter*, as too much Judaizing, at *Antioch*; For they think *Peter* understood well enough, it was not serious; and in the mean, care was had for the infirmity of the By-standers. Thirdly, as oft as it is certain, He, to whom the speech is, will not take in evill part the impairing of his liberty in judging, yea will give thanks for the same, by reason of some commodity he attains thereby; then also, a ly strictly called so, that is, injurious, is not made: as, He would not commit Theft, who, upon presumption of the Masters will, should spend some small matter of his, to the end he might thence gain him great profit. For, in these things which are so certain, the will presumed is accounted for the express. And to a willing man,

Liv. lib. 34. Appian. Hisp.

* *Adde Cyrillum adversus Julianum lib. 9. circa finem. nec multo aliter Tertull. 1. & 3. cont. Marcionem.*

man, 'tis certain, injury is not done. So then, he seemeth not to sin, who either comforteth a sick friend with a perswasion not true, as *Arria* comforted *Pætus*, his son being dead; which History is in *Plinie*'s Epistles: or addeth courage to one ready to lose the battell, by a false report; that revived by it, he may get victory and safety to himself, and being so deceived may not be taken *, as *Lucretius* speaks. *Democritus*: *We must by all means speak the truth, where it is better.* Xenophon; *We may deceive our friends for their good.* And *Clemens Alexandrinus* grants, *We may use a ly for a remedy*: Maximus Tyrius: *The Physician deceives his Patient, the General his Soldiers, and the Master of the ship the Saylers: nor is there any hurt in this.* *Proclus* on *Plato* gives the reason: *For that which is good, is better than the truth.* Such is that in *Xenophon*, *That the Confederates are at hand*: and that of *Tullus Hostilius*, *That by his command the Albans wheel'd about*: and that wholsomely, as Histories call it, of the Consul *Quinctius*, *That the enemies fled in the other wing*: and the like every where in the Historians†. And in this kind, it is to be noted, the hurt of

Plin. epist. 3. 16.

* *Ac sic deceptus non capiatur.* Lucret.

Xenoph. 4. *Socr.*

Livius lib. 34.

† Agesilaus being come into Bœotia, having understood that Pisander was overthrown at sea by Pharnabazus and Conon, commanded a contrary report to be dispersed among his Soldiers, and putting on a Crown offered Sacrifice for the victory; *Plutarch. Agesil.* [*See the History of the famous Montross, in the battell of Aldern, Lat. p.*112.]

the judgment is so much less, because most part it is momentany, and within a little while the Truth is manifest. A *Fourth* Instance and neer to the former is, as oft as He that hath a right supereminent * over all the rights of Another, useth that right for his good, whether proper or publick. And this especially *Plato* seemeth to have regarded, who grants to those that have command, to speak false. When he seemeth to grant the same sometimes to Physicians *, and sometime to deny it, we may perhaps reconcile him to himself by this distinction, making him understand in the first place Physicians publickly called to this office, in the Later them that privately assume it to themselves. Yet God, though he hath supreme power over men, cannot ly, as the same *Plato* rightly acknowledges, because it is a mark of infirmity to have such a refuge. An example of unblamable false speaking may perhaps be given in *Joseph*† (*Philo* approving it) who being *Vice-Roy* of *Egypt* feignedly accuseth his brethren, first as spies, then as theeves, not having such an opinion of them: And in *Salomon*, who gave a *Specimen* of the wisedom given him by God, when, before the women contending about the Child, he pronounced those words, which signified a will of dividing the Child, and yet meant nothing less, but intended to render her Child to the true Mother. It is a saying of

* Iliad. 2. Agamemnon Græcorum Imp. *Ante tamen Danaos verbis tentabo (sinit fas) utq; cite fugiant ærata classe monebo.* Plato 3. de rep.

* Examples of Physicians are alleged by Chrysostom, l. 1. *de Sacerdotio.*

† *Cum fratribus dispensatoria severitate crimen explorationis inureret,* ait Cassiod. de amicitia.

of *Quintilian*, *Sometimes common utility exacteth of us, to defend also what is false.* A *Fift* may be, as oft as the life of an innocent person, or something equal to it, cannot otherwise be saved; and Another cannot otherwise be averted from perfecting some wicked enterprize †. Such was the fact of *Hypermnestra* *, who is wont to be praised upon this score.

Lib. 2. 18.

† Aug. in 5. ps. relatus à Gratiano in causam 22. quæst. 2. c. ne quis.

Duo vero sunt genera mendaciorum in quibus non est magna culpa, sed tamen non sunt sine culpa, cum aut jocamur, aut proximo consulendo mentimur. Illud autem primum in jocando ideo non est pernitiosum, quia non fallit; novit enim ille cui dicitur, causa jocandi fuisse dictum. Secundum autem ideo minus est, quia retinet nonnullam benevolentiam. Tertullian in his De pudicitia, among the sins of daily incursion, to which we are all exposed, putteth, to ly upon necessity.

* *Splendide mendax, & in omne virgo*
Nobilis ævum. Horat. 3. Carm. 2. Ubi scholiastes, *Decenter: pulchrum est enim pro justitia mentiri.* Chrysostom of Rahab: O brave ly, O laudable deceit, of one not betraying Divine things, but preserving true piety. Augustin of the Egyptian Midwives: O the great wit of Humanity, O pious ly for to save life! Hierom commendeth the same Midwives, and believes, rewards, and those eternal, were given them: upon Ezech. 17. and Es. 56. Augustin is doubtful, upon Exod. lib. 2. So is Aquinas 2. 2. q. 110. a. 54. and Cajetan there. Tostatus saith, They did not sin. See the learned Masius on Josua, 2. 5.

XII. *False speaking, whether lawful toward enemies.*

A Larger license, than this we have spoken of, is given by many wise writers, that determine it to be lawful to use false speech to enemies. So, to the Rule of not lying, this exception, *unless to enemies*, is added by *Plato*, *Xenophon*, *Philo* among the Jews; among the Christians *Chrysostom* *. Whither perhaps you may not amiss refer, that extent in holy Scripture, the ly of the *Jabusites* * in the siedge, and something like it of the Prophet *Elisha* *; and of *Valerius Levinus*, who boasted he had slain *Pyrrhus*. To the third, fourth and fift of those observations newly set down, perteins a place of *Eustratius Metropolitan* of *Nicæa* upon the sixt of the *Ethicks*: *Who rightly consulteth is not one who necessarily speaketh truth; for it may be that one rightly consulting may consult how he may ly on purpose, either to his enemy, to deceive him; or to his friend, to rescue him from evil: examples whereof Histories are full of.* And *Quintilian*, If a Robber is to be averted from killing a man, or an enemy to be deceived for the safety of our Country, saith, that which otherwise is to be reprehended in servants, will be commendable in a wise man. Those sayings do not please the Schools of later Ages, who

Lib. 2. *de repub*, *Lib.* 2. *de Cyri inst.* & 5. *Socrat. Philo de migr. Ab.*

* *Chrys. l* 1. *de Sacerd.* Where he saith, If you cal the Actions of the most noble Captains to the rest, you shall find most of their trophies to be rais'd by fraud; and that such have more praise than Conquerours by open force.

* 1 Sam. 11.

* 2 Reg. 6. 18. & 8. 10. as the Maforets and the vulgar Latin read it.

Tho. 2. 2. *q* 110. *art.* 1. & 3. *Co var. in c. quamv. de pactis in* 6. *p.* 1 §. 5. *n.* 15. *Soto de justitia* 5. *q.* 6. *art.* 2. *Tolet lib.* 4. *c.* 21. *l.* 5. *c.* 58. *Less. l.* 2. *de justit. c.* 42. *dub.* 9.

who have chosen S. *Augustin* † of all the Antients, to be followed by them almost in all things. But the same Schools do admit tacit interpretations, so abhorrent from all use, that it may be doubted, whether it is not better to admit false speaking against some, in the cases mention'd, or in some of them, (for I take not upon me here to define any thing) than so indiscreetly to exempt from false speaking these sayings: as when they say, *I know not*, it may be understood, *to tell thee*: And, *I have not*, it may be understood, *to give thee*: and the like, which common sense, rejecteth and which if they be admitted will effect, that one affirming may be said to deny the same thing, and denying to affirm. For, it is most true, that there is no word but may receive a doubtful interpretation *, seeing all, beside the significat of the first notion, as they call it, have another of the second †, and that various, according to various arts, and other senses too by Metaphor or the like figures. Neither do I more allow of their Device, who, as if they did abhor the word not the thing, call them *jests*, which are utterd with a countenance and pronuntiation most serious.

† Against whose after-sentence in this matter, wrote Rupertus Abbas.

* Id. Chrysippus defendit apud Gellium l. 9. c. 12. Et Seneca de Benef. 2. c. 34. *Ingens est copia rerum sine nomine, quas non propriis appellationib. notamus, sed alienis commodatisq;.*

† Augustinus de Magistro: *Nullum nos signum comperisse, quod non inter cætera quæ significat, se quoq; significet.*

XIII.

XIII. *This is not to be extended to promising words, nor to Oaths.*

MOreover, we must know, what we have said of false speaking is to be referd to *asserting* speech, and such as hurteth none but a publick enemy, not to *promising* †. For, upon promise, as afore we began to say, a special and new right is confer'd to him, to whom the promise is made: and that hath place even amongst enemies, without any exception of hostility now being; nor only in *express* promises, but also in *tacit*, as in calling for parly; as we shall declare, when we come to that part, which is of keeping faith in war. And further, that is to be repeated out of our former Dissertation of Oaths, whether an *oath* be *assertive* or *promissive*, it hath the vertue to exclude all exceptions, which might be derived from the person of him with whom we deal: because we have to do, not with man only, but with God, to whom we are bound by our Oath, although no right arise to man. In the same place we have also said, that it is not in an Oath as in other words; wherein, that we may be excused from a ly, are admitted any Interpretations not altogether unusual; but truth is exactly requir'd in that sense, which the man that hears it, is supposed verily

† Agesilaus and with him Plutarch distinguish so. To violate leagues is to contemn the Gods. Otherwise to deceive the enemy with words, is not only just, but glorious, profitable and delightful.

verily to underſtand. So that, their impiety is very much to be deteſted, who doubted not to aſſert, that as Childern with toys, ſo men are to be deceived with Oaths.

XIV. *It is more grievous and agreeable to Christian ſimplicity, to abſtein from falſe ſpeech alſo againſt an enemy.*

WE know alſo, that ſome kinds of frauds, which we have ſaid to be allowed naturally, were refuſed by ſome Nations or men: but that was, not out of an opinion of injuſtice, but by reaſon of a certain magnamity, and ſometime confidence of their own ſtrength. In *Ælian* is extant a ſaying of *Pythagoras*, That man comes neereſt unto God in two things: in ſpeaking truth always, and in doing good to others: and in *Jamblichus*, Veracity is ſaid to be the Guide to all good both Divine and human. *Ariſtotle*'s Magnanimous man *loves to ſpeak truth, and boldly*. *Plutarch* ſaith, *It is a ſervile thing, to ly*. *Arrianus* * of *Prolome: To him, being a King, it was more diſhonourable to ly, than to any other.* *Alexander* * in the ſame hiſtorian; *It is unworthy of a King, to ſpeak any thing to his Subiects, but the Truth.* *Mamertinus* of *Julian*: *Admirable in our Prince,* is

Ariſt. ὁ μεγαλόψυχος παῤῥησιαστικὸς καὶ ἀληθευτικός. Nic. 4. 1. Τὸ ψεύδεσθαι δουλοπρεπές. Plutarch.

Philo in his book, That every honeſt man is a free man, ſaith, They are wont to call deceitfull & double-dealers, men of an illiberal and ſervile mind.

* *Lib.* 1.

* *Lib.* 8.

is the concord of his mind and tongue; He knows a ly is a sin, not only of a low and little mind, but servile too: and seeing that poverty indeed, or fear, make men lyars, the Emperour that lyes understands not the greatness of his fortune. Plutarch commends *Aristides, for his constant nature, holding fast that which is just, and abhorring to ly, though in sport. Probus* of *Epaminondas: He was so studious of truth, that he would not ly, no not in jest.* Which indeed is the more to be observed by Christians, because simplicity is not only commanded them, but vain speech forbidden, and He is proposed for an example, in whose mouth was found no guile. *Lactantius; That true and just Traveller saith not that of* Lucilius, *It is not my property to ly to my friend and familiar: but also to an enemy and stranger, he will think he must not ly: nor will he commit at any time, that his tongue the interpreter of his mind should disagree with his meaning.* Such a one is *Neoptolemus* in *Sophocles* *, *excelling in a generous simplicity*, as *Dion Prusaensis* hath well noted. So, *Alexander* said he would not steal the victory. And *Polybius* saith, the *Achaians* abhorred from all fraud against the enemies, because they esteemed that only to be a true victory, which drew a confession of it from the enemies themselves. Such were the *Romans* till the end of the second *Punick* war.

Mat. 10. 16.
Mar. 12. 36.

* In Philoctete Sophoclis, Neoptolemus Ulyssi ad dolos hortanti sic respondet:

Ego

Ego audiens quæ doleo, Laerta sate,
Implere factus oaerim multo magis:
Nam sic nec ego sum natus, ut fallacias
Secter, nec olim genitor, ut perhibent meus:
At sum paratus vi mera, non fraudibus
Pertrahere raptum. De Genitore ejus, Achille, Hor. carm. lib. 4. Ode 6.

Ille non inclusus equo Minervæ
Sacra mentito, male feriatos
Troas & lætam Priami choreis
Falleret Aulam:
Sed palam captis gravis, &c. Ubi Scholiastes dicit, Achillem *nihil fraude, sed semper palam Virtutis fiducia dimicasse.* Euripides Rheso:

Generosus animus hostibus furtim necem
Inferre nescit.

Ælian: *Valour is proper to the Romans, not victory gotten by fraud and cunning.* Whence, when *Perseus* King of *Macedon* was deceived by hope of Peace, the old Senators said, Those were none of the Roman arts; Their Ancestors never waged war to shew their wit but their valour; They left such deceits to the *Carthaginians* and *Greeks*, who accounted it more glorious to ensnare the enemy than to beat him. And then they added: *At present perhaps Deceit may be more profitable than valour, but a perpetual victory is obteined over his mind, who is forc'd to a confession, that he is overcome, neither by art nor chance, but by plain battell in a just and pious war.* And in after-times, we read in *Tacitus*, *That the* Annal. lib. 2. *Romans were wont to revenge themselves of their enemies, not by fraud, not secretly,*

Scholiastes ad 2. Apollon.

ly, but openly and in arms. Such also were the *Tibarens*, who did agree with the enemy about the place and time of battell. And *Mardonius* in *Herodotus* saith the same of the *Grecians* in his time.

XV. *It is not lawful to make a traitor; it is, to use him.*

LAstly, to the manner of acting this is pertinent: Whatsoever is not lawful for any one to do, to impell or sollicite him to do it is not lawful neither. For example; It is not lawfull for a subject to kill his King, nor to yield up Towns without publick Counsell, nor to spoil the Citizens. To these things therefore, it is not lawfull to tempt a subject, that remaineth such. For always, he that gives cause of sinning to another, sins also himself. Nor may any reply, that to Him, who impelleth such a man to a wicked act, that act, namely the killing of his enemy, is lawfull. He may indeed lawfully do it, but not in that manneer. *Augustin* well: *It is all one, whether your self commit a sin, or set another to do it for you.* It is another thing, if, to effect a matter lawful for him, one use the offerd service of a man sinning without any other impulse but his own: That this is not unjust we have proved elswhere by the example of God himself. *We receive a fugitive by the Law of War,* saith

ſaith *Celſus* †; that is, It is not againſt the Law of War, to admit him, who, having deſerted the enemies part, electeth ours *.

† *L. Transfugam. D. de acq. rerum dom.*

* Nor are ſuch to be rendred; except it ſhall be agreed in the peace, as in the peace with Philip, the Ætolians, Antiochus. *Polyb. in excerp. Legat. 9. 28. 34. Menander protector idem nos docet.*

XVI. Goods of Subjects bound for the Rulers debt. *Naturally, none is bound by anothers deed but the Heir.*

Cap. 2.

LEt us come to thoſe things, which deſcend from the Law of Nations. They belong partly to every war, partly to a certain kind of war. Let us begin with generals. By the meer Law of nature, no man is bound by anothers act, but the ſucceſſor of his goods: for, that Goods ſhould paſs with their burthens, was introduced together with the dominion of things. The Emperor *Zeno* ſaith, It is contrary to natural equity, that any ſhould be moleſted for other mens debts. Hence the Titles in the *Roman* Law, That neither the wife be ſued for the Husband, nor the husband for the Wife; nor the Son for the Father, nor the Father or Mother for the Son. Nor do particular men owe that which the Community owes, as *Ulpian* hath it plainly: to wit, if the Community hath any Goods: for otherwiſe, particulars are bound as they are a part of the

L. unica. c. ut null. ex vicaneis c. ne uxor pro mar. & ne fil. pro patre, totis titulis.

L. ſicut. §. 1. D. quod cujuſq; univerſ. nom.

the whole. *Seneca*; *If one lend my Country mony, I will not call my ſelf his debtor: yet will I pay my ſhare.* He had ſaid afore, *Being one of the people, I will not pay as for my ſelf, but contribute as for my Country.* And, *Every one will owe, not as a proper debt, but as a part of the publick.* Hence it was ſpecially conſtituted by the *Roman* Law, that none of the Villagers ſhould be tyed for the other debts of Villagers: and elſwhere, no poſſeſſion of any man is charged with the debts of others, no not with the publick debts: and in the Novell of *Juſtinian*, *Pignorations* † for others are prohibited, the cauſe being added, that it is againſt reaſon for one to be charged with anothers debt: where alſo ſuch exactions are called odions. And King *Theodoricus* in *Caſſiodore** calls this Pignoration of one for another a wicked licence.

Lib.6. de Benef. c. 20. & c. 19.

Vide Leges Siculas in fine l. 1.

D. L. unica. c. ut null. ex vicun. l. 11. l. nullam. c. de execut. & exact. lib. 12. Novel. 52. & 134.

† C. unico de injuriis in ſexto: *Pignorationes, quas vulgaris elocutio repreſſalias nominat.* Rectius ſcribas ut libri quidam, *reprenſalias*. Id enim voci Saxonicæ Withernamii ad amuſſim reſpondet, ſed uſus alterum recepit.

* Lib. 4. Var. epiſt.

XVII. *By*

XVII. *By the Law of Nations Subjects are tied for the debts of the Ruler.*

ALthough these things be true, yet by the voluntary Law of Nations it might by induced, and it appears to have been induced, that, for that which any Civil Society, or the head thereof, ought to make good, either by it self primarily, or because in anothers debt it hath also made it self lyable by not doing right; for that, I say, are tyed and bound all corporal and incorporal Goods of them that are subject to the same society or head. And it was a certain necessity that effected this; because without this, great licence would be given to the doing of injuries, seeing the Goods of Rulers oftentimes cannot so easily come to hand, as of private men who are more. This then is among those Laws, which *Justinian* saith were constituted by the Nations, upon the urgency of human needs. Howbeit, this is not so repugnant to nature, that it could not be induced by custome and tacit consent, when even without any cause sureties are bound by consent alone. And there was hope, that the members of the same society might more easily obtain mutual right, and provide for their own indemnity, than foreiners, who in many places are very little regarded.

Justinian. de jure nat. Tho.2.2.q. 40. art. 1. Molin. disp. 120. & 121. Valentia disp. 3. qu. 16. n. 3. Navar. c. 27. n. 136.

ded. Besides, the benefit of this obligation was common to all Nations, so that they which were one time grieved with it, another time might be eased by the same. Moreover, that this custome was received, appears not only out of full wars, which Nations wage against Nations (for in these, what is observed may be seen in the forms of denuntiation *, and in the proposal *, and the decree * it self;) but also, where matters are not come to that fulness of war, yet there is need of a certain violent execution of right, that is, imperfect war, we see the same to be used †. *Agesilaus* of old, said to *Pharnabazus*, a subject of the King of *Persia* *, *We, O Pharnabazus, when we were the Kings friends carried our selves like friends towards all his, and now being become his enemies we carry our selves like enemies. Wherefore, seeing you will be one of the things that are His, we do justly oppose him in you.*

* *Populis priscorum Latinorum, hominibusq; priscis Latinis bellum indico facioq;.* Liv. l. 1.
* *Vellent, juberent Philippo Regi Macedonibusq; qui sub regno ejus essent bellum indici.* lib. 31.
* *Populus Romanus cum populo Hermundulo, hominibusq; Hermundulis bellum jussit:* Gell. l. 16. c. 4. quod ex Cincio est in re militari: & alibi: *Hostis sit ille, quique intra præsidia ejus sunt.* Liv. lib. 38. & alibi.
† A prudent man Nicolaus Damascenus distinguisheth wars from these pignorations, where he shews, that Herod, to whom it was not lawful to make war against the Arabians, might lawfully use pignoration for the Debts due unto him by contract. *Joseph. 6. ant. hist.* ubi hæc verba. *Cum narrasset quingenta Herodi talenta debita, cautionemq; de iis expositam id continere ubi dies præstituta transiisset, posse ipsum ex omni Arabum terra pignora capere, hanc expeditionem expeditionem non esse dicebat, sed justam debiti exactionem.* * Plutarch. Agesil. & Xenoph. hist. Gr. 4.

XVII.

XVII. *An example hereof in the Apprehension of men, and of goods.*

ONe *species* of that execution which I speak of, was that which the *Athenians* called * Apprehension of men: * ἀνδροληψία. of which the *Attick* Law thus, *If one have force offerd him, and dy, his Kinsman and friends may apprehend men, till either the Man-slayers be duly punisht, or yielded: but it is lawful to apprehend only three men, and no more.* Here we see, for the debt of the City, which is bound to punish her subjects that have hurt others, is tyed a certain incorporal right of the subjects, that is, the liberty of staying where they please, and doing what they will; so that they may be in servitude, until the City do what she is bound to do, that is, punish the Guilty. For, though the *Epygtians*, as we learn out of *Diodorus Siculus*, argued, that the body or liberty ought not to be bound for a debt, yet therein is nothing contrary to nature; and the custome, not of the *Greeks* only, but of other Nations prevailed on the other side. In like manner, to recover a Citizen taken captive by manifest injury, are the Citizens of that City where the injury was done, reteined. Wherefore some at *Carthage* would not suffer *Ariston* the *Tyrian* to be taken, *For*, said they, *the same will befall the Carthaginians at Tyre and in other towns of Trade, wherto they often resort.* Another *species* of violent execution is * *Pignoration among divers Nations*; which the later Lawyers * call the right of *Reprizals*; the *Saxons* and the English, *Withernam*; and the French, even when it is obtained of the King, *Letters of Marc*. And this hath place, say the Lawyers, where right is denyed.

Liv. lib. 34.

* ἐνεχυρασμὸς, *Justin. novell.* σύλας *id dicit Demosth. in orat. pro corona, & Arist. œcon.* 2.

* *Bald.* 3. *cons.* 58. *Bart. de repress. q.* 5. *ad* 3. *n.* 9.

XVIII. *Of Reprizals, after right denyed. Life is not engaged.*

Right of Reprizals cometh, not only if Judgment cannot, within fit time, be obtained against the guilty part, or Debtor; but also if in a matter not doubtful (for in a doubtful matter there is a presumption for them who are elected to publick judgments:) judgment be given plainly against right. For, the authority of the judge is not of the same value over foreiners, as over subjects. Even amongst subjects, it taketh not away what was truly owed: *A true Debtor, though he be absolved, yet by nature * remains a Debtor*, saith *Paul* * the Lawyer: *And when, by the injury of the judge, the Creditor had taken away from the owner a thing which was not the debtors, as engaged to him; and the question was put, whether, the debt being paid, the thing ought to be restored*

* *Spectant huc quæ habet Gail. de pace pub. l.* 2. *c.* 8. *n.* 7.

* *L. Julianus D. de cond. indeb. L. rescriptum.* §. 1. *D. de distr. pign.*

restored to the Debtor, *Scævola prov'd it ought to be restored.* There is this difference, that subjects cannot by force hinder the execution, even of an unjust sentence; nor lawfully pursue their right by force by reason of the efficacy of the power over them: but foreiners have right to compell, which yet they cannot use lawfully, so long as they may obtein their own by judgment. Upon such a ground then, that either the bodyes or movables of his subjects, who renders not right, may be taken, 'tis not introduc'd indeed by nature, but commonly received by custome. The most antient example whereof is in *Homer*, where *Nestor* is related, for horses taken from his father, to have driven away the Catteil of the *Elidenses*: and in the same narrations, All they were by proclamation call'd together, to whom the *Elidenses* were any thing endebted; to the end, that every one might have his part. But, that the life of innocent subjects should be engaged for such a cause, perhaps was believed amongst some people, upon this principle, that they believ'd every man had full right over his own life, and that might be transferd on the Commonwealth: which, we have said elswhere, is not probable, nor consentaneous to founder Theology. Neverthelefs it may fall out, not by intention, but by accident, that they may be slain, who by force will hinder the execution of right.

Iliad. λ.

 But

But if this be foreseen, by the Law of charity (we have shewed other where) the prosecution of right is rather to be omitted; seeing, by that law, the life of man ought to be more esteemed (among Christians especially) than our Goods, as we have demonstrated already *.

* Part. 2. 10.

XIX. *A distinction, in this matter, 'twixt the Law Civil, and the Law of Nations.*

Dec. conf. 352. Bal. l. 3. de offic. assess.

But, in this matter as well as in others, we must beware, that we confound not those things which are properly of the Law of Nations, and those which are constituted by the Civil Law or the agreements of people. By the Law of Nations are under pignoration all subjects doing injury, who are such by a permanent cause, whether they be natives, or strangers; not they, that are in any Countrey, passing through it, or staying a little while. For, pignorations are introduced after the example of burthens, which are brought in for discharging of publick debts: from which they are freed, who only for a time are subject to the Laws of the place. Yet, from the number of subjects, are exempted, by the Law of Nations, Embassadors, not sent unto our enemies, and their Goods. But by the Civil Law of States are usually excepted the person persons of women and Infants; and the Goods also of Scholars, and Merchants. By the Law of Nations, every one hath the right of pignoration, as also at *Athens* * in the apprehension of men. By the Civil Law of many Countries it is wont to be asked, in some places of the Highest power, in some of the Judges. By the Law of Nations, *ipso facto*, the dominion of the things taken is acquired, to the sum of the debt and costs, so that the residue ought to be restor'd †. By the Civil Law, they that are concernd, are wont to be cited; and the things are to be sold by publick authority, or addicted to those that are concern'd. But, these and other points are to be learned of the Civil Lawyers, and namely of *Bartolus*, who hath written *Of Reprizals*. Onely this I will here add, because it belongs to the mollifying of this right, rigid enough of it self, That whosoever, by not paying what they owed, or by not doing justice, gave cause to pignorations, they are obliged, by natural and Divine Law, to repair their losses * who are dammaged thereby.

* ἐν ἀνδρωληψίᾳ.

† The Venetians used this equity, having taken the ships of Genua, as Gregoras relates in his 9. Book, saying, They did not spoil any of the lading, which was corn and fish; but preserved all very carefully, till, the debt being received, they restored what they had taken, entirely. * Plutarch in his Cymon concerning the Scyrians: very many of them would not contribute monies, but bade them that either received or had taken away other mens goods, repair the loss. *Vide Ægid. Regium de actib. supernat. disp. 13. du. 7. n. 117.*

Cap. 3.

XX. Of just and solemn War by the Law of Nations. *Between whom this war is : and, that it must be denounced.*

* Part. 1. 38.

ABove * we began to say, that a just war, in approved authors, is often called so, not from the cause whence it ariseth, nor from the greatness of the actions, but by reason of some effects of Law. What this war is, is best understood by the definition of enemies in the *Roman* Lawyers. *Enemies are they, who against us, or against whom we do publickly decree war : the rest are theeves or robbers,* saith *Pomponius*: and so saith *Ulpian* too. Where, what they speak of the *Roman* people, we must understand of every supreme power. *He is an enemy*, saith *Cicero*, *who hath a Commonwealth, a Court, a Treasury, consent and concord of Citizens, and some way, if occasion be, of peace and league.* Yet doth it not presently cease to be a Commonwealth or City, if it commit some unjust act, even in Common; nor is a company of Pirats or Robbers a Commonwealth, though perhaps they keep a kind of equality among themselves, without which no company is able to consist. For, These associat themselves to do mischief *: They, although sometimes they are not without fault, yet hold society to maintain right, and they do

L. hostes de verb. signif.
L. hostes. D. de captivis.

Philip. 4.

* *Turba hominum non lege congregata, sed injustitiæ causa in unum coacta.* Procopius 2. Vandalicor.

do right to others, if not in all things according to the Law of Nature (which, among many people, is in part obliterated:) at least according to agreements made with every other Nation, or according to customs. So the *Greeks*, at what time it was accounted lawful to take spoil at Sea, absteined from slaughters and populations by night, and from stealing Oxen that plowed, as the *Scholiast* upon *Thucydides* observes. And other Nations living also upon the spoil, when they were come home from Sea, sent unto the owners to * redeem (if they pleased) at an equal rate, what they were robbed of, as *Strabo* saith. Now the principal, in moral matters, is instead of the form; and, as it is rightly said by *Cicero*, and *Galen*, *The denomination is given from the greater part.* Wherefore the same *Cicero* speaketh too crudely, saying in his third *De Republicâ*, where is an unjust King, or unjust Senators, or an unjust people, there is not now a vitious, but no Commonwealth. Which sentence S. *Augustin* correcting saith, *Yet I shal not therefore conclude it to be no people, nor Commonwealth, so long as there remaineth a rational multitude joyned together in a sociable Communion of things which they love* *. A diseased body is nevertheless a

Lib. 1.

* *Tales & illi quorum Saxo meminit, libro* 14.

Lib. 11.

Cic. de finib. 5. *Ex eo quod maximas partes continet, latissimeq; funditur, res tota appellatur.*

Galenus talia vocat ὀνομάζεσθαι κατ' ἐπικρατοῦν.

De Civit. Dei l. 19. *c.* 24.

* Aristotle saith, if one too far stretch the power of a Few, or of the people, the Commonwealth at first becomes vitious, afterward none. 5. *de rep. c.* 9.

body:

body: and a City, though very ſick, is a City, as long as Laws remain, Courts of Juſtice remain, and other things neceſſary, that foreiners may there obtain right, as well as private men among themſelves. Better ſpake *Dion Chryſoſtom*, who ſaid, the Law (that eſpecially which makes the right of Nations) is in a Commonwealth, as the ſoul in the body of man: which being taken away, 'tis no longer a † Commonwealth. And *Ariſtides* in that Oration wherein he exhorts the *Rhodians* to concord, ſhews that many good Laws may conſiſt, even with Tyranny. Now, although there be ſo great a difference between a people how wicked ſoever, and them that being not a people come together for wickedneſs, yet may a change happen, not only in ſingle perſons (as *Jephtha*, *Arſaces*, *Viriatus*, of Captains of Robbers became juſt Captains) but in companies alſo, as, they that were only Robbers, embracing another kind of life may become a Commonwealth*, Moreover, who they are that have the Higheſt power, we have ſaid above; whence it may alſo be underſtood, If any have it in part, for that part they may wage a juſt war: and much more they, who are not ſubjects, but unequally confederate †, as, between the *Romans*

† Cicero l. 10. epiſt. 1. *Nec leges ſunt, nec judicia, nec omnino ſimulacrum aliquod aut veſtigium Civitatis.*

* *Exemplum in Mamertinis. Diodorus Siculus in Fragmentis.* Auguſtin. de latrocinio locutus: *Hoc malum ſi in tantum perditorum hominum acceſſibus creſcit, ut & loca teneat, ſedes conſtituat, civitates occupet, populos ſubjuget, regni nomen aſſumit.* † Ut Dux Lotharingiæ, apud Crantzium Saxonicis, 12, 13.

and

and their Fellows, though inferiour in League, the *Volscians*, *Latins*, *Spaniards*, *Carthaginians*, all things of a just War were exercised, as the Histories inform us. But, that war may be just in this sense, it sufficeth not, that it be waged between Highest powers on both sides: but it is requisite, as we have heard, that it be publickly decreed, and truly so decreed publickly, that the signification thereof be made by the one party to the other †: whence *Ennius* calls them *promulgata prælia*, promulged battells. *It is a just war which is waged by edict*, (saith an antient writer in **Isidore*) *things being requir'd, or for resistance of Enemies*: and *Livy* put it in the description of a just war, that it be commenced with an Edict, and in an open manner †.

Cajet. 2. 2. q. 40. art. 1.

† Cic. Offic. 2. *At belli quidem æquitas sanctissime feciali populi R. jure perscripta est; ex quo intelligi datur, nullum bellum esse justum, nisi quod aut rebus repetitis geratur, aut denuntiatum ante sit & indictum.* Jos. Antiqu. lib. 15. πόλεμον ἀκήρυκτον ἐπάγειν, ἀσεβεία. Vide Crantzium Saxonic. 11. Nicet. l. 3. & 4. * Lib. 1. † Liv. lib. 31. Idem cum narrasset Acarnanas agrum Atticum esse populatos: *Irritatio animorum ea prima fuit: postea justum bellum decretis civitatum ultro indicendo factum.*

XXI. *In denouncing war, what is of the Law of Nature, what proper to the Law of Nations.*

FOr the underſtanding of the places laſt cited, and other like, about the promulgation of war, we muſt accurately diſtinguiſh, what things are due by the Law of Nature, what by nature are not due, but honeſt; what things by the Law of Nations are requir'd to the proper effects of the ſame Law, and what proceed from the peculiar inſtitutes of ſome Nations. By Natural Law, where either force offerd is repelled, or puniſhment exacted of one that hath offended, no denuntiation is required there. And this is that which *Stenelaidas* the *Ephor* ſaith in *Thucydides: We muſt not ſtand debating with words and arguments; being injur'd beyond words*. And *Latinus* in *Halicarnaſſenſis: He that is aſſaulted with war is wont to repell his enemy*. And *Ælian* out of *Plato* ſaith, *War undertaken to reſiſt violence is indicted, not by an Herald, but by nature*. Hence *Dion Chryſoſtom* affirms *, *Moſt wars are made without proclamation*. And for no other cauſe *Livy* objects to *Menippus* prefect of *Antioch*, that he had ſlain certain *Romans*, war being neither proclam'd, nor ſo begun, that they had heard of ſwords or any blood

Lib. 1.
Idem lib. 3 in Placenſium orat. *Fas eſt arcere eum à quo hoſtiliter impetimur.* Flaminius apud Diodorum Siculum in excerptis Peireſianis: *Omnes Deo homineſq; teſtabatur, inceptum à Rege bellum.*
* *Orat. ad Nicomedienſes.* πόλεμοι ἐπὶ τὸ πλεῖστον ἀκήρυκτοι γίγνονται.

blood as yet drawn : thereby ſhewing,either of theſe two might ſuffice for a defenſe of his deed. Neither is *Indiction* more neceſſary by the Law of Nature, if a Lord will lay hands upon his own goods. But, as oft as one thing is invaded for another, or the debtor's goods for the debt; and much more, if one will ſeiſe upon the goods of them that are ſubject to the debtor, *Interpellation* is required, whereby it may appear, we had no other way to come to our own, or that which is due unto us. For, that right is not primary, but ſecondary and ſurrogate. So alſo, before the Supreme Governour may be invaded by war for the debt or the offenſe of the ſubject, there ought to intercede an Interpellation, that may conſtitute him in a fault, whereby he may be eſteemed to do a dammage, or to be delinquent; according to what we have diſcourſed above. Yet further, where the Law of Nature commandeth not ſuch an interpellation to be made, it is honeſtly and commendably * interpoſed, to wit, that the adverſe party may abſtein from offending any more, or the offenſe given may be expiated by repentance and ſatisfaction; according to what we have ſaid of uſing means to avoid war*. Pertinent here is that Precept * which God gave unto the *Hebrews*, that they ſhould make offer of Peace to the City that was to be aſſaulted : which precept, being ſpecially given

* *Vide Marianam* 27. 13.

* Part 2.

* Et illud: *Extrema primo nemo tentavit loco.*

given to that people, is, by ſome, *ill* confounded with the Law of Nations. Nor indeed was that any other peace, but on condition of ſubjection and Tribute. *Cyrus*, when he had marched into the *Armenians* Country, before he did hurt any man, ſent Meſſengers to the King to demand Tribute due upon the League, and ſoldiers: *Suppoſing that to be more friendly and courteous, than to lead on farther, and ſay nothing*; As *Xenophon* ſpeaks in that Hiſtory. But, by the Law of Nations, to thoſe peculiar effects in all caſes is requir'd denuntiation, not on both, but on the one party. This denuntiation is either *Conditionate*, or *Pure*. Conditionate, where it is join'd with Remanding of Things. And, in the name of *Res repetitæ* the * Heralds Law comprehended, not only vindication by right of dominion, but alſo the proſecution of that which is due upon a Civil or Criminal cauſe, as *Servius* explains it rightly. Thence was that in the forms, *To be rendred*, *To be ſatisfyed*, *To be yielded*: Where, *To be yielded*, as we have ſaid elſwhere, is to be underſtood, unleſs they that are call'd upon, will rather puniſh the guilty themſelves. This requiring of Things, *Pliny* teſtifies, was named *Clarigation*. That denuntiation in *Livy* is conditionate: *That they will with all their power depell that injury, except it be remedied by thoſe that did it*: And in *Tacitus*: *Unleſs they ſpeedily*

Jus feciale.

Ad 10. *Æneid.*

Lib. 8.

dily bring the offenders to punishment, He will make promiscuous slaughter *. Pure denunciation is that which is specially Indiction, or Edict, where either the other hath already begun the war (this is that which in *Isidore* is called war to beat off men) or himself hath committed such faults as deserve † punishment. But sometime the Pure follows the Conditionate, though that be not necessary, but *ex abundanti*. Hence is that form : *I testify, that people is unjust, and will not do right* *. This also is an argument of supervacuous observation, that war hath oft been proclamed on both sides, as the *Peloponnesian* by the *Corcyraans* and *Corinthians*, when it is sufficient that it be indicted and proclamed by either. Furthermore, from the custom & institutes of some Countries, not from the Law of Nations are the White Rod * among the *Greeks*, the Turfs and bloody spear, among the *Æquicolæ* first, and by their example among the *Romans*; the renouncing of friendship and society, if there had been any; thirty solemn days after demaund made; the throwing of the spear, again † and other things of like kind, which ought not to be confounded with those that properly belong to the Law of Nations. For a great part of these

* Simile est apud Papinium: *Aut Danais edice rogos, aut prælia 7 bebis.* Polybius hoc vocat, ῥῆμα κα-ταγγέλλειν: Romani veteres, *Condicere.*

† *Exemplum vide apud Bembum lib. 7.*

* Et altera : *Quarum rerum, litium, causarum condixit Pater patratus populi Romani Quintium Patri patrato populi Priscorum Latinorum, hominibusq; priscis Latinis, quas res nec solverunt, nec dederunt, nec fecerunt, quas res dari, fieri, solvi oportuit, puro pioq; duello quærendas censeo, consentio, consciscoq;.*

* Caducæus. Unde ejus origo disces ex Plinio, 29. 3. & Servio ad 4. & 8. Æneidos.

† Vide Servium ad 9. Æn. Ammianum 19. & quæ ad eum notata à doctissimo Lindenbrogio.

ceased

Arnob. l. 2. cont. Gentes. ceased to be used, saith *Arnobius*, in his *Varro. l. 4. de L. L.* time; yea, in *Varro*'s time, some of them were omitted. The third *Punick* War was at once indicted and begun. *Mecenas* in *Dion* will have some of them to be proper to a popular State.

XXII. *War proclamed against any one includes his Subjects and Adherents: But, not as considerd by Themselves.*

MOreover, War indicted against him, who hath the highest power over the people, is withall suppos'd to be indicted against all His, not only subjects, but those too who will join themselves unto him, as being an accession to his party: and this is that which the later Lawyers say, *The Prince being diffyed, his Adherents also are diffyed.* *Diffidato principe, diffidati sunt ejus adhaerentes. Bald. ad l. 2. c. de serv. n. 70.* For, to indict war, they call *To diffy*. Which is to be understood of that same war, which is waged against him to whom it is indicted: As, when war was denounced against *Antiochus*, They were not pleased to denounce it against the *Ætolians* apart, because they had openly join'd themselves with *Antiochus*: The Heralds answerd, *Liv. lib. 36.* *The Ætolians have declared war of their own accord against themselves.* But, that war being ended, if another People or King, for supply of aids, is to be warred against, that the effects of the Law of Nations

tions may follow, there will be need of a new Indiction. For now, he is not lookt upon as Accessory, but Principal. Wherefore it is rightly said, that, by the Law of Nations, neither the war of *Manlius* upon the *Gallo-Greeks*, nor of *Cæsar* upon *Ariovistus*, was * Lawfull: for they were not assalted now, as an accession of a Neighbours War, but principally: to which purpose, as by the Law of Nations Indiction, so by the *Roman* Law a new command of the *Roman* people was necessary. For, what was said in the proposal against *Antiochus*: *Was it their will and pleasure, that War should be enterd with King* Antiochus, *and those that followed his party*: (which was observed too in the Decree against King *Perseus*:) seemes truly understood, so long as the War continued with *Antiochus* or *Perseus*, and of those that really immixed themselves in that War.

* *Idem dici potest de bello sociorum Ulyssis in Ciconas Priamo quondam auxiliatos, de quib. Hom. Odyss. 1. & ibi Didymus.*

Livius lib. 36.

Lib. 42.

XXIII. *The Cause why Denuntiation is requisite to some effects, which are not found in other Wars.*

NOw, the cause why Nations requir'd Denuntiation to that war, which we have said to be just by the Law of Nations, was not that which some allege; that

Alb. Gent. l. 1. c. 2.

that they might do nothing privily or by deceit; for that perteins rather to the excellence of their valour, than to right; as some Nations are read to have appointed their enemies the day and the place of battell *; but, that it might certainly appear, the War was not waged by a private undertaking, but by the will of either people, or their Heads. For, thence are sprung those peculiar effects, which have place, neither in war against Robbers, nor in that which a King wageth against his Subjects. Therefore *Seneca* spake distinctly; *Wars were indicted against Neighbours, or waged against Citizens.* As to that, which is noted by some, and shew'd by examples, That even in such wars the things taken become theirs that take them; it is true, but on the one part onely, and that by natural right, not by the voluntary right of Nations; as that, which provides for Nations only, not for those which are no Nation, or a part of a Nation. Besides, they erre in this, that they think, War undertaken for defense of ones self or ones Goods, needs no indiction; for it doth need, not simply, but in regard of those effects which we have begun to speak of, and shal explain anon.

* As the Romans to Porsena, saith Plutarch in Publicola. The Turks, two days before battell, make very many Fires, saith Chalcochond. 7.

Lib. 3. *de ira.* c. 2.

Ayala.l. 1. c. 5. Capta fieri capientium.

Alb. Gent. d. l. 2. c. 2.

XXIV.

XXIV. *War may be indicted and waged together. War indicted for violation of Embassadors.*

NEither is that true, that War may not be waged presently as soon as it is indicted, which *Cyrus* did against the *Armenians*, the *Romans* against the *Carthaginians*, as we said even now. For, Indiction, by the Law of Nations, requireth no time after it. Yet may it come to pass, that, by natural right, some time may be required according to the quality of the business; to wit, when things are remanded, or punishment requir'd upon the guilty, and that is not denyed. For then, such time is to be allowed, wherein that which is requir'd may commodiously be done. And, if the right of Embassages be violated, it will not therefore be unnecessary to *denounce* War; but it will suffice to do it as it may be done *safely*, that is, by Letters: as also citations and other denuntiations are usually made in places not safe.

Cap. 4.

XXV. The right of killing enemies in a solemn War. *The effects of that War in generall.*

TO that of *Virgil* *, *Then it will be lawful to hate, and fight, and to take spoil* : *Servius Honoratus*, when he had deduced the Original of the Heralds law from *Ancus Martius*, and farther from the *Æquicolæ*, saith thus : *If at any time men or beasts were by any nation taken away from the people of Rome, the Pater patratus went with the Heralds, that is, Priests who have authority in making of Leagues; and standing before the bounds, with a loud voice, pronounced the cause of the War; and, if they would not restore the things taken; or deliver up the Authors of the injury, he threw a spear, which was the beginning of fight; and thenceforth it was lawful, after the manner of War, to take the spoil* †. Whereby we learn, that there are certain proper effects * of War indicted between two Nations or their heads, which effects do not follow war, as it is considered in its own nature. This agrees very well with what we noted afore out of the *Roman* Lawyers.

* *Tum certare odiis, tum res rapuisse licebit.*

† Ante dixerat: *Veteres lædere*, res rapere *dicebant, etiamsi rapinæ nullum crimen existeret: similiter satisfacere* res reddere *dicebant.*

* *Crantzius Saxonicorum*, 11. 5.

XXVI.

XXVI. *Lawful is distinguisht into that which is done without punishment, and that which is done without fault.*

But *Virgil's Licebit, it will be lawful*, Let us consider what importance it hath. For, sometime that is said to be lawful which is right and pious intirely, though perhaps another thing may be done more laudably; as in that saying of S. *Paul* the Apostle, *All things are lawful for me, but all things are not expedient* (All things: that is, *all* of that kind, of which he had begun to speak, and would speak more.) So, it is lawful † to contract matrimony, but more laudable is single Chastity proceeding from a pious design, as S. *Augustin* discourses to *Pollentius* out of the same Apostle. It is also lawful to marry again; but it is more lawdable to be content with one marriage, as *Clemens Alexandrinus* † rightly explains this question. A Christian husband lawfully may leave his Pagan

1 Cor. 6. 17.

† Tertullianus adv. Marcion. 1. *Vacat abstinentiæ testimonium, si licentia eripitur.* Vide de hac re, & de fuga in persecutione eund. l. 1. ad ux. Hieronym. ad Helvid: *Virgo majoris est meriti, dum id contemnit, quod si fecerit, non delinquit.* Ad Pammach. *Semper grandia in audientium ponuntur arbitrio. Non tibi imponitur necessitas, ut voluntas præmium consequatur.* Chrysost. *ad* 1 Cor. 7. βελτίονα δείκνυσι τὴν ἐγκράτειαν. † In the fourth of his Stromatea: where among other things he saith of one that marries again, He doth not indeed offend against the Law, for there is no Law to forbid it, but he falls short of that most excellent perfection of the Evangelical life.

* *August. lib.* 1. *de adulterinis conjug. ad Pollentium cap.* 13. *&* 18.

* *L.* 1. §. *licet. D. de peric. & com. rei vend.*

wife, as S. *Augustin* * thought : (with what circumstances this is true, is not proper to determine here ;) but he may also keep her lawfully. *Ulpian* *, of a Seller, to whom 'tis lawful, after appointed day to pour forth the wine : *If yet*, saith he, *when he may pour it forth, he doth it not, he is the more to be praised.* But sometime a thing is called lawful, not which may be done without violating the rules of piety and duty, but which among men is not subject unto punishment†. So, among many people, it is lawful to commit fornication: among the *Lacedemonians* and *Egyptians* it was also lawful to steal. In *Quintilian* we read * : *There are some things not laudable by nature, but granted by Law, as in the XII. Tables, The Creditors might divide the Debtors body among them.* But this signification of the word, *lawfull*, is less proper (as *Cicero* observeth well in the fift of his *Tusculans*, speaking of *Cinna* : *To me, on the contrary, he seemeth miserable, not only in that he did such things, but in that he so behaved himself that it might be lawful for him to do them : though indeed it is lawful for none to do amiss, but we erre in our language, calling that lawful, which is permitted to any one* :) nevertheless it is received, as when the same *Cicero* for *Rabirius Posthumus* thus bespeaks the Judges ; *Ye ought to consider, what becomes you, not how much is lawful*

† Tertull. in exhort. ad castitatem: *Licentia plerumq; tentatio est disciplinæ.* Ibid. *Omnia licent, sed non Omnia pro salute.* Chrysost. de poenit. 8. ἐκ ἔξεςί σοι ἢ τῷ ἰδιώτῃ βασιλεῖ πάντα ἐξεῖναι. Columella præf. l. 8. *Nec sane est vindicandum nobis quicquid licet : Nam summum jus antiqui putabant summam crucem.* Hieronym. ad Jovinian. *Et ô vere jus summum, summa malitia.*

* Lib. 3. c. 8.

ful for you: for if ye seek only what is lawful, you may take away out of the City whom you please. So, all things are said to be lawful for *Kings*, because they are * *exempt from human punishments*. as we have said elswherere. But *Claudian* informing a King or Emperour rightly saith:

* ἀνυπεύθυνοι.

—* *Have in your thought,*
Not what you may effect, but what you ought.

* Claud: *Nec tibi quid liceat, sed quid fecisse decebit, Occurrat.*

And *Musonius* * reproveth Kings, *who use to say, This is lawful for me; not, This becomes me.* And in the same sense we often see opposed, What is lawful, and What ought to be done, as by *Seneca* the Father * in his controversies more than once †.

* Ded. lib. 3. & 5.

* *Contr. l.* 4. *c.* 4.

† Ammian. Marcell. *Sunt aliqua quæ fieri non oportet, etiamsi licet. lib.* 30. Plin. in epist. *Oportet quæ sunt inhonesta, non quasi illicita, sed quasi pudenda vitare. lib.* 5. Cicero ipse orat. pro Balbo: *Est enim aliquid quod non oporteat, etiamsi licet.* Idem pro Milone, fas esse ad naturam, licere ad leges refert. Et in declamatione Patris, Quintiliani est, *Aliud esse jura spectare, aliud justitiam*, Declam. 251.

XXVII. *The effects of solemn War generally consider'd are referrd to the later sense of lawful, in respect of impunity: And, why such effects were introduced. Testimonies.*

IN this sense then, it is lawful for an Enemy to hurt his Enemy, both in his person, and in his Goods: that is, not only for him who upon a just cause wageth war, and who hurteth within that measure, which we have said to be naturally granted, in the beginning of this book; but lawful on both sides and without distinction: So that, for that cause, he can neither be punisht, being perchance deprehended in another territory, as an homicide, or theef; nor can War be made against him by another, upon that account. Thus we read in *Sallust: To whom all things in victory were lawful by the Law of War.* The cause, why it pleased the Nations to have it so, was this; It had been dangerous for other Nations to take upon them to pronounce and determine about the Right of War between two Nations: for, by that means, they would be engaged in the War of others; as the *Massilians* said in the cause of *Cesar* and *Pompey*, *That it was above their Judgment, and above their power, to discern whether side had the juster cause.* Moreover,

Sallust: *Cui omnia in victoria lege belli licuerunt.*

Moreover, even in a just War, it can hardly be known by external marks, what is the just measure of self-defense, of recovering ones own, or of exacting punishments; so that, it is much better, to leave these things to be examined by the Conscience of those that War, than to reduce them under the judgment of others†. Besides this effect of licence, that is, of impunity, there is another also, to wit, of dominion, concerning which we shall speak hereafter. As to that licence of hurting, which we have now begun to handle, it extendeth first to Persons: of which licence many Testimonies are extant in good Authors. It is a *Greek* proverb out of a Tragedy of *Euripedes*, *That the blood of an enemy leaves no stain.* Therefore, by the old custom of the *Greeks*, it was not lawfull to bathe, to drink, to sacrifice much less, in their company, who had slain a man out of the time of war; but in theirs that had done so in war, it was lawfull. And commonly, *to kill*, is calld the right of War. *Marcellus* in *Livy*; *Whatsoever execution I have done upon the enemy, the right of War defends.* In the same historian *Alcon* saith to the *Saguntines*, *I think it better for you to suffer these things, than your bodies to be slain, your wives and children to be dragd and ravisht before your eyes, by the right of War.* The same elswhere, when he had related how the *Astapenses* were put to the sword, addeth,

† Achæi in orat. ad Senatum apud Livium, lib. 39. *Quonam modo ea quæ jure belli acta sunt, in disceptationem veniunt?*

Eurip. Ione. καθαρὸς ἅπας τοι πολεμίους ὃς ἂν κτάνῃ.

Lib. 26.

Lib. 21.

Lib. 28.

addeth, It was done *jure belli*, by the right of War. *Cicero* for *Deiotarus*: *Why should he be an enemy to you, by whom he might have been killed by the Law of War; by whom he remembred he was made King, and his sons.* And for *M. Marcellus*: *When, by the condition and right of Victory we were all dead men, we were preserved by the judgment of your Clemency.* *Cæsar* to the *Hæduans* signifies, *They were saved by his favour, when the Law of War gave him leave to destroy them.* *Josephus*, in the war of the Jews; *It is honourable to fall in War; but, by the Law of War, and by the hand of the Conquerour* †. Now, whē these writers speak of the Law or right of War, it appears by other places, they must be understood, not of that which frees the act from all fault, but of the impunity before mentioned. *Tacitus* said, *Causes and merits are considerd in peace; in War, the innocent and the guilty fall together.* The same, in another place: *Neither did the right of men suffer them to honour that slaughter; nor the course of War, to revenge it.* Nor is the right of War to be taken otherwise when *Livy* tells, how the *Greeks* spared *Æneas* and *Antenor*, because they had always perswaded unto Peace†

Comment.l.7.

† Papinius: *Nec querimur cæsos: hæc bellica jura vicesq; Armorum.* Servius in excerptis Fuldens. ad 2. Æn. *Jure belli Politen Pyrhus occiderat: sed cur ante oculos patris?* Spartianus Severo: *præter eos quos jus belli absumpsit.*

Peace †. *Cyprian**; *Manslaughter, when private men commit it, is a crime: when it is publickly done, 'tis call'd a vertue. Not respect of innocence, but greatness of the cruelty gives impunity to wicked Actions.* So *Lactantius* saith, *The Romans did Legitimate their injuries by their power.* And *Lucan's Jusq; datum sceleri,* is of the same sense, † *Law was given to wickedness.*

†Senec. Troad. *Quodcunq; libuit facere, victori licet.* Et in epist. 96. *Quæ commissa capite luerent, tum quia paludati fecerunt laudamus.* * Cypr. epist. 2. *Consensere jura peccatis, & cœpit esse licitum quod publicum est.* Ibidem. † *Pharsal.* 1.

XXVIII. *Of Strangers found in an Enemies Country.*

THis Law of Licence is of large extent: for first, it comprehends not only them that actually bear arms, or are subjects to him that maketh war, but also all that are within the enemies Country: which is manifest by the very form in *Livy*, *Let him be our Enemy, and they that are within his guards.* For, danger may be feard from them too, which, in a continued and universal war, sufficeth to make way for that right of which we speak: otherwise than in pignorations, which, as we have said, after the example of burthens imposed, were introduced for the discharge of publick debts: wherefore it is no wonder, if, as *Baldus* notes, much more licence be in war than in the right of pignoration. And this which I have said, hath

Liv. l. 37. & alibi passim. *Hostis sit ille, & qui intra præsidia ejus sunt.*

Ad L. 1. *de justitia.*

hath no doubt indeed, as to strangers, who after the beginning and notice of the War, come into the enemies quarters. But, they that went thither before, seem by the Law of Nations to be accounted for enemies after some small time *, wherein they might have departed. For so the *Corcyræans* about to besiege *Epidamnum*, first allowed strangers liberty to go away, denouncing otherwise they should be taken for enemies.

* *Bembus 7. hist.* Cicero uses that defense in his oration for Ligarius. You have an example in Livy l. 25. of the Citizens of Campania. Other examples in Thucyd. lib. 1. & 5.

XXIX. *The enemies subjects may every where be offended. This right extends to Infants and Women, to Captives, and such as yield themselves without conditions.*

But, they that are truly subjects of the enemies, to wit, upon a permanent cause, may be offended every where, by this right of Nations, if we respect their own persons. For, when War is proclamed against any one, it is withall proclamed against all his men, as we shewd above in the form of indiction: and so in the decree; *Was it their will and pleasure, war should be denounced against King* Philip *and the* Macedonians *which are under his Government* *. Now, he that is an enemy, may every where according

Liv. l. 31.
* *Vellent juberent Philippo regi Macedonibusq; qui sub eius regno essent bellum indici.*

ding to the Law or Nation's be assalted †. Enemies therefore may be slain on their own ground, on the enemies ground, on that that belongs to none, on the Sea. But, that it is not lawful to kill or violate them in a peaceable territorie, proceeds not from their own person, but from his right who hath Empire there *. For, civil societies might constitute, that nothing should violently be done against men in such a Country, unless according to process of Law †. And, where the Law is open, there are weighed the merits of persons, and that promiscuous right of hurting ceaseth, which we have said was introduc'd among enemies. *Livy* relates, that seaven Ships of the *Carthaginians* were in a Haven under the *Syphax's* dominion, who had peace at that time both with the *Carthaginians* and *Romans*; that *Scipio* arrived there with two ships, and before he entred the Haven they might easily have been opprest by the *Carthaginians*, but being born in with a strong winde before the *Carthaginians* could weigh anchor, they durst not fight with them in the Kings Haven. But to return, how far that licence reacheth, is hence understood, that the slaughter of Infants too, and women goes unpunished, and is comprehended in this right of war. I will not

† Eurip. *ubicunq; prensum jura lædi hostem sinunt*. Marcian. IC. *Transfugas licet ubicunq; inventi fuerint, quasi hostes interficere*. l. 3. in fine D. ad l. Corn. de sicar.

* *Vid. Alberic. Gentil. Hispan. Advocat. l. 1. 6. wechner. in consl. Franconico 92.*

† Apud Euripidem est: *Si crimen istus aliquod hospitibus struis, Jus impetrabis: vi quidem hinc non abstrahes.*

Liv. lib. 28. See the like deed of the Venetians hindring the Greeks from hurting the Turks in a Haven under the Venetian Government, in Chalcocondyl. l. 9 Of the Venetians and Turks at Tunis, See Bemb. lib. 4.

Deut. 2.34. 20.16.

† As the Amalekites, of whom Josephus in the life of Saul, l. 6. 8. He proceeded to the slaughter of women and children, thinking he did nothing cruel or adverse to human nature; first, because they were enemies against whom it was done, &c.

Psal. 137.

not allege here, that the *Hebrews* slew the women and children of *Heshbon*, and that the same is commanded to be done upon the *Canaanites*, and upon them whose cause was connexed † with the *Canaanites*; These are the works of God, whose right over men is greater than that of men over beasts, as we have said other where. That comes neerer to shew the common custom of Nations, that in the Psalm he is called blessed who shall dash the Infants of *Babylon* against the stones*. The *Thracians* of old, as *Thucydides* relates, having taken *Micalessus*, put the women also and children to the sword. *Arrian* tells the same of the *Macedonians*, when they had taken *Thebes*. The *Romans* † did the like at *Ilurgis* a town of *Spain*, as *Appian* saith. *Germanicus Cæsar* is said by *Tacitus* to have laid wast with sword and fire the Villages of the *Marsi*, a people in *Germany*, and it is added, *Neither sex, nor age mov'd compassion*. *Titus* proposed also the women and children of the Jews for a spectacle, to be torn by wild-beasts. And yet these two are supposed to have been of no cruel disposition. So customary was that cruelty becom. The less marvel 'tis to hear of old men slain, as of

* Parallel whereto is that of Homer,

—— illisaq; corpora terræ
Infantum, sævus dum concutit omnia Mavors.

Out of the same Homer Severus used these words against the Britains. *Nec qui latet abditus intra Viscera matris adhuc, fugiet crudelia fata.*

† Scipio also at the taking of Numantia; Julians soldiers against the women left at Dacir. Zozim. 3. The same Julian at the taking of Majozamaltha, without difference of sex or age furiously destroyed all. Ammian. l. 14. Annal. l. 1.

Priam

Priam by *Pyrrhus*. Nor were Captives † exempted from this licence. *Pyrrhus* in *Seneca* according to the custom then receiv'd: *No Law spares a captive, or hinders his punishment* †. So the *Corcyraeans* slew the captives out of *Epidamnum* *; and five thousand captives were slain by *Annibal**. A *Centurion* of *Caesar's* thus addresses himself to *Scipio* in *Hirtius* of the *African* war, *I give you thanks that you promise me life, being your Captive by the Law of War*. Nor at any time is excluded the power of killing such as are taken in War, as to the Law of nations; though by the Lawes of Cities it is restrained, in some places more, in some less. Moreover, there are frequent examples of suppliants also slain, as by *Achilles* in *Homer*, in *Virgil* of *Mago* and *Turnus*: which we see are so related, that they are withall defended by that right of war which we have said. For†, S. *Augustin* also praising the *Gotths*, who had spared suppliants and such as fled to sanctuaries, saith, *What had been lawful to be done by the Law of War, they judged unlawful for them to do*. Nor are they always receiv'd that yield themselves; as, in the battel at *Granicum*, the *Greeks* that serv'd the *Persian*; the *Uspenses* in *Tacitus*, as yet free, begging Mercy: *but the Victors would not hear*, saith he, *and so they fell by the Law of War*. Note here again, the Law of War. So also, you may read, they that yielded and

† Elizaeus in Josephus said it was just to kill captives, by the Law of War. Therefore Virgil brings in a captive supplicating *per patrios manes, per spes surgentis Iuli.* Withikind. l. 2 tells of seventy thousand Slavonians taken and slain by Otto.

† Troad. In Ciri Virgil: *At belli saltem captivam lege necasses.* Horat: *Vendere cum possis captivum, occidere noli.* Ponit licere. Et Donatus, servos dictos qui servati essent, *quum eos occidi oporteret jure belli*: ubi illud *oporteret*, improprie pro *liceret*, positum videtur. *Adelph. act. 2. sc. 1*

* *Thucyd. lib. 1.*

* *Ap. Annib.*

†. 1. *De Civitate Dei.* 2.

Annal. 12.

and were received without any condition, were slain †; as the Princes of *Pometia* by the *Romans*, the *Samnites* by *Sulla*, the *Numidians* by *Cæsar*, and *Vercingetorix*: yea this was almost the perpetuall custom of the *Romans* upon the Commanders of the enemies, whether taken or yielded, to kill them on the day of triumph *, as *Cicero* *, *Livy* *, *Tacitus** and many others teach us. In the same *Tacitus*, *Galba* commanded them to be *decimated*, every tenth man slain, to whom he had given quarter. And *Cæcina* having accepted *Aventic* yielding to him, put to death *Julius Alpinus* one of the Princes, as the raiser of the War, the rest he reserved for the mercy, or the cruelty of *Vitellius*.

† *Vide Thuanum l. 70. in an. 1580. in rebus Hibern.*

* *Simile apud Reginonem, in an. 905.*
* *Cic. 5. Verrin.*
* *Liv. lib. 28.*
* *Tacit. Annal. 12.*

XXX. *That right ill referd to other causes. It reacheth also to hostages.*

HIstorians * are wont sometimes to refer the cause of killing enemies, captives especially or suppliants, either to talion, or to pertinacy in resisting: but these causes, as we have elswhere distinguished, are rather *suasory* than *justifick*. For a just talion † and properly so called is

* *Chalcocondylas lib. 8*

† Diodor. Sic. *Neq; enim ignorabant ipsis rebus edocti, cum bellantium par sit fortuna, alterutris, si male rem gessissent id expectandum quod ipsi in victis statuissent.* Apud eundem Philomelus Dux Phocensium: *Pari pœna exacta effecit ut hostes à superbo & insolenti supplicio temperarent.* Vide eundem Diod. de Spendio & Amilc. in exc. Peiresc.

is to be exercised upon the same person that offendeth, as may be understood by what we have said above, of communication of Punishment. But on the contrary, from war, for the most part, that which is called talion, redounds to the evil of those, who had no hand in that which is accused. And as to a pertinacious affection to one side, no man judges that worthy of punishment, as the Neapolitans in *Procopius* * answer *Belisarius*: * Procop. 1. Gotth.
which is then most true, when that side is either assigned by nature, or chosen upon good ground. Yea, so far is this from being a crime, that it is a crime to quit a Garrison, especially by the old military *Roman* Law, which here admitted not lightly any excuse of fear or danger. *To depart from a Garrison*, saith *Livy*, *is capital.* Wherefore every one as he pleaseth, makes use of that highest rigour for his own Interest; and that rigour is defended among men by that right of Nations, of which we now speak. The same right hath been also used against Hostages, nor against them only who had obliged themselves, as by agreement, but against them too, that were deliverd by others. Two hundred and fifty were once slain by the *Thessalians*, by the *Romans* three hundred of the *Volsci*. We must note, that Children also were wont to be given for Hostages, as by the *Parthians*; which we read was also done by *Simon* one of the *Maccabees*;

Polyb. l. 1. *&* 6.

Lib. 24.

Plutarch. de claris mul.

Dionys. 16.
Tacit. An. 1.
1 *Maccab.* 13. 17.

Maccabees; and women, as by the *Romans* in the time of *Porsena*, and by the *Germans*, as *Tacitus* relateth.

4. Histor.

XXXI. *By the Law of Nations, it is forbidden to kill with Poyson. Of poysoning weapons and waters.*

NOw, as the Law of Nations permitteth many things, by that way of permission afore explained, which are prohibited by the Law of Nature; so it prohibiteth some things, which by the Law of Nature are permitted. For to kill a man, whom it is lawful to kill, whether with the sword or with poyson is no matter, if you respect the Law of Nature: I say, the Law of Nature: for indeed it is more generous to kill so, that he who is killed may have leave to defend himself: but this is not due to any one, who hath deserv'd to dy. But the Law of Nations, if not of all, yet of the best, is of old, that an enemy may not be kill'd with poyson; which consent hath its rise from a regard of common advantage; that dangers of war, which began to be many, might not be too much hightned. And it is credible, that this proceeded from Kings, whose life above others is defended from arms, but is less secured from poyson than the life of other men, unless it be defended by some reverence of Law and fear of infamy †.

famy †. *Livy* calls it *Clandestin wickedness*, speaking of *Perseus*: *Claudian*, *a heinous act*, speaking of the treachery against *Pyrrhus* rejected by *Frabricius*; and *Cicero*, *wickedness*, touching the same history. For common examples sake no such thing is to be admitted, say the *Roman Consuls* in their letter to *Pyrrhus* * *with arms not with poyson are wars to be waged*, is in *Valerius Maximus*: and, as *Tacitus* relates, when a prince of the *Catti* promised the death of *Arminius* by poyson, *Tiberius* rejected him, equalling himself in that glory with the old Generals. Wherefore, they that hold it lawful to kill an enemy by poyson*, as *Baldus* out of *Vegetius*, respect the meer Law of Nature, but oversee that which derives it self from the will of Nations. It is a little distant from such poysoning and comes neerer to force, to infect darts with poyson, and double the causes of death; which *Ovid* hath deliverd of the *Getes* †, *Lucan* of the *Parthians*, *Silius* of some *Africans*, and namely of the *Ethiopians* *Claudian*. But this too is against the Law of Nations*, not the universal, but of the *Europaeans*, and of such as conform to the Civility of better *Europe*. This is well observ'd by *Salisberiensis*, in these words: *Although I see it used sometimes by Infidels, yet I do not find the licence of poyson by any law ever indulged to us.* Therefore *Silius*'s phrase is, *To infame steel by poy-*

† The Senators to Pyrrhus: That we may not get infamy, if any thing befal you.
Liv. lib. 42.
Cic. Offic. 3.
* *Gellius ex Cl. Quadrigario, l. 3. c. 8.*
Val. Max. 5. 5.
Tac. An. 3.

* *Vide de Venetis Bembum fine libri 3.*
Bald. 2. Cons. 188.
† De Scythis Plin. *l.* 11. 53. *Scythae sagittas tingunt viperina sanie, & humano sanguine, irremediabile id scelus mortem illico adfert Levi tactu.*
De Servis v. supp. Helmoldi cap. 4.
* Ideo Ilus Mermerides in Odyss. α. Ulyssi negat venenum ad spicula, *Veritus vim Divum morte carentum.*
Salisb. 8. 20.

ſon: for, to poyſon fountains alſo (and this too is not kept ſecret, or not long) *Florus* ſaith, is not only *contra morem majorum*, againſt the manner of the Antients, but againſt the right of the Gods, that is, againſt the Laws of Nations, which were wont to be aſcribed to the Gods as Authors. Nor ought this to ſeem ſtrange, if to leſſen dangers there be ſome ſuch tacit agreements of Warriours, when of old the *Chalcidians* and *Eretrians*, during the War, conſented together *to make no uſe of darts*. But, the ſame is not to be determined of corrupting waters without poyſon †, ſo that they may not be potable, which *Solon* and the *Amphictyones* are read to have thought juſt againſt *Barbarians*, and *Oppian* relates as uſual in his time. For that is eſteemed all one, as if the ſtream be averted, or the Veins of the Spring intercepted *, which both by Nature and Conſent is lawfull.

Lib. 2.

Strab. lib. 10.

† Cadaveribus, asbeſto, quibus uſus in obſidione Auximi Beliſarius. Procop. Got. 2. calce, ut Turcæ ad Dibibram. Nicet. lib. 1.

De piſcatu 4.

* Vide Priſcum in excerptis legationum.

XXXII.

XXXII. *Whether it be against the Law of Nations, to use Murtherers.*

WHether it be lawful by the Law of Nations, to kill an enemy, a *, Murtherer being sent against him, is wont to be enquired. To be sure we must make a difference between Murtherers, who violate their faith, either express or tacit, as Subjects toward a King, vassalls toward their Senior, Soldiers toward him whom they serve, men received as suppliants, or strangers, or fugitives toward their Receivers; and between those that are not bound with any faith; as *Pipin* father of *Charles the Great* attended with one Soldier, passing the *Rhene*, is related to have slain his Enemy in his Chamber; which *Polybius* saith was in like manner attempted against *Ptolemy* King of *Egypt* by *Theodotus* an *Etolian*, and he calls it *a manly boldness*. Such also was that enterprize of *Q. Mutius Scævola* * commended by Historians, which himself thus defends: *Being an enemy, I purposed to kill an Enemy.* *Porsena* himself, in this act, acknowledges nothing but valour. *Valerius Maximus* calls it a pious and valiant design, and *Cicero* praiseth it in his Oration for *P. Sextius*. It is indeed lawful to kill ones Enemy every where, not only by the Law of Nature but of Nations too, as we have said above: nor is it

* Immisso percussore.

Vide Paulum Warnafredi l. 6.

Liv. lib. 2.

* Qui Plutarcho ἀνὴρ εἰς πᾶσαν ἀρετὴν ἀγαθός.

Lib. 3. c. 3.

it material, what the number is of those that do, or suffer. Six hundred *Laconians* with *Leonides* entring the Enemies camp, go on straight to the Kings tent. Fewer might lawfully have done so †. Few were they, that killed the Consul *Marcellus* being secretly circumvented *; and that were very neer stabbing *Petilius Cerialis* in his bed * *Ambrose* commends *Eleazar* † for setting upon an Elephant bigger than the rest, supposing the King sate thereon. Nor onely they that do these things, but they that appoint others to do them, are accounted without fault by the Law of Nations. *Scævola*'s boldness* was authoriz'd by those old *Roman Senators*, so religious in their Wars. Nor ought any one to be mov'd with this, that such being taken are wont to be extremely punisht: for that proceeds not from their having offended against the Law of Nations, but from this, that by the same Law every thing is lawful against an enemy: and every one, as it is for his own profit, determineth, either more rigourously, or more gently. For so also Spies, who doubtless by the Law of Nations may be sent, such as *Moses* sent, such as *Joshua* himself was, being deprehended, were used very ill (*The custom is to put spies to death*, as *Appian* saith:) justly sometimes, by these that manifestly have a just cause of Warring; by others, by that licence which the Law of war granteth. As to those

Justin. lib. 2.
† Valens promised money to him that would bring the head of a certain Scythian, and so obtained peace. Zozi. 4.
* Liv. lib. 27.
* Tacit. hist. 5.
† Et Joseph antiq. 15. 14. Factum non dissimile Theodosii in Eugenium est apud Zosimum l. 4. Gallorum in regem Persarum apud Agathiam: Persarum decem in Julianum apud Ammianum 24 & Zosimum 3. Alexii Comneni in Tousen apud Nicetam Chroniaten lib. 4. de Manuele. Bulgarorum in Nicephorum Imp. apud Zonarum.
* Liv. lib. 2.
Lib. 3. §. *ult. ad l. corn. de Sicariis pun.*

those that have refused such offerd service, their refusal is to be referd to their noble-ness of mind, and their confidence in their known strength, not to any opinion of just or unjust. But, concerning those Murtherers, whose act hath perfidiousness in it, we must make another judgment. Nor do they themselves only act against the Law of Nations, but they also that use their service. For, though in other things, who use the service of wicked men against an Enemy, are judged to sin before God, not before Men (*i. e.* against the Law of Nations:) because in that point, *customes have overpowred Laws*, and *to deceive after the manner of the times* (as *Pliny* speaks) *is Prudence:* Neverthelefs, that custome hath stayed beneath the right of killing. For, here, who useth anothers treachery is believ'd to have violated the Law, not of Nature only, but of Nations. This is signified by those words of *Alexander* to *Darius: Ye undertake impious wars; and though ye have arms, ye bid mony for the heads of your enemies.* And a little after, *Ye have not kept the Laws of War with me.* Elswhere, *He is to be pursued by me to his utter ruine, not as a just Enemy, but as a Murtherer and Poysoner.* That of *Valerius Maximus* is pertinent*: *The death*

Vide Crocerum p. 113.

Lib. 8. epist. ad Ruf.

Curt. lib. 4. & lib. 14. Apud Livium est de Perseo: *Non justum apparare bellum regio animo, sed per omnia clandestina grassari scelera latrociniorum & veneficiorum. lib. 42.* Marcius Philippus de iisdem factis Persei agens lib. 44. *Ea omnia quam Diis quoq; invisa essent, sensurum in exitu rerum suarum.* * *Lib. 9. c. 7.*

of Viriatus hath a double charge of perfidiousness; one against his friends, because he was slain by their hands; another against Q. Servilius Cæpio the Consul, because he was the Author of this wickedness, having promised impunity: and so deserved not the victory, but bought it †. The cause why it was determined so in this case, and not in others, is the same we set down before, concerning poyson; *viz.* lest dangers should be too much heightend, especially theirs who are most high. *Eumenes* said *, *he did not believe any Commander would be willing to overcome so, as to give a very bad precedent against himself.* And in the same Historian, when *Bessus* had laid hands upon *Darius*, it is said a matter of example and the common cause of all Kings †. This therefore is not lawful in a solemn war, or among them who have right to proclame a solemn War: but without that, it is accounted lawful by the same Law of Nations. So *Tacitus* saith, the treachery against *Gannascus* a revolter was not degenerous. *Curtius* saith, the perfidiousness of *Spitamenes* might be the less odious, because nothing seemed impious against *Bessus* the Murtherer of his King. So also, to be perfidious to Theeves and Pirats, though not

† Scriptor de viris illust: *Quæ victoria, quia emta erat, à Senatu non probata.* Eutropius: *Cum interfectores ejus præmium à Cæpione Consule peterent, responsum est, Nunquam Romanis placuisse Imperatorem à suis militibus interfici.* Ubi forte legendum, à *Cœpione Consule promissum.* Sic quod in Sertorium admissum est, damnat Marcellinus. lib. 30.

* *Justin. l.* 14. *lib.* 12.

† Seneca: *Regi tuenda est maxime Regum salus.* Consules Rom. in epist. ad Pyrrhum: *communis exempli & fidei visum est, ut te salvum velimus. Tac. Lib* 11. *Curt. lib.* 7. Sic laudatur Artabanes occiso Gontharide apud Procopium, fine Vandal. c. 2.

without

without fault, is unpunisht among the Nations, because such rogues are hated.

XXXIII. *Of ravishing of Women in War.*

RAvishing of Women you shall often read in war, both permitted and not permitted. They that have permitted it considered only the injury offerd to anothers body; to which, they judged it meet for the Law of arms, whatever is the enemies, should be subject. Better minded were others, who considered here not the injury alone, but the very act of inordinate wild lust, and that it perteins neither to security nor to punishment; and therefore, it ought not to be unpunisht, no more in war than in peace. This latter is the Law, not of all Nations, but of the best. So, *Marcellus* * before he took *Syracuse*, is related to have taken care of preserving chastity even in the enemy. *Scipio* saith in *Livy*, *It concern'd him and the people of Rome, that nothing which is any where sacred should be violated by them:* any where; *i. e.* among the more vertuous and Civil Nations. *Diodorus Siculus*, of the Soldiers of *Agathocles*: *They did not abstain, no not from dishonouring and forcing Women* †. *Ælian*, when he had told how the *Sicyonian* conquerors had prostituted the *Pellenæan* women and

* And Lucullus, as Xiphilin relates. See the edict in Procop. Vand. 1. *Aug. de Civit. Dei lib.* 2. *Liv. lib.* 26.

† Appian. Mithrid. de Chiis captis: *Mulieres & pueri barbarum in morem ab iis qui ducebant stuprati.* *Lib.* 6. *Var. hist.*

and virgins, exclames, *Cruel acts, O ye Gods of Greece, and so far as I can remember, dishonest even in the sight of Barbarians!* And it is fit to be observed among Christians *, not only as a part of military disciplin, but also as a part of the Law of Nations, that whosoever hath violently injur'd Chastity, though in War, should every where be obnoxious unto punishment. For, neither by the *Hebrew* Law should any such offender have escaped, as may be understood by that part of it *, constituted about marrying a Captive, and not selling her afterward. Upon which place *Bacchai* the *Hebrew* Master: *It was Gods will, that the Camp of the Israelites should be holy, not polluted with whoredomes and other abominations, like the campes of the Gentiles.* *Arrian*, when he had related, how *Alexander*, taken with the love of *Roxane*, *would not abuse her as a captive through lust, but vouchsafed her the honour of Marriage*, addes a commendation of the deed. *Plutarch*, of the same deed; *He did not lustfully abuse her, but, as became a Philosopher, took her for his wife.* And one *Torquatus*, because he had offerd violence to a Virgin of the enemies, was carried away into *Corsica* * by decree of the *Romans*, as the same *Plutarch* has it.

* Belisarius observ'd it every where, and Totilas when he took Comes and Rome. Procop. Gott. 3.

Deut. 21. 10.
* Which Philo eloquently expounds in his book of Humanity. Josephus, in his second against Appian, saith, The Law took care for captives in war, that they should not be put to shame, specially women.

* But the Persian King Chosroes affixt him to the Cross who had ravished an Apamean maid. Procop. Persic. 2.

XXXIV.

XXXIV. Of Wast. *The Enemies things may be spoyled.* Cap. 5.

CIcero said, *It is not against nature to spoil him, whom it is lawful to kill.* No wonder then, that the Law of Nations permitted the goods of enemies to be spoiled, when it had permitted themselves to be slain. *Polybius* in the fift of his Histories saith, it is comprehended in the Law of war, that the fortifications, Havens, Towns, Men, Ships, Fruits of the Enemies, and all things like, may either be carryed away or destroyed. And in *Livy* we read, *There are certain Laws of War, which are right to be done or sufferd; namely, for fields to be burnt, houses ruin'd, spoiles of men and cattell to be brought away.* You may find in Historians, almost in every page, whole Cities overthrown, or walls levelled with the ground, populations and burnings of the Countrey. And we must note, such things are lawful also upon those that yield. *The Townsmen*, saith *Tacitus*, *opening their gates submitted themselves, and all they had, to the Romans: Themselves were spared, the Town was fired.*

Offic. 3. Sueton. Nerone 40. *tanquam occasione nata spoliandarum jure belli opulentissimarum provinciarum.* Cypr. de Mortalit. *Sic cum irruptione hostili civitas aliqua possessa est, omnes simul captivitas vastat.* Lib. 31.

Annal. 13.

XXXV. *Of spoiling things sacred and religious.*

NOr doth the meer Law of Nations (the consideration of other duties laid aside, of which we shall speak below) except sacred things, *i. e.* Such as are dedicated to God, or to the Gods. *When places are taken by the enemies, all cease to be sacred* *, saith *Pomponius* the Lawyer †, *The sacred things of the Syracusians, Victory made profane*, saith *Cicero* *. The reason whereof is this, because the things which are called sacred, are not indeed exempted from human uses, but are publick *; and they are named sacred from the end to which they are appointed. A sign of this which I say, is, that when any people yield themselves to another people or King, then also they yield those things which are call'd divine, as appears by the *formula*, which we have cited afore * out of *Livy*: and therefore *Ulpian* saith, publick Right consisteth also in sacred things †. *Pausa-*

* Tertullian in his Apologetick: Wars and victories, most part, consist in taking and overthrowing Cities. Which work is not done without injury of the Gods. The walls of Cities, and Temples of the Gods partake in the same ruine: the Citizens and Priests equally slaughtered: nor is the rapine of sacred riches and profane unlike. So many therefore are the sacriledges of the Romans, as their trophies; So many are their triumphs over Gods, as Nations, &c. † *Pompon. l. cum loca. D. de religiosis.* * *Cic. Verrina* 4. * *Marsil. Patavinus in defensore pacis c.* 5. *p.* 2. *Nicol. Boerius Decis.* 69. *num.* 1, *Bossius in crim. de foro competente num.* 101. *Cothman. cons.* 100. *num.* 30. * *Part.* 1 *n.* 42. *pag.* 88. Cui convenit illud in Amphitruone Plauti: *urbem, agrum, aras, focos, seq; uti dederent.* Deinde: *Dedentq; se, divina humanaq; omnia.* † In the necessity of times sacred things were converted to uses of war, by Pericles, under promise of making

king restitution. Augustus borrowed money out of the Treasury of Temples. Appian Civil. 5. Heraclius in extreme need turned the Church-plate into coyn: but afterward restored the price, as Theophanes relates. See the Oration of Laurent. in Bemb. l. 6.

nias † saith, It was a custom common to *Greeks* and *Barbarians*, that sacred things should be in their power, that had taken Cities. And the same Author notes, that the consecrated Gifts were wont to be taken by the Conquerours: and *Cicero* calls it *the Law of War*. So, *Livy* saith, the ornaments of the Temples which *Marcellus* brought from *Syracuse* to *Rome* were gotten *by the Law of War*. And *Cato* in his Oration in *Salust*, relating what things are wont to happen to the conquered, puts among them *the spoiling of Temples* *. Notwithstanding, this is true, if any divine power be believ'd to be in any Image, to violate that, is high impiety in them, that agree in such perswasion; and in this sense of impiety, or of the Law of Nations broken, are they sometimes accused, who have committed such things; *viz.* on supposition of such perswasion. 'Tis otherwise, if the enemies are of another opinion; as, the Jews were not only permitted, but commanded to abolish the Idols of the Nations: for, that they are forbidden to take them to themselves, is upon this ground, that the *Hebrews* might the more detest the superstitions of the Heathens, being admonisht of their impurity by the interdict of a *touch*; not, as if the

† *Pausan. Arcadicis.*

* *Vide cromerum lib. 17. Procop. Persic. 2.*

Deut. 7. 5.

Antiquæ hist. 4. 8. & *libro contra Ap. altero.* the sacred things of Aliens were spared, as *Josephus* expounds it, in favour of the *Romans*, no doubt; as also, in the exposition of another precept, of not *naming* the Gods of the Nations; which he so explains, as if they were forbidden to speak against them; when in truth the Law sufferd them not to mention them for honours sake, or without abomination. For, the *Hebrews* knew, by the infallible Word of God, that in those Images neither dwelt the Spirit of God, nor good Angels, nor the vertue of Stars, as the deluded Nations thought; but wicked Devils, enemies of Mankind; so that *Tacitus* rightly said, in describing the Jewish Institutions, *All things are there profane, which with us are sacred.* No wonder then, if we read more than once, that Temples of profane worship were burnt by the *Maccabees*. And *Xerxes* too, when he destroyed the images of the *Grecians*, did nothing against the Law of Nations (though the *Greek* writers much exaggerate the fact to bring it into hatred.) For, the *Persians* † believed not any Deities to be in Images, but that the Sun was God, and the Fire some portion of him. By the *Hebrew Law*, as the forecited *Tacitus* rightly, *All were kept from entring into the Temple, beside the Priests.* But *Pompey*, as he saith, *entred the Temple by the right of victory*; or, as *Augustin*, *not with the devotion of a supplant*,

Tacit. hist. 5.

1. *Macc.* 5. & 10.

Ascon. pæd. in Verr. 3.

† Diogenes Laertius in his beginning, saith, Images are condemned by the Magi.

De Civit. Dei l. 18. *cap.* 45.

pliant, but by the right of a Conquerour. Well did he, that he spared the Temple, and the Things of the Temple, though (as *Cicero* plainly) for shame and fear of obtrectators, not for Religion; he did ill, that he entred, as in contempt of the true God, wherewith also the Prophets do upbraid the *Chaldaeans*; for which cause too, some think it came to pass by the singular providence of God, that the same *Pompey* was slain even in the view of *Judaea*, at *Cassium* a Promontory of *Egypt*. Howbeit, if you look upon the *Romans* opinion, Nothing was therein done contrary to the Law of Nations. So *Josephus* relates, how the same Temple was given up to destruction by *Titus*; and addeth, *It was done by the Law of War* *. What we have said of sacred things ought to be understood also of religious. For these too are not in the possession of the dead, but of the living, whether a people, or family. Wherefore, as sacred places taken by the enemies, so religious likewise cease to be such, as *Pomponius* hath written in the place afore, and *Paulus* the Lawyer*; *The Sepulchers of the enemies are not religious to us, and therefore the stones taken thence we may convert into any use.* Which yet is so to be understood, that the bodies of the dead be not treated ill, because that is against the right of buriall, which was introduced by the Law of Nations, as we have demonstrated above *.

Pro Flacco.

Dan. 5. 23.

* *Bell. Jud. l. 6. c.* 24. & 34. Τῷ ἐν πολέμῳ νόμῳ.

* *L. Sepulchra. D. de sepulc. violato.*

* Part. 2. n. 73.

XXXVI.

Cap. 6.

XXXVI. About acquisition of things taken in war. *What is the Law of Nature: what, of Nations.*

BEside the impunity of some acts against men, of which we have spoken, there is also another effect in solemn War, properly arising out of the Law of Nations. And truly by the Law of *Nature*, in a just War, those things are acquir'd to us, which either are equal to that, which being due unto us we cannot otherwise obtain; or also, which do infer damage to the guilty part, within fit measure of punishment, as hath been said above. By this right *Abraham*, of the spoyles he had taken from the five Kings, gave the Tithe to God *, as the Divine Writer to the *Hebrews* explains the History extant in *Genesis*. After the same manner, the *Greeks* too, the *Carthaginians*, and *Romans*, consecrated the Tenth of the spoyle to their Gods, as to *Apollo*, *Hercules*, *Jupiter*, *Feretrius*. And *Jacob* bequeathing a Legacy to *Joseph* above his brethren, saith, *Moreover I give to thee one portion above thy brethren, which I took out of the hand of the Amorite with my sword, and with my bow.* In which place*, *I took*, seemeth by a Prophetick way of speaking, to mean, *I will certainly take*; and here is attributed to *Jacob* that which

* And food to his servants, and part of the spoyl to his companions. *vide Josephum in hac historia.* Hebr. 7. 4. Gen. 14.

Gen. 48. 22.

* The Chaldee interprets it done by Prayers to God, who by a singular favour preserved Sichem for Jacob and his posterity.

which his posterity called by his name should do afterward; as if the person of the progenitor and his children were the same. For, this is righter, than with the *Hebrews* to draw these words to that spoyle of the *Sichemites*, which was made before by the sons of *Jacob*: which being joyned with perfidiousness was condemned by the piety of *Jacob*, as we may see in the Story. Now, that the right of taking spoyle was approved of God, within those natural bounds which I have mentiond, is manifest also in other places. God in his Law speaking of a City conquerd after the refusal of peace, saith thus: *All the spoil thereof shalt thou take unto thy self, and thou shalt eat the spoil of thine enemies, which the Lord thy God hath given thee.* The *Reubenites, Gadites*, and part of the *Manassites* are said to have conquerd the *Ituraans* and their neighbours, and to have taken from them much spoil, this reason being added; because they called upon God in the war, and God had heard them graciously: As also that pious King *Asa* is said, after prayer to God, to have gotten both victory and spoil of the *Ethiopians*, that provoked him by unjust war: which is the more to be observed, because those arms were taken, not by special mandate, but by common right. And *Joshua* encouraging the said *Reubenites, Gadites*, and *Manassites*, saith, *Be yee*

Gen. 34. 30. 49. 6.

Deut. 20. 14.

1. Par. 5. 20, 21, 22.

2. Par. 14. 13.

Jos. 22. 8.

ye partakers of the spoil of the enemies together with your brethren. And *David*, when he sent of the spoils gotten from the
1 Sam. 30. 26. *Amalikites* to the Elders of the *Hebrews*, addeth in commendation of his present, *Behold, this is a Gift for you of the spoil of the Lord's enemies.* For verily, as *Seneca* saith, it is the glory of military men 'to enrich one with the enemie's spoils. And there are extant divine Laws about dividing the spoil, *Numb.* 31. 27. And *Philo* saith, it is among the Threats of the Law, that the field should be reaped by their enemies, whence would follow *their own famine, and their enemies plenty.* But, by the Law of *Nations*, not only he' that wageth war on a just cause, but every one, in solemn War, and without end and measure, is made Master of all he takes from the enemy, in that sense, that by all Nations both himself, and they that have Title from him, are to be maintained in the possession of such things; Which, as to external effects, we may call Dominion. *Cyrus* in *Xenophon*: *It is an everlasting Law among men, that, the enemies City being taken, their goods and money should be the Conquerors. Plato* said, *The Conquerors get all that the Conquer'd had*; who in another place, among the kinds of acquisition, that are as 'twere natural, puts the *Polemical* for one, having therein the assent of the forecited *Xenophon*; in whom *Socrates* by interrogations

De benef. 3. 37.

Philo de diris.

Xen. 5. de instit. Cyri.

Sophist. Com. 4.

terrogations brings *Euthydemus* to a confession, that 'tis not always unjust to spoil, namely, an enemy. *Aristotle* also saith, *The Law is as a common agreement, wherby the things taken in War become the Takers* †. *Philip* in his Epistle to the *Athenians*: *We all do hold Towns left us by our Ancestors, or gotten by the Law of War.* Æschines: *If in War made against us you have taken the City, by the Law of War you possess it rightly.* *Marcellus* in *Livy* saith, what he took from the *Syracusians*, he took away by the same Law. *Things taken from the enemies presently become theirs that take them, by the Law of Nations*, saith *Caius* the Lawyer. *Theophilus* in the *Greek* Institutions calls this acquisition *Natural*: for, not any cause but the naked fact is considered, and thence a right springeth: as also *Nerva* the son (the Lawyer *Paulus* reporting it) said, the dominion of things began from natural possession, and some print thereof remains in the things taken in the Land, the Sea, & the Air; and in things taken in War; all which instantly become theirs, who first laid hold on the possession. From the enemy are judged to be taken away, those things also, which are taken away from the subjects of the enemy. So *Dercyllides* argueth in *Xenophon*, when *Pharnabazus* was the enemy of the *Lacedemonians*, and *Mania* subject to *Pharnabazus*, the Goods of *Mania* were in such

1. Polit.

† Apud Plutarch. in vita Alex. *Ea quæ victi fuerant, & esse & appellari debent Victoris.* Ibidem. *Vincentes etiam ea quæ hostium sunt, sibi acquirere.* Diodorus Siculus excerptis Peiresian. n. 467. *Quæ armis quæsita essent & parta belli jure, non dimittenda.* Etiam Clemens Alexand. ait, *res hostium rapi & acquiri belli jure.* Strom. 1.

Liv. lib. 39.

L. naturalem. §. *ul*. D. *de acq. rerum dom. tit. de rer. div.*

Hist. Gr. 3.

a case, that they might be rightly seized on by the Law of War.

XXXVII. *When Movable Goods are by the Law of Nations judged Taken: When Lands.*

Moreover, in this question of War it hath pleased the Nations, that he may be understood to have taken a thing, who so deteins it, that the other hath lost all probable hope of recovery, *that the thing hath escaped pursuance*, as *Pomponius* speaketh in a like question. And this so proceeds in movable goods, that they are said *Taken*, when they are brought within the bounds, that is, the guards of the enemy. For in the same manner a thing is lost, as it returns by *Postliminium*. It returns, when it comes within the bounds of Empire, *i. e.* within the guards. And *Paulus* saith plainly of a man, that he is lost, when he is gone beyond our bounds: and *Pomponius* interprets him *Taken* in War, whom the enemies have taken out of ours, and brought within their own guards; for, before he is brought into their guards he remains a Citizen. Now, in this Law of Nations, there was the same reason of a man and of a thing. Whence it is easy to be conceived, that elswhere things taken are said presently to become the Takers, ought to be understood with some condition, to wit, of continuing

L. Pomponius. D. de acq. rer. dom. L. postlim. ¶. postliminio. D. de capt. l. ult. Ib. l. postlim. ¶. in bello. d. tit. Inst. de rer. divis. ¶. item ea. Inst. d. loco. l. naturalem. ¶. item de acq. rer. dom.

continuing the possession so far; whence it seemeth to follow, that on the Sea, ships and other things may then be thought taken, when they are carried away into the Haven, or the place where the Navy lies: For then, the recovery seems to begin to be past hope. But, by the newer Law of Nations among the people of Europe we see 'tis introduc'd, that such things are supposed taken, when they have been in the enemies power for the space of four and twenty hours *. As for Lands or Fields, they are not conceiv'd presently to be taken, so soon as they are sate upon. For, though it be true, that that part of the field, which an Army hath entred with great force, is for the time possessed by it, as *Celsus* hath noted; Yet, as to that effect which we speak of, every possession is not sufficient, but a firm possession is requir'd. Wherefore the *Romans* were so far from judging the field which *Annibal* encamped in without the Gate, to be lost, that at the very same time it was valued at the same price it was sold before. That field then will be supposed taken, which is so included with lasting fortifications, that without overcoming them the other party can have no access. Whence it is a very probable derivation * of the word *Territory*, from terrifying the enemies. So *Xenophon* saith, the possession of land in the time of War is reteined by *Forts or muniments*.

Consulatu maris c. 283. & 287. Constit. Gallicæ lib. 20. tit. 13. art. 24. Corn. de Lap. in Gen. c. 14. Molin. disp. 118. L. quod meo. D. de acq. vel amit. poss.

* By land also the same is observed, as you may learn out of Thuanus l. 113. in an. 1595. *Vid. & Alb. Gent. Hispan. Adv. l.* 3.

* *Territorium à terrendis hostibus.* Sic. Flac. *à terendo.* Var. *à terra.* Frontin. *à terrendi jure.* Pomp.

Xen. lib. de Vectigal. τεῖχη καὶ ἐρύματα.

XXXVIII. *Things that are not the enemies are not acquir'd by war. Of Goods found in the Enemies Ships.*

AND this is manifeſt, that a thing may be made ours by the Law of war, 'tis requir'd, that it have been the enemies; For, things that are with the enemies, that is, in their Towns, or within their guards, but whoſe Owners are neither the enemies ſubjects, nor of an hoſtile mind, thoſe things cannot be acquir'd by war, as appears, among other arguments, by that ſaying of *Æſchines*†, that *Amphipolis*, a City of the *Athenians*, by the war of *Philip* againſt the *Amphipolitans* could not become his. For, both Reaſon faileth, and this Right of changing Dominion by force is ſo odious, that it is not fit to be produced. Wherefore, what is wont to be ſaid, *that the Goods are the enemies, which are found in the Enemies ſhips †, ought not to be ſo underſtood, as if it were a certain Rule of the Law of Nations, but that it may ſhew

† *De malè obita legatione.*

* *Conſul. maris c.* 273.

† Neither are the ſhips of friends to be made a prey becauſe of the enemies goods, unleſs it be by conſent of the Maſters of the ſhip. *L.* [illegible]*otem. D. de Publicanis. Rodericus Zuarius li. de uſu maris, Conſil.* 2. *n.* 6. And ſo I think the Laws of France are to be underſtood, which ſubject ſhips and goods to the prey for one another. Otherwiſe the things alone become a prey. *Meurſ. Danic. lib.* 2. So in the War of the Venetians with the Genuans, the Greek ſhips were ſearched, and the enemies hidden there drawn forth. *Gregoras lib.* 9. *vide & Crantzium Saxon.* 2. *& Albericum Gentilem Advoc. Hiſpan. lib.* 20.

a

a presumption, which yet by strong proofs to the contrary may be overthrown. So, in our *Holland*, long since, *Anno* 1338. in the heat of War, I have found it was judged in full Senate, and upon that judgment passed into a Law.

XXXIX. *By the Law of Nations the things are made ours, which our enemies took from others by war.*

AND this is without Controversy if we respect the Law of Nations, Things taken by us from the enemies cannot be challenged by them that had possessed them before our enemies, and had lost them by war: because the Law of Nations made the enemies first masters by external dominion, and then us. By which right, among other arguments, *Jephtha* defends himself against the *Ammonites*, because that Land which the *Ammonites* challenged, by the Law of war had passed from the *Ammonites* to the *Hebrews*; as also another part, from the *Moabites* to the *Amorites*, and from the *Amorites* to the same *Hebrews*. So *David* accounteth that for his own, and divides it, which he had taken from the *Amalekites*, the *Amalekites* formerly from the *Philistins* †. *Titus Largius* in *Dionysius Halicarnassensis*, when the *Volscians* requested to have their old posses- sions

Jud. 11. 23, 24, 27.
1 Sam. 30. 20.
† So Resin King of Syria gave a City which was the Idumæans not to them, but to the Syrians to be inhabited, as the Masorets read, 2 Reg. 16. 6.
Halicarnass. l. 6.

sions again, gave his opinion, in the *Roman Senate*, thus: *We Romans believe those possessions to be most honourable and just, which we have taken by the Law of War, nor can we be induced, by a foolish facility to part with the monuments of our valour, and restore them to those that were not able to keep them. Nor do we judge such possessions to be communicated only to our Countrymen now living, but to be left to our posterity. So far are we from relinquishing what we have got, and dealing with our selves as if we were our own enemies*. And in the answer of the *Romans* given to the *Aurunci*: *We Romans are of this Judgment, what one hath gotten of his enemies by valour, he may transmit to his posterity by right. Livy*, after his narration how the land neer *Luca* was divided by the *Romans*, notes, *That Land was taken from the Ligures, and had been formerly the Ethruscians*. By this right was *Syria* reteined by the *Romans*, as *Appian* notes, and not restored to *Antiochus Pius*, from whom *Tigranes* the *Romans* enemy had forced it: and *Justin* out of *Trogus* makes *Pompey* answer the same *Antiochus* in this manner: *As he did not deprive him of his Kingdom when he had it, so would he not restore him to the Kingdom he had lost to* Tigranes, *and knew not how to keep*. And likewise those parts of *Gallia* which the *Cimbrians* had taken from the *Galls*, the *Romans* took for their own.

De Veiis idem in Romulo narrat Plutarchus.

Halic. l. 8.

Lib. 41.

Mithrid. Civil. 1.

Lib. 40.

XL.

XL. Of the Right over Captives. *Their Condition, and the reason of it.* Cap. 7.

IN the Primitive state of Nature, no men are servants; yet is it not repugnant to Natural Justice that by the fact of man, that is, by Covenant or transgression, servitude should come in. But, by that Law of Nations, of which we now speak, servitude is of larger extent, both as to *persons*, and as to *effects*. For, if we consider Persons, not only they that give up themselves or promise servitude are accounted for servants, but all indeed that are taken in publick solemn War, after they are brought within the guards, as *Pomponius* saith. Nor is Transgression necessary, but the lot of all is equal, even of them, who by their ill fortune *, after war is on the suddain begun, are deprehended within the bounds of the enemies. Nor are they servants only themselves, but also their posterity for ever: to wit, they that are born of a mother being a servant after servitude †. Now, the effects of this right are infinite, so that, as *Seneca* the Father said, there is nothing which is not lawful to a Master over his servant. No suffering, which may not freely be imposed on him; no work which may not every way be commanded or extorted from him: so that even the cruelty of

L. Libertus §. 1. *D. de statu hom.*

L. postlim. ¶. 1. *D. de captiv.* *L. in bello D. de captivis.*

* Philo: *Multi viri boni variis casibus nativam libertatem amiserunt.* Pueros bello captos abducere πολέμου νόμῳ vocat Oppian.

† *L. & servorum* ¶. 1. *D. de statu hominum.* 1 Cor. 5.

of Masters toward servile persons is unpunished, unless so far as the Civil Law sets a measure and a penalty for cruelty, *We may observe*, saith *Caius*, *that Masters, among all Nations equally, have had power of life and death over their servants.* Then he addeth, that limits were appointed to this power by the *Roman* Law, to wit, on *Roman* ground. Moreover, all things which are taken with the persons are acquir'd to the Master. The servant himself, who is in the power of another, saith *Justinian*, can have nothing as his own. Whence is refelled, or at least restrained, their opinion, who say incorporal things are not acquired by the Law of War. For, it is true, they are not primarily and by themselves acquired, but by means of the person whose they were. Yet here are to be excepted those things which flow from a singular propriety of the person, and therefore are unalienable, as the right paternal. For these, if they can remain, remain in the person; if not, they are extinguished. Now, all these things were introduc'd by the Law of Nations, for no other cause, but that the Takers tempted by so many commodities might willingly abstein from that extreme rigour, whereby they might kill those they had taken, both at the instant, and afterward, as we have said afore. *The appellation of servants*, saith *Pomponius*, *is derived hence, that Commanders are accustomed*

L. 1. D. de his qui sui sunt iuris Instit. de his qui sui.

Donat. ad Ter. And. A. 1. S. 1. *Quid non justum domino in servum?*

Instit. per quas person. ¶. item vob.

L. Pupillus. D. de V. S. vide & Servium ad 1. Æn. ubi originem vocis salsem explicat.

stomed to sell Captives, and so preserve and not kill them. I said, that they might *willingly* abstein: for here is nothing like a Covenant whereby they may be *Compeld* to abstain, if you look upon this Law of Nations, but a manner of perswading from consideration of that which is more profitable. And for the same cause, this right is also transcribed to others, just as the dominion of things. The reason why this dominion was extended to the Children, is, because otherwise, if the Takers should use their highest right, they would not be born. Whereto is Consequent, that the Children born before that calamity, unless they be taken too, become not servants.. And, the reason why it pleasd the Nations, that the Children should be of their Mothers condition, is, because servile copulations were neither regulated by Law nor by certain custody, so that no sufficient presumption could shew the Father. So is that of *Ulpian* to be understood, *The Law of Nature is this, that he which is born without lawfull Matrimony, should follow the Mother.* That is, The Law of general custom drawn from some natural reason, as we have elswhere shewed that the word *Natural Law* is taken. Now, that these rights were not in vain introduced by the Nations, may be understood by example of Civil Wars; wherein, for the most part, we see those that are taken

L. Lex Naturæ. D. de statu hom.

Caius JC. lib. 2. rerum quotidian. *Item quæ ex hostib. capiuntur jure gentium statim capientium fiunt adeo quidem ut liberi homines in servitutem deducantur.*

slain,

ſlain, becauſe they could not be brought under ſervitude: which *Plutarch* alſo hath noted in the life of *Otho*, and *Tacitus* in the ſecond of his Hiſtories.

XLI. *This right over Captives prevailed not among all Nations, nor doth it prevail among Christians.*

NOtwithſtanding, we muſt know, this Law of Nations concerning Captives hath not been always receiv'd, nor among all Nations; though the *Roman* Lawyers ſpeak univerſally, ſtyling the more notable part by the name of the whole. So, among the *Hebrews*, who were ſegregated by ſpecial Ordinances from the community of other people, refuge was granted unto ſervants, namely thoſe (as Interpreters righly obſerve) who fell into that calamity by no fault of their own. And Chriſtians † have generally agreed, that ſuch as are taken in War between them ſhould not become ſervants, to be ſold, to be forced to work, and ſuffer the like ſervile things. Very juſtly; becauſe they had, or ought to have, learned better of the Commendator of all Charity, than not to be kept from the killing of miſerable men, except by conceſſion of a leſs cruelty. And that this hath paſſed heretofore from the Anceſtors to their poſterity, among profeſſors of the ſame Religion,

Deut. 23. 15. *Vide praeceptorum vetantium* 180.

Bart. in l. hoſtes, D de capt. Covar. in c. peccatum p. 2. ¶. 11. n. 6.

† The Eſſenes alſo, from whom the firſt Chriſtians took beginning See Joſephus.

ligion, *Gregoras* † hath written; nor, was it proper to the Subjects of the *Roman* Empire, but common with the *Thessalians*, *Illyrians*, *Triballians* and *Bulgarians*. Thus hath the reverence of the Christian Law effected this at least, though it be but small, which *Socrates* of old, when he would have perswaded the *Greeks* to observe toward one another, could not obtein *. The same do the *Mahumetans* also observe among themselves in this point *, which the Christians do. Yet, even among the Christians, hath remained a custom to keep the Captives, until a ransom be paid, whose valuation is at the pleasure of the Conquerour; unless a certainty were agreed on. And this right of keeping the Captives is usually granted all that have taken them, except the persons of eminent place and dignity; for, over these, the manners of most Nations give a right to the Commonwealth, or to the head thereof.

† Greporas, lib. 4. *Mos hic est ab antiquo deductus, ad posteros, propter fidei consortium, ut res quidem in prædam vertere liceat, homines autem nec captivos facere, nec interficere extra prælii tempus.*

* *Plato 5. de Repub.*

* Chalcocondyl. lib. 3. Leunclav. lib. 3. & 17. Busbequius epist. exoticarum, 3.

Bart. in l. nam. & serv. D. de Reg. gestis. Boër. decis. 178. Const. Reg. Hisp. lib. 8. tit. 26. pag. 2.

XLII.

Cap. 8.

XLII. *Of Empire over the Conquered.*

HE that can ſubject unto himſelf particular men by perſonal ſervitude, no wonder if he can ſubject unto himſelf a community, whether it be a Commonwealth, or part thereof, by a ſubjection either meerly Civil, or meerly berile, or mixt. Therefore *Tertullian* ſaid, Empires are got by arms, and propagated by victories. *Alexander* in *Curtius*; Laws are given by Conquerors, receiv'd by the Conquered †. *Arioviſtus* in *Cæſar* * ſaith, It is the Law of War, that they who have overcome ſhould govern thoſe whom they have overcom, as they pleaſe. *Juſtin* * out of *Trogus* relates, that the Warriors before *Ninus* ſought not Rule for themſelves but Glory, and being content with honour abſteined from dominion; but *Ninus* was the firſt that enlarged the bounds of his empire, and ſubdued other Nations; whereupon, it went into a Cuſtom. *Bocchus* in *Salluſt*, ſaith, *He took arms to defend his Kingdom; for, part of Numidia, whence he had expelld* Jugurtha, *was become His by the Law of War.* Now, Empire may be acquired to the Conqueror, either only as 'tis in a King †

Apologet.

† Minio in orat. ad Romanos, apud Liv. l. 35. *Cur Syracuſas atq; in alias Siciliæ Græcas urbes Prætorem quotannis cum Imperio & virgis & ſecuribus mittitis? Nihil aliud profecto dicatis, quam armis ſuperatis vos iis has leges impoſuiſſe.*

* De De bell. Gall.

* Lib. 1.

† Alexander after the Battell at Gaugamel was ſaluted King of Aſia. The Romans ſaid, what Syphax had was theirs by the Law of War. Appian. But, when the Hunni ſaid, the Gepidæ were theirs, becauſe they

they had taken their King, the Romans denyed that, because the Gepidæ had rather a Prince than a King, nor were they in his Patrimony. Menander Protector.

or other Governour, and then He succeeds only into his right, and no farther; or also as 'tis in the people; in which case, the Conqueror hath Empire so, that he may also alienate it, as the people might. And so it came to pass, that some Kingdoms were in patrimony, as we have said afore †. Farther, it may be, that the Commonwealth that was, may cease to be a Commonwealth; either so, that it may be an accession of another Commonwealth, as the *Roman* Provinces; or, that it may adhere to no Commonwealth, as, if a King waging War at his own charge, so subject a people to himself, that he will have it governd, not for the profit of the people chiefly, but of the Governour; which is a property of Heril Empire, not of Civil. *Government*, saith *Aristotle*, *is either for the utility of the Governour, or for the utility of the Governed; this hath place among fiee men, that among Masters and servants.* The people then, that is kept under such command, will be for the future, not a Commonwealth but a great Family*. And hence may be understood, what kind of empire is that which is mixt of Civil & Heril, to wit, where servitude is mingled with some personal liberty. So we read, people have been deprived of arms, and commanded

† Part. 1. n. 47.

Lib. 7. de rep.

* Alexandrides ἐκ ἴσι δύλων αἰγαθ' ὡδὲ μὲν πόλις.

Tacitus; *non dominationem & servos sed rectorem & cives cogitaret.*

Xencphon saith of Agesilaus, that when he conquerd Cities, he governd them as free, and did not enslave them.

commanded to have no iron, but for agriculture; and others have been compeld to change their language and course of life. Moreover, as things which did belong to particular men, are acquir'd by the right of war to them, who subject those men to themselves; so also the things of a Community become theirs who subject to themselves the Community, if they please. *Annibal* in his Oration to
Liv. lib. 43. his Soldiers: *Whatsoever the Romans do possess, being gotten and heaped up with so many triumphs, All that together with*
Strabo lib. 12. *the masters will be ours.* So *Pompey*, what *Mithridates* had taken and added to his Empire, subdued to the *Roman* people. Wherefore also incorporal rights of a community will become the Conqueror's, so
Dionys. 3. far as he pleaseth. So, *Alba* being conquer'd, the *Romans* challenged to themselves the rights of the *Albans*. Whence it follows, that the *Thessalians* were wholly freed from the obligation of the hundred talents; which sum, due from them to the *Thebans*, *Alexander the Great*, having conquerd *Thebes*, forgave them by the right of victory. Nor is that true which in *Quintilian* is alleged on behalf of the *Thebans*, that that only is the conqueror's which he holds himself: and, incorporal right cannot be holden; and that the condition of an heir and of a conqueror is different, because the right passeth to the former, the thing to the later. For, he

he that is Master of the Persons, is also Master of the things, and of all right which belongs to the Persons. He that is possessed, doth not possess for himself; nor hath he any thing in his power, who hath not himself. Yea, if one leave the right of a Commonwealth to a conquered people, he may take to himself some things which were the Commonwealths; for, it is at his pleasure, to appoint what measure he will to his own favour. The fact of *Alexander* was imitated by *Cesar*, when he forgave those of *Dyrrachium* the debt which they owed to some one of the adverse party. But here might be objected, that the War of *Cesar* was not of that kind of which this Law of Nations was established †.

L. qui in servitute est. de reg. juris. L. sic eveniet. D. ad leg. Jud. de adult.

Cic. ep. ad Brut. 6.

† Antonius commanded the Tyrians to restore what they possessed of the Jews, not granted to them by the Senate, and possessed before the War of Cassius. *Josephus. vide & Bezarum Genuensis histor. lib.* 20.

XLIII. Admonitions *about things done in an unjust War.*

Cap. 10.

I Must now return, and take away from those that wage War almost all that I have seemed to give them, and yet have not given. For I said at first, when I began to explain this part of the Law of Nations, that many things are lawfull or of right, in that they are done *impunè*, without punishment, and partly because coactive judgments do lend them their authority;

authority; which things yet, either are exorbitant from the rule of right; whether that rule be placed in right strictly so call'd, or in the precept of other vertues; or els at least may be omitted better and with more commendation among good men. In *Seneca's Troades*, when *Pyrrhus* saith, *No law spares a captive, or hinders his punishment*. Agammenon replies, *What Law forbiddeth not, Pudor forbids to be done*. Where *Pudor* (or, Modesty) signifies not so much respect of men and reputation, as of Right and Good, or at least, of that which is righter and better. And in that sense you may often see Justice joyn'd with Pudor, *Plato*; *Justice is call'd the companion of Pudor, and that deservedly*. And in another place; *God fearing the destruction of mankind, gave unto men Justice and Pudor, the ornaments of Cities, and bonds of friendship*. *Cicero* so distinguisheth between Justice and Modesty, that he makes it the part of Justice, not to violate men; of modesty, not to offend them. With that which we brought out of *Seneca* well agrees a saying of the same Author in his Philosophic writings; *How narrow is that Innocence, to be good according to Law*? How much larger is the rule of duties than of Law? How many things doth piety, humanity liberality, justice, faith require? all which are without the Statute-book*. Where you see *Law* is distinguished from *Justice*; because

Lib. 12. de leg.

Ad ineruditum præsidem.

Offic. 1.

Lib. 1. de ira. cap. 27.

*Cic. de Offic. 3. *Aliter leges, aliter Philosophi tollunt astutias. Leges quatenus manu tenere res possunt; Philosophi quatenus ratione & intelligentia.*

because *Law* conteins that which is of force in externall judgments. The same difference *Aristotle* intimates, disputing whether the servitude be to be called just, which ariseth from War. *Some respecting one kind of just (for the Law is a certain just thing) say, servitude arising from war is just: yet not perfectly; because it may happen, that the cause of Warring was unjust.* So also the *Roman* Lawyers, what oftentimes they call the right of captivity, they elswhere call injury, and oppose it to natural equity; and *Seneca* saith, the name of servant came from injury, respecting that which oft happens. And the *Italians* in *Livy*, retaining the things they had taken from the *Syracusians* in War, are called pertinacious to confirm their injury. *Dion Prusaensis*, when he had said, Captives in war, if they returned to their own, receiv'd their liberty, addes, *as men that were injuriously kept in servitude. Lactantius* * speaking of the Philosophers; *When they discourse of offices perteining to war, they accommodate their words neither to justice nor to true vertue, but to this life and the custom of Commonwealths.* And a little after he saith, *the Romans did injury by Law.* First, then we say, If the cause of war be unjust, although war be undertaken after a solemn manner, all acts that have their rise thence, are unjust by *internal* injustice: so that they, who *knowingly* do such acts, or do

Arist. pol. 1. c. 6.

L. postlim. in pr. D. de cap.

Epist. 32.

Lib. 28.

Orat. 15.

* Austin in his 4. Epistle, which is to Marcellinus, saith, If this earthly commonwealth would keep Christs precepts, even wars would not be waged without kindness. *Apud veros Dei cultores etiam ipsa bella pacata sunt.* Idem.

cooperate to them, are to be reckoned in their number, who, without Repentance, cannot enter into the Kingdom of heaven. And, true Repentance, if time and ability be not wanting, by all means requires, that he who hath given the damage, whether by killing, or by spoiling things, or by taking the prey, repair the same*. Therefore God saith, he hates the fasts of those that detein the prisoners not justly taken *; and to the *Ninivites* their King proclames, that they turn every one from the violence that is in their hands, seeing this by natures light, that without such restitution repentance would be feign'd and fruitless. And thus we find not only Jews † and Christians to have judged, but the *Mahumetans* too †. Now, to restitution are the Authors of war (whether by right of power, or by counsil) bound, concerning all the things that usually follow war; yea such things as are not usual, if they have commanded any such, or perswaded, or when they could hinder, have not hindred. So also Leaders are bound concerning the things done by their Command; and all soldiers fully, who have concurred to any common act, as namely the burning of a town; in divided acts, every one for the damage whereof himself is the only cause, or at least one of the causes. Nor can I think, that exception is to be admitted, which is added by some, concerning them that

1 Cor. 6. 10.

Num. 5. 6.

* Hieron. ad Rust. *Nec dissertur ultionis sententia, si non reddantur universa.* August. in epist. ad Maced. quæ est 54. *Si res aliena propter quam peccatum est, reddi possit & non redditur, pœnitentia non agitur sed simulatur.*

* *Es.* 58. 5, 6, 7.

† Vide Canones pænitentiales Maimonidæ cap. 2. §. 2.

† Vide Leunclav. Turcic. 5. & 17.

Less. l. 2. c. 13. dub. 4.

Vasquez. lib. 1. controv. ill. c. 9. n. 17. Molin. disp. 118. §. ut vero.

that do ſervice unto others, if in them be any part of the fault. For the fault ſufficeth to reſtitution without deceit. Some there are, who ſeem to be of opinion, that things taken in war, though the cauſe of war was not juſt, are not to be reſtored; becauſe Warriors, when they enter into war againſt each other, are underſtood to have allowed thoſe things to the Takers. But, no man is eaſily preſumed vainly to expoſe his own, and war of it ſelf is far diſtant from the nature of Contracts. And, that peaceable people might have ſomewhat certain which they might follow, and not be entangled in war againſt their will, it ſufficed to introduce that external dominion of which we have ſpoken. Which alſo the ſaid Authors ſeem to determine in the Law of the captivity of perſons. Therefore the *Samnites* in *Livy*, *We have ſent back*, ſay they, *the things of our enemies taken in prey, which ſeemed ours by the right of War.* They ſay, *ſeemed*, becauſe that war was unjuſt, as the *Sammites* had before acknowledged. Not unlike is this, that from a contract entred without deceit, wherein is inequality, by the Law of Nations there ſprings a certain faculty of compelling him who hath contracted, to fulfil his Covenants; and yet notwithſtanding is he bound by the office of an honeſt and good man, who hath covenanted for more than is right, to reduce the matter to equa-

Lib. 9.

Lib. 8.

lity. Moreover, He that hath not himself given the damage, or hath given it without all fault, but hath in his hand a thing taken by another in unjust war, is bound to restore it; because, why the other should go without it, there is no cause naturally just, not his consent, not his ill desert, not compensation. There is an history pertinent to this in *Valerius Maximus: The people of Rome*, saith he, *when* P. Claudius *had conquer'd the Camerini by his fortunate conduct, and had sold them under the spear, though they saw the treasury encreas'd with money, and the bounds of their fields enlarged, neverthelesse, because the action seemed not to be done by their General upon a clear account, with very great care they sought them out, and redeemed them, and restored their lands**. Likewise to the *Phocenses*, by decree of the *Romans*, was also that publick liberty rendred, and the fields that had been taken away. And afterward the *Ligures*, who had been sold by *M. Pompilius*, the price being repaid to the buyers, were restor'd to liberty, and care had for the restitution of their goods. The same was decreed by the Senate concerning the *Abderites*, the reason being added, because an unjust War is waged against them. Howbeit, if he that keepeth the thing hath laid out any cost or pains, he may deduct as much as was worth to the master to attain a possession despair'd of; but

Lib. 6. c. 5.

*Mahumet the Turk commanded them to be freed, that were in the town of S. Mary in Achaia. Chalcocond. l. 9.

Liv. lib. 28.

Liv. lib. 42.

Lib. 63.

but if he that had the thing, being without fault, hath consumed or alienated it, he will not be bound, but for so much as he may be esteemed richer for it.

XLIV. *A Temperament about the right of killing in a just War.* General rules.

Cap. 11.

BUt, neither in a just War is that to be admitted which is said, *He gives all, that denyes me right*. Better said Cicero: *There are some offices to be done even to them, from whom you have received injury; For revenge and punishment must have a measure* †. The same Author praiseth the old times of the Romans, when the Issues of Wars were, either mild, or necessary. *Cruel they are,* saith Seneca, *which have cause of punishment, but have no measure. They may,* saith Aristides, *they may also, who revenge themselves be unjust, if they exceed the mean. For, he that in punishing goes farther than is meet, is the second author of injury* †. Now, when killing is just in a just war, according to internal justice, when it is not, may be understood by what we have said in the beginning of this Book. For it happens, that one is slain,* on purpose, or without purpose.

Omnia dat, qui justa negat. Lucan.

Offic. 1.

Offic. 2.

2. *De Clem.* c. 4.

Leuctrica 1.

† Tacit. 3. Annal. *Pompeius gravior remediis quam delicta erant.* Ausonius; *Vindictaq; major Crimine visa sue est.*

† Laudatur Propertio Minos; *Victor erat quamvis, aequus in hoste fuit.* Sed & Ovidio: *Leges captis justissimus auctor Hostibus imposuit.* * *Vict. de jure belli. num. 36. & 45.*

On purpose no man can be slain justly, unless either for just punishment, or as without it we cannot defend our life and our goods; though this, to kill a man for perishing things, however it be not contrary to justice strictly so called, departeth from the Law of Charity. That punishment may be just, it is necessary that he who is slain have offended; and that so much, as may be avenged with the punishment of death in the sentence of an equall Judge. Whereof we shall say the less now, because we have said so much afore about punishments. And afore, when we spake of suppliants (for there are suppliants as well in War as in Peace)
ἀτυχήματα καὶ ἀδικήματα.
we distinguished 'twixt misfortune and injury. *Gylippus* in that place of *Diodorus* enquires, in which ranck the *Athenians* ought to be placed, whether of the unfortunate, or of the unjust; and saith, They cannot be accounted unfortunate, who of their own accord, provoked by no injury, had begun a war upon the *Syracusians*: whence he infers, Being they had of themselves undertaken the war, they must also be content to bear the evils thereof. An example of the unfortunate are They, who are with the enemies, without an hostile mind; such as the *Athenians* were in the times of
Vell. Pat. l. 2.
Mithridates, of whom *Velleius* thus; *If any one impute to the Athenians this time of rebellion, wherein Athens was besieged*

sieged by Sulla, *he is too ignorant of truth and antiquity. For*, *So sure was the Athenians fidelity toward the Romans, that always and in all things, whatever was done sincerely, the Romans said was done* fide Attica, *with Attick faith. But, at that time the Athenians were in a miserable condition, opprest by the force of* Mithridates: *They were possest by their enemies, and besieged by their friends: They had their minds without the walls, and their bodies within, yielding to necessity.* Which last clause seems taken out of *Livy*, in whom *Indibilis* the *Spanyard* saith, Lib. 26.
his body only was with the *Carthaginians*, his Soul with the *Romans*. *Verily*, as *Cicero* speaketh, *all men having their* Pro Quintio.
life in anothers hand, more often think, what he can do, in whose power they are, than what he ought to do. The same for *Ligarius*; *The third time is, when after the coming of* Varus *he stayd in Africa: which, if it be a crime, is a crime of necessity, not of will*. And *Julian* considered this in the cause of the *Aquileians*, as Lib. 21.
Ammianus testifies, who, when he had related the punishment of a few, addeth, *The residue, all, went off free; whom necessity, not their will, had engaged in the tumult* *. The old Commentator upon the place of *Thucydides* about the *Corcyraans* Captives sold; *He shews the clemency worthy of Grecian Natures: for tis hard to kill Captives after fight, servants especially,*

* Halicarnass. l. 1. ἅπαν συγγνώμης ἄξιον τὸ ἀκούσιον.

especially, who do not war of their own accord. Moreover we must note, between full injury and meer misfortune often intercedes some Mean, which is as 'twere compos'd of both: so that it can neither be call'd the act of one knowing and willing, nor meerly the act of one ignorant or unwilling. *Aristotle* put the name ἀμάρτημα upon this kind; we may call it *some fault*. The same *Aristotle*; *Equity commands, that we equal not injuries and faults, nor faults and misfortunes; misfortunes are they, which could not be foreseen, nor are admitted with a wicked mind; faults, which might be foreseen, yet are not done with a wicked mind; injuries, which are done with a wicked mind and purposely* †. This distinction, by *Themistius* in the praise of the Emperor *Valens*, is applyed to our argument, thus: *You have made a difference 'twixt an injury, a fault, and a misfortune. Although you neither study* Plato, *nor read* Aristotle, *yet you put their doctrin into practice. For, you have not thought them worthy of equal punishment, who from the beginning perswaded the War, and who afterward were carried with the stream, and who at last*

Moral. 5.

De arte Orat. lib. 1.

†Tria hæc notarunt veteres, & in illo Homeri versu de Achille, Iliados postremo; ὄυτε γὰρ ἔσ' ἄφρων, ὄυτ' ἄσκοπος, ὄυτ' ἀλιτήμων. Philo, autem in leg. spec. explicatione sic ait: *Dimidiatum esse facinus, ubi non accessit longa animi deliberatio.* Thucydides lib. 4. *Credibile est apud Deum quoq; paratam esse veniam his qui bello aut qua simili necessitate tracti aliquid admittunt.* Cærites apud Livium l. 7. *Ne appellarent consilium, quæ vis ac necessitas appellanda esset.* Aristides Leuctr. 2. *Difficilia tempora excusationem aliquam dant desciscentibus.*

submitted

submitted to him that now seemed to have the highest power. But, the first you condemned, the next you chastised, the last you pityed *. So, in *Josephus*, (*lib.* 5. *belli Jud.*) *Titus* inflicts real Punishment upon the Leader in the Crime, verbal upon the following multitude. Meer misfortunes, neither deserve punishment, nor oblige to the restitution of the damage, unjust actions, to both; A mean fault, as it is liable to restitution, so it often deserves not punishment, especially capital. What *Themistius* notes, that the Authors of war are to be distinguisht from the Followers, is frequently Exemplified in Histories. *Herodotus* * relates, how the *Grecians* took revenge of those, who were Authors to the *Thebans* of a defection to the *Medes*. So were the Princes of *Ardea* beheaded, as *Livy* * tells us; And in the same Author *, *Val. Lævinus*, *Agrigentum being taken, beat with rods and beheaded those that were Chief in the business; the rest, with the spoil, he sold.* The *Athenians*, in *Thucydides* *, repented of their decree against the *Mitylenæans, to put to the sword the whole City, and not the Authors of the defection only*. And *Diodorus* saith, *Demetrius* having taken *Thebes*, put to death only ten of

* Idem Themistius alibi adolescentem Imperatorem vult discere, quid distet ἀδίκημα, καὶ ἁμάρτημα καὶ ἀτύχημα, est quomodo regem deceat istius misereri, hoc corrigere, postremum vero solum ultione prosequi. *Such was Trajan, eminent among the Roman Princes, not exactly learned in words, but one that knew what to do, and did it.* Xiphil. *M. Aurelius, a singular Prince, shewing wisdom, not in words and opinions, but in temperance and gravity of manners.* Herod. *Macrinus did not know the Laws so exactly, as he executed them faithfully.* Xiphil. *O God! Give us but such Princes in our times!* * Vide Gail. l. 2. de pace pub. n. 18. * Herod. Cal. * Liv. lib. 4. * Liv. lib. 26. * Thucyd. lib. 3.

of the principal offendors. Again, in the Authors of War, causes are to be distinguished: for some, though not just, yet are such, that they may impose upon men not wicked. The Writer to *Herennius* puts this as a most favourable cause of deprecation, if one hath offended, not out of hatred or cruelty, but out of duty and right affection. *Seneca's* wise man, *will dismiss his Enemies safe, and sometimes commended, if they took Arms for honest causes, for faith, for league, for liberty.* In *Livy*, the *Cærites* ask pardon for their errour, that they aided their Kinsmen the *Phocenses*. The *Chalcidians* and others, that helped *Antiochus* according to their league, had pardon granted them by the *Romans*. *Cicero* saith, they are to be saved, who were not cruel and barbarous in the War: And, that Wars made for the glory of Empire, are to be waged with less bitterness. That hath place often, which is in *Cicero*, concerning the war of *Cæsar* and *Pompey*: *It was a dark War: a Contention 'twixt most famous leaders: many doubted what was best.* And, what he saith elswhere: *Though we were in some fault of human error, yet certainly we are free from wickedness**. Just as in *Thucydides* things are said worthy of pardon, which are done, *not out of malice, but rather by mistake.* What *Brutus* wrote of Civil, I think may be well referd to most wars, *They are more sharply to*

Vict. de jure belli. n.59. l.2.

Lib.2.de clem. cap. 7.

Lib. 7.

De offic. 1.

* De Deiotaro ille Cicero: *Non ille odio tui progressus, sed errore communi lapsus est.* Sallust in Hist. *Cætera multitudo, vulgi more magis quam judicio, post alius alium quasi prudentiorem secuti.*

to be forbidden, than prosecuted. And where Justice doth not exact this, yet 'tis agreeable to Goodness, agreeable to Modesty †, agreeable to Magnanimity. *By pardoning was increased the Greatness of the Roman People*, saith Sallust. Tacitus: *No less Gentleness is to be used toward suppliants, than stifness toward an enemy.* It is a memorable passage in the fourth Book to *Herennius*: *Well did our Ancesters observe this, to deprive no King of life, whom they had taken in War. Why so? Because it was not meet to use the power fortune had given in the punishment of them, whom the same fortune so lately had placed in the higest dignity. But did he not lead an Army against us? I will not remember that. Why so? Because it is the part of a valiant man to take them for enemies, that contend for victory; and to look upon the conquered, as men: that valour may diminish the danger of War, and Courtesy may encrease the honour of Peace. But would he have done so, had he overcom? Why then do you spare him? Because I use to contemn such folly, not to imitate it* †. *Perseus*, *Syphax*, *Gentius*, *Juba*, and in the time of the *Cesars*, *Caractacus* and others, escaped capital Punishment; so that it may appear, both the causes of

† King Theuderichus in Cassiodor 2. 41. saith, Those wars succeeded best with him, which were accompanied with most moderation: for He is a perpetual Conqueror, who is temperate in all things.

† In panegyrico tamen qui dictus est Constantino Constantii filio: *—cæteri in vinculis luce privati aliis regibus dedere documentum, ut mallent amicitiam colere Romanorum quam exasperare justitiam.* Nolim reduci hunc morem; tamen & Josua reges captos interfecit. Nimium hæc documenta sunt regibus ad modestiam.

War

war and the manner of waging it were considerd by the *Romans*: whom yet *Cicero* and others do confess to have been somewhat too sharp in the use of Victory. VVherefore *M. Æmilius Paulus*, in *Diodorus Siculus*, not amiss admonisheth the *Roman Senators*, in the Cause of *Perseus*: *If they feared nothing human, yet they should fear divine revenge, imminent over them that use their victory with too much pride and insolence.* And *Plutarch* notes, in the wars among the Greeks, the very enemies held their hands from the *Lacedemonian* Kings, in reverence of their dignity. An enemy therefore, that will regard, not that which human Laws permit, but that which is his duty, that which is good and pious, will spare even an Enemies blood: and will put none to death, but to avoid death himself, or somewhat like death, or els for sins proper to the person, which amount to capital offences. And yet, to some that deserve death, he will forgive, either all punishment, or that of death; either for humanity sake, or for other probable causes. Excellently saith the now-cited *Diodorus Siculus*: *Expugnations of Cities, prosperous fights, and whatsoever is in War successfull, more often proceed from fortune than from valour: but, in the highest power, to bestow mercy upon the Conquered, is the work of Providence alone**. Now, concerning the slaughter of them, who

Agide.

Lib. 27.

* Curtius; *Alexander, quamquam belli auctoribus poterat irasci, tamen omnibus venia data.*

who are killed by chance, not on purpose, we must remember, it is a part of mercy, if not of Justice, not without great causes and such as conduce to the safety of many, to enterprize such a thing, whence destruction may come upon the innocent. *Polybius* is of this mind, saying: *It is the part of good men, not to wage a destructive War, no not with the bad; but so far, that offences may be repaird and amended: not, to involve the innocent with the guilty in the same ruine; but for the innocent, to spare the guilty also.* Lib. 5.

XLV. *Children, Women, old Men, Priests, Scholars, husbandmen, are to be spared.*

UPon those premises, 'twil not be hard to determine of the specials that follow. *Let age excuse a child, sex a woman*, saith *Seneca* in the Books where he is angry with Anger. God himself, in the wars of the *Hebrews*, even after peace offerd and refus'd, will have women and infants spared; besides a few Nations excepted by special command; against which the war that was, was not of men, but of God; and so 'twas called. And when he ordered the *Madianitish* womē to be slain, for a proper crime of theirs, he excepted Virgins that were untoucht. Yea, when he had very severely threatned the *Ninivites* with destruction for their most heinous

Lib. 3. 24.

Deut. 20. 14.

nous sins, he suffered himself to be restreined by compassion upon many thousands of that age, that knew not good from evil. Like whereunto is that sentence of *Seneca : Is any one angry with children, whose age † doth not yet discern the differences of things ?* If God hath done and determined thus, who may without injustice slay any men of what sex or age soever without any cause, being the giver and Lord of life*; what is fitting for men to do, to whom he hath given no right over men, but what was necessary to human safety and the conservation of society ? Add here, concerning children, the judgment of those Nations and times wherein equity most prevailed. *We have Arms* (saith *Camillus* in *Livy*) *not against that age, which even in taking of Cities is spared, but against armed men. And this is among the Laws of War* : he means the Natural Laws.† *Plutarch* speaking of the same thing : *There are* (saith he) *among good men, certain Laws of War too.* VVhere note that, *among good men*, that you may descriminate this Law from that which is customary and consisteth in impunity. So *Florus* saith, * It could not otherwise be, without violation

De ira 2. 9.
Lucan. *crimine quo parvi cædem potuere mereri.*
† Pliny in his natural history 8. 16. saith : A Lyon, when he rageth, rageth upon men sooner than women, and not upon infants, unless provoked by great hunger. Philo of special laws 2. Many pretences may be found out against men of mature age, but against infants calumny it self can find nothing to say, as being clearly innocents. Josephus notes it in Manaem, as extreme cruelty, or rather barbarity, that he spared not Infants. Add that which Beda hath l. 2. c. 20. of the ferity of Carævolla: and a good Law of the Helvetians in Simler, and the pious commands of Q. Elizabeth in Camden in anno 1596. **Vict. de jure bell'i, n.* 36. † *Vita Camilli.* **Lib.* 1.

of

of integrity. In another place of *Livy*: *An age, from which Soldiers in their anger would abstein.* And elsewhere: *Their cruel wrath went on, even to the slaughtering of infants.* Now, that which hath place in children always, that have not attained the use of reason, for the most part prevails in women; that is, unless they have committed something peculiarly to be avenged, or do usurp manly Offices. For it is a sex, as *Statius* speaks, *that hath nothing to do with the sword* †. *Alexander* in *Curtius* *; *I am not used to wage war with Captives and Women.: he must be armed, to whom I am an enemy.* Grypus in Justin *. *None of his Ancestors, among so many domestick and external wars, did ever after victory shew cruelty to women, whom the softness of their sex exempteth from perils of War, and the rough handling of the Conquerors.* Another in *Tacitus*: *He carried arms against armed men, not against women.* *Valerius Maximus* * calls it barbarous and intolerable cruelty which *Munatius Flaccus* shewed to Infants and Women. *Latinus Pacatus* saith, *Women are a sex which wars do spare.* *Papinius* hath the same of old men: *They are a company violable by no arms.* The same is to be determined universally of males, whose course of life abhorres from war. *By the Law of War, they that are armed and resist are slain*, as *Livy* speaketh: that is, by

Lib. 24.

† *Sexus rudis insciusq; ferri.* Statius. Neroni hostem vocanti Octaviam in Trag. reponit præfectus, *Fœmina hoc nomen capit.* Ideo Tucca & Varus delendos censuere in 2. Æn. versus, ubi deliberat Æneas, an Helenam occidat.

* Lib. 5.

* Lib. 38.

* Lib. 9. c. 1.

Papin: *Nullis violabilis armis Turba senes.* *Vict. d. loco.*

Lib. 28.

by that Law which agrees with Nature. So *Josephus* saith; It is meet, that in fight they be punisht that use weapons, no hurt must be done the guiltless. *Camillus* at the taking of *Veia* proclamed, that the unarmed should not be touched. In this rank are first to be placed, Ministers of Sacred things: for these by the antient custom of all Nations abstein from arms, and therfore no force was offerd them. So the *Philistins*, enemies of the Jews, did no harm to the College of the Prophets * that was at *Gaba*, as we may see, 1 *Sam.* 10. 5, 10. And so, to another place, where was the like College, as secluded from all injury of arms, *David* fled with *Samuel*, 1 *Sam.* 19. 18. The *Cretians*, † *Plutarch* tells us, when they were embroiled in Civil War, saved the Priests * from all harm, and those whom they called κατακαῦται, men that had the care of burials. *Strabo* † notes, when all *Greece* in old time was enflam'd with war, the *Eleans*, as being sacred to *Jupiter*, and their guests, lived in secure peace. With Priests are justly equald in this respect, they that have chosen a like kind of life, as *Monks* and *Penitents*; whom therefore, as well as Priests, the Canons following naturall equity, will have spared *. To these you may deservedly add those, who give

Antiq. 12. 3.

Liv. lib. 5.

* Hircanus besieging Jerusalem sent Sacrifices to the Temple, as the Hebrews relate. So the Goths are praised by Procopius, who spared the Priests of Peter and Paul without Rome. *Gotth. 2. vide Legem Longobard. l. 1, t. 11. 14.*

† Quæst. Gr.

* Serv. ad 7. Æn. *Nam eum defendebat à bello, si non ætas, saltem religio Sacerdotis.*

† *Et Polyb. l. 4. & Diod. Siculus in exc. Peiresc.* Likewise they that went to the Olympian, Pythian, Nemean, Isthmian Games, in the time of War, had safeguard and security. *Thucyd. l. 5. & 8. Plutarch. Arato.* * *C. de treug. & pace.*

give themselves to the studies of good learning, and sciences useful to mankind. After these, Husbandmen; whom the Canons also adscribe. *Diodorus Siculus** reports of the *Indians* to their praise: *In battells the Enemies kill one another, but they meddle not with Husbandmen, as men that are profitable to the publick.* Of the antient *Corinthians* and *Megareans*, *Plutarch*: *None of them did Husbandmen any harm.* And *Cyrus* sent a message to the King of *Assyrians*, *That he was ready to save those that tild the ground, from all indemnity.* *Suidas*, of *Belisarius*: *He was so tender of the Countrymen, and took so much care of them, that, whilst he commanded, none of them ever had any violence offerd him.* The Canon addes Merchants; which is not only to be understood of them that stay for a time in the enemies quarters, but of perpetual subjects: For their life hath nothing to do with Arms. And under this name are conteind also other Workmen and Artificers, whose gain loves not War, but Peace.

* Lib. 2. Bibl.

Xenoph. de Cyri. inst. 5.

XLVI. *Captives, and They that yield, are not to be killed.*

THat we may come to them that have born arms, we have afore related the saying of *Pyrrhus* in *Seneca*, that we are forbidden by *Pudor*, *i. e.* by respect of equity, to take away a Captives life; a like sentence of *Alexander* we had, wherein Captives are joind with women. Let that of S. *Augustin* be added: *Let not Will, but Necessity* † *slay a fighting Enemy. As violence is rendred to him that warreth and resisteth, so to one conquerd*

Ad Bonifac. epist. 1.

† *Plutarchus Marcello*: Epaminondas and Pelopidas, neither killed any after victory, nor brought Cities into servitude; and the Thebans, it is believ'd, would not have done what they did against the Orchomenians, if they had been present. Marcellus followed their example, having taken Syracuse, as Plutarch there saith. See the same Plutarch in his Cato Uticensis. *Procopius Persic.* 1. When Cabad King of Persia had taken Amida by force, and much slaughter was made, an old Priest told him, it was not royal to kil those whom he had taken. *Idem Persic.* 2. To rage against captives is contrary to piety. In the same Author is an excellent oration of Belisarius to his Soldiers, *Gott.* 2. The Emperor Alexius in Annas Comnenas saith to one, perswading him to kill the Scythian Captives: Though Scythians, yet they are Men; though enemies, yet are they worthy of compassion. *Gregoras lib* 6. What is done in the heat of battell is capable of pardon, whatever it be, because at that time the hand is not governd by reason; but when the danger is past, and there is time to examin and judge, to let the hand be unruly, and do things undecent, is a token of an evil mind. See Chalcocondylas, of the laudable custom of the Polonians. Julian in his second Laudation of Constantin, under whose person he describes a good Prince: Being Conqueror in battell, he eased the sword of any further work, thinking it great impiety to take away life from one that ceaseth to defend himself.

or

or taken, mercy is now due, especially to one not likely to trouble our Peace. Xenophon of *Agesilaus*: *He charged his Soldiers, that they should not punish Captives, as guilty, but keep them, as men.* Diodorus Siculus: *All* (the Greeks) *oppose themselves to such as resist; and spare such as submit.* In the judgment of the same Author, The *Macedonians* under *Alexander* dealt more extremely with the *Thebans*, than the Law of War would permit. *Sallust*, in his *Jugurthin* History, having related the slaughter of the yong men after they had yielded, saith, *It was done against the Law of War*: which is, against the nature of Equity, and the manner of milder persons †. *Tacitus* * commends *Primus Antonius* and *Varus*, *Flavian* Commanders, because they never shewed cruelty after battell †. The Prophet *Elisha* speaks about Captives to the King of *Samaria*, thus *: *Wouldst thou smite those whom thou hast taken captive with thy sword, and with thy bow* †? The *Byzantians* and *Chalcedonians*, because they had killed a good number of Captives, are marked with this Elogy in *Diodorus Siculus* *: *They did acts of exceeding great Cruelty.* The same Author elswhere calls it *Common-right* to spare Captives †: whosoever do other-

Lib. 13.

Lib. 17.

† Lactantius l. ✠ *Parcitur Victis, & est locus inter arma Clementiæ.*

* Histor. 4.

† Aristides de Pace, 2. *Hominum est nostri ingenii resistentes armis coercere, prostratos tractare leniter.*

* 2 Reg. 6. 22.

† Apud Euripidem in Heraclidis quærenti nuntio,

Hostem perimere vestra Lex ergo verat?
Respondet Chorus,
Quem Mars reliquit prælio superstitem.

Ibidem Euristheus Captivus :

Quæ me necabunt , non erunt puræ manus.

* Lib. 12. † Capitol. M. Antonio. *Æquitatem etiam circa captos hostes custodivit.*

wise , without controversy (saith he) they do amiss. To spare Captives , 'is a command of Goodness and Equity, saith *Seneca* *; and in Histories we find them every where commended, who, when too great a number of Captives might be burdensome or dangerous , chose rather to let them all go, than to slay them. For the same causes, they that yield up themselves, covenanting for the saving of their lives ; whether in battell or in a siege, are not to be rejected †. Therefore *Arrian* saith, the slaughter made by the *Thebans* upon those that yielded , was not according to the manner of the *Grecians*. Likewise in *Thucydides* * : *Ye receiv'd us willing, and stretching forth our hands : and the Grecians use not to kill such.* The *Syracusian* Senators in *Diodorus Siculus*; *It is worthy of a Noble mind, to spare a suppliant.* Sopater : *To save suppliants , is a custom in Wars.* In towns besieged, 'twas observed by the *Romans* , before the *Ram* had smitten the wall. *Cæsar* * denounceth to the *Advatici* , He would save their City, if, before the *Ram* had touched the wall , they yielded. Which is still in use , in weak places , before the Great Guns are fired : in stronger places , before an Assalt is made upon the walls. But *Cicero* *, not so much respecting what is done , as what

* De benef. 5. c. 18.

† The Romans to the Persians in the fort of *Petra, Goth*.4. We take pity on you, while you strive with your yoke, and we would spare you though you desire death, and save you against your wills , as becomes Christians and Citizens of the Roman Empire. *Vide Serranum in rebus Franc. 1. & Henrici 2.*

* *Thucyd. lib.* 3.

* *Cæs. l.* 2. *de bello Gallico.*

* *Cic. Offic.* 1.

what ought to be done, delivers his judgment thus; *As you must consult for the good of those whom you have subdued by force, so are they to be receiv'd into protection (though the* Ram *hath smitten the wall) who lay down their arms, and fly to the mercy of the Generals.* The *Hebrew* Interpreters observe, That their Ancestors had a custom, when they besieged a City, not to engirt it round, but to leave one part open for those that would fly †, to the end the less blood might be shed at Taking of it. The same Equity commands, that They be spared, who without conditions submit themselves to the Conqueror, or become suppliants. *To kill them that call for mercy, is cruel*, saith *Tacitus* *. *Sallust* * also, of the *Campsanians*, who yielded themselves to *Marius*, when he had related the slaughter of the yong men, addes, *It was done against the Law of War*, that is, the Natural Law. The same elswhere *, *Not men armed, nor in battell according to the Law of war, but suppliants were slain* †. Yea, This is also to be endevoured, that they may rather be constrained through fear to yield, than be slain. This is prais'd in *Brutus*; *who sufferd not his men to do execution upon his Adversaries, but surrounded them with his Horse, commanding them to be spared, as those that would presently be His.*

† So Scipio Æmilianus at the overthrowing of Carthage, proclamed, They should fly that would. *Polybius.*

* Annal. 12.

* Bello Jug.

* L. 1. de ord. Rep.

† Livio; *jure belli in armatos repugnantesq; cædes*. & alibi; *qui deditis contra jus ac fas bellum intulisset* lib. 45.

XLVII. *Objections answered.*

AGainst these Precepts of equity and Natural Law, are wont to be brought exceptions very unjust: to wit, if talion be exacted, if there be need of error, if there was an obstinate resistance. But, that these things are not sufficient to justify slaughter, he will easily conceive, who remembreth what we have set down afore about the just causes of killing. From
Vide Vict. de jure belli, n. 49. & 60. Captives, and those that yield or desire to yield, there is no danger: that therefore they may be justly killed, there must be some antecedent Crime, and that such a one, as an equal judge would think worthy of death. And so we see sometimes great severity shewed to Captives, and those that have yielded; or, their yielding on condition of life not accepted; if, after they were convinced of the injustice of the War, they had nevertheless persisted in arms; if they had blotted their enemies name with unsufferable disgraces; if they had violated their faith, or any right of Nations, as of Embassadors; if they were fugitives. But, Nature admits not talion, except against the same persons that have offended; nor doth it suffice, that the enemies are by a fiction conceived to be as it were one body, as may
P. 2. n. 113. be understood by what is said above *, of the Communication of punishments. We

read

read in *Aristides, Is it not absurd to imitate, what you do condemn?* *Plutarch* for this accuseth the *Syracusians*, that they slew the wives and children of *Hicetas*, only for this reason, because *Hicetas* had slain the wife, sister, and son of *Dion*. Moreover, the benefit which is hoped from terror for the future, perteins not to the giving of a right to kill; but, if there is a right, it may be among the causes for which that right is not remitted. And, For a more obstinate affection to ones own side, if the cause maintained is not at all dishonourable, that deserves not punishment, as the *Neapolitans* discourse in *Procopius*: or, if there is any punishment thereof, it ought not amount to death; for an equal Judge would not so determine. *Alexander*, at a certain town, when he had commanded all the youth to be slain; because they made so sharp resistence, seemed to the *Indians* to wage war after the manner of Robbers: and the King fearing such a blemish of his Name began to use his victory more mildly. It was better done by the same King, to spare the *Milesians*: *because he saw they were gallant men, and faithful to their own party*: which are the words of *Arrian*. *Phyto* Governor of *Regium*, when, for defending the town so stoutly, he was by command of *Dionysius* drawn to torture and death, cryed out, He was punisht, because he would not break his trust

De pace 2.

Plut. Timon. & Dione.

Lib. 1. Gotth.

Polyan. lib. 4.

trust and betray the place, but God would suddenly revenge it. *Diodorus Siculus* styleth these ἐκνόμους τιμωρίας, unlawfull punishments. I am very much pleas'd with that vote in *Lucan* †.

† Lucan.

——— ———Vincat quicunq; necesse
Non putat in victos sævum distringere ferrum,
Quiq; suos cives, quod signa adversa tulerunt,
Non credit fecisse nefas.— ——— ———

May he be Conqueror, who means to spare
His Fellow-Citizens, that adverse are:

Provided, by the Name of Fellow-Citizens we understand, not those of this or that Nation, but of that common Countrey of all Mankind. Least of all is Slaughter justifyed by grief and anger for some overthrow receiv'd, as we read *Achilles*, *Æneas*, *Alexander*, sacrificed to their friends the blood of Captives and such as yielded †: Wherfore *Homer* justly saith of *Achilles* on this occasion: *He resolved on a wicked act.*

† This seemed cruel to after-ages, as Servius notes upon the 10. of the Æneis.

XLVIII.

XLVIII. *The Multitude spared. Hostages spared. Needless fights to be avoided.*

MOreover, where offenses are of that nature, that they may seem worthy of death, it will be a point of Mercy, because of the Multitude of them, to remit somewhat of extreme right. Of which clemency we have God himself for Author, who was pleased, that Peace should be offerd to the *Cananites* and their neighboring Nations, offenders in the highest degree; such a Peace, as allowed them life on condition of being tributaries. Pertinent here is that of *Seneca*: *The Severity of a General shews it self against particulars: but pardon is necessary, where the whole Army is revolting. What takes away Anger from a wise man? The Multitude of Transgressors* †. And that of *Lucan* *:

2. *De ira. cap.* 10.

† *Quicquid multis peccatur, inultum est.* Scholiastes Inv. ex Lucano. August. epist. 64. *Magis monendo, quàm minando: Sic enim agendum est cum multitudine peccantium: severitas autem exercenda est in peccata paucorum.*

* *Tot simul infesto juvenes occumbere letho,*
Sæpe fames, pelagiq; furor, subitæq; ruinæ,
Aut cœli terræq; lues, aut bellica clades,
Nunquam pœna fuit. Lucan.

Plagues,

Plagues, Famine, Ruines, Storm, or
Fights have sent
So many to their grave: not Punishment.

. *Casting of Lots was ordained*, saith Cicero, *that too many might not be punished.* Sallust to Cesar: *No man exhorteth you to cruel punishments, or bitter sentences, whereby a City is rather wasted than reformed.* As to Hostages, what is to be determined out of the Law of Nature may be seen above. Of old, when it was commonly believed, that every one had as much power over his own life as over other things within his propriety; and that that power, by consent either tacit or express, was devolved from every particular person upon the Commonwealth; it is the less to be admir'd, if we read, Hostages (though in themselves innoxious) were put to death for the offense of the Commonwealth, either as by their own peculiar, or as by the publick consent, wherein their own was included also. But after that the more true and perfect Wisedom
Vict. de jure belli. n. 43. hath taught us, that Dominion over life is excepted by God, it follows, that by consent alone no man can give to any, power and right over the life either of himself, or of his Citizen. And therefore it seem'd atrocity to *Narses* a good General, to take punishment of innoxious
Lib. 1. Hostages, as *Agathias* tells us: (and other

ther Authors say the like of others :) even by *Scipio*'s example, who said he would not shew his displeasure upon harmless Hostages †, but upon those that had revolted : and, that he would not take revenge of the unarmed, but of the armed enemy. Now, that among the later Lawyers some of great name, say such agreements are of force, if they be confirm'd by custom, I admit it, if by *right* they mean *impunity* only, which in this argument often comes under that appellation : But, if they suppose them free from sin, who by agreement alone take away any ones life, I fear they are deceiv'd themselves, and by their perilous authority deceive others. Clearly, if he that comes an Hostage, be, or were before, in the number of grievous delinquents; or, if afterward he hath broke his faith given by him in a great matter ; possibly, the punishment may be free from injury. But *Clodia*, who came not an Hostage of her own accord *, but by Order of the City, when she had passed *Tyber* and escaped, was not only safe, but praised for her Vertue by the *Etruscian* King, as *Livy* * speaks in this History. We must here add this, all combates which are of no use to obtein right, or end the War, but have meer ostentation of strength proposed to them *, are contrary, both to the office of a Christian man, and to Humanity it self. Therefore Rulers ought seriously

† Livius, lib. 28. The same saith Julian, in Nicetas. l. 2.

Menoch. arb. q. 7.

* Compare the story of Hostages refusing that burthen, and punisht for it, in Nicetas, l. 2.

* *Liv. lib.* 2.

† *Id est, ut Græci loquuntur,* ἐπίδειξιν ῥώμης μᾶλλον ἢ πρὸς πολεμίους ἀγῶνα.

Art. 1.

ously to forbid them, being to render an account for blood unprofitably shed, to Him in whose stead they bear the sword. Surely, *Sallust* also hath commended Generals, that bought their victories at the least expence of blood; And *Tacitus* saith of the *Catti*, a people of approved valour: *Their excursions and fortuitous fights were seldom* †.

† Plutarch reprehends Demetrius for exposing his soldiers to dangers, and thrusting them into battells, rather out of a desire of glory, than for any Advantage.

Cap. 12. XLIX. A Temperament about wast, and the like. *What wast is just. When not to be made.*

THat one may destroy the Goods of another, one of these three things is a necessary antecedent: either such a necessity which ought to be understood excepted in the first institution of dominion, as, if one to avoid his *danger*, throw away down the river a third man's sword, which a mad man is about to use; in which very case yet, it is the truer opinion, that there remains an obligation of repairing the loss: or, some *debt* proceeding from inequality, to wit, that the thing wasted or lost may be reckoned for that debt, as receiv'd; for otherwise there were no right: or, some evil *desert*, whereto such a punishment is meet, or whose measure the punishment doth not exceed; for, as a a Divine of sound judgment rightly notes, that for cattel driven away, or some houses fir'd, a whole Kingdom should be laid wast, is no equity; which also *Polybius* saw, who will have punishment in war not run on *in infinitum*, but so far, that Offenses may be in fit manner expiated.. And these causes truly, (and only within these bounds,) bring it to pass, that there is no injury. Notwithstanding, unless the cause of *Profit* perswade, it's folly to hurt another without Good to himself. Wise men therefore use to be mov'd by their own Interests. The chief is that, observed by *Onesander*; *Let him be sure to wast the Enemies Countrey, to burn and populate; for scarcity of money and fruits minishes war* *, *as much as plenty encreases it*. Wherewith agrees that of *Proclus*, '*Tis the part of a good General to cut off the enemies provisions on every side*. *Curtius*, of *Darius*: *He supposed, by want to overcome his enemy, having nothing but what he got by rapine*. And that population truly is to be born with, which doth in short time humble the enemy to a petition for Peace; which kind of war *Halyattes* used upon the *Milesians*, the *Thracians* upon the *Byzantians*, the *Romans* upon the *Campanians Carpenates*, *Spaniards*, *Ligures*, *Nervians*, *Menapians*; But, if you rightly weigh the matter, you shall find such things done more often out of hatred, than

Vict. de jure belli, n. 52. & 56.

Polyb. lib. 5.

Strat. c. 6.

* Philo de vita contemplativa: *Solent hostes vastare & arboribus nudare terram hostilem, ut hostes eo facilius se dedant, rerum necessariarum penuriâ.* Idem de diris: *Duplex sibi malum acquirunt, inopiam amicis, copiam hostibus.*

Herod. l. 1. Pol. l. 4. Front. strat. 3. cap. 4. Liv. l. 5. 3. 34. 40. Cæs. de bel. Gal. lib. 6.

than prudence. For, most commonly it happens, that either those moving causes cease, or other causes move the other way more strongly. *First*, This will come to pass, if we our selves so possess a fruitful thing, that it cannot bring any fruit to the enemies. Whereunto properly that Law Divine hath respect, which will have wild Trees bestowed upon works of war, but the fruitful kept for food, the cause being added, that Trees cannot, as Men do, rise against us in a battell. Which, by similitude of reason, *Philo* enlarged also to fruitful fields †. And *Josephus* upon the same place saith, Trees, if they had a voice, would cry out that they do unjustly bear the punishments of war, being not the causes of war. Nor hath that of *Pythagoras* (if I mistake not) any other rise, in *Jamblichus*: *Do not hurt, nor cut up any mild and fruit-bearing Tree.* And *Porphyry* describing the manners of the Jews, extends this Law * (custom as I think in terpreting it) even to beasts serving for Countrey-work. For these also must be spared in war, as *Moses* hath commanded.

† Philo de creat: ubi legi hæc verba affingit: *Quid rebus inanimis quæ & mites sunt & mites fructus ferunt irasceris? An vero in morem hominum qui hostes sunt, inimicitiæ significationem arbores prodant, ut pro his quæ faciunt aut facere minantur stirpitus evellendæ sint? Quin prosunt victoribus præbentq; copiam rerum quas necessitas exigit, imo, & voluptatem. Non soli homines tributa ferunt, sed meliora arbores statis temporibus, ac talia ut sine iis vivere non detur.* Alter ejusdem locus de Humanitate: *Æquitatem suam etiam largius dispensans Moses valde ea ubertim ac liberaliter utitur, discedens à ratione utentibus ad muta animantia, ab his verò ad ea quæ è terra nascuntur, &c.* * Porphyr: *Parci etiam jubet lex, in terra quamvis hostili, animantibus operum socius, ita ut ea occidere non liceat.*

But

But the *Talmud*-writings and the *Hebrew* Interpreters add, that this Law is to be stretched * to every thing, which may perish without cause, as, if buildings be burnt, things to be eaten and drank be corrupted. Agreeable to this Law is the prudent moderation of *Timotheus* the *Athenian* Captain, who, as *Polyænus* relates, *suffer'd no house to be pull'd down, nor fruit-tree to be cut up.* There is a Law of *Plato* in his fift *De repub. That no ground be wasted, no house fired.* Much more will this have place after complete victory. *Cicero* * approves not the overthrow of *Corinth*, though the Embassadors of the *Romans* were shamefully treated there: and the same *Cicero* in another place, saith, it is a horrible, nefarious, odious War, that is made with walls, roofs, pillars, posts. *Livy* praiseth the lenity of the *Romans*, because having taken *Capua*, they were not furious† in firing and ruining the innocent walls and building. *Agamemnon* in *Seneca* saith, *He was willing Troy should be conquerd, not levell'd.* Indeed, the sacred History tells us that some Cities were by God condemned to destruction: and, that against the former general Law the trees of the *Moabites* were commanded to be cut up. But, that was not done by hostile hatred, but in just detestation of

* Yet with this exception, unless trees in suburbs hinder the shooters.

* *De Offic.* 1. *Pro domo sua ad ad Pont.*

† Excellent to this purpose is the letter of Belisarius to Totilas, wherein he saith, It was thought a part of wise and civil men, to erect fair buildings; to demolish them was the part of those that blush not to leave to posterity marks of their foolish cruelty, &c. *Vide Procop. Gotth.* 3.

Equidem fatebor (pace dixisse hoc tua Argiva tellus liceat) affligi Phrygas Vincique volui; ruere & æquari solo Etiam arguissem. Seneca Troad.

Jos. 6.
2 Reg. 3. 19.

of their Iniquities, which were either publickly known, or ſentenc'd to ſuch puniſhment by the Judgment of God himſelf. *Secondly*, That which we have ſaid will alſo come to paſs, in a doubtful poſſeſſion of a Countrey, if there be great hope of a ſpeedy victory, whoſe reward will be both the Countrey and the fruit. So the Great *Alexander*, as *Juſtin* * relates, kept his ſoldiers from the population of *Aſia, Bidding them ſpare their own* †, *and not ſpoil what they came to take poſſeſſion of*. So *Quintius*, when *Philip* ſpoiled *Theſſaly* with a running Army, exhorted his ſoldiers, as † *Plutarch* ſaith, to march as through a Country granted them, and now becom their own. * *Craſus* perſwading *Cyrus*, not to give up *Lydia* to be pillaged by his men, tells him, *You will not ſpoil my City, not my Goods: For they are not mine now. They are yours, and the plundering ſoldiers prey upon you* *. *Thirdly*, it will be ſo, if the enemy can have elſwhere wherewith to ſupport himſelf: to wit, if the Sea, or another Country be open to him. *Archidamus* in *Thucydides* in his oration wherein he dehorteth his *Lacedemonians* from a war upon the *Athenians*, asketh what hopes they have. *Do you hope eaſily to lay waſt the Attick fields by your nu-*

* *Juſtin. l.* 5.

† Gelimer and the Vandals beſieging Carthage, neither took the prey, nor waſted the land, but were as careful of it, as of their own: *Procop. Vandalic.* 2. Apud Helmoldum lego, l. 1. c. 66. *Nonne terra quam devaſtamus terra noſtra eſt, & populus quem expugnamus populus noſter eſt? Quare ergo invenimur hoſtes noſtrimet, & diſſipatores vectigalium noſtrorum?* Vide Bembum. l. 9. Parutam hiſt. 6.

† *Vit. Flamin.* * *Herod. lib.* 1. * Sen. Theb. *Nemo ſic vaſtat ſua. Quæ corripi igne, quæ meti gladio jubes, Aliena credis.*

merous

merous Army? Suppose you do: Yet have they, both other Lands under their command (Thracia & Ionia) *and the Sea brings them in all things necessary.* Wherfore in such a case it is best, that agriculture also in the very frontiers be secured. Which we have lately seen was long done in the *Low Countrey Wars*, on condition of paying Contribution to both sides. And that is consentaneous to the old custom of the *Indians*, among whom, as *Diodorus Siculus* saith, *The Husbandmen are untoucht, and as it were sacred; yea, nigh to the Camps and Troops, they do their work without danger.* He addes, *They neither burn the Enemies fields, nor cut up the trees.* After: *No Soldier doth any wrong to any Husbandman; but that kind of men, labouring for the common good, is protected from all injuries.* And, between *Cyrus* and the *Assyrian* was an Agreement, saith *Xenophon*, *That they should have Peace with the Plough-man, war with the Soldier.* So *Timotheus* † let out to Husbandmen the most fruitful part of the land, as *Polyænus* saith: Yea, as *Aristotle* addes, he sold the fruits themselves to the enemy, and paid his soldiers with the money. Which *Appian* testifies was done in *Spain* by *Viriatus*. And the very

Lib. 2.

† Plutarch in his Greek questions hath the same of the Megareans: Procopius in the third of his Goth. of Totilas when he besieged Rome, saith

He did no hurt to the Husband-men through all Italy, but commanded them, as they were wont, to till the earth with safety, so that they brought him tribute. This saith Cassiodor, is the greatest praise. 12. 15.

ſame, in the *Belgic* war now mention'd, we have ſeen done with very great reaſon and advantage, to the admiration of ſtrangers. Theſe manners, the Canons * being teachers of humanity do propoſe to the imitation of all Chriſtians, as thoſe that owe and profeſs more humanity than other men: and therefore will have not husbandmen only, but alſo the plowing catell and the ſeed which they carry to the field, plac'd without the danger of war: upon ſuch like ground, as the Civil Laws * forbid the inſtruments of husbandry to be taken for a pledge; and among the *Phrygians* and *Cyprians* of old, afterward among the *Atticks* and *Romans* *, to kill the plowing Oxe was a heinous matter. *Fourthly*, it happens that ſome things be of that nature, that they have no moment to make or continue war: which things reaſon will have ſpared, even while the war laſts. Hither belongs that ſpeech of the *Rhodians* to *Demetrius* * the Town-taker, for the picture of *Jalyſus*, expreſt by *Gellius* after this manner: † *What madneſs is it for you to deſtroy that image by firing of the houſes? for if you overcome us and take the town, the Image alſo ſafe and ſound will be the reward of your victory: but if you beſiege us in vain, pray conſider how diſhonourable it will be for you, becauſe you cannot conquer the Rhodians, to ſhew your ſpight againſt a * dead Painter.* Po-

* *C. 2. de treug. & pace. Nic. Damaſc. Ælian. 5. 14. Dion. Chry. orat. 64.*

* *L. execut. C. quæ res pign.*

* Etiam in Peloponneſo. *Varr. 2. de re ruſt. Columel. princip. lib. 6. Plin 8. 45. Ælian. de hiſt. anim. 2. cap. ult. Porphyr. 2. de abſtinen. Veget. 3. de arte veterin.*

* *Vide Plin. Hiſt. Natur. 8. 38. & 35. 10. & Plutarchum Demetrio.*

† *Gell. l. 15. 31.*

* *Protogenes. Polyb. l. 5.*

lybius

lybius saith, it is the part of a raving mind to spoil things, which diminish not the enemies strength when they are spoild, nor add any emolument to the spoiler, such as are Temples, Galleries, Statues, and the like. *Marcellus spared all the Houses of the Syracusians both publick & private, sacred and profane, as if he had come thither with an Army not to conquer, but to defend them.* *Cicero* speaks it to his praise; and the same *Cicero*, after: *Our Ancestors left unto the Conquered, what seemed pleasing to them, light to us.* *Verrin. 2.*

L. *Things Sacred and Religious are not to be spoyled.*

NOw, as this hath place in other ornaments for the reason above mentiond, so a special reason is added in things dedicate to holy uses. For, although these things also, as hath been said, are after their manner publick, and therefore by the Law of Nations are impunely violated; yet, if no danger may come thence, the reverence of things Divine requires *, that

* *Polybius in excerp. Peires.* When thou art angry with men, to be impious therefore against the gods is a sign of the greatest folly. Better it is, said Severus, that God should be any way worshipt there, than it should be turnd into a stable. *Lampr.* Annibal, for religion sake, spared the temple of Diana at Saguntum. *Plin. Nat. Hist.* 16. 2. We do not take away their Temples from enemies and foreiners. *Appian.* Of the Religion of Agesilaus, See the Latin writer of his life, and Plutarch; Who communicateth this praise to many Romans, in Sulla. *Vid. Brodæum* 5. *Miscel.* Cabao the Moor, being no Christian himself, honoured the

Churches of Christians, which the Vandals had profaned, against whom he hoped the Christians God, who ere he was, would shew his displeasure. *Procop. Vand.* 1. Chosroes the Persian, no Christian, spared the Christians Church at Antioch. *Pers.* 2. Justinian also durst not retein the things Vespasian had brought to Rome out of the Temple at Hierusalem, and being found at Rome Gizerichus had carried into Africa. *Vandal.* 2. How the Mahumetans sav'd the holiness of that place, where the bones of Ezechiel and Daniels three fellows were buried, is testified by Benjamin the Jew in his Itinerary.

such buildings and the things perteining to them be conserved; specially among them, who worship the same God according to the same Law, though perchance in some opinions and rites they differ *. *Thucydides* saith, it was the Law among the *Greeks* of his time, that the Invaders of their Enemies should abstein from holy places. *Alba* being overthrown by the *Romans*, *Livy* saith, they spared the Temples of the Gods †. Against *Q. Fulvius* the Censor, *Livy* * relates, it was said: *He engaged the people of Rome in sacrilege by the ruins of Temples, as if the immortal Gods were not the same every where, but some were to be worshipped and adorned with the spoils of others.* But *Marcius Philippus* *, when he came to *Dium* to encampe under the walls of the Temple, gave command, that nothing should be violated in the holy

* *Silv. de bello. p.* 3. *n.* 5.

† De Romanis Capua capta sic Silius lib. 13.
Ecce repens tacito percurrit pectora sensu
Religio, & saevas componit numine mentes,
Ne flammam taedasq; velint, ne templa sub uno
In cinerem sedisse rogo.

* *Liv.* 42.

* *Lib.* 44.

ly place. *Strabo* * relates, that the *Tectosages*, who with others had taken away the *Delphic* treasure, to pacify the God at home dedicated the same with an additament. That we may come to Christians, *Agathias* commemorates, that the *Franks*, being of the same Religion with the *Greeks*, spared their Temples. Yea, and men were usually spared for the Temples sake: which (not to allege the many examples of profane Nations, this being the common custom * among the *Greeks*) S. *Augustin* thus commends in the *Gotths* † that took *Rome*: *Witness the places of the Martyrs, and the Royal structures of the Apostles, which in that Vastation entertain'd the Conquered, their own and aliens, flying to them. Hitherto did the bloody enemy rage: here his furious slaughter was bounded: hither were led by the compassionat enemies, they that had been spared other where, that they might not fall into their hands that had not the like compassion. Who yet, though elswhere cruelly raging, after they came to these places* *, *where that was forbidden which had been permitted elswhere by the Law of War, all the immanity of their rage was refrained, and their desire of taking Captives cooled.* What I have said of Sacred places, is likewise to be understood of Religious, even of those that are built for the honour of the dead. For also these, though the Law of Nations indulgeth im-

* *Stra. l.* 4.

Lib. 2.

* *Diod. lib.* 19.

L. 1. *de C.D.*

† Under Alarichus: of whom Cassiodore relates this memorable act, 12. 20. That when the Vessels of S. Peter were brought to him by his men, he sent them back by the same hands, that they might blot out their sacrilege by their devotion.

* Not only Christians but Barbarians have been allowed the benefit of Sanctuary. *Vid. Zosim. l.* 4. *de Tomit. barb.*

 punity

punity to anger exercised therein, cannot be violated without contempt of Humanity. Greatest is that reason, say the Lawyers, which makes for Religion. *Euripides* hath a pious sentence, as well for Religious as sacred places:

L. sunt personæ. D. de religios.
Eurip. Troad.

> *Who Cities, Sepulchers and Temples wast,*
> *Are Fools, and ruinate themselves at last.*

Apollonius Tyanaus did thus interpret the Fable of the Giants oppugning heaven: *They offerd force to the Temples and seats of the Gods. Statius* accuseth *Annibal* of sacrilege, *who set fire on the Altars of the Gods. Scipio* having taken *Carthage* rewarded his Soldiers with gifts, *Those excepted, who had inur'd the Temple of Apollo* *. *Cæsar*, as *Dion* * saith, durst not take away the Trophy raised by *Mithridates, being sacred to the Gods of War.* His Religion would not suffer *Marcus Marcellus* to touch the things that victory had profan'd, saith *Cicero*: and he addes, There are some enemies, who in war retein the rights of Religion and of customs. The same elswhere saith, the war of *Brennus* against *Apollo's* Temple was nefarious. The deed of *Pyrrhus*, who had robbed the Treasury of *Proserpina*, *Livy* calls a foul deed and done in contempt of the Gods. Such another act of *Hamilco*

** Appian. Pun.*
** Lib. 42.*
Verrina 4.

Hamilco is call'd impiety and ſin againſt the Gods, by *Diodorus*. The war of *Philip* the now cited *Livy* calls nefarious too, as waged againſt the Gods both above and below; wickedneſs alſo, and madneſs. *Florus* of the ſame: *Philip, beyond the right of victory, ſpar'd neither Temples, Altars, nor Sepulchers* *. *Polybius* touching the ſame ſtory, addes his judgment thus: *To ſpoil things which will neither be profitable to us for war, nor hurtful to our enemies, Temples eſpecially, and Images, and the like ornaments in them, is undeniably the work of a mind miſchievous and madded with anger.* And in the ſame place he admits not the excuſe of *Talion*, or rendring like for like.

Lib. 14.

* The like fact of Pruſias is detected by Polybius, whoſe words Suidas hath preſerved, in vocab. Pruſ.

LI. *The utilities of Moderation.*

ALthough it be not properly a part of our deſign here to inquire what is uſeful, but to reſtrain the looſneſs of warring to that which is lawful by Nature, or among things lawful is better; yet will Vertue herſelf, vile in this evil Age, be pleaſ'd to excuſe me, if, ſeeing ſhe is contemned by herſelf, I add eſteem to her from the Conſideration of profit. Firſt then, that Moderation in preſerving things which do not retard the war, deprives the Enemy of a mighty weapon, deſperation. It is *Archidamus*'s ſaying in *Thucydides*, *Think the Enemies Country no other than* *a hostage, and so much the better, as it is more fertile; wherefore also spare it as much as is possible, lest despair make them more hard to be conquerd.* The same was the Counsil of *Agesilaus*, when, against the opinion of the *Achaians*, he left the *Acarnans* a free seeding time, saying, the more they sowed, the more desirous would they be of Peace. The *Satyrist* to our purpose *:

Xen. hist. Gr. 4. & Plutarch. Agesilao.

* Spoliatis arma supersunt.

——After such harms,
And losses suffer'd, what remains but
Arms?

Livy speaking of the City taken by the *Galls*: *It pleased* (saith he) *the Chief of the* Galls, *that all the houses should not be fired: that the remainder of the City might be a means to soften and bow the heart of the enemy.* Add, that this Moderation, while the war continues, maketh shew of great confidence of the victory: and that clemency is apt of it self to move and win the mind. *Annibal* in *Livy* makes no spoil in the fields of *Tarentum*: *It appeared* (saith he) *'twas not done out of the modesty either of the Soldiers or of the Captain, but to gain the affections of the Tarentines.* For like cause *Augustus Cæsar* in *Pannonia* absteind from rapine. *Dion* tells us, why: *He had hope by this means to win them without violence. Timotheus*, by that care of his aforemen-

Lib. 34.

Lib. 49.

tion'd

tion'd, beside other things, *aimed at the good will of his Enemies*; as *Polybius* observeth. Lib. 3. Of *Quintius*, and the *Romans* with him, *Plutarch*, when he had related what we have said of him above, addeth; *Titus Quintius Flaminius.* *They had the fruit of this Moderation a little after; For they were no sooner come into Thessaly, but the Cities yielded to him: and the Greeks inhabiting between* Thermopilæ *wished for him with ardent desires: but the* Achaians *renouncing the friendship of Philip associated themselves to the* Romans *against him.* Of the City of the *Lingones*, which in the war waged against *Civilis* the *Batavian* and his fellows, by the conduct of *Cerealis*, under the Authority of *Domitian*, had escaped a feared spoil, *Frontinus* saith: *Because*, Lib. 5. 3. *beyond expectation, it was inviolate and lost nothing, being reduced to obedience it gave him seventy thousand armed men.* Contrary Counsels have also contrary events. Lib. 26. *Livy* gives us an example in *Annibal: His mind Precipitous to avarice and cruelty, carryed him to the spoil of what he could not keep himself, that the enemy might not enjoy it. That policy was dishonorable and disprofitable to him, both at the beginning and the end; For, not only the minds of them that sufferd unworthy things were alienated from him, but of others too; for the example reached unto more than the calamity did.* Surely, it is most true, which is noted by *Ægid. Regius de act. supernat. disp. 31. dub. 7. n. 127.* some

ſome Divines, that it is the office both of the Higheſt powers, and of Captains, who will be accounted Chriſtians, both in the judgment of God and men, to ſuperſede the violent direptions and ſpoiling of Cities, and all like violences, as thoſe that cannot paſs without the calamity of many Innocent perſons, and oft-times litt'e avail to the main of the War: So that Chriſtian-Goodneſs almoſt always, even Juſtice it ſelf for the moſt part abhors them. Greater certainly is the bond of Chriſtians to one another, than that of the *Grecians* was: by whoſe wars, that no City of *Greece* ſhould be deſtroy'd, was provided by a Decree of the *Amphictyons*. And the Antients deliver, that *Alexander* of *Macedonia* never did repent him more of any thing he had done, than of the overthow and ruine of *Thebes*.

Cap. 13.

LII. *A Temperament about things taken.*

NEither ought the Capture of hoſtile Goods in a juſt War be judged without ſin, or free from the charge of reſtitution. For, if you look upon what is done rightly *, it is not lawful to take or have farther than the enemy is indebted: except, that alſo for neceſſary ſecurity things may be detein'd; but, to be reſtored in themſelves or the price, after the hazard is

* *Vide quod judicavit Innocentius Pontifex apud Bembum*, 1. *Victor. de jure belli n.* 55, 56.

is past. Now, the Goods of subjects may be taken, not only for the obteining of the primary debt, whence the war began, but of a debt arising after it, according to what we said in the beginning of this part. And so is it to be understood, which some Divines write; *Things taken in war are not equalled with the Principal debt*: that is, there must be also satisfaction made, according to a true Judgment, for that damage that was done in the war it self. So, in the disceptation with *Antiochus*, the *Romans*, as *Livy* * relates, judged it equal, that the King, by whose fault the war was raised, should pay all the cost †. Tis in *Justin* *, *To bear the charge of the war, by a just Law.* In *Thucydides* the *Samians* are condemned *to pay the expences of War.* And elswhere often. Now, that which is justly imposed upon the Conquered, is also by a war extorted from them justly. But yet we must know, as we have mention'd afore, the rules of Charity are of larger compass than the rules of Law: He that has a flourishing estate will be guilty, if he thrust his needy debtor out of all he hath, that himself may be paid to the utmost farthing; and much more, if that same debtor came into that debt through his own goodness, as, if he hath been Surety for his friend, and himself hath converted none of the mony to his own use. For, as *Quintilian*'s Father * saith, *a Sureties danger is to commiserated.*

Silv. verb bell. n. 10. *Vict. n.* 51.

* *Lib.* 27.

† The King of Polonia alleges this custom for himself in Thuanus, *l.* 73. *an.* 1581. *Sic apud Hom. Il.* γ' *vocem* νίκην *Scholiastes interpretatur* περίτημα τοῦ πολέμου.

* *Lib.* 33.

* He addeth, that a Creditor cannot come with any modesty to the surety, except he cannot recover of the debtor. *Vide Cic. ad Att.* 16. 15.

miserated. And yet, so hard a Creditor doth nothing against right strictly taken. Wherefore Humanity requires, that to those who are without fault of the war, and who are bound no otherwise than as sureties, such things be left, as we can want more easily than they: especially, if it be evident, that they shall not recover from their Commonwealth, what they have in that manner lost*. Hither perteins that saying of *Cyrus* to his Soldiers, after he had taken *Babylon*: *It will not be unjust for you to possess what you have gotten, but it will be your Humanity to leave something to the enemyes*. This is also to be noted, seeing this right over the goods of innocent Subjects is introduced for relief, so long as there is hope we shall get our own easily enough from the principal debtors, or from them who, by not doing right, do of their own accord make themselves debtors, that while, to come unto them who are without fault (though it be granted not repugnant to strict right) doth depart from the rule of humanity. Examples of this humanity are frequent in history, especially in the *Roman*; as, when Lands were given to the Conquered on condition they should come into the Commonwealth: or, when a small part of the Lands for honor sake was left to the old Possessor *. So, *Livy*

Ægid. Regius de act. supern. disp 31. *dub*. 7. *n*. 117

* Ptolomy remitted to Demetrius the son of Antigonus his tent and all pertinents to the care of his body, with his money, too, saying, Their quarel was not for every thing, but for Empire and honour. *Plut. in Demet.*

* Appian. Civil. 2. The old Romans did not take away all from the conquer'd, but divided their Lands with them So did the Vandals in Afric, and the Goths in Italy, as History shews. † *Arrian l*. 3.

saith,

ſaith, the *Veientes* were mulcted a part of their lands by *Romulus*: So *Alexander* the *Macedonian* † gave the *Uxians* the Lands they had been maſters of, for Tribute: So you ſhal often read of Cities deliverd up and not ſpoiled: and above we have ſaid, not the perſons only but the goods of the Inhabitants, are commendably and according to the pious preſcript of the Canons, ſpared, at leaſt under tribute; and under the like tribute, is wont alſo to be granted unto wares, immunity from war.

† *Arrian. l.* 3.

LIII. *A Temperament about Captives.*

Cap. 14.

WHere Captivity of men, and Servitude is in uſe, if we reſpect internal juſtice, 'tis to be limited firſt after the likeneſs of things, *viz.* that ſuch acquiſt may be lawful ſo far as the quantity of the debt, either primary or ſecondary, doth admit: except perhaps in men themſelves be ſome peculiar fault, which equity will bear to be puniſht with the loſs of liberty. Hitherto then, and no farther, He that wageth a juſt war hath a right over his enemies ſubjects being taken, and doth validly transfer it upon others. But, it will be the part of equity and goodneſs here alſo to apply thoſe differences, which were noted above, when we ſpake of killing. *Demoſthenes* in his Epiſtle

Vict. de jure belli. n. 41. *Dec. l.* 2. *c.* 5. *dub.* 4. *Covar. c. peccatum.* §. 2. §. 1.

Epistle for the Children of *Lycurgus*, praiseth *Philip* of *Macedon*, that he had not made all that had been among his enemies, to be servants †. *For*, saith he, *he did not think it meet to deal with all alike, but judged of every one according to his merit*. But first we must note, the right which springs as 'twere from suretyship for a City, is not so large as that, which springs from a fault, against them who are made servants by way of punishment. Whence a *Spartan* said, *He was a Captive, not a Servant* *. For, if we look rightly into the matter, this general right over Captives in a just war, is like to that right, which Masters have over them, who, being compeld by poverty, have sold themselves into servitude: except that their calamity, is the more to be pityed, who come not into that condition by any special fact of their own, but by the fault of Governours. '*Tis a most sad thing*, saith *Isocrates*, *to be made a prisoner of War*. This servitude then, is a perpetual obligation to work, for maintenance likewise perpetual. *Chrysippus* his definition is very fit for this kind of servants: * *A servant is a perpetual mercenary*. And him, who hath sold himself being compeld by poverty, the *Hebrew* Law plainly compares to a mercenary: and in his redemption, it will have his work so profit him,

† His son Alexander, Thebes being taken, exempted from servitude, both the Priests, and those who had not assented to the Decrees made against him. *Plutarch*.

* Philo saith, Fathers for their children, and children for their Fathers have often paid a ransome, when they were either taken away by robbers, or made prisoners of war: whom truly, the Laws of Nature, stronger than these Laws made on earth, write free-men. Helena saith in Theodectes; Who dare call me a servant, that am on both sides descended from the Gods? * *Sen. de benef.* 3. c. 22.

as fruits received of a field sold should profit the old possessor. Much difference therfore there is 'twixt what is done impunely against a servant by the Law of Nations, and what natural reason suffers to be done. That of *Philemon* tendeth to this.

> *He that is born a man, although*
> *He serve, is stil a man, I trow.*

Seneca: *They are servants, yea Men: they are servants, yea our Companions: they are servants, yea our friends: they are servants, yea our fellow-servants.* Which also you may read in *Macrobius*, agreeing in sense with that of S. *Paul*; *Masters, give unto your servants that which is just and equal, knowing that ye also have a Master in Heaven.* And in another place, he would have Masters *forbear threatning*, upon the same argument, *knowing that their Master also is in heaven*, who regardeth not such differences of qualities. In the Constitutions ascribed to *Clemens Romanus* we read, *Thou shalt not be imperious over thy man-servant or thy maid-servant in bitterness of mind**: *Clemens Alexandrinus* † would have us use our servants as our other selves, seeing they are men as well as we; following the sentence of the *Hebrew* wise-man, *If thou hast a servant, use him as a brother, for he is such a one as thy self.* The right therefore which is called of life and death over

Sen. Epist. 47.

Coloss. 4. 1.

Eph. 6. 9.

Lib. 7. c. 14.

* Sic & in ep. Barnabæ est: *Noli acerbè imperare servo aut ancillæ tuæ in Christum sperantibus, ne eo ipso ostendas non timere te communem tibi & ipsis dominum.*

† Pæd. ult.

over a servant gives the Master a dome-
stick Jurisdiction, but such as must be exer-
cised with the same religious care , as the
1. De Clem. 18. publick is exercised. This was *Seneca's*
Epist. 47. meaning when he said , *In a bondman is*
to be considered, not how much may be in-
flicted on him impunely , but how much e-
quity permits ; which commands us to
spare even Captives and those whom we
L. 3. *de benef. cap.* 18. *have bought with money.* And again ,
What matter is it , under what command
one is , if it be the highest ? Where he
compares a subject to a servant, and saith,
under a divers title the same is lawful
over them : which in respect of taking a-
way the life and of what is pertaining to
it , is most true. *Our Ancestors*, saith the
Epist. 43. same *Seneca , judged our House to be a*
little Commonwealth : and Pliny , *The*
house is unto servants a certain Common-
wealth , and as it were a City. Cato Cen-
sorius, as *Plutarch* relates , if any servant
seemed to have committed a capital crime,
did not punish him, till after he was con-
demned by the judgment also of his fel-
low-servants. Wherewith may be com-
par'd the words of *Job* , 31. 13. &c. A-
bout the lesser punishments too , namely
stripes and beating of servants, equity, yea
Vide Mosem de Kotzi pracept. jubent. 147. 175. 178. & *collat. leg. Mosis & Roman. tit.* 3. and clemency is to be used. *Thou shalt not*
oppress him ; thou shalt not rule hardly
over him, saith the Divine Law of an *He-*
brew servant , which, the force of neigh-
bourhood being now enlarged, ought to
be

be extended to all servants: *Deut.* 15.17, 45, 53. Upon which place *Philo : Servants are indeed inferior in fortune, but in nature equal to their Masters : now, to the Divine Law that is the rule of justice, not which agrees to fortune but to nature. Therefore it becomes not Masters to use their power over servants frowardly, nor to make it matter for their pride and insolence and cruelty. For these are signes of an ill disposed and tyrannical mind.* Seneca: *what is more foolish than to be furious against men, and yet use dogs and horses gently?* Hence in the *Hebrew* Law, to a servant man or maid, not for an eye only, but a tooth injuriously struck out, liberty was due*. Moreover, work is to be exacted of them moderately*, and a human respect is to be had to the health of servants. Which very thing, beside other, the *Hebrew* Law provides for, in the institution of the Sabbath : *viz.* that some breathing space might be allowed Labourers. *Seneca* observes in the word, *Paterfamilias*, the humanity of the antients. *Do you not see, how our Elders have taken off all envy from Masters, all contumely from servants? They named the Master the Father of the family, the servant familiars*. The like piety hath *Ser-*

Philo de special. legib. 2. Cyprian. ad Demetr. *Non agnoscis miser dominum Deum tuum, cum sic exerceas ipse in hominem dominatum.*

Exod. 21. 26, 27.

* Vide Philonem dicto loco.

Exod. 20. 10. 23. 12. Deut. 10. 14.

* Sen. epist. 47. *Non tanquam hominibus, sed tanquam jumentis abutimur.*

Of the Athenians lenity to their servants, See Xenoph. *de repub. Athen.* Epist. 47.

* Epicurus, friends, *Sen. epist.* 107. Dion Prus. optimum regem describens; *Domini nomen adeo in homines liberos non usurpat, ut & in servos eo abstineat.* Tertullian: *Gratius est nomen pietatis quam potestatis.* Hieronym. ad Celantiam: *Benignitate potius quam severitate exige reverentiam.*

vius † noted in they word *pueri Children*, by which they signified servants. For their work, as we have said, maintenance is due to servants. *Cato: Provide well for the family; cloaths against cold, food against hunger. There is somewhat*, saith Seneca †, *which a Master ought to afford his servant, as food and apparell* *. The cruelty of the *Sicilians* †, who famished the *Athenian* Captives, is condemn'd by the historians. Farther, *Seneca* in the same place proves, a servant is free in some respect, and has wherewith to do a benefit, if he hath done, what exceeds the measure of servile duty, what is done not upon command but voluntarily, where service is turn'd into the affection of a friend, which he explains at large. Whereto agrees, if a servant (as it is in *Terence*) defrauding his Genius hath saved any thing, or by his diligence at spare times hath gotten any thing, that in some sort is his own *. Nor is it material, that the Master may, at his pleasure, take away or diminish his servants stock; for, he will not do what is right, if he do it without cause; by *Cause* I understand not only punishment, but the necessity of the Master; for the profit of the servant is subordinate to the profit or interest of the Master; yea, more than the wealth of a Citizen to the City. Therefore, as we read, that Clients have contributed to the use of their Patrons, and subjects of their Kings; so

† Servius ad illud Maronis: *Claudite jam rivos, pueri.*

† *Sen. l. 3. de Benef.*

* Cicero: *opera exigenda, justa praebenda.* Arist. δίκαιο μισθὸς τροφή 1. Oecon. 5 Sirach. 33. 25. ἄρτος καὶ παιδεία καὶ ἔργα οἰκέτῃ.

† *Et Isaaci Angeli in Siculos captivos memorante Niceta lib.* 1.

Phorm. act. 1. *sc.* 1.

* Varro de servis; *Studiasiores ad opus fieri liberalius tractando, aut cibariis aut vestitu largiore, aut remissione operis, concessioneq; ut peculiare aliquid in fundo pascere liceat.*

so have servants to the uses of their Masters *; if a daughter be to be preferred, if a Captive son to be redeemed, or if any like occasion had fallen out. *Pliny*, as himself saith in his Epistles, granted leave to his servants to make certain testaments as it were, that is, to divide, to give, to bequeath within the family. Among some Nations a fuller right of getting an estate was granted unto servants, as there were several degrees of servitude. To this internal justice which we expound, the Laws, among many Nations, have also reduced that external right of Masters. For among the Greeks, it was lawful for servants ill used *, *to demand that they might be sold*; and at *Rome*, to fly unto the statues, and implore help of the Governors against rigour, or hunger, or intolerable injury. But, 'twill proceed not from strict right, but from humanity and beneficence (yet such as is due sometimes) that after long service and very great, Liberty be given to a servant. After that by the Law of Nations servitude came in, there followed the benefit of manumission, saith *Ulpianus*. An example whereof, we have in that of *Terence*:

Thou wast my servant: and I made
thee free,
*Because thou didst thy service * Liberally.*

*Salvian** saith, it is a thing of daily use, that servants, though not of the best, yet of

* Seneca: *Nunquid dubium est, quin servus cum peculio domini sit? Dat tamen domino suo munus.*

* πρᾶσιν αἰτεῖν.

Instit. de his qui sui vel al. L. manumiss. D. de just. & ju.

* Andr. act. 1. 1. *Servibas liberaliter.* Ita MS. recte.

* Lib. 3.

of honeſt diligence, be ſet at liberty; He addes: *and be not forbidden to carry with them out of their maſters houſe, what they gained in their ſervice.* Of which benignity there are many examples in the Martyrologies. And here alſo is to be praiſed the benignity of the *Hebrew* Law, that commands an *Hebrew* ſervant, after a certain time fulfill'd, to be manumitted; and, not without gifts *; of the contempt of which Law, the Prophets make a heavy complaint. *Plutarch* reprehends *Cato* major, becauſe, when his ſervants were aged, he ſold them, unmindful of that common nature of mankind. A queſtion here is incident, whether it be lawful for him to fly, who is taken Captive in a juſt war. (We ſpeak not of him, who by his own proper fault hath deſerv'd that puniſhment, but of one that by publick action is fallen into this fortune.) It is the truer anſwer, that it is not lawful: becauſe, by the common agreement of Nations, he owes his ſervice in the Name of the Commonwealth. Which yet is ſo to be underſtood, unleſs intolerable cruel uſage impoſe upon him this neceſſity. Another doubt is, whether, and how far, they that are born of ſervants are under Dominion by internal right: a doubt, which may not be omitted here, by reaſon of the ſpecial conſideration of Captives in war. If the parents by any crime of theirs had deeſerv'd the puniſhment of death,

Deut. 15. 13.

* *Conſuetudo id interpretata, ne minus 30. Siclis detur. vide prae. jubente 84.*

Silv. verbo ſervitus, §. 3. Fortunius in l. manumiſ. D. de juſt. & ju.

Leſs, l. 2. c. 5. dub. 5.

death, their Children which they hoped for, might, to save their lives, be bound over to servitude: because otherwise they would never be born. (For, even for maintenance, which they would otherwise want, parents may sell their Children.) Such is the right, which God alloweth the *Hebrews* over the posterity of the *Canaanites*. Deut. 15. 13. But, for the debt of the Common-wealth, they which were already born, as a part of the Common wealth, might be bound, no less than the Parents themselves. Howbeit, as to them who are not yet born, this cause seemeth not sufficient, but another is required: either from Parents express consent together with a necessity of maintenance, and that for ever; or from the allowance of maintenance, and that only till the work hath paid for all that was layd out. If any further right is given the Master over these, it seemeth to proceed out of the Civil Law, favouring Masters more than is enough. Among the Nations, with whom that Law of servitude by war is not in use, it will be best, that Captives should be exchanged; next, that they should be dismissed at a reasonable rate. What this is, cannot precisely be determined; but Humanity teacheth, it ought not be so heightned, but that the residue of the Captives estate may supply him with all Necessaries. In some places, this is defined by Covenants and Customs; as, a-among the *Greeks* of old *Mina* *, now among Soldiers a months pay goes for a ransome. *Plutarch* relates, that heretofore wars were waged between the *Corinthians* and *Megareans* *mildly, and so as became men of the same blood.* If any one were taken, he was entertained by the Taker, as a Guest, and sent home upon promise of a price for his deliverance. That of *Pyrrhus* † commended by *Cicero*, argues a more noble mind:

* In the war of the French with the Spaniard in Italy, a horsman was redeem'd for the fourth of his yeerly pay, See Mariana l. 27. 18. Qu. Græc.

† The like goodness of Tiberius a Christian Emperor toward the Persians is commended by Menander Protector: of Sisebutus by Mariana, and of Sanctius King of Castile, *Lib.* 11,

Nec mî aurum posco, nec mî pretium dederitis:
Ferro non auro vitam cernamus utrique,
Quorum fortunâ belli fortuna pepercit,
Eorundam libertati me parcere certum est.

Apud Ciceronem de Offic.

No gold for me, no price do I require:
To fight it out with steel is my desire.
The valiant men, to whom good fortune gave
Their life, by my gift Liberty shall have.

Pyrrhus, no doubt, believed his war just: nevertheless, he thought fit to spare their liberty, who on probable cause were engag'd gag'd against him. The like act of *Cyrus* is celebrated by *Xenophon*, of *Philip* the *Macedonian* after his victory in *Chæronea* by *Polybius*, of *Alexander* toward the *Scythians* by *Curtius*, of *Ptolomy* the King and of *Demetrius*, contending with one another not more in war than in benignity toward Captives, by *Plutarch*. And *Dromichætes* King of the *Getes*; having taken *Lysimachus** in war, made him his guest, and prevaild on him so far, that having experience both of the *Getick* poverty and courtesy, he chose rather to have such men for his friends than enemies.

2. Cyropæd. *Vita Dem. Strab. l. 7.* * *Diod. Sic. in excerpt.*

LIV. *A Temperament about acquisition of Empire.* Cap. 15.

THat Equity which is requir'd, or that Humanity which is commended, toward particular persons, is so much more requir'd or commended toward Nations or the parts of Nations, by how much more signal is the injury and the benefit done to many. By a just war, as other things may be acquired, so also the right of a Ruler over people, and the right which the people themselves have in the empire: but (to be sure) so far as the measure either of the punishment arising from the fault, or the measure of some other debt will bear. To which is to be added the cause of avoiding extreme danger.

Vict. de jure belli. n. 38. & 59.

ger. But this cause for the most part is mixed with other, which yet is it self most considerable, both in constituting peace, and in using victory. For the rest happly may be remitted out of compassion: but in publick danger, to be secure beyond measure is unmercifulness. *Isocrates* writes to *Philip: The Barbarians are so far to be subdued, as it shall be sufficient to secure your own Countrey.* *Crispus Sallustius*, of the old *Romans: Our Ancestors, being most religious men, took nothing from the Conquerd, but the licence to do injury.* A sentence worthy to be spoken by a Christian: wherewith agrees that of the same Author, *Wise men wage war for the sake of Peace, and sustein labour in hope of ease.* *Aristotle* said more than once, *War is ordaind for peace, and business for rest.* *Cicero*'s meaning is the same, whose most pious saying 'tis: *War must be so undertaken, that nothing else but peace be aimed at.* And another like it; *For this cause are wars to be waged, that we may without injury live in peace.* Nothing different are these fron what the Doctors of true Religion teach us, That the end of war is to remove things that trouble our Peace. Before the times of *Ninus*, as we have noted out of *Trogus*, it was the manner to defend * the bounds of Empire, rather than to enlarge them; Every King was contented to reign in his own Countrey; they did not so much seek their own

Jugurth.

De repub. l. 7. c. 14. & 15. Nic. 10. c. 7.

De offic. 1.

Tho. 1. 2. q. 40. art. 1. ad 3.

* Alexand. Imp. Artaxerxi Persæ: *Manendum cuiq; intra suos fines nihil novando, neq; debere quenquam incerta spe sublatum bella incipere, sed suo esse contentum.*

power

power, as their peoples glory: being satisfied with victory, they refused Empire. To which moderation S. Augustine earnestly recalls us, when he saith, Let them consider, lest perhaps it be not the part of good men, to rejoice † in their Empires latitude. He addeth: 'Tis greater felicity to have a good neighbour for ones friend, than to subdue an evil neighbour that is an enemy. And the Prophet Amos, in the Ammonites themselves, severely reprehends this desire of extending dominion by War. To this exemplar of antient innocence, the prudent modesty of the Romans made the neerest approach. What were our Empire at this day, saith Seneca, unless wholsom providence had mixed the conquer'd with the Conquerours? Our Founder Romulus (they are Claudius's words in Tacitus) was of so prevailing wisedom, that he made many people Citizens, the same day, they had been his enemies: He adds, that nothing else undid the Lademonians & Athenians, but their keeping off the conquered, as Aliens. Livy saith, the State of Rome was advanced by receiving their enemies into the City. In histories are extant, examples of the Sabins, Albans, Latins, and the rest of Italy: till at last, Cæsar triumph'd over the Galls, and enfranchiz'd them. Cerialis in Tacitus, in his Oration to the Galls: Ye your selves for the most part command our Legions; ye govern these and other Provinces;

De Civit. Dei li. 4. 15.

† Cyril in his 5. against Julian commends the Hebrew Kings for this, that they were content with their own bounds.

Am. 1. 13.

Lib. 2. de Ira. cap. 34.

Annal. 5.

vinces; Nothing is separate and shut from you. And then; *Wherefore, Love and embrace that Peace and life, which you the conquerd and we the Conquerours enjoy with equal right.* At length, which is most to be admir'd, They that are in the *Roman* world, by the constitution of the Emperour *Marcus Antonius*, are made *Roman* Citizens; which are the words of *Ulpian*. After that time, as *Modestinus* saith, *Rome* is the Common Countrey. *Claudian*;

L. in orbe. D. de stat. hom. L. Roma. D. ad munic.

Claudian; *Hujus pacificis debemus moribus omnes, Quod cuncti gens una sumus.*

> *We all owe this to his pacifick mind:*
> *One Nation hath united all Mankind.*

Another kind of moderate victory, is, to leave unto the Conquerd, either Kings or People, the Empire which they had. So *Hercules* dealt with *Priamus* *; and having overcome *Neleus* he committed the Kingdom † to his son *Nestor*. So the *Persian* Kings left the Kingdom to the Kings they had conquerd †. So *Cyrus* to the *Armenian*. So *Alexander* to *Porus* *. *Seneca* commends it: *To take nothing from the Conquerd King, but Glory.* And *Polybius* celebrates the goodness of *Antigonus*, who having *Sparta* in his power, left them *the Commonwealth and liberty of their Ancestors*, Whereby he obteined great praises thorough *Greece*, as it is there related.

* Seneca Troad. *Hostis parvi victus lacrymis, Suscipe dixit rector habenas, Patrioq; sede celsus solio: Sed sceptra fide meliore tene.*

† *Æl. l. 4. 5.*

† *Herod. lib. 7.*

* Pipinus to Aistolphus Longobard.

* *De clem.* 1. 21. The whole place is worth reading, where he also calleth it a triumph after victory. Pompey left Tigranes a part of his Kingdom. *Eutrop. l. 6.*

ted. So the *Cappadocians* were permitted by the *Romans*, to use what form of Commonwealth they would; and many States, after war, have been left free: *Carthage is free and enjoyes her own Laws*, say the *Rhodians* to the *Romans*, after the second *Punick* War. *Pompey*, saith *Appian*, *left some of the subdued Nations free* *. And to the *Ætolians*, saying, there could be no firm peace, unless *Philip* the *Macedonian* were driven out his Kingdom, *Quintius* answer'd, That they had given their opinion, unmindful of the *Romans* custom to spare the Conquerd, adding: *The Greater the Conqueror is, the more gentle mind he beareth toward the conquer'd.* Sometime, together with the concession of Empire, provision is made for the conquerors security. So 'twas decreed by *Quintius* *, that *Corinth* should be rendred to the *Achaians*, and a Garrison be put in the Fort; that *Chalcis* and *Demetrias* should be deteind, till they were quitted of the care of *Antiochus*. Imposition of Tribute also perteineth oft, not so much to the restitution of charges, as to the security both of the Conquerour and Conquered. *Cicero*, of the *Greeks*: *Also, let Asia consider, she had no way to avoid the calamity, both of forein war, and discord at home, but by adhering to this Empire: and seeing this Empire cannot be maintaind without Tribute,* Let her be content to buy a firm and lasting peace with

Liv. lib. 32.

Mithridat.

* *Vid. Polybium, exc. Legat. n. 6.*

Apud Tacitum est: *Zonfini victo nihil ereptum.* Annal. 12.

* Yet was that remitted afterwards. *Plut. Flaminio.*

Lib. 1. *ad Q. fr. epist.* 1.

Hist. 4.

with some part of her revenues. *Petilius Cerialis* in *Tacitus*, speaks for the *Romans* to the *Lingones* and other *Galls*, after this manner: *We, though so often provok'd, by the right of Victory, have only laid this upon you, that was necessary to preserve peace. For, neither can the quiet of Nations be procured without arms, nor arms without stipends, nor stipends without tributes.* Pertinent here are other things also, which we have said afore, when we spake of an unequal league; to deliver up arms *, ships, not to have any weapons, not to have an Army. But, that their Empire may be left unto the Conquered, is not only a point of humanity, but oftentimes of Counsil. Among the institutes of *Numa*, this is praised, that he sacrific'd to *Terminus* without blood, signifying, there is nothing more profitable to a safe peace, than to keep within ones own bounds. *Florus* excellently: *It is more hard to keep, than to make Provinces; they are got by force, they are kept by Justice* *. The Embassadors of *Darius* to *Alexander*: *A forein Empire is ful of danger: 'tis difficult to keep that which is too great: 'tis more easy to conquer some countries, than to hold them: much more readily do our hands receive, than retein.* *Appian* observes, that many people who desir'd to put themselves under the *Roman* power, were refus'd by them: and others had Kings by their appointment. In the judgment

* *Vide de Persis Agathiam lib. 4.*

Plutarch. qu. Rom. 15.

* Livius; *facilius parari singula quam teneri universa.* Augusti dictum apud Plutarchum: μεῖζον τῦ ἀτ... μεγάλην ἡγεμονίαν τὸ διατάξαι τὴν ὑπάρχουσαν.

jugment of *Scipio Africanus*, in his time, *Rome* possessed so much, that 'twas greediness to desire more, being abundantly happy, if she lost nothing of what she had already. Wherefore, that form of prayer, whereby the Gods were entreated to advance the State of *Rome*, he amended *, praying that they would be pleased, but to preserve it, as it was. The *Lacedemonians*, and (at first) the *Athenians*, challenged to themselves no Empire over the Cities they had taken: only, they required them to use a form of Government accommodate to theirs, the *Lacedemonians* under the power of the Chief, the *Athenians* at pleasure of the people; as *Thucydides*, *Isocrates*, *Demosthenes* declare: and *Aristotle* too, in his fourth *De repub.* The like was done, as *Tacitus* relates, by *Artabanus* at *Seleucia*: *He committed the common people to the Chief men, according to his own use: for a popular Government is free, the domination of a few more neer to royalty.* But, whether such Changes make for the Conquerors security, is not of our inspection. If it be less safe to abstein from all Empire over the Conquered, the matter may be temper'd so, that some part of the government may be left to them or their Kings. *Tacitus* calls it a custom of the *Roman* people, to have Kings also for instruments of servitude †.

* Augustus is prais'd in Dion, that he was not ambitious of more, but to keep what he had.

Thuc. 1. *Isoc. Pan. Demosth. orat. de Chers.*

Annal. 6.

Hist. 2.

† *Eidem Antiochus inservientium regum ditissimus.* Strabo Βασιλεῖς Ῥωμαίων ὑπήκοοι. Lucanus *Atq; omnis Latio quæ servit purpura ferro.* Vid. Panegyr. Maxim. dict.

So

So, among the Jews, the Scepter remained in the *Sanedrin*, also after the confiscation of *Archelaus*. *Evagoras* King of *Cyprus*, as 'tis in *Diodorus*, said He would give obedience to the *Persian*, but as a King to a King. And *Alexander* several times offerd to *Darius* † being overcome, this condition; that he should rule over others, and be subject unto *Alexander*. We have spoken of mixed Empire elswhere *. To some, one part of the Kingdom hath been left, as a part of their Lands to the old Possessors. Again, when all Empire is taken from the Conquerd, there may be left them, about private affairs, and publick to of less moment, their own Laws * and customs, and their own Magistrats. So, in *Bithynia*, a proconsular Province, the City *Apamæa* had the privilege to administer the Commonwealth their own way †, as *Pliny* tells us in his Epistles; and in other places the *Bithynians* had their own Magistrats, their own Senate. And so in *Pontus*, the *Amisen*'s City used their own Laws, by the favour of *Lucullus*. The *Gotths* also left to the *Romans* the *Roman* Laws. A part of this indulgence is, not to deprive the Conquerd, against their perswasion, of the use of their old Religion *. Which as very grateful to the Conquerd, so to the

† Such Kings were of old in Italy, under the Empire of other Kings. *Serv. ad* 10. *Æn.* So among the Turks. *Leuncl. lib.* 18.

* Part. 1.

* Philo in his Embassy to Caius, saith, Augustus had as much care to keep the Laws proper to every Nation, as the Roman.

† *Vid. ep.* 93. *Plin. & seq. Traj. lib.* 10. *Cic. l.* 6. *ad Attic. epist. &* 5. 21.

* *Melius est ibi aliquem coli Deum, quam nullum.* Severus. So the Gotths in Procop. Gott. 2. say, they forced none to their Religion.

Conqueror

Conqueror it is not hurtful, as *Agrippa* proves in his Oration to *Caius*, related by *Philo* in his *Embassy*. And in *Josephus*, both *Josephus* himself, and *Titus* the Emperor object to the rebells of *Jerusalem*, that by the indulgence of the *Romans*, they had so much privilege in their own Religion, as to keep out Aliens from the Temple, even at the peril of their lives. But, if the Conquer'd have a false Religion, it will belong to the Conquerors care, that the True be not opprest: which was the care of *Constantin*, when he had broken the party of *Licinius*, and after him of the *French* and other Kings. The last Caution is, that even in the fullest and (as 'twere) herile Empire, the Conquered be us'd with Clemency, and so that their Interest be taken in with the Interest of the Conquerour. *Cyrus* bade the overcom *Assyrians* be of good cheer: They should be in as good case as they had been, their King only changed; They should have their Houses, Lands, Wives and Children, as in times past: and if any one should injure them, He and His would right them. In *Sallust* we read; *The people of Rome conceived it better to get friends, than servants; and they thought it safer to rule over willing men, than forced*. The *Britains*, in the times of *Tacitus* did cheerfully come to the musters, and pay tribute, and perform offices injoind

Xenoph. Cyrop. lib. 4.

Vit. Agric.

join'd them, if they were not injur'd: Injuries they could not endure, being subdued into obedience, not yet to servitude.
Liv. lib. 8. That man of *Privern*, being asked in the *Roman* Senat, what peace the *Romans* could expect from them, answerd: *If you grant us a good Peace, faithful and firm: if an evil Peace, not lasting.* He adds a reason: *Believe it, no people, no man will abide, longer than he must needs, in that*
Liv. lib. 8. *condition that is not pleasing.* So *Camillus* said; It is the firmest Empire, wherewith the subjects are best contented. *Hermo-*
Diod. lib. 13. *crates* in *Diodorus*: *It is not so honorable to overcome, as to use the victory with gentleness and moderation* †.

† Scythæ Alexandro: *Inter Dominum & servum nulla amicitia; etiam in pace, belli tamen jura servantur. Curt. lib. 7.* Salubri Taciti Sententia: *Bellorum egregii fines, quoties ignoscendo transigitur.* In Cæsaris Dictatoris epistola est: *Hæc nova sit ratio vincendi, ut misericordia & liberalitate nos muniamus.* The Lacedemonians in Thucydides lib. 5. We are of opinion, quarels are turned in firm concord thus; not if one, in revenge and taking advantage by his success, impose upon others a necessity of swearing to unequal articles: but if, when he is able to do so, he use as much equity now, as valour before, and compose matters with as much moderation as may be.

LV. Restitution *of things unjustly taken away. Objections answer'd.*

THings gotten by unjust War are to be restored, as we have said above; and not onely by those that took them, but also by others to whom the things by any means are come. For, no man can transfer upon another more right than he had himself, say the Authors of the Roman Law; which *Seneca* briefly explains, *No man can give what he hath not.* He had not dominion *internal,* who was first Taker: wherefore, neither will he have it, who derives his title from him; the second then, or the third Possessor, hath received that dominion, which we call *external;* that is, this benefit, that every where he is by judiciary authority and power to be maintained as the Owner: which yet, if he use against him, from whom the things were by injustice taken away, he will do dishonestly. Such things therefore are to be rendred to those from whom they were taken away: which, we see, hath been oft times done. *Livy,* when he had related how the *Volsci* and *Æqui* were conquer'd by *L. Lucretius Tricipitinus,* saith, the spoyl was expos'd in *Campus Martius,* that every one for the space of three daies might know and receive his

L. traditio D de acq. dom.

Lib. 5. de benef cap. 12.

Liv. lib. 3.

Tt own.

own. The ſame Hiſtorian, when he had ſhewed, that the *Volſci* were overthrown by *Poſthumius* the Dictator, *Part of the ſpoyl* (ſaith he) *was reſtored to the Latins and Hernicians, knowing their own goods; part the Dictator ſold* ſub haſta. Elſwhere: *Two daies were given the Owners to find out their Goods.* *Polyb. hiſt. l. 3.* *Polybius* ſaith of *L. Æmilius*, Conquerour of the Galls: He rendred the prey to thoſe from whom 'twas taken. *Plut. Apoph. App. Pun. Adde Valer. Max. l. 1. c. 1. n. 6.* That *Scipio* did the ſame, *Plutarch* and *Appian* teſtifie, when, having taken *Carthage*, he had found many Donatives there, which the *Carthaginians* had brought thither out of Cities of *Sicily* and other places. This act of *Scipio's* is expreſſed at large by *Cicero*. *Verrina de ſignis.* The *Rhodians* reſtored to the *Athenians* four Ships of theirs, which they had recovered from the *Macedonians*. Goods alſo, in *Strabo, l. 13.* former times conſecrated at *Epheſus*, which the Kings had appropriated, the *Romans* reduced into their antient ſtate. But, what if ſuch a thing hath paſſed to any one in the way of Commerce, may he charge the firſt owner with the price he paid for't? It ſeems he may, ſo far as the recovery of his deſperate poſſeſſion was valuable to him, who had loſt the thing. And if ſuch coſt may be requir'd, why may not alſo the eſtimation of labour and hazard, juſt as if one by diving had brought up ſomething of another man's loſt in the Sea? Appoſite to this queſtion,

queſtion, methinks, is the hiſtorie of *Abraham*, when being Conquerour of the five Kings, he return'd to *Sodom*, *He brought back* (ſaith *Moſes*) *all the goods*, *viz.* which the Kings had taken: appoſite is the condition which the King of *Sodom* offers to *Abraham*, *Give me the perſons, and take the goods to thy ſelf*, *viz.* for his pains and danger. But *Abraham*, a man not onely of a pious, but a noble mind *, would take nothing for himſelf, ſave onely of the goods (for of them is this narration) as by his own right, he gave a tenth to God, he detracted neceſſary charges, and was pleaſed ſome portion ſhould be alotted to his partners in the action. Now, as Goods are to be rendred to the Owner, ſo alſo people † and their parts, are to be reſtored to thoſe who had right of Government; or to themſelves, if they were in their own power before the unjuſt force. So, we learn out of *Livy**, that *Sutrium* was regained and reſtored in the time of *Camillus*. The *Æginetes* and *Melians* had their Towns reſtored to them by the *Lacedemonians*; the Grecian Cities, invaded by the *Macedonians*, were freed by *Flaminius*. The ſame *Flaminius* alſo,

Gen. 14. 16.

Gen. 14. 21.

* Benè hoc notavit Jacchides ad Daniel, 5. 17. Sulpitius de Abrahamo: *Reliquis quibus erepta erant reddidit.* Ambroſ. lib. 1. de Patriarchis: *Ideo, quoniam ſibi mercedem ab homine non quæſivit, à Deo accepit.* Non multum hinc diſtant facta Pittaci & Timoleontis: *Pittacus Mitylenæus cùm recuperati agri dimidia pars conſenſu omnium offerretur, avertit animum ab eo munere, deforme judicans virtutis gloriam magnitudine prædæ minuere.* Val. Max. l. 6. c. 5. n. 1. De Timoleonte Plutarch. vid. † The Exiles of *Saguntum*, after ſix years, were reſtored by the *Romans*. *Antonius* ſet at liberty thoſe who were brought into ſervitude in the War of *Caſſius*, and reſtor'd their Goods to the Owners. * *Liv. l. 2. Id. l. 72. Xenoph. Hiſt. Gr. 3. Liv. lib. 34.*

in a Conference with the Embassadours of *Antiochus*, thought it fit, the Cities of *Asia*, which were of the Grecian name (which *Seleucus* the Ancestor of *Antiochus* had taken by war, *Antiochus* had recover'd being lost) should be freed: *For*, said he, *the Colonies were not sent into* Æolis *and* Ionia, *to be in servitude under the King; but to the end their Race might be increased, and the most antient Nation propagated through the world.* There is also a question made of the space of time, wherein the internal obligation of restoring a thing may be extinguished. But this question, between Citizens of the same Empire, is to be determined out of their Laws (if they grant an internal right, and do not consist onely in the external; which is to be gathered out of the words and purpose of the Laws by prudent inspection:) and, among them that are foreiners to each other, by sole conjecture of dereliction, of which elswhere. Lastly, if the right of War be very ambiguous, 'twill be best to follow the counsel of *Aratus Sicyonius* *, who partly perswaded the new Possessors to accept of money rather, and yield the Possessions; partly perswaded the former Owners to think it more commodious to have a just price for it, than to recover what they had lost.

Cicero Offic. 2.

* *Quod fecit rex Ferdinandus memorante* Mariana, l. 29. c. 14.

LVI.

LVI. Of Neuters in War. *How they are to be used; and, how to behave themselves.* Cap. 17.

IT might seem superfluous to speak of them, who have nothing to do with War, seeing it is manifest there is no right of War over these: Yet because by occasion of the VVar, many things are wont to be done against these, borderers especially, on pretence of necessity, we must here repeat what we have said a- Part. 2.
fore, that Necessity ought to be extreme, that it may give a right over what belongs to another man: 'tis requir'd moreover, that the Owner himself be not in equal necessity: and, where the necessity is manifest, no more is to be taken than the necessity exacteth; that is, if the custody suffices, the use of the thing is not to be taken; if the use, not the abuse: if the abuse be necessary, yet is the price of the thing to be restored. *Moses*, when the highest necessity urged him and the people, to pass through the Land of the *Idumæans*, first he saith, he would pass along the high way, and not divert into their Corn-fields or Vineyards: if he had need but of their water, he would pay a price for it. The worthy Captains, both Greek and Roman, have done the like. In *Xenophon*, the *Greeks* with *Clearchus* promise the *Persians* to march

march away without any damage to the Countrey; and if they might have necessaries for money, they would take nothing by force. *Dercyllides* in the same *Xenophon*, *led his Army through peaceable places without any detriment to his friends*. *Livy* of King *Perseus*: *Through* Phthiotis, Achaia, *and* Thessalia, *without doing any harm in the fields through which he passed, he returned into his Kingdome*. *Plutarch* of the Army of *Agis* the Spartan: *They were a spectacle to the Cities, marching through* Peloponnesus *fairly, and without hurt, and almost without noyse* *. *Velleius* reports the like of *Sulla*: *Cicero* of *Pompey* †: *Frontinus* of *Domitian*: *Lampridius* of the Parthick Expedition of *Alexander Severus*. Concerning the *Gotths* *, *Hunnes*, *Alans*, that served *Theodosius*, the Panegyrist: *No tumult, no confusion, no pillaging, as Barbarians use: but if at any time he had scarsity, he patiently endured want, and by parsimony enlarged the provision, which was streighten'd by* number. *Claudian* † gives the same praise to *Stilico*, and *Suidas* to *Belisarius* *. This was effected by the exact

* The like testimony *Plutarch* gives to *Titus Q. Flaminius*.

† And *Plutarch* saith, when he heard of his Souldiers license, he sealed up their Swords, and punisht every one that brake the Seal.

* *Cassiodor.* 5. 10. & 2. 13, 25. & 9. 25.

† Claudian:
Tanta quies, tantusque metus servator honesti
Te moderante fuit, nullus ut vinea furtis
Aut seges erepta fraudaret messe colonum.

* This virtue is oft commended in *Belisarius* by *Procopius*, his Companion,

and

and witness of his actions. See to this purpose his excellent speech to his Souldiers near *Sicily*, when he marched into *Africk*, and the narration of his march through *Africk*, *Vandal.* 1. The like praise of the *Almains* in their expedition to the Holy Sepulcher, see in *Nicetas*, *Manuele Comneno. Gregoras*, *l.* 9. commends the same in the *Venetians*.

care to provide † Necessaries, and by good Pay, and strict Discipline, which *Ammian* tels us of, *That none should tread upon the Lands of quiet men.* And *Vopiscus* *: *Let no Souldier steal a Chick, touch a Sheep, pluck a Grape, exact Oil, Salt, Wood.* And *Cassiodore*: *Let them live in the Province, in a civil manner: nor let their Arms make them over-bold, because the Shields of our Army ought to save the* Romans *from all trouble.* Adde to these that of *Xenophon* *: *A friendly City's not to be compell'd to give any thing against their will.* Out of these Sayings you may best interpret that Advice of the great Prophet, yea one greater than a Prophet: *Do violence to no man, neither accuse any man falsly, but be content with your wages* *. Parallel is that of *Aurelian*, in *Vopiscus* now cited: *Let the Souldier be content with his provision: let him live of the spoyl of the Enemy, not of the tears of the Province.* Nor has any one reason to think these things are well

† Plin. Hist. Nat. 26. 4. *Curæ Romani duces primam semper in bellis commercium curam habuêre?* Cassiod. 4. 13. *Habeat quod emat, ne cogatur cogitare quod auferat.* Simi-lia habet, 5. 10, & 13. * *L.* 18. *Vide & Ammianum lib.* 21. * *Vop. Aurel.* * *Xenoph. Exped. lib.* 6. *Luk.* 3. 14. * Ambrof. ad hunc Lucæ locum: *Iccirco stipendia constituta militiæ, ne dum sumtus quæritur, prædo grassetur. Sunt egregiæ ad hanc rem Constitutiones apud* Greg. Turon. lib. 2. 27. *Frederici primi legem sic refert Guntherus:*

Si quis pacificæ plebis villasve domosve
Usserit, ab rasis signabitur ora capillis,
Et pulsus castris post vulnera multa recedet.

 spoken,

ſpoken, but cannot be performed. For, neither would that divine man have given ſuch a charge, nor wiſe Law-givers have requir'd it, if it had been in their conceit impoſſible. Beſides, we muſt neceſſarily grant it may be done, which we ſee has been done†. Therefore have we brought examples: whereunto this eminent one is worthy to be added, which *Frontinus* * mentions out of *Scaurus*: That a Fruit-bearing Tree, encloſed within the bounds of the Camp, the next day after the Armies removal was found ungather'd. *Livy*, when he had related the ill deportment of the Roman Souldiers in the Camp at *Sucron*, and that ſome of them went abroad by night pillaging the quiet people of the Countrey, addeth, All this was done by the luſt and licence of the Souldier, nothing by Military Diſcipline. In one of *Cicero's* Orations againſt *Verres*: *Thy care hath been to pillage and vex the Towns of our peaceable friends.* I cannot here omit the opinion of Divines, which I think moſt true: That a King, who pays not his Souldiers duely, is not onely bound to the Souldiers for the loſſes following thence, but alſo to his Subjects and Neighbours, whom the needy Souldiers have plundered and abuſed. On the other ſide, it is the duty of thoſe that abſtain from VVar, to do nothing for the ſtrengthening of him who maintains a bad Cauſe; or,

† *Sic & Guiciard. differit, lib.* 16.

* *Lib.* 4. *c.* 1. See *Spartian* of *Niger's* ſeverity for a ſtoln Cock.

De Præt. Urb.

Ægid. Regius de act. ſupern. diſp. 31. *dub.* 7. *n.* 95.

or, whereby the motions of him, that wageth a just VVar, may be retarded. And in a doubtfull case, they ought to shew themselves equal * to both, in permitting passage, in affording provision for the Legions, in not relieving the besieged. The *Corcyreans* in *Thucydides* say, It is the duty of the *Athenians*, if they would not side with any party, either to prohibite the *Corinthians* from raising Souldiers out of *Attica*, or permit them to do the same. It was objected by the *Romans* against *Philip* King of the *Macedonians*, that the League was violated by him two waies, both because he did injuries to the fellows of the Roman people, and because he assisted the Enemy with aids and money. The same things are urged by *Titus Quintius* in his Conference with *Nabis*: *Yet, thou sayst, I have not properly violated you, and your friendship and society. How often shall I prove the contrary? In short, Wherein is friendship violated? By these two things especially: If thou hast my friends for enemies: if thou art a friend to my enemies.* In *Agathias* we read, He is an enemy, who doth what pleaseth an enemy. And in *Procopius*, He is reckoned in the Enemies Army, who supplyeth them with what is properly usefull for the VVar *. *L. Æmilius* Prætor * ac-

* *Exemplum nobile vide apud Parutam, lib. 8.*

Lib. 1.

Lib. 3.

Gotth. 1.

* Demosthenes: *Qui ea facit & machinatur, quibus ego capi possim, etiamsi nec feriat, nec jaculum emittat, hostis mihi est.* * *Liv. lib. 37.*

cused

cused the *Teians* for victualling the Enemies Navy, and promising them Wine; adding, unless they would do the like for the Navy of the *Romans*, he would account them for his Enemies. *Augustus* said: *The City that receives my Enemy, is become my Enemy*. It will be also profitable to mingle League with both sides waging war, so that, with the good will of both, it may be lawfull to abstain from war, and exhibit the common offices of humanity to both. 'Tis in *Livy*: *Let them, as becomes neutral friends, desire peace, not interpose themselves in the war*. *Archidamus* King of *Sparta*, when the *Eleans* seemed to encline to the *Arcadians* party, wrote an Epistle to them containing onely this: * *It is good to be quiet*.

Plut. Bruto.

Liv. lib. 35.

* καλὸν ἡσυχία.

Cap. 18.

LVII. *Of things done* privately *in publick War*.

WHat we have hitherto said, most part, concerns them, who either have command in chief, or execute publick orders. We must also see, what is lawfull privately in War, by the Law of Nature, of God, or of Nations. *Cicero* relates, that the Son of *Cato Censorius* served in the Army of General *Pompilius*, and when, after the dismission of that Legion wherein he served, the Young Man, in love with war, had remained

Offic. 1.

mained in the Army, *Cato* wrote unto *Pompilius*, that if he would have him ſtay, he ſhould give him an oath the ſecond time; adding this reaſon, becauſe being diſ-engaged from the firſt, he could not juſtly fight with the Enemy. *Cicero* ſetteth down the very words of *Cato* to his Son, whereby he admoniſheth him, not to enter into Battel; for it is not lawfull, ſaith he, for one to fight the Enemy, that is no Souldier. So alſo we read the praiſe of *Chryſantas*, one of *Cyrus*'s Souldiers, who being upon his Enemy, withdrew his Sword, hearing a retreat ſounded. *Seneca* ſaith: *He is call'd an unprofitable Souldier, who hears not the ſign given for a retreat*. But they are deceiv'd, who think this comes from the external Law of Nations: for if you regard that, as it is lawfull for every man to ſeize upon the Enemies goods, ſo alſo to kill the Enemy; for by that Law the Enemies are of no account. Wherefore, that which *Cato* adviſed, comes from the Military Diſcipline of the *Romans*: wherein it was a Law, noted by *Modeſtinus*, that whoſoever obeyed not his Orders, ſhould be puniſht with death, though the matter ſucceeded well. Now, he alſo was ſuppos'd not to have obeyed, who out of order, without the command of the General, entred into any fight, as the Manlian commands do teach

Xenoph. Cyrop. Plut. Quaest. Rom. 39. & Marcello.

De ira, c. 9.

L. deſertorem. D. de re milit.

Liv. l. 7. Manliana Imperia.

teach us. For truly, if that were lawfull, either ſtations would be deſerted, or (licenſe proceeding) the Army, or part thereof, would be engaged in unadviſed Battels *, which by all means is to be avoyded. Therefore *Salluſt*, when he deſcribes the Roman Diſcipline, ſaith, *In war they have been often puniſhed, who againſt Authority had fought againſt the Enemy, and who being recall'd made no haſt out of the Battel.* A certain Laconian, when, being upon his Enemy, and hearing the ſign of retreat, he had repreſſed the blow, gave the reaſon thus: *It is better to obey my Commander, than to kill my Enemy.* And *Plutarch* ſaith, They that are disbanded cannot kill the Enemy, because they are not bound by Military Laws, wherewith they ought to be bound that are to fight. And *Epictetus* in *Arrian* relating the now-mention'd fact of *Chryſantas*, addeth, *So much did he prefer the execution of his Commanders will before his own.* Neverthelefs, if we reſpect natural and internal right, it ſeems granted to every man, in a juſt War, to do thoſe things, which he is confident will, within the juſt meaſure of warring, be advantageous to the innocent party: not alſo to appropriate to himſelf things taken, for nothing is owing to him; unleſs perchance he exact puniſhment by the common right

* Ita Avidius Caſſius cauſam ſententiæ ſuæ reddebat: *Evenire potuiſſe ut eſſent inſidiæ.* Volcatius.

Arrian. l. 6.

right of men. Which laſt, how it is reſtrain'd by the Goſpel-law; may be underſtood by what we have ſaid afore. *Part.* 2. Now, a mandate may be either general, or ſpecial. General, as in a tumult among the *Romans*, the Conſul ſaid, *Whoſoever would have the Common-wealth ſafe, follow me.* *Serv. ad. 8. Æn.* Yea, and to all particular Subjects is ſometimes granted a right of killing, beſides in the way of ſelf-defence, when 'tis publickly expedient. Special mandate, not onely they may have that receive Pay, but they alſo that go to war at their own charge, *C. quando liceat unicuiq. l. 1, & 2.* and that (which is more) adminiſter at their charge a part of the VVar: as they that provide Ships, and maintain them by their own expences; to whom, inſtead of Pay, is wont to be granted leave to keep what they can take. And how far that may go, without violation of internal juſtice and charity, is not without cauſe enquir'd. Juſtice either reſpects the Enemy, or the Common-wealth it ſelf wherewith one has contracted. From the Enemy, we have ſaid, may be taken away the poſſeſſion of all things which may feed the VVar; and this, for ſecurity ſake, on condition to reſtore it: and the dominion too may be taken away, ſo far as to the compenſation of that, which, either from the beginning of the war, or by what

fell

fell out after, is owing to him that wageth a juſt war; whether the things belong to the hoſtile Common-wealth, or to particular men, and thoſe in themſelves innocent: but the goods of the nocent, even by way of puniſhment, may be taken away and poſſeſſed by the Takers. So then, hoſtile goods will become theirs, who adminiſter part of the war at their own charge, ſo far (as to the Enemies) that the meaſure I have expreſſed be not exceeded; and this is to be determin'd by an equal judgement. But, as to the Common-wealth, the ſame will be juſt by internal juſtice, if there be equality in the contract; that is, if the charges and the dangers be as great, as the probability of the prey. For, if this hope be of much more value, the overplus muſt be rendred to the Common-wealth; juſt as if one had, at too cheap a rate, bought a Caſt, uncertain indeed, but eaſy, and of great hope. Yet further, when Juſtice ſtrictly ſo call'd is not offended, there may be a tranſgreſſion from that office which conſiſteth in the love of others, eſpecially ſuch as the Chriſtian Law preſcribeth: as, if it appear that ſuch predation will chiefly hurt, not the generality of the Enemies, nor the King, nor thoſe that are in themſelves nocent, but the innocent; and that ſo much, that it will caſt them into very

great

great calamities; into which, to cast even them that are privately indebted to us, were unmercifulness. But, if moreover that depredation be not of much moment, neither to end the war, nor to weaken the Enemy; in such a case, an honest man, especially a Christian, ought to think it an unworthy gain, which is made onely of the infelicity of the times †. Sometimes also it happens, that, by occasion of publick war, private war ariseth, *viz.* if one chance to fall among ones Enemies, and come into hazard of life or goods: in which case, the same things are to be observ'd, which we have elswhere said of the lawfull manner of self-defence. There is wont also to be joyn'd with private utility, publick authority: *viz.* if one, upon great damage receiv'd from the Enemy obtain a right to recompence his losses out of the Enemies goods: which right is to be defined by what we have said above, of Reprizals. But, if any Souldier or other, even in a just war, hath fir'd the Enemies houses, wasted their fields, and done other damages of the like sort, without command, and when their was no necessity, nor just cause; it is rightly deliver'd by Divines, that he is bound to repair the damages. Justly have I added, what they omitted, *without cause*: for, if there be cause, he will be

Silv. in verbo bellum, n. 8. vers. 5.

† *Plutarch* blames *Crassus* for this, that he got his wealth out of the fire and war, turning the common calamities into private gain.

Part. 2.

Silv. in verbo bellum, p. 1.

be bound perhaps to the Commonwealth, whose Laws he hath transgressed, not to the Enemy, whom he hath not wronged. Not impertinent is that which a Carthaginian gave in answer to the *Romans*, when they requir'd *Annibal* to be yielded to them: *Whether* Saguntum *was set upon by private or publick counsel, is not the question: but, whether justly or unjustly. For, we have this controversy with our Citizen, By what authority he did it; our onely question with you, is, Whether it was against the League or no.*

LVIII.

LVIII. *Admonitions touching Faith and Peace. The Conclusion.*

AS when I treated of undertaking War, I annexed ſome Admonitions about declining War, as much as is poſſible: So will I now alſo, before I diſmiſs the Reader, adde a few *Adviſoes*, which are uſeful both in war and after war, tending to the care of Faith and Peace; and firſt of Faith, both for other reaſons, and for this eſpecially; that the hope of Peace may not be loſt. For, by Faith, not only every Commonwealth is conſerved, as *Cicero* ſaith, but alſo that greater ſociety of Nations. This being taken away as *Ariſtotle* truly, *Commerce is taken away from among men.* Therefore the ſame *Cicero* ſaith, It is a wicked thing, to break ones Faith, without which there is no life. *It is* (as *Seneca* ſpeaks) *the moſt ſacred thing that is ſeated in the breaſt of Man.* And this Faith is ſo much more religiouſly to be kept by the ſupreme Rulers of the world, by how much more they are exempted from the puniſhment of their ſins here, than other men. Take away Faith, they will be like unto wild beaſts, whoſe violence all are afraid of. And Juſtice truly, in its other parts, hath oft-times ſomewhat of obſcurity: but the bond of Faith is manifeſt by it ſelf, yea is therfore

Cicero Offic. 3.

Ariſtoteles Rhetor ad Theodect. 1. 15.

Seneca epiſt. 88.

Cic. pro Q. Roſc.

used that all obscurities may be cleared. The more are Kings to embrace it; First, for Conscience sake, and then for their Credit sake and Reputation, upon which depends the Authority of their government. Wherefore, let them be assured, that such as instill into them the arts of deceiving, do that very thing which they teach. That doctrin cannot long be profitable, which maketh man insociable with man; add also, odious to God. Next, in the whole administration of War, the mind cannot be kept serene and confident in God, unless it always make a prospect toward Peace. For it is most truly said by *Sallust*: *Wise men make war, to obtein Peace.* Wherewith agrees that sentence of S. *Augustin*: *Peace is not sought, that war may be exercis'd; but War is waged, that Peace may be acquir'd.* *Aristotle* himself, more than once, accuses the Nations, that propos'd to themselves actions of War, as their ultimate end. Force is a thing that belongs to wild beasts: and this, in War, is most eminent: the more diligent care must be us'd, to temper it with humanity, lest by too neer imitation of those beasts, we forget that we are men, and lose the softness of our nature †. If then a safe Peace may be had,

Sallust. Orat. ad Caes.

Augustin. epist. ad Bonifac.

Arist. 7. pol. 2. & 14.

† The Embassadors of Justinian in Procopius (*Persic. 2.*) address their speech to Chosroes after this manner: Did we not see you here with our own eyes, and pronounce these words in your ears, we should never have believed that Chosroes the son of Cabades would bring his Army, and enter forcibly into the Roman bounds, contrary

contrary to his Oath; the firmest bond of Truth among men; contrary to his League, the only hope left to those that are afflicted with war: For what is this, but to change the life of men into the life of wild beasts. Take away Leagues, there will be eternal Wars. And Wars without end have this effect, to put men beside themselves, and devest them of their nature.

it is well worth the forgiveness of injuries, and losses, and charges: especially among Christians, to whom their Master hath bequeath'd his Peace. Whose best Interpreter will have us, as far as is possible, and as much as in us lyeth, live peaceably with all men. Rom. 12. 18. It is the property of a good man, as we read in *Sallust*, to begin war with an unwilling mind, and to prosecute it no farther than he needs must. This one consideration may be enough, but for the most part also mens Interest and profit carryes them to this end: first them; who are inferiour in strength; because long strife with one more mighty is full of danger; And, as on shipboard, a greater calamity is to be redeemed with some loss; leaving off anger and hope, deceitful counsellers, as *Livy* rightly call'd them. This sense is thus exprest by *Aristotle*: *Better it is, to yield some of our goods to those that are more potent, than to contend with them and lose all**. And as to the more potent, Peace is for their Interest too: because, while their affairs are prosperous (as the now-cited *Livy* saith no less truly) Peace is honorable to those that give it; and better and safer than the victory hoped for. For the Common Chances of

*Philo de constitutione principis: *Pax, quamvis cum magno detrimento, bello utilior.*

Communis Mars.

War muſt be conſidered. So ſaith *Ariſtotle*, *We muſt think how many and how unexpected alterations do happen in war.* And in *Diodorus*, in a certain Oration for Peace, they are cenſur'd, *who glory in the greatneſs of their actions, as if it were not Fortunes cuſtom, to diſpenſe her favours, and ſucceſſes, by turnes.* And beſides, there is one thing more, which may be feared moſt, the Boldneſs of deſperate men, like unto the fierceſt biting of dying beaſts †. But, if both Parties ſeem to themſelves equal, that indeed, in *Caeſars* judgment, is the beſt time to treat of peace, whileſt they have Both ſome confidence in their own ſtrength. And, when Peace is made, on whatſoever terms, it is by all means to be preſerved by reaſon of that ſanctimony of Faith aforeſaid: and with all care muſt be avoided, not only perfidiouſneſs, but alſo whatever exaſperates the mind. For, what *Cicero* ſaid of private, you may apply as well to theſe publick friendſhips, As they are all to be maintained with exact fidelity and Religion, ſo thoſe eſpecially which after enmities are made up again and reſtored.

† *Quippe timenda etiam morientis luſtra Leonis.*

God

GOd (who alone can do it) inſcribe theſe things in their hearts, who have the Affairs of Chriſtendom in their hands; and grant them a Mind intelligent of Divine and Human Right, and ever remembring that ſhe is elected by God to govern man, a creature moſt dear unto himſelf †.

† Chryſoſt. ſerm. de Eleemoſyna; ἄνθρωπος τὸ περισπούδαστον ζῶον τῷ θεῷ.

THE END.

OUT OF THE LIFE OF

S. LUDOVIC,

HIS CHARGE

To his Son.

IF any Controversy or action be rais'd against thee, inquire into the *Truth*, as well on the contrary part as on thy side. If thou hast any thing of anothers, taken by thy self, or by thy Ancestors, *Restore* it quickly. Wage no War against any *Christian*, but by the Counsel of *Many*, and when War is unavoidable. And in War, do no hurt to *Church-men*, and those that have done thee no wrong. If *Seditions* rise among thy subjects, quiet them as soon as thou canst. See often what thy *Officers* do, and examin their ways, and reform what is amiss. Let no foul sin reign within thy Kingdom.

Out

Out of the same King's life written by Joinvil, chap. 89.

THe King's great Counsellors reprehended him oft for taking so much pains to make *peace* among his *neighbours:* saying, He did ill to end their wars, which would be for his Advantage. The King answerd, *You say not well. For, if my neighbouring Princes did see me cherish their Wars, they would say I had a plot upon them, and hate me, and take a time to do me and my Kingdom a mischief. Moreover, I should provoke the wrath of God against me, who blesseth the Peacemakers.* Certain it is, the *Burgundians* and *Lorainers*, perceiving the Kings *Goodness* and *Justice*, were so loving and observant of him, that they referred then differences to his *Arbitration*. I have often seen them come to him, for that purpose, to *Paris*, and other places, where the King was resident.

MEMO-

MEMORIALS OF THE LIFE AND DEATH OF H. GROTIUS.

LONDON,
Printed by *T. Warren* , for *W. Lee* , And
are to be ſold at his ſhop, at the ſign
of the *Turks-head* in *Fleet-ſtreet* , 1654.

Memorials of the Authors Life and Death.

HE that hath surveyed with a judicious eye the various & choyce Learning conteined in this Book, cannot but desire to know more of the Author, than what the Title shews him, That He was, The Illustrious Hugo Grotius. *Men are naturally apt to enquire (as He* observes) and to know as much as they can can of the person whose Actions or writings have any way drawn their attention. Who is this man, that hath written such things? To write the life of this Man perfectly, were an enterprize for one more versed both in Books and Men: For Me, it will be enough, to collect out of the Authors own Writings (And indeed, to describe* Grotius, *who is so able as* Grotius?) *and of some of his friends, what may represent (in some sort) so excellent a person to my Readers view, and conduce to the perpetuating of his happy Memory among us Englishmen, to whom he bare a special*

* The writer of Mr. Medes Life.

ſpecial Affection. And firſt we will repreſent that ſummary of his firſt years, which we find in Meurſius's *Athenæ Batavæ, to this effect.*

Athenæ Bat. Anno 1583. *Hugo Grotius* was born at *Delf* in *Holland*, 4. *eid. April. Anno* 1583. He was of an Antient, and Noble Houſe. His Grandfather of the ſame name was learned above the model of thoſe darker times, and well skild in the three principal Languages, *Latin*, *Greek* and *Hebrew*. His Uncle *Cornelius Grotius* was profeſſor of the Civil Law at *Leyden*, where he flouriſhed in the good eſteem and favour of the beſt men. His Father was *Joannes Grotius*, Curator of that Univerſity: whoſe Poems are extant, with *Lipſius* Letters to him, and *Douſa's* verſes: whoſe name alſo hath adorned many learned Mens Books dedicated to Him. Being bleſt with this Hopeful ſon, he uſed all pains and care in his good education, and cheriſhed this great Wit ſo well, that when he was but eight years

Anno 1591. old, *viz. Anno* 1591. He did *fundere verſus*, make verſes *ex tempore*, and diſputed twice publickly in queſtions of Phi-

Anno 1598. loſophy. *Anno* 1598. *æt.* 15. He travelled into *France* in the train of that incomparable perſon, *Joannes Oldenbarneveldius*, Embaſſador from the States to the Great *Henry*; and returned honour'd with Royal Bounty, and the Friendſhip of Illuſtrious Men; having before that time

begun

begun to ſet forth notes upon the ſeven Liberal Arts of *Martianus Capella.* When he had after ſtudied ſome years at *Leyden,* much endeared unto *Scaliger,* his Father fearing the yong Scholars mind ſhould, by the Amenity and delight of human literature and Poeſy, be drawn away from more profitable employment; he was taken off, and aſcribed among the Advocates at the *Hague*, *Anno* 1599. and Anno 1599.
ſoon after pleaded Cauſes. Yet did not he addict himſelf ſo much to that profeſſion, but that his Genius led him back, and made him often reviſit his former ſtudies of Humanity. For which, he was moſt dear to the *French* Embaſſador *Buzanvall,* to *Janus Douſa* the Father, and many other Perſons of Honour. About this time the States of *Holland* began to uſe his ſervice, in penning the Hiſtory of the moſt famous War in the whole world. Afterward *Anno* 1607. Com- Anno 1607.
mended by the Suffrages of the Courts, nominated by the States, and elected by the moſt potent Prince, the Admiration of all other Princes, *Grave Maurice*, he became *Fiſci Advocatus*, Advocate of the Treaſury, and behaved himſelf ſo well in this moſt weighty office, that he received from his ſuperiours a moſt ample teſtimony of his diligence and integrity. Here perceiving the Trade into *India* of great Importance to his Countrey, that he might ſtir up the ſpirits

of

of his Countrymen thereto, he wrote a Book, *De Jure Commercii Indicani. Again*, observing, after the Truce with the *Spaniard*, the peace of the Commonwealth began to be disturbed by certain dangerous Innovators, judging it to be the Duty of a good Patriot, to oppose himself against their Designs, and to commend unto All the present State, he set out a Dissertation, entituled, *De Antiquitate Reipublicæ Batavia*. After the death of *Elias Olden Barneveldius*, a man not less Noble for his good parts, than his family, Our *Grotius* sufferd himself to be chosen into his place, *Syndic of Roterdam*, and so was advanced from the Bar to the Bench. And then was he sent into Great *Britain* to accommodate the difference about the *Indian* Trade: whence he was dismist not without eminent marks of favour from that King of Learning and Religion, and from the most learned and pious men of that Iland, together with this most pleasing fruit of his Journey, that he there had found the Great *Isaac Casaubon*, whom he reverenced before at a distance, and had now enjoyed a more intimate and familiar conversation with him. About that time the Church being very sick of the Controversies of *Predestination*, and of the contention of some Pastors with the Magistrates about the right of Church-Government: in so much that the States of *Holland* were by some

Contu-

Contumeliouſly reproached : Our Author thought it his Duty to vindicate the Right of the State , and offer his Medicines for the Cure of thoſe Diſtempers , and ſhew the way to Peace in thoſe and other Differences that diſturb the Chriſtian World.

Thus far out of Athenæ Batavæ , *a Book conteining the Lives of the moſt eminent profeſſors and learned men that have flouriſhed in that Univerſity,and much tending to the honour of it. Wherfore it may be a good precedent for our two famous Univerſities , and for* London (*that perhaps may not improperly be ſtiled a third Academy) and ſtir them up to do the like. For* England *hath in this laſt Age produced men as worthy, as any other, though not ſo much known abroad. But , to reflect a little upon what is ſaid already, before we go on : That ſo laſting a Wit as* Grotius *had, ſhould be ſo ſoon ripe, is not a little to be admired.* Odi puerulum præcoci ingenio , *ſaith the Poet of ſentences ; Precocity is a token of a ſhort-liv'd wit: but 'twas not ſo in Him. Well did a great man in* France *apply to him, what* Turnebus *formerly had ſaid of* Joſeph Scaliger, *that he was* portentoſi ingenii Juvenis ; *And* Daniel Heinſius *a great wit too (me thinks 'tis happy when ſuch men bear a fair reſpect to one another,and do not turn ingenuous Emulation into envious Detraction:) hath honoured him with this elogy *:*

* *Heinſius ad Grotium cum ab eo Adamo exule Tragœdia donaretur.*

Natura

Natura nutrix, obstetrixq; , quæ prius
Noverca cunctis, Grotio Mater fuit.
Senex Ephebus ille, quem Batavia
Miratur omnis , optat Hetruscus sibi
Omnisq; Gallus. Ille dum puer fuit
Vir esse cœpit. Namq; relliqui viri
Tandem fuere : Grotius *vir natus est.*

Nature, the stepdame to us all,
Grotius may his Mother call.
That old Yong man Holland admires,
Italy and all France desires.
We grow up slowly : would you see
One born full Man? *Grotius* is He.

*As he became a man very quickly , and did all things like a Man , so did he last long , and was never idle. Another Poet * speaks thus, of that eminent Pair* Grotius *and* Heinsius *:*

Vobis Dei favore nomen obtigit
Livore majus , & senecta temporum ,
Exsorsq; lethi : Parca nullum jus habet
In secla vatum, quos Perennitas sacrat.
Cœlestis aura morte deleri nequit ,
Nec interire sanguis Heroum potest.
Nihil precari majus aut vobis licet ,
Aut sæculo , quam possit ut diu frui
Tanto Deorum munere. O cultum mihi
Par, & colendum semper antiqua fide !
Sublime cœlo latus efferam caput ,
Votisq; nulla summa desiet meis ,
Si me benignus eruditorum chorus,
Consentiensq;

* *Dominicus Baudius in carm. ad Dan. Heins. Idem Baudius ad Grot. & Heins.* O par gemellum amoris antiqua fide, Morumq; nexu, heroicisq; laudibus, &c.

Consentiensq; postuma gentis favor
Tali jugo accensere tertium velit.

Of our Author's *Martianus Capella* which he set forth before he was fifteen years old, hear the divine *Scaliger* *

* *Jos. Scalig. in Martianum Capellam Hugonis Grotii.*

Hugo soboles Grotius *optimi parentis,*
Qui limina nondum tetigit puberis avi,
Sed mente senili teneros pravenit annos;
Magnum meditans, auspiciis noluit illis
Praludere, qua vesticipum postulat atas,
Sed maluit à grandibus inchoare cœptis.
Nam qui penus est, omnis & arca disciplina,
Sed quem horridulum injuria squallore vetustas
Omni studiorum nitido abdicarat usu,
Illius ab incude profectus, atq; amæno
Splendore micans, purpurea veste decorus,
Cultusq; novo pumice Martianus exit.
Cernisne, ut ovantem lepido flore juventa,
Commendet eum gratia luminis recentis?
Quam sive habuit, restituit Grotius *illi;*
Seu non habuit, contulit hanc Grotius *illi.*

The Author himself maks a modest mention of his Capella *and some other writings of his about the same time, in an Epistle to his great friend (and indeed the*

 great

great friend of all learned men) *Jacobus Augustus Thuanus* *: I was exceedingly glad (faith he) when I understood, my *Capella*, *Aratus*, and *Epithalamium Regium*, were not only come to your hands, but also well taken ; not that I think those poor endeavours of my Youth do merit the honour of your suffrage, but that I am confident, you have rightly esteem'd the Donour's Affection. My own opinion of *Martianus* & the other Syntagm is only this, that they are capable of some excuse from my Age : for I wrote them when I was very yong *. But you are pleas'd to go farther, and upon these beginnings ground a judgment of Greater Hope and Growth hereafter. This , I must confess , is my desire , this is my greatest ambition, to be prais'd by the prais-worthy. As to the *Epithalamium* , I am sorry many things are mistaken , of which I have since had better intelligence : for I compos'd it by conjecture. And I wish I had inserted some things of the *Allobrogick* War , in the place of some other. I know not how it comes to pass, which I find in my self, that my yonger writings are condemn'd by the judgment of my riper years, and yet I cease not, but have a minde to compose what will afterward displease my self. I have now some pieces done , others designed, which , when they are set forth, shall carefully be conveyed to you. My chief care is at present , to collect something

* *Grot. epist. ad Ja. Aug. Thuan. Anno 1601.*

* *Diu ante plenam pubertatem.*

thing

thing that may be useful to you in your *Annals* of *France*, believing it to be of much concernment to my Country, if the Actions thereof, by occasion of the Neighbouring Affairs, be eterniz'd in so glorious a Work. And I will take the best care I can, to answer your desire, by informing you, what time and place was fatal to the learned Men of our Countrey. Happy are you, who at your spare hours (which I am perswaded are but few) can do things above the Abilities of other men, who make it their only Business. Happy is *France*, govern'd by the Counsil of Men, that liberally bestow upon the Commonwealth of learning, the Remainder of their Time which they can borrow from the publick Affairs of the Kingdom. And would I might be so happy once, as to enjoy the presence and friendship of such men, which I do not despair of, especially hoping for your Favour. *An.* 1601. *In another Epistle of the same year to the same Thuanus, wherewith he presented him his* Adamus Exul *(concerning which, by the way, take this of Janus Douza* *: * *Jan. Dous. in Hug. Grot. Adamum Exulem Tragœd.*

Mortiferum hic vetita decerptum ex
arbore pomum,
Adami lapsus exiliumq; Leges,
Nunc primum en Latio donati atq; urbe
Quiritum;
Debita quæ Civi gloria sola meo;

Qui Phœbo Delphisq; suis, nec consule tantum
Patre, sed & Magni nomine dignus ovat.)

Grot. in epist. ad Jacobum Aug. Thuan. *To the same* Thuanus, *I say, our Author thus addresses himself:* To You is this offer'd, most illustrious President, who after that light of *Scotland* have revived Tragedy. Indeed *Buchanan*, in other points most excellent, seemeth to degenerate from the hight of the *Buskin*, so that I may say, You are the first by whose conduct the old Majesty of the Stage is brought back again, from that Prince of Tragœdians *Æschylus*. Give me leave to adore your footsteps, and receive here a Tragedy, and that a sacred one; to the writing whereof as Your example invited, so my manifest inequality might have deterred me. For no sober man, where he desires to excell, would follow *Thuanus*: to whom who doth not so give the first place, as not daring to aspire unto the second? As for me, I contend not with any one for Glory, but pleased my self in this sacred Argument; fearing not censure, while I am unsollicitous of praise.

Anno 1608. *Anno.* 1608. *He published another Tragedy entitled* Christus patiens, *and dedicated it to* Petrus Janninus, *the King of France's Embassador to the States. A* Grotii epist. ad Petrum Janninum. *part of his dedicatory Epistle is very fit to be read here.* Suffer, I pray, the noblest name, and that which will be perpetually ly celebrated in the Annals of *France*, to be inſcribed upon this Book : that Men, by this ſign may ſee, though I cannot be thankful enough, I have not willingly been unthankful. The trueſt praiſe of the *French-Nation* is Humanity, eſpecially toward ſtrangers : but your Humanity hath exceeded all former limits, and is not common to the Nation, but proper to your ſelf. You have new-ſpirited a yong man, commendable for nothing but his love of good learning, and admiration of eminent perſons, and you have not only countenanced him & encouraged him with gracious words, (which was much:) but of your own accord, have admitted him (let me not offend your honour in ſaying ſo) into your boſom, as an intimate friend. Moreover, You have laid hold on all occaſions to advance me, with a bountiful, prone, and (I had almoſt ſaid) Paternal Affection. Whenſoever the Affairs of *France* and greater cares ſhall recall you from us, it will be a ſad time to All, moſt to Me; For it will deprive me of the chiefeſt part of my felicity: Yet tis a comfort, that it ſhall never be able to extinguiſh, either the memory which you are pleaſed to retein of me, or the honour which I have received from ſo illuſtrious a Friendſhip. And, ſeeing it much concern'd me to have it known, I thought it meet upon that account to make this publick Addreſs, and offer you this Tragedy for a teſtimony of a moſt devoted Heart. That it might be worthy of you, ſeeing I could not give it value from my ſelf, I have taken it from the matter, moſt woeful in in the fact, moſt joyful in the effect and fruit, moſt ſacred every way. This alone unites the divided minds of Chriſtians, ſtriving with one another as much in hatred as they ought in love, and keeps them ſtil almoſt invincible, not permitting their differences to be infinite. No other Argument could be found more agreeable to your Mind, who long mourn for the lamentable diſtractions of this Age, and ſtudy to procure, as much as is in you (and very much is in you) the Peace of the Church; a thing that we can only wiſh for. For, that, Truth neceſſary to ſalvavation being eſtabliſht, due liberty 'twixt unjuſt Domination and unbridled Licence being granted in other points, the Parties much inflam'd by ambition, avarice, private Intereſts, and impunity of ſpeaking & doing evil brought in by wars, may by degrees be reconciled and cloſe in a League; to this end (*I ſay*) the Authority of your King, the Prince of Chriſtian Princes, and next unto that your lenity and moderation, and of ſuch as you are, yieldeth us the greateſt Hope. Which Hope, may He at length, bring unto an Iſſue, who is our Common Redeemer, and hath bought us with his own blood, the memory of which ineffable Benefit, we have

have expressed in this Tragedy, if not with happy success, yet with a pious endeavour.

This last passage I was the more willing to communicate to the Christian Reader, because it shews, that our Author very early entred into that pious care of the Churches Peace, which he carried with him all along the course of his life, even to his grave, as we shall observe in that which follows. In his studies of Piety and Religion he had the domestick Assistance of the learned and peaceable Divine Franciscus Junius; *whose Opinions yet, our* Grotius *did not so obstinately embrace, (as the manner of some is to follow their Masters beyond reason) but that he had an ear for* Arminius, *one of the publick professors at* Leyden *about the same time. Because I have mention'd a name hated by many (more through prejudice, than upon any true ground) I shall here annex our Authors Verses upon his death*, not so much out of an intention to praise the man, as to set forth the Temper of our Author in his own lively words;* * Anno 1609.

** Scrutator altæ Veritatis Armini*
Sublime pectus, anima fœta doctrinæ,
Solertiæq; perspicacis exemplum,
Tu nunc ademptus sæculo tenebricoso
Et semicœcæ palpitantium turbæ
Claros beatæ lucis incolis campos:
Et sive multum debuit tibi verum,

* *Grot. Farrag. libro 3. In mortem Jacobi Arminii.*

Seu

Seu parte in aliqua, more gentis humanæ,
Et neſcientis multa ſorte naturæ,
Te cepit error (Judicent, quibus ſacri
Juris poteſtas, viſq; tanta naſcendi)
Certe ſuperni codicis frequens Lector,
In verba certe non adactus humana
Labi timentis, nec rebellis in ſeſe,
Fers teſte cœlo conſcientiæ laudem,
Ibi ſatur quiete, gaudii plenus,
Quæſita quondam diſcis, & vides, quanta
Involvat homines inſcientiæ nubes:
Quam nil ſit illud, quod vocamus hic ſcire,
Quo nos ſuperbi tollimus caput cœlo,
Calcamus alios, invicemq; calcamur.
Hinc tanta bella ſæviunt magiſtrorum,
Hinc odia plebis: interim fugit longè,
Nec ſe videndam dimicantibus præbet
Amica ſancta ſancta Veritas Pacis.
Unde iſta rabies, & libido pugnandi
Inſedit animos? Cur placet Deus, belli
Materia? Quo tot ſtudia, tot novæ partes?
An hoſtis atra nocte peſtilens Chriſti
Inſparſit agro ſemen? an furor pugnax
Mortalitatis, ingeniq; corrupti
Alimenta quævis ſumit, & Dei cauſâ
Permiſcet hominem? curioſus an mundus
Dum nil latere patitur, & ſequi gaudet
Sciri negata, jure ſentit hanc pœnam?
Ut illa quondam, dum viam parat cœlo,
Structrix ſuperbæ molis inſolens turba

In

In mille linguas abiit, atq; aberranti
Sermone priscum vocis exuit fœdus.
Heu quid paramus? Lectus orbe de toto
Grex ille parvus lancinamur heu fœde
Iterumq; & iterum, scindimurq; discordes,
Ridente Turca, nec dolente Judæo,
Felix remota factionibus Vulgi
Religio simplex, arte non laborata:
Quæ morte Christi certa dilui culpas,
Hic spem fidemq; ponit, & dari credit
Gratis salutem, promerentibus pœnam:
Sanctiq; amoris lene munus exercens
Non curat altum sapere, nec nimis quærit,
An lege certa veniat omne Venturum:
Exsors malorum quomodo malum nolit,
Velitq; Rector: summa quatenus causa
Potente nutu velle temperet nostrum.
Felix & ille quisquis ambitu liber,
Nec vana captans lucra, nec leves plausus,
Cœlestiores excitatus ad curas
In astra tendit, & Deum studet nosse,
Qua se ipse pandit, ambulatq; suspensis
Periculosas gressibus per ambages,
Non mentientis fila persequens libri:
Cui charitate temperata libertas
Certat manere dissidentibus concors:
Piaq; purus æquitatis affectus
Damnatus aliis, ipse neminem damnat:
Modestiaq; limitem premens, donat
Nunc verba vero, nunc silentium paci.
Hæc sæpe populo teste, sæpe privatim,
Hæc

Hæc ipsa fato jam propinquius, Armini,
Adhuc monebas, cum laboribus vitæ
Longis fatiscens, sæculiq; pertæsus
Fastidiosi, pertinacis, ingrati,
Indigniore parte fractus & languens;
Meliore sospes; illa millibus multis
Monstrata per te regna totus arderes.
Et nunc paterno sidus additum templo
Deum precaris, Det gregi suo lucem.
Hic quanto satis est, hac det esse contentum:
Det non loquentes sua reperta Doctores:
Det consonantes semper omnium linguas,
Aut corda saltem: præpotente vi flammæ
Caliginosas litium fuget sordes:
Ut spiret unum tota civitas Christi,
Vitamq; terris approbet, fidem cœlo.

Did we all follow what is here so well exprest; that is, humbly submit to plain Scripture, not boldly enquire into things unrevealed; more exercise our charity, and less quarrel about opinions; walk in sincerity of heart before God, and in uprightness of conversation before men; Certainly it would be much better with Christendome, than it is at this day. But, the great fault is, that men lay out their zeal upon a sect, or side; and study not to improve the Common Truths to the Advancement of Peace and Charity †.

† See Dr. *Hammonds* Treatise of Fundamentals.

But

But more of this hereafter. Among our Author's first works, above is mention'd his De Republica Batav. *of which Himself speaks in an Epistle to* Thuanus, An. 1610. *thus:* *An. 1610.*

* This Book of our Common-wealth I send to you, that have framed together not the French Historie onely, but the Historie of the whole World, with such variety of matter, and such elegance of stile, that no man could ever have expected the like from one at greatest leisure. But I send you a slender work if you look upon the matter, containing not the affairs of all mankind, no nor of some great Kingdome, but of one Nation included within narrow bounds: nor all the affairs of this, but a breviate onely of the Government. Plainly, here is nothing for you to love, nothing to praise, besides a mind like yours, *viz.* most affectionate to my Country, and not addicted to Innovation. I embrace that saying of *Thucydides: That scheme of Government which every one hath received, it is good for him to preserve.* That's your care in a great Kingdome, ours in a little Common-wealth. Your immortal work, though it may please all by the antient elegance of words, and variety of matter, yet doth it not deserve better of the Readers in any respect, than that it makes them both good men, and good Subjects. We also will be

* *Grot. Epist. ad Jac. Aug. Thuanum.*

be among the Disciples of this Institution, and will labour after your example, that our fidelity and liberty in all things may be approved.

In England *our Author began the thirtieth year of his Age on Easter day,* An. 1612.* *and celebrated the same with these following Verses :*

* *In Pascha, Anni 1612. Natalem trigesimum. Farrag. l. 3.*

**Christe tui quondam testis de morte triumphi;*
In lucem reduci quæ tibi prima fuit;
Hæc quoque nascentem me post tot sæcula vidit
Sancta piis semper, bis mihi sancta dies:
Scilicet ut nequeam, geminato munere, donec
Sum memor ipse mei, non memor esse tui.
Olim quindecimum cum Sol mihi conderet annum,
Ostendit mihi ver Gallia, *vere meo.*
Contigimus dextram, qua nulla potentior armis,
Quæ quod regnabat debuit ipsa sibi.
Nunc bis quindecimum luces mihi noctibus æquans
Phrixeæ Phœbus vellera lustrat ovis:
Natalisq; meus me ditibus aspicit arvis,
Quæ Tamesis puro vitreus amne rigat.
Vidimus hic illum, qui regno maximus, unus
Est regum regno celsior ipse suo:
Qui postquam terris datus est, sapientia vera

Pri-

Privatum posthac se decus esse negat.
Hactenus ista. latet sors indeprensa futuri:
Scit, qui sollicitum me vetat esse, Deus.
Duc Genitor me Magne: sequar quocunque vocabor,
Seu tu læta mihi, seu mihi dura paras.
Sistis in hac vita? maneo? partesq; tuebor
Quas dederis. Revocas optime? promtus eo.
Post reges visos, da regum cernere Regem,
Natalemq; mihi, sed sine nocte, diem.

A little before he came into England, *he had correspondence with* Casaubon, *and consulted him about the Churches peace, proposing some expedients to that purpose.* Casaubon *in one Epistle returns him this Answer:*

* You have made me happy with your Letters which I lately receiv'd: and I cannot express the pleasure I take in your cares and studies of Peace and Concord. You see in your Country, how easy a thing it is to stir up contentions among brethren, how hard to allay them. Think every Country to be *Holland.* So great store is there of the lovers of Contention every where: who account it a matter indifferent, or not so much, whether the Church have any peace or no. 'Tis a small thing, not to love

* *Casauboni Epist.* 220. *Hugoni Grotio. Lond.* 15. *Kal. Feb.* 1612.

love concord: I know many, that do suspect and hate no men more than peace-makers. The more have I admir'd the piety of King *James*, who doth so embrace the study of Truth, that he recedes not from the study of Unity. *The same* Casaubon *in another Epistle to* Grotius: * The most wise King, most studious of Peace and Concord, having read your Letter, exceedingly praised your piety joyn'd with equal prudence. His Majestie could wish, that all They, who have any hand in the Government of Christian Kingdomes and Commonwealths, were of your mind: and, he doubteth not, it would be for the great good of God's Church. He also wonderfully approves the counsel you suggest, of procuring concord by all means, at least among our own. If this, any way, through Gods mercy, could be effected, the King assures himself, Many good men, who at this day knowing not whither to turn themselves amidst our so great discords, do groan under the Popes Tyrannie, would provide for the liberty of their Consciences. I will pronounce nothing of the Papists of other Countryes: but of my Countrymen of *France* I think I may truly say, the best of them do wait for the day of the Lord, and from their souls detest the maintainers of empty superstitions, and of Papal Tyrannie. I say more, and I say it upon good

* *Casaub. Epist.* 221. 6. *Kal. Febr.*

good ground: If in our *France*, Reformation had been carried on, without so much varying from the form of the Antient Church, many thousands more, now most averse from the Doctrine of our Churches, had been converted. When I have said thus to our Ministers in *France*, I found but few, who preferred not their own preciseness before gentle and moderate counsels. Here, far otherwise minded are both the King, and every most learned man of the English Clergy. Many of the Bishops in this Kingdome, men excelling in learning and piety, I have found; who day and night study the same thing with you, and give themselves continually to the same Cogitations. And I doubt not, if a beginning were made, or if any occasion did arise of effecting that, of which you have most prudently written, both his most excellent Majestie, and the whole Church of *England*, and especially the most reverend Bishops, would try all things, to promote so good a work. His Majestie commanded me, to let you understand so much, requesting you to continue in the same mind, and to communicate your counsels to us.

Being in England, *our* Grotius *persisted in his endeavours of Reconciliation, and presented to the learned Dean of St*. Pauls, *Dr*. Overal; *a little Tract, (of late * published) entituled*, Con- ** Cum aliis opusc. Amstelod. 1652.*

ciliatio

ciliatio diffidentium de re prædeftinaria & gratia opinionum : *which the Dean having perufed, returns, with this judgement upon it :*

Jo. Overallus Hug. Grotio, Maii 16. 1613.

Remitto ad Te, &c. I return to you your Conciliation, which is very much approv'd by me, but I fear you will not approve it to your Antagonifts, efpecially the more rigid Sectators of *Calvin's* way: That Zenonian Sect will hardly yield to moderate fentences in thefe matters, but will tooth and nail adhere unto that fatal doctrine of Predeftination, in the pure mafs, or at leaft in the corrupt, the Reprobates (that is, All men befides their abfolutely Elect) being excluded from the Redemption of Chrift, and from fufficient Grace, in the intention of God and of Chrift.

After his return into Holland *he profecuted his Confultation for Peace by Letters to his friends in* England, *and fent over a Copy of the Decree of the States for the ending of thofe Difputes: as appears in another Epiftle of* Cafaubon's, 1614.

* *Cafauboni ad Grotium epift. Lond. 6. Kal. Maii. 1614.*

* Yours to Dr. *Overal* I will deliver him my felf this day, and ask his counfel about your Bufinefs. He is now, not Dean of St. *Pauls*, but Bifhop of *Lichfield*, which preferment was conferr'd on him by the moft gracious King, a month fince. But, fuch Accidents befall men, this Acceffion of honour was made

the

the leſs joyfull to him, by the Stone, or ſome like diſeaſe, wherewith he was taken that very day whereon he obtain'd his place. I will prevail with him to write you an Anſwer, or, if I cannot, I will fully declare unto you his opinion. The Edict of the moſt illuſtrious States, I read ſo ſoon as I had opened your Packet, and noted therein one or two expreſſions, which I would have wiſhed a little otherwiſe conceived. But I will expect the judgement of others; and then I will diligently write unto you both my own and their Obſervations. In the mean, I cannot ſufficiently praiſe the Deſign of the moſt illuſtrious States, in putting a reſtraint upon curious Heads by this Edict †. The Lord bleſs their work. I have long been perſwaded, that the immoderate deſire of men to peirce into the ſecret Counſels of God, beyond what the eternal Wiſdome hath revealed to us in Scripture, is one of the moſt grievous Evils of our Time. The antient Church firmly believ'd, there are many myſteries in Chriſtian Religion, of which it is better to be ſilent, eſpecially among the Common People, than to diſpute ſubtilly. I have written much of that

† Et in Epiſt. ſeq. *Neque vero conſilium duntaxat Rex iu- [illegible] & alii viri graviſſimi probavere, ſed & formulam quoque ipſam juſſit ordinum conceptam. Apparet enim id eſſe actum, ut à duobus ſcopulis in hac doctrina æque periculoſis, hinc Manichæorum, inde Pelagianorum, popul avertantur: & in ea doctrina confirmentur, quæ ſalutis noſtræ proram & puppim, principium, inquam, progreſſum & τελείωσιν, uni Deo adſcribens contemptum tamen bonorum operum non inducat.* See the late Kings Decree, ſet before the 39. Articles, to the like purpoſe.

 opi-

opinion of the Antients, when I expounded why the Sacraments are called Myſteries. Which Argument when I handled, and thought upon the modern Controverſies, I could not forbear to ſay ſomewhat of the matter. See, if you pleaſe, the beginning of the 564. page.

The Book now cited by Caſaubon, *is his Exercitations againſt* Baronius, (Lond. 1614.) *upon which Work here follow* Grotius'*s Verſes, which I ſet down for the better demonſtration of that moderate way theſe great Scholars followed in the buſineſs of Religion, wiſhing their example may help to reduce others from extravagancies.*

* *Hugonis Grotii carmen in Exercit. Baronianas Iſ. Caſaubon.*

* *Annales docti nimium ſervire* Baroni
Qui legis, &c. Thus in Engliſh:
The Annals of the great *Baronius*,
Approv'd at *Rome*, too too obſequious,
Believe not raſhly: The Laborious Book
Was over-aw'd by an Imperious look:
Errours cloakt under purple Robes: No hope,
This long time, that plain Truth ſhould pleaſe the Pope.
O Piety, where art! where is the Man
So valiant againſt this Age, that can
Defend thy Cauſe; when Schiſm and Faction,
Paſſions and Luſts reign o'r Religion?

Some

Some to impose one as the Head of All,
To raise Him up, consider not who fall.
Reverend Antiquity, without her choyce,
Is forc'd against her self to give her voyce.
Kings to deprive both of their Life and Crown,
For private Interest, to throw Justice down,
New falshood to commend with an old Name,
This is the way to Riches and to Fame.
Some others too, guilty of Innovation,
Call this a free and a pure Reformation:
To these, received Rites displeasing are;
Lest that to *Rome* they should approach too near.
Thus Piety afflicted, and long hid,
(Which alwaies to speak Falshood doth forbid,
And sometimes, to conceal Truth;) weeping past
From place to place to find some aid at last,
Other hands failing, *Casaubon* divine,
She was not dis-appointed seeking thine.

I have no wealth to give ; not the
  Red Hat :
Alas (said she) my Enemies have
  that :
Yet have I great Rewards , Good
  Conscience ,
Gratefull Posterity, Gods Beneficence.
Thou heardst , and fearedst not this
  evil Age ,
That Wars against Peace with per-
  petual Rage.
Hence *Athenæus*, and *Polybius* now ,
Those Glorious and younger Works ,
  which thou
Hast wrought : and let thy *Strabo*
  yield his place ,
And all thy Sons of Roman or Greek
  race.
One more Heroick comes. The former
  were
Labours of Learning : Piety is here.

Near the same time, he wrote an Epistle to Joannes Hotmannus Vellerius, *which, because it touches Concord and the Decree above mention'd, may fitly be added in this place.*

* *Hugo Grot. Jo. Hotman. Vellerio, 26. Aug. 1614.*

* I received by the hand of the Right Honourable the French Embassadour your worthy Present, *viz.* Books of excellent Men written on behalf of the best thing (yet most despair'd of) the peace of divided Christianity. To speak my opinion briefly , I think, if *Luther* had

had had the mind of *Melancthon*, and the Patriarch of the West the mind of *Cassander*, it had fared better with the Affairs of *Europe*, which is now, for a whole Age almost, miserably shaken with bloody wars, under the Title of the Gospel. And now, when even those who have deserted the Roman party, do for a few Controversies so implacably disagree, what hope can there be of Concord in the whole Body? Nevertheless, Endeavours in so good a thing are not without praise, even when they are without success, But, if the present Age deserve this punishment, to be given up to their own madness, and will not admit any wholsome Counsels, the next Age perchance will be more happy, and either be studious of peace, or weary of contention. God often brings matters about unexpectedly. I suppose you have read my Book*. 'Tis doubtfull whether my own Countrymen or the Jesuits are more displeased with it: the Former, because I defend that paradox (as it seemeth to them) That in every Church, they may be tolerated, who differ about things not simply necessary: the Latter, because I call Princes to the inspection and care of matters of Religion. Both which Points are such, that, if they be not stated so, we shall neither be able to recover our lost unity, nor to retain this

* *Cui tit. Pietas Ordinum Hollandiæ, ni fallor.*

this which we have. That the States of *Holland* are of the same Judgement with me, you shall perceive by their Decree. I have taken some pains, that it might not go forth without testimonies, not onely that the Authority thereof might be more sacred, but also that I might accustom our men to yield somewhat to pious Antiquity, which by some is frowardly despised. *Adde unto this what he wrote the next year to* Thuanus:

Grotius Thuano, 1515.

I engaged in this contentious kind of writing, not moved thereunto by my own disposition, (for that is not quarrelsome) but impelled by a certain greater force, *viz.* by the counsel of prudent men, and by a desire to serve both my Country and the Church: and truly the Church more than my Country. For, to tell you the very truth (and who better deserves to hear the truth?) ever since I began to consider diligently of the Affairs of Religion, I found their complaints, who called for amendment in doctrines, in rites, in government, to be most just; but (as it commonly happens) they went too far, and erred a little on the other hand *. So, whil'st they departed from the dangerous confidence of Merits, there crept in opinions contemning Good Works: in hatred of Superstition, they were dis-affected to all Liturgie, and order of Divine Service: and for fear

* διὰ τὸ τῆς ἀνθολκῆς ἁμαρτάνειν.

fear of Tyrannie (which had been intolerable) they proceeded to the confines of Anarchy. VVherefore I have alwaies thought it the duty of all good men on our side, to do their utmost, that by little and little, whatsoever was exorbitant might be reduced to a Golden mediocrity. VVhich cogitation I see was fixed in the mind of *Melancthon*. Now, there is nothing objected, I will not say, to our Churches, but to the most famous Doctours of our Churches, more odious, than that by too much urging certain rigid doctrines, and savouring more of *Zeno's* Porch than *Salomon's*, they assign unto God the causes of sinning, and * by an idle word evert the care of piety. The learned *Melancthon* saw this, and having been carried upon these rocks by the violence of *Luther*, afterward, by the admonition of *Erasmus*, steered a better course. VVhose footsteps, when some of our Pastors insisted in, but being prest by the vehemence of their Colleques, had their onely refuge in the goodness of the Magistrates, I associated my self to them, who conceiv'd it intolerable, that a most pernicious thing should from this beginning go into example, and that the VVorld should know, Moderate men could not be suffered in our Churches. VVhen some sharp Doctours in the Neighbourhood made

* διὰ τὸν ἀργὸν λόγον.

made ſtrong oppoſition againſt this pious deſign, and mixed other matters with this buſineſs, onely to raiſe an *odium* againſt the Magiſtrates purſuing peace; it ſeemed good, that it ſhould be ſhewed how unjuſt thoſe turbulent clamors were, in the confutation of one moſt eminent among his fellows, who had in ill manner implored the aid of external power. To this ſervice was I choſen, not but that many might have done it better, but becauſe it ſeemed proper to the office which I then did execute. Nor was I ignorant what 'twas to provoke VVaſps; but being armed with a good Conſcience, I adventured to expoſe my ſelf to calumnies, which they ſhall never eſcape that will oppoſe vices aged and robuſtious. But I give you thanks, and acknowledge your good will to me, and your wiſdome, when you perſwade me to abſtain for the future from ſuch contentions. I will indeed, in compliance with your Authority, and my own inclination both, carefully avoyd all unneceſſary quarrels; becauſe I ſee it is (as you write) of very great moment, as well to the health of body, (which to me is but weak) as to tranquillity of mind. *After this he comes to ſpeak of his hiſtorical writings, thus:* The Hiſtorie of our VVar I have continued to the end, that is, to the Truce.

There

There remains now the labour of revising and correcting it, almost more trouble-some than the writing: I see, when I had leisure to write more heedfully, I was not well provided with solid know-ledge of affairs: now, when I am able to get a better understanding of matters, my employments (being many rather than great) do not afford me time to select words fit for the Historie. And I much fear, that the work will be un-eaven and broken, and being composed at divers times, will not resemble the same Author. VVhat I have written, upon your encouragement I will revise and amend as perfectly as I can, and then lay it up where it shall have no commerce with this Age; for it is dan-gerous to contract with it. Posterity is better trusted; not because it will be better, but because it will be more kind to the deceased; for there will arise o-ther objects for envy and malice to work upon.

Anno 1616. Gulielmus Grotius, *our Author's brother, published a Collection of his Poems. Concerning which our Author, in an Epistle of his prefixed, saith:*

Some

* Hugo Grotius Gulielmo Grotio fratri.

* Some will accuse the Variety and desultorious kind of writing. The work indeed is not of one age. Spring and Summer are several seasons. And a mans mind is not always in the same temper: sometimes free and at its own command; sometimes weary, and seeking where to breath; often by request of friends bound and confined to a certain subject. Neither do I think it the part of a constant man, to put the same countenance upon jest and earnest. Moreover, my wit and *Genius* being ductile and apt to follow, as it was warmed with the reading of any Poet, was easily led in the way of imitation. I acknowledge my self in some places full of *Lucans* spirit, in other very studious of *Manilius*, and in other attempting somewhat more castigate after the pattern of *Statius* and *Claudian*, &c. But for the edition of these poems, I neither say *yea*, nor *nay*, but leave you to your self, and to the Counsils of those, who are most able to judge thereof. Such as are those Princes of this Art *Heinsius* and *Rutgersius*, and the most honest and most learned *Vossius*. However, I rejoyce in having such a brother, who loveth not my person only but my writings so fraternally.

We are now coming neer to that Ecclipse of honour, which overtook this great light in his own Countrey: but, before we give you the story of that, you shall, if you please, behold

behold him shining in his full splendor, in that happy Elogy or character bestowed on him by his most worthy and most dear friend now-mentiond, Gerardus Vossius:

** O quam te memorem, optimi parentis*
Proles maxima ter-beate Groti!
Tu Pharsalica bella detonantem
Vitæ restituis: tuum est quod æger
Felix nomine Marcianus ille
Jam felix iterum vigere cœpit:
Vivunt per te Avienus atq; Aratus
Et Germanicus. Alter Æsculapi
Das vitam & simul accipis perennem.
Sed ne summa tuæ sit ista laudis,
** En silvas similes Papinianis,*
En pares elegos Tibullianis;
Non cedunt Senecæ tui cothurni,
Nec cedunt Epigrammatum libelli
Musæ Bilbilicæ aut Catullianæ.
Ludunt singula singuli Poetæ:
Hæc tu cuncta potes, Poeta noster †.
Quis non hoc stupeat Batava Siren?
Nondum diximus. Explicas futuris
Bella Belgica seculis suavi
Ex virtutibus utriusq; cinno,
Contendens Taciteq; Livioq;
Gratior Themidi nec est sacerdos,
Et sollertior expedire cæca
Legum ænigmata. Charta testis illa,
Qua præstas mare liberum Batavis,
Et quæ post aliæ sequentur illam.
Testis innumera illa, cui fuisti
Salus perfugiumq;, turba. Testis

* *Jo. Gerardi Vosii carmen ad Hugonem Grotium.*

* *H. Grotii Poemata.*

† The best Poems of these later Ages were written by the best Scholar, the immortal Hugo Grotius. *The editor of Mr. Cartwright.*

Cata

Cata Hollandia, qua ſui Patronum
Fiſci legerat. Ipſa Diva teſtis
Quindeno ſibi te ſacrans ab anno.
Ad hac plura praſtites ſacrorum
Ipſos ſacra doces. Negare livor
Hoc unquam velit ? Obſtruet ſed ora
Virtus, & triplici triplex ſuperſtes
*Mundo pagina : * quâ pios tueris*
*Primores patria : atq; * quâ ſacrorum*
Iſdem poſt Dominum Deumq; noſtrum
Jus ſummum imperiumq; vindicaſti :
*Et * qua Chriſtiadûm docens ſalutem*
Diſpellis nebulas Socinianas.
Hac mirabitur, hac ſtupebit orbis :
Imprimis quibus ingenî ignea illa
Vis neſcitur, & ut ſacros libellos,
Et Patrum monumenta diverſes,
Inde à tempore, quo ſagacis, annos
Ante veſticipes, ab ore Junî,
Divini hoſpitio fruens magiſtri,
Nectar eloquii ſacri bibiſti.
Nec annis gravis otioq; abundans
Facis talia; publicis ſed uſq;
Diſtrictiſſimus : rebus ante fiſci :
At nunc meſſibus haut quater novenis
Viſis, cor oculuſq; civitatis,
Natali celebris qua Eraſmiano eſt :
Et magnatibus, imperî Batavi
Inclinata ſuper quibus recumbit
Nec Alcida humeris ferenda moles,
Curarum ſocius comeſq; fidus.
Felici omine dicte Magne, quid Te
Sol majus videt ? O decus tuorum
Delfî gloria patrii, Batavûm

* *Pietas Ordinum Hollandiae,*
* *De imperio ſummarum poteſtatum circa Sacra.*
* *De ſatisfactione, contra Socinum.*
That *de Imperio*, was tranſlated into Engliſh, and printed, An. 1651. Of the Autherity of the Higheſt power in matters of Religion.

The Author.

Splendor inclyte, Belgices ocelle,
Orbis delicium, Deiq; amores.

Now, the story of his Trouble and Imprisonment I shal deliver you as I have received it from his own pen, in the preface to his Apologetick, written and published by himself, after his safe arrival in France, *as followeth:*

* I have this onely way left me to open and declare the Truth to all those that have not their mind subject to their passions. And the plain Truth is this.

* ***Hollandiæ, Westfrisiæ, vicinarumq; nationum Rectoribus superioris atq; inferioris gradus, populoq; omni, Hugo Grotius.***

Among the Doctors of that Religion, which obteins the name of Reformed, both among us and in other places, hath been a variety of opinions, about Divine Prædestination, the amplitude of Grace, and the manner of its efficacy, and about certainty of perseverance, as appears by the Books published. The number of them that hold Predestination conditionate, Grace universal and resistible, and peseverance conditionate likewise (some such in former time had been at *Utrecht*, *Goad*, *Horn*, and elswhere :) by inquiring diligently into those points was much encreased. Against these other opposed themselves, preaching, that that Opinion was contrary to the Word of God and the confessions of the Church, attempting also to out them of their Pastoral office, and bring them under other Ecclesiastical censures. The accused and prosecuted party were

were not wanting to themselves in making their defence, both by their tongues and pens. The States of *Holland* and *West-frisia* following the Counsil, first of the Judges of their own upper *Bench*, and then also of the King of *Great Britain*, deliverd by word of mouth and by writing: (when 'twas clear, that the determination of those Controversies by most voices of the Pastors would make a rent, and much afflict both the body of the Reformed Religion, and the Commonwealth too, and that many of the Magistrats (to say nothing now of a great number of private Citizens, lovers of Vertue and of their Countrey) were so well affected to the accused party, that they could not think the condemnation therof could consist with the safety of Religion, nor could they use their power to that purpose:) They judged it best to set forth a Decree of mutual Toleration, charging the Pastors, that in those Controversies they should bear with one another, and not handle that Argument, but temperately, and only in order to Godlyness, preserving among themselves the bond of Christian Charity unbroken. And that all abrupt points of those questions might be shunned, and no new ones started, more and more Decrees were made, which pleased very many Godly-learned Men, both at home and abroad. But, some of the Pastors, assuring themselves of certain victory

ctory by a definitive sentence, and not able to attain unto it lawfully, the way being obstructed by the said Decrees, did, by Clandestine Meetings and secret combinations, move the common people to a Church-separation; and, to gain the countenance of Authority, laboured with some Towns and neighbouring Nations, to bring the businese to a Common Synod; which themselves, as if the seven Confederate Nations were one Nation, call National: which was against the will of most of the Rulers of *Holland*, against the will of the *Trajectins* and *Transisalans* and part of *Geldria*, being afraid of the ill effects usually caused by determining and defining Questions. The same were of opinion, that they could not be compell'd by those Nations which were less molested with those controversies, to joyn with them in the indiction of a Synod for the said definition: because, every Nation, even after the *Trajectin* league had excepted for it self, as other points of supremacy, so also the right of ordering the Church and publick divine service; witness the league it self, and the succeeding Acts, and the practice continued to these last times. Nevertheless they affirmed, They would persist in the Reform'd Religion, on these terms, that a liberty of dissenting in those Controversies should be permitted: for the use of which liberty in a moderate way with-

out

out commotions of the people, divers expedients were propofed. But, whileft this was under debate, the Adverfaries of mutual peace, in fome places, invaded the Temples, caft out their Diffenting brethren, and moreover ftood againft that Right, which the Magiftrates, in *Holland* as well as among their neighbours, had exercifed of old, and did exercife to that time, *viz*. Of having their voices in the election of Paftors. There were fome alfo, who by their bitter Declamations and libells defaming the Rulers expos'd them to the hatred of the people, and alfo ufed violence againft them. *Maurice* Prince of *Aurange*, having long kept himfelf quiet in thefe Controverfies, by the fecret arts of fome men is exafperated more and more againft *Oldenbarneveld* Affeffor (or, Advocate) of *Holland*, a man of moft flourifhing Authority in the Affembly, from whom long fince at the making of the Truce he had diffented: Withall, he is poffeft with fuch things concerning the form of the Commonwealth (which he had not been very much converfant in hitherto, being taken up with military affairs:) which were neither agreeable to the Laws, nor Cuftoms. He then, at length begins to difallow the Decrees made by the States of *Holland* for toleration of diverfity of opinions, to forfake the publick Churches, and affociate himfelf to the feparating Congregations. And further, without the know-

knowledge of the States of *Holland*, he gave Command to the ordinary Soldiers, not to stir in any businesses arising from those Controversies; when as the States of *Holland* were of another Judgment, *viz*. That obedience from the Soldier was due to their Decrees, and safeguard to the Rulers of Towns and to publick places against all force and sedition whatsoever. Upon this motive, some Magistrates of Towns, that had either no Garrisons at all, or such as were, for the said causes, suspected by the Rulers, by the Decree of the States of *Holland* encreased and ordered the Guards of their Town. which right also they had heretofore often used, without contradiction of the States confederate, or the Governour, who is the Commander of the ordinary Soldiers. The same was done by the *Trajectin* Rulers and as well these as the other professed, they would entertain these Soldiers at at their own charge, over and above the common burdens of the War. About the same time, the two Benches of Judges, to whom lyes an Appeal from the Towns, begin to decree against the Decrees of the States of *Holland*, in those writs whereby they call'd whom they pleas'd into question. That, the States of *Holland* pronounce to be unjustly done, and the limits of their judiciary power to be exceeded, as it was often before these times. Some Nations are impelled by

Prince *Maurice* and others, to call a common Synod (which we have said was stiled National) in the name of the Assembly of the Confederates, and to disband the military guards of the Towns. Both the *Hollandian* and *Traectin* Rulers oppose themselves against this attempt, testifying, that 'twas not Lawful for the Confederates, themselves interceding, to constitute any thing in those matters by the vote of the major part. They go on to call the Synod inviting also the Divines of other Nations, but no other than they knew would joyn in those opinions, to which the victory was destin'd. The proposals of the *Hollanders* and others for a fair accommodation of the matter were rejected. And in the mean time Prince *Maurice* with some Legates (or, Deputies) of the Assembly of Confederates goes to *Trajectum*, and against the will of the Rulers there disarms the Guard: though the Deputies from *Holland* did what they could (but all in vain) to hinder it; for they were commanded by their Superiours, to assist the *Trajectin* Rulers to their utmost, and if need were, to admonish the ordinary Soldiers in their service that they should attempt nothing against the will of the said Rulers, by force, in the things pertaining to the internall government of that Nation, and to the security thereof, being such as every Nation by it self had

reserved

reserved in their own power. The King of *France* having receiv'd intelligence of the Differences of his friends, dispatcheth *Bossizius* to them; who in consequence to the things treated on already by *Maurerius*, the same King's Leiger, might pursue all means of reconciliation. In hope whereof, the Rulers of the *Hollandian* Towns dismissed their Guards. This was no sooner done, but eight men, in the name of the Confederate States, from whom they had no such Commission, commanded *Oldenbarnveld* (whom the States of *Holland* a little before had taken into their protection) and *Hogerbet* and Me to be apprehended. Against this, the States of *Holland* and the Rulers of our Towns make their complaints. When we were long detein'd in prison, and oft examin'd; Judges at last, in the name of the Confederate States, are given us. Nor did it avail us, to shew out of our Country Laws and Customs, that the Confederate States have no Jurisdiction over them, and that the Judges themselves, for many reasons, were suspected. They go on in their Design, and give us not leave, neither to revise what things we written in our examination, nor to lay open the justice of our cause, nor to prove matters of fact pertaining to our defense, nor to refute the witnesses, nor to use Counsil: Sentence of death is pronounc'd upon

Oldenbarneveld, of perpetual imprisonment upon Us, of publication of Goods upon all Three. A year after, without hearing us, followed an Interpretation of the sentence, whereby we are pronounced Traitors. I can truly profess, in the sentence against Me, many things were set down beside the truth, many things expressly denyed by Me, some things whereof I was wholly ignorant, some things of which I was not so much as examind; so far was I from being allowed a fair Tryal. This, and much more would be very evident, if my Answers to every Interrogatory in my examination might come to light intire and sincere, as I do earnestly intreat. Before we were apprehended, at *Trajectum* the Noble men and Rulers of the City; whilst we were kept prisoners, all over *Holland*, the Decurions, Consuls, Oppidan Judges are removed before their time, others being put in, against the most sacred Laws, established of old by the Oaths of the Earles of *Holland*, and religiously observed many Ages. Before the Synod (which they call'd National) and in the time of it, many Pastors who taught prædestination conditionate (whom they call'd Re-
Anno 1618. monstrants) are put out of office. Others of them being summoned to the Synod are requir'd to plead their cause before their Adversaries, who had before condemned them by their secession, by their declamation

declamation in the Church, by the Synod, and by their writings: neither yet is it granted them to defend their own, and to oppugn the contrary opinion, otherwise than it seemed good unto the Synod, that is, unto their Adversaries. They are cast out of the Synod and condemned. There follow cruel Decrees against the Congregations of the condemned opinion, and against Collection of Alms for the feeding of Pastors, who being expeld or banisht from their Country, if they return, are clapt up in perpetual prison, their Accusers being invited by Rewards. Congregations are scattered more unmercifully than the Edicts would bear, by force, and oftentimes not without blood; to the great grief of a huge number of very good Men, lovers of Christian piety and of their Countrey. This is a true Relation of what was done. Now, I profess I cannot possibly approve that contempt of the Equity of the *Hollandian* States in their Decrees for a mutual Toleration, nor the condemnation of the Pastors and the things that followed. All which I suppose had been better prevented upon fair terms, seeing those things could not be profitable to the publick and to Prince *Maurice*, whose safety and glory (if I mistake not) consists in the good Affection of the people, those especially, who are devoted and addicted to their Countrey, such as I judge them that were cast out of their Magistracy, and many thousands of the overthrown opinion. But, in all those things whereof I am accus'd, nothing was acted by Me on my one head, but by command both of the States of *Holland*, and of the Rulers of the Town of *Rotterodam*, to whom, and to no other man living, was I bound by my Oath. To whom therefore, when I shewed my Obedience, I was a Traitor to none, but gave that respect both to the highest and to the inferior powers, which Nature and my Office did require. If any one thought he had to complain of that which I had done as the Minister of other men, He was not to proceed against me; but against my superiors. And, if I had done any thing by my own private undertaking (which is not so) yet was I not to be judged by my Adversaries, nor by Judges found of purpose against me, nor by any one who had receiv'd power of judging from the Confederate States, but by the perpetual and my proper Judges, as the Common Laws of our Countrey and the proper Laws of Towns (for which Laws we at first took Arms) appoint. As to my mind and intention, I testify before God and the world, it was no other, than to maintain that lawful form of Commonwealth under which I was born and bred, and to procure the unity of the Church by a loving Composure agreeable to the divine Precepts: to which end, many things I proposed, and many I had in readiness, when I was carryed away to prison. Whosoever judge otherwise of my Intention, do me injury, and have no just ground of their mistake. My life hath been without stain or spot. The Rulers of *Rotterodam*, in the time of my Office, know what Labours I did undergo for the safety and interests of that town. The Curators of the Treasury can witness, how exactly and without favour or fear I defended the rights thereof. The Benches of the Judges in *Holland* have good experience of my integrity in the prosecution of offences. They that have seen me in the Assembly of the States of *Holland*, and in the Sessions of the Curators of that Commonwealth, can remember what pains I took, that by parsimony and improvement of the Tribute there might be a supply of Money. Nor is Prince *Maurice* ignorant, how I satisfyed his desires in private businesses which he was pleased to commend unto my care. And, They that were together with me in the Assembly of the Confederates, are intreated to call to mind, how I omitted nothing that might conduce, to secure the Publick against the enemies force, to advance the Trade through *India*, and *America*, to continue a fair Amity and correspondence with Kings and other our Confederates and Allies. How heartily I affected the glory of our Commonwealth,

and

and of all things done valiantly in defense of it, and peculiarly favour'd the renown of Prince *Maurice*, my Books may testify; which I have partly divulged, and partly communicated to my friends. For these Offices, if I had expected a Reward, truly it had not been without example: but I never regarded that, being content with my salary, and the recompense of a good Name. What Return had I, after all my service? That for the space of nine months, being grievously sick, I was kept under a most streight custody, so as I could not so much as once have the comfort to see my wife or any friend: That, in the habit of a guilty person I was brought into that Auditory, wherein I had upheld the honour of Publick Justice. That, being shut up afterward in one chamber, I was so closely guarded with Soldiers, that my wife sometimes had not liberty to go abroad: That those few Goods I possessed, and (if ever any man) had gotten honestly, were taken from me and my five Children. Than all which, yet, This one thing is more grievous, that the eares of my Countreyman and of foreiners are filled with a false rumour, as if I had conspired and plotted against my Countrey; because, it is incredible to most men, that any Man of truth and honesty should be so used, as I have been. Neither is the injury confined to my person alone, but part

part of the *odium* and Calumny redounds to those that are allied to me by blood or marriage: who, as publick enemies and traitors, in several places, are persecuted by evil words and deeds. Against all these things, my comfort is in God, and in a good Conscience, and in the example of very many excellent Patriots, who for no sin but for solid vertues sake have endured the like Afflictions. Of late, there is come forth a Latin Book of an unknown Writer, who saith, that, by reason of the iujuries done me, I will be in affection, if not in body, with the King of *Spain.* This is far from Truth. I know all desire of Revenge is forbidden Christians. To the King of *Spain* I am not obliged, nor do I desire to be obliged. My Body is in *France*: there I live; and so long as I remain there, I will be faithful and obedient to the King, as tis my duty. Toward my Countrey in the mean time, which hath special need of the Kings friendship, I will preserve the same Affection I ever had, sollicitous for her safety, liberty and profit, and ready to do Her service, if she can make any use of me. For which Affection I desire nothing, but that You All of what Order and degree soever (for I know, many among the Rulers too, by the cunning of others, are depriv'd of the true understanding of what was done in our Case) laying aside prejudices, would be pleas'd to judge of mine and other mens

mens Doings, ſo, as you would have your own to be judged. And, to that purpoſe, I humbly beſeech God to cleer the eye of your mind, that you may ſee the Truth, and every one for his part do that which Equity requires; eſpecially, that you may find out the way of Peace, which at this time is moſt neceſſary.

By this Narration, the charitable Reader cannot but be well perſwaded of our Author's Innocency and Patience: Vertues happily conjoyned in him, and appearing alſo in that Epiſtle which he ſent out of priſon to his great friend Du Maurier *the French Embaſſador, as followeth:*

** Hugo Grotius Ben Aub. Maurerio. 15. Jan. 1621. ex carcere Lupiſteni.*

* To the moſt Chriſtjan King, to his moſt wiſe Council, and namely to you I acknowledge my ſelf more indebted than can be expreſt, for the labours undertaken to eaſe my calamities, into which I am fallen by the fate of our Commonwealth. And, although as yet the matter is come to no effect, 'tis no ſmall refreſhment to me to ſee ſo good and ſo great Men compaſſionating our ſufferings. The decreed Embaſſy into *France* yieldeth now ſome better Hope: but, that again is abated by conſidering how ill-affected they, who are ſent thither, are to us; and how eaſy it is, with all ſorts of calumny, to traduce thoſe, who have their voice ſtopt by the walls of a priſon, for this reaſon chiefly, that the world may not hear, what it concerns them to be concealed. Having thus long

long examined my Cause in the Auditory of my own Conscience (more sacred to me than all Tribunals) in the inmost recesses of my own Soul I find onely this, that my constant purpose was (liberty of opinions in things disputable being preserved) to retain the Unity of the Church; a thing wanting neither old nor new examples. I never meant to innovate any thing in the Commonwealth: it was my hearty endeavour, to maintain their Right, to whom Nature hath made me a Subject, and my office a Servant, and to whom I was sworn: that Power remaining in the hand of the Confederates, and of the Prince, which hitherto they had enjoy'd, being conferr'd on them by publick suffrages. They that know the matter, easily understand this to be our onely crime, that we did not act in the Commonwealth according to those Laws which they were about to constitute for their own Interest. If, upon that account, we are depriv'd of our Goods, Honours, Fame, this also is not without example. But the worst of all is, that, both the infirmity of my body is denied the free air, and the sadness of my mind the comfort of my friends. Yet, by Gods assistance, I will endure this and whatsoever can be imagined more cruel, rather than ask pardon of those things wherein my mind acknowledges no fault.

If

If there be any honeſt way of getting liberty, I would owe it to none more willingly than to your King and Kingdome; whoſe infinite merits towards our Common-wealth, I alwaies have extolled, whoſe friendſhip I have commended, whoſe wholſome Counſels I have defended from the calumniation of Enemies, both at liberty, and in my captivity, and the like I ſhall never ceaſe to do. And, God grant I may live to tranſmit unto Poſterity, together with thoſe publick benefits, this private one conferr'd on me, by ſome Monuments of Learning. That certainly will be to me the greateſt fruit both of my life and liberty. But, if that be above our Hope, yet whatever ſhall be performed for me and *Hogerbet* (whoſe cauſe being moſt near to mine, I equally commend) will, among our Countrymen of the higheſt, midſt and loweſt order, be moſt gratefull and glorious.

* Tranſlated into Engliſh, and printed, Anno 1652.

*I ſhall here mention alſo another Epiſtle *, a very large one, which he wrote in Priſon to the ſame* Du Maurier, *to comfort him after the death of his Wife. A rare Soul he had, who could adminiſter ſuch excellent conſolations to Another, when his own Condition ſeemed to be moſt uncomfortable. But he had a treaſure of the beſt Learning laid up in his memory, whence he drew as oft and as much as he pleaſed. That golden work,* Of the truth of of Chriſtian Religion, *was one of his exerciſes while he was a Priſoner, which he then wrote in Dutch verſe for the uſe of his Countrymen that trade among the Infidels, and afterward put the ſubſtance of it into* * *Latin proſe. Another fine piece he wrote likewiſe in Dutch verſe, in the time of his Captivity*, (An Inſtitution of Children baptiz'd) *which was done too by himſelf afterward in* † *Latin verſe. I find moreover in one of his Epiſtles* *, *that in his Reſtraint at the* Hague , *before the uſe of his Pen was taken from him, he was come to the* 49. *Title of his* Florilegy * , *which Title* (*ſaith he*) *contains an expreſs character of that Time. Thus was he wont* (*to ſpeak in his own phraſe*) triſtiſſimum tempus fallere , *to ſweeten the bitter daies of his Impriſonment. His happy eſcape out Priſon by an Ingenious Device of his noble and virtuous Wife, is recorded by himſelf in one Of his Poems, in theſe Divine Verſes:*

* Two Diſcourſes out of it were printed in Engliſh, Anno 1653. 1. Of God and his Providence. 2. Of Chriſt and his Miracles.

† And is of late elegantly tranſlated, and publiſhed both in Greek and in Engliſh.

* *Epiſt.* 75. *Maurerio*, p. 176.

* *Dicta Poetarum e Stobæo.*

* *Nos quoque ſi quiſquam multum debere fatemur*
Conjugio. memini , poſt tot tua vota preceſq́ ,
Cynthia cum nonum capto mihi volveret orbem ,
Qualem te primum , conjux fidiſſima, vidi
Carceris in tenebris : lacrymas obſorperat ingens

* *Grot. Silva ad Franciſcum Aug. Thuan.*

Vis

Vis animi, neque vel gemitu te luctus adegit
Consentire malis. rursus nova vincula, sed quæ
Te socia leviora tuli, dum milite clausos
Nos Mosa & tristi Vahalis circumstrepit unda.
Hic patriam toties & inania jura vocanti,
Et proculcatas in nostro corpore leges,
Tu solamen eras. heic jam te viderat alter,
Et post se media plus parte reliquerat annus,
Cum mihi jura mei per te, sollerte reperto,
Reddita. tu, postquam jam cæca acceperat alvus
Dulce onus, oppositis libabas oscula claustris:
Atque ita semoto foribus custode locuta es.
Summe pater, rigido si non adamante futurum
Stat tibi, sed precibus potis es gaudesq; moveri,
Hoc quod nostra fides lucem servavit in istam
Accipe depositum, tantisq; exsolve periclis.
Conjugii testor sanctissima jura, meaq;
Spem sobolis, non huc venio pertæsa malorum,

Sed

Sed miſerata virum: poſſum ſine Conjuge, poſſum
Quamvis dura pati. Si poſt exempla ferocis
Ultima ſævitiæ nondum deferbuit ira,
In me tota ruat. vivam crudele ſepulcrum:
Me premat & triplicis cingat cuſtodia valli,
Dum meus ætheriæ ſatietur paſtibus auræ
Grotius, & caſus narret patriæq; ſuoſq;.
Dixerat, atque oculis fugientia vela ſecutus,
Addit; Abi Conjunx, neque te niſi libera cernam.
Quod mea ſi auderet famam ſpondere Camæna,
Acciperet quantis virtutem laudibus iſtam
Poſteritas? nomen non clarius illa teneret,
Admeto regina ſuos quæ tradidit annos,
Quæque ſuper cineres jecit ſe arſura mariti,
Dignaq; tam Bruti thalamis, quam patre Catone
Porcia, & in letum magno comes Arria Pæto.

Being ſecretly conveyed out of Priſon in a Cheſt, he was brought to a Friends

houſe,

house, and so away to Antwerp, *and thence to* France. *From* Antwerp *he writes to his good Friend* Du Maurier, *thus:*

Grotius Maurerio. 30. Martii, 1621. Antuerpiæ, Hagam.

* Assure your self, I shall ever be indebted to you for your good will, as much as if you had brought the business of my Liberty to effect. Your Affection was never the less, though God prevented you, and took unto himself the Glory of the Work. And now, the Favours you do me, and offer me, are so great, that if any could be equall'd with the Good of Liberty, They might, which are of much concernment to my life, safety, and honour. I have chosen my first Refuge in this City, that I might here explore, whether it be a seasonable time for me to go into *France*, while the Embassie of our Countrymen, (I cannot say, of our Friends) is there. For that reason, I have written to the most honour'd, the President *Janninus*. But, what I expected from him, I find abundantly in your Letter. Wherefore, by Gods blessing, I will follow your Counsel. Thither will I betake my self, and render Thanks to my good Friends, that have labour'd so much to procure my Liberty. *In the next Epistle* (from *Paris*) *to the same Person, he saith:* * I learn chiefly by you, how great is the constancy of Goodness, not swimming in the surface, but sunk into the heart. So incessant are you,

Grotius Maurerio. 22. Apr. 1621. Lutetiæ.

you, in your favours and graces toward me. This I perceive by their love, whom your love chiefly hath made to be my Friends. *Putean* and *Peiresc*, so soon as they heard of my comming, ran presently to bid me welcome, and obliged me by their extreme courtesy. The President *Janinus* sent his Letters to me, while he suppos'd I stay'd at *Antwerp*, overflowing with Kindness, and (which I esteem greatest) giving as large a Testimony of our Innocence, as could be wisht. Thus kind I found *Boissizius* also, whom I met at his own house, where he stay'd for me, being about to go to Court. By the advice of them Both, I rest at *Paris*, ready to follow that way for the future, which they shall think good, to whose wisdom, fidelity, and friendship, I do entirely commit my self.

At Paris *he was recompenced for his tedious restraint by the sweet conversation of his learned Friends,* Tilenus, Cordesius, Petrus *and* Jacobus Puteanus, Franciscus Thuanus, *and others of great note. Among whom he dispersed certain Epigrams concerning his fortunate escape; to One, a most eminent Person, he sends this following Epistle with them:*

* Liberty, the greatest Good of this life, and most convenient to Nature, hath this incommodity, that unwary Mortals can scarce keep a mean in the

* *Grotius N.N. Lut. 8. Maii,* 1621.

use thereof. This, I think, happen'd to me, when I sent abroad the Epigrams, wherewith I gratulated my self; as if they ought not to be Captives, when I was freed. So, they came first into the hands of my Friends, then to yours, most Eminent Sir, whose censure the most serious works may be afraid of. 'Twas much, you read them once: but your Desire is to keep them, written with my own hand. Truly, the most pleasant Flowers have but a short beauty: and things that commend themselves at first sight, if you eye them much and oft, eed satiety and disdain. Yet I must lfill your desire, seeing without any esert of mine, you have so engaged me y your Humanity, that I ought rather to be immodest than disobedient. Take therefore what you ask: but take them, I pray, not as Verses, but as a testimony of the divine favour and mercy to me, that was pleas'd I should spring from a Chest as from the Womb, and rise again, as 'twere out of my Coffin, and gave me an auspicious token of the life to come, by delivering me from the confines of a most miserable death.

How joyfully he past his time in France, *what a concourse of learned men there was unto him, what favour he found among the Nobility and Great Officers of State, and with the King him-* [illegible], *from whom he had Protection, and* *a Pension for divers years; what correspondence he held by Letters with his absent learned Friends*, Peireskius, Salmasius, *and others; How he was admitted into the bosom of the Great Chancellor of* Suedia, Oxenstern, *and advanced to be Embassador into* France *for that Kingdome; these things (that I may not retard the Press) I shall leave the Able Reader to pick out of our Author's Epistles**. *Onely, you shall hear him tell his Friend* Peireskius † *the news of his Advancement, in this loving manner:*

* Epist. ad Gallos ex officina Elzevir. 1648. *Quemadmodum autem has ad Gallos jam habes meo beneficio, si vicissim alicui, Grotiani nominis, & bonarum rerum studioso, libeat, quas ad Belgas, Germanos, Suecos, Danos, Anglos, Italos, aliosq; scripsit ferè infinitas, investigare, nec literatis invidere, ingens bonæ frugis, & nobis plurimas ex diversis Europæ oris acceptas jam possidentibus, ac ad edendas omnes paratis, gratissimus futurus est acervus.* Præf. ad Lect. † *Vide, si placet, summi literatorum Amici, Nicolai Peireskii vitam, per Gassendum.*

* You that have heretofore afforded compassion and faithfull comforts to my Adversity, have heard of the Amendment of my Fortunes with joy, I doubt not. Though the Fame hereof hath prevented my Letter, yet I thought it was my duty to signifie to One who hath merited so much of Me, and of all Learning and Learned Men, that I am sent hither, Embassadour of the Queen and Kingdome of *Sueden*: and so being extricated out of the discords both of my Coun-

* *Epist. 165. ad Nic. Fabricium Peirescium, Lut. 23. Martii, 1635.*

try, and of *Germany*, and out of the evils of ſo long and ambiguous a War, I enjoy the ſweetneſs of the French air, and of my old Friends: So that nothing is wanting to my Happineſs (as in mortal life) beſides the ſight of your face, and the fruition of your diſcourſe. Yet may this want partly be repaired by epiſtolical commerce, and partly by ſerene thought of the ſecure poſſeſſion of this our friendſhip, &c.

I need not tell the Reader, that hath any Acquaintance in the Commonwealth of Learning, of our Author's Controverſy with Dr. Rivet: *let their Books be compared: nor of his Annotations in five or ſix Folio's upon the whole Bible: (the largeſt of them, upon the Evangeliſts, is by our learned and judicious Engliſh Annotator *, ſtil'd* Admirable.) *Nor need I reckon up other leſſer pieces of our* Grotius *not yet mentioned, or not yet come forth into the light. As to this noble Work, out of which we have tranſlated theſe large Selections, (and left enough to exerciſe the diligence of ſome better hand) the Author mentioning it to* Franciſcus Thuanus*, *acknowledgeth the help he had from Books out of his Library. And he had need of the Aid of good Libraries, the Work being ſo dif-*

* *Dr.* Hammond *in his Advertiſement to the Reader of his Paraphraſe:* The moſt learned and judicious *Hugo Grotius*, in his admirable Comments on the Goſpels, as alſo in the poſthumous Annotations on the other parts of the New Teſtament, which for a great part bear his ſignature upon them.

* *Epiſt. 73. Fran. Aug. Thuano, An. 1623.*

fuſed,

sused. Nor could he more freely borrow elswhere, than from that Library, which was furnished by Thuanus *the Father* *, *for the benefit of all Learned Men.*

* *Vide Testamentum Jac. Aug. Thuani, in Com. de vita sua.*

How much the Author was addicted to the waies of Peace and Reconciliation, appears afore. That the Reader may see his Constancy in such Christian Endeavours, and that his example may encline our men to Moderate courses, 'twill be worth the pains to translate hither what he wrote to Joannes Duræus, *a man that laboured much to establish an union of the Evangelical Churches.*

* I have alwaies wished, and will never cease to wish, that the Churches, which for most weighty causes have departed from the Pope of *Rome*, may come to a nearer Agreement one with the other, and may testifie the same conspicuously. Nor am I ignorant, having also had some experience, how many rubs there are in the way, and difficulties, from Reasons of State, from the suspicions of Divines, from the love every one beareth to his own opinions, and the desire of advancing his own way, and of separating himself from others, and keeping a large distance under pretence of purity. But all these things ought to deterr no man from effecting a most excellent work, if he be able: if he cannot effect it, certainly he may have comfort of his Conscience, and

* *Grotius ad Duraum, 11. Sept. 1637. Lutetiæ.*

please himself in the thought of so noble an Attempt. *Again to the same* Duræus. Both the Embassadors of *England* think, as I also do, that these Times will not permit a General Assembly of Protestants: Times, wherein they do not enjoy so much as that common peace of humane Society: That it will therefore be best, as the Kingdome of *Sueden* and *England* are joyned together in Friendship, and haply e're long will be confederate; So also that the Churches of these Kingdomes set forth a publick profession of their Concord, and first give the Neighbours of *Sueden*, the *Danes*, and *Norwegians*, and then others too, an example for them to imitate. Such a Body of Churches being once constituted, there is hope, their Neighbours, one after another, will by degrees close with them. And this is the more to be desir'd by Protestants, because Many do every day forsake them, and joyn with the Romanists, for no other Reason, but because they are not one Body, but distracted parties, separated Congregations, having every one a peculiar Communion and Rites, and moreover striving one to disgrace the other with reproaches. That it concerns the Protestants, these things should be remedied, especially seeing so great a Conspiracy of their Adversaries against them, who doth not perceive?

Grotius Duræo, Lut. 21. Nov. 1637.

Nor

Nor was our Author zealously affected onely to the peace of Protestants, but of all Christendome, witness his Via ad pacem Ecclesiasticam*, *in the entrance whereof he hath a sweet Epigram in praise of Moderators, to this effect,* Qui gaudes Batavis, &c. * *Edit.* 1642.

That Roterdam Erasmus *stands in Brass;*
(Yet this Reward to's worth inferiour was:)
That mild Cassander's *Works are published,*
(Thanks to Cordesius*) and by thee are read:*
That Nectar drops from sweet Melancthon's *vein;*
Wicel *and* Modreve *write in the same strein:*
That in Spalato's *Books good Votes are seen*
For Unity: (ill lost are Two of Ten:)
*That Great Great-*Britains *King hath wisely done,*
In signifying his mind by Casaubon:
Who joy'st in all this, view with gentle look
Our way of Reconcilement in this Book,
Good, if not best: 'Twill please thou mayst presage,
Though not the Present, yet the Future Age.

Adde

Add only this passage of His out of his Answer to Dr. Rivet , *where he hath words of this sense :*

* In Animadv. Grotii pro notis ad Cassandrum. De discrim. pecc.

* I have always loved Peace , and do love it , and to it do I direct my labours both publick and private , that we may obtein it : first , between Empires professing Christ , and then in the Church , which Christ would have to be One. And I mean Peace without injury to that Truth, which the Scripture and perpetual Tradition consign unto us. And seeing Peace, though it were made , cannot be kept without a certain Order of Government , I love also that order, which the long experience of old times hath approved. It cannot be, but the Lovers of these things, must incur the hatred of them that seek advantage by wars and discords , such as our Age abounds with. Such enemies of Peace I well foresaw would rise up against Me and my endeavour of Peace. I easily suffer it , and comfort my self with the Conscience of my good Design. For the promoting whereof I have said that, which seemed to me most profitable , according to the measure of my understanding and Reading, with some Regard also to the times wherein we live. *To the order of Government here named pertains what he speaks elsewhere :* '. For , if the perpetual Custom of the Universal Church , introduced (as we may believe , and the Antients did believe) by the Apostles them-

[A]nimadvers. . de cœlibatu [S]acerdotum.

selves

ſelves, be of any value, neither can a Presbyter be ordained but by a Biſhop, nor a Biſhop but by two or more Biſhops. The Contempt of this Holy Order hath brought in ſo much Licence, that whoſoever can lead the common people by the ears, maketh to himſelf a right of gathering a new Church †.

† *Novum cœtum, & ut nunc loqui mos eſt, Eccleſiam colligere, Mihi, etiamſi liceret, non liberet. Video quam male id aliis ceſſerit. Multiplicarunt numerum, non lætitiam.* Grotius in Voto p. 40.

Here ſhall I inſert that Elogy of our Grotius *which I received from a learned man* * *that had the honour to be acquainted with him in France.* He was a Man wonderfully courteous and affable, very free in communicating his knowledge in any point of learning, very ready to give his advice touching any courſe of ſtudy, what Authors were fitteſt to be read. His *Latin* in his diſcourſe was altogether ſuch as we ſee in his Books, ready, fluent, eaſy and unaffected: ſo that I verily think, no man ever ſpake more fluently in his Mother tongue. He was a moſt indefatigable Student, and a man of a ſingular ready memory, and clearneſs of judgment: A great Lover of the Union and Peace of the Church*, an Approver of the Church of *England* *, as moſt orderly reformed. He was of a moſt ſweet *Chriſtian* diſpoſition, far from any thought of revenge for any Injury. One time coming

† Mr. M. T. Chaplain to the (then) Engliſh Embaſſadour, the truly Noble L. Scudamore.

* See the beginning of his *Votum pro pace.*

* See, of Authority, p. 103.

ming from an Audience at S. *Germans*, the Secretary of Ceremonies being in the Coach with him, it chanced that in one place a great number of people were in the way ſeeing an execution. His Coachman and Poſtilion driving boldly through the company, the Archers, which uſe to attend executions with ſhort pieces, being angry to ſee the execution diſturb'd, made after the Coach, ſhot his Poſtilion and Coachman, and through the Coach, even through his Hat: And the King offering to hang three or four of them at his gate, if he pleaſed, he pardoned them All. In his Journey between *France* and *Sueden* he dyed, putting off Miniſters that came to him with, *Non novi vos*, as they ſay.

But, how little of probability there is in that ſaying, or any ſuch like, may appear by this Narrative of his Death, which I have tranſlated out of Dr. Caſaubon,* *as followeth*:

* *Mericus Caſaub. de uſu verborum, Lond.* 1647.

Becauſe we deſire the Memory of this Great Man ſhould be dear to all Lovers of Vertue and Learning, according to his moſt High Deſerts toward the Commonwealth of Good Letters, I have eaſily obtained of My ſelf, to inſert here, and to communicate to the candid and ingenuous Reader, what hath come unto my hands by the help and favour of ſome Friends, concerning the End of ſo excellent a Perſon, in a Letter of *Quiſtorpius*, the primary Profeſſor of Theology at *Roſtoch*

stoch, set forth at *Amsterdam*.

* You are earnest with me, to relate the last act of that Phœnix of learned men *Hugo Grotius*, and how he behaved himself, when he took his leave of this world. Here take it, briefly thus. He took ship at *Stockholm*, bound for *Lubec*. At Sea he met with a great Storm, and having been beaten with it, and tossed for the space of three dayes, he suffers Shipwrack, and is cast upon the shore of *Cassubia* sick and weak: Thence, in a very incommodious Journey, and a rainy season, passing sixty miles and more, he is brought at length to *Rostoch*. He diverts to *Balemannia*, and sends for *Dr. Stochman* the Physician; who observing the weakness of his body, by reason of age, shipwrack, and the incommodities of the journey, presageth the end of his life to be at hand. The next day after his entrance into this City (which in the old style was the XVIII. of *August*) about IX. at night he requesteth me to visit him. I came, and found the Man approaching neer to the agony of death: I saluted him, and signifyed how happy I should have been to have had conference with him, had he been in health. His answer was, *Ita Deo visum fuit*: Thus it hath pleased God. I go on, and advise him to compose himself to a happy departure, to acknowledge himself a sinner, and repent of whatsoever he had done amiss

* *J. Quistorpii Epistola. Rostoch. Sept.* 1645.

miſs : and when , as we diſcourſed, I had mentioned the *Publican* confeſſing himſelf a ſinner , and praying God to be mercifull unto him , He anſwers ; *Ego ille ſum Publicanus* : I am that Publican. I proceed, and remit him to Chriſt , without whom there is no ſalvation. He replyes : *In ſolo Chriſto omnis ſpes mea eſt repoſita :* In Chriſt alone is placed all my Hope. I rehearſed with a loud voice that *German* Prayer in the *German* tongue , **Herr Jesu. wahrer Mensch und Gott,&c.** He , with cloſed hands and a low voice ſaid after me. When I had done , I asked whether he had underſtood me : He anſwers , *Probe intellexi* : I underſtand you well. Afterward , I repeated ſome paſſages out of the Word of God , which dying men are wont to be put in minde of , and I ask again , whether he underſtood me : *I hear your voyce*, ſaith he , *but hardly underſtand what you ſay.* Then he became ſpeechleſs , and in a ſhort time after gave up the Ghoſt , juſt at twelve, midnight. Thus have you the Cataſtrophe of *Grotius* , the laſt end of this excellent Man's Life. His dead Body was committed to the Phyſicians. His Bowells were put in a Veſſel of Braſs,and that they might be laid up in the moſt honourable place of our principal Church dedicate to the Virgin *Mary* , I eaſily obtained of the Governours. *Let him reſt in Peace.*

I

The Author.

I have received from a good hand, that our Author *, a little before his death, declared his Affection to the* Church of England *, and his Desire to end his dayes in the Communion of the same.*

These Collections *put together in some haste (til One more Able arise to do honour to this* Great *Man's Memory) be pleased, Gentle Reader, favorably to accept from the* Translator ,

Clement Barksdale.

THE END.

ERRATA.

PAg. 1. lin. 1. * State. p. 6. l. 3. are often, l. 4. *dele* *. pag. 94. l. 6. was included in. p. 400. CXIII. and ſo reſtore the following numbers. p. 448. l. ult. joyning.

SCRIPTURES EXPLANED.

Rom.

Scriptures Explaned.

Gen.

Scriptures Explaned.

An

An Alphabetical Table of the principal Matters.

Fugitive.

Law

Power.

Spies

THE END.

Books printed for *William Lee*, and are to be sold at his shop, at the Turks-Head in Fleetstreet together with the Prices of some of them.

ANnotations upon all the New Testament, by *Edward Leigh* Esquire Master of Arts of *Magdalen*-Hall in *Oxford*. 1650.

A Systeme or *Body of Divinity* in ten Books, wherein the Fundamental and main grounds of Religion are opened, by *Edward Leigh* Esquire Master of Arts in *Magdalen*-Hall in *Oxford*, in Folio 1654. about 240. Sheets.

The Saints Encouragement in Eviltimes, in 12. 1651. written by the said Author *Edward Leigh*.

An Exposition of the Prophecy of Haggee, in fifteen Sermons, by that famous Divine *John Reynolds* D. D. in 4. 1649.

An exposition of the Psalms of degrees.

The Young mans Tutor, both writ by *T. Stint*, in 8.

Heresiography, or a *Description of all the Heresies & Sectaries of these later times*, of *Ranters* and *Quakers*, by *Eph. Pagit*. 4. with new Additions 1654.

Contemplations, Sighs and groans of a Christian, published by *W. Stiles* Esquire, of the Inner Temple. 12.

The Saints Comfort in evill times. 12.

Gods revenge against Murther, in *thirty Tragical Histories*,

[*]

Histories, by *J. Reynolds*, in Fol.

Sylva Sylvarum, or *a Natural History in ten Centuries*. Whereunto is newly added, *The History of Life and death*, or the *Prolongation of Life*: both written by the Right Honorable *Francis* Lord *Verulam*. in Fol. 1651.

The { Magnetique cure of Wounds. / Nativity of Tartar in Wine. / Image of God in Man.

Also another Treatise of the Errors of Physicians Concerning *Defluxions*: both published in English by *Dr. Charleton* Physician to the late King. 4. 1650.

The darkness of Atheism dispelled by the light of Nature, written by the said Author, in 4. 1653.

A Discourse concerning the King of Spains *Surprizing of the Valtoline*, Translated by the Renowned Sir *Thomas Roe*, many times Embassador in Forein parts. 4.

The Roman Foot and Denaries, from whence as from two principles, the measure, and weights may be deduced, by *John Greaves* of *Oxford*. 8. 1647.

A Treatise of the Court, Written in *French*, by that great Counsellour *De Refuges* many times Embassador for the two last *French* Kings, Englished by *John Reynolds*. 8.

Aminta. A Pastoral Translated out of *Tarquata Tasso*. 4.

The Hebrew Commonwealth Translated out of *Petrus Cuneus*, in 12. 1653. both Translated by *Clem. Barksdal*.

Hugo Grotius, his two Treatises, *Of God and his Providence*, *and of Christ and his Miracles*; together with the said Authors judgment of sundry points controverted, in 12. 1653.

Certamen Religiosum, or a Conference between the late

late King of *England*, and the late Lord Marquess of *Worcester* concerning Religion. 4. 1652.

The Battel of Agincourt, fought by Henry *the fift, the miseries of Queen* Margaret, *with other Poems*, by *Mic. Drayton* Esquire. 8.

The Odes of Horace, Selected and translated by Sir *Thomas Hawkins*, in 12.

The Spanish Gallant, instructing men in their Carriage to be beloved of the People.

Youths Behaviour, or *Decency in conversation amongst men*; with new Additions of a Discourse of Powdering of Hair, of black Patches, and naked Brests, 8. 1651.

The Tillage of Light, A Treatise of *The Philosophers stone*. 8.

The Right of Peace and War, in three Books, written in Latin by the Illustrious *Hugo Grotius*, together with the life of the said Author, in English. 8. large. 1654.

A Sermon of the Nature of Faith, by *Barten Holyday* Doctor of Divinity, 1654.

The Innocent Lady, or the Illustrious Innocent, written Originally in French by the learned Father *de Cerizeirs* of the Company of Jesus, rendred into English by Sir *William Lower*, Knight, 1654.

A Disputation at *Winchcomb* in *Glocester-shire*, wherein is much satisfaction given in many fundamental points of Religion, in the presence of many Eminent Persons, 1654.

A brief discourse of changing Ministers Tithes into Stipends, or into another thing. 1654.

Books printed for *W. Lee* (and ſome others) and are to be ſold at the Turks Head in Fleetſtreet, together with the prices of the ſaid Books.

THe *Chriſtians Warfare againg the Devil, World, Fleſh*, by *John Downam*. Fol. 16 s.

Second Epiſtle of Saint *Peter*, by *Tho. Adams*. Fol. 1633. 20 s.

A ſixfold Commentary upon Geneſis, wherein ſix ſeverall Tranſlations are compared, by *Andrew Willet*, in Fol. 16 s.

The Theater of Plants, or a large Herbal, by *John Perkinſon* Apothecary. 2lb.

Orlando Furioſo, Engliſhed by Sir *John Harrington*, with the Tranſlators additions of his Epigrams, in Fol. 8 s.

Mare Clauſum, by *John Selden* Eſquire, of the beſt Impreſſion, in Fol. 6 s.

Books printed for *William Lee*, *M. Walbanck*, *D. Pakeman*, and *G. Bedell.*

REports *or new Caſes of Law*, by *John March* of *Grayes-Inne* Barreſter. 4. 1648. 2 s. 8 d.

The Attorneys Academy, being the manner of Proceeding in all the Courts of Records at *Weſtminſter* and other Courts of Law or Equity. 4. 1647. 3 s.

The learned Argument upon the three learned Readings, 1. By the Lord *Dyer*, 2. By Sir *J. Brograve*, 3. By *Th. Riſden* Eſquire.

Writ

Writ of *Habeas Corpus*, in Court of Upper Bench, with the opinion of the Court thereupon.

The Touchstone of Common assurances, by *W. Shepheard* Esq; of the midde-Temple. 4. 1651. 5 s. 6d.

The book of Oaths, and the several Forms thereof, both Antient and Modern, in 8. 1649.

Fleta, an antient Manuscript of the Laws of *England*, published in print by *John Selden* Esq; and is to be sold by *W. Lee*, *M. Walbanck*, and *D. Pakeman*. 4. 1647. 8 s. 6 d.

Books printed for *W. Lee*, *D. Pakeman*, and *G. Bedell*, and are to be sold at their Shops in Fleet-street.

BIblia Sacra sive Testamentum vetus ab Jun. Tremelio & Fra. Junio ex Hebrao Latinè redditum, & Testamentum Novum à Theod. Beza è Græco in Latinum versum, Argumentis Capitum additis versibusque singulis distinctis, & seorsum expressis, cum Indice, in 12. 1640. 5 s.

The History of the Civil Wars of France, written in *Italian* by *H. C. Davila*. Translated out of the Original. Fol. 1647. 8 s.

De Priscis Anglorum Legibus, being the Antient Laws of England, in Saxon and Latin, out of the Author (Mr. *Lamberts*) own Manuscript Copie. 1645. 8. shillings.

Divine Essayes, by the honourable *Walter Mountague* Esq; 4. 1648.

Reports or *Cases* in *Chancery*, Collected by Sir *George Cary* one of the Masters of the Chancery.

The

The whole Office of a Countrey Justice of Peace, with an Abridgment of all the Acts and ordinances, which any ways concern a Justice of Peace, by *William Shepheard* Esq; 1650. 2 s. 9 d.

The Compleat Lawyer.

A perfect abridgment of the Eleven Books of Reports of the Reverend and Learned Knight Sir *Edward Coke*, sometime Chief Justice of the Upper-Bench, written in French by Sir *John Davis*, and now Englished. 1651. 1 s. 6 d.

The History of the Life and Reign of Richard *the third*, by *George Buck* Esq; Fol. 1646.

Learned Reports, perused and approved by Justice *Godbole*. 4. 1652.

The Office and duty of Executors. 4. 2 s. 4 d.

The Grounds and Maxims of the Law of England, by *W. Noy* Esquire, both printed for *W. L. D. P.* and others. 1 s.

For the sacred Law of the Land, a learned book, written by *John White* Esq; 8. 1653.

A general Table to all the Reports of my Lord Coke *in English*, 8. 1652.

These Books following are to be sold by *W. Lee*, and *D. Pakeman* at their Shops in Fleetstreet.

A Collection of all the Statutes frequent in use, with Notes in the margent and references to the Book-Cases, with an Abridgment of the Residue which be expired or repealed, by Ferdinando Pulton of Lincolns-Inne, in large Fol. 1640. 38 s.

The

The first part of the Institutes of the Laws of *England*, or a Commentary upon *Littleton*. 17 s.

The second part of the Institutes, containing the Exposition of many antient, and other Statutes of *Magna Charta*. 12 s.

The third part of the Institutes concerning Pleas of the Crown and Criminal Causes. 5 s. 9 d.

The Fourth part of the Institutes, concerning the Jurisdiction of Courts. 7 s. 6 d. all written by *Edward Coke Milite* sometimes Chief Justice of the Upper Bench. Fol. 148.

The Reports of that Reverend and Learned Judge Sir *Henry Hobard* Lord Chief Justice of the Common-Pleas, being inlarged and perfected by his own Copie, in Fol. 1650. 7 s. 6 d.

The 1, 2, 3, 4, 6, 7, and 11. Parts of the Reports of my L. *Coke* in Fol.

The Abridgment of my *L. Coks* 11. Reports, by *Ed. Tratman*. 8. 4 s. 6 d.

The year-Book of *Edward* the fourth, also, Long *Quinto* of *Edward* the 4. both Fol.

The Register of Writs. Fol. 1634. 17 s.

Henric. De Bracton, De Legibus & Consuetudinibus Angliæ. 4. 1640. 12 s.

Presidents, the first and second part, by *W. West*, in large 4. 10 s.

Crumptons Jurisdiction of Courts. 4.

The Elements of the Laws of England, by Sir *Francis Bacon* sometime Lord Chancellor of *England*. 4. 1639. 2 s.

The Judges Arguments about Ship-money. 4. 1 s. and 2. pence.

Natura Brevium, by *Fitz-Herbert*.

The Office of Sheriffs, by *Wilkinson*. 8. 2 s. 2 d.

Four Books of Law, by Sir *H. Finch*. 8. 3 s.

Doctor

Doctor and *Student*. 8. 1 s. 6 d.

A Book of Presidents. 8. 1 s. 2 d.

Littleton and *Perkins*; together, or single. 16.

The Compleat Copie-holder, with the Reading of Copyholds, the first by Sir *E.Coke* the second, by *C.Caltrop* Esquire. 4. 2 s. 6 d.

The order of keeping of a Court-Leet, and Court Baron. 4.

A little Treaſe of Bail and Mainprize, by *E.C.* Knight.

A Declaration of Nuſance, concerning dwelling-Houſes, with the reſolutions of the Judges of Aſſizes, upon Queſtions touching Pariſhes.

Speciall and Selected Law Caſes, out of the Reports and year-Books, concerning the perſons and eſtates of all men whatſoever. 2 s.

Analecta, formerly called the *Country Justice*, the ſixth Edition, carefully and truly corrected from the groſs Errors of the former Impreſſions, in 12. 1648. 1 s. 6 d.

Statuta Pacis, containing all the Statutes in order of time, as concern a Juſtice of Peace, in 12. 1 s. 6 d.

Kelaways Reports. Fol. 8 s.

The Laws Reſolutions concerning Womens rights, in 4. 3 s.

The Engliſh Lawyer by Judge *Dodridge*. 4.

Viceſimo primo Jacobi & primo & tertio Caroli. Fol.

An ancient learned Book of the Law called *Britton*.

FINIS.

www.ingramcontent.com/pod-product-compliance
Lightning Source LLC
LaVergne TN
LVHW102102300926
849161LV00001B/2
* 9 7 8 1 6 1 6 1 9 2 7 9 2 *